PREFACE

THE papers that I venture to offer the reader of this book were all published between 1948 and 1960. In other words, they relate to work undertaken since the Second World War and it is my hope that they may serve as an illustration of the development of British medicine, since that time, in one special but broad aspect. I have been encouraged to bring them together in this volume not only by a continuing demand for reprints, much of which I have long been unable to meet, but also by a knowledge that a number of them are being used, here and abroad, as required reading in undergraduate and postgraduate medical teaching.

One thing I must instantly make plain. Many of these papers are not my own. Many of them relate to joint work that I have carried out with others—mainly with my colleagues in the Medical Research Council's Statistical Research Unit—all of whom have most kindly allowed me to include them here. Others, concerning the trials of new treatments and of vaccines, are the reports of Medical Research Council Committees and therefore the work of a great many persons. With all these I have indeed been myself intimately concerned but they are in no sense my own work. I am privileged to be able to include them in this book and I am deeply indebted to the Medical Research Council for permission to do so.

My aim in bringing these various papers together is not, of course, to produce yet another textbook of statistical method. In this respect I have already endeavoured to meet the needs of the non-mathematically minded worker in my *Principles of Medical Statistics*, while for the more mathematically minded many excellent texts are available. Here I attempt to show the method in daily use in research and thus to expound a 'philosophy', a means of seeking answers to the questions that typically arise in clinical and preventive medicine. There is, I seek to show, more to the statistical method than a familiarity with formulae, a test of significance and an electronic computer. There are the fundamental, and usually far more difficult, problems of how to plan observations and experiments, how best to carry them out and how with accuracy and clarity to present the results. I cannot, alas, claim that any of the papers included here can serve as models in any of these respects. I can claim that they are all honest down-to-earth attempts to carry out research by the statistical method and (particularly with hindsight) they may, I believe, be instructive in their failings as well as in their virtues.

The book falls naturally into three sections. The first deals with the problems of simple but strictly controlled clinical trials of new (or old) treatments of the sick, a proper knowledge of which is a *sine qua non* in clinical medicine. The second part discusses the corresponding problems that arise in the field trials of vaccines designed to prevent disease. The third takes up the most difficult problems of all—the epidemiology and aetiology of disease where almost invariably we are powerless to experiment and, proceeding by observation, must usually endeavour to disentangle an involved chain of causation and thus reach most probable conclusions. In each section I have first included my own published lectures or addresses in which I have attempted to expound the 'philosophy' and the methodology. I then illustrate the application of such philosophy and methodology to various problems in medicine by an appropriately selected series of papers. In selecting these papers I have made no attempt to give a complete picture of the subject nor to include all the relevant studies that have been published. My aim has been to give a sample that is both sufficient and apt to illustrate the particular thesis, whether it be clinical trial, field trial or epidemiological conundrum. For those who wish to seek further I have added a bibliography of my own published papers and also of those Medical Research Council trials with which I have myself been most closely concerned.

To the gratitude that I have expressed above to my co-authors and to the Medical Research Council I must add my thanks to the various editors of journals and others who have given me permission to reproduce these papers. For this courtesy and aid I am much indebted to the Director of the National Institutes of Health of the Public Health Service of the U.S.A., the Council of the Royal Institute of Public Health and Hygiene (for permission to include my Harben lectures in full), the Controller of H.M. Stationery Office, and the editors, or honorary editors, of the *British Journal of Industrial Medicine*, the *British Journal of Preventive and Social Medicine*, the *British Medical Bulletin*, the *New England Journal of Medicine*, the *Proceedings of the Royal Society of Medicine* and the *Quarterly Journal of Medicine*. Finally, my gratitude to the Editor of the *British Medical Journal* calls for a sentence to itself since as many as 14 of the 25 papers here presented first appeared in its pages.

AUSTIN BRADFORD HILL

August, 1962

CONTENTS

PART III

THE EPIDEMIOLOGICAL APPROACH

PART I

CLINICAL TRIAL OF TREATMENT

CHAPTER 1

THE PHILOSOPHY OF THE CLINICAL TRIAL

TAKING the expression 'clinical trial' in its widest possible sense—that is, to cover the test of any therapeutic procedure applied to a sick person—it is obvious that the clinical trial must be as old as medicine itself. Even the witch-doctor trying out for the first time a new and nauseating compound must surely, like Alice nibbling at the mushroom in Wonderland, have murmured to himself 'which way?'—though he would no doubt have concealed his anxiety from his patient with the customary bedside manner. Such personal observations of a handful of patients, acutely made and accurately recorded by the masters of clinical medicine have been, and will continue to be, fundamental to the progress of medicine. Of that, however statistically minded this age may be or may become, there can be no doubt whatever. What *can* happen, what *does* exist, quite regardless of the *frequency* of occurrence and irrespective of causation or association, may be observed even on a sample of one. For instance, as I have stressed elsewhere, if

'we were to use a new drug upon one proven case of acute leukaemia and the patient made an immediate and indisputable recovery, should we not have a result of the most profound importance. The reason underlying our acceptance of merely one patient as illustrating a remarkable event—not necessarily of cause and effect—is that long and wide experience has shown that in respect of acute leukaemia human beings are *not* variable. They one and all fail to make immediate and indisputable recoveries. They one and all die. Therefore although it would clearly be most unwise upon this one case to pass from the particular to the general, it would be sheer madness not to accept the evidence presented by it' (Hill, 1952).

There is not, therefore, in my view, the unbridgeable gap between the statistical and the clinical approach that some persons seem to observe or would wish to create.

On the other hand one has to remember that in many respects the reactions of human beings to most diseases are, under any circumstances, extremely variable. They do not all behave uniformly and

Reprinted from *The National Institutes of Health Annual Lectures*—1953, Washington, D.C.

decisively. They vary, and that is where the trouble begins. 'What the doctor saw' with one, two, or three patients may be both acutely noted and accurately recorded; but what he saw is not necessarily related to what he did. The assumption that it is so related, with a handful of patients, perhaps mostly recovering, perhaps mostly dying, must, not infrequently, give credit where no credit is due, or condemn when condemnation is unjust.

The field of medical observation, it is necessary to remember, is often narrow in the sense that no one doctor will treat many cases in a short space of time; it is wide in the sense that a great many doctors may each treat a few cases. Thus, with a somewhat ready assumption of cause and effect and, equally, a neglect of the laws of chance, the literature becomes filled with conflicting cries and claims, assertions and counterassertions. It is thus, for want of an adequately controlled test, that various forms of treatment have, in the past, become unjustifiably, even sometimes harmfully, established in everyday medical practice. To take a specific instance, to what extent do the salicylates benefit the patient with rheumatic fever? They were introduced for that purpose very many years ago, yet even today doubt still prevails.

It is this belief, or perhaps state of unbelief, that has led in the last few years to a wider development in therapeutics of the more deliberately experimental approach. That development has, of course, been overwhelmingly reinforced by the phenomenal production of one new treatment after another—with the modern antibiotics and drugs. With so many competing claimants to the throne and, no doubt, more than one young pretender amongst them, there can often be no other answer than a designed and accurately recorded trial of strength.

AN EIGHTEENTH CENTURY TRIAL

Such controlled trials are, however, by no means wholly new as the following quotation from the writings of James Lind (1753) will show.

On the 20th of *May*, 1747, I took twelve patients in the scurvy, on board the *Salisbury* at sea. Their cases were as similar as I could have them. They all in general had putrid gums, the spots and lassitude, with weakness of their knees. They lay together in one place, being a proper apartment for the sick in the fore-hold; and had one diet common to all, viz. water-gruel sweetened with sugar in the morning; fresh mutton-broth often times for dinner; at other times puddings, boiled biscuit with sugar etc. And for supper, barley and raisins, rice and currants, sago and wine, or the like. Two of these were ordered each a quart of cyder a day. Two others took twenty-five gutts of *elixir vitriol* three times a day, upon an empty stomach; using a gargle strongly acidulated with it for their mouths. Two others took two spoonfuls of vinegar three times a day, upon an empty stomach; having their gruels and their other food well acidulated with it, as also the gargle for their mouths. Two of the worst patients, with the tendons in the ham rigid (a symptom none of the rest had) were put under a course of sea-water. Of this they drank half a pint every day, and sometimes more or less as it operated, by way of gentle physic. Two others had each two oranges and one lemon given them every day. These they eat with greediness, at different times, upon an empty stomach. They continued but six days under this course, having consumed the quantity that could be spared. The two remaining patients, took the bigness of a nutmeg three times a day of an electuary recommended by a hospital-surgeon, made of garlic, mustard-feed, *rad. raphan*, balsam of *Peru*, and gum myrrh; using for common drink barley-water well acidulated with tamarinds; by a decoction of which, with the addition of *cremor tartar*, they were greatly purged three or four times during the course.

The consequence was, that the most sudden and visible good effects were perceived from the use of the oranges and lemons; one of those who had taken them, being at the end of six days fit for duty. The spots were not indeed at that time quite off his body, nor his gums sound; but without any other medicine, than a gargle of *elixir vitriol*, he became quite healthy before we came into Plymouth, which was on the 16th June. The other was the best recovered of any in his condition; and being now deemed pretty well, was appointed nurse to the rest of the sick.

The essence of any trial, as that classical experiment by Lind in the treatment of the scurvy makes clear, is comparison.

PAST EVENTS AS A STANDARD OF COMPARISON

Occasionally it may be possible to plan a trial with *past* events and observations as this standard of reference. In so doing one is necessarily presuming that everything—except the new treatment under test—has remained constant in time. In other words it is presumed that the type of case brought into the trial, the severity of the illnesses, the ancillary treatment given, and so on, are all just the same as in the past group, or groups, for which there are similar measurements. That does not often happen in practice though an example of that type of trial can occasionally be found. An instance lies in the early tests of the value of streptomycin in the treatment of tuberculous meningitis. With this disease in the pre-streptomycin days a fatal conclusion was invariable. Taking recovery as the criterion of success it was then merely necessary to collect a reasonably large group of proven cases and treat them. If any recoveries took place, that is if the fatality rate fell below its past and invariable 100 per cent, there was clear evidence of some value in the antibiotic in that situation.

Rarely, however, does that dramatic situation, so beloved of the cinema, prevail. More often the question at issue is much more mundane—whether we can reduce a fatality rate of, say, 10 per cent; whether we can speed up the normal rate of recovery of patients by a week or so; whether we can reduce the incidence of complications in a disease. Not much it may seem and yet of considerable importance to patients and doctors. For that purpose impressions of the past are frequently unreliable while past observations are usually insufficient—even if they exist at all. One invariably finds that such past records do not contain all the information that it is thought necessary to collect in the trial of a new treatment, or that it has been recorded in a different form, or at different time intervals, and so on. It is rarely too that one can feel wholly sure that these past observations do relate to a precisely similar group of patients. This is a most difficult thing to prove to one's own satisfaction or to the satisfaction of a critic. Yet it is a *sine qua non* if the comparison is to have any validity.

CONCURRENT 'CONTROLS'

The basic requirement of most clinical trials, therefore, is *concurrent* 'controls'—a group of patients corresponding in their characteristics to the specially treated group but not given that special treatment. Here, however, lies a difficulty that is unique, or almost unique, in the field of scientific experiment. The would-be experimentalist has to contend with an ethical problem. Is it proper to withhold from any patient a treatment that might conceivably give benefit? Admittedly the treatment is unproven—otherwise there would be no need for a trial. But on the other hand there must be some basis for it—whether it be *in vitro*, in animals, or, on a small scale, in patients. There must be some basis to justify a trial at all. The duty of the doctor to his patient and scientific requirements may then clash. The problem will clearly turn in part—often very considerably—upon what is at stake. If it is a question of, say, treating the common cold and seeing whether its departure can be hastened, then the ethics of a rigidly controlled trial perhaps need not disturb us unduly. On the other hand taking a more immediate issue of the day, should one withhold in serious cases of young adult phthisis the present established treatment—streptomycin and PAS, streptomycin and isoniazid, whatever it may be—so as to obtain a true measure of the value of any new drug that the chemist may produce tomorrow? Every proposed trial must according to its own circumstances be weighed in this balance, and one must accept a scientifically imperfect trial rather than run any risks. (It will be well to remember, however, that the risks do not lie all on one side of the balance. What is new is not always the best and, as recent history has shown, is not indeed always devoid of danger.)

There is a second point that flows from this peculiar situation and that is that it may be quite impossible to repeat a trial. Suppose one does some experiment in the laboratory, with animals or in the test-tube, or in an agricultural field plot trial, or in industry. And suppose this experiment gives a suggestive but not a decisive answer. If the matter were important one would repeat the experiment—the initial experiment, indeed, is often planned merely to give a lead and with a repetition or extension in mind. But supposing one does a clinical trial and in the specially treated group 10 per cent die, and in the orthodoxly treated group 25 per cent die. That difference of 15 per cent may lie well below the technical level of significance that statisticians adopt; but 'not significant' is not the equivalent of 'there is no difference'. It corresponds merely to 'not proven'—that there is insufficient material to allow one to dismiss chance as an alternative explanation. In other words, the trial has not clearly proved that the new treatment is likely to be of value; but it has not proved that it is not of value. In such a position the ethics of repeating the trial to make more certain will call for a great deal of hard thinking. It may well be out of the question and an unproven treatment be inevitably accepted.

It follows that the design of a clinical trial should, whenever possible, comprise a scale of events which it is estimated will give a decisive answer, one way or the other, to a basic question—as decisive an answer as can be foreseen or that the statistical approach can ever give. In many cases too, it will be wise to have a relatively simple design. Too often an attempt to answer many questions at one time results in answering none wholly or none clearly. Also, as a statistician one has to remember that the persons who carry out clinical trials are not usually statisticians or biometricians. They are clinicians who, rightly, like to know what they are doing, and why.

and what the answer means. They have not invariably got at their finger tips the latest methods of statistical design and analysis, and an easily understood experiment and an easily understood analysis of results are more likely to ensure their co-operation and interest. This is not necessarily a lowering of the sights. It has been rightly observed that while it does not take a great mind to make simple things complicated it takes a very great mind to make complicated things simple.

THE PATIENTS TO BE ADMITTED

It is with such views in mind that the clinical trials set up by the Medical Research Council in the United Kingdom have so far all been quite simple in their design. The first aim has been to define precisely the type of patient who is to be brought into the trial. This denotes not only such elementary points as age and sex—which are relatively easy to determine—but also what, in fact, the patient is suffering from, which is, quite often, not so simple. In testing, for example, the relative effects of cortisone and ACTH upon patients with rheumatic fever, it is important as a first step to make sure they all have rheumatic fever. The present Anglo-American trial in this field has therefore endeavoured to lay down exact criteria to govern the type of case which is to be entered for that trial. They must have such-and-such signs, they must have such-and-such symptoms.

It is, unfortunately, possible, one should observe, that these necessary criteria may sometimes lead to the exclusion of important cases. For example, the very early case with indefinite signs might, under these criteria, be excluded until the signs have become definite—when it is no longer in those desirable early stages. That is a dilemma which may need careful consideration in setting up a trial.

On the other hand, the groups involved may be made just as narrow or just as wide as one pleases. There is no limitation. The crucial point is that each group be clearly defined, and, as far as possible, be not open to such errors of inclusion, or exclusion, by different observers as must lead to incomparabilities. If the group is too narrow then clearly the generality of the answer reached by means of it must be severely limited; we cannot necessarily pass from the particular to the general—for instance from the advanced case of rapidly progressing phthisis treated in a particular way to the patient with an early lesion. If, on the other hand, the group is made too wide there may be too many variables involved, all of which may influence the course of disease, for example, the grade of disease (the advanced and minimal lesion) the age of the patient and so on. In deciding upon a happy mean between these extremes the wise experimenter will first of all decide *exactly* what it is he hopes to learn from his experiment. Precision in the question is likely to lead to precision in seeking the answer.

THE DIVISION INTO GROUPS

The appropriate cases having been accepted, they are allocated *at random* to one or another of the treatments under study—usually by the use of random sampling numbers. When the body of patients under study is fairly homogeneous—for example the bilateral and rapidly progressing phthisis in the young adult that has been used in Great Britain in a number of trials—then the patients may be allocated according to a predetermined random order to a specific treatment (for instance to streptomycin + PAS; streptomycin + isoniazid; PAS + isoniazid). With more heterogeneous material, for example cases of rheumatic fever, it may be better to 'stratify' the patients, in other words, to put them first into more homogeneous sub-groups (*e.g.*, by age and duration of illness). Within each of these sub-groups they will then be randomly allocated to treatment, *e.g.*, to cortisone, ACTH, or salicylates. In some trials it may be advisable, while randomizing, to ensure that the number of patients on each treatment will be equal at specified points, *e.g.*, that there will be four of them on each of three treatments when the twelfth patient is admitted.

For this purpose we can first list these three treatments, A, B, and C, with the first 12 numbers attached to them, as follows: 1A, 2A, 3A, 4A, 5B, 6B, 7B, 8B, 9C, 10C, 11C, 12C. These numbers 1 to 12 can then be placed in a new and *random* order by taking the order in which they happen to turn up in the columns of a page, or pages, of a book of random sampling numbers. Thus, using Kendall and Babington-Smith's book of numbers, starting (randomly) on page 33 and looking at the last two digits of each column, the order in which the numbers 01 to 12 appear is as follows: 5, 2, 6, 8, 11, 12, 4, 9, 3, 7, 1, and 10. The order of treatments to be used then is B, A, B, B, C, C, A, C, A, B, A, C, the treatments originally attached to the first 12 numbers.

This is merely a trick, and there are many of them, for securing a random order. What matters is the philosophy underlying the tricks—in other words underlying this random allocation of the patients to the treatment groups. It may be summarized thus:

> Strictly adhered to—and I need hardly say that that is a *sine qua non*—this method ensures three things: it ensures that neither our personal idiosyncrasies (our likes or dislikes consciously or unwittingly applied) nor our lack of balanced judgment has entered into the construction of the different treatment groups—the allocation has been outside our control and the groups are, therefore, unbiased; it removes the danger, inherent in an allocation based upon personal judgment, that believing we may be biased in our judgments we endeavour to allow for that bias, to exclude it, and that in so doing we may overcompensate and by thus 'leaning over backwards' introduce a lack of balance from the other direction; and, having used a random allocation, the sternest critic is unable to say when we eventually dash into print that quite probably the groups were differentially biased through our predelictions or through our stupidity. Once it has been decided that a patient is of the right type to be brought into the trial the random method of allocation removes all responsibility from the clinical observer (Hill, 1952).

So, too, that the observer may not be influenced in his decision as to whether or not a patient should be brought into the trial—or be influenced in his decision as to the order in which two patients should enter—it is sometimes wise to deny him any prior knowledge of the treatment which the patient will receive in the event of acceptance. For this purpose the treatment order may be given in sealed numbered envelopes, each to be opened appropriately after a patient has been brought into the trial; alternatively the order may be held by a third party and divulged as each patient is entered.

THE TREATMENT SCHEDULE

In nearly all the large-scale co-operative trials carried out under the Medical Research Council a specific treatment schedule has been laid down in advance (or schedules allowing for variations in the patients in age and weight, etc.) and this must be rigidly followed by the clinicians concerned.

In an earlier paper (Hill, 1951) I wrote that 'if clinicians taking part in a trial are free to vary the treatment just as they will, then it must be clear that no specific question has been propounded and therefore no specific answer can be expected.' Perhaps that statement is a trifle too positive, a trifle too general. Certainly it is often most desirable to lay down a fixed schedule and, except under exceptional, *e.g.*, ethical, circumstances, this schedule should be adhered to by all taking part in the trial. Often very little is known of the possibilities of a new drug—both for good and evil—and in a co-operative trial involving many persons it will usually be better to ask some precise question—what, for example, are the effects of isoniazid and streptomycin given in a particular dosage for a particular length of time. If dozens of people are free to vary the dosage as they think fit, it may be very difficult to extract a clear answer from the experiment.

On the other hand there may well be instances in which the clinician should be allowed to adjust the dosage according to the progress and responses of the patient—to 'individualize' the treatment. That may clearly be the case in dealing with, say, rheumatoid arthritis, under treatment with cortisone. One man's meat is another man's poison. With this disease, therefore, various trials are under way in which the physician may select his treatment over a wide range of dosage and from time to time. This does not necessarily prohibit the use of the customary measures of progress—fever, sedimentation rate, etc. —even though the physician may, of course, base his selected treatment upon their level and variation in time. The question asked of the trial has merely been changed. What after X months are the clinical conditions, the degrees of fever, the levels of the blood sedimentation rate, the X-ray appearances of *two groups* of patients, namely (*a*) a group treated with, say, cortisone, and (*b*) a group treated with, say, salicylates, the treatment having varied within both groups at the will of the clinician? Do they differ? Emphasis must be placed upon the *two groups* for the fundamental point lies there. There is no error so long as the comparison is confined to those two whole groups. We may thereby prove whether what the doctors chose to do with cortisone has given a better average result after X months than what they chose to do with aspirin.

It may be argued that what they chose to do was foolish but that is quite another matter, though such an argument may well favour the adoption of one rigid schedule. It must be argued that no further dissection of the two groups can be made to see how well patients fared on the different régimes of treatment. The physicians have deliberately varied these régimes in accordance with the patient's responses; it is not reasonable, then, to turn round at the end of the trial and observe the responses in relation to the régimes. To measure the effect of different régimes there can be no other way than the setting up of a trial to that end by, as before, randomizing the patients to different régimes.

THE RESULTS OF THE TRIAL

Turning to the results of a clinical trial, we have sought, in those with which I have been concerned, to base them, as far as possible, upon objective measurements. Thus we have noted the level and duration of fever, the level of the sedimentation rate, the presence or absence of infecting organisms, the change in body weight, and so on. Less objective but highly important measurements are to be found in the clinician's detection of, say, heart murmurs and in X-ray pictures. With the latter we have endeavoured to eliminate any possible bias, or any accusation of bias, by having the serial films read and interpreted by an expert, or experts, with no knowledge of the treatment given to any patient.

On the other hand it can be argued and, indeed, has been argued that all these objective measurements are so many 'bits and pieces' and that the addition of 'bits and pieces' does not necessarily make the whole. For example, the patient's sedimentation rate fell to normal, his fever abated, his haemoglobin and white blood count gave no grounds for complaint and his blood pressure was irreproachable. Everything was fine—except that the patient died. What, therefore, one needs, it is said, is the whole judgement of the patient's condition at any time and of its changes—the judgement of the clinician. That may well be true for there is no convincing evidence that the 'bits and pieces' are always sufficient. Sometimes it is possible to set up a trial so that the clinician's judgement is given without him having any knowledge of the treatment given. In that way any possible bias can be removed. Sometimes that technique is quite out of the question. In each instance therefore it must be considered whether clinical intuition and judgement can be brought effectively into the picture, whether, if so, it can be wielded 'blind', whether a 'dummy' treatment is called for. That form of trial clearly raises still more ethical issues—when is it proper to give a patient a 'dummy' treatment, when is it proper for the clinician in charge of the patient not to know the treatment? The answers will clearly depend upon the circumstances of each trial; there can be no rule of thumb.

By whatever procedure the results are measured it is important to remember that they show the comparative reactions of groups. The statistical approach is not concerned with individuals. As a specific example one may take the Medical Research Council's early trials of treatment of acute cases of phthisis in young adults. Of 52 patients treated by bed rest (in the days when supplies of streptomycin were severely limited) only 8 per cent showed considerable radiological improvement after six months. For 59 patients treated with PAS only (20 g. daily), the corresponding figure was 22 per cent. For 53 patients treated with streptomycin and PAS (1 g. and 20 g. daily), it was 51 per cent (Daniels and Hill, 1952). The relative position of the groups is clear. On the average there is a great advantage in a particular procedure; but with the individual we clearly cannot invariably, or even often, predict the upshot or say that a treatment is necessary. But no approach except, perhaps, second sight or crystal-gazing, would at present appear to answer that problem.

CONCLUSION

In summary, the philosophy of the clinical trial lies rather in the experimental versus the observational approach. Thus, in its rigorous form it demands concurrent controls on an orthodox treatment. It demands replicates, that is, that the experiment should include a number of different patients, sufficient to measure with reasonable precision what we seek to measure; such numbers will be dependent upon the variability of the responses and the magnitude of the differences observed between the groups. It demands an experimental design that will ensure, as far as possible, that groups of similar characteristics are built up, differing only in their treatments. Within this framework it demands the random allocation of patients to one or another group so that no personal bias can effect construction. Lastly it demands to the greatest possible extent objective measurements of the results and the use of subjective assessments only under a strict and efficient control which will ensure an absence of bias. Sometimes those requirements can be met; sometimes it is quite impossible. Sometimes we must accept that limitation and be content in this particular field with something much less than the best. But the basic ideas of the statistical-experimental approach in the trial of new (or old) treatments are of quite general applicability. It happens that so far the method has been almost entirely confined to acute diseases of short duration or to the acute phases of diseases of long duration. But that is because for one reason, such diseases are more easily observed, and therefore more appropriate to pioneering ventures, and secondly because the modern forms of treatment have been largely directed against them. There is, however, no reason why the method should not be applied to a chronic disease; in fact, the present trial of cortisone and ACTH in rheumatic fever does look far beyond the initial acute phase of the illness. It envisages a follow-up for at least several years to observe the incidence and nature of residual heart disease in the various groups. An efficient organization and a philosophical and patient outlook are the only extra features called for.

Further, there is no true basis at all for the suggestion that this experimental technique should be usually limited 'on grounds of cost and labour' to 'treatments which give reasonable promise of importance, that is, to those which are applicable either to a serious disease or to large numbers of patients' (Medical Research Council, 1952). This is loose thinking and its wide acceptance would be lamentable. The statistical approach, and the ideas lying behind it, are quite general. Application of the method does not necessarily call for the widely organized trial of the type sponsored by the British Medical Research Council; it does not necessarily demand large numbers; it does not necessarily lie beyond the financial means or intellectual capabilities of the individual. The technique of the controlled therapeutic trial is applicable on any scale, in the numerically unimportant diseases as well as in the important diseases, and in the slight misfortunes that befall mankind as well as in the more lethal. That is already becoming apparent in the literature (Sevitt, Bull, Cruickshank, Jackson and Lowbury, 1952; Fisher and Whitfield, 1952). With its more extensive, but careful, use, that same literature may in time become slightly less cluttered up by the seemingly interminable arguments regarding therapeutic procedures.

REFERENCES

Daniels, Marc, and Hill, A. Bradford (1952). *Brit. med. J.* **i**, 1162.
Fisher, O. D., and Whitfield, C. R. (1952). *Brit med. J.* **ii**, 864.
Hill, A. Bradford (1951) *Brit. med. Bull.* **7**, 278.
Hill, A. Bradford (1952). *New Engl. J. Med.* **247**, 113.
Lind, James (1753). *A Treatise of the Scurvey*. Reprinted 1953. Edinburgh: University Press.
Medical Research Council (1952). *Annual Report, 1951–52*. London: Medical Research Council.
Sevitt, S., Bull, J. P., Cruickshank, C. N. D., Jackson, D. M., and Lowbury, B. M. (1952). *Brit. med. J.* **ii**, 57.

CHAPTER 2

THE CLINICAL TRIAL—I

'THERAPEUTICS', said Professor Pickering in his Presidential Address to the Section of Experimental Medicine and Therapeutics of the Royal Society of Medicine,

'is the branch of medicine that, by its very nature, should be experimental. For if we take a patient afflicted with a malady, and we alter his conditions of life, either by dieting him, or by putting him to bed, or by administering to him a drug, or by performing on him an operation, we are performing an experiment. And if we are scientifically minded we should record the results. Before concluding that the change for better or for worse in the patient is due to the specific treatment employed, we must ascertain whether the result can be repeated a significant number of times in similar patients, whether the result was merely due to the natural history of the disease or in other words to the lapse of time, or whether it was due to some other factor which was necessarily associated with the therapeutic measure in question. And if, as a result of these procedures, we learn that the therapeutic measure employed produces a significant, though not very pronounced, improvement, we would experiment with the method, altering dosage or other detail to see if it can be improved. This would seem the procedure to be expected of men with six years of scientific training behind them. But it has not been followed. Had it been done we should have gained a fairly precise knowledge of the place of individual methods of therapy in disease, and our efficiency as doctors would have been enormously enhanced' (Pickering, 1949).

It would be difficult to put the case for the clinical trial more cogently or more clearly. It is the gradual development of this attitude of mind coupled with the concurrent introduction of one antibiotic, one modern drug, after another, that has led in the past few years to the highly organized and efficiently controlled therapeutic trial of new remedies. For instance, as Marc Daniels (1950) wrote of one field, 'it is now becoming generally accepted that scientific appraisement of new drugs in tuberculosis is a fundamental necessity, but it is hard to realize that this particular progress has been made almost entirely within the past five years'. Its absence in the past led, he suggests, to the many years of inconclusive work on gold therapy, while Pickering stresses the much earlier and positively dangerous

Reprinted from *British Medical Bulletin*, 1951, **7**, 278.

methods of therapeutics, such as blood-letting, purging and starvation, of which the dangers could not have failed to be exposed by comparative observations, impartially made. In more recent years much work has, of course, been done on the efficacy of methods of treatment, *e.g.*, the use of artificial pneumothorax in pulmonary tuberculosis. But many of these studies, as was pointed out in the review of fifty years of medicine published by the *British Medical Journal* (1950), suffer from the handicap that no comparative observations were made, sometimes for ethical reasons, but too often because their importance was not appreciated.

IMPERFECT CONTRASTS

As a result of this situation very many second-best, or even much inferior, 'controls' have been put forward. Thus the following ways and means have been used from time to time, and are still used:

(*a*) The treatment of patients with a particular disease is unplanned but naturally varies according to the decision of the physicians in charge. To some patients a specific drug is given, to others it is not. The progress and prognosis of these patients are then compared. But in making this comparison in relation to the treatment the fundamental assumption is made—and must be made—that the two groups are equivalent in all respects relevant to their progress, except for the difference in treatment. It is, however, almost invariably impossible to believe that this is so. Drugs are not ordered by doctors at random, but in relation to a patient's condition when he first comes under observation and also to the subsequent progress of his disease. The two groups are therefore not remotely comparable and more often than not the group given the specific drug is heavily weighted by the more severely ill. No conclusion as to its efficacy can possibly be drawn.

(*b*) The same objections must be made to the contrasting of volunteers for a treatment with those who do not volunteer, or between those who accept and those who refuse. There can be no knowledge that such groups are comparable; and the onus lies wholly, it may justly be maintained, upon the experimenter to prove that they are comparable, before his results can be accepted. Particularly, perhaps, with a surgical operation the patients who accept may be very different from those who refuse.

(*c*) The contrast of one physician, or one hospital, using a particular form of treatment, with another physician, or hospital, not adopting that treatment, or adopting it to a lesser degree, is fraught with much the same difficulty—apart from the practicability of being able to find such a situation (with, it must be noted, the same forms of ancillary treatment). It must be proved that the patients are alike in relevant group characteristics, *i.e.*, age, sex, social class, severity of illness, before they can be fairly compared and their relative progress, or lack of progress, interpreted. That proof is clearly hard to come by.

(*d*) The 'historical' control relies upon a contrast of past records of the pre-drug days with those of the present treated patients. Of the former group 10 per cent, say, died and 90 per cent recovered while for the present group the ratios are 5 and 95 per cent. If everything else remained constant in time, this comparison would clearly be valid. But does it? The specific treatment may be given only to certain patients and thus a selected group is being contrasted with the previous unselected group. Or, if all patients are given the treatment, then we must be sure that there has been no change in those presenting themselves for treatment—a change that the treatment itself may sometimes promote, *e.g.*, by bringing in the intractable case with renewed hope of cure. We must be sure that there has been no change in the severity of the disease itself. We are invariably faced with the question: Were these two groups fundamentally similar? The answer is rarely certain.

(*e*) Lastly, the worker may have no controls at all but may rely upon his clinical impressions and general knowledge of the past. Sometimes, not often, controls are indeed unnecessary. If in the past a disease has invariably and rapidly led to death there can be no possible need for controls to prove a change in the fatality rate. Thus the trial of streptomycin in tuberculous meningitis needed no control group. Given a precise and certain identification of the case, the success of treatment could be measured against the past 100 per cent fatal conclusion. No controls, too, are essential to prove the value of a drug such as penicillin which quickly reveals dramatic effects in the treatment of a disease. Such dramatic effects occurring on a large scale and in many hands cannot be long overlooked.

Unfortunately these undeniable producers of dramatic effects are the exception rather than the rule, even in these halcyon days of the antibiotics. Also, it must be noted that the position has been reached in which we are often no longer contrasting older orthodox methods of treatment with a potent modern drug, but one modern drug with another. To prove that a fatality rate of the order of 60 per cent (*e.g.*, meningococcal meningitis) has fallen to 15 per cent is a very much easier task than to prove that with a new treatment the 15 per cent can be reduced to 10 per cent. Even a poor clinical trial could hardly destroy the evidence of the former profound change; it may take a very efficient one to prove the latter. Yet, in the saving of life, that improvement is a very important change.

For such reasons, we have come to the highly organized controlled clinical trial of today.

AIMS AND ETHICS

The first step in such a trial is to decide precisely what it is hoped to prove, and secondly to consider whether these aims can be ethically fulfilled. It need hardly be said that the latter consideration is paramount and must never, on any scientific grounds whatever, be lost sight of. If a treatment cannot ethically be withheld then clearly no controlled trial can be instituted. All the more important is it, therefore, that a trial should be begun at the earliest opportunity, before there is inconclusive though suggestive evidence of the value of the treatment. Not infrequently, however, clinical workers publish favourable results on three or four cases and conclude their article by suggesting that this is the method of choice, or that what is now required is a trial on an adequate scale. They do not seem to realize that by their very publication they have vastly increased the difficulties of that trial or, indeed, made it impossible. For if it be a question of recovery or death, then the ethical situation produced by even inconclusive evidence may at times be such that the treatment cannot be withheld. It can, of course, be argued that more lives will be saved in the long run than are lost in the trial, but such an argument must, in my view, be advanced with very great caution. On the other hand, where life and death (or serious after-effects) are not at issue the problem is clearly eased. It is also eased, more often than not, by the state of our ignorance. For, frequently, we have no scientific evidence that a particular treatment will benefit the patients and, as Pickering points out, we are often, willy-nilly, experimenting upon them. It may well be unethical, therefore, *not* to institute a proper trial.

Returning to the aims of the trial, it is essential that these should be laid down in every detail at the outset. For example, the object in one of the Medical Research Council's trials of streptomycin was to measure the effect of this drug upon respiratory tuberculosis (Medical Research Council, 1948). This illness may, however, denote many different things: the minimal lesions just acquired by the patient, the advanced and progressive disease that offers a poor prognosis, or the chronic and relatively inactive state. Equally, its course, its rapidity of development or the recovery of the patient may differ with age, whether early childhood, adolescence or old age. The question, therefore, must be made more precise. It was, in fact, made precise by restricting the trial to 'acute progressive bilateral pulmonary tuberculosis of presumably recent origin, bacteriologically proved, unsuitable for collapse therapy, age group 15 to 25 (later extended to 30)'. Thus it was ensured that all patients in the trial would have a similar type of disease and, to avoid having to make allowances for the effect of forms of therapy other than mere bed-rest, that the type of disease was one not suitable for such other forms. In such cases the chances of spontaneous regression were small but the lesion, on the other hand, offered some prospect of action by an effective chemotherapeutic agent. In short, the questions asked of the trial were deliberately limited and these 'closely defined features were considered indispensable, for it was realized that no two patients have an identical form of the disease, and it was desired to eliminate as many of the obvious variations as possible'.

This planning, as already pointed out, is a fundamental feature of the successful trial. To start out upon a trial with all and sundry included, and with the hope that the results can be sorted out statistically in the end, is to court disaster. It is, of course, usually possible to sort out the results by segregating them in groups according to, say, age and sex; but with a trial of the customary size it will almost invariably be found that the numbers in such sub-groups are quite insufficient to answer the many questions put to them.

As a general principle, therefore, it must be emphasized that it is wise to limit the questions strictly to a few and to be absolutely precise upon those few. The loss in so doing lies, of course, in the fact that the answers are limited to very specific questions and clearly cannot be generalized upon outside their field.

THE CONSTRUCTION OF GROUPS

The next step in the setting up of the trial is the allocation of the patients to be included in the treatment and the non-treatment groups (or to more than two groups if more than one treatment is under test). It should be noted that by non-treatment is not implied *no* treatment. Almost always, the question at issue is: does this particular form of treatment offer more than the usual orthodox treatment? The contrast is not, and usually cannot ethically be, with no treatment. The aim, therefore, is to allocate the patients to the 'treatment' and 'control' groups in such a way that the two groups are initially equivalent in all respects relevant to the inquiry. Individuals, it may be noted, are not necessarily equivalent; it is a group reaction that is under study. In many trials this allocation has been successfully made by putting patients, as they present themselves, alternately into the treatment and control groups. Such a method may, however, be insufficiently random if the admission or non-admission of a case to the trial turns upon a difficult assessment of the patient and if the clinician involved knows whether the patient, if accepted, will pass to the treatment or control group. By such knowledge he may be biased, consciously or unconsciously, in his acceptance or rejection; or through fear of being biased, his judgement may be influenced. The latter can be just as important a source of error as the former but is more often overlooked. For this reason, recent British trials have avoided the alternating method and adopted the use of random sampling numbers; in addition, the allocation of the patient to treatment or control is kept secret from the clinician until after he has made his decision upon the patient's admission. Thus he can proceed to that decision—admission or rejection—without any fear of bias. One such technique has been for the statistician to provide the clinician with a set of numbered and sealed envelopes. After each patient has been brought into the trial the appropriately numbered envelope is opened (no. 1 for the first patient, no. 2 for the second and so on) and the group to which the patient is to go, treatment (T) or control (C), is given upon a slip inside. Alternatively a list showing the order to be followed is prepared in advance, *e.g.*, T, T, C, T, C, C, T, T, T, C, etc., and held confidentially, the clinician in charge being instructed after each admission has been made.

A further extension of this method is frequently made, to ensure a final equality of the groups to be compared. Separate sets of envelopes, or of lists, are provided for sub-groups of the patients to be admitted, *e.g.*, for each sex separately, for specific age-groups or for special centres of treatment, and in each sub-group the number of T cases is made equal to the number of C. Thus we may have allocation lists, or envelopes based upon them, as follows:

TABLE **2,** 1

Patient's number in each sub-group	Male		Female	
	20–29 years	30–39 years	20–29 years	30–39 years
1	T	T	C	T
2	C	T	T	C
3	C	T	T	C
4	T	C	T	T
5	T	C	C	C
6	C	T	C	T
7	T	C	C	T
etc.				

It is often argued that these fine sub-divisions are unwarranted, since the numbers within the sub-groups will finally be far too small to justify any comparisons. This overlooks, however, the fundamental aim of the technique which, since the trial is not being confined to a narrowly defined group, as discussed previously (section 2), is to ensure that when the *total* groups, T and C, are compared they have within themselves equivalent numbers of persons with given characteristics. Thus in the above example when the T and C experiences as a whole need to be compared, it will be found that there are eight males and seven females in the T group and six males and seven females in the C group, and seven T and seven C persons are aged 20–29, eight T and six C are aged 30–39. On the whole, therefore, the T and C groups have been automatically equalized, a result which —and particularly with small numbers—would not necessarily have been achieved with a single allocation list which ignored age, sex and place. With large numbers, equality of characteristics in the two groups will result in the long run; with small numbers, it is wise to ensure equality as much as possible by design.

Another technique, of very great value when circumstances allow it, is to keep the clinician uninformed throughout the trial as to the actual treatment given—drug or placebo. Thus, he can make his assessment of the patient's progress and condition uninfluenced by any such knowledge. This method was used in the Medical Research Council's clinical trials of antihistaminic drugs in the prevention and treatment of the common cold (Medical Research Council, 1950a). Here it was important to make sure that no bias should enter into the assessment of the results, and essential that neither patient nor clinician should be aware whether antihistamine tablets or control tablets had been given in a particular case. To ensure this result, numbered boxes of tablets and similarly numbered record sheets were issued to the centres, each box to be used in conjunction with the appropriate sheet. Box no. 1, for instance, might contain anti-histamine tablets, box no. 2 the control tablets and so on, as deter-mined beforehand from randomly constructed lists. Neither box had any label indicating its contents. In the final analysis, therefore, record sheet no. 1 must relate to the antihistaminic group, record sheet no. 2 to the comparative group, record sheet no. 3 to the com-parative group and so on. But neither patient nor investigator in the field could know that.

THE TREATMENT

Before the clinical and co-operative trial is actually set in train close consideration must be given to two aspects: (a) what is to be the treatment, and (b) what are to be the measures of its effects?

On the first point it is essential that the dosage to be used in the trial, or other details of treatment, should be specifically laid down beforehand and to the greatest possible extent adhered to. If clinicians taking part in a trial are free to vary the treatment just as they will, then it must be clear that no specific question has been propounded and therefore no specific answer can be expected. It must be con-sidered whether such a trial is worth while at all. It is, too, quite out of the question to compare, one with another, the results given by the various treatments adopted by the clinicians. For these treatments would not have been given randomly but often in accordance with the condition and progress of the patient, e.g., those given an in-creased dosage might well be the more severely ill, while those progressing favourably receive a lower dosage. This is a fundamental point. The contrasting of dosages can come only from a specifically designed trial and not from the haphazard production of a trial designed for a broader or other purpose. In the long run, therefore, it is preferable to have a standard treatment procedure and to abide by it.

Consideration must also be given to the treatment of the control group. In such a trial as that of streptomycin in phthisis in young adults (quoted above), involving frequent injections of the drug, it would be quite impossible to institute any corresponding procedure for the controls. They were, therefore, treated as they would have been in the past, precautions being taken that neither those treated nor the controls knew they were part of a controlled trial.

On the other hand, in the treatment of the common cold a dummy treatment was essential, for one cannot invite volunteers for a trial, obviously keep half as 'guinea-pigs', and then hope for co-operation and good records. The fact that they would be taking part in a trial was therefore made clear to the participants but they were not told which treatment they would receive. The importance of the control treatment in this experiment is shown by the results: *e.g.*, of colds of under one day's duration at the start of treatment, 13.4 per cent were cured, and 68.2 per cent cured or improved, on the second day following administration of the antihistamine compound; but with the placebo, the corresponding figures were 13.9 and 64.7 per cent.

Another example of the necessity for a control treatment is shown by Quin, Mason and Knowelden (1950) in their study of the clinical assessment of rapidly acting agents in rheumatoid arthritis. Following the administration of deoxycortone and ascorbic acid, one patient out of 43 observed a marked reduction in pain within an hour and 12 observed a moderate reduction. Of the same 43 patients, however, one of them observed a marked reduction in pain and 11 a moderate reduction after the injection of saline. In most cases, therefore, a placebo treatment is desirable and its practicability must be considered.

MEASURING THE RESULTS

One great advantage of a placebo which is used in such a way that the clinician cannot recognize it is that the clinical impression can be given full weight in the analysis. If, in other words, two groups of patients are being treated, one T and one C, and the clinician does not know the components of these groups, then he can without fear or favour assess the progress and condition of every patient. And thus clinical opinion, as well as more strictly objective measures, can be used to assess the result—a very valuable addition to the trial.

In the adoption of other measures of the effect of treatment, detailed planning must as usual play its part. Before the trial is set under way it must be laid down, for example, precisely when and how temperatures will be taken, when full clinical examinations will be made and what will be specifically recorded, how often and at what intervals X-rays will be taken. Standard record forms must be drawn up, and uniformity in completing them stressed. Unless these rules and regulations are well kept and observed by the clinicians in charge of the trial, many and serious difficulties arise in the final analysis of the results, *e.g.*, if some X-ray pictures were not taken at the required monthly interval, or if some erythrocyte sedimentation rate (E.S.R.) tests were not made. In fact every departure from the design of the experiment lowers its efficiency to some extent; too many departures may wholly nullify it. The individual may often think 'it won't matter if I do this (or don't do that) just once'; he forgets that many other individuals may have the same idea.

It is fundamental, too, that the same care in measurement and recording be given to both groups. The fact that some are specially treated and some are not is wholly irrelevant. Unless the reactions of the two groups are equally noted and recorded, any comparisons of them must clearly break down. For the same reason, if a follow-up of patients is involved it must be applied with equal vigour to all. Experience in recent trials has shown the advantage of making, whenever possible, 'blind' assessments of the patient's condition or progress. Thus in the trial of streptomycin in young adult phthisis the chest radiographs of all patients were viewed, and changes assessed, by three members of a special radiological panel working separately and not knowing whether the films came from treated or control patients. The setting up of a team whose members worked independently gave an increased accuracy to the final result; the 'blind' assessment removed any possibility of bias or over-compensation for bias. Similarly in the trial of deoxycortone and ascorbic acid one worker injected the patient with the compound or with saline, the other, not knowing the nature of that injection, assessed or measured the results of compound or saline in the patient. Such a technique, faithfully observed, removes all possibility of clinical enthusiasm (or scepticism) producing the result desired. It should invariably be considered in every therapeutic trial.

REPORTING THE RESULTS

A high standard must be set in reporting the results of clinical trials, particularly, as Daniels (1950) suggests, in these 'pioneering investigations' which 'may in many ways serve as a model and lesson to future investigators'. He rightly lays down that 'just as in a laboratory experiment report, it is at least as important to describe the techniques employed and the conditions in which the investigation was conducted, as to give the detailed statistical analysis of results'. In short, a statement must be made of the type of patient brought into the trial and of the definitions governing the selection of a case; the process of allocating patients to treatment and control groups should be exactly defined; the treatment should be precisely stated; the assessments and measurements used must be clearly set out and it must be shown whether they were made 'blind' or with a knowledge of the treatment given. In other words, the whole plan and its working out should be laid before the reader so that he may see precisely what was done.

Secondly, even if a random allocation of patients has been made to the treatment and control groups, an analysis must be made to show the equality of the groups at the start of the trial. With large numbers such an equality will almost invariably be present but with small numbers the play of chance will not invariably bring it about. It is important therefore to see whether there is an equality or an inequality for which allowance must be made (*e.g.*, by sub-division of the records or by standardization). In the trial of the antihistamine drug in the treatment of the common cold, for example, there were 579 persons given the drug and 577 a placebo. Of the former group 34.8 per cent had had symptoms for less than a day before treatment, of the latter 30.0 per cent; 55.4 per cent of the former had a blocked nose as a presenting symptom, and 53.2 per cent of the latter; 7.6 per cent of the former and 8.0 per cent of the latter said at entry that they 'felt ill' (Medical Research Council, 1950a).

With the much smaller-scale trial of streptomycin in young adult phthisis a reasonable degree of equality was also reached. Of 55 patients in the treatment group 54 per cent were in poor general condition at the start of the trial; of 52 patients in the control group 46 per cent were in a similar condition. Twenty and 17 respectively were desperately ill, 32 and 30 had large or multiple cavities, 19 and

19 showed radiological evidence of segmental atelectasis (Medical Research Council, 1948). To such an extent can a carefully designed and deliberately limited inquiry bring about equality in even quite small groups. But that it has achieved that aim must be shown. (See also the Medical Research Council's trial (1950b) of streptomycin and para-aminosalicylic acid in young adult phthisis and Daniels, 1951).

The experience of co-operative trials in Great Britain has been wholly in favour of the protocols being centralized for analysis and a report drawn up by one or two persons for submission to all the principal investigators. Revision is then made in the light of their comments. It is too much to hope that individual investigators at numerous centres can carry out a precisely uniform analysis and report in precisely the same terms. Central analysis safeguards the standards, and with its larger numbers and wider view may also suggest matters of importance which would be overlooked at points on the periphery, each with its handful of cases.

GENERAL CONCLUSIONS

One advantage of the co-operative trial is that sufficient numbers of patients can be treated uniformly, though in different centres, to give a precise answer to the questions at issue. Statistically speaking, most diseases are seen relatively infrequently by any one physician working in any one centre. The personal experience is therefore frequently too slender to allow a safe passage from the particular to the general. For instance, Spence and Court (1950) show that of 127 children with acute intussusception seen by 121 family doctors in Newcastle-upon-Tyne in the years 1944–9, 15 doctors saw three or more cases, while 50 doctors saw none, 44 saw only one case, and 12 saw two. On the other hand the well-controlled and well-reported experiment does not, as is sometimes thought, necessarily demand vast numbers. Indeed as Margaret Merrell has wisely observed: 'large numbers in themselves are worse than useless if the groups are not comparable, since they encourage confidence in an erroneous opinion' (Merrell, 1949). If the groups are strictly comparable, then often a total of 50 to 100 cases, and sometimes very much less, will provide decisive evidence. (The actual numbers must, of course, depend upon the problem at stake and upon the magnitude of difference between the treatment and control groups that is to be expected or is actually observed.)

On the other hand it appears sometimes to be thought that there is some necessary antagonism between the clinical assessment of a few cases and the 'cold mathematics' of the statistically analysed trial dealing with a larger number. It is difficult to see how in fact there can be any such antagonism. The clinical assessment, or the clinical impression, must itself be numerical in the long run—that patients are reacting in a way different from the way the clinician believes was customary in the past. In the controlled trial an attempt is made to record and systematize those impressions (and other measurements) and to add them up. Standard errors, alarming as they may be to some persons, are wholly subsidiary, being merely tests, when the answer has been reached, as to whether it is safe to generalize from that answer. The result reached is, of course, a group result, namely, that *on the average* patients do better on this treatment than on that. No one can say how one particular patient will react. But that, clearly, is just as true (to say the least of it) of the approach *via* clinical impressions and two cases, as it is *via* a controlled and objectively measured trial and 100 cases.

In general it will be seen that the essence of a successful controlled clinical trial lies in its minutiae—in a painstaking, and sometimes very dull, attention to every detail. As Lord Macmillan (1937) wrote in another field (the art of advocacy), 'all this, you may say, is very elementary, not to say menial. But, believe me, it is of real importance. Attention to these apparently trivial details has a much greater effect on the fortunes of a case than is imagined'. So it is here, and one cannot over-emphasize it. It is often, indeed, that very lack of attention to detail and the resulting lack of uniformity, that makes it impossible to draw comparisons between the results of one local centre and another. As Daniels (1950) has said, for clinicians to be 'willing to merge their individuality sufficiently to take part in group investigations, to accept only patients approved by an independent team, to conform to an agreed plan of treatment, and to submit results for analysis by an outside investigator involves a considerable sacrifice'. But the sacrifice is being made on an increasing scale. The reason is, that it can be seen to lead rapidly to those therapeutic advances for which Pickering pleaded.

REFERENCES

British Medical Journal (1950), **i,** 68.

Daniels, M. (1950). *Amer. Rev. Tuberc.* **61,** 751.

Daniels, M. (1951), *Brit. med. Bull.* **7,** 320.

Macmillan (1937). *Law and other Things.* Cambridge: University Press.

Medical Research Council, Streptomycin in Tuberculosis Trials Committee (1948). *Brit. med. J.* **ii,** 769.

Medical Research Council, Special Committee (1950a). *Brit. med. J.* **ii,** 425.

Medical Research Council, Streptomycin in Tuberculosis Trials Committee and the British Tuberculosis Association Research Committee (1950b). *Brit. med. J.* **ii,** 1073.

Merrell, M. (1949). *Bull. Johns Hopk. Hosp.* **85,** 221.

Pickering, G. W. (1949). *Proc. R. Soc. Med.* **42,** 229.

Quin, C. E., Mason, R. M., and Knowelden, J. (1950). *Brit. med. J.* **ii,** 810.

Spence, J., and Court, D. (1950). *Brit. med. J.* **ii,** 920.

Chapter 3

THE CLINICAL TRIAL—II

IT is with mixed feelings that I stand, a layman, before the medical faculty of one of the world's most famous universities. In the past century, or more, statisticians have, it is true, been recognized as having a right of entry to the field of public health, and to its related sciences of epidemiology and preventive medicine. They have been closely associated with medical officers of health. They have worked with all who have been concerned with the promotion and maintenance of the wellbeing of the community. But it is clear that the health of the community—the group—essentially requires the statistical approach. For we are concerned with the herd rather than with the individual and so we need community measures. I might hope to speak on matters of mutual interest to your School of Public Health. I might, of course, prove boring to it, but I should speak as a bore, not as a stranger. I should promote sleep rather than catcalls; that belief gives me courage. What, however, of your university's medical school? Dare the statistician now pass from the well-tilled (perhaps I ought to say well-drained) fields of public health to those more exclusive upland meadows in which are practised the arts of the clinician—arts that appear to cultivate the individual approach and sometimes even an air of infallibility? It is a bold step. In my own country I have been fortunate enough to be able to take it and can, even at the worst, still exclaim, with the poet Henley, 'my head is bloody but unbowed'. Over a fairly wide expanse of clinical medicine in Great Britain the statistical approach has been accepted as useful; it is being increasingly applied. But here, like Ruth 'amid the alien corn' I stand, if not tearfully, at least a trifle fearfully.

Before setting out I sought support in an anonymous article on Statistics in Medicine that formed part of the *British Medical Journal's* instructive review of the progress of British medicine in the first half of the present century. Between statistician and clinician there had been, it confesses, antagonism: 'The medical man charged

Reprinted from the *New England Journal of Medicine*, 1952, **247,** 113.

with responsibility for the patient was contemptuous of the statistician's fundamental approach through the group; and the statistician took a jaundiced view of the conclusions light-heartedly drawn by the practitioner from a handful of cases without allowance for the play of chance '. (Anon., 1950.) The only comforting thing about that statement is its use—an apparently deliberate use—of the past tense. Has, then, the antagonism gone? I believe it is undoubtedly very much less than it used to be. But I could not lay my hand upon my heart and say it has vanished wholly. There are still noticeable from time to time, in medical journals and at meetings of medical societies, various kinds and degrees of mutual misunderstanding and even scorn. Before launching out upon the philosophy of a clinical trial, I think it would be well to consider them.

MISUNDERSTANDINGS AND MISTAKES

The Statistician

Let me first place in the dock those of my own profession. The statistician, and particularly those not in close contact with clinical medicine, may tend to forget that the physician's first duty is to his patient—to do all in his power to save the patient's life and restore him, as rapidly as possible, to health. That fundamental and ethical duty must never be overlooked—though with the introduction of better, brighter and ever more toxic drugs, and with the wide prevalence of surgical procedures such as tonsillectomy, the onlooker may perhaps with good reason sometimes ask the clinician 'are you sure you know where that duty lies?' It seems to me sometimes to be unethical *not* to experiment, not to carry out a controlled clinical trial. But we must never forget the issues. Basically, too, the statistician is concerned with things that can be counted. 'In so far as things, persons, are unique or ill-defined, statistics are meaningless . . . ; in so far as things are similar and definite . . . they can be counted and new statistical facts are born . . . Our arithmetic is useless, unless we are counting the right things. (Bartlett, 1951.) Clearly, until that happy day arrives when every clinician is his own statistician, we need a close collaboration to ensure that the statistician *is* counting the right things—for instance, that he is devising satisfactory groups into which patients can be classified, and that he is setting up the most appropriate and definite measures of the patient's condition before and after treatment. I have seen friction arise through the statistician's inability to do this through a lack of knowledge of the medical problem and of its details.

The art of applied statistics is, needless to day, compounded of two things—a knowledge of statistical methodology and a wide and detailed knowledge of the data to which that methodology is to be applied. I should hesitate to allocate a relative importance to each of these two aspects, but I hold firmly that both are essential and that the use of the methodology, however erudite, without a parallel and exact knowledge of the data under study can be, indeed is likely to be, most dangerous. It follows that the statistician, if he is to play his proper part in a clinical trial must be in it 'up to his neck'; he must be in it from its very start—that is, at the initial planning level. If he is a layman he must endeavour to learn and understand its medical as well as its statistical aspects—and should, I believe, be as intensely absorbed and interested in the one as in the other. As a corollary he should almost invariably decline to be brought in at the end of a trial merely to sort out and add up the results or, even worse, to calculate as a kind of super bookmaker, the odds for or against some event of whose pros and cons he is largely ignorant and about which he could not care less. Too often, he makes the mistake of accepting such a task. In short, the statistically designed clinical trial is above all a work of collaboration between clinician and statistician, and that collaboration must prevail from start to finish.

Finally, in my indictment of the statistician, I would argue that he may tend to be a trifle too scornful of the clinical judgement, the clinical impression. Such judgements are, I believe, in essence, statistical. The clinician is attempting to make a comparison between the situation that faces him at the moment and a mentally recorded but otherwise untabulated past experience. There clearly may be gain in the introduction of more objective and more quantitative methods of assessment, which can be recorded, than can be supplied by this clinical instinct. Certainly no harm will be done, as Sir Henry Dale (1951) has pointed out, if these newer and more objective methods of observation 'are used primarily to supplement, and only by careful stages and with proved advantage to replace, the older and subjective ones. The loss, if any, would arise from haste to discard a coherent though impressionistic picture, and to replace it by a collection of precise but as yet uncoordinated details'. At present I would argue that we should, whenever possible, endeavour to harness the clinical impression to our measurements of the results of a therapeutic trial. To that I shall return again.

The Clinician

Turning now to the other side of the picture—the attitude of the clinician—I would, from experience, say that the most frequent and the most foolish criticism of the statistical approach in medicine is that human beings are too variable to allow of the contrasts inherent in a controlled trial of a remedy. In other words, each patient *is* 'unique' and so there can be nothing for the statistician to count. But if this is true it has always seemed to me that the bottom falls out of the clinical approach as well as the statistical. If each patient is unique, how can a basis for treatment be found in the past observations of other patients? In fact, of course, physicians do not act like that. They base their 'method of choice' upon what they have seen happen before—whether it be in only two or three cases or in a score. But even if human beings are not each unique in their responses to a given treatment they are certainly likely to be variable, sometimes extremely variable. Two or three uncontrolled observations may, therefore, give merely through the customary play of chance, a favourable picture in the hands of one doctor, an unfavourable picture in the hands of a second. And so the medical journals, euphemistically called the 'literature', are cluttered up with conflicting claims—each in itself perfectly true of what the doctor saw, and each insufficient to bear the weight of the generalization placed upon it.

Far, therefore, from arguing that the statistical approach is impossible in the face of human variability, we should realize that it is because of that variability that it is often essential. It does not follow, to meet another common criticism of the statistical approach, that it invariably demands large numbers. It may do so; it depends upon the problem. But, it should be recognized, the responses to treatment of a single patient are clearly a statement of fact—so far as the observations were truly made and accurately recorded. And that single case may give, in certain circumstances, evidence of vital importance.

If, for example, we were to use a new drug in a proved case of acute leukaemia and the patient made an immediate and indisputable recovery, should we not have a result of the most profound importance? The reason underlying our acceptance of merely one patient as illustrating a remarkable event—not necessarily of cause and effect—is that long and wide experience has shown that in their response to acute leukaemia human beings are *not* variable. They one and all fail to make immediate and indisputable recoveries. They one and all die. Therefore, although it would clearly be most unwise upon this one case to pass from the particular to the general, it would be sheer madness not to accept the evidence presented by it. No statistician (no statistician, let me say, who knew his subject matter) would object to that sample on the grounds that it was too small to be informative.

If, on the other hand, the drug were given to a patient suffering from acute rheumatic fever and the patient made an immediate and indisputable recovery, the statistician might suggest (with customary diffidence) that we have little basis for remark. That recovery may clearly have followed the administration of the drug without the slightest probability of a related cause and effect. With this disease human beings *are* variable in their reactions, some may die, some may have prolonged illnesses but recover eventually with or without permanent damage, some may make immediate and indisputable recoveries, whatever treatment we may give them. We must, therefore, have more cases before we can reasonably draw inferences about cause and effect.

I have somewhat laboured this point of numbers of observations because the old and fallacious gibe still lingers on, even among persons who should know better: that statisticians would if given the opportunity, have rejected—or even suppressed, though I am never quite sure how—some of the original and fundamental observations in medicine, on the grounds of their small number. For example, *fragilitas ossium*, I was once told, was originally described in just two cases; and this number I was also informed, a trifle tartly, 'statisticians would regard as useless evidence'. Why on earth should they? My retort ran as follows (Hill, 1950):

If 'exact descriptions' were given of these two cases and 'beautiful water colours' were supplied to illustrate them, then of course they are scientific evidence, and undeniable evidence of an occurrence—whether it be of one case or two. It would only be in relation to any subsequent appeal from the particular to the general that the statistician—and equally any trained scientific worker—could object. If on the basis of these two cases the clinician (in practice, let us say, near Smithfield Market) should be so unwise as to argue that the condition was specific to butchers, then the statistician might suggest that the experience was both too select and too slender in size to justify any such generalization.

In short there is, and can be, no magic number for either clinician or statistician. Whether we need one, a hundred or a thousand cases turns upon the setting of our problem and the inferences that we wish to draw. Faced with the rapid recovery of a single patient with rheumatic fever under a new drug what, I suggest, the careful clinician would do is not to generalize but to test the treatment on a second case. If it worked well again—or, perhaps, if it did not—he would test it on a third. And, without being accused of undue caution, or even of mathematical leanings, he might go so far as to seek a fourth. Thus, with somewhat halting steps, he unwittingly directs himself up the statistical garden path. I believe he might sometimes fare better if he straightaway walked boldly up the path and without any ado opened the gate to a designed and controlled clinical trial.

The Controlled Trial

The essence of such a trial is comparison. To the dictum of Helmholtz that 'all science is measurement', we should add, Sir Henry Dale (1951) has pointed out a further clause that 'all true measurement is essentially comparative'. Usually, therefore, but again not always, we need not only the group of patients to be submitted to a special treatment, or treatments, under investigation but another group differently treated—by, usually, the older and, at the time, more orthodox methods. The first step in the statistical technique, then, is the *random* allocation of patients to one or other of these groups. (I am, of course, assuming that the ethical situation has first been most carefully considered and the decision reached that such a trial is both proper and possible; if it is not it may yet be possible to devise some other, though probably less informative, type of trial, but with that I am not here concerned.)

There are various ways in which the random allocation of the patients to the treatment groups can be carried out. Most often today and, I think, preferably, it is done by the construction of an order of allocation, unknown in advance to the clinician, and based upon random sampling numbers—a modern substitute for tossing up, and one that is a trifle less embarrassing in the ward or office. Thus using OT to stand for orthodox treatment and NT for new treatment (without necessarily any confession of faith therein) we may have as the order for patients consecutively brought into the trial OT, NT, NT, OT, OT, OT, NT, and so forth. We may easily introduce a device to equalize the number of patients on the new and old treatments at, for example, every dozen—since otherwise by the play of chance we may occasionally be embarrassed by too many of one kind and too few of another. I do not think it necessary to spend time now upon these minutiae. What I would emphasize are the advantages of this random and unpremeditated distribution of patients to groups. Strictly adhered to—and I need hardly say that this is a *sine qua non*—this method ensures three things: it ensures that neither our personal idiosyncrasies (our likes or dislikes consciously or unwittingly applied) nor our lack of balanced judgement has entered into the construction of the different treatment groups— the allocation has been outside our control and the groups are therefore unbiased; it removes the danger, inherent in an allocation based upon personal judgement, that believing we may be biased in our judgements we endeavour to allow for that bias, to exclude it, and that in so doing we may overcompensate and by thus 'leaning over backward' introduce a lack of balance from the other direction; and, having used a random allocation, the sternest critic is unable to say when we eventually dash into print that quite probably the groups were differentially biased through our predilections or through our stupidity. Once it has been decided that a patient is of the right type to be brought into the trial the random method of allocation removes all responsibility from the clinical observer.

It may sometimes, however, be argued—and with truth—that this random allocation gives too much freedom to the play of chance and thus fails to provide groups that are sufficiently alike, or as alike as they could have been if we had used a more deliberate method of distribution. The likelihood of such a failure is clearly dependent upon two things: the size of the groups that we set up and the variability of the patients we bring into them. Often one can effectively meet the difficulty by first dividing the somewhat heterogeneous group of patients who are to be brought into the trial into more homogeneous sub-groups, and then making the random allocation to treatment O, treatment N and so forth within each of the sub-groups. This has been the technique adopted in the joint trials of cortisone and ACTH versus salicylates in rheumatic fever now being carried out to a common plan in a number of centres in the

United Kingdom, the United States and Canada. Thus we have six sub-groups. Rheumatic fever runs, on the average, a different course in young children and in adolescents. We have, therefore, a sub-division by age into patients under sixteen years old and patients aged sixteen years or over. Apart from age, however, the course of the disease in relation to treatment, particularly with regard to any permanent damage that may occur to the heart, may well be influenced by the speed with which, after the onset of an attack, treatment can be instituted. We have, therefore, within each of the two age groups, three divisions by the duration of time that had elapsed between the recorded onset of attack and the start of treatment: treatment begun within the first two weeks of the illness; treatment begun between two and six weeks after onset; and treatment not begun until more than six weeks had elapsed. Every patient must first satisfy certain criteria of diagnosis, which have been laid down. Being thus eligible for entry to the trial, he is first allocated to whichever of the six sub-groups he belongs. He is then allocated to a specific treatment, whether with cortisone, ACTH or salicylates, by means of random orders set up for each of the six sub-groups and, separately, for each centre taking part in the trial.

It may be, and indeed it is highly likely, that we shall not have enough cases in each of these six more homogeneous sub-groups to allow firm conclusions to be drawn. But we shall at least be in the position to amalgamate the six sub-groups, if it is justifiable, knowing that the three treatment groups in total will have the same distribution of patients by age and by duration of illness. By the design of the trial we have ensured equality in the treatment groups in these respects, and by a random allocation applied to the sub-groups we have ensured an absence of personal bias.

Such designs, simple though they may be, are of importance. They may often require smaller numbers of patients for the solution of a problem and allow a wider range of questions to be simultaneously tackled. I would usually, however, myself sooner seek a decisive answer to one or two questions than cast my bread upon the waters and be faced finally with seven 'not statistically significant' differences. 'Not statistically significant,' one should always remember, is the equivalent of the 'non-proven' of the Scots law rather than the 'not guilty' of the English courts. I also emphasize that in spite of the random construction of the treatment groups that I have envisaged, it will in practice be essential to prove that the groups of patients under each treatment have, in fact, turned out to be similar in their features at entry—that is, in such features as may be relevant to a patient's response to treatment. For example, an analysis of the patients at entry to the trial must reveal the level of their temperatures and their blood sedimentation rates, the frequency of their heart murmurs and their bacteriologic companions, and so on. No method of random allocation can absolutely ensure the equality of the groups in all these respects. The goddess of chance may prevent it, particularly when we are concerned with small groups. It is therefore our first and imperative job to show that the groups we have set up are reasonably alike or, if not, to make such allowances as are possible for the differences that have occurred. Such allowances after the event are not always easy to make, and therefore the 'stratifying' by sub-groups that I have touched upon has considerable advantage in ensuring equalities in major characteristics.

THE TREATMENT

In the great majority of the controlled clinical trials with which I have been associated a specific treatment schedule has been laid down. It may, needless to say, be varied with age or body weight or some other characteristic of the patient; but apart from that it has been rigidly defined in advance and must be adhered to by the clinician (except for the usual overriding ethical reasons). Clearly, however, in regard to treatment there are an infinite number of questions we can ask of a trial. We can choose one dose out of many; we can vary the interval of administration; we can give it by different routes; we can exhibit it for different lengths of time; and so on. In testing a new form of treatment knowledge at first is necessarily scanty, being usually based upon laboratory work and a few scattered clinical observations. In Medical Research Council trials we have thought it proper, therefore, to choose such a régime as promised to reveal the potentialities (and often the dangers) of the drug (or whatever may be concerned). Thus we have a tidy question—for example, if to a defined type of patient 2 g. of drug X are given daily in four divided doses by intramuscular injection and for three months, what happens?

But perhaps the question is too tidy. We can, of course, extend it after its answer has been reached by experimenting with variations upon the original theme. It may, however, be argued, and some-

3   S.M.M.

times, I think, legitimately, that allowance should have been made during the basic trial for individual idiosyncrasies, that the clinician should have been free to vary the dosage according to his own judgement of the patient's needs as shown by the latter's responses. Statistically, I see no reason why that should not be done so long as two things are observed and remembered. The first is that we have deliberately changed the question asked of the trial; it now runs 'if competent clinicians in charge of defined types of patients use drug X in such varying amounts and for such varying durations of time, and so forth, as they think advisable for each patient, what happens?' The moot point is which question in given circumstances, is the better one to ask. The second point is that at the conclusion of such a trial we can *in no circumstances* compare the effects of the different régimes of treatment that have been used. These régimes have been determined by the conditions and responses of the individual patients; to observe then, at the end of the trial, the patients' differential conditions and responses in relation to their treatments is merely circular reasoning. We cannot possibly measure thus the advantages and disadvantages of different régimes but only, by an expansion of the controlled trial, by including groups randomly allocated to such treatments. The main danger of this free-for-all trial is the apparently almost overpowering attraction to some clinicians of circular motion.

THE ANSWERS

These are the opening gambits of the clinical trial—the definition of the patients, their random allocations to the treatment groups, the laying down of the treatment schedule. At the end of play we shall have to add up the score. Clearly the more objective we can make our means of so doing, the safer we shall be from criticism. Naturally, therefore, we turn first to measurable characteristics. Stone-dead has no fellow, and pre-eminent, therefore, stands the number of patients who die. No statistician, so far as I know, has in this respect accused the physician of an over-reliance upon the clinical impression. Fortunately, however (except statistically speaking), many diseases upon which we must test new treatments are not particularly lethal. Other objective characteristics must be sought and are usually found in such features as the duration of fever, the level of the blood sedimentation rate and the presence of infecting organisms. The appropriate measures vary from one disease to another, and I shall not dwell on them now. I would, however, stress that it is essential to decide *before* the trial begins exactly what measurements will be taken, how they will be taken and precisely when. Without those prior decisions chaos will reign. Working under them we shall have measurements by means of which we can see whether the different treatment groups show differences in their average levels of, for example, body temperature or body weight on specified days—and in their ratios, such as the proportion of patients who become afebrile after a given duration of treatment and the proportion who have a raised blood sedimentation rate. Even with prior thought, it is not always a quite simple task to lay down requirements. In another field, that of the law, Lord MacMillan notes that a statute of the reign of King George III enacted that the penalities under the Act were to be given one half to the informer and one half to the poor of the parish. Neither the informer nor the poor would, however, he points out, be likely to be grateful for this benefaction since the only penalty prescribed was fourteen years' transportation to the colonies. If lawyers, with their care for words, can so err, how much more the doctor!

Returning to our answers from the clinical trial, they present, it will be noted, a *group* reaction. They show that one group fared better than another, that given a certain treatment patients, *on the average*, get better more frequently or more readily, or both. We cannot necessarily, perhaps very rarely, pass from that to stating exactly what effect the treatment will have on a particular patient. But there is, surely, no way and no method of deciding that. Also it is well to remember that observation of the group does not inhibit the most scrupulous and careful observation of the individual at the same time—if it is believed that more can be learnt that way.

'WHEREAS I WAS BLIND, NOW I SEE'

Passing now from such measurable to the less measurable characteristics of disease processes we shall have, in some cases, X-ray evidence and in all of them the clinical assessment to which I referred above. The difficulties inherent in making unbiased and reliable assessments of X-ray films we have endeavoured to meet in some Medical Research Council trials, and I think with much success, by having the films read and the radiologic changes assessed by one or more persons, who have in so doing been kept in ignorance of the treatment groups to which the patients belonged. That process resolves to a large extent the problem of bias, and it does not subject the clinician in charge of the case to hardship. The clinical assessment of the patient's progress and of the severity of the illness he has suffered presents considerably greater difficulties. If it is to be used effectively, without fear and without reproach, the judgements must be made without any possibility of bias, without any over-compensation for a possible bias, and without any possibility of accusation of bias. In other words, the assessment must, whenever possible, be 'blind'—the assessing clinician must not know the treatment of the patient. And that, of course, is a difficult procedure to carry out—indeed it is sometimes quite impossible. Thus, in the Medical Research Council's trials of streptomycin in young adult patients with phthisis, in the early days of that antibiotic, the group on streptomycin had to undergo repeated injections—at least twice a day for several months. It would have been out of the question, for very obvious reasons, to give the contrasting group similar injections of an inert substance. There could be no way of disguising the treatment from the clinical observer (in fact, in that particular situation it was not very necessary to do so, for we could judge on the mortality and the radiologic changes that were assessed 'blind').

On the other hand, in the Medical Research Council's trial of an antihistaminic drug in the 'cure' of the common cold, feelings of enthusiasm or scepticism may well run high in the bosom (or should I say nasal mucosa?) either of the recipient of the drug or of his clinical observer, or indeed of both. If either were allowed to know the treatment that had been given, I believe that few of us would without qualms accept the result that the drug was of value —if such an answer came out of the trial. Here a group given a placebo was essential; here complete ignorance in both patient and doctor of the treatment actually given was essential. It was not very difficult to incorporate both features in the trial (and in passing it is interesting to note that the placebo produced not only the same number of 'cures' as the drug but almost as many 'side-effects').

Sometimes another possible approach is by means of the administration of a known treatment, such as an injection, by one person and the clinical assessment of the results by another kept in ignorance of that treatment. In short, given a problem of sufficient importance and given sufficient faith in the method, some means of making a 'blind' clinical assessment can frequently, if not usually, be devised. It is thus, I suggest, that we may effectively give the 'coherent though impressionistic picture' its rightful place in the therapeutic trial.

RESPONSIBILITIES

Without demanding this 'blind approach', or even accurate measurement, it is certainly likely that the mental contrasting of one treatment with another or of a new treatment against the old will give, at least in the hands of able observers, a truthful, if not precise, answer *if* a treatment has a real and considerable effect. Without a strictly controlled trial the merits of a penicillin could not (and, in fact, did not) fail to come to light. With 'winners' it is very easy for the critics of the statistical approach to be wise after the event and to say that the general evidence available at the start of a long, and perhaps tedious, trial made it unnecessary or pedantic. They tend—conveniently to themselves—to forget the occasions when the trial has shown that a treatment has little, if any, value—in spite of the general 'evidence' that was available. The history of medicine is, surely, sullied by the reigns of such vulgar upstarts whose prestige, lacking a scientific test, lingered on, to the detriment of human welfare.

It is easy to point out to critics, too, that it is difficult to determine through clinical impressions whether a drug is quite useless or of some slight but undoubted value, and that it is even more difficult to determine with uncontrolled and unco-ordinated observations whether, today, one powerful antibiotic is more valuable than another in particular situations. For instance, I do not think the relative values of aureomycin, chloramphenicol and penicillin in the treatment of clinical pneumonias could have been clearly determined without a fairly large-scale and carefully controlled trial. (Medical Research Council, 1951.) In particular, it is frequently important that negative results be proved and proved without undue delay.

These particular criticisms are not difficult to meet. The real difficulty to my mind lies, or may lie, in the charge that a trial is unethical. For instance in a letter to the *British Medical Journal* (1951) a writer protesting—in part, I think, justifiably—against present ways of writing scientific papers referred to 'the replacement of humanistic and clinical values by mathematical formulae', the degradation of patients 'from human beings to bricks in a column, dots in a field, or tadpoles in a pool' and 'the eventual elimination of the responsibility of the doctor to get the individual back to health'. This appears to me to be in essence an attack upon the clinical trial, though the writer at the same time admitted that 'since science is mensuration, a sound statistical survey of any particular form of treatment is of importance'. I am impressed by the editorial comment in the same issue of the *British Medical Journal*, a comment that expresses what I feel and could not myself, I am sure, have put more clearly:

It is difficult to see how the results of this 'sound statistical survey' can be analysed other than by a 'sound statistical method' and presented otherwise than in a 'sound statistical table', with, if necessary, mathematical formulae. By so doing, in what way are we degrading the patients and shirking our responsibility as doctors to get the individual back to health? The whole essence of the survey is to see whether a new treatment will benefit patients. There appear to be two ways of going to work. We may try it on John Smith and Mary Robinson and report the results— that John Smith got well quickly and Mary Robinson, poor soul, died. We have done our best for both. Or we may try it on 30 John Smiths and 20 Mary Robinsons and report the numbers that lived and died. It is likely that the larger numbers will be found more informative than the smaller. But have we done any less for the 50 than we did for the two? Further, if there be no ethical reasons to forbid—a paramount and over-riding proviso—we may contrast the 30 John Smiths and 20 Mary Robinsons with an equal number of men and women not given this new and wholly unproved drug. Wherein have we shirked our duties? In treating patients with unproved remedies we are, whether we like it or not, experimenting on human beings, and a good experiment well reported may be more ethical and entail less shirking of duty than a poor one.

As R. A. McCance (1951), professor of experimental medicine at Cambridge University, has pointed out, 'the medical profession has a responsibility not only for the cure of the sick and for the prevention of disease but for the advancement of knowledge upon which both depend. This third responsibility can be met only by investigation and experiment'. The statistically guided therapeutic trial is not the only means of investigation and experiment, nor indeed is it invariably the best way of advancing knowledge of therapeutics. I commend it to you as *one* way, and, I believe, a useful way, of discharging that third responsibility to mankind.

REFERENCES

Anon. (1950). *Brit. Med. J.* **i,** 68.
British Medical Journal (1951), **ii,** 1088.
Bartlett, M. S. (1951). Some remarks on the theory of statistics. *Trans. Manchr. statist. Soc. 1950–51.*
Dale, H. (1951). *Brit. med. Bull.* **7,** 261.
Hill, A. Bradford (1950). *Brit. med. J.* **ii,** 1114.
McCance, R. A. (1951). *Proc. R. Soc. Med.* **44,** 189.
Medical Research Council, Antibiotics Clinical Trials (non-tuberculous) Committee (1951). *Brit. med. J.* **ii,** 1361.

CHAPTER 4

STREPTOMYCIN TREATMENT OF PULMONARY TUBERCULOSIS

WHEN a special committee of the Medical Research Council undertook in September, 1946, to plan clinical trials of streptomycin in tuberculosis the main problem faced was that of investigating the effect of the drug in pulmonary tuberculosis. This antibiotic had been discovered two years previously by Waksman (Schatz, Bugie, and Waksman, 1944); in the intervening period its power of inhibiting tubercle bacilli *in vitro*, and the results of treatment in experimental tuberculous infection in guinea-pigs, had been reported; these results were strikingly better than those with any previous chemotherapeutic agent in tuberculosis. Preliminary results of trials in clinical tuberculosis had been published (Hinshaw and Feldman, 1945; Hinshaw, Feldman, and Pfuetze, 1946; National Research Council, 1946); the clinical results in pulmonary tuberculosis were encouraging but inconclusive.

The natural course of pulmonary tuberculosis is in fact so variable and unpredictable that evidence of improvement or cure following the use of a new drug in a few cases cannot be accepted as proof of the effect of that drug. The history of chemotherapeutic trials in tuberculosis is filled with errors due to empirical evaluation of drugs (Hart, 1946); the exaggerated claims made for gold treatment, persisting over 15 years, provide a spectacular example. It had become obvious that, in future, conclusions regarding the clinical effect of a new chemotherapeutic agent in tuberculosis could be considered valid only if based on adequately controlled clinical

A Medical Research Council investigation planned, directed and reported by the Streptomycin in Tuberculosis Trials Committee, composed of the following members: Dr. Geoffrey Marshall (chairman), Professor J. W. S. Blacklock, Professor C. Cameron, Professor N. B. Capon, Dr. R. Cruickshank, Professor J. H. Gaddum, Dr. F. R. G. Heaf, Professor A. Bradford Hill, Dr. L. E. Houghton, Dr. J. Clifford Hoyle, Professor H. Raistrick, Dr. J. G. Scadding, Professor W. H. Tytler, Professor G. S. Wilson, and Dr. P. D'Arcy Hart (secretary).

Reprinted from the *British Medical Journal*, 1948, ii, 769.

trials (Hinshaw and Feldman, 1944). The one controlled trial of gold treatment (and the only report of an adequately controlled trial in tuberculosis we have been able to find in the literature) reported negative therapeutic results (Amberson, McMahon, and Pinner, 1931). In 1946 no controlled trial of streptomycin in pulmonary tuberculosis had been undertaken in the U.S.A. The Committee of the Medical Research Council decided then that a part of the small supply of streptomycin allocated to it for research purposes would be best employed in a rigorously planned investigation with concurrent controls.

The many difficulties of planning and conducting a trial of this nature are important enough to warrant a full description here of the methods of the investigation.

PLAN AND CONDUCT OF THE TRIAL

Type of Case

A first prerequisite was that all patients in the trial should have a similar type of disease. To avoid having to make allowances for the effect of forms of therapy other than bed-rest, the type of disease was to be one not suitable for other forms of therapy. The estimated chances of spontaneous regression must be small. On the other hand, the type of lesion should be such as to offer some prospect of action by an effective chemotherapeutic agent; for this reason old-standing disease, and disease with thick-walled cavities, should be excluded. Finally the age-group must be reasonably limited, since the total number of patients in the trial could not be large.

Such closely defined features were considered indispensable, for it was realized that no two patients have an identical form of the disease, and it was desired to eliminate as many of the obvious variations as possible. For these several reasons the type of case to be investigated was defined as follows: acute progressive bilateral pulmonary tuberculosis of presumably recent origin, bacteriologically proved, unsuitable for collapse therapy, age-group 15 to 25 (later extended to 30).

The selection of this type of disease constituted full justification for having a parallel series of patients treated only by bed-rest, since up to the present this would be considered the only suitable form of treatment for such cases. Additional justification lay in the fact that all the streptomycin available in the country was in any case being used, the rest of the supply being taken up for two rapidly fatal forms of the disease, miliary and meningeal tuberculosis.

Recruitment and Admission of Cases

Co-operation in the trial was obtained in the first place from Brompton Hospital (drawing on London County Council cases), Colindale Hospital (London County Council), and Harefield County Hospital (Middlesex County Council). The L.C.C. and the M.C.C. gave full co-operation, permitting recruitment of suitable cases from the areas served by them, covering a population of nearly six million persons. Accordingly letters were sent, through the tuberculosis departments of these authorities, to tuberculosis officers and to medical superintendents of general hospitals outlining the proposed trial and asking that particulars and X-ray films of possibly suitable patients be sent to the co-ordinator of the trials for consideration. Visits were paid to the tuberculosis clinics and hospitals to show by representative X-ray films the type of case sought and to explain in detail the nature of the controlled trial. When cases were submitted the clinical particulars and X-ray films were taken to the Committee's selection panel for consideration. When a patient had been accepted as suitable, request was made through the local authority for admission to one of the streptomycin centres; in spite of long waiting-lists these patients were given complete priority, and the majority were admitted within a week of approval.

The first patients to be accepted were admitted to the centres in January, 1947. At first the impression was that cases of the type defined are seen often. In fact, such cases are not common. As it became evident after three months that enough cases could not be found in the London and Middlesex areas, other authorities were approached. The Welsh National Memorial Association, the Department of Health for Scotland, and the Leeds Tuberculosis Service made available centres at Sully, Bangour, and Killingbeck, and cases were recruited to those centres from the respective areas. In addition, another centre was opened in the London area, at the Northern Hospital (L.C.C.).

By September, 1947, 109 patients had been accepted, and no more were admitted to this trial. Two patients had died within the pre-preliminary observation week; these are excluded from the analysis. Of the remaining 107 patients 55 had been allocated to the streptomycin group and 52 to the control group.

The Control Scheme

Determination of whether a patient would be treated by strepto-mycin and bed-rest (S case) or by bed-rest alone (C case) was made by reference to a statistical series based on random sampling numbers drawn up for each sex at each centre by Professor Bradford Hill; the details of the series were unknown to any of the investigators or to the co-ordinator and were contained in a set of sealed envelopes, each bearing on the outside only the name of the hospital and a number. After acceptance of a patient by the panel, and before admission to the streptomycin centre, the appropriate numbered envelope was opened at the central office; the card inside told if the patient was to be an S or a C case, and this information was then given to the medical officer of the centre. Patients were not told before admission that they were to get special treatment. C patients did not know throughout their stay in hospital that they were control patients in a special study; they were in fact treated as they would have been in the past, the sole difference being that they had been admitted to the centre more rapidly than was normal. Usually they were not in the same wards as S patients, but the same régime was maintained.

It was important for the success of the trial that the details of the control scheme should remain confidential. It is a matter of great credit to the many doctors concerned that this information was not made public throughout the 15 months of the trial, and the Com-mittee is much indebted to them for their co-operation.

By definition, cases accepted for the trial were unsuitable for collapse therapy; clinicians were therefore asked to adopt collapse therapy only if the course of the disease so changed that some collapse measure became indispensable and urgent. In the S cases collapse therapy was in fact never applied during the four treatment months. It was given to five of the 52 C cases during that period.

Observation and Treatment Period

Each patient was to remain in bed at the centre for at least six months, and the results were to be assessed on the clinical status at the end of that period. In addition to the usual hospital records, clinical observations were entered on standard record forms designed particularly for this trial; these forms provided for details of history, criteria of acceptance, examination on admission, monthly routine re-examinations with assessment of progress since last examination, observation of toxic reactions, temperature and treatment records, and finally a pathological record form. Instructions on required frequency of examinations were given.

Clinicians' and pathologists' meetings were held during the trials to discuss the work as it proceeded. The co-ordinator visited centres and was constantly in touch with the clinicians concerned to discuss the progress of the trial and the problems arising. The working sub-committee of pathologists established the technical laboratory procedures, discussed the findings at intervals, and arranged for independent checking of sensitivity tests of tubercle bacilli and streptomycin levels in the blood.

Analysis of Results

The general trend of results during the course of the trial was followed through the monthly reports from the centres. The analysis of results up to six months after the patient's admission is presented here; it is based on information from the standard record forms completed for each patient and on the X-ray films which have been made available by the hospitals concerned.

The films have been viewed by two radiologists and a clinician, each reading the films independently and not knowing if the films were of C or S cases. One of the radiologists had been attached to a centre taking part in the trial; the other two specialists had not been connected with the trial in any way. There was fair agreement among the three; at a final session they met to review and discuss films on which there had been a difference of interpretation, and agreement was reached without difficulty on all films. The results of radiological assessment presented in the main analyses are the agreed results, but the separate reports and their differences are discussed under the heading 'Changes in Radiological Picture'.

Condition on Admission

Each patient was under observation at a centre for at least one week before streptomycin treatment or observation proper for the trial started. Data in Table **4,** 1 reflect the condition on admission.

Thirty patients (54 per cent) in the S group and 24 (46 per cent) in the C group were in poor general condition at the start of the trial; of these, 20 and 17 respectively were considered to be desperately ill. Twenty-four S patients (44 per cent) and 19 C patients (36 per cent) had during the preliminary observation week maximum evening temperatures of 101° F. (38.3° C.) or over. In 36 S patients (65 per cent) and 29 C patients (56 per cent) the sedimentation rate (Westergren, 200 mm. reading at one hour) was over 50.

TABLE **4**, 1

Condition on Admission

General Condition	S Group	C Group	Max. Evening Temp. in First Week *	S Group	C Group	Sedimentation Rate	S Group	C Group
Good	8	8	98–98·9° F. (36·7–37·15° C.)	3	4	0–10	0	0
Fair	17	20	99–99·9° F. (37·2–37·75° C.)	13	12	11–20	3	2
Poor	30	24	100–100·9° F. (37·8–38·25° C.)	15	17	21–50	16	20
			101° F. (38·3° C.)+	24	19	51+	36	29
Total	55	52	Total	55	52	Total	55	51†

* Temperature by mouth in all but six cases.
† Examination not done in one case.

These data reflect the fairly acute clinical condition of most of the patients, though obviously the clinical picture was far from uniform in the 107 patients admitted to the trial. The data show also that random distribution has equalized the groups; if anything, there are more severe cases in the S group. There were 22 men and 33 women in the S group, 21 men and 31 women in the C group.

X-ray Classification

All cases conformed more or less to the type defined, but within the possible limits of the definition there were wide variations. All films showed opacities representing extensive infiltration of apparently recent origin; where there was room for doubt the length of history was taken into consideration as evidence of the age of the lesions.

It was thought at first that gross cavitation should be excluded, but this view was abandoned, as many otherwise suitable cases had large cavities. Thirty-two of the 55 S cases and 30 of the 52 C cases showed large or multiple cavities in the film taken on admission (tomography was not used as a routine); it must be stressed, however, that from their radiological appearance these seemed to be of recent development and that the lesions predominating in the lungs were bronchopneumonic in type.

In 19 S cases and in 19 C cases there was radiological evidence of segmental atelectasis.

TREATMENT

All S patients were given streptomycin* by the intramuscular route. The dose was 2g. per day, given in four injections at six-hourly intervals. This dosage was adopted following exchange of correspondence with Dr. H. C. Hinshaw of the Mayo Clinic, to whom the Committee is indebted for advice during the planning of the trial.

The original intention was to continue streptomycin treatment for six months. However, reports from observers in the U.S.A., and a growing impression in our own centres, indicated that the maximum effect of streptomycin was reached within the first three or four months, and it was therefore decided in July, 1947, to treat patients for four months only, but to continue observation to the end of six months from admission as for C patients. (One patient was treated with streptomycin for 6 months, 2 for $5\frac{1}{2}$ months, 6 for 5 months, 5 for $4\frac{1}{2}$ months; the remainder, 41 patients, were treated for 4 months.)

Patients in both groups were on bed-rest during the period of the trial, and were allowed up only to the toilet where the general condition allowed. As already indicated, although patients admitted were considered unsuitable for collapse therapy, it was agreed that when the course of disease had so changed that collapse therapy was strongly indicated such treatment should be given. In 11 C patients collapse measures (artificial pneumoperitoneum with phrenic paralysis in 10 cases, pneumothorax in one) were induced at some time during the six months—three in the third month of observation, two in the fourth month, two in the fifth, and four in the last observation month. In seven of the 11 the course of the disease appears not to have been affected; in four there was deterioration before and improvement after induction of artificial pneumoperitoneum. Col-

* The streptomycin used was in the form of the hydrochloride, obtained from one American producer. For technical particulars of the product see article in *Lancet*, 1948, **i**, 582.

lapse therapy was induced in 11 S patients during the fifth or sixth month; in all but two the course of the disease was apparently unaltered.

RESULTS AT END OF SIX MONTHS

Four of the 55 S patients (7 per cent) and 14 of the 52 C patients (27 per cent) died before the end of six months. The difference between the two series is statistically significant; the probability of it occurring by chance is less than one in a hundred.

Assessment of condition at the end of the six-months period should be based on a judicious combination of changes in the radiological picture, changes in general condition, temperature, weight, sedimentation rate, and bacillary content of the sputum. We have not attempted a numerical evaluation of the relative importance of each of these, and changes in them will be reported in turn. Appreciation of the clinical effects of the drug have not been lacking in the many reports published within the past two years. So far as possible, the analysis in this report will deal with the more readily measurable data only.

The following preliminary analysis is based on changes in the radiological picture alone, this being in our opinion the most important single factor to consider; it will be seen later that in the great majority of cases clinical and radiological changes followed similar trends.

The overall results given in Table **4**, 2 (extracted from Table **4**, 9) show differences between the two series that leave no room

TABLE **4**, 2

Assessment of Radiological Appearance at Six Months as Compared with Appearance on Admission

Radiological Assessment	Streptomycin Group		Control Group	
Considerable improvement	28	*51%*	4	*8%*
Moderate or slight improvement	10	*18%*	13	*25%*
No material change	2	*4%*	3	*6%*
Moderate or slight deterioration	5	*9%*	12	*23%*
Considerable deterioration	6	*11%*	6	*11%*
Deaths	4	*7%*	14	*27%*
Total	55	*100%*	52	*100%*

for doubt. The most outstanding difference is in the numbers who showed 'considerable improvement' in the radiological picture— *i.e.*, those for whom at the end of the six-months period there was a reasonable prospect of recovery. Twenty-eight of the S patients (51 per cent) and only four of the C patients (8 per cent) were considerably improved (the probability of such a difference occuring by chance is less than one in a million).

Results in men and women were similar, and need not be tabulated here. There was a higher mortality among males in both S and C groups; two of 22 male S patients died and eight of 21 male C patients, compared with two of 33 female S patients and six of 31 female C patients, but the difference is not significant.

RESULTS RELATED TO CONDITION ON ADMISSION

The next point to be considered is whether the prognosis was worse in those most acutely ill, and whether the difference between the S and C groups applies to the less or more acutely ill patients.

Temperature

TABLE **4**, 3

Results at Six Months Related to Temperature on Admission

Max. Evening Temp. during First Observation Week		Radiological Assessment at 6 Months			Deaths	Total
		Improvement	No Change	Deterioration		
98–98·9° F. (36·7–37·15° C.)	S	3	0	0	0	3
	C	3	1	0	0	4
99–99·9° F. (37·2–37·75° C.)	S	9	1	3	0	13
	C	7	2	2	1	12
100–100·9° F. (37·8–38·25° C.)	S	13	0	2	0	15
	C	5	0	7	5	17
101° F. (38·3° C.)+	S	13	1	6	4	24
	C	2	0	9	8	19

The results in Table **4**, 3, represented graphically in Fig. **4**, 1, show first what was to be expected—*viz.*, in both groups the most grave prognosis was in the patients most febrile on admission; indeed, in the S group the only deaths were in patients who had on admission evening temperatures of 101° F. (38.3° C) or over. A

second, more important, point that emerges is that the superiority
of results in the S group as a whole over the C group is almost
entirely accounted for by the most febrile patients. Only seven (19
per cent) of 36 C patients with a temperature of 100° F. (37.8° C.)
or over were improved at the end of six months, compared with 26

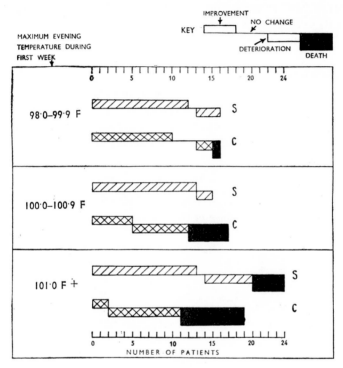

FIG. **4,** 1

Results at six months (radiological assessment) related to temperature
on admission

(67 per cent) of 39 S patients. Further analysis reveals that eight of
the 24 S patients with a temperature of 101° F. (38.3° C.) or over
showed considerable improvement, and none of the 19 C patients.
In less febrile and in afebrile patients there is little difference in
results between the two groups, though analysis shows that the
number showing considerable improvement was greater in the S
group.

Sedimentation Rate (E.S.R.)

Relation of results to the E.S.R. on admission shows the same trends. Of patients with an E.S.R. not higher than 50, 13 (68 per cent) of 19 S patients were improved, compared with nine (41 per cent) of 22 C patients. Eighteen (50 per cent) of 36 S patients with E.S.R. over 50 were improved, compared with seven (24 per cent) of 29 C patients.

Radiological Assessment on Admission

The data in Table **4,** 4 show that in both S and C groups the results were better where there was no gross cavitation on admission. In the S cases with no gross cavitation the results were outstandingly good, with no deaths and 17 of 23 patients showing considerable improvement.

TABLE **4,** 4

Radiological Assessment at Six Months Related to
Presence or Absence of Gross Cavitation on Admission

X-Ray on Admission	Group	Total Cases	Radiological Assessment at 6 Months					Deaths
			Improvement		No Change	Deterioration		
			Con-siderable	Slight or Moderate		Slight or Moderate	Con-siderable	
Cases with large or multiple cavities	S	32	11	7	2	4	4	4
	C	30	1	8	2	6	2	11
Other cases	S	23	17	3	0	1	2	0
	C	22	3	5	1	6	4	3

CLINICAL CHANGES DURING PERIOD OF TRIAL

General Condition

Assessment of changes in general condition is based on a combination of clinical facts, clinician's general impression, and patient's feeling of well- or ill-being. As such, it is mentioned only briefly here.

At four months after admission the general condition had improved in 40 (73 per cent) of the 55 S patients, compared with 26 (50 per cent of 52 C patients; only seven (13 per cent) S patients were worse, whereas 10 (19 per cent) C patients had died and another 13 (25 per cent) were worse than on admission. At six months after admission the difference between the two groups was less; in 33 (60 per cent) S patients and in 24 (46 per cent) C patients the general condition was better than on admission: 13 S patients (24 per cent) were worse and four others (7 per cent) had died; 12 C patients (23 per cent) were worse and 14 others (27 per cent) had died.

Temperature

Three S patients and four C patients were afebrile on admission to the trial. The three S patients remained afebrile throughout, with the exception of a short slight pyrexial episode in one case. Two of the four C patients remained afebrile throughout; the other two had occasional low pyrexia, and one was still pyrexial at the end of the six months. Temperature changes in the febrile patients at two months, four months, and six months after admission are shown in Table **4, 5**.

TABLE **4, 5**

Temperature Changes in Patients Febrile on Admission

Highest Evening Temp. During Week following Admission	Group	Total	No. of Patients whose Temperature was Normal at end of			No. of Patients Showing Temp. Fall (including Fall to Normal) at end of		
			2 Mos.	4 Mos.	6 Mos.	2 Mos.	4 Mos.	6 Mos.
101°F. (38·3°C.) or over	S	24	1	5	6	15	14	11
	C	19	0	2	3	7	6	8
99–100·9° F. (37·2–38·25° C.)	S	28	8	15	18	12	19	24
	C*	28	5	10	10	10	11	12

* Temperature for one C case not available.

The difference between S and C series at any one point of time is not statistically significant, but appears at every stage—*i.e.*, at every stage more S patients than C patients show a temperature drop to normal or to a degree of pyrexia lower than that on admission. A common effect of streptomycin not obvious in the above simplified presentation of data is a rapid temperature drop in the first weeks of therapy, followed sometimes by a rise to a level usually lower than the level on admission. Among the less acutely febrile patients (temperature 99–100.9° F.; 37.2–38.85° C.) an increasing number of S cases show falling temperature; at six months 18 of the 28 were apyrexial and six others had temperatures lower than on admission; 10 of 28 similar C cases were apyrexial and two others had temperatures lower than on admission.

There is thus a consistent difference between S and C groups. It is important to note, however, that in 20 of 47 febrile patients treated by bed-rest without streptomycin the temperature was lower at the end of six months than on admission; in 13 of the 20 it was within normal limits. For the type of lesions selected, these results serve to emphasize both the value of prolonged bed-rest and the need of controls in an investigation of this type.

In seven of the 13 C patients with normal temperature at the end of six months an artificial pneumoperitoneum had been induced at some time during the trial, but in every case the temperature had come down to normal previous to the induction of artificial pneumoperitoneum. The temperature fall in the C patients can be attributed to the effect of bed-rest alone.

Weight (Table 4, 6)

In the first four months 20 S patients had gained weight (5 lb.—2.27 kg.—or more), with a total weight gain between them of 253 lb. (114.76 kg.), mean 12.6 lb. (5.71 kg.). The weight gains in the C group are very similar: 20 patients gained weight, with a total gain of 255 lb. (115.67 kg.), mean 12.7 lb. (5.76 kg.). At the end of six months 24 S patients had gained weight, with a total gain of 451 lb. (204.57 kg.), mean 18.8 lb. (8.53 kg.). Eighteen C patients had gained weight, with a total gain of 313 lb. (141.97 kg.), mean 17.4 lb. (7.89 kg.).

These facts reveal, first, that many patients with a severe form of tuberculosis gained weight on treatment by bed-rest alone; indeed, 12 at the end of six months had gained a stone (6.35 kg.) or more in weight. Secondly, the weight gains in the S group in the first four months were no greater than in the C group, and therefore do not reflect the important improvement observed in other respects; on the other hand, there was more weight gain in the last two months— i.e., after treatment had stopped. It is certain that some patients

TABLE **4,** 6

Weight Changes

Weight Changes	4 Months After Admission		6 Months After Admission	
	S	C	S	C
14 lb. (6.35 kg.) or more gain	8	6	19	12
5–13 lb. (2.27–5.89 kg.) gain	12	14	5	6
Less than 5 lb. (2.27 kg.) gain or loss	15	9	12	10
5 lb. (2.27 kg.) or more loss	13	7	11	5
Deaths	0	10	4	14
Total*	48	46	51	47

* Information not available for all cases; some patients too ill to be weighed.

failed to gain weight, or gained little weight, during the course of streptomycin treatment, and this may be at least partly ascribed to the gastric disturbances, which were severe in a few cases and in others were mild but sufficient to reduce appetite and retard weight gain.

Menstruation

In 10 of 32 female S patients and in 12 of 31 female C patients menstruation was normal on admission and remained normal. In nine S patients and 12 C patients amenorrhoea persisted throughout. In 11 S patients and seven C patients menstruation appeared at some time during observation and remained normal subsequently; in addition two S patients had a temporary return of menstruation.

Sedimentation Rate

The data in Table **4,** 7 show two main differences between groups S and C. If one takes into account the patients who died, in the C group the number of patients with a very high sedimentation rate (over 50) was never reduced; in the S group the number fell from 36 to 19 (including four deaths). Secondly, at six months in only four C patients had the E.S.R. fallen to within normal limits; in the S group the corresponding number was 17.

TABLE **4,** 7

Sedimentation Rate

E.S.R.	Group	On Admission	At 2 Months	At 4 Months	At 6 Months
0–10	S	0	0	6	17
	C	0	1	2	4
11–50	S	19	31	23	17
	C	22	10	15	18
51+	S	36	24	26	15
	C	29	37	23	14
Deaths	S	—	0	0	4
	C	—	2	10	14
Total*	S	55	55	55	53
	C	51	50	50	50

* Totals do not correspond in all columns, as results were not available in all cases.

CHANGES IN RADIOLOGICAL PICTURE
DURING PERIOD OF TRIAL

After the close of the trial the chest radiographs of all patients were viewed, and changes assessed, by the three members of the radiological panel working separately. They were not told whether films were of patients from S or C series. Radiographs of each patient had been taken on admission and at monthly intervals subsequently. It was decided to make as simple an assessment as possible, reviewing progress at two-monthly intervals, each two-monthly film being compared with the film taken two months previously and with the initial film. Thus the comparisons on which report was requested were: 0 with 2 (initial film with film two months after admission), 2 with 4, 0 with 4, 4 with 6, and 0 with 6. Assessments were required to fall under one of the five headings 'considerable improvement', 'moderate or slight improvement', 'no change', 'moderate or slight deterioration', 'considerable deterioration'. A report 'no change' might signify no appreciable change in the radiological picture or improvement in one part of the lung offset by deterioration in another.

So simple a classification invited difficulties, and these were soon evident. How should atelectasis be classified? Some films showed considerable clearing of infiltration concurrently with enlargement of cavities—radiologically they were both better and worse. The analysis in Table **4,** 8 shows the separate results of readings by the three assessors. Two most important readings have been chosen for this analysis: 0 with 4 (comparison of initial film with film four months after admission) and 4 with 6.

TABLE **4,** 8

Comparison of Radiological Assessments by Three Assessors

Interval	Group	Total Cases	Assessor	Radiological Assessment				
				Improvement		No Change	Deterioration	
				Con-siderable	Slight or Mod.		Slight or Mod.	Con-siderable
Admission to end of 4th month	S	55	X	18	24	4	5	4
			Y	27	17	3	4	4
			Z	27	15	1	6	6
	C	42	X	0	11	4	18	9
			Y	2	10	11	10	9
			Z	3	8	8	15	8
End of 4th month to end of 6th month	S	51	X	2	17	11	15	6
			Y	5	18	10	8	10
			Z	3	12	11	19	6
	C	38	X	0	11	18	7	2
			Y	2	9	19	5	3
			Z	1	10	11	14	2

It can be seen from Table **4,** 8 that there was some disagreement among the three members of the panel, but the outstanding differences between results in S and C groups remain unaffected.

Where reports were identical they were adopted as the final agreed report. Where the reports on a case by the three members fell in two adjoining columns of the classification (*e.g.,* 'considerable improvement' and 'slight or moderate improvement') the majority of two was taken as the final agreed report. In all other cases there was held to be disagreement. Thus in the comparisons between radiograph on admission and radiograph at four months there was agreement in 76 cases and disagreement in 21. In the comparisons

TABLE **4**, 9.   *Changes in the Radiological Picture*

Interval	Group	Total		Improvement		No Change		Deterioration		Deaths	
				Considerable	Slight or Mod.			Slight or Mod.	Considerable		
Admission to end of 2nd month	S	55	100%	8 14%	34 62%	7 13%		5 9%	1 2%	0	
	C	52	100%	0	3 6%	27 52%		14 27%	6 11%	2	4%
Admission to end of 4th month	S	55	99%	25 45%	18 33%	4 7%		4 7%	4 7%	0	
	C	52	99%	0	11 21%	9 17%		14 27%	8 15%	10	19%
Admission to end of 6th month	S	55	100%	28 51%	10 18%	2 4%		5 9%	6 11%	4	7%
	C	52	100%	4 8%	13 25%	3 6%		12 23%	6 11%	14	27%

TABLE **4**, 10.   *Changes in the Radiological Picture*

Interval	Group	Total		Improvement		No Change		Deterioration		Deaths	
				Considerable	Slight or Mod.			Slight or Mod.	Considerable		
Admission to end of 2nd month	S	55	100%	8 14%	34 62%	7 13%		5 9%	1 2%	0	
	C	52	100%	0	3 6%	27 52%		14 27%	6 11%	2	4%
End of 2nd month to end of 4th month	S	55	100%	6 11%	30 54%	8 15%		8 15%	3 5%	0	
	C	50	100%	0	9 18%	13 26%		16 32%	4 8%	8	16%
End of 4th month to end of 6th month	S	55	99%	3 5%	16 29%	15 27%		10 18%	7 13%	4	7%
	C	42	100%	1 2%	9 21%	17 41%		9 21%	2 5%	4	10%

between radiographs at four months and at six months there was agreement in 75 cases and disagreement in 14.

At a final session the three members of the radiological panel met for discussion and review of films on which there had been disagreement. After a short discussion it was agreed that changes in the prognosis for the patient should be taken as the base-line of assessment. In a comparison of two radiographs of a patient the question should be, judging from these films alone: Has the outlook for the patient become better or worse? On this basis the films in question were reviewed, and agreement was reached on all of them. The analysis which follows is based on the agreed results. The overall results under the five different headings are given for each of the three assessments 0:2, 0:4, and 0:6 in Table **4,** 9 and Fig. **4,** 2, and for each of the three assessments 0:2, 2:4, 4:6 in Table **4,** 10 and Figs. **4,** 3 and **4,** 4.

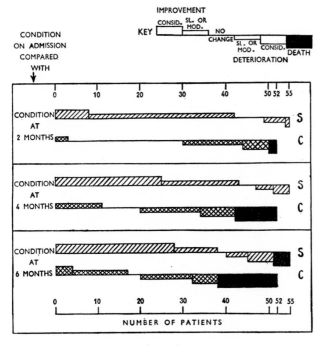

FIG. **4,** 2

Condition on admission compared with condition at two, four, and six months (radiological assessment)

It is evident that at every stage there is between the two groups a great difference in the course of the disease.

At two months 76 per cent of S patients showed radiological

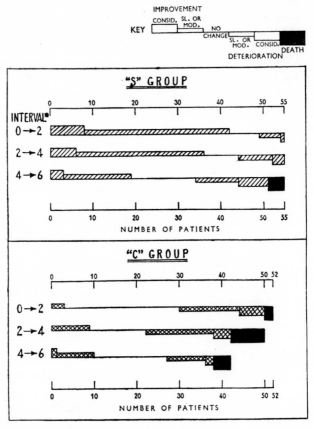

Fig. **4**, 3

Changes in the radiological picture in succeeding two-monthly periods. $0 \to 2$, admission to end of second month; $2 \to 4$, end of second month to end of fourth month; $4 \to 6$, end of fourth month to end of sixth month.

improvement, and in 14 per cent the improvement was considerable; only 6 per cent of C patients were improved, and in none was the improvement considerable. Of C patients 4 per cent had died and another 38 per cent were worse than on admission; 11 per cent of S patients were worse, and none had died.

From the end of the second month to the end of the fourth month the proportion of S patients who improved (65 per cent) was slightly lower than in the first two months and the corresponding proportion of C patients (18 per cent) was higher, but the difference between

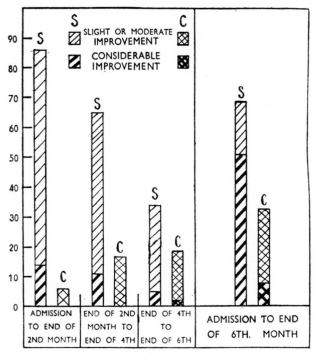

FIG. 4, 4

Percentage of total patients admitted (*not* of survivors at beginning of each period) showing improvement in radiological picture in succeeding two-monthly periods and in six months.

the two groups is still marked. Considering the overall change in the first four months, 78 per cent of S patients were improved and only 21 per cent of C patients; in none of the latter and in 45 per cent of S patients the improvement was considerable. Of C patients 19 per cent had died and another 42 per cent were worse than on admission; no S patients had died and only 14 per cent had deteriorated.

The proportion of S patients who improved in the fifth and sixth months was again lower than before (34 per cent compared with 65 per cent in the third and fourth months and 76 per cent in the first two months); this can be seen clearly in Figs. **4,** 3 and **4,** 4. Of S patients 7 per cent died in that period and another 31 per cent deteriorated (the total 38 per cent compares with 20 per cent in the preceding two months and 11 per cent in the first two months); 10 per cent of C patients surviving at four months died and another 26 per cent deteriorated. Despite the setback in S patients in later months, the result at six months compared with the condition on admission shows, as we saw in the preliminary analysis, a remarkable difference between the two groups.

It is of interest to analyse in greater detail the changes that occurred from period to period. The analysis in Tables **4,** 11 and **4,** 12 relates results in succeeding two-monthly periods.

TABLE **4,** 11

Radiological Changes in Succeeding Periods (S Cases)

Admission to End of 2nd Month	Total	End of 2nd Month to End of 4th Month			
		Improvement	No Change	Deterioration	Deaths
Improvement	42	31	6	5	0
No change	7	4	1	2	0
Deterioration	6	1	1	4	0
Total	55	36	8	11	0
End of 2nd Month to end of 4th Month	Total	End of 4th Month to End of 6th Month			
Improvement	36	17	12	7*	0
No change	8	1	1	5†	1
Deterioration	11	1	2	5	3
Total	55	19	15	17	4

* One case had begun to deteriorate in the fourth month, though the overall assessment 2:4 was improvement.

† Two cases had begun to deteriorate in the fourth month, though the overall assessment 2:4 was no change.

Thirty-one of 42 S patients who improved in the first two months continued to improve in the third and fourth months, but less than half of those who improved in the third and fourth months made further good progress subsequently. Nearly all S patients who deteriorated in the first months continued to get worse subsequently; only one of the six in the first two months and one of the 11 in the third and fourth months improved subsequently; the improvement in the latter case began only after induction of pneumoperitoneum.

Considering now the 17 S patients who deteriorated and four who died in the fifth and sixth months, eight had been getting worse during the preceding two months, six more had shown 'no change', and seven had improved in the preceding two months. These cases are analysed in detail later.

Analysis of radiological changes in the C group (Table **4**, 12) shows that here patients who improved did so much more slowly. Only three patients improved in the first two months, and they did

TABLE **4**, 12

Radiological Changes in Succeeding Periods (C Cases)

Admission to End of 2nd Month	Total	End of 2nd Month to End of 4th Month			
		Improvement	No Change	Deterioration	Deaths
Improvement	3	0	2	1	0
No change	27	9	9	8	1
Deterioration	20	0	2	11	7
Total	50	9	13	20	8
End of 2nd Month to end of 4th Month	Total	End of 4th Month to End of 6th Month			
Improvement	9	2	7	0	0
No change	13	5	4	4	0
Deterioration	20	3	6	7	4
Total	42	10	17	11	4

not continue to improve subsequently. Nine patients showed improvement in the third and fourth months. In all nine the condition had been stationary in the first two months; the improvement was attributable to bed-rest alone—only one of these patients had collapse therapy, three and a half months after admission. None of the nine deteriorated in the fifth and sixth months, contrary to what was seen in the S group. On the other hand, as in the S group, nearly all patients who deteriorated in the first two months continued to deteriorate subsequently—*i.e.*, for those who showed no response to the first two months of bed-rest and streptomycin, or bed-rest alone, the outlook was poor.

Six of the 10 C patients who improved in the fifth and sixth months received collapse therapy; in four of them the improvement was considered due to these measures.

CLINICAL OBSERVATIONS ON CASES SHOWING IMPROVEMENT

In the preceding sections various clinical and radiological changes have been analysed separately, the analysis showing for each factor differences between S and C groups. Below are additional data and some representative case histories to give a more complete picture of patients' progress under treatment.

Considerable Improvement in S Cases

Of the 28 S patients who radiologically had improved considerably at the end of six months 11 had been regarded as desperately ill on admission. All 28 improved from the first month of treatment. In none could the improvement even in later months be ascribed to collapse therapy.

(*a*) Twenty-one of the 28 improved clinically in all respects—*i.e.*, their general condition and symptoms improved, they gained weight, temperature and E.S.R. fell, 18 were apyrexial at the end of six months, and 16 had gained more than 14lb. (6.35kg.) in weight. In eight cases the sputum had become negative to all examinations for tubercle bacilli.

Case 69.—A man aged 25 had been ill for four months and had been in hospital since shortly after the clinical onset. Artificial pneumothorax had been attempted, but failed; on complete bed-rest throughout the four months he continued to deteriorate. On admission to the centre he was exceedingly ill, wasted, with laryngitis, with swinging temperature 99.4–103.4° F. (37.4–39.7° C.), sedimentation rate 66, sputum heavily positive. The chest radiograph showed confluent opacities of bronchopneumonic type throughout both upper and mid-zones, and scattered foci in the lower zones (Plate **4**, 1). During the first two months there was slight clinical improvement: fever persisted, though at a lower level; the sedimentation rate was unchanged; the sputum was negative on direct examination and positive on culture. The chest radiograph showed little change. During the next months there was a striking turn for the better: symptoms regressed, the laryngitis improved; from the end of the fourth month he was apyrexial; he gained 42 lb. (19.05 kg.) weight from the third to the sixth month (on admission he had been too ill to weigh). The sedimentation rate had fallen to 22. Sputum was still positive, though on culture only. Radiologically there was remarkable clearing of lesions (Plate **4,** 2).

Case 90.—A woman aged 24 had been ill for two months; her condition had been aggravated by recent parturition and post-partum haemorrhage. She was in hospital for two weeks before admission to the streptomycin centre. She was desperately ill on admission, wasted, and had a pyrexia varying from 99–103.4° F. (37.2–39.7° C.); sedimentation rate 150. On the chest radiograph were dense confluent opacities throughout the left lung, with some cavitation, and less extensive lesions in the right lung (Plate **4,** 3). She remained critically ill during the first week of treatment, after which there was marked improvement in her general condition and symptoms. The evening temperature fell to 100° F. (37.8° C.) at the end of the second month, and from the end of the fourth month she was apyrexial. Weight gain was only 4 lb. (1.8 kg.). The sedimentation rate fell progressively to 20 at the end of six months. The sputum and material from gastric lavage were negative to all methods of examination for tubercle bacilli from the fifty-ninth day onwards. There was considerable radiological clearing of lesions (Plate **4,** 4). 'The result on discharge must be regarded as dramatic' (report by clinical registrar).

(*b*) Seven of the 28 patients improved clinically in most respects, but six were still pyrexial at six months, and the other, though apyrexial, remained in poor general condition, with no weight gain and a high E.S.R. (Case 39, Plates **4,** 5 and **4,** 6).

Considerable Improvement in C Cases

Considerable improvement in the radiological picture was reported for only four C patients. None was acutely ill on admission. In none of them had the sputum become negative at the end of six months.

In Case 73 there was general clinical improvement, beginning in the first month, but the marked radiological improvement dated only from the induction of artificial pneumoperitoneum three and a half months after admission. In Case 80 also there was improvement in all respects, but only after induction of pneumoperitoneum two and a half months after admission.

In the two others, Cases 81 and 96, the improvement was attributable to bed-rest alone. Both improved clinically but retained a low pyrexia.

Case 81.—A woman aged 22 had a six-months' history of illness, and had been in bed at home for six weeks. On admission she looked ill and wasted, and had a low pyrexia (97.4–99° F. (36.3–37.2° C.)) and a sedimentation rate of 110. Chest radiography showed scattered nodular shadows throughout both lungs, denser at the apices, with a large cavity in the right upper zone (Plate **4**, 7). From the first weeks her general condition improved, and in the six months she gained 28 lb. (12.7 kg.). She retained, however, a low evening pyrexia, the sedimentation rate at the end of six months was 85, and the sputum was positive on culture. Radiologically there was considerable regression and shrinkage of lesions, and the cavity system in the right upper zone was less obvious (Plate **4**, 8).

Slight or Moderate Improvement in S Cases

At the end of six months, of 10 S patients who showed radiologically slight or moderate improvement five were apyrexial, four had sedimentation rates not above 10, and two had gained over 14 lb. (6.35 kg.) in weight. In none of the 10 cases was the sputum negative, though in two it had been negative at some time during treatment and became positive again later.

Case 95.—A woman aged 25 was extremely ill when admitted. She had a history of symptoms for about five months, and had been in bed at home for four weeks. On admission she had a temperature swinging between 99 and 102.4° F. (37.2 and 39.1° C.), and was very weak and wasted. The sedimentation rate was 28, the sputum heavily positive. There was extensive infiltration in the lungs, particularly in the right lung, where there were large cavities; a calcified primary complex was clearly definable on that side (Plate **4**, 9). Clinically she made excellent progress throughout the six months, with remarkable improvement in the first two months of treatment, and she gained 28 lb. The evening temperature had fallen to 99° F. (37.2° C.) at the end of two months, and shortly after became normal and remained normal. The sedimentation rate fell to 5. The sputum was negative at four months, but subsequently was occasionally positive. Radiologically there was little change in the first two months and improvement subsequently, with clearing at the right base and cavities much less obvious at the right apex (Plate **4**, 10).

Slight or Moderate Improvement in C Cases

Of 13 C patients who showed slight or moderate improvement radiologically at the end of six months, eight had improved clinically in all respects; three of the eight had been clinically very ill on admission. In two the sputum became negative (in one of the two after artificial pneumoperitoneum). Ten were apyrexial at six months, and six had gained over 14 lb. In most of these cases the clinical improvement was much greater than that seen in the lung radiographs.

CASE DEMONSTRATING 'CONSIDERABLE IMPROVEMENT'

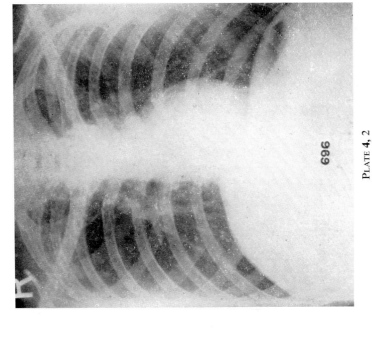

PLATE **4**, 2
case 69(S). November 17, 1947

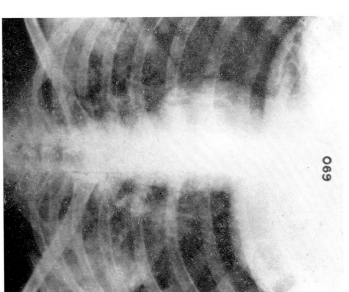

PLATE **4**, 1
case 69(S). May 12, 1947

4

CASE DEMONSTRATING 'CONSIDERABLE IMPROVEMENT'

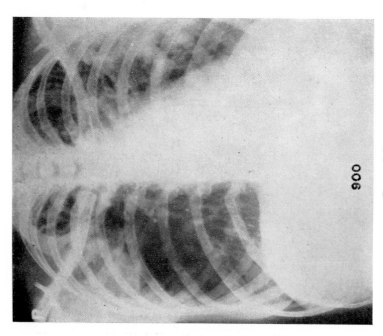

PLATE 4, 3

PLATE 4, 4

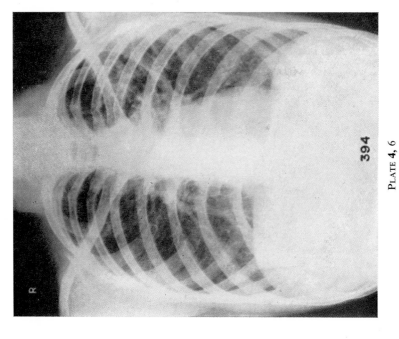

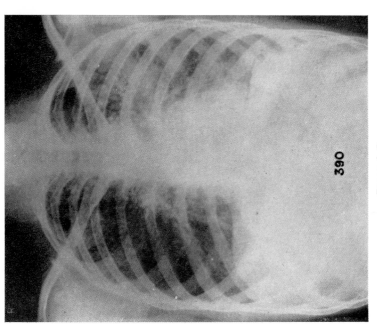

PLATE 4, 5
case 39(S). June 21, 1947

PLATE 4, 6
case 39(S). October 20, 1947

CASE DEMONSTRATING 'CONSIDERABLE IMPROVEMENT'

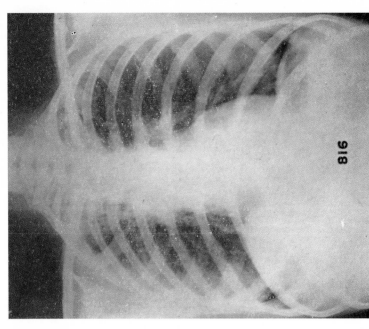

PLATE 4, 7
case 81(C). February 27, 1947

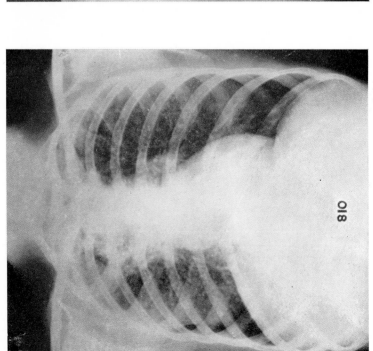

PLATE 4, 8
case 81(C). August 27, 1947

CASE DEMONSTRATING 'MODERATE IMPROVEMENT'

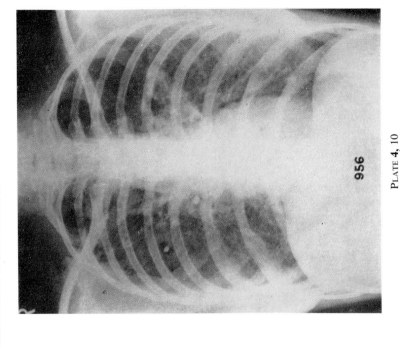

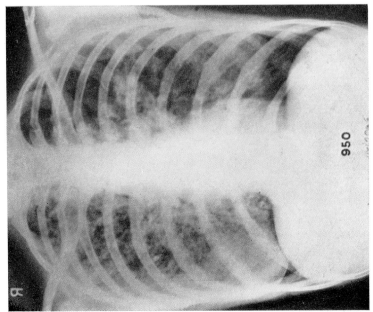

PLATE 4, 9
case 95(S). May 21, 1947

PLATE 4, 10
case 95(S). November, 21, 1947

CASE DEMONSTRATING 'MODERATE IMPROVEMENT'

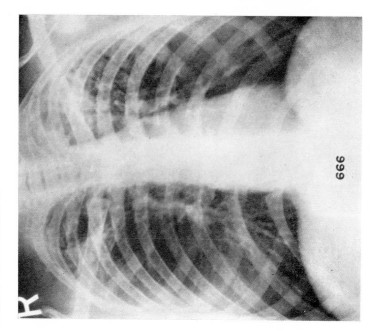

PLATE **4**, 12
case 66(C). October 15, 1947

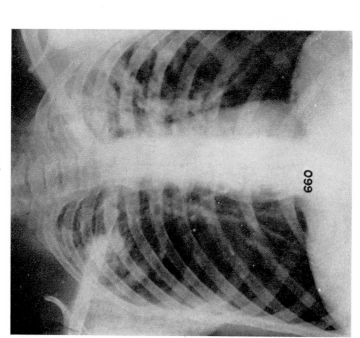

PLATE **4**, 11
case 66(C). April 11, 1947

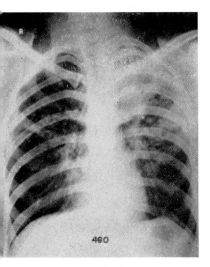

PLATE **4,** 13
case 46. January 30, 1947

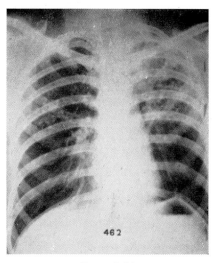

PLATE **4,** 14
case 46. March 26, 1947

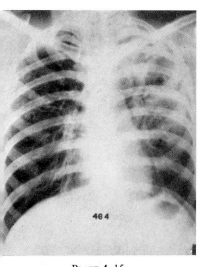

PLATE **4,** 15
case 46. May 23, 1947

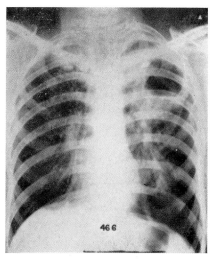

PLATE **4,** 16
case 46. July 21, 1947

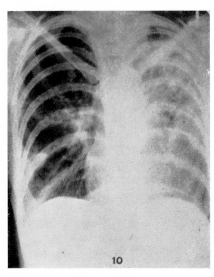

PLATE **4,** 17
case 1. June 2, 1947

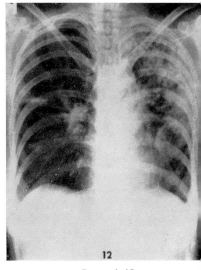

PLATE **4,** 18
case 1. July 25, 1947

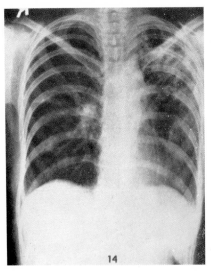

PLATE **4,** 19
case 1. September 29, 1947

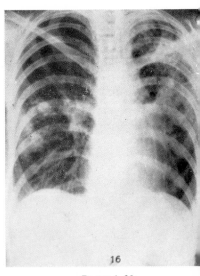

PLATE **4,** 20
case 1. November 21, 1947

Case 66.—A man aged 23, ill for about six weeks, had been admitted to a general hospital as a case of appendicitis one month before his admission to the centre. His general condition was fairly good, symptoms were slight, the temperature ranged from 97.6–100.2° F. (36.4–37.9° C.), the sedimentation rate was 70. There was shadowing throughout the upper and mid-zones of both lungs, particularly dense and with cavitation on the left side (Plate **4**, 11). During the six months of observation there was slow but progressive overall improvement; he put on 24 lb. (10.88 kg.) in weight, symptoms improved, he was afebrile after the third month, three consecutive sputum specimens at the end of the fifth and sixth months were negative. Radiologically there was moderate improvement, with some shrinkage of lesions particularly on the right (Plate **4**, 12).

DETERIORATION IN S CASES

(*a*) In six patients there was radiological deterioration in the first two months. In two of these (Cases 87 and 99) there was no clinical response to treatment, and they continued to deteriorate until death in the fifth or sixth month. Two others (Cases 22 and 40) continued to deteriorate radiologically; clinically there was temporary improvement in the general condition, but temperature and E.S.R. remained high; one (Case 22) died in the fifth month. One (Case 16) continued to deteriorate radiologically (deterioration confined to one lung), but the temperature fell to normal limits, the patient gained weight, and felt much better until after treatment stopped; E.S.R. remained high, over 70. The sixth of these patients improved subsequently in the opinion of the radiologists' panel, but deteriorated clinically. Four of the six had gross cavitation on admission.

(*b*) In seven patients other than those just mentioned there was radiological deterioration through the third and fourth months. Five (Cases 46, 49, 60, 64 and 86) had improved radiologically in the first two months, and there had been temporary clinical improvement; in Case 60 there was marked clinical improvement until a spontaneous pneumothorax occurred three months after admission.

Case 46.—A man aged 25 had been ill for six weeks with cough, dyspnoea, lassitude, loss of weight. He had been resting in bed at home for five weeks before admission to the streptomycin centre. On admission his condition was fair, his temperature ranged from 97.6–102° F. (36.4–38.9° C.), the sedimentation rate was 40. Chest radiograph showed extensive scattered lesions in upper and mid-zones of both lungs and a large cavity in the left mid-zone. There was slight clinical improvement in the first two months of treatment, symptoms regressed, the temperature fell to a range of 97.8–99.4° F. (36.55–37.4° C.); the sedimentation rate was unchanged and weight was stationary. The clinical change was not of the same order as the change in the radiological picture, which showed considerable improvement (Plates **4**, 13 and **4**, 14). During the third month the clinical condition was stationary except that the temperature began to rise again, and radiologically there was extension and more cavitation of the lesions in the left lung. He then began to lose weight (7 lb.—3.18 kg.—in the fourth month), to feel tired again, and radiographs showed further deterioration with extensive cavitation; a spontaneous pneumothorax occurred in the sixth month (Plates **4**, 15 and **4**, 16). The sputum had remained positive throughout; on the 65th day of treatment and subsequently strains of tubercle bacilli from the sputum were 8,000 times less sensitive to streptomycin than the strains isolated before treatment.

In the other two of the seven patients (Cases 54 and 105) the pulmonary condition was stationary radiologically in the first two months; one (Case 105) deteriorated clinically throughout the first months and until after induction of artificial pneumoperitoneum in the fifth month, after which there was radiological improvement also; the other was slightly better clinically in the first months of treatment, but the radiological worsening was rapidly followed by clinical deterioration, and she continued to go downhill. All seven of these cases which deteriorated radiologically for the first time in the third and fourth months had gross cavitation on admission, and five also had some atelectasis.

(c) Three other patients (Cases 11, 26, and 59) on whom the radiological report for the second two-month period was 'no change' or 'improvement' had begun to deteriorate radiologically in the fourth month—i.e., before treatment stopped. In Case 26 spontaneous pneumothorax was diagnosed in the fifth month. In Cases 26 and 59 clinical deterioration also began in the fourth month; in Case 11 only in the sixth month, after a haemoptysis. All three continued to get worse in the last months. Case 59 was the only one of these to have gross cavitation on admission.

(d) In nine cases radiological deterioration did not occur until the last two months. In three of these (Cases 28, 77, and 101) the radiological report for the third and fourth months was 'no change'; two of them had improved in the first two months, but at the end of the fourth month all three were still febrile and had a high E.S.R. In Case 28 the temperature fell to normal in the first two months and the patient gained 11 lb. (4.98 kg.) in weight, but the temperature rose in the third month, and there was subsequently continued clinical deterioration.

Finally, radiological deterioration in the fifth and sixth months was seen in six patients who had improved radiologically to the end of the fourth month. In two of these (Cases 7 and 24) there had been little or no clinical response to streptomycin treatment; at four months they were pyrexial, had lost over a stone in weight, and had a high E.S.R.; both had gross cavitation on admission. The others (Cases 1, 4, 29, and 71) had improved clinically to the end of the fourth month, though at that date three were still pyrexial and none had an E.S.R. below 40. Only one of these four had gross cavitation on admission.

Case 1.—A woman, aged 24, had been ill for about 10 weeks, and for six weeks before admission had been in bed at home. She was very ill when admitted, pale, wasted, with severe dyspnoea and lassitude; the tempera-ture ranged from 100–104.2° F. (37.8–40.1° C.), the sedimentation rate was 98, the sputum was strongly positive. The chest radiograph showed exten-sive shadowing of bronchopneumonic type throughout both lung fields, more dense in the left lung than in the right (Plate **4,** 17). In the first month the temperature dropped to a range of 99–101° F. (37.2–38.3° C.), and remained at this level during the rest of the four months of treatment. In the first month also there was definite improvement both in symptoms and in general appearance, and she gained 7 lb. (3.18 kg.) in weight. At the end of two months the sputum was negative to direct examination and culture, and radiologically there was some clearing of the lesions, especially on the right. In the third and fourth months she began to lose her feeling of well-being, appetite deteriorated, and she lost 5 lb. (2.27 kg.) in weight; sputum became again heavily positive (strains were 250 times less sensitive to streptomycin than strains isolated before treatment). Radiographs, how-ever, showed further considerable clearing of lesions (Plates **4,** 18 and **4,** 19). After treatment was stopped she felt better for a short time, but in the sixth month the condition deteriorated, symptoms were worse, the tem-perature rose to the same level as on admission, and radiographs at the end of the sixth month showed increased cavitation in the left lung and fresh lesions in the right (Plate **4,** 20).

This analysis has shown that though 21 S patients deteriorated radiologically in the fifth and sixth months—*i.e.*, at a time when no streptomycin was being given in most cases—there is much evidence of commencing deterioration or arrested improvement before the end of the fourth month. Only six of the 21 had been improving radiologically throughout the preceding two months; two of the six had lost weight, and five had remained pyrexial since admission.

Moreover, it is noteworthy that in patients who received strepto-mycin for more than four months results were similar to those for patients treated for four months only; deterioration in the fifth and sixth months was seen in five of 13 patients treated for more than four months, compared with 16 of 42 patients treated for four months only. However, in one patient treated for five months deterioration started in the sixth month. While there is suggestive evidence in a few cases that deterioration was related to cessation of treatment, it is very probable that some factor other than this is responsible in the majority of cases that deteriorated.

Gross cavitation may be a factor in determining relapse after first improvement. Of 16 patients who deteriorated at some time after first improvement, 11 (69 per cent) had large or multiple cavities on admission; of 30 patients who improved throughout, 14 (47 per cent) had large or multiple cavities. The difference is not statistically significant.

Spontaneous pneumothorax occurred in four S patients. In Case 60 it occurred at three months; the patient had been much improved until then, but subsequently went downhill rapidly and died. In two other cases deterioration had begun before the pneumothorax occurred. At first the impression was that this was a particular risk in the S group, but pneumothorax occurred spontaneously also in three C cases.

TOXICITY

Toxic effects of streptomycin therapy were observed in many patients, but in no single case did they necessitate cessation of treatment. For this reason and because toxic effects of this anti-biotic have already been fully described by other investigators—*e.g.*, Veterans' Administration (1947)—they will be mentioned here only briefly.

By far the most important toxic effect was the damage to the vestibular apparatus. Giddiness was a frequent first symptom; it was noticed by 36 of the 55 patients, and first appeared on sitting up in bed or turning the head suddenly. It appeared usually in the fourth or fifth week of therapy, and persisted for periods varying from one week to several months. Spontaneous nystagmus on lateral vision was another frequent sign of vestibular disturbance; blurring of vision was less common. Tests for vestibular dysfunction were not carried out in all centres with sufficient regularity and uniformity to permit analysis of grouped results, but it is possible to say that absence or reduction of caloric response was not found with the frequency reported in many American investigations, and that in some patients loss of response was temporary only. No standard functional tests at the end of treatment were performed; many patients are reported as having unsteadiness of gait, which improved gradually with visual compensation but remained a handicap in the dark. Possibly many of these patients retain a disability revealed in a dangerous ataxia on such occasions as walking downstairs in the dark, crossing a congested street, or walking in a moving train. It is highly desirable that standard tests be adopted for assessment of vestibular dysfunction.

No loss of hearing was reported, except for two cases of high-tone deafness. Many patients suffered from nausea and vomiting, symptoms which were often relieved by antihistamine therapy. Albuminuria and casts in urine, raised blood urea, pruritus and urticarial rash, eosinophilia, 'yellow vision' after injection, and circumoral numbness are among other transient effects reported. All subsided spontaneously—*i.e.*, without stopping treatment.

BACTERIOLOGY

(1) Bacterial Content of Sputum

Sputum was tested by direct-smear examination and by culture; where there was no sputum, material from laryngeal swab and/or gastric lavage was cultured. Examinations were done on admission and again at intervals of not more than one month.

In Table **4,** 13 the results in the third month and at the end of six months are related to the results on admission. Results of direct smear are recorded as 'strongly positive' where one or more acid-fast bacillus per 1/12in. (0.2cm.) field was seen or where the result was recorded as + + + or + + ; 'weakly positive' includes results with less than one acid-fast bacillus per field or results recorded as +. For one hospital where only direct-smear examinations were done, and where degrees of positivity were not recorded, positive results in both groups have been tabulated in column 1, 'strongly positive'; one C case and one S case (Nos. 3 and 107), positive on admission and negative to direct examination (no culture) at six months, have been excluded from the analysis; another (Case 62) has been excluded because no results were recorded for the third month.

TABLE **4**, 13

Presence of Tubercle Bacilli

Results on Admission	Total	Deaths	Results in Third Month			
			Direct Smear		Smear Negative Culture Positive	Culture Negative
			Strongly Positive	Weakly Positive		
S Cases:						
Smear strongly positive	40	0	16	12	10	2
Smear weakly positive	11	0	1	3	1	6
Smear negative, culture positive	3	0	1	0	0	2
C Cases:						
Smear strongly positive	29	5	19	3	1	1
Smear weakly positive	17	1	6	8	2	0
Smear negative, culture positive	4	0	1	1	2	0
			Results at End of 6 Months			
S Cases:						
Smear strongly positive	40	4	24	1	7	4
Smear weakly positive	11	0	3	3	2	3
Smear negative, culture positive	3	0	1	0	1	1
C Cases:						
Smear strongly positive	29	11	15	2	0	1
Smear weakly positive	17	3	4	7	3	0
Smear negative, culture positive	4	0	0	1	2	1

Considering the results in the third month, one C case and 10 S cases were negative to all examinations for tubercle bacillus. Apart from these cases of 'sputum conversion', six C cases and 23 S cases were positive at a lower level than on admission. The differences between the two series are significant. There is no doubt here of the pronounced effect of streptomycin on the tubercle bacillus.

The results at the end of six months also show a difference, though less marked, between the two groups; two C cases and eight S cases had become negative to all examinations. These final results signifying 'sputum conversion' are based on repeated examinations, in most cases of sputum; the case with least satisfactory evidence had negative results from one gastric lavage and two laryngeal swabs. Besides these cases five C cases and 10 S cases were at six months positive at a lower level than on admission. Taking together cases becoming negative or positive at a lower level, the difference between the two series is significant.

In the S group the results are best in cases without gross cavitation; six of 23 became negative, compared with two of 31 cases with large or multiple cavities.

If in order to get an overall evaluation of changes we give a numerical score to each category of results (4 = negative; 3 = smear negative, culture positive; 2 = smear weakly positive; 1 = smear strongly positive; 0 = death), the total in each group is as follows:

	On Admission	During Third Month	At end of Six Months
S cases	71	124	98
C cases	75	69	62

In the S group these results confirm the impression already gained of maximum improvement in the first months and subsequent deterioration.

The following numerical scores on the same basis are obtained from data for 51 of the S group analysed in greater detail (examinations for the C group were not frequent enough to provide comparable data).

Months after Admission	0	1	2	3	4	5	6
Bact. 'score'	66	111	115	127	105	104	94

This overall evaluation shows the marked improvement during the first three months, followed by a steep fall in 'score' in the fourth month and further decline later.

(2) Streptomycin Sensitivity

Strains from 42 cases were tested for streptomycin sensitivity on primary isolation and during the course of treatment. Details of the technique adopted will be given in a subsequent report by the Pathological Subcommittee.

A. Degree of Sensitivity

All strains isolated before streptomycin therapy was begun showed sensitivity to the drug equivalent to that of the standard strain H37Rv (obtained from the American Depot, Trudeau Sanatorium, Saranac Lake); this was usually at a level of 0.1 to 0.5 µg. per ml., using the Tween-albumin medium.

Sensitivity after Start of Streptomycin Treatment.—(1) In one patient (Case 90) there was not full opportunity to detect streptomycin resistance, as all cultures were negative after the fifty-ninth day. (2) In six cases resistance did not emerge at a level above 10 times that of H37Rv. (3) In five cases strains were isolated which showed streptomycin resistance from 32 (one case) to 64 times (four cases) that of H37Rv. (4) In 17 cases resistance between 100 and 256 times that of H37Rv was demonstrated. (5) In 13 cases the resistance demonstrated was more than 2,000 times that of H37Rv; in four of these it was over 8,000 times.

Summarizing, strains with resistance over 10 times that of H37Rv were found in 35 of the 41 cases.

B. Time of Emergence of Streptomycin Resistance

In the majority it was not possible to detect with any great precision the date at which resistant strains could be first isolated, as specimens were not taken at frequent enough intervals. The date is taken as that midway between the date of the last sensitive culture and the date of the first resistant culture. In a few cases this interval was only a few days; in one it was five and a half months. Where it was possible to isolate strains at frequent intervals, it was seen that resistance rose rapidly to a maximum level at which it persisted subsequently with only minor fluctuations.

The results are shown in Fig. **4,** 5. Of 35 cases showing resistance over 10 times H37, this resistance emerged in five cases in the first month, in 21 in the second month, four in the third, four in the fourth, and one as late as the fifth month. Taking all observations, the mean date of emergence of resistance is the fifty-third day after starting streptomycin therapy. The median is the forty-fifth day.

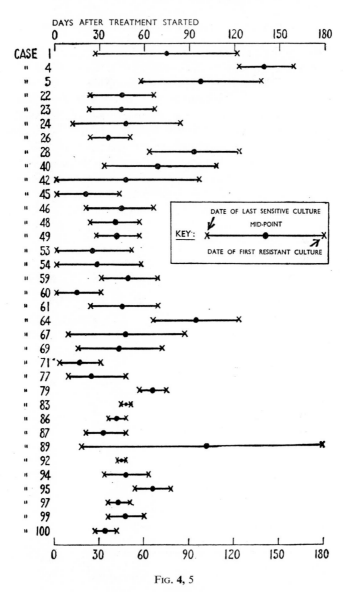

FIG. 4, 5

Showing date of emergence of streptomycin resistance (over 10 times
that of H37Rv)

RESULTS RELATED TO RESISTANCE DEVELOPMENT

The results given in Fig. **4, 6** raise an important point: the radiological results at six months compared with condition on admission
seem to be related to the degree of streptomycin resistance found
during observation. Of six patients from whom strains isolated did
not show resistance greater than 10 times that of the standard
H37Rv, all had improved at six months. Twenty-two patients
developed streptomycin resistance over 10 and less than 1,000 times
H37Rv; five of them, or just under one in 4, had deteriorated at six
months (one of the five had died). Of 13 patients in whom the drug-
resistance developed was over 1,000 times H37Rv, eight or over
one-half had deteriorated (three of the eight had died). The differences in results in the three groups are statistically significant.

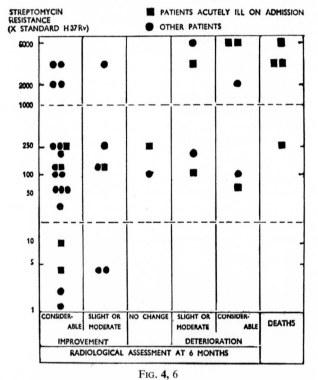

FIG. 4, 6

Radiological assessment at six months related to degree of streptomycin
resistance

If we consider not only the result at six months but deterioration at any time during the six months, it is interesting to note that the six patients who did not develop resistance over 10 times H37Rv improved throughout, without setback at any time in the six months.

Of the 22 cases with resistance 32 to 256 times H37Rv, deterioration occurred in six in the fifth and sixth months after continuous improvement in the first four months (but only two of these were worse at the end of six months than on admission); in two deterioration began after two months' improvement; one began to deteriorate in the third month, the condition having been stationary in the first two months; one died after continuous deterioration throughout. The remainder, 12 patients, did not deteriorate at any time.

In the cases with resistance over 1,000 times H37Rv, deterioration began earlier: within the first two months in four cases, in the third and fourth months after initial improvement in three cases, and only in the final months in two cases.

Before accepting degree of streptomycin resistance as a major factor in prognosis it is important to determine if among the cases with high streptomycin resistance there is a higher proportion of initially severe cases than in the others, as if so this might account for the worse prognosis. Six of the 13 patients from whom were isolated strains over 1,000 times more resistant than H37Rv were very acutely ill on admission (had high pyrexia and large or multiple cavities), compared with nine of the 28 other patients. The difference is small. Moreover, there is both in the patients very ill on admission and in the others the trend to bad prognosis with increasing levels of streptomycin resistance. Thus in those very ill on admission the proportion deteriorating was 0/2 where resistance was not more than 10 times H37Rv, 3/7 where it was more than 10 and not more than 1,000 times (one of the three died), and 6/6 where it was above 1,000 times (three of the six died). In the other patients it was 0/5 where resistance was not more than 10 times H37Rv, 2/14 where it was more than 10 and not more than 1,000, and 2/7 where it was over 1,000 times. However, while the trend to bad prognosis with increasing levels of drug resistance is seen in both groups, the trend is greater in the patients very ill on admission than in the others; there is a possibility of relationship between severe clinical condition and development of high degrees of streptomycin resistance. In conclusion, one can say that the results were outstandingly good in cases in which little or no drug resistance was demonstrated, but for the others it remains difficult to assess the relative importance and the interdependence of the two factors—clinical condition at start of treatment and degree of drug resistance developed during treatment.

DISCUSSION

This planned group investigation has demonstrated both the benefit and the limitations of streptomycin therapy in pulmonary tuberculosis. The trial—the first controlled investigation of its kind to be reported—was designed to give a negative or affirmative answer to the question, Is streptomycin of value in the treatment of pulmonary tuberculosis? It was not designed to determine in what types of pulmonary tuberculosis streptomycin could be effective, nor to determine optimal dosage or duration and rhythm of treatment.*

Analysis of the results at the end of the first six-month period has shown that the course of bilateral acute progressive disease can be halted by streptomycin therapy; 51 per cent of the streptomycin-treated patients showed considerable improvement radiologically when comparison was made with their chest radiographs taken on admission. That streptomycin was the agent responsible for this result is attested by the presence in this trial of the control group of patients, among whom considerable improvement was noted in only four (8 per cent), and two of these four patients had improved only after collapse therapy. In other words streptomycin therapy was effecting what the patients' tissues alone could not do—checking the spread of the tubercle bacillus in one of its most favourable *milieux*.

Among the treated patients radiological improvement occurred most often in those who, though having extensive infection, did not have large or multiple cavitation. Nevertheless in one-third of those with gross cavitation considerable improvement also occurred, principally by resolution of recent infiltrative spread; some cases thus became suitable for collapse therapy. Streptomycin therapy alone did not lead to closure of large cavities.

The need of a control group in trials of a new drug for pulmonary

* Since this investigation was begun a number of notable publications on the effect of streptomycin in pulmonary tuberculosis have appeared. As, however, the prime objective of the Medical Research Council trial was a comparison of treated cases with controls, other investigations have not been referred to here.

tuberculosis is underlined by the finding that impressive clinical improvement was seen in some of the patients treated by bed-rest alone: 12 gained more than 14lb. (6.35kg.) in weight, and in 13 of 47 febrile patients the temperature was within normal limits at the end of six months. It was to be expected that in many of these patients with gross lesions who until recently had been at work the constitutional symptoms would be temporarily improved by bed-rest, although the lesions were so advanced that bed-rest alone could not be expected to effect corresponding improvement in the radiological picture. Nevertheless it should be noted that some radiological improvement was recorded in one-third of the C patients. The improvement in these patients was mainly among those least acutely ill on admission, and it is in this group that the treated series shows the least advantage over the control series. In such cases, with little or no pyrexia, relatively low sedimentation rate, and little cavitation, the patient's natural recuperative power added to bed-rest may in itself arrest the progress of the infection, and the advisability of using streptomycin in such cases may well be doubted. The major advantage is among the acutely ill patients. Although the only deaths that occurred in the S series were in this group, it is in these patients that the striking difference between the S and C series is most clearly demonstrated.

While stressing the good results in the streptomycin group, it is important to note, first, that no clinical 'cures' were effected, and that only 15 per cent were bacteriologically negative (to direct examination and culture) at the end of six months, and, secondly, that this trial presents at the time of writing only a short-term evaluation.* The major improvement in patients treated with streptomycin was seen in the first two to three months; in the latter half of the six-month period numbers of them began to deteriorate. Thus 21 S patients deteriorated radiologically in the fifth and sixth months, and four of them died. Streptomycin therapy had been stopped at the end of four months, and it is natural to ask whether the deterioration is attributable to stoppage of treatment. This seems unlikely for the majority; most had begun to deteriorate radiologically before the end of four months; only six of the 21 had improved radiologically throughout the four months, and two of these six had deteriorated clinically.

---

* An addendum gives the results at one year after admission to the trial.

Strains of tubercle bacilli resistant to high concentrations of streptomycin were isolated by the end of the second month of treatment from most patients whose sputum was still positive; this fact may account for at least a part of the deterioration witnessed in treated patients. Strains showing streptomycin resistance over 10 times that of the original strain or of the standard H37Rv were isolated from 35 of 41 patients for whom data are available; in 13 of the 35 cases the strains had a resistance over 2,000 times that of the control organism.

Therapeutic results appear to be related to the degree of drug resistance developed; thus the best results were seen in cases in which little or no drug resistance was demonstrated, and the worst results were in the group of 13 patients from whom were isolated strains of tubercle bacilli with a drug resistance over 2,000 times that of H37Rv; at the end of six months three of the 13 had died and five were radiologically worse than on admission. The relation between a bad prognosis and a high degree of streptomycin resistance applies particularly to patients most acutely ill at the start of treatment. The numbers involved are small, but the differences between the groups at different levels of resistance are suggestive. Probably both initial severity of clinical condition and development of drug resistance during treatment are factors responsible for deterioration, and the two factors may be interdependent. Even with the aid of a powerful chemotherapeutic agent healthy tissue reaction on the part of the host is necessary for complete destruction of the invading parasite. It is reasonable to suppose that, where a high degree of streptomycin resistance is demonstrable by the method used (which is qualitative and not quantitative), this may have occurred by rapid proliferation of resistant strains in tissues that have a poor natural defence against tuberculous infection.

On knowledge at present available, the development or emergence of streptomycin-resistant strains of tubercle bacilli is a fundamental factor to be taken into consideration when contemplating a course of streptomycin therapy. The technique of measuring sensitivity used in this investigation is so slow as to be of little immediate use in estimating, say at the end of one or two months of therapy, whether the course can be usefully continued or not. Organized investigations will be needed to determine whether emergence of streptomycin-resistant strains can be prevented by association of streptomycin with another drug or by a special rhythm of treatment. Until such time as this problem has been solved it seems fair to assume that after two to three months of streptomycin treatment in a patient with open pulmonary tuberculosis further treatment or a repeat course later is unlikely to be effective. Moreover, the possible dangers to the public health of dissemination of streptomycin-resistant strains, with the possible subsequent production of fresh cases (including cases of miliary or meningeal tuberculosis) which would not respond to streptomycin treatment, must be borne in mind.

One must add to this disadvantage of streptomycin therapy the information on the drug's toxic effects on the vestibular apparatus. These are frequent when the dose employed in this trial, 2 g. a day, is given; recent American reports indicate reduced toxicity with a dosage of 1 g. a day, but even then the effects are far from negligible.

These considerations must dictate a full measure of caution before prescribing streptomycin for any particular patient. They must be weighed in the balance against possible advantages of streptomycin therapy, particularly when contemplating its use for tuberculous lesions likely to improve by other known forms of treatment; and they render undesirable its administration for tuberculous lesions which, by reason of their age and pathological type, are unlikely to benefit by any form of chemotherapy.

The investigation reported here has demonstrated the value of streptomycin in one not very common form of tuberculosis. The type of result obtained indicates that the drug is probably of greatest value in cases of pulmonary tuberculosis in which the lesions requiring treatment are acute and of recent development. Its use may be recommended in acute contralateral spreads after artificial pneumo-thorax or after thoracoplasty. It probably has a place in the treatment of rapidly advancing pulmonary tuberculosis in which immediate collapse therapy would be dangerous or impracticable; in fact its most effective use may be in preparation of such lesions for collapse therapy. It has probably little place in the treatment of the more common chronic fibro-caseous forms of the disease. These conclusions are of necessity lacking in precision; much organized work is yet required to determine the precise indications of streptomycin and the best schemes of dosage in pulmonary tuberculosis.

ADDENDUM

Before going to press it has been possible to collect data regarding the condition of each patient one year after admission to the trial. The data are based on a general assessment by the clinicians concerned. Radiological evaluation by a panel was not possible, and therefore, although the data give a provisional impression of the course of the disease in these patients, the figures are not comparable with those based on independent radiological assessment, for example, in Table **4**, 2.

TABLE **4**, 14

Condition at 12 Months Related to Condition on Admission

Group	Total	Improvement	No Change	Deterioration	Death
S	55 100%	31 56%	4 7%	8 15%	12 22%
C	52 100%	16 31%	5 10%	7 13%	24 46%

The difference in mortality between the two groups is statistically significant.

SUMMARY

One hundred and seven patients with acute progressive bilateral pulmonary tuberculosis, unsuitable for collapse therapy, were studied in a clinical trial of streptomycin.

The supply of streptomycin available during the investigation was limited. The type of disease selected was one considered hitherto unsuitable for any form of treatment other than bed-rest. Bed-rest accordingly was the treatment given to one group of 52 patients (C), while 55 patients were treated with bed-rest plus streptomycin (S). Patients were assigned to one or the other group by random selection, and only after acceptance as suitable for the trial.

The period of observation for each patient, under conditions laid down for the trial, was six months.

S patients received 2g. of streptomycin intramuscularly daily in four injections at six-hourly intervals. No toxic effects necessitated stopping treatment, but vestibular disturbance was common.

At the end of six months 7 per cent of S patients and 27 per cent of C patients had died. Considerable improvement radiologically was noted in 51 per cent of S cases and 8 per cent of C cases. Slight or moderate improvement was noted in 18 per cent of S cases and 25 per cent of C cases. Apart from those who died, deterioration was seen in 18 per cent of S cases and 34 per cent of C cases.

The main difference between S and C series is among the patients clinically acutely ill on admission: thus, among patients having on admission evening temperatures of 101° F. (38.3° C.) or over, 13 of 24 S patients and two of 19 C patients showed improvement radiologically.

More S patients than C patients showed clinical improvement, but the difference between the two series is smaller than in respect of radiological changes.

Improvement in S cases was greatest in the first three months. After the end of this period many S cases began to deteriorate.

At the end of six months examinations for tubercle bacilli were negative in eight S cases and two C cases. The best results in S cases were seen in the first months of treatment.

Results of tests for streptomycin sensitivity of infecting strains are given for 41 cases. In 35 cases tests revealed *in vitro* resistance from 32 to over 8,000 times that of the original strain or the standard H37Rv. In most cases streptomycin resistance emerged in the second month of treatment. It seems probable that streptomycin resistance is responsible for much of the deterioration seen in S cases after first improvement.

An addendum gives the results at one year after admission.

REFERENCES

Amberson, J. B., jun., McMahon, B. I., and Pinner, M. (1931). *Amer. Rev. Tuberc.* **24**, 401.

Hart, P. D'Arcy (1946), *Brit. med. J.* ii, 805, 849.

Hinshaw, H. C., and Feldman, W. H. (1944). *Amer. Rev. Tuberc.* **50**, 202.

Hinshaw, H. C., and Feldman, W. H. (1945). *Proc. Mayo Clin.* **20**, 313.

Hinshaw, H. C., Feldman, W. H., and Pfuetze, K. H. (1946) *Amer. Rev. Tuberc.* **54**, 191.

National Research Council Committee on Chemotherapeutic Agents (1946). *J. Amer. med. Ass.* **132**, 70.

Schatz, A., Bugie, Elizabeth and Waksman, S. A. (1944). *Proc. Soc. exp. Biol. N.Y.* **55**, 66.

Veterans' Administration (1947). *Amer. Rev. Tuberc.* **56**, 485.

CHAPTER 5

CHEMOTHERAPY OF PULMONARY TUBERCULOSIS IN YOUNG ADULTS

DURING the period 1947 to 1951 three trials of chemotherapy of pulmonary tuberculosis in young adults were made under the direction of the Medical Research Council's Streptomycin in Tuberculosis Trials Committee. The first of these trials was designed to assess the efficacy of streptomycin itself. At that time the drug was available in only very small quantities, and it was thus possible to contrast the patients given streptomycin with similar patients treated by rest in bed only (Medical Research Council, 1948). In the second trial the newly discovered drug P.A.S. was brought under study, and its effects when used either alone or in combination with streptomycin were compared with the results given by streptomycin alone. It was clearly proved that the dose of 20 g. of P.A.S. daily would frequently prevent the development of streptomycin-resistant organisms (Medical Research Council, 1950). However, this dose often produced undesirable side-effects in the patient—nausea and vomiting—and a third trial was therefore set up to determine whether smaller doses of P.A.S. (5 or 10 g. daily) would be as effective as 20 g. in preventing the emergence of streptomycin-resistant strains. With the completion of this third trial (Medical Research Council, 1952) it is now possible to consider together the results of all three investigations.

The three trials were all designed in the same way. Clinicians and pathologists of several hospitals co-operated. The patients admitted to the trial had to conform to a particular definition (acute progressive bilateral pulmonary tuberculosis, believed to be of recent origin, bacteriologically proved, unsuitable for collapse therapy, age group 15–30); after acceptance by a panel the cases were randomly allocated to one or another treatment group; in each trial the different treatment groups were treated and observed concurrently; the clinical

An analysis of the combined results of three Medical Research Council trials, prepared and published in conjunction with Marc Daniels.

Reprinted from the *British Medical Journal*, 1952, **i**, 1162 and radiological examinations and record-keeping were made according to a plan previously agreed by all concerned; and, finally, the results of each trial were analysed by the Tuberculosis Research Unit of the Medical Research Council.

The groups involved in the three trials are shown in Fig. **5,** 1. There were 107 cases in Trial A, 166 in Trial B, 115 in Trial C: a total of 388 cases. An important feature of each study was that the groups on different treatments were observed concurrently. On the other

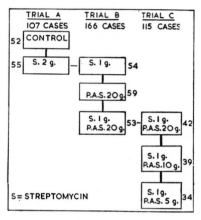

FIG. **5,** 1

Diagram showing groups involved in the three trials

hand, although the three trials took place at different points of time, a comparison between the non-concurrent groups is justifiable, since the methods of study were so similar and the type of case, as defined, remained the same. Also a link between the successive trials was deliberately introduced: Trial A and Trial B each had a group treated with streptomycin only (though in the first the daily dose was 2 g. and in the second 1 g.); Trials B and C each had a group treated with streptomycin, 1 g., and P.A.S., 20 g., daily. This 'overlap' of a similarly treated group from one trial to the next should reveal whether it is fair to make comparisons between differently treated patients in the different trials.

Larger numbers are made available by bringing the three trials together. The main objects of this analysis are therefore: (1) to compare the clinical results of the different treatments employed in the three trials; (2) to analyse the effect of different treatments on streptomycin sensitivity; and (3) to assess the clinical significance of streptomycin resistance.

Comparability of Cases in the Three Trials

In Table **5,** 1 are given data, for each of the three trials, concerning the condition of patients before treatment started. The results are

TABLE **5,** 1

Condition Before Treatment Started. Comparison of Patients in Three Trials

Condition on Admission to Trial		Trial A		Trial B		Trial C	
		No.	%	No.	%	No.	%
Total cases		107	*100*	166	*100*	115	*100*
Average evening temperature in first week	Afebrile	7	*7*	16	*10*	19	*17*
	Less than 90° F. (37·2° C.)	31	*29*	50	*30*	30	*26*
	99–99·9° F. (37·2–37·75° C.)	39	*36*	55	*33*	45	*39*
	100° F. + (37·8° C. +)	30	*28*	45	*27*	21	*18*
Sedimentation rate (Westergren)	0–10	0*	*0*	3*	*2*	2	*2*
	11–20	5	*5*	6	*4*	8	*7*
	21–50	36	*34*	67	*41*	50	*43*
	51 +	65	*61*	89	*54*	55	*48*
X-ray: gross cavitation		62	*58*	87	*52*	61	*53*

* Examination not done in one case

shown diagrammatically in Fig. **5,** 2. The analysis shows that the groups are very similar, though there is a suggestion that the cases admitted were somewhat less acute in successive trials. The proportion with average evening temperature of 100° F. (37.8° C.) or more in the pre-treatment observation week was 28 per cent in Trial A, 27 per cent in Trial B, 18 per cent in Trial C; 7 per cent were afebrile in Trial A, 10 per cent in Trial B, and 17 per cent in Trial C. The figures for sedimentation rate show a similar trend. Gross cavitation was found in 58 per cent of patients in Trial A, compared with 52 per cent in Trial B and 53 per cent in Trial C. These dif-

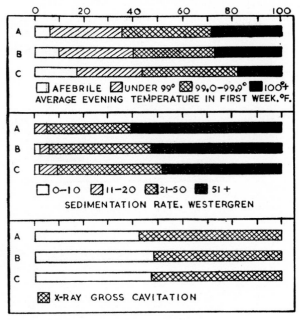

FIG. 5, 2

Condition before treatment started. Comparison of patients in three trials

ferences are small enough to justify comparisons of results, but the question of initial condition will be referred to in respect of certain analyses.

RESULTS

Radiological Assessment

The most important measure of clinical results for each of the trials is the radiological assessment of changes between the condition just before treatment started and the condition six months later. The data for each of the eight groups are brought together in Table 5, 2. In Table 5, 3 and Fig. 5, 3 the two groups treated with streptomycin only (A2 and B1) have been combined; so also have the two groups receiving streptomycin plus 20g. of P.A.S. (B3 and C1), and the groups receiving streptomycin plus 5 or 10g. of P.A.S. (C2 and C3).

Table **5,** 2 reveals, it is important to note, that in each of the pairs thus grouped together the results were strikingly similar. In other words, there is good evidence of a constancy of conditions in these three trials—ample justification, therefore, for adding groups together and for making cross-comparisons between the trials.

The results given in Table **5,** 3 show clearly a gradation in the

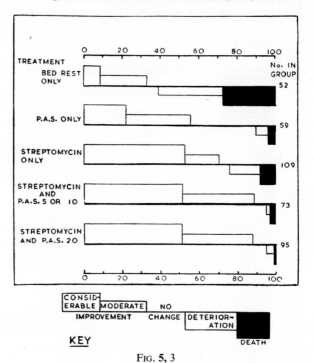

FIG. 5, 3

X-ray assessment at six months. Combined results of three trials

frequency of improvement, from 33 per cent for the cases treated by rest in bed only (the original comparative group) to 56 per cent for those treated by P.A.S. alone, 71 per cent for those treated by streptomycin alone, and, finally, nearly 90 per cent for those on combined treatment with streptomycin and P.A.S.

Clearly, all groups receiving either P.A.S. or streptomycin, or both, showed results very much better than the groups treated by rest in bed alone.

All groups receiving streptomycin had similar numbers showing

TABLE **5**, 2.   *Radiological Assessment at Six Months: Results in Three Trials*

Trial Group	Treatment (Daily Dose) Strepto-mycin	Treatment (Daily Dose) P.A.S.	Total No.	Total %	Improvement Considerable No.	Considerable %	Improvement Moderate No.	Moderate %	No Change No.	No Change %	Deterioration No.	Deterioration %	Death No.	Death %
A1	Nil	Nil	52	100	4	8	13	25	3	6	18	34	14	27
A2	2 g.	Nil	55	100	28	51	10	18	2	4	11	20	4	7
B1	1 g.	Nil	54	100	30	56	10	18	3	6	6	11	5	9
B2	Nil	20 g.	59	100	13	22	20	34	20	34	4	7	2	3
B3	1 g.	20 g.	53	101	27	51	19	36	3	6	3	6	1	2
C1	1 g.	20 g.	41*	100	22	54	14	34	4	10	1	2	0	0
C2	1 g.	10 g.	39	100	19	49	15	38	4	10	1	3	0	0
C3	1 g.	5 g.	34	100	19	56	11	32	2	6	0	0	2	6

* X-ray films of one patient not available

TABLE **5**, 3. *Radiological Assessment at Six Months: Results in Three Trials*

Trial Group	Treatment (Daily Dose) Strepto-mycin	Treatment (Daily Dose) P.A.S.	Total No.	Total %	Improvement Considerable No.	Improvement Considerable %	Improvement Moderate No.	Improvement Moderate %	No Change No.	No Change %	Deterioration No.	Deterioration %	Death No.	Death %
A1	Nil	Nil	52	100	4	8	13	25	3	6	18	34	14	27
B2	Nil	20 g.	59	100	13	22	20	34	20	34	4	7	2	3
A2) B1)	1 or 2 g.	Nil	109	100	58	53	20	18	5	5	17	16	9	8
C2) C3)	1 g.	5 or 10 g.	73	101	38	52	26	36	6	8	1	2	2	3
B3) C1)	1 g.	20 g.	94*	99	49	52	33	35	7	7	4	4	1	1

* X-ray films of one patient not available

TABLE **5, 4**   *Radiological Assessment at Six Months Related to Clinical Condition on Entry*

Condition on Entry	Treatment	Total		Improvement				No Change		Deterioration		Death	
				Considerable		Moderate							
		No.	%	No.	%	No.	%	No.	%	No.	%	No.	%
Acutely febrile	S only	34	100	11	32	6	18	2	6	6	18	9	26
	S + P.A.S.	34	100	12	35	12	35	3	9	4	12	3	9
Not acutely febrile but with gross cavitation	S only	39	100	18	46	11	28	3	8	7	18	0	0
	S + P.A.S.	65	100	32	49	26	40	6	9	1	2	0	0
Others	S only	36	99	29	80	3	8	0	0	4	11	0	0
	S + P.A.S.	68	100	43	63	21	31	4	6	0	0	0	0

S = Streptomycin

considerable improvement (52–53 per cent), results very much better than for the group given P.A.S. alone (22 per cent).

The groups treated with streptomycin and P.A.S. had significantly greater numbers improving and significantly less deteriorating than those treated with streptomycin only. Deterioration (including those with a fatal ending) occurred in only 5 per cent of those on combined therapy, against 24 per cent in patients on streptomycin alone. In view, however, of the indication in Table **5,** 1 that cases were rather less severe in the later trials than in the earlier, the comparison between groups on combined therapy and those on streptomycin alone has been related to the condition before treatment started; the data are set out in Table **5,** 4. It is clear that the differences already observed apply regardless of initial condition.

It will also be seen that among the groups on combined chemo-therapy the radiological results are almost the same whether they received 5, 10, or 20 g. of P.A.S. (see Tables **5,** 2 and **5,** 3).

Results in Men and Women.—Of male patients, 12 per cent were in the early group treated by rest in bed only, 17 per cent were on

TABLE **5,** 5

Radiological Assessment at Six Months: Men and Women

	Total		Improvement				No. Change		Deteri-oration		Death	
			Consi-derable		Mode-rate							
	No.	%	No.	%	No.	%	No.	%	No.	%	No.	%
All cases:												
Men	175*	*99*	69	*39*	51	*29*	21	*12*	18	*10*	16	*9*
Women	212	*100*	93	*44*	61	*29*	20	*9*	26	*12*	12	*6*
All cases on chemotherapy:												
Men	154*	*99*	68	*44*	45	*29*	20	*13*	13	*8*	8	*5*
Women	181	*100*	90	*50*	54	*30*	18	*10*	13	*7*	6	*3*

* X-ray films of one patient not available

P.A.S. alone, 24 per cent on streptomycin alone, and 47 per cent on streptomycin plus P.A.S. Of the corresponding female patients 15 per cent were on rest in bed, 14 per cent on P.A.S. alone, 32 per cent on streptomycin alone, and 40 per cent on combined therapy. These proportions are fairly similar. The results for men and women separately, for all groups, and for all groups on chemotherapy— that is, excluding the control group—are shown in Table **5, 5**. The small difference in favour of the women is not statistically significant.

Sputum Examination

After radiological assessment the effect of chemotherapy on bacterial content of sputum is one of the most important measures of efficacy. The results for five groups are set out in Table **5, 6**. They show the same gradation of results as did the X-ray examinations, and again there is no significant difference between the groups on combined therapy but with different amounts of P.A.S.

TABLE **5, 6**

Sputum Examination: Results from Three Trials

Treatment Group	Total Cases in Trial	Cases Sputum-Negative Throughout 3rd Month		Cases Sputum-Negative Throughout 6th Month	
		No.	%	No.	%
Rest in bed only	52	1	*2*	2	*4*
P.A.S. only	59	5	*8*	4	*7*
Streptomycin only	109	16	*15*	17	*16*
Streptomycin + P.A.S. 5 or 10g.	73	16	*22*	18	*25*
Streptomycin + P.A.S. 20g.	95	27	*28*	22	*23*

Streptomycin Sensitivity Related to Treatment

For the purpose of the analysis of streptomycin sensitivity the results have been set out in four groups:

S2:   The group in Trial A, treated with streptomycin only, 2g. daily (55 patients).

S1:   The group in Trial B, treated with streptomycin only, 1g. daily (54 patients).

SP 5/10: Groups in Trial C, treated with streptomycin 1g. daily plus P.A.S. 5 or 10g. (73 patients).

SP 20:   Group in Trials B and C treated with streptomycin 1g. daily plus P.A.S. 20g. (95 patients).

The grouped data are shown in Table **5, 7** and represented graphically in Fig. **5, 4**. In each successive month there is a clear

gradation in results, from the highest percentage resistant in the
S2 group to the lowest in SP 20. The differences are very striking,
especially in respect of the proportion with strongly resistant strains
(R.R. 100+); in the second month the proportion was 35 per cent
in the S2 group, 16 per cent in the S1, 2 per cent in the SP 5 or 10,

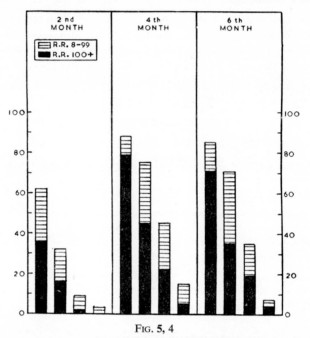

FIG. 5, 4

Percentage of cases with streptomycin-resistant strains in second, fourth, and
sixth months after treatment started. Results from three trials. S2 = Daily
streptomycin 2 g. S1 = Daily streptomycin 1 g. SP5/10 = Daily streptomycin
1 g. + P.A.S. 5 or 10 g. SP20 = Daily streptomycin 1 g. + P.A.S. 20 g.

and *nil* in the SP 20 group. In the fourth month it was 78 per cent
in the S2 group, 45 per cent in the S1, 21 per cent in the SP 5 or 10,
and 4 per cent in the SP 20.

The great difference between those receiving streptomycin only
and those receiving streptomycin plus 20 g. of P.A.S. has been
previously noted and discussed. So also has the difference between
those receiving low doses of P.A.S. (5 or 10 g.) and those receiving
20 g. of P.A.S. daily. It is important, however, to note from the
present analysis that, though the effect of 5 or 10 g. of P.A.S. is less

TABLE 5, 1. *Streptomycin Resistance in Successive Months after Start of Treatment: Results from Three Trials*

| Month After Treatment Started | Treatment Group | Total Cases with Positive Cultures Examined for Sensitivity | | Streptomycin-resistance Ratio* (Highest Recorded During the Month) | | | | | |
| | | | | Less than 8 (Sensitive) | | 8–99 (Mod. Resistant) | | 100+ (Strongly Resistant) | |
		No.	%	No.	%	No.	%	No.	%
First	S2	24	100	24	100	0	0	0	0
	S1	44	100	41	93	3	7	0	0
	SP 5 or 10	59	100	57	97	2	3	0	0
	SP 20	77	100	76	99	1	1	0	0
Second	S2	26	100	10	38	7	27	9	35
	S1	43	99	29	67	7	16	7	16
	SP 5 or 10	53	100	49	92	3	6	1	2
	SP 20	75	100	73	97	2	3	0	0
Third	S2	28	101	8	29	5	18	15	54
	S1	47	100	15	32	15	32	17	36
	SP 5 or 10	43	100	35	81	5	12	3	7
	SP 20	55	100	51	93	3	5	1	2
Fourth	S2	23	100	3	13	2	9	18	78
	S1	40	100	10	25	12	30	18	45
	SP 5 or 10	38	100	21	55	9	24	8	21
	SP 20	52	100	45	86	5	10	2	4
Fifth	S2	26	101	3	12	2	8	21	81
	S1	40	100	11	27	13	33	16	40
	SP 5 or 10	47	100	31	66	9	19	7	15
	SP 20	60	100	54	90	3	5	3	5
Sixth	S2	21	99	3	14	3	14	15	71
	S1	34	99	10	29	12	35	12	35
	SP 5 or 10	45	101	30	67	7	16	8	18
	SP 20	58	99	54	93	2	3	2	3

* The ratio of the minimum concentration of streptomycin to which the tubercle bacilli of the patient are sensitive, to the corresponding figure for the standard strain H37Rv

97

than that of 20 g. in preventing emergence of streptomycin resistance, it is nevertheless quite considerable. Among those who received 5 or 10 g. of P.A.S. in addition to 1 g. of streptomycin daily, the proportion producing strongly resistant strains by the fourth to sixth month was only half that in the group receiving 1 g. of streptomycin without P.A.S. It is also noteworthy that in those receiving P.A.S. resistance developed at a somewhat later date.

Another important finding was the more frequent reduction of drug resistance in cases on combined therapy than in cases on streptomycin alone. In five of the 12 patients (42 per cent) receiving streptomycin plus 20 g. of P.A.S. daily from whom resistant strains were isolated, the final cultures obtained in the six months were sensitive. Corresponding figures for the SP 5 and SP 10 groups are 13 out of 30 (43 per cent), while in the group receiving 1 g. of streptomycin daily without P.A.S. only four out of 39 cases (10 per cent) had subsequently sensitive cultures.

Clinical Significance of Streptomycin Resistance

In each of the trials it was found that the clinical results were least good in the cases with streptomycin-resistant strains. It was, however, difficult to dissociate this from the fact that streptomycin resistance was observed most frequently in patients most severely ill on admission. There was some indication, nevertheless, that streptomycin resistance was of some importance in determining the course of the disease. The amalgamation of data from the three trials makes it possible now to analyse this problem more effectively.

For the analysis set out in Table **5,** 8, the results of streptomycin-sensitivity tests have been combined for 163 cases from four groups: those receiving streptomycin only and those receiving streptomycin plus P.A.S., 5 or 10 g. The percentage with resistant strains is so low in the groups receiving 20 g. of P.A.S. that their inclusion would weight the figures excessively with those for sensitive strains.

Of the 44 patients who were acutely febrile on admission, 27, or 61 per cent, later produced strongly resistant strains, compared with 40 per cent of the 63 not acutely febrile but with gross cavitation, and 21 per cent of the 56 others.

Looking first at the results for all cases it is obvious that results were worst in those who produced strongly resistant strains at any time: 16 per cent of them died, and no deaths occurred in the others; 36 per cent died or deteriorated, against only 2–5 per cent of the

TABLE 5, 8. *X-ray Assessment at Six Months Related to Clinical Condition on Entry and Streptomycin Resistance. Combined Results (from Three Trials) for Patients who Received Streptomycin Alone or Streptomycin Plus 5 or 10 g. P.A.S., and for whom Sensitivity Results are Available from Specimens Taken after the First Month of Treatment*

Condition on Entry	Streptomycin-resistance Ratio*	Total		Improvement				No Change		Deterioration		Death	
				Considerable		Moderate							
		No.	%	No.	%	No.	%	No.	%	No.	%	No.	%
Acutely febrile (average evening temperature 100° F. (37·8 C.) or over during first week)	Less than 8	7	100	6	86	0	0	0	0	1	14	0	0
	8–99	10	100	3	30	4	40	1	10	2	20	0	0
	100+	27	100	5	19	6	22	2	7	4	15	10	37
	Total	44	101	14	32	10	23	3	7	7	16	10	23
Not acutely febrile but with gross cavitation	Less than 8	23	100	11	48	11	48	1	4	0	0	0	0
	8–99	15	101	7	47	7	47	1	7	0	0	0	0
	100+	25	100	11	44	4	16	4	16	6	24	0	0
	Total	63	101	29	46	22	35	6	10	6	10	0	0
Others	Less than 8	27	101	21	78	5	19	1	4	0	0	0	0
	8–99	17	100	12	70	4	24	1	6	0	0	0	0
	100+	12	100	8	67	1	8	0	0	3	25	0	0
	Total	56	100	41	73	10	18	2	4	3	5	0	0
All cases	Less than 8	57	101	38	67	16	28	2	4	1	2	0	0
	8–99	42	100	22	52	15	36	3	7	2	5	0	0
	100+	64	100	24	38	11	17	6	9	13	20	10	16
	Total	163	101	84	52	42	26	11	7	16	10	10	6

* Highest recorded during the 6 months

others; 55 per cent improved, compared with 88–95 per cent of the others. There is little difference between those with sensitive strains and those with moderately resistant strains, though the results slightly favour the former.

To assess the effect of initial condition in relation to the sensitivity results, the cases have been divided into three groups according to clinical condition on entry, and the results then related to sensitivity tests within each of those groups.

High fever has been taken as the main indicator of a severe condition on admission. The 10 deaths that occurred were all in the group of 44 patients who were acutely febrile before treatment started. But it will be noted that these deaths were all in those 27 who produced strongly resistant strains—a fatality rate of 37 per cent; furthermore, only 11 of the 27 in this group improved, against 13 of the 17 others. The results were less good in those with moderately resistant strains than in those remaining sensitive: three of 10 in the former group showed considerable improvement, compared with six of the seven in the latter. The difference is significant.

Among patients not acutely febrile on admission, but having gross cavitation, the only deterioration observed was in those with strongly resistant strains. Improvement was seen in 60 per cent of these, compared with 94–96 per cent of the others. There is no difference between those remaining sensitive and those with moderately resistant strains.

Among patients who were neither acutely febrile nor had gross cavitation, again the only deterioration observed was in those with strongly resistant strains, and in this group improvement was seen in 75 per cent, compared with 94–97 per cent of the others. Here again there is no difference between those remaining sensitive and those with moderately resistant strains.

Summarizing this analysis, it can be said that the relatively poor results in those who became strongly drug-resistant were not due solely to their initial severe condition. Among those acutely ill at the start of treatment the results were markedly worse in those who became strongly drug-resistant than in the others. In other clinical groups also the worst results were in the group with strongly resistant strains; nine out of 37 deteriorated, and none of the 82 others, but the difference is less great than in those acutely febrile. Moderate drug resistance appears to be of much less clinical significance than resistance at higher levels.

DISCUSSION

The discovery of streptomycin six years ago, and later of other specific drugs for tuberculosis, has changed radically many concepts of treatment and prognosis of this disease. To evaluate these drugs and determine how they can be used most effectively has been the task of many workers since that time. A series of chemotherapy trials organized by the Medical Research Council has contributed to that end. It is appropriate, at a time when claims are being made for other newly discovered drugs (Robizek and Selikoff, 1952), to look back over the series of Medical Research Council trials and to attempt, by amalgamating the results, to define the potentialities and limitations of the two drugs investigated. Evaluation of new drugs in the future can the more profitably be set against the background of established knowledge.

The three main trials undertaken were concerned with the effect of streptomycin and then of P.A.S. in pulmonary tuberculosis. All three were based on comparison of concurrently observed treatment groups, the placing of each case in one or another treatment group having been made by random allocation. In the first trial the value of streptomycin was compared with that of treatment by bed-rest alone; in the second, P.A.S. was assessed by comparing it with streptomycin alone and in combination with that drug; the third was designed to determine the smallest dose of P.A.S. which, in association with streptomycin, would delay or prevent emergence of streptomycin resistance. A well-defined form of pulmonary tuberculosis was chosen for these investigations and served throughout the trials, giving them a uniformity which has made possible the present review of the combined results. Analysis of the condition on admission of the 388 patients in these trials shows that the various treatment groups are very similar in this respect, and the overlap of similarly treated groups from each trial to the next provides further justification for considering as one whole these three investigations, which took place at different points of time.

Radiologically all groups treated with streptomycin or P.A.S., or both, fared much better than the group treated by bed-rest alone. Of the groups on chemotherapy, those treated with P.A.S. alone fared least well; results were much better in all groups treated with streptomycin, and best in those receiving P.A.S. in addition to streptomycin. Among the latter, the radiological results were the same whether the daily dose was 5, 10, or 20 g. of sodium P.A.S. Similar results apply to sputum conversion in the various treatment groups. It is clear that, on this assessment alone, the best chance of getting quickly effective action with streptomycin in pulmonary tuberculosis lies in its use with P.A.S.

Analysis of the levels of drug sensitivity adds weight to these findings. Streptomycin resistance developed more rapidly and more frequently in patients receiving streptomycin alone than in those treated with streptomycin plus P.A.S. In the fourth month after the start of treatment the proportion of cases with highly resistant organisms was 78 per cent in the group treated with 2 g. of streptomycin daily, 45 per cent in those on 1 g. of streptomycin daily, 21 per cent in those treated with 1 g. of streptomycin plus 5 or 10 g. of P.A.S., and only 4 per cent in those receiving 20 g. of P.A.S. with 1 g. of streptomycin. Further, reversion to drug sensitivity was seen frequently in cases on combined therapy, but relatively rarely in those treated with streptomycin only.

Though since 1946 much information has been obtained concerning emergence of streptomycin-resistant strains—and this has generally been assumed to worsen the prognosis—assessment of the clinical significance of bacterial drug resistance has been difficult. Certainly the best results were seen in patients who did not develop resistant strains, but on the whole these patients were at the start of treatment less ill than those from whom resistant organisms were later isolated. Many patients with streptomycin-resistant strains continue nevertheless to improve—whether under the influence of continued treatment or by their own resources is not clear. It is known also that drug-resistant organisms may be excreted into the bronchi from one lesion while other lesions in the same lung harbour streptomycin-sensitive bacilli (Canetti and Rocher, 1950). Because of the many complexities it has been difficult in relatively small investigations to judge the weight of this factor in prognosis. The present analysis has made it possible to disentangle some of the elements.

The relatively unfavourable prognosis in patients with highly resistant organisms was found to be due only in part to the fact that on admission they were very acutely ill; the clinical results were better in patients equally ill but who did not develop resistant strains. The analysis shows that, regardless of the initial clinical condition, the prognosis is, on the average, adversely affected by the emergence of strongly resistant organisms; moderate drug resistance seems to be of much less significance. Similar conclusions have been reached in a statement by the American Trudeau Society (1952).

It is true that in the groups on combined therapy there was no measurable difference in clinical results between those on 20g. of P.A.S. and those on smaller doses, though drug resistance emerged in a greater proportion of the latter. However, the results in all groups on combined therapy were so good (87–88 per cent showing radiological improvement) that differences are unlikely to show in groups of the size available. The one death that occurred in the 95 patients on 20g. of P.A.S. and the two deaths in the 73 patients on lower doses were all three in cases from which strongly resistant strains were isolated. In view of the outstanding results in all groups on combined chemotherapy, and of the finding that even small doses of P.A.S. reduce appreciably the risk of drug resistance (compared with streptomycin alone), it is not possible to lay down absolute recommendations on dosage. The clinician must in each case weigh the lessened risk of drug resistance when high doses of P.A.S. are used against the greater digestive discomfort these doses may produce in the patient. The best working rule is probably to continue to give the maximum dose of 20g. of sodium P.A.S. unless it is not tolerated by the patient.

The findings reported here relate to short-term results only (it is proposed later to analyse the results in the same cases at two years after the start of treatment), but they will help, it is believed, to determine the direction of work in connexion with new antibacterial agents in tuberculosis and possibly with drugs which may affect the host's reaction to the organism (Hart, Long, and Rees, 1952). Of the need of such scientific assessment as that produced by these trials there is no doubt: after each new advance assessment becomes the more difficult since each new drug must be measured against higher standards. The analysis of the results here presented has been made possible by the uniformity of the relatively small investigations from which they were derived, and by methods of planning which, now well proved, can be rapidly set in motion for the assessment of any new drugs.

SUMMARY

The results of three Medical Research Council trials of chemotherapy in pulmonary tuberculosis have been amalgamated to provide material for a detailed analysis. Three hundred and eighty-eight patients with similar forms of acute progressive bilateral pulmonary tuberculosis have been studied in these trials: 52 were treated by rest in bed only, 109 by streptomycin alone, 59 by P.A.S. alone, 73 by streptomycin plus 5 or 10 g. of P.A.S. daily, and 95 by streptomycin plus 20 g. of P.A.S. daily.

The results at six months after the start of treatment were much better in all groups on chemotherapy than in the group on rest in bed alone. They were much better in groups receiving streptomycin than in the group having P.A.S. only, and better in groups on combined therapy than in those on streptomycin alone. There was no apparent difference between the groups having different daily doses of P.A.S. plus 1 g. of streptomycin daily. There was no difference between the results in men and those in women.

The percentage of patients developing streptomycin-resistant strains was much higher in patients treated with streptomycin only than in those on combined therapy; among the latter it was higher in those patients for whom the daily dose of P.A.S. was 5 or 10 g. than in those receiving 20 g. daily. The clinical significance of streptomycin resistance is discussed. In patients with a similar initial condition the results were worst in those who developed high degrees of drug resistance. Moderate drug resistance seems to be of less clinical significance.

REFERENCES

American Trudeau Society (1952). *Amer. Rev. Tuberc.* **65**, 103.

Canetti, G., and Rocher, G. (1950). *Bibl. tuberc.*, *Basle* (fasc. 3) 30.

Hart, P. D'Arcy, Long, D. A., and Rees, R. J. W. (1952). *Brit. med. J.* **i**, 680.

Medical Research Council, Streptomycin in Tuberculosis Trials Committee (1948). *Brit. med. J.* **ii**, 769.

Medical Research Council, Streptomycin in Tuberculosis Trials Committee and the British Tuberculosis Association Research Committee (1950). *Brit. med. J.* **ii**, 1073.

Medical Research Council, Streptomycin in Tuberculosis Trials Committee and the British Tuberculosis Association Research Committee (1952). *Brit. med. J.* **i**, 1157.

Robitzek, E. H., and Selikoff, I. J. (1952). *Amer. Rev. Tuberc.* **65**, 402.

CHAPTER 6

CLINICAL TRIALS OF ANTIHISTAMINIC DRUGS IN THE PREVENTION AND TREATMENT OF THE COMMON COLD

THE investigations of Brewster (1947, 1949), Gordon (1948), Murray (1949), Arminio and Sweet (1949), Phillips and Fishbein (1949, 1950), and Tebrock (1950) suggested that antihistaminic drugs had beneficial effects in the prophylaxis and treatment of the common cold. On the other hand, these observations could not be confirmed by Paton, Fulton and Andrewes (1949), Hoagland, Deitz, Myers, and Cosand (1950), Feller, Badger, Hodges, Jordan, Rammelkamp, and Dingle (1950), and Cowan and Diehl (1950). A critical review by the Council on Pharmacy and Chemistry of the American Medical Association (1950) cast serious doubt on the validity of the conclusions and the interpretation of the results of some of the earlier investigations, referred to above, which had seemingly shown favourable effects.

In view of the great practical importance of the favourable findings, if confirmed, the Medical Research Council undertook, at the request of the Ministry of Health, to investigate in this country the value of the treatment. A special committee was appointed early in 1950, and the results of the tests arranged by the committee are reported here.

The trials have been of two kinds: (1) small-scale tests of two powerful antihistaminic drugs—promethazine hydrochloride (Phenergan, May & Baker, Ltd.) and chlorocyclizine hydrochloride (Histantin, Burroughs Wellcome & Co.)—in the prevention of inoculated colds in volunteers at the Common Cold Research Unit,

Report by a special committee of the Medical Research Council, the members of which were Dr. F. H. K. Green (chairman), Dr. C. H. Andrewes, Professor W. A. Bain, Professor A. Bradford Hill, Dr. W. C. Cockburn, Dr. P. D'Arcy Hart, Dr. J. Faulkner, Dr. N. L. Lloyd, Group Captain T. C. MacDonald, Dr. L. G. Norman, Dr. J. P. Sparkes, Dr. T. Sommerville, and Dr. J. A. Harrington (who was appointed secretary and co-ordinated the trials).

Reprinted from the *British Medical Journal*, 1950, **ii**, 425

Harvard Hospital, Salisbury; and (2) large-scale trials of the much weaker antihistaminic thonzylamine (also known in America as 'neohetramine' or 'anahist') for the treatment of colds occurring naturally among volunteers drawn from the general adult population —workers in the Civil Service, industrial establishments, universities, and the like.

I. THE PROPHYLACTIC EXPERIMENT AT SALISBURY

The object of this experiment was to see whether antihistamines given before, and for a few days after, nasal instillation of common-cold washings to human volunteers would prevent the development of a cold. Histantin and Phenergan were selected as the drugs for test, as the antihistaminic activity of both was known to be high. The volunteers were isolated in pairs throughout the trial—in the same way as has previously been described by Andrewes (1949). Half the subjects received the drug under test; the other half received dummies indistinguishable from it and containing $\frac{1}{4}$ g. (16 mg.) of phenobarbitone. It was felt that the latter would, in the dosage employed, have a mild sedative effect and so be acceptable as a control medication against which the efficacy of the antihistamine could be measured. Tablets were given at approximately 10 a.m. and 7 p.m., swallowing being supervised by the matron. Two members of a pair were given the same substance. Whether they were to be given the drug or the dummy was decided randomly, and neither the patient nor the clinical observer knew which any particular patient had received.

Trial 1: Histantin (January 18–28, 1950)

A 50 mg. tablet of Histantin (or of the dummy) was given twice daily, beginning 48 hours before the cold inoculation and continuing until 72 hours after it. The virus inoculum was a one in three dilution of an unfiltered washing from patient G., who had developed a cold after receiving passage material from one of the Common Cold Research Unit's 'pedigree' strains, Harrow. The results are shown in Table **6,** 1. The incidence of colds is seen to be the same in the treated and control groups; there was no clinical difference from the usual course of experimental colds. One spontaneous cold

TABLE **6,** 1

Results of Trial 1

Drug Administered	Cold	No Cold
Histantin	4*	4
Control tablet	4*	4
Total	8	8

* Includes one spontaneous cold developing
during quarantine period before inoculation.

developed in a subject who had been taking Histantin for 24 hours;
a similar case occurred in the control group.

Trial 2: Phenergan (February 1–11, 1950)

A 20 mg. dose of Phenergan (or of the dummy) was given twice
daily, beginning 60 hours before virus inoculation and continuing
for 72 hours after. Two test viruses were used—unfiltered G diluted

TABLE **6,** 2

Results of Trial 2*

Drug Administered	Cold Washing	Cold	No Cold
Phenergan	G	5	0
	Pool 82	2	2
Control	G	3	4
	Pool 82	1	3

* In the phenergan experiment two volunteers of opposite sex were unpaired;
these were treated as singletons, one getting the drug and one not. In addition
one volunteer and her partner inoculated with the G virus have been excluded
since she developed influenza in the course of the experiment.

one in three, as in Trial 1, and a filtrate of pool 82 (also virus of
Harrow passage series). Table **6,** 2 shows the results. As in Trial 1
there is no evidence of prevention with the antihistaminic drug.

SIDE-EFFECTS

Subjects were not warned that some side-effects of the drugs might
be apparent, but may well have read of this possibility in the lay
press. In the first trial, of the eight persons taking the drug only one

complained of 'fuzziness in the head' half an hour after her fourth dose of Histantin; it lasted ten minutes. In the second trial four patients complained of drowsiness; two were in the Phenergan and two in the control group. In assessing the significance of this low incidence of side-effects it must be remembered that the volunteers in this trial were leading a very leisurely existence and were under no kind of strain.

DISCUSSION

Some claims to a beneficial effect of antihistamines in curing colds have emphasized the need for beginning treatment within a few hours of onset. It is thus particularly noteworthy that the results at Salisbury with experimental colds showed no effect even when the drugs were given for two to three days *before* infection. Clinical observation of the volunteers revealed no difference in the nature and duration of experimental colds in those who received antihistaminic treatment and those who did not. The results with the two antihistamines tested were clear cut, and there seemed to be no good reason for repeating the experiment with other drugs of a similar kind.

II. LARGE-SCALE THERAPEUTIC FIELD TRIAL

Plan of Investigation

To assess the value of antihistaminic drugs in the treatment of the common cold it was necessary to compare the experience of treated individuals with that of a similar group not treated; for this purpose it was decided to plan the inquiry on similar lines to those adopted by a committee of the Council in investigating the value of patulin for the same purpose during the war (Medical Research Council, 1944).

Choice of an Antihistamine for Test.—The antihistaminic drugs vary considerably in their properties, potency, and toxicity, but it clearly was impracticable to carry out field tests of more than one product if sufficiently large groups for statistical analysis were to be obtained within a reasonable period. The available evidence indicated that thonzylamine would be the most appropriate choice in the first instance, as it was generally accepted as having a low toxicity (Friedlaender and Friedlaender, 1948; Criep and Aaron, 1948; Schwartz, 1949) and had been claimed as very effective against the common cold by Arminio and Sweet (1949) and Tebrock (1950).

Organization of Trials at Individual Centres.—The supervision and conduct of the investigation at the individual centres were carried out by medical officers who had been visited by the secretary of the committee and instructed in the standard procedure proposed; at some centres the conduct of the test was delegated to a trained industrial nurse working under the supervision of a medical officer. The existence of the trial was brought to the notice of potential volunteers by means of posters, notices, etc., the details of publicizing the scheme being left to the medical officer in charge. Volunteers were told of the experimental nature of the inquiry and the desirability of attending for treatment as soon as possible after the onset of symptoms of a cold.

Selection of Cases.—Admission to the trial was limited to volunteers over the age of 15 years in whom there was good evidence of the presence of the common cold. As it was important to obtain uniformity in different areas, the following definition of a common cold was given as a guide to the observers: 'A catarrhal inflammation of the upper respiratory passages usually without pyrexia but with a watery or mucous discharge from the nose and associated with sneezing, fullness in the head and nose, and sometimes with cough, headache, sore throat, hoarseness, and running eyes.' Reliance was placed mainly on the subjective diagnosis, and cases were accepted on the basis of the patient's description of his symptoms; clinical examination, other than the recording of temperatures, was carried out only to exclude other conditions. All volunteers whose conditions fell into any of the following categories were excluded: chronic catarrh or sinusitis; acute tonsillitis; suspected influenza; any person whose temperature was found to exceed 100° F. (37.8° C.); those who, on inquiry, seemed likely to have taken an antihistaminic drug for any purpose within the previous week; those with a *present attack* of hay-fever or allergic rhinitis. Persons with a *previous history* of allergic states were included, but a note to this effect was made in the appropriate column of the record sheet.

Design of Trial

To ensure that no bias could enter into the assessment of results it was essential that neither the patient nor the investigator should be aware whether antihistaminic tablets or control tablets had been given in a particular case. For this purpose, those who were to be

Trial Centre	**RECORD SHEET**			Serial Number
	Trials of Antihistaminic Drugs in the Treatment of the Common Cold			
	(MEDICAL RESEARCH COUNCIL)			

Surname (BLOCK CAPS.) Initials:	Mr. Mrs. Miss	Age (years)	Clock No.	Department	Occupation

A

FIRST EXAMINATION

(*To be filled in by a doctor: please put a ring round the appropriate items*)

Is there any previous history of: Hay-fever Allergic Rhinitis Asthma

Has patient been previously treated in these trials? Yes No

Other Allergic Manifestations (*State nature*):

Date of first examination	Time

Duration in days of Head Cold before first examination $\frac{1}{4}$ $\frac{1}{2}$ 1 2 3 4 5 6 7 or more days

Blocked Nose Fullness in Head Sneezing Sore Throat Hoarseness Cough Headache Feeling Ill

Nasal Discharge: Watery Mucoid Purulent Temperature (if taken) . . . .

Are you satisfied that this is a case of Common Cold? Yes No Uncertain

B (Enter progress at 24 hours, 48 hours, and after a week) PROGRESS RECORD (*Please put a ring round appropriate items*)

Date	Time	Number of Tablets Since Previous Recordings	Progress				Temperature (if taken)	Doctor's Comments
			Cured	Improved	Unchanged	Worse		
			Cured	Improved	Unchanged	Worse	Recurred	
			Cured	Improved	Unchanged	Worse	Recurred	
			Cured	Improved	Unchanged	Worse	Recurred	
			Cured	Improved	Unchanged	Worse	Recurred	
			Cured	Improved	Unchanged	Worse	Recurred	

treated and those who were to be 'controls' were prearranged in random order by the use of random sampling numbers, with the one restriction that each batch of 50 volunteers should include 25 treated (T) and 25 controls (C), a restriction not known at the centres.

These lists were numbered consecutively, so that, for example, a series might run as follows: 1T, 2T, 3C, 4T, 5C, 6C, and so on, randomly. Such lists were constructed, in the Council's Statistical

---

Reverse Side of Record Sheet

SIDE-EFFECTS

(*Please do not ask* DIRECT QUESTIONS *about specific side-effects as this may give misleading results*)

1. Has the treatment agreed with the patient?   Yes   No
2. If 'No', what symptoms does the patient attribute to the tablets?
   (*State nature and severity as 'mild', 'moderate', or 'severe'; and date of occurrence*)

Off work* from............to............   Reason:
   * (*Delete if not off work during trial*)

ANY FURTHER COMMENTS

Research Unit, for each centre. Record sheets and cartons containing the appropriate tablets were then marked (in the Statistical Research Unit) with the serial number—namely, 1, 2, 3, 4, 5, 6, etc., but with no reference to (T) or (C)—and sent to the local centres; thus at the local centre one carton and one record sheet, *the serial numbers of which corresponded*, were used for each patient. They were used in strict order of serial number; thus if the last patient on one day was recorded on record sheet '15' and received tablets from carton '15', the first patient on the next day was recorded on record sheet '16' and received tablets from carton '16'. The key to the identity of the serial numbers was kept centrally and secret until the end of the investigation.

This somewhat novel method was adopted in place of the more usual one of merely labelling one product X and the other Y and giving them in random order, in view of the side-effects to be expected with the antihistaminic drug. If decisive side-effects were observed with even one patient then the nature of X (and Y) would ever after be known (or suspected). With the method chosen the identity of one carton might well be suspected in the patient with side-effects, but no evidence would thereby be given regarding the treatment of any other patient.

Course of Treatment

At the first attendance the medical officer, having satisfied himself that the patient was suffering from a common cold and was not within one of the excluded categories previously defined, completed Part A of the record sheet (reproduced p. 110) and then proceeded to dispense the tablets.

Each patient, it was laid down, should receive one tablet three times a day for three days—that is, a total of nine tablets. The individual and numbered carton for each patient held three envelopes, each containing three tablets: one envelope was issued each day—that is, on reporting, on the next day, and on the day following that. Antihistaminic tablets contained 50 mg. of thonzylamine; control tablets contained 5 mg. of quinine sulphate in a lactose base. All tablets were sugar-coated, and those which contained the antihistamine were indistinguishable in appearance from those which did not. Volunteers were told to swallow the tablets whole, to remove the possibility of detection by taste if they were bitten or chewed. Each patient was given an instruction leaflet (explaining the details of the treatment and follow-up) and a note to hand to his family doctor if the latter was consulted during the period of the test.

Follow-up and Assessment of Progress

Patients were instructed to report progress at the end of 24 hours, 48 hours, and after a week. At these attendances the volunteers were requested to state quite frankly whether they thought the treatment given had been effective; assessments of progress were recorded by ringing the words 'cured', 'improved', 'unchanged', 'worse', or 'recurred' as appropriate. The definitions of these categories had been laid down as follows:

'*Cured.*'—Only those persons who, after questioning, are found to be *completely* free from symptoms and who, on examination, are found to be without objective signs.

'*Improved.*'—Persons who, on questioning and examination, are found to be improved but not cured since the previous examination.

'*Unchanged.*'—Persons in whom, on questioning, the symptoms and signs are found to be unchanged since the previous examination. (*All cases in which there was doubt regarding progress were included in this category.*)

'*Worse*'.—Persons in whom, on questioning and examination, the symptoms and signs are found to have increased since the previous examination.

'*Recurred.*'—Patients, previously classified as 'cured', and who report with another cold within 14 days of recovery from the previous one.

Assessment of Side-effects.—Direct questions about side-effects were avoided during treatment lest the investigator might surmise from the answers whether the patients were on the antihistaminic or the control treatment. Where, however, side-effects were spontaneously complained of, details were noted, including the nature, date of onset, and severity. In all cases the patient was asked at his *last* attendance, and after the assessment of progress, whether the tablets had affected him adversely in any way; if the answer was in the affirmative the symptoms attributed by the patient to the tablets were noted.

Results

These therapeutic trials were set up at 19 widely distributed centres with a total population of approximately 58,000. They were carried out in each area between the middle of March and the middle of May, 1950, though not invariably over the whole of that period.

In total, 1,550 volunteers at the various centres were treated in the investigation—775 with the drug and an equal number with the control tablets. However, 394 record sheets had subsequently to be rejected from the analysis for such reasons as failure to complete the treatment or to report progress on the required days. These rejects came about equally from the treated and control groups (196 and 198 respectively), and thus show no differential bias. Deducting the rejects, 1,156 record sheets were available for analysis—579 for patients who received antihistaminic treatment and 577 for patients who had the alternative treatment. Since analysis of the results from each centre revealed no significant difference between them, only the combined results from all centres need be given here. It may also be noted that a special analysis was made according to the number of records that had to be rejected. The centres were grouped in three categories: under 10 per cent of records rejected, 10–19 per cent rejected, 20 per cent or more rejected. No differences in results were revealed, showing again that the lapses did not bias the inquiry.

TABLE **6,** 3

Duration of Cold Before Treatment was Begun

Duration of Symptoms Before Treatment (in Days)	Persons Given Anti-histaminic Treatment		Persons Given Alternative Treatment	
	No.	%	No.	%
$\frac{1}{4}$	64	11·1	60	10·4
$\frac{1}{2}$	137	23·7	113	19·6
1	180	31·1	213	36·9
2	96	16·6	84	14·6
3	49	8·5	42	7·3
4	22	3·8	25	4·3
5	7	1·2	10	1·7
6	8	1·4	1	0·2
7+	16	2·8	29	5·0
Total	579	100·2	577	100·0

The comparable nature in regard to initial symptoms of the volunteers who received antihistaminic treatment and those who did not is shown in Tables **6,** 3 and **6,** 4. It will be seen that the method of random allocation used resulted in two groups which were closely alike in relevant respects.

The results at the end of the first day, second day, and one week for different durations of colds before treatment are given in Table **6,** 5. None of the differences is individually statistically significant for each duration of cold before treatment, and indeed the similarity in response of the two groups seems more remarkable than any dissimilarity. For instance, of those who came for treatment within the first day of their onset of symptoms, 13.4 per cent and 13.9 per cent of the treated and controls, respectively, reported a cure on the second day; 48.8 per cent and 46.8 per cent were cured at the end of the week. It may, however, be noted that the treated group had consistently a slightly higher proportion of cured and improved on the first day of treatment than had the controls.

By combining all results, irrespective of duration of cold before treatment, 48.0 per cent of the treated and 42.1 per cent of the control group were found to be improved (including nine treated and five control cases who were cured) at the end of the first day's treatment. The difference, 5.9±2.9, is just significant in a technical

TABLE **6, 4**

Frequency of Presenting Symptoms at First Visit

Symptoms	Persons Given Anti-histaminic Treatment		Persons Given Alternative Treatment	
	No.	%	No.	%
Watery nasal discharge	359	62·0	337	58·4
Mucoid nasal discharge	114	19·7	118	20·5
Purulent nasal discharge	49	8·5	42	7·3
Blocked nose	321	55·4	307	53·2
Fullness in the head	385	66·5	390	67·6
Sneezing	413	71·3	408	70·7
Sore throat	217	37·5	231	40·0
Hoarseness	183	31·6	177	30·7
Cough	242	41·8	226	39·2
Headache	196	33·9	207	35·9
Feeling ill	44	7·6	46	8·0

sense, but even if it be real it is so small that it clearly has no practical importance. Also, this small difference, it will be seen, vanished on the second day, when, taking all the group together, the proportions of cured and improved were respectively 8.8 per cent and 53.0 per cent in the treated and 8.5 per cent and 51.3 per cent in the control group. Possibly the apparent small difference at the end of the first day's treatment can be accounted for by a slight sedative effect in some few subjects who received thonzylamine or by the unwitting inclusion of some individuals who were suffering from hay-fever or an allergic rhinitis and not from the common cold.

It has been mentioned that volunteers with a present attack of hay-fever or allergic rhinitis were, so far as possible, excluded, but persons with a previous history of allergic conditions were included

TABLE **6, 5**

Percentage Cured or Improved at the End of the First Day, Second Day, and One Week for Different Durations of Cold Before Treatment

<table>
<tr><th rowspan="2">Day of Observation</th><th colspan="12">Duration of Cold Before Treatment</th></tr>
<tr><th colspan="3">Under 1 Day</th><th colspan="3">1 Day</th><th colspan="3">2 Days</th><th colspan="3">3 Days or More</th></tr>
<tr><td></td><td>T
201 Obs.</td><td>C
173 Obs.</td><td>Difference</td><td>T
180 Obs.</td><td>C
213 Obs.</td><td>Difference</td><td>T
96 Obs.</td><td>C
84 Obs.</td><td>Difference</td><td>T
102 Obs.</td><td>C
107 Obs.</td><td>Difference</td></tr>
<tr><td>First day—improved*</td><td>47·8</td><td>45·1</td><td>2·7±5·2</td><td>47·2</td><td>38·5</td><td>8·7±5·0</td><td>50·0</td><td>40·5</td><td>9·5±7·4</td><td>48·0</td><td>45·8</td><td>2·2±6·9</td></tr>
<tr><td>Second day { Cured</td><td>13·4</td><td>13·9</td><td>−0·5±3·6</td><td>7·8</td><td>6·6</td><td>1·2±2·6</td><td>3·1</td><td>4·8</td><td>−1·7±2·9</td><td>6·9</td><td>6·5</td><td>0·4±3·5</td></tr>
<tr><td>Cured or improved</td><td>68·2</td><td>64·7</td><td>3·5±4·9</td><td>58·3</td><td>55·4</td><td>2·9±5·0</td><td>59·4</td><td>57·1</td><td>2·3±7·4</td><td>57·8</td><td>62·6</td><td>−4·8±6·8</td></tr>
<tr><td>One week { Cured</td><td>48·8</td><td>46·8</td><td>2·0±5·2</td><td>42·2</td><td>37·1</td><td>5·1±5·0</td><td>31·3</td><td>33·3</td><td>−2·0±7·0</td><td>29·4</td><td>36·4</td><td>−7·0±6·5</td></tr>
<tr><td>Cured or improved</td><td>80·6</td><td>74·6</td><td>6·0±4·3</td><td>77·8</td><td>77·5</td><td>0·3±4·5</td><td>70·8</td><td>79·8</td><td>−9·0±6·5</td><td>70·6</td><td>78·5</td><td>−7·9±6·0</td></tr>
</table>

T = Antihistaminic treatment. C = Alternative treatment. Obs. = Number of patients observed.
* Including the few patients (9 T and 5 C) who said they were cured on the first day.

116

provided they were believed to be suffering from a cold. From Table **6**, 6 it will be seen that a previous history of hay-fever, allergic rhinitis,

TABLE **6**, 6

Distribution of Results at the End of the First Day, Second Day, and One Week for Persons with a Previous History of Allergic Conditions

	1st Day		2nd Day		Week	
	T	C	T	C	T	C
Previous history of hay-fever						
Cured	2	—	4	3	6	13
Improved	13	13	13	14	12	12
Unchanged	10	16	8	14	8	6
Worse	3	5	3	3	1	1
Recurred	—	—	—	—	1	2
	28	34	28	34	28	34
Previous history of allergic rhinitis						
Cured	1	—	3	3	3	7
Improved	12	7	10	12	12	8
Unchanged	9	10	10	6	7	4
Worse	3	6	2	2	2	1
Recurred	—	—	—	—	1	3
	25	23	25	23	25	23
*Previous history of other allergic manifestations**						
Cured	—	—	4	5	15	13
Improved	25	17	22	17	20	12
Unchanged	17	10	12	9	8	5
Worse	2	7	6	3	1	3
Recurred	—	—	—	—	—	1
	44	34	44	34	44	34

T = Antihistaminic treatment.   C = Alternative treatment.
* Including asthma, urticaria, and other conditions believed to have an allergic basis.

and other allergic manifestations had no striking influence on the results obtained with the treatment, but the numbers in each of the treated and control groups are small. By combining all these allergic manifestations the figures shown in Table **6**, 7 are obtained.

TABLE **6**, 7

Percentages Cured or Improved

	1st Day	2nd Day	One Week
Treated	54·6	57·5	70·1
Controls	40·7	59·3	71·4
Difference	13·9 ± 7·3	−1·6 ± 7·2	−1·3 ± 6·6

There is a suggestion that the antihistaminic drug gave some relief to these subjects during the first day of treatment, but later results do not differ at all.

Side-effects.—Side-effects attributed to the treatment were reported by 121 (20.9 per cent) subjects receiving the test drug, while the comparable figure for those receiving the alternative treatment was 111 (19.2 per cent); details are given in Table **6**, 8. It is most unlikely that

TABLE **6**, 8

Side-effects Attributed to Treatment

Main Symptoms	Persons Given Antihistaminic Treatment	Persons Given Alternative Treatment
Drowsiness, lassitude, listlessness	26	35
Dizziness, giddiness, vertigo	21	13
Headache	21	16
Headache and other nervous symptoms	11	6
Depression with or without other nervous symptoms	2	5
Insomnia	3	1
Gastro-intestinal	13	12
Combined gastro-intestinal and nervous symptoms	8	7
Miscellaneous	16	16
Total	121	111

the large number of side-effects attributed to the alternative treatment can have been due to the small doses of quinine given in the control tablets. It seems much more probable that many of the symptoms described as side-effects were, in fact, symptoms of the cold itself. On the other hand, when, as here, efforts were made to avoid direct questions about specific side-effects, prior knowledge of the possibility of reactions may have led to a spurious increase in their incidence through psychogenic factors.

CONCLUSIONS

In a small but carefully controlled experiment two antihistaminic drugs—promethazine hydrochloride and chlorocyclizine hydrochloride—showed no evidence of having any value in the prevention of experimentally induced colds.

A large-scale clinical trial of thonzylamine in widely separated areas in Great Britain and Northern Ireland, carried out between the middle of March and the middle of May, 1950, showed that, in the dosage employed, this antihistaminic drug had little if any value in the treatment of the common cold.

REFERENCES

Andrewes, C. H. (1949). *Lancet*, **i**, 71.
Arminio, J. J., and Sweet, C. C. (1949). *Industr. Med.* **18**, 509.
Brewster, J. M. (1947). *Nav. med. Bull. Wash.* **47**, 810.
Brewster, J. M. (1949). *Industr. Med.* **18**, 217.
Council on Pharmacy and Chemistry, American Medical Association (1950). *J. Amer. med. Ass.* **142**, 566.
Cowan, D. W., and Diehl, H. S. (1950). *J. Amer. med. Ass.* **143**, 421.
Criep, L. H., and Aaron, T. H. (1948). *J. Allergy*, **19**, 215.
Feller, A. E., Badger, G. F., Hodges, R. G., Jordan, W. S., jun., Rammelkamp, C. H., jun., and Dingle, J. H. (1950). *New Engl. J. Med.* **242**, 737.
Friedlaender, S., and Friedlaender, A. S. (1948). *J. Lab. clin. Med.* **33**, 865.
Gordon, J. S. (1948). *Laryngoscope*, **58**, 1265.
Hoagland, R. J., Deitz, E. N., Myers, P. W., and Cosand, H. C. (1950). *J. Amer. med. Ass.* **143**, 157.
Medical Research Council, Patulin Clinical Trials Committee (1944). *Lancet*, **ii**, 373.
Murray, H. G. (1949). *Industr. Med.* **18**, 215.
Paton, W. D. M., Fulton, F., and Andrewes, C. H. (1949). *Lancet*, **i**, 935.
Phillips, W. F. P., and Fishbein, W. I. (1949). *Industr. Med.* **18**, 526.
Phillips, W. F. P., and Fishbein, W. I. (1950). *Industr. Med.* **19**, 201.
Schwartz, E. (1949). *Ann. Allergy*, **7**, 770.
Tebrock, H. E. (1950), *Industr. Med.* **19**, 39.

CHAPTER 7

A COMPARISON OF CORTISONE AND ASPIRIN IN THE TREATMENT OF EARLY CASES OF RHEUMATOID ARTHRITIS—I

IN 1951 the Medical Research Council and Nuffield Foundation Joint Committee on Clinical Trials of Cortisone, A.C.T.H., and Other Therapeutic Measures in Chronic Rheumatic Diseases decided that, for an effective assessment of the value of cortisone within its field of study, it was essential to carry out relatively small-scale but carefully controlled clinical trials. One of these trials, it was agreed, should deal with the important problem of the treatment of patients in the early stages of rheumatoid arthritis. The aim would be to measure the therapeutic effects of cortisone treatment upon the rheumatoid process while that process is still uncomplicated, either by severe anatomical changes in the joints or by metabolic or endocrine disturbances resulting from a prolonged and debilitating disease. In short, such a trial would have two objects: first, to compare the relative efficacy of cortisone and another drug usually regarded as efficacious in relieving symptoms and in improving the patient's functional capacity; and, secondly, to study the evolution of the rheumatoid process during prolonged therapy with these different agents. A scheme for this trial was drawn up by a sub-committee of the Joint Committee, and six centres in England and Scotland agreed to take part.

A report by the Joint Committee of the Medical Research Council and Nuffield Foundation on Clinical Trials of Cortisone, A.C.T.H., and Other Therapeutic Measures in Chronic Rheumatic Diseases, the members of which were: Sir Henry Cohen (chairman), Dr. E. G. L. Bywaters, Dr. W. S. C. Copeman, Sir Charles Dodds, Dr. J. J. R. Duthie, Professor A. Bradford Hill, Mr. H. Osmond-Clarke, Dr. F. T. G. Prunty, Dr. J. Reid, Dr. H. F. West, Professor J. H. Kellgren and Mr. W. A. Sanderson (joint secretaries).

Reprinted from the *British Medical Journal*, 1954, **i**, 1223

Type of Patient

It was agreed that the patients to be included in the trial must (*a*) be within the ages of two to 59 years inclusive; (*b*) have a polyarthritis of rheumatoid type affecting at least four joints and bilateral involvement of either hands or feet, ankles, or wrists; and (*c*) have had the disease at their time of entry to the trial for not less than three months and not more than nine months. In deciding upon this duration it was required that the initial symptoms of the present illness, which had brought the patient to the centre, should be the first evidence of any rheumatoid disease in the patient—except that a previous episode of polyarthritis suggestive of rheumatoid disease would not exclude the patient from the trial provided that this episode had been of less than 12 months' duration, had left no residual signs, and had resolved completely at least one year before the onset of the present illness. A previous history of a painful incident of up to three weeks' duration would not be considered evidence of previous rheumatoid disease.

No other diagnostic criteria were considered necessary, but centres were asked to make every effort to exclude other diseases such as rheumatic fever, Reiter's disease, and neisserian infection. In addition the sheep-cell agglutination test first described by Rose, Ragan, Pearce and Lipman (1948) was performed in most of the patients, and usually on several occasions.

Allocation to Treatment

In a long-term trial of this nature it was obviously out of the question, on ethical grounds, to set up a control group on a dummy treatment. The contrast must lie between treatment by cortisone and another drug usually regarded as efficacious in the treatment of rheumatoid arthritis. The two modes of treatment adopted, and allocated at random, were therefore (1) cortisone and (2) aspirin, with both groups receiving the same basic régime of splints, physiotherapy, etc. No patient would, of course, be brought into the trial unless he or she could be regarded as a suitable case for treatment by *either* of these agents.

Because clinicians at the participating centres would have to select patients for admission to the trial it was necessary to ensure that they would not know whether each patient, in the event of being brought in, would be on cortisone or on aspirin. The procedure adopted was as follows. The clinician at the centre accepted a patient as suitable on the basis of the criteria laid down. Having done so he applied to a central office to know whether the treatment of that patient should be with cortisone or aspirin. At the central office a register had been constructed showing the order in which the treatments were to be applied. It was held by one person. Such a random order of treatments was constructed separately for each of 48 small sub-groups of patients—namely, according to whether they were (a) male or female, (b) aged 2–16 or 17–59 years, (c) had a duration of symptoms of three to five months or six to nine months, and (d) were treated at one or other of the six centres. Within each of these small sub-groups random sampling numbers were used to give approximately equal numbers of patients on cortisone and aspirin. In summation, therefore, the cortisone and aspirin groups would be very similar in these four characteristics—sex, age, duration of illness, and treatment centre.

In detail, the technique was that on admitting a patient a treatment centre would send particulars of the sex, age, and duration of illness to the holder of the register. The prepared list for a person of that sex, age, and duration would be consulted, the patient's name entered on the next available line, and the nature of the treatment already inscribed on that line would, with supplies of hormone or aspirin, be sent to the treatment centre.

Treatment

Each patient was admitted to hospital for a minimum period of four weeks, but subsequently could be treated and observed as an out-patient. It proved impossible to make up cortisone and aspirin suspensions to look alike. The aspirin was therefore given in brown tablets with a bitter flavour so that they would be unrecognizable by the patient as 'merely aspirin'. They were labelled 'Tabs. Rheumatic C'. Cortisone acetate was given orally either in tablet form or as a suspension made up in syrup. It was labelled 'Tabs. (or Mist.) Rheumatic A'. Patients were asked not to take additional drugs or tablets. For the first year of treatment it was laid down that therapy would be given in twelve-weeks' courses separated by one week off treatment. Each course would start with a standard dosage, after which the physician was free to adjust the dose to suit the requirements of individual patients. The specified courses for adult patients,

given in divided doses not fewer than three times a day, were as
follows:

		Cortisone	Aspirin
First week:	Day 1	300 mg.	6 g.
	Day 2	200 mg.	6 g.
	Day 3 to day 7 ..	100 mg. daily ..	6 g. daily
Second week:	Day 8 to day 14 ..	50 mg. daily ..	2 g. daily
Third to			
twelfth week:	Day 15 to day 84 ..	Individualized at 25 to 200 mg. daily with graded withdrawal in week 12	Individualized at 1 to 8 g. daily with graded withdrawal in week 12

In the 'free' period—that is, the third to twelfth week—the
physician was asked to employ the minimum dosage that would
restore maximal functional efficiency without producing serious
side-effects. In the thirteenth week no treatment by cortisone or
aspirin was given, observations and measurements being made (in
this week analgesics other than aspirin could, if necessary, be given).
If symptoms recurred the twelve-weeks' course was repeated, except
that the selected dose for the individual patient replaced the standard
dose of the second week.

Assessment of Patient

Clinical assessment of each patient (including measurement of the
haemoglobin level and blood sedimentation rate) was required one
week before and also immediately before the start of treatment. After
therapy had begun, an assessment of some or all characteristics was
called for at the end of the first, second, fourth, eighth, twelfth, and
thirteenth weeks of the first course, and at the end of the first, eighth,
and thirteenth weeks of the second and subsequent courses.

The clinical assessment included (a) a defined judgement of the
patient's general functional capacity (for the five grades laid down,
see Table 7, 7); (b) a judgement of the activity of the disease as
inactive, slightly active, or very active; and (c) a statement whether
the patient appeared to be in remission. In addition to these subjective assessments the clinician was required to measure the strength
of grip for each hand. (The patient had to squeeze an oblong rubber
bag 5in. by 3in. (12.5cm. by 7.5cm.) inflated at a pressure of
10mm. Hg, and the figure recorded was the average of three grips.)
Two tests of dexterity were applied—namely, in patients with

affected hands the time taken to tie six double knots with 12-in. (30-cm.) pieces of household string, and in patients with affected legs the time taken to go up and down 10 steps. Estimates were also made of joint tenderness and of range of movement, and the number and site of any new joints involved were recorded as well as of previously affected joints which had recovered. Complications and side-effects were noted. The only obligatory laboratory tests were the blood sedimentation rate and the haemoglobin level.

The Analysis of the Data

In total, 62 adult patients (aged 17 to 59) and 14 children were admitted to the trial. The latter are too few to be informative, and the present report is confined to the adult group. One of these patients, allotted to the aspirin group, refused to co-operate, so that the numbers available are 30 on cortisone and 31 on aspirin. In 53 cases the results of a sheep-cell agglutination test are available. They are lacking for three patients on aspirin who were lost to the trial at an early stage (see below) and for five other patients who were followed up for the first year but never tested (three on aspirin and two on cortisone). The cases admitted at Edinburgh, Sheffield, and Manchester were tested by the method of Ball (1950), the test being regarded as positive if agglutination occurred in a titre of 1:4 or higher when read at one hour, or 1:32 or higher when read at 18 hours: a positive result was obtained on at least one occasion in 29 out of 40 patients (73 per cent). The cases admitted at Hammersmith and West London were tested by the original method of Rose, in which the test is considered positive if the two titres recorded show a ratio of 1:16 or higher: in nine out of 13 cases a positive result was obtained on at least one occasion (69 per cent). In view of the close similarity of the results given by the two methods the data from the different centres may be added in comparing the two treatment groups. It is then found that 18 of the 28 patients on cortisone who were tested were positive at one time or another (64 per cent), and 20 of the 25 patients on aspirin who were tested (80 per cent). In other words, each treatment group had a high proportion of positive tests and there is no statistically significant difference between them.

Ball, whose method was principally used in this trial, has reported 50 per cent of positive results in a large unselected series of out-patients diagnosed as suffering from rheumatoid arthritis; and in a carefully selected series of typical cases of varying duration admitted to the Manchester Royal Infirmary for special study 41 out of 61 (67 per cent) gave a positive test (Ball, 1952). Scott (1952), using the Rose method, has reported positive results (a ratio of 1:16 or more) in 60 per cent of an unselected series of 124 confirmed rheumatoid arthritis patients. The 38 positive results in 53 patients in the present trial (72 per cent) compare very favourably with these various figures. They are good evidence of the accuracy of the diagnosis of rheumatoid arthritis in the patients admitted to the trial.

Details of the patients by centre, sex, age, and duration of symptoms are given in Table 7, 1. The data show how effective the

TABLE 7, 1

Comparison of the Patients on Cortisone and Aspirin at Start of Treatment

Treatment Centre	No. of Patients on			Male		Female	
	Cortisone	Aspirin		No. of Patients on		No. of Patients on	
				Cortisone	Aspirin	Cortisone	Aspirin
1	2	5	Age:				
			17–39 years	5	5	4	6
			40–59 years	8	6	13	14
2	5	4					
			Total	13	11	17	20
3	1	—					
4	8	8					
			Duration of symptoms:				
5	6	6	3–5 months	5	4	6	8
6	8	8	6–9 months	8	7	11	12
Total	30	31	Total	13	11	17	20

method of allocation has been in equalizing the two treatment groups in these respects. Their initial equalities or inequalities in other characteristics will be seen in each of the tables that follow, where these initial assessments are set alongside the subsequent observations.

It must be noted that during the first year of treatment and observation three patients, all on aspirin, were lost to sight. The reasons were as follows:

(1) Male aged 48, West London Centre. After some preliminary improvement his condition deteriorated and he did not, after six months, feel that he was gaining any benefit from the tablets.

(2) Female aged 53, Sheffield Centre. Relapsed on leaving hospital, had a psychological breakdown and declined to return (at week 12).

(3) Female aged 60, Edinburgh Centre. Left the country for New Zealand (at week 30).

The first two must clearly be counted as failures of treatment and must be remembered in considering the results. The third patient was responding satisfactorily up to week 30, and subsequent information has confirmed that she continues to do well on aspirin. For the remaining 58 patients assessments were available towards the end of the first year. The centres, however, were not able invariably to fulfil the agreed schedule, and it was found that the number of patients off treatment in week 52, as required by it, was not sufficient to allow an effective analysis at that point (only about half had the off-treatment week at the end of the year). On the other hand, assessments were available for all 58 patients at some point close to the end of the year while they were still on their personal dosage. The week chosen for analysis, therefore, was, for each patient, that week of personal dosage which provided assessments and was nearest to week 52—with the proviso that it must lie at least four weeks before an off-treatment week—that is, before any 'tapering off' of dosage would have begun. There were six patients (four on cortisone and two on aspirin) who at the end of the year had been off treatment for periods varying from nine to 26 weeks. In these cases the personal dosage was taken to be nil and the week nearest to the end of the year was chosen for inclusion. The actual points taken lay between the forty-sixth and fifty-fourth week in all but three cases (which were at the forty-second, forty-fourth and forty-fifth week).

RESULTS

(a) Joint Tenderness

The changes in joint tenderness are shown in Table **7,** 2. In reaching the figures there set out an overall 'tenderness' index was first computed separately for each patient by taking the average of his recorded joints. The mean of these averages gave, at each point of time, an index for the treatment group as a whole. It will be seen that the average position at the start of treatment is almost identical in the two groups—1.91 cortisone and 1.89 aspirin. In both there is a significant and considerable reduction in pain in the first week of treatment, when the averages fall by 0.80 and 0.72 respectively. This fall continues, though more slowly, up to week 8, and very slightly thereafter, between week 8 and the end of the year. As a result the final averages are still almost identical, though at a much lower level (0.74 cortisone and 0.76 aspirin); the reduction over the year has been some 60 per cent in each group.

In the second and third rows of Table 7, 2 similar figures are given separately for the wrist-joints and the small joints of the hand.

TABLE 7, 2

*The Average Changes Observed in the Joint Tenderness Index**

Joints Measured	Treatment Group	Average Joint Tenderness in Week 0	Average Changes in Joint Tenderness			Joint Tenderness at 1 Year	
			Week 0 to Week 1	Week 1 to Week 8	Week 8 to 1 Year	Average	As % of Average at Week 0
All relevant joints (including wrist and hand, given below)	Cortisone	1·91	−0·80†	−0·29	−0·09	0·74	39
	Aspirin	1·89	−0·72	−0·21	−0·15	0·76	40
Wrist-joints	Cortisone	1·80	−0·83	−0·10	+0·13	1·00	56
	Aspirin	1·93	−0·79	−0·21	+0·08	0·96	50
Small joints of hand	Cortisone	2·25	−0·93	−0·50	−0·25	0·58	26
	Aspirin	2·05	−0·82	−0.24	−0·34	0·53	26

* Tenderness was graded on the scale 0 for no pain, 1 for slight pain, 2 for wincing, and 3 for wincing and withdrawal. The records have been used as an ordinary numerical scale.

† In this and subsequent tables, values in italics are statistically significant changes between specified times, and in the penultimate column between the beginning and end of the year (P < 0·05).

Though the changes are not statistically significant, it appears that with each of the treatments the average levels of pain tended to continue to decrease up to the end of the year in respect of the small joints of the hand, but to show some increases after week 8 in the wrist-joints. In both instances, however, the initial and final averages are closely similar for the cortisone- and aspirin-treated groups.

(b) Range of Movement and Strength of Grip

Table **7, 3** gives the figures for range of movement in the wrists and strength of grip. In these respects the cortisone group reveals, by chance, some advantage before treatment was started—the

TABLE **7, 3**

The Average Changes in (a) Range of Wrist Movement and (b) Strength of Grip

Character-istic Measured	Treat-ment Group	Average Measure-ment in Week 0	Average Changes in Measurement			Measurement at 1 Year	
			Week 0 to Week 1	Week 1 to Week 8	Week 8 to 1 Year	Aver-age	As % of Average at Week 0
Range of wrist movement (in degrees)	Corti-sone	99*	+13·9	+4·6	+1·1	120*	121
	Aspirin	78	+23·2	−1·8	+2·3	103	132
Strength of grip (in mm. Hg) left hand	Corti-sone	138	+33·3	+17·8	+12·2	202*	146
	Aspirin	111	+35·3	+8·5	+0·4	164	148
Strength of grip (in mm. Hg) right hand	Corti-sone	134	+46·7	+2·5	+3·7	187	140
	Aspirin	116	+34·5	+15·1	−7·1	166	143

* The mean of the cortisone group was significantly greater than the mean of the aspirin group.

average range of movement and average strength of grip were greater. (The difference in the average range of movement is statistically significant.) It is not possible, however, to detect any material difference between the two groups in their responses to treatment. There is, in each characteristic, a substantial improvement in the first week of treatment; week 1 to week 8 and week 8 to 1 year reveal, on the whole, some further increases, but the changes are much smaller and very variable. At the end of the year the average for the cortisone group, compared with the aspirin group, is significantly greater for the range of movement in the wrists but by no more than it was initially. In respect of strength of grip the averages for the cortisone group at the end of the year are also above those for the aspirin group, but once again by no more than they were initially. In other words, the mean percentage changes have been remarkably similar—an increase of 20–30 per cent in range of wrist movement and of 40–50 per cent in strength of grip.

(c) Tests of Dexterity

Table **7, 4** gives the results of the timing tests. The average starting-points of the two groups are reasonably alike, and the progression under treatment and the end-results are again very similar. Each treatment group shows an average improvement of some 20–25 per cent.

TABLE **7, 4**

The Average Changes in Time Taken to (a) Tie Six Knots and (b) Go Up and Down Ten Steps, by Patients with Affected Hands and Legs Respectively

Character-istic Measured	Treat-ment Group	Average Measure-ment in Week 0	Average Changes in Measurement			Measurement at 1 Year	
			Week 0 to Week 1	Week 1 to Week 8	Week 8 to 1 Year	Aver-age	As % of Average at Week 0
Time (in seconds) to tie 6 knots	Corti-sone	38	−4·2	−0·2	−4·2	29	76
	Aspirin	41	−3·0	−3·9	−0·8	34	83
Time (in seconds) to go up and down 10 steps	Corti-sone	14	−1·3	−2·6	+0·6	11	79
	Aspirin	18	−4·5	+0·8	−0·2	13	72

(d) Haemoglobin Level and Blood Sedimentation Rate

The changes in the level of haemoglobin and in the blood sedimentation rate are shown in Table **7, 5**. In both these respects there is apparent some difference between the cortisone- and aspirin-treated groups. In haemoglobin level they start alike with mean values of 12.2 and 12.1 g. per cent. Under treatment the patients on cortisone show, on the average, an improvement, and at the end of the year the mean has reached 13.1 g. per cent. The corresponding

TABLE 7, 5

The Average Changes in (a) Haemoglobin and (b) Blood Sedimentation Rate

Character- istic Measured	Treat- ment Group	Average Measure- ment in Week 0	Average Changes in Measurement			Measurement at 1 Year	
			Week 0 to Week 1	Week 1 to Week 8	Week 8 to 1 Year	Aver- age	As % of Average at Week 0
Haemoglobin (in g. %)	Corti- sone	12·2	+0·2*	+0·6	+0·1*	*13·1**	107
	Aspirin	12·1	−0·4	+0·4	−0·8	11·3	93
E.S.R. (mm./hr.)	Corti- sone	42	−18·1*	−4·4	+5·5	*27*	64
	Aspirin	42	−1·4	+0·4	−6·1	35	83

* The averages shown by the cortisone and aspirin groups differ significantly.

changes under aspirin are erratic and statistically insignificant, with the final average of 11.3 g. per cent, rather below the initial level and significantly below the average for the cortisone group.

The mean blood sedimentation rate at the start of treatment was identical—42 mm./hour in each group. In the first week of treatment there was a pronounced fall in the cortisone group and an insignificant fall in the aspirin group. Subsequent mean changes were slight and at the end of the year of observation the final averages of 27 mm./hour for patients on cortisone and 35 mm./hour for patients on aspirin do not differ appreciably, though still slightly favouring the former group. On the other hand, in each treatment group five patients had a value of 10 mm./hour or below at the end of the year.

(e) Clinical Assessments

At the end of the year two patients on cortisone and three on aspirin were reported to be in remission (though two of those of aspirin were still on maintenance doses of 4g. and 1.7g. respectively). There were a further two patients on cortisone and a further one on aspirin who had not been on treatment for 10, 40, and 20 weeks respectively. Thus four patients in each group were regarded as either in remission or as not requiring treatment at that time. The overall assessments of condition and progress at the end of the first year are shown in Table 7, 6, and reveal little difference between the two groups. If the two aspirin patients who progressed un-favourably and were lost to view are included as 'very active' the picture would not be materially altered.

TABLE 7, 6

Clinical Assessments of Activity at One Year

Grade	Cortisone No.	Aspirin No.
Inactive	2	2
Slightly active	21	19
Very active	7	7
Total	30	28

The assessments of functional capacity are given in Table 7, 7, and once again the two treatment groups are more remarkable for their similarity than for their dissimilarity. At the start of treatment the majority of patients were placed in grade 3—not employed and unemployable, no physical recreations. By the eighth week many had been moved to the higher grades—full or light work, etc. In the week off treatment, the thirteenth, a number returned to the lower grades, but by the close of the year about four-fifths of the patients were capable of either full (grade 1) or light work (grade 2). Division of these patients into grades 1 and 2 separately gives 13 and 10 patients on cortisone and 11 and 10 on aspirin, or approximately 40 per cent, with full functional capacity in each treatment group. Only two patients, both on cortisone, were bedridden at the end of the year. The two missing aspirin cases may be set against these—that is, putting the most unfavourable complexion upon them.

TABLE 7, 7

Number of Patients with Given Functional Capacity at Different Points of Treatment *

Treatment Group	Time of Assessment	Functional Capacity			Total
		1 or 2	3	4 or 5	
Cortisone	Week 0	4	18	8	30
Aspirin		5	18	6	29†
Cortisone	Week 8	18	11	1	30
Aspirin		15	11	3	29
Cortisone	Week 13	10	16	4	30
Aspirin		10	13	5	28
Cortisone	1 Year	23	5	2	30
Aspirin		21	5	0	26

* Functional capacity grades were:

Grade 1: Fully employed or employable in usual work and able to undertake normal physical recreation.

Grade 2: Doing light or part-time work and only limited physical recreation. For housewives, all except the heaviest housework.

Grade 3: Not employed and unemployable. No physical recreations. Housewives, only light housework and limited shopping.

Grade 4: Confined to house or wheel-chair, but able to look after themselves in essentials of life. Hospital patients confined to bed.

Grade 5: Completely bedridden.

† No record was made in this respect for two patients, and, as stated previously, three were subsequently lost to view.

(f) Side-effects

Side-effects were recorded for 19 patients in the cortisone group and 21 patients in the aspirin group. Most of these patients had more than one complication, the most frequent in the cortisone group being moon-face or rubicundity (11 patients), depression (five patients), and euphoria (four patients), and in the aspirin group tinnitus (11 patients), deafness (10 patients), nausea, dyspepsia, or anorexia (13 patients). There were no severe complications in the cortisone group necessitating discontinuance of treatment despite a final personal dosage at the end of the year of between 100 and 125 mg. a day in 11 of the 26 patients.

The numbers of patients showing side-effects in each consecutive three months of this first year's treatment were 14, 15, 11, and 12 in patients on cortisone, and 16, 10, 6, and 6 in patients on aspirin. In other words, the numbers with these minor complications were equal in the early months of treatment, but became less in the aspirin group as time passed.

DISCUSSION

This trial, as emphasized in the early paragraphs of the report, was designed to answer a specific but very important question— namely, in early and uncomplicated cases of rheumatoid arthritis is it possible to maintain the patient's well-being more efficiently by treatment with cortisone than by treatment with aspirin? Simultaneously, if the trial can be continued into a second or third year, as is envisaged, light may be thrown upon the evolution of the rheumatoid process during prolonged therapy with these different agents. While scientifically it would obviously be of much value to be able to compare the changes in both these treated groups with those taking place in a group receiving neither cortisone nor aspirin, ethically such a course is impossible. One or other agent, it was held, must be administered—together with any other basic treatment that might be required (splints, physiotherapy, etc.).

It was, however, decided that treatment should be tapered off at the end of each three-months' period and then withheld for one week to allow of assessment of the patient's condition. Analysis of the data thus provided at the end of the first course—that is, at the thirteenth week—revealed a distinct 'relapse' in some of the patients, though an equal degree of 'relapse' occurred on the two forms of treatment. For example, the average joint tenderness at the start of treatment was 1.91 in the cortisone group and 1.89 in the aspirin group (Table 7, 2). By week 8 the average had declined by 1.09 in the cortisone group and by 0.93 in the aspirin group. In the week off treatment it increased again by 0.49 and 0.31 respectively, giving average levels in the thirteenth week of 1.32 on cortisone and 1.29 on aspirin.

Very similar reversals were seen in all the other characteristics measured or observed. In Table 7, 7 they have already been shown for the functional capacity. It is, however, apparent that the two treatment groups have, on the whole, kept remarkably in step. They closely parallel one another in their immediate and favourable reaction to the first week of treatment; in the continuation of that reaction, but at a much slower rate, up to the observations made at week 8; in their unfavourable response to the cessation of treatment in week 13; and, finally, in their position at the end of the first year of the trial.

The haemoglobin levels and blood sedimentation rates have responded rather more favourably to cortisone than to aspirin. In all other respects there has been little to choose between the two agents. On each form of treatment joint tenderness is substantially reduced; on each form the disease is judged at the end of one year to be inactive, or only slightly active, in three-quarters of the patients; on each form two-fifths of the patients were regarded at the end of one year as capable of normal work and activity. As usual with cortisone treatment, certain more intangible differences have been observed. Some patients appear to experience a sense of well-being, and sometimes an almost excessive and inappropriate cheerfulness during therapy, followed by a swing to a mood of depression during the periods off treatment. On the other hand, the patients receiving aspirin tend to have changes in mood which are more in keeping with the increase and decrease in their symptoms. For practical purposes, however, there seems to have been surprisingly

TABLE 7, 8

Daily Maintenance Doses being Administered at the End of the First Year (Before any Tapering-off)

Cortisone (mg./day)	No. of Patients on Given Dose	Aspirin (g./day)	No. of Patients on Given Dose
125	2	6	8
100*	9	5	2
75†	7	4	13
62½	2	3	1
50	4	2	1
37½	1	1·7	1
25	1		
Total	26	Total	26
Nil (off treatment)	4	Nil (off treatment)	2
Mean value for those on treatment	80 mg.	Mean value for those on treatment	4·5 g.

* Including 1 at 105 mg.   † Including 1 at 80 mg.

little to choose between cortisone and aspirin as adjuvants in the management of these 61 early cases of rheumatoid arthritis. The maintenance doses that were being employed at the end of the first year to produce these results are shown in Table 7, 8.

In the second year of the trial it is intended that treatment shall be continuous—unless the patient is in remission or is held to require no maintenance dose.

SUMMARY

Sixty-one patients in the early stages of rheumatoid arthritis, and regarded as suitable for treatment with either cortisone or aspirin, have been allocated at random to treatment with one or other agent (cortisone 30 cases, aspirin 31 cases). Two comparable groups of these early cases were thus constructed and have now been treated and observed for one year. For most of the year treatment was 'individualized' by the physician in charge of the patient at a level sufficient to restore maximal functional efficiency without producing serious side-effects.

Observations made one week, eight weeks, 13 weeks, and approximately one year after the start of treatment reveal that the two groups have run a closely parallel course in nearly all the recorded characteristics—namely, joint tenderness, range of movement in the wrist, strength of grip, tests of dexterity of hand and foot, and clinical judgements of the activity of the disease and of the patient's functional capacity. The haemoglobin level and blood sedimentation rate were slightly more favourably influenced by cortisone, but in no other respect do the two groups differ materially.

On each form of treatment the disease was judged at the end of one year to be inactive, or only slightly active, in about three-quarters of the patients, and on each treatment some two-fifths of the patients were regarded as capable of normal work and activity. For practical purposes, therefore, there appears to have been surprisingly little to choose between cortisone and aspirin in the management of these 61 patients in the early stages of rheumatoid arthritis.

REFERENCES

Ball, J. (1950). *Lancet*, **ii**, 520.
Ball, J. (1952). *Ann. rheum. Dis.* **11**, 97.
Rose, H. M., Ragan, C., Pearce, E., and Lipman, M. O. (1948). *Proc. Soc. exp. Biol. N.Y.* **68**, 1.
Scott, F. E. T. (1952). *Lancet*, **i**, 392.

CHAPTER 8

A COMPARISON OF CORTISONE AND ASPIRIN IN THE TREATMENT OF EARLY CASES OF RHEUMATOID ARTHRITIS—II

THE therapeutic trial here presented was designed to answer a specific but important question—namely, in early and uncomplicated cases of rheumatoid arthritis is it possible to maintain the patient's well-being more efficiently by treatment with cortisone than by treatment with aspirin? At the same time it was hoped to study the evolution of the rheumatoid process during prolonged therapy with these two different agents. In other words, the aim was to measure the therapeutic effects upon the rheumatoid process of a long-term treatment initiated while that process was still uncomplicated, either by severe anatomical changes in the joints or by metabolic disturbances resulting from a prolonged and debilitating disease.

For this purpose 61 adult patients, regarded as suitable for treatment with *either* agent, were admitted to six centres in England and Scotland. Thirty of these patients were treated with cortisone and 31 with aspirin, their allocation to one or other treatment being made entirely at random (within each centre and for patients of each sex and duration of illness). By such means two comparable groups of these early cases were constructed. Observations of the groups made one week, eight weeks, thirteen weeks, and approximately one year after the start of treatment showed that they had run a closely parallel course in nearly all respects—for example, in joint tenderness, strength of grip, tests of dexterity of hand or foot, clinical assessments of the activity of the disease and of the patient's

A second report by the Joint Committee of the Medical Research Council and Nuffield Foundation on Clinical Trials of Cortisone, A.C.T.H., and Other Therapeutic Measures in Chronic Rheumatic Diseases, the members of which were: Sir Henry Cohen (chairman), Dr. E. G. L. Bywaters, Dr. W. S. C. Copeman, Sir Charles Dodds, Dr. J. J. R. Duthie, Professor A. Bradford Hill, Mr. H. Osmond-Clarke, Professor F. T. G. Prunty, Dr. J. Reid, Dr. H. F. West, Professor J. H. Kellgren and Mr. W. A. Sanderson (joint secretaries).

Reprinted from the *British Medical Journal*, 1955, **ii**, 695 functional capacity. 'For practical purposes, therefore,' the first report concluded, 'there appears to have been surprisingly little to choose between cortisone and aspirin in the management of these 61 patients in the early stages of rheumatoid arthritis.' In the present report the comparison is extended to approximately two years from the beginning of treatment.

Full details of the trial were given in the first report but will be briefly recapitulated here.

The Patients

Each patient included in the trial (a) had a polyarthritis of rheumatoid type affecting at least four joints and bilateral involvement of either hands or feet, ankles or wrists; (b) had had the disease for not less than three and not more than nine months; and (c) was aged between 17 and 59 years. A sheep-cell agglutination test was performed in most of them during the first year of observation (53 of the total 61) and gave a positive result in nearly three-quarters.

The two groups of patients, on cortisone and aspirin respectively, were initially almost identical in the numbers of men and women, in the numbers aged 17–39 and 40–59 years, and in the numbers with a duration of symptoms of three to five or six to nine months. In each of the six centres the cases admitted were almost equally divided between cortisone and aspirin. The initial equalities or inequalities in the characteristics studied will be seen in the tables that follow.

Treatment

For the first year of treatment it was laid down that therapy would be given in twelve-weeks' courses separated by one week off treatment. Each course would start with a standard dosage, after which the physician was free to adjust the dose to suit the requirements of individual patients. The specified courses, given in divided doses not fewer than three times a day, were:

		Cortisone	Aspirin
First week:	Day 1	300 mg.	6 g.
	Day 2	200 mg.	6 g.
	Day 3 to day 7	100 mg. daily	6 g. daily
Second week:	Day 8 to day 14	50 mg. daily	2 g. daily
Third to twelfth week:	Day 15 to day 84	Individualized at 25 to 200 mg. daily with graded withdrawal in week 12	Individualized at 1 to 8 g. daily with graded withdrawal in week 12

In the 'free' period—that is, the third to twelfth week—the physician was asked to employ the minimum dosage that would restore maximal functional efficiency without producing serious side-effects. In the thirteenth week no treatment by cortisone or aspirin was given, observations and measurements being made (in this week analgesics other than aspirin could, if necessary, be given). If symptoms recurred the twelve-weeks' course was repeated, except that the selected dose for the individual patient replaced the standard dose of the second week.

During the second year these twelve-weeks' courses were replaced by continuous treatment—unless the patient was in remission or was thought to require no maintenance dose. The dosage throughout the year was entirely at the physician's discretion, but the aim was again to employ the minimum that would produce maximum functional efficiency and relief of symptoms without producing serious side-effects.

Assessments

The clinical assessment included (a) a defined judgement of the patient's general functional capacity (for the five grades laid down, see Table **8**, 10); (b) a judgement of the activity of the disease as inactive, slightly active, or very active; and (c) a statement whether the patient appeared to be in remission. In addition to these subjective assessments the clinician was required to measure the strength of grip for each hand. (The patient had to squeeze an oblong rubber bag 5in. by 3in. (12.5cm. by 7.5cm.) inflated at a pressure of 10mm. Hg, and the figure recorded was the average of three grips.) Two tests of dexterity were applied—namely, in patients with affected hands the time taken to tie six double knots with 12-in. (30-cm.) pieces of household string, and in patients with affected legs the time taken to go up and down 10 steps. Estimates were also made of joint tenderness and of range of movement. Complications and side-effects were noted. The only obligatory laboratory tests were the blood sedimentation rate and the haemoglobin level.

Towards the end of the second year X-ray pictures of the hands and feet were taken and the amount of porosis and erosion revealed in each was assessed.

The Data

During the first year's observation three patients were lost from the trial—all three from the group treated with aspirin, reducing the number in that group to 28. It was concluded in the first report that two of these ought to be regarded as failures of treatment and should be remembered as such in considering the results (a male who deteriorated after some preliminary improvement, and, feeling after six months that he was gaining no benefit, was taken out of the trial and given other treatment; and a female who relapsed on leaving hospital, had a psychological breakdown, and did not attend further. The third patient, who did well on aspirin, went to New Zealand at week 30). No losses took place in the second year, and observations are available for all the 58 patients previously reported. It must be noted, however, that during the second year six patients (one on cortisone and five on aspirin) were known to have received some treatment other than that laid down (there was, however, no transfer from one treatment group to the other). These were:

(a) Two patients on aspirin (Postgraduate Medical School Centre) who did not attend regularly in the second year.

(b) Two patients on aspirin (West London Centre) who had their aspirin therapy discontinued in weeks 55 and 72.

(c) One patient on aspirin (Edinburgh Centre) who had severe side-effects and the drug discontinued in week 55.

(d) One patient on cortisone (Edinburgh Centre) who had severe side-effects and the hormone discontinued in week 55.

These patients have been retained in their original groups, which are thus composed of 30 patients on cortisone, one of whom was given some other treatment (not aspirin), and 28 patients on aspirin, five of whom were given some other treatment (not hormone).

The treatment schedule laid down for the second year required continuous therapy until the last four weeks (except in cases already in remission or thought not to require any maintenance dose). In weeks 100 to 104 a gradual 'tapering off' was called for, followed by four weeks without treatment and an assessment at the end of this period—that is, in week 108. The centres were not, however, able to fulfil this schedule in all cases, and for about one-third of each group no 'off-treatment' assessment was made (nine of each treatment group). In some cases the withdrawal of treatment was regarded as unjustifiable, and in others signs of relapse following a reduction of dosage caused the full amount required for maintenance to be restored. On the other hand, assessments were available for all 58 patients at some point close to the end of the year while they were still on their personal dosage. The week chosen for analysis, therefore, was, for each patient, that week of personal dosage which provided assessments and was nearest to week 104—with the proviso that it must lie at least four weeks before an off-treatment week— that is, before any 'tapering off' of dosage would have begun. There were six patients (three on cortisone and three on aspirin) who had been off treatment for all or part of the second year; in these cases the personal dosage was taken to be nil and the week nearest to the end of the year was chosen for analysis. The actual points taken lay between the ninety-sixth and one hundred and twelfth weeks in all cases.

RESULTS

In the first report the changes under treatment were shown for each group between the start of treatment and the end of the first week, between week 1 and week 8, and between week 8 and one year. It has not been thought necessary to present the intermediate data again, and the tables that follow show the picture at the start of treatment and the end of the first and second years.

(a) Joint Tenderness

In reaching the figures for joint tenderness set out in Table **8**, 1 an overall 'tenderness' index was first computed separately for each patient by taking the average of his recorded joints. The mean of these averages gave, at each point of time, an index for the treatment group as a whole. It will be seen that the average position at the start of treatment was almost identical in the two groups—namely, 1.91 cortisone and 1.89 aspirin—and that the decline in tenderness during the first year was considerable and strikingly similar—to 0.74 cortisone and 0.76 aspirin. During the second year the average for the cortisone group has remained almost the same (0.72), while for the aspirin group the figure has declined further to 0.58. Division of the joints into those of the wrists and of the hand (the main components of the total index) gives a very similar picture in each group—that is, equality at one year and a lower figure in the aspirin

TABLE 8, 1

The Average Levels of the Joint Tenderness Index*

Joints Measured	Treatment Group	Average Joint Tenderness		
		Start of Treatment	End of 1 Year	End of 2 Years
All relevant joints (including wrist and hand, given below)	Cortisone	1·91	0·74	0·72
	Aspirin	1·89	0·76	0·58
Wrist-joints	Cortisone	1·80	1·00	0·93
	Aspirin	1·93	0·96	0·73
Small joints of hand	Cortisone	2·25	0·58	0·63
	Aspirin	2·05	0·53	0·31

* Tenderness was graded on the scale 0 for no pain 1 for slight pain, 2 for wincing, and 3 for wincing and withdrawal. The records have been used as an ordinary numerical scale.

TABLE 8, 2

Joint Tenderness Index (all relevant joints) at the End of Two Years Related to the Initial Levels of Tenderness. Number of Patients

Joint Tenderness at Start of Treatment	Treatment Group and No. of Patients		Joint Tenderness at End of 2 Years				
			0	Under 1	1–	2–	3
Under 1	Cortisone	1		1			
	Aspirin ..	3	1	2			
1–	Cortisone ..	13	2	6	4	1	
	Aspirin ..	7	4	3			
2–	Cortisone ..	11	3	4	3	1	
	Aspirin ..	13	3	5	4	1	
3	Cortisone ..	5	2	2	1		
	Aspirin ..	5	1	3			1
Total	Cortisone ..	30	7	13	8	2	0
	Aspirin ..	28	9	13	4	1	1

group at two years. The differences at two years are not, however, statistically significant, and too much emphasis must not be placed upon them. Table **8,** 2 gives the numbers of patients with different levels of joint tenderness at the start of treatment and at the end of two years. The equality of the two groups is again noticeable. Thus, for the joints recorded at the start of treatment, 7 of the 30 patients on cortisone had no remaining joint tenderness at all at the end of two years, in 13 it was slight, and in 10 it was more definite. The corresponding figures for the 28 observed patients on aspirin were 9, 13, and 6. The numbers available are small, but the same equality of trend is suggested in each sub-division of the table.

(b) Range of Movement and Strength of Grip

Table **8,** 3 gives the figures for range of movement in the wrists and strength of grip. In these respects the cortisone group had, by

TABLE **8,** 3

The Average Measurements of (a) Range of Wrist Movement and (b) Strength of Grip

Characteristic Measured	Treatment Group	Average Measurement		
		Start of Treatment	End of 1 Year	End of 2 Years
Range of wrist movement (in degrees)	Cortisone	99*	120*	111
	Aspirin	78	103	103
Strength of grip (in mm. Hg) left hand	Cortisone	138	202*	187
	Aspirin	111	164	158
Strength of grip (in mm. Hg) right hand	Cortisone	134	187	186
	Aspirin	116	166	164

* The mean of the cortisone group was significantly greater than the mean of the aspirin group.

chance and on the average, some advantage over the aspirin group when treatment was started. At the end of one year both groups had improved considerably. At this point of time the averages of the cortisone group remained above those of the aspirin group, but the advantage was no greater than had been observed at the start of treatment. At the end of two years even that gap has narrowed, both groups having shown a very slight deterioration during the second

TABLE **8, 4**

Range of Movement (Wrists) at Two Years Related to the Initial Range of Movement. Number of Wrists Involved

Range of Movement (Degrees) at Start of Treatment	Treatment Group	Range of Movement at End of 2 Years (Degrees)			
		0–	50–	100–	150+
0–	2 Cortisone		2		
	9 Aspirin		5	3	1
50–	12 Cortisone	1	5	5	1
	13 Aspirin		6	6	1
100–	12 Cortisone		2	6	4
	11 Aspirin		6	4	1
150+	3 Cortisone			1	2
	0 Aspirin				
Total	29 Cortisone	1	9	12	7
	33 Aspirin	0	17	13	3

year and there being no significant difference between them at the end of the second year. The frequency with which various ranges of wrist movement were observed are shown in Table **8,** 4, and the changes in strength of grip in Table **8,** 5. Neither table reveals any clear advantage to one or other treatment.

TABLE **8, 5**

Number of Patients Showing Given Improvement or Deterioration in Their Strength of Grip (in mm. Hg) Between Start of Treatment and End of Two Years

Treatment Group and No. of Patients	Improved by 100mm. or More	Improved by up to 100mm.	No Change	Deteriorated by up to 100mm.	Deteriorated by 100mm. or More
Left hand:					
30 Cortisone	7	14	1	6	2
28 Aspirin	4	15	3	6	—
Right hand:					
30 Cortisone	11	12	1	5	1
28 Aspirin	7	14	1	6	—

(c) Tests of Dexterity

Table **8,** 6 gives the results of the timing tests. The improvement noted at the end of one year has been maintained, but not increased, during the second year of treatment. The two treatment groups remain very similar in these respects.

TABLE **8,** 6

The Average Time Taken to (a) Tie Six Knots and (b) Go Up and Down Ten Steps by Patients with Affected Hands and Legs Respectively

Characteristic Measured	Treatment Group	Average Time (in Seconds)		
		Start of Treatment	End of 1 Year	End of 2 Years *
Time to tie 6 knots	Cortisone	38	29	29
	Aspirin	41	34	33
Time to go up and down 10 steps	Cortisone	14	11	11
	Aspirin	18	13	11

* 8 patients (5 cortisone, 3 aspirin) included in the earlier averages had no recording for either dexterity test at two years.

(d) Haemoglobin Level and Blood Sedimentation Rate

During the first year of the trial it was found that the haemoglobin level and blood sedimentation rate responded, on the average, rather more favourably to cortisone than to aspirin. During the second year this advantage to the cortisone group has not been maintained (Table **8,** 7). While its average values for the haemoglobin level and erythrocyte sedimentation rates have both remained practically unchanged, the average haemoglobin value in the aspirin group has risen and the average E.S.R. has fallen. As a result the two treatment groups differ little in the average haemoglobin level and negligibly in the average E.S.R. at the end of two years. Looking beneath the averages to individual levels of the E.S.R., the same picture of close similarity is revealed (Table **8,** 8). Taking under 20mm./hour as the level of

TABLE **8,** 7

*The Average Levels of (a) Haemoglobin and (b) Blood
Sedimentation Rate*

Characteristic Measured	Treatment Group	Average Measurement		
		Start of Treatment	End of 1 Year	End of 2 Years
Haemoglobin (g. %)	Cortisone	12·2	13·1*	13·0
	Aspirin	12·1	11·3	12·3
E.S.R. (mm./hr.)	Cortisone	42	27	29
	Aspirin	42	35	28

* The averages shown by the cortisone and aspirin groups differ significantly.

TABLE **8,** 8

*Number of Patients with Given Blood Sedimentation Rates at the
End of Two Years Related to Their Rates at the Start of Treatment*

E.S.R. (mm./hr.) at Start of Treatment	Treatment Group and No. of Patients	E.S.R. (mm./hr.) at End of 2 Years			
		0–	20–	40–	60+
0–	9 Cortisone	6	3		
	5 Aspirin	3	2		
20–	6 Cortisone	1	3	2	
	11 Aspirin	5	4	2	
40–	9 Cortisone	2	5	1	1
	7 Aspirin	2	5		
60+	6 Cortisone	1		3	2
	5 Aspirin	1	1	2	1
Total	30 Cortisone	10	11	6	3
	28 Aspirin	11	12	4	1

normality, 10 of the 30 patients on cortisone and 11 of the 28 on
aspirin had a normal E.S.R. at the end of two years of treatment,
while 11 and 12 respectively had an elevated rate (20–39) and nine

and five had a considerably elevated rate (40 or over). Within the sub-groups with different levels at the start of treatment the trend also appears to have been remarkably similar in the two groups.

(e) Clinical Assessments

At the end of the second year four patients on cortisone and four on aspirin were reported to be in remission. The overall clinical assessments of condition at the end of the first and second years are shown in Table **8**, 9.

TABLE **8**, 9

Clinical Assessment of Activity at End of One Year and End of Two Years

Grade	End of 1 Year		End of 2 Years	
	Cortisone	Aspirin	Cortisone	Aspirin
Inactive	2	2	4	4
Slightly active	21	19	20	19
Very active	7	7	6	5
Total	30	28	30	28

The assessments of functional capacity are given in Table **8**, 10, and at the end of two years the two treatment groups still remain, as was noted at one year, more remarkable for their similarity than for their dissimilarity. In each treatment group 21 patients were regarded as capable either of full work (grade 1) or of light work (grade 2), and sub-division of them shows 14 patients in grade 1 in the cortisone group and 13 in the aspirin group. Seven of the 30 patients on cortisone remained seriously incapacitated (grade 3), compared with five of the 26 patients on aspirin. Only two patients, both on cortisone, were still grossly incapacitated, and against this may be placed the two aspirin cases who progressed unfavourably in the first year and were lost sight of—that is, putting the most unfavourable complexion upon them.

TABLE **8**, 10

Number of Patients with Given Functional Capacity
at Different Stages of the Trial*

Treatment Group	Time of Assessment	Functional Capacity			Total
		1 or 2	3	4 or 5	
Cortisone	Start of treat-	4	18	8	30
Aspirin	ment	5	18	6	29†
Cortisone	End of 1 year	23	5	2	30
Aspirin		21	5	0	26
Cortisone	End of 2 years	21	7	2	30
Aspirin		21	5	0	26

* Functional capacity grades were:

Grade 1: Fully employed or employable in usual work and able to undertake normal physical recreation.

Grade 2: Doing light or part-time work and only limited physical recreation. For housewives, all except the heaviest housework.

Grade 3: Not employed and unemployable. No physical recreations. Housewives only light housework and limited shopping.

Grade 4: Confined to house or wheel-chair, but able to look after themselves in essentials of life. Hospital patients confined to bed.

Grade 5: Completely bedridden.

† No record was made in this respect for two patients, and three were lost sight of during the first year of the trial. The two patients not assessed at the start of treatment had functional capacities at the end of two years of 1 and 2 respectively.

(f) X-ray Observations

X-ray films of the hands were taken for all 30 patients on cortisone and for 27 of the 28 patients on aspirin during the second half of the second year of the trial. For the feet, films were available for 26 patients on cortisone and 24 on aspirin. All these films were read independently by three observers (a clinician at one of the centres and two radiologists), who assessed the degree of porosis and erosion present in each case without knowing the treatment group to which it belonged. The results are shown in Table **8**, 11 and **8**, 12. It is clear that while observers B and C were similar in their interpretations of the films, observer A had a quite different standard—

particularly in porosis. For instance, no or doubtful porosis of the hands (grades 0 and 1) was recorded for 20 and 21 patients on cortisone by observers B and C, but for only 14 by observer A. An analysis of variance shows these differences between the observers, in their gradings of both porosis and erosion, to be highly significant (P < 0.001).

Comparison between the treatment groups shows that for each observer the mean figures for porosis and erosion of the hands and feet are rather higher in the aspirin group than in the cortisone group. The differences are very small for porosis but more marked for erosion. The analysis of variance shows that they are not

TABLE **8,** 11

X-ray Films of the Hand. Number of Patients with Given Gradings at the End of Two Years by Three Independent Observers

Grade*	Cortisone			Aspirin		
	Observer			Observer		
	A	B	C	A	B	C
Porosis						
0	5	16	13	4	10	7
1	9	4	8	6	4	11
2	8	7	7	11	10	8
3	5	2	1	4	3	1
4	3	1	1	2	0	0
Total	30	30	30	27	27	27
Average grade	1·73	0·93	0·97	1·78	1·22	1·11
Erosion						
0	6	7	9	3	5	3
1	5	7	5	3	4	4
2	11	12	12	8	7	16
3	5	3	4	11	10	4
4	3	1	0	2	1	0
Total	30	30	30	27	27	27
Average grade	1·80	1·47	1·37	2·22	1·93	1·78

* Gradings of porosis and erosion were: 0 = Nil. 1 = Doubtful. 2 = Slight. 3 = Moderate. 4 = Severe.

TABLE **8,** 12

*X-ray Films of the Feet. Number of Patients with Given Gradings
at the End of Two Years by Three Independent Observers*

Grade	Cortisone			Aspirin		
	Observer			Observer		
	A	B	C	A	B	C
	Porosis					
0	5	18	14	3	14	12
1	8	3	9	6	6	8
2	5	3	1	10	3	2
3	6	1	2	4	1	2
4	2	1	0	1	0	0
Total	26	26	26	24	24	24
Average grade	1·69	0·62	0·65	1·75	0·63	0·75
	Erosion					
0	9	7	7	5	6	3
1	4	10	9	0	3	6
2	7	4	9	10	7	12
3	4	4	1	5	8	3
4	2	1	0	4	0	0
Total	26	26	26	24	24	24
Average grade	1·46	1·31	1·15	2·13	1·71	1·63

statistically significant. A simple summation of the readings of the
three observers gives the following proportions with some degree of
porosis or erosion (grades 2, 3, and 4):

	Porosis		*Erosion*	
	Cortisone	*Aspirin*	*Cortisone*	*Aspirin*
Hands ..	39% ..	48% ..	57% ..	73%
Feet ..	27% ..	32% ..	41% ..	68%

The differences are again relatively slight (except, perhaps, for
erosion of the feet), and, with the numbers of patients involved,
none of them is significant. It is not possible to compare the *changes*
that have taken place in these respects in the two treatment groups,
since X-ray films were not one of the requirements at the start of the

trial. X-ray films were, however, taken initially in some patients, and it is possible to make use of these. Thus there were 16 patients in the aspirin group and 25 in the cortisone group for whom X-ray films of the hands were available at the start of treatment and at the end of two years, and eight and 11 respectively with X-ray films of the feet. The latter are too few to be of any value, and examination suggests also that they may well be an unrepresentative group. On the other hand, the 16 patients on aspirin for whom X-ray pictures of the hands were available had at the start of treatment average measurements in joint tenderness, grip, etc., very similar to the total aspirin group. In these respects, therefore, those whose hands were X-rayed do not appear to be a biased group. To allow comparison of the recorded changes in porosis and erosion in these 16 patients on aspirin each has been matched with a cortisone patient with the same initial degree of porosis or erosion. (Where more than one appropriate cortisone patient was available a random choice was made.) This comparison of the 16 matched patients shows that at entry to the trial some degree of porosis (slight, moderate, or severe) was recorded as present in 45 per cent of the readings in each treatment group. At the end of two years the percentage was 40 in the cortisone group and 55 in the aspirin group, slight and not significant changes. In erosion the initial percentage was only 6 in each treatment group, but at the end of two years this had increased to 65 in the cortisone group and 74 in the aspirin group. The change here is large, but is similar in both groups. On the basis of these admittedly limited figures for the hands there is clearly no material difference between the progression of the two treatment groups.

(g) Side-effects

During the first year of treatment side-effects were recorded for 19 patients in the cortisone group and 21 in the aspirin group. During the second year the numbers were 19 and 12. Most of these patients had more than one side-effect, the most frequent in the cortisone group being oedema of the ankles (eight cases), moon-face or rubicundity (six), depression (five), euphoria (four), and obesity (three); in the aspirin group the most frequent were nausea, dyspepsia, or anorexia (six), tinnitus (four), and oedema of the ankles (three). In only two cases, one in each treatment group, were these side-effects severe enough to necessitate the discontinuance of treatment. The patient on cortisone, a woman aged 36, suffered from persistent and severe headache, depression, dyspepsia, and vomiting, and had occasional casts of red blood cells in the urine. The patient on aspirin, a man aged 40, had marked dyspepsia and vomiting.

THE MAINTENANCE DOSES

The maintenance doses that were being employed at the end of the second year are set out in Table **8**, 13. They do not differ appreciably from those in use at the end of the first year, when the average values were 80 mg. of cortisone and 4.5 g. of aspirin.

TABLE **8**, 13

Daily Maintenance Doses Being Administered at the End of the Second Year (Before any Tapering off)

Cortisone (mg./day)	No. of Patients on Given Dose	Aspirin (g./day)	No. of Patients on Given Dose
125	1	6·7	2
100	6	6	2
75	11		
62½	3	5*	4
50	3	4	9
37½	1	3·3	1
25	1	2·7	1
		2	1
Total	26	Total	20
Mean value	75 mg.	Mean value	4·5 g.
Not receiving cortisone	4	Not receiving aspirin	8

* Including 1 at 5·3

DISCUSSION

In the first year of this trial of the treatment of early cases of rheumatoid arthritis it was decided that the treatment should be tapered off at the end of each three-months' period and then withheld for a week to allow an assessment of the patient's condition.

At the end of the first of these courses of treatment it was found that there was distinct 'relapse' in some of the patients, though, it is important to note, an equal degree of 'relapse' occurred on the two forms of treatment, cortisone and aspirin. Such 'relapses', even though minor in degree, were clearly undesirable, and it was therefore decided that treatment should be continuous throughout the second year of the trial (and, indeed, in a number of cases it became continuous before the end of the first year). At the end of this continuous treatment, which allowed a maintenance dose entirely at the physician's discretion, an assessment was made, usually while the patient was on a maintenance dose (or on no dose if in remission). Thus comparisons can now be made between the two groups at approximately the end of two years of treatment (between weeks 96 and 112 from the start of treatment), the second year's treatment having been uninterrupted.

In total, 61 patients were admitted to the trial, 30 being allocated at random to cortisone and 31 to aspirin. Three of the patients in the aspirin group were lost sight of during the first year, of whom two could be regarded as failures of that treatment and one, who migrated, as a success so far as it went. During the second year none has been lost to sight, and measurements and assessments are available for all 58 patients in most respects. On the other hand, it must be noted that the aspirin group contains four patients who had some additional therapy (not hormone) during the second year, while there was also one patient in the aspirin group and one in the cortisone group whose treatment was discontinued as a result of severe side-effects. These few changes are hardly sufficient to disturb materially the comparison of the two groups. It may be added, too, that a separate analysis has been made, for several of the features given in the tables above, for the patients on cortisone and aspirin who were at the three centres where the only changes were the discontinuance of treatment in one cortisone and one aspirin case. Here there could be no bias, and the results were found to parallel closely those set out in full for the total groups. Attention may therefore be confined to these total groups.

The results of the trial continue at the end of two years to show a similarity between the two treatment groups that is almost remarkable. In some respects the average values for the two groups have come even closer together than they were at the end of one year—either by slight improvement in the aspirin group or by a slight falling-off in the cortisone group. This applies to the range of wrist movement, the strength of grip, and the tests of dexterity. In joint tenderness the cortisone group shows no change in its average index, while the aspirin group shows a reduction. None of these differences, however, is statistically significant. At the end of one year, on the other hand, it was shown that the haemoglobin level and blood sedimentation rate had, on the average, responded rather more favourably to cortisone than to aspirin. This advantage of the cortisone group has vanished during the second year. The mean and frequency distribution of the sedimentation rates are almost identical and the mean haemoglobin levels no longer differ significantly.

A new measure has been introduced to the trial by means of X-ray films of the hands and feet of the patients, assessed independently and 'blindly' by three observers. Their estimates of the degree of porosis and erosion shown by each patient reveal very little difference between the two treatment groups in respect of porosis, but some excess of erosion in the aspirin group. This excess, however, is not more than might fairly easily arise by chance. The relative position of the two groups in this respect at the start of treatment is unknown, since X-ray examinations were not demanded at entry. A study of such X-ray films of the hands as were available suggests, however, that neither group has changed appreciably in the incidence of porosis. Both groups show a very considerable rise in the recorded incidence of erosion, but differ little from one another.

Clinical assessments of the patient's condition continue to show no difference between the two groups. With almost equal numbers at risk, four in each group were in remission, six on cortisone and five on aspirin were 'very active', 14 on cortisone and 13 on aspirin were regarded as capable of doing their usual work and of taking normal physical recreation, nine on cortisone were still gravely incapacitated and seven on aspirin (including here the two unsuccessful cases lost to sight in the first year). As at the end of one year the two groups retain their equality.

SUMMARY

A further report is made on 61 patients who were allocated at random to treatment with either cortisone (30 cases) or aspirin (31 cases) while they were still in the early stages of rheumatoid arthritis. In their second year of therapy, treatment with one or other agent has been continuous, and 'individualized' by the physician in charge of the patient to meet each patient's needs. At approximately the end of two years of treatment 58 of the original 61 patients have been reassessed clinically, submitted to some simple objective tests, had X-ray films taken of their hands and feet, and had their haemoglobin levels and blood sedimentation rates measured. In no respect do the two groups differ by more than might easily be due to chance, and in most respects they are distinguished more by their equalities than by their differences. At the end of two years, therefore, as previously reported at the end of one year, it appears that for practical purposes there has been remarkably little to choose between cortisone and aspirin in the management of this group of patients.

CHAPTER 9

A CONTROLLED CLINICAL TRIAL OF LONG-TERM ANTICOAGULANT THERAPY IN CEREBROVASCULAR DISEASE

THE assessment of any treatment of cerebrovascular disease is greatly handicapped by lack of knowledge of fundamental aspects of the condition. It is beyond the scope of the present paper to consider these difficulties at length, but the design and purpose of this clinical trial require that they be briefly summarized. The pathogenesis of cerebrovascular accidents is the subject of considerable disagreement among clinicians. Arterial spasm, thrombotic occlusion, embolic occlusion derived from atheromatous plaques in the great vessels of the neck, and insufficiency (the reduction of blood-flow through vessels narrowed, but not occluded, by atheroma), have all been advanced as possible causes of cerebral infarction. All these mechanisms may occur, but their relative frequency is unknown. Thus the clinician, faced with the individual patient, is unable with certainty to make a pathological diagnosis; indeed he has considerable difficulty even in making so gross a pathological distinction as between infarction and haemorrhage. The application of the criteria enumerated by Merritt and Aring (1937) on the basis of their clinico-pathological study, although of value, still leaves an uncomfortably large proportion of cases in which diagnostic certainty is lacking. Furthermore, the variation in the clinical pattern of the disease and the uncertainty of its natural history add difficulties to the appraisal of any form of treatment.

In addition to these factors relating to the disease itself, there are problems inherent in the application of the form of treatment under study which may complicate the assessment of its efficacy. In cerebrovascular disease the effect of anticoagulant therapy upon a recently established lesion is not entirely predictable. Thus it has been suggested (Brain, 1954; Symonds, 1956) that anaemic infarcts may become haemorrhagic under the influence of anticoagulants, and experimentally induced infarction in animals has been shown to

(With John Marshall and David A. Shaw). Reprinted from the *Quarterly Journal of Medicine*, 1960, **29** (N.S.), 597.

behave in this way (Wood, Wakim, Sayre, Millikan, and Whisnant, 1958). On the other hand, Sibley, Morledge, and Lapham (1957) have failed to observe this effect in their experiments, nor can we be certain that experimentally induced infarction necessarily parallels naturally occurring thrombotic occlusion. Apart from the particular case of cerebrovascular disease, the precise mode of action of anti-coagulant drugs, and their influence on the course of occlusive vascular disease generally, are not fully understood, and consequently the definition of 'effective anticoagulation' is debatable. Further-more, the treatment carries a risk of haemorrhagic complications; the frequency of these varies in different reported series, but their occurrence has always to be weighed against the possible benefit which the treatment may confer. The history of the use of anti-coagulants in disease of the coronary arteries, which constitute a vascular system less complex than the cerebral arteries, bears out the reluctance of these drugs to yield to clinical appraisal.

In spite of all these foreseeable difficulties, there is a need in cerebrovascular disease for a trial of a form of therapy which theoretically might improve the outlook for the immense number of patients for whom, at present, we have so little to offer. In the presence of so many unpredictable factors the only satisfactory approach is by a strictly controlled clinical trial, in which the progress of patients receiving the treatment is compared with that of a similar group not so treated, but managed in the same way in all other respects over the same period of time. This we have en-deavoured to do in our present study of the place of long-term anticoagulant therapy in the treatment of cerebrovascular disease.

PREVIOUS STUDIES

Apart from a single patient treated with heparin and described by Denber (1945), the first attempt to use anticoagulants as a long-term prophylactic measure in cerebrovascular disease was recorded by Rose (1950). Three patients suffering from hypertensive heart disease and 'spasm' of cerebral arteries were treated with dicoumarin. Since one patient had severe haematuria, and the other two had further minor disturbances of cerebral function within five and eight weeks respectively, the method of treatment was not considered to be of use, and was abandoned. Campbell (1953) described the beneficial effects of long-term anticoagulant therapy in a male patient aged 74 suffering from basilar artery thrombosis. Most previous studies have come from the United States, where comparisons of progress in patients during periods on and off treatment have been regarded as an acceptable method of control (Wright, 1957). Fisher and Cameron (1953) reported on a patient with basilar artery thrombosis whose fleeting attacks of ischaemia were absent for several months while on treatment with anticoagulants, and who relapsed on two occasions when they were withdrawn. At the first Princeton Conference on Cerebral Vascular Diseases, Fisher (1954) referred to 12 patients similarly treated, in whom results were promising, and the same author (1958) reported a series of 58 patients with symptoms and signs of the various stages of cerebral thrombosis due to atherosclerosis. Results suggested that 'anticoagulant therapy abolishes transient ischaemic attacks and prevents or postpones the arrival of a threatening stroke'. The group included 22 patients with internal carotid–middle cerebral involvement and 22 with vertebral-basilar disease; of the remainder, four had posterior cerebral and three lateral medullary syndromes, and in seven cases the anatomical diagnosis was uncertain. Benefit was measured by comparing the frequency of ischaemic manifestations during periods on and off treatment, but in addition comparison was made with 37 untreated patients, whose progress was found to be much less satisfactory than that of the treated group. In the latter group anticoagulant control was not uniform, and some patients also received hypotensive drugs. The author stated that the data did not provide incontrovertible evidence of the therapeutic efficacy of anticoagulants, because of the lack of satisfactory control patients.

Millikan, Sickert, and Shick (1955a) reported on the use of anticoagulant drugs in 26 patients suffering from basilar artery disease. Five showed features of intermittent insufficiency and, in all these patients, attacks ceased on therapy. The other 21 were thought to have thrombosis within the basilar arterial system, and three of them died in spite of treatment, whereas there were 10 deaths in a group of 23 untreated patients. The same authors (1955b) described the absence of ischaemic attacks in seven patients with intermittent insufficiency of the internal carotid arterial system treated by anticoagulants. In 1958 Millikan, Sickert, and Whisnant reported their experience in a much larger group of patients, totalling 317, all of whom received anticoagulants; 94 were classified as having intermittent insufficiency in the vertebral-basilar system, and 85 in the carotid system; 107 had irreversible vertebral-basilar thrombosis, and 31 had actively advancing carotid thrombosis. Treatment appeared to confer striking benefit in stopping ischaemic episodes in the 'insufficiency' groups and in reducing, in the 'thrombotic' groups, the mortality anticipated on the basis of the authors' observations of untreated patients. McDevitt, Carter, Gatje, Foley, and Wright (1958) summarized their 10-year experience in the use of anticoagulants in 100 cases of cerebral vascular disease; basing their observations on a comparison of periods on and off treatment, they concluded that anticoagulants substantially reduced the incidence of thrombo-embolic episodes; but, as 51 of their patients had rheumatic heart disease, and the authors did not differentiate in their analysis between embolism and thrombosis, their data cannot be interpreted in specific relation to the latter condition. It is considered that embolic infarction of cardiac origin is not strictly comparable for therapeutic purposes with thrombotic occlusion, because in the former case the cerebral vascular tree is not necessarily diseased. Schäfer (1959) also treated a group of 60 patients with cerebral thrombosis or embolism with anticoagulants but, comparing their progress with that of an untreated group, concluded that there was no significant difference.

There is thus a considerable weight of evidence to support the use of anticoagulants in chronic cerebrovascular disease, yet none of the studies referred to fulfil the criteria required in a strictly controlled trial. In particular, the use of the patient as his own 'control' is regarded as unsatisfactory in a disease in which we have so little knowledge of the natural history, and in which the course is so variable and unpredictable (Marshall and Shaw, 1959). Furthermore, most authors have confined their attention to certain sharply defined diagnostic categories of cerebrovascular disease, though the issue that confronts the general physician, to whom the vast majority of patients with cerebrovascular disease is referred, is a broader one. In our experience the recognition of specific categories may be extremely difficult, and facilities for carotid and vertebral angiography are not everywhere available, even if such investigation were considered desirable. Patients of the type which is alleged to respond best to anticoagulant treatment are numerically few in proportion to the total number of cases of cerebrovascular disease, and reference to hospital at the stage of transient ischaemia, without established neural damage, is relatively uncommon. For these reasons we have based our study on a broader plan, by including a wide range of cerebrovascular cases commonly encountered in general medical practice. We have attempted to answer the questions as to whether or not long-term anticoagulant therapy (1) increases the expectation of life, or (2) decreases the incidence of further cerebrovascular accidents, or (3) influences the functional capacity of patients with cerebrovascular disease in general, or in specific sub-groups thereof. In the present paper only the first two considerations will be discussed.

METHOD

Patients were considered for inclusion in the trial who were under 70 years of age, and in whom there existed past or present evidence of neurological disturbance lasting for more than 24 hours, and judged by the clinician caring for the patient at the time, and by ourselves subsequently, to be attributable to non-haemorrhagic cerebral, carotid, or vertebral arterial disease. Admission was permissible at any time in relation to such disturbance, provided 14 days had elapsed since the last acute episode. Patients with a clinical diagnosis of cerebral aneurysm or angioma were excluded, as were patients suffering from intercurrent disease which presaged death within two years, or in which anticoagulant therapy was contra-indicated. Thus a history of peptic ulceration, haemorrhagic disease or recurring haemorrhage from any site, syphilis, malignant hypertension, and renal or hepatic disease, was regarded as grounds for exclusion. Patients who were pregnant, or in whom a need for intensive salicylate therapy was anticipated, were likewise not considered. Patients were also excluded if for personal, occupational, or geographical reasons it was thought that they would be unable or unwilling to co-operate sufficiently or to attend regularly for the necessary supervision. Candidates for the trial attended hospital on a day-patient basis for one day. The history was taken, and a full clinical examination made. The following investigations were carried out: X-rays of skull and chest, electrocardiography, blood-grouping and Wassermann reaction, blood urea and cholesterol, chemical and microscopic examination of the urine, and a water dilution test. Six records of resting blood pressure were made at hourly intervals with the patient supine; levels of blood pressure referred to subsequently are the mean of these readings.

To obtain uniformity in the application of the criteria of selection, the decision as to whether or not a patient was eligible for admission to the trial was taken by one of us (D.A.S.). The decision was made without knowledge of the treatment group to which the patient would be allocated. Patients admitted to the trial were differentiated by sex, and allotted by pairs to one of two groups by a randomization table. One group (high-dosage) received tablets containing 50 mg. phenindione (Dindevan), the other group (low-dosage) received apparently identical tablets containing 1 mg. phenindione, an amount insufficient to interfere with the clotting mechanism. Patients did not know to which group they belonged, and were given the same advice regarding the possibility of haemorrhage and the action to be taken in the event of their requiring urgent medical or surgical treatment. Each was issued with a card stating his blood group and the address and telephone number of the hospital. It will be noted that no attempt was made to match the pairs in such features as age, blood pressure, anatomical and pathological diagnosis, duration of symptoms, and frequency of ischaemic episodes. It was anticipated that with a large number of patients randomization would produce similarity in the two groups. The method does not, of course, preclude study of the data for defined sub-groups as well as for the total.

THE CONTROL OF THERAPY

All patients, in both high- and low-dosage groups, attended at one of four anticoagulant clinics, staffed by three doctors, at a frequency which varied between once weekly and once in four weeks, and at each attendance blood was taken for prothrombin estimation. The patients were seen regularly by the same doctor, but the dosage of tablets in both groups was controlled by one of us (D.A.S.), and was intimated to the patient, along with the time of the next visit, by postcard. The aim of treatment in the high-dosage group was to maintain the prothrombin time, estimated by the Quick one-stage method, at a level of two to two and a half times the control value. The prothrombin estimations were made by the same two technicians throughout the trial. When a further cerebrovascular accident occurred in a patient in the trial, treatment was continued with high- or low-dosage tablets according to the patient's group, unless there was indication of haemorrhage as shown by blood in the spinal fluid. In the latter case treatment was permanently stopped, as it was in the event of major extracerebral haemorrhagic complication, but the patient continued to be observed. In the case of minor haemorrhage the patient resumed therapy if it was deemed safe, provided the period of interruption of treatment had not exceeded 28 days. The same limit was set for patients whose therapy had to be interrupted for surgical treatment. If the period of interruption exceeded 28 days, treatment was not resumed, but the patient was followed up as usual. With regard to general measures, there was uniformity of management in the two treatment groups. Many of the criteria for selection and details of control and management, described above, were based on the plan of the Medical Research Council (1959) trial of anticoagulant therapy in coronary thrombosis, to which access was kindly granted, and we gratefully acknowledge the help thus received.

CASE MATERIAL

Between 11 October, 1957, and 5 June, 1959, 142 patients were admitted to the trial, 71 (47 men and 24 women) to the high-dosage group and 71 (47 men and 24 women) to the low-dosage group. The age distribution is given in Table 9, 1. The average age in the high-

TABLE **9**, 1

Age and Sex Distribution

Age (years)	High-dosage group				Low-dosage group			
	Male	Female	Total	%	Male	Female	Total	%
40–44	3	2	5	7·0	1	—	1	1·4
45–54	7	7	14	19·7	13	6	19	26·8
55–64	31	9	40	56·4	22	14	36	50·7
65–69	6	6	12	16·9	11	4	15	21·1
Total	47	24	71	100·0	47	24	71	100·0

dosage group was 57.9 years (S.D. 6.9) and in the low-dosage group 58.2 years (S.D. 6.6). Table **9**, 2 gives the distribution of patients according to the anatomical site of lesion. When there was a history of more than one previous acute episode, the diagnosis was based on the most recent; Table **9**, 3 shows the frequency of previous attacks in the two groups. Table **9**, 4 indicates the incidence of

TABLE **9**, 2

Clinical Diagnosis

Site of lesion	High-dosage group				Low-dosage group			
	Male	Female	Total	%	Male	Female	Total	%
Hemisphere focal	29	19	48	67·6	33	16	49	69·0
Hemisphere diffuse	4	2	6	8·5	5	—	5	7·1
Brain stem	12	3	15	21·1	7	6	13	18·3
Internal carotid	2	—	2	2·8	2	2	4	5·6
Total	47	24	71	100·0	47	24	71	100·0

TABLE **9**, 3

Frequency of Previous Attacks

Number of previous attacks	High-dosage group				Low-dosage group			
	Male	Female	Total	%	Male	Female	Total	%
1	34	18	52	73·2	33	22	55	77·5
2	9	5	14	19·7	8	2	10	14·1
3 or more	4	1	5	7·1	6	—	6	8·4
Total	47	24	71	100·0	47	24	71	100·0

TABLE **9**, 4

Incidence of Hypertension

Diastolic blood-pressure	High-dosage group				Low-dosage group			
	Male	Female	Total	%	Male	Female	Total	%
110mm. Hg or above	13	11	24	33·8	14	10	24	33·8
Below 110mm. Hg	34	13	47	66·2	33	14	47	66·2
Total	47	24	71	100·0	47	24	71	100·0

hypertension, patients being classified as hypertensive who had a mean diastolic pressure of 110 mm. Hg or above, on the basis of the average of the six resting readings taken before admission to the trial. The rate of admission to the trial was fairly uniform as is shown in Fig. **9,** 1. The differences in the duration of treatment of patients in the two groups (Table **9,** 5) are accounted for by the

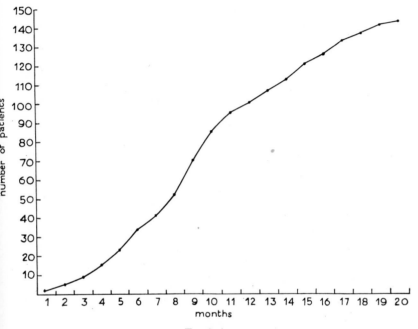

FIG. **9,** 1

Rate of admission of patients to the trial

unequal distribution of deaths, haemorrhagic complications, and other causes of stoppage of treatment (Tables **9,** 7 and **9,** 8). The analysis of the case material has been given in these tables and the figure in some detail since, as mentioned earlier, a valid assessment of the results must depend upon the high- and low-dosage groups being homogeneous in respect of many variable features. Examination of the Tables shows that the randomization has, in fact, brought about two very similar and, therefore, comparable groups.

TABLE **9,** 5

Duration of Treatment

Months	High-dosage group				Low-dosage group			
	Male	Female	Total	%	Male	Female	Total	%
0–	5	3	8	11·3	6	3	9	12·7
3–	10	5	15	21·1	7	4	11	15·5
6–	8	5	13	18·3	6	6	12	16·9
9–	13	7	20	28·2	14	6	20	28·2
12–	6	3	9	12·7	9	4	13	18·3
15–	3	1	4	5·6	2	1	3	4·2
18–20	2	0	2	2·8	3	0	3	4·2
Total	47	24	71	100·0	47	24	71	100·0

RESULTS

The trial began on 11 October, 1957, and was brought to an end in its present form on 5 June, 1959. The results are summarized in Table **9,** 6. During the period of observation there were five non-fatal recurrences of cerebrovascular accidents in four patients in the high-dosage group, and four similar recurrences in three patients in

TABLE **9,** 6

Summary of Results

	High-dosage group			Low-dosage group		
Total number of patients	Male *47*	Female *24*	Total *71*	Male *47*	Female *24*	Total *71*
Non-fatal cerebrovascular accidents	3	2	5	4	–	4
Fatal cerebrovascular accidents	2	2	4	–	–	–
Deaths possibly attributable to treatment	1	–	1	–	–	–
Deaths from other causes	2	1	3	1	–	1
Progressive deterioration	–	1	1	1	–	1
Defaulters	–	–	–	1	1	2*

* One died of myocardial infarction, and one is alive and has had no further cerebrovascular accidents.

the low-dosage group, a difference which is clearly not significant. On the other hand, in the high-dosage group there were four fatal cerebrovascular accidents, and in the low-dosage group there was none. Since all four deaths were due to cerebral haemorrhage, it must be questioned whether they have not arisen as complications of treatment rather than as incidents in the natural history of the disease. In addition there was one non-cerebrovascular death which must be similarly questioned, though the explanation of the cause of death in this patient (No. 8 in Table **9, 7**) was not entirely satis-factory. His condition on admission to hospital suggested a diagnosis of myocardial infarction, but at post-mortem examination this was not confirmed. Nevertheless, a moderate amount of blood, which was not measured, was found in the pericardial sac, and although there was no other evidence of spontaneous haemorrhage, and the prothrombin time was within the therapeutic range, it was felt that the death must be added to those possibly attributable to treatment. The probability of observing by chance five deaths in the one group and none in the other is 0.058 (exact test) or odds of about 17 to 1. In other words it does not quite meet the customary 20 to 1 signi-ficance level.

The causes of death are listed in Table **9, 7**. Five of them, Nos. 4, 65, 78, 91, and 137, are regarded as not directly related to the primary disease or to treatment and, of these deaths, three occurred in the high-dosage group and two in the low-dosage group (including the defaulter), an insignificant difference. In only one of the four patients who died from cerebral haemorrhage (No. 43) was the last recorded prothrombin time outside the therapeutic range, but, at 3.1 times the control, it was not excessive. Three of these four patients had diastolic blood pressures above 110 mm. Hg, and in two of them post-mortem examination suggested that the original lesion had been due to haemorrhage and not to thrombosis. Reviewing their case histories, it was not possible to discern any clinical features which might have indicated a diagnosis of haemorrhage rather than thrombosis, yet in retrospect it seems probable that they were ad-mitted to the trial on the basis of an erroneous diagnosis.

The patients who defaulted, and those in whom treatment had to be abandoned owing to progressive deterioration in their general condition, have all been traced. One (included in the comparisons of deaths) had died from myocardial infarction, but none had sustained a further cerebrovascular accident, so that they do not influence the

TABLE **9, 7.** *Causes of Death*

	Case number	Age (years)	Sex	Blood-pressure	Prothrombin time*	Diagnostic group	Duration of treatment	Cause of death
High-dosage group	8	58	M	180/100	×2·2	Hemisphere diffuse	11 months	Haemopericardium†
	30	57	M	170/114	×1·8	Hemisphere focal	3 months	Cerebral haemorrhage†
	43	69	F	200/134	×3·1	Hemisphere focal	11 months	Cerebral haemorrhage†
	46	68	M	155/100	×2·3	Hemisphere focal	4 months	Cerebral haemorrhage†
	78	62	M	168/100	×2	Hemisphere focal	5 months	Myocardial infarct†
	91	46	F	220/120	×3	Brain-stem	6 months	Congestive heart failure†
	134	56	F	230/122	×2·4	Brain-stem	2 months	Cerebral haemorrhage†
	137	63	M	144/84	×4	Hemisphere focal	2 weeks	Carbon monoxide poisoning† (suicidal)
Low-dosage group	65	68	M	156/100	×1	Hemisphere focal	7 months	Myocardial infarct
	4‡	67	M	150/95	×1	Hemisphere focal	1 month	Myocardial infarct

* Last recorded reading expressed as multiplication factor of control time.
† Confirmed by autopsy.   ‡ Patient defaulted and subsequently died.

analysis. Haemorrhagic complications were not excessive as compared with other series, but in two instances treatment had to be abandoned (Table 9, 8).

TABLE 9, 8

Complications of Treatment

Total number of patients	High-dosage group			Low-dosage group		
	Male 47	Female 24	Total 71	Male 47	Female 24	Total 71
Haemorrhage; treatment interrupted	5	8	13	1	–	1
Haemorrhage; treatment abandoned	2	–	2	–	–	–
Hypersensitivity; treatment abandoned	–	1	1	–	–	–
Intercurrent illness; treatment abandoned	–	–	–	–	1	1

DISCUSSION

The trial was stopped in its present form earlier than had been anticipated, because of the emergence of a disturbing picture. Non-fatal cerebrovascular accidents were distributed about equally to the two groups (5 to 4), and so were deaths due to unrelated causes (3 to 2). On the other hand, the haemorrhagic fatalities that might be due to the treatment were very unevenly divided (5 to 0). While this difference does not quite reach the 0.05 level of significance, it so closely approaches it as to pose a serious ethical problem.* It may well be that long-term anticoagulant therapy in patients with cerebrovascular disease carries a significant hazard of cerebral haemorrhage. Previous workers with anticoagulants in this field have not been unaware of such occurrences. McDevitt, Carter, Gatje, Foley, and Wright (1958) encountered five instances of cerebral haemorrhage, three of which were fatal, and two instances of

* If it be believed that to such a group of patients the anticoagulant treatment could bring no benefit but could conceivably do harm, then the adverse difference in mortality between the treated and control groups would certainly be significant (P approximately 0.03 in the appropriate one-tail test).

subarachnoid haemorrhage. Fisher (1958) mentioned two fatal cases of cerebral haemorrhage, but they were not included in his series of 58 patients. Schäfer (1959), whose 60 patients were treated for only a short period, also had three fatal cases of cerebral haemorrhage. Our figures are thus comparable, but are thrown into bolder relief by comparison with the low-dosage group, emphasizing that without a controlled trial the implications of such an incidence are liable to be overlooked.

There are several possible explanations as to why patients with cerebrovascular disease on anticoagulant therapy should be prone to cerebral haemorrhage. Firstly, it might be argued that they were instances of thrombotic infarction in which bleeding was induced; but one would then expect to have encountered a comparable group of thromboses in the low-dosage group. Secondly, it may be that anticoagulant therapy *per se* tends to cause cerebral haemorrhage; yet only one case of cerebral haemorrhage occurred in the large series of patients with coronary artery disease so treated in the Medical Research Council's trial (1959). Thirdly, it could be argued that the deaths in our series were attributable to inadequate control of therapy; that an 'effective' therapeutic range was achieved is borne out by the fact that a difference between the two groups emerged, but the comparatively low incidence of extracerebral haemorrhagic complications confirms the view that the high-dosage group were not overtreated. A fourth, and in our view the most likely explanation, is that small contained haemorrhages are a commoner cause of transient cerebrovascular accidents than has formerly been supposed, such lesions being indistinguishable by present methods from non-haemorrhagic infarcts. It would appear that recurrences of the latter have been evenly distributed to the two groups, but that there is an increased liability for haemorrhagic lesions to recur in the presence of anticoagulant therapy, and for these to be devastating in their effects. A cerebral haemorrhage, once started, is unlikely to be self-limiting in a patient receiving anti-coagulant therapy, so that one would not expect a corresponding increase in non-fatal recurrences. A striking example was seen in Case 43 (Table **9**, 7). In May 1958 the patient suddenly developed dysphasia and weakness of the right upper limb, with no headache, vomiting, or loss of consciousness. She was admitted to another hospital, where she was found to have dysphasia and a right hemiparesis, and recovered within 48 hours. A month later, when she was admitted to the trial, there were no residual signs. Eleven months later she suddenly lost consciousness, and died within 24 hours. Autopsy (Professor W. Blackwood) showed the cause of death to be a massive cerebral haemorrhage in the right hemisphere. In the left hemisphere, however, there was the residuum of an old small haemorrhage. It seems clear that this was the cause of her transient symptoms in May 1958.

Of the four fatal cases of cerebral haemorrhage, three came from the 24 patients who were hypertensive by our definition, and one from the 47 who were not hypertensive; the difference is not statistically significant. Carter (1957) and others, however, have suggested that anticoagulants carry a higher risk of haemorrhagic complications in elderly and in hypertensive patients; yet in the Medical Research Council's trial (1959) only those hypertensive patients who were in the malignant phase were excluded, and the incidence of complications was not high. In view of the present results, however, it was decided to bring the present trial to an end, and to restrict the further use of anticoagulants to diagnostic groups for which particular claims of efficacy have been made.

On the basis of some of the results already reported from the United States, when this trial was set up it might perhaps have been argued that it was unethical to withhold the treatment from half the patients. The wheel has turned so far that we feel it is unethical to proceed with the treated group without making the modification described. Although this result has emerged from the mortality figures, no conclusion can be drawn from the comparison of the non-fatal recurrence rates in the two groups. The low incidence of further non-fatal cerebrovascular accidents in the high-dosage group regarded in isolation might well give rise to the clinical impression that treatment had been beneficial. Yet comparison of the results with those in the low-dosage group clearly shows that this is not so. Indeed, the recurrence rate in the latter group is so low over the period of follow-up that any form of treatment would require to be almost 100 per cent effective, and devoid of serious hazard, before it could claim to be of definite value. A longer period of follow-up, however, will be required before this point can be settled.

In conclusion, the present study strongly indicates that the general use of anticoagulant therapy in patients with cerebrovascular disease, who are selected and managed along the lines adopted in this trial, is hazardous, because of the risk of cerebral haemorrhage.

This risk is present even when the anticoagulant therapy is carefully controlled, and the prothrombin time maintained at a level which is generally accepted to be safe. It may be that certain restricted types of cerebrovascular disease gain benefit from anticoagulant therapy, but, in view of the many variable factors present in the condition, this can be ascertained only by properly designed and strictly controlled clinical trials.

SUMMARY

A controlled clinical trial of long-term anticoagulant therapy in chronic cerebrovascular disease has been described. One hundred and forty-two patients were included in the study, and were divided by random allocation into two groups; one of these, the high-dosage group, was treated with phenindione, the prothrombin time being maintained at two to two and a half times the control. The other, the low-dosage group, received identical tablets containing a quantity of phenindione insufficient to alter the clotting mechanism, but in all other respects was managed in the same way as the high-dosage group.

The incidence of further non-fatal cerebrovascular accidents did not differ significantly between the two groups, but there were four deaths from cerebral haemorrhage and one from haemopericardium in the high-dosage group, compared with none in the low-dosage group. (The difference is not quite formally significant.) It has been concluded that, although anticoagulant therapy may be of benefit in certain restricted types of cerebrovascular disease, its general use in cerebrovascular disease may carry a definite hazard of cerebral haemorrhage.

We are most grateful to the Nuffield Foundation for their generous support of this investigation at all its stages.

The Hospital Case Numbers of the patients referred to were as follows: No. 8, 39985; No. 30, 77964; No. 43, 79129; No. 46, 79520; No. 78, 69655; No. 91, 20508; No. 134, 85107; No. 137, 85882; No. 65, 80100; No. 4, 39732.

REFERENCES

Brain, W. R. (1954). *Lancet*, **ii**, 831.
Campbell, M. H. (1953). *Canad. med. Ass. J.* **69**, 314.
Carter, A. B. (1957). *Quart. J. Med.* **26**, 335.
Denber, H. C. B. (1945). *Schweiz. med. Wschr.* **75**, 192.
Fisher, C. M. (1954). In *Cerebral Vascular Diseases*, p. 94, ed. Luckey, E. H. London: Grune and Stratton.
Fisher, C. M. (1958). *Neurology (Minneap.)* **8**, 311.
Fisher, C. M., and Cameron, D. G. (1953). *Neurology (Minneap.)* **3**, 468.
McDevitt, E., Carter, S. A., Gatje, B. W., Foley, W. T., and Wright, I. S. (1958). *J. Amer. med. Ass.* **166**, 592.
Marshall, J., and Shaw, D. A. (1959). *Brit. med. J.* **ii**, 1614.
Medical Research Council Working Party (1959). *Brit. med. J.* **i**, 803.
Merritt, H. H., and Aring, C. D. (1937). *Res. Publ. Ass. nerv. ment. Dis.* **18**, 682.
Millikan, C. H., Siekert, R. G., and Shick, R. M. (1955a). *Proc. Mayo Clin.* **30**, 116.
Millikan, C. H., Siekert, R. G., and Shick, R. M. (1955b). *Proc. Mayo Clin.* **30**, 578.
Millikan C. H., Siekert, R. G., and Whisnant, J. P. (1958). *J. Amer. med. Ass.* **166**, 587.
Rose, W. M. (1950). *Med. J. Aust.* **1**, 503.
Schäfer, von R. (1959). *Schweiz. med. Wschr.* **89**, 236.
Sibley, W. A., Morledge, J. H., and Lapham, L. W. (1957). *Amer. J. med. Sci.* **234**, 663.
Symonds, C. P. (1956). *Practitioner*, **176**, 130.
Wood, M. W., Wakim, K. G., Sayre, G. P., Millikan, C. H., and Whisnant, J. P. (1958). *Arch. Neurol. Psychiat.* **79**, 390.
Wright, I. S. (1957). In *Cerebral Vascular Diseases*, p. 132, ed. Millikan, C. H. London: Grune and Stratton.

PART II

THE FIELD TRIAL OF VACCINES

CHAPTER 10

THE EXPERIMENTAL APPROACH
IN PREVENTIVE MEDICINE

I.—THE PROBLEMS OF EXPERIMENTS IN MAN

ACCORDING to Voltaire—and a passage in 'Candide' is my authority—there has been in dispute in Islam a very delicate piece of doctrine. The question at issue is whether the prophet Mahomet plucked from the angel Gabriel's wing the pen which he used for the writing of the Koran, or whether Gabriel made him a present of it. On this point, says Voltaire, two of the most learned of the Mahometan doctors disputed for three days and three nights with a warmth worthy of the noblest ages of controversy. At the end of which time each, fully persuaded of the truth, returned to his home, the one satisfied, like all the disciples of Ali, that the Prophet had plucked the quill, the other convinced, like the rest of Omar's followers, that the Prophet was incapable of committing any such rudeness. It is said that there was at that time at Constantinople a certain free-thinker who insinuated that it would be proper first to examine whether indeed the Koran was written with a pen taken from the wing of an angel. He was stoned.

A generation ago a like fate might well have been met by the experimental or statistically minded scientist venturing into the field of medicine. At the best, with the decline in physical violence, he would have encountered the stony stare of incredulity. Even though, with a sustained effort of control, he avoided the customary Hunterian cliché, he would surely have been welcome neither to the protagonists nor to the antagonists of the pharmaceutical preparations advertised in the pages of the *British Medical Journal* and *Lancet* of 30 years ago. With the passage of time most of those remedies have completely disappeared. Yet, as Lord Cohen (1953) has pointed out, the eulogies than appended to them were certainly no less than those appended to drugs today. I would believe that the

The Harben Lectures, 1957. Reprinted from the *Journal of the Royal Institute of Public Health and Hygiene*, 1958, **21**, 177, experimentalist might at least have hastened their passing, if not unsung perhaps with a trifle less clamour.

Similarly, in the preventive field, with a suggestion for a strictly controlled trial in the *human* population, he would, I suspect, have been unwelcome equally to the vaccinationist as to the antivaccinationist. The disputation over B.C.G., also conducted with a warmth worthy of the noblest ages of controversy, may have been enlivened by the statistician's entry thereto; it showed very little sign of being enlightened.

I believe I do not exaggerate. In 1949, Sir George Pickering, the present Regius Professor of Medicine in the University of Oxford, grumbled that

'modern medicine still preserves much of the attitude of mind of the school men of the Middle Ages. It tends to be omniscient rather than admit ignorance, to encourage speculation not solidly backed by evidence, and to be indifferent to the proof or disproof of hypothesis. It is to this legacy of the Middle Ages that may be attributed the phenomenon which Wilfrid Trotter used to call "the mysterious viability of the false". And it is, above all, to this habit of mind so inimical to scientific inquiry that we may trace the fact that the experimental method has found so small a place in clinical studies' (Pickering, 1949).

Ten years earlier, in 1939, Sir John Ledingham, discussing prophylactic immunization against infectious diseases, complained that this country had been a follower in this field, and rather a tardy follower. 'Though our laboratory workers have contributed very materially to the knowledge of methods, we have left to other countries the task of trying them out seriously and intensively in the field' (Ledingham, 1939).

However just these accusations may be, then or now, we have, nevertheless, always to recognize, and to remember in part extenuation, one special difficulty. Experiments in medicine, in its preventive as well as its clinical aspects, must often be carried out upon *man*. What has been proved for one species may not hold for another. As a result we are always faced with an ethical problem and, very frequently indeed, with considerations of experimental practicability.

With regard to clinical medicine I have elsewhere discussed these problems at length (Hill, 1955) even, perhaps, *ad nauseam*, and I shall not concern myself with them here. I would merely add two footnotes. The first is that in my experience of the lay scientific world some of the most vociferous critics of the doctors' lack of enthusiasm for experiment might well prove to be, when sick, the most vociferous in defence of their own rights. The second is that the readier admission today of the statistician to the clinical field is sometimes, I suspect, on a par with the answer of the French woman to the question did she believe in ghosts. 'No,' she replied, 'but I am afraid of them.'

Before turning to the particular issues raised by human experimentation in preventive medicine it would be helpful, I think, first to consider briefly what is implied by the expression 'experimental approach'. The essence of experimentation lies in a power to make a *planned* intervention. One seeks to exert complete power over both treatment and subjects—using those two words in their widest and most general sense. One seeks power to allocate treatments, to use subjects, in any way that will yield the maximum amount of information from the resulting observations. We thus may learn what happens to A when we deliberately manipulate B, excluding—so far as can be—the possible effects of all unknown extraneous factors. In other words the basis of a successful experiment is the ability to exert active interference and to control the conditions.

In the fields covered by preventive medicine that ability is often, and inevitably, lacking.

Take, for example, the problem of retrolental fibroplasia. In the early days of treating prematurely born babies with high concentrations of oxygen, one might conceivably have made an experiment to test the advantages, and to reveal any possible but unknown dangers, of that procedure. To control the conditions adequately would have required a random distribution of the infants (or of sub-groups of them) to oxygen or no oxygen (or to differing concentrations). But the procedure was regarded as life-saving, the risk of producing blindness was, at that time, quite unknown. In such circumstances could one ethically have withheld the treatment at all? On the other hand *after* the observation of the occurrence of retrolental fibroplasia, after the indication that a high or prolonged oxygen concentration was likely to be its cause, could one ethically have conducted an experiment to prove that that was so? Could one now properly allocate babies at random to the procedure to see whether, indeed, it led to blindness? The wheel had turned full circle. The risk involved in an experiment depends very much, suggests McCance (1951), on whether the investigator knows that he will always retain control of the situation. In neither of these situations could he have had that assurance.

Again, there are scattered observations in the literature reporting congenital defects in the infant which followed an attack of mumps in the mother during pregnancy. Obviously such 'double events' must occur by chance from time to time, whether we are concerned with mumps, housemaid's knee or the sight of a dark man run over by a tram. It is merely more fashionable today to report the mumps. But supposing there are more such double events than are readily attributable to chance? It does not automatically follow that we have detected cause and event. Maybe the adult woman who is still susceptible to mumps, and who goes about her pregnancy contracting it, differs also in some other respects from the woman who is not susceptible or sits at home and knits, unexposed to infection; she may differ in other constitutional or environmental respects that could affect the incidence of congenital malformations. Yet there can be no question here of making an experiment to clarify the answer, to exclude the possible effects of unknown extraneous factors. We cannot set up comparable groups of pregnant women and give one group the mumps. We must adopt the most reasonable interpretation of the facts as presented by the course of events in nature (the most reasonable interpretation being that mumps has no such effect).

Similarly, we cannot submit mankind to a large-scale smoking experiment. We cannot randomize large numbers of young men and women to cigarette smoking or no smoking and then, in the course of their lives, measure the relative frequencies of cancer of the lung. For those who disbelieve the present evidence of the association there is clearly no ethical problem; but, whether we disbelieve it or not, the experiment is impracticable. No large population would submit to the experimental requirements over the 20 to 30 years required.

It is not, I would add, a corollary of that situation that we throw up our hands in despair, settle the cigarette in the corner of our mouths and decline to draw any conclusions from the available *observational* data. That is not the way in which science and the public health have advanced. Indeed while medicine may be unique in the ethical problems that it presents to its would-be experimental students, it is certainly not unique in problems of practicability. If experimentation were the only way of advancing knowledge, and of deducing cause and effect, the outlook would be hardly encouraging for such a subject as, say, human genetics. The advance may well be slower and more difficult without experiment but it can be made and has thus been made in the past. We have but to study the history of medicine. The modern experimental design may ask questions of nature more efficiently than the old, possibly it may lead to still faster progress, possibly, but by no means certainly, to fewer mistakes of interpretation. However that may be, such an approach is quite certainly not all-embracing; it cannot be demanded as a *sine qua non* in all circumstances. The conquest of typhoid fever did not hinge upon a Latin square nor call for the analysis of variance.

As Cornfield (1954) has pointed out, the observational and experimental types of evidence do not really differ in kind. They do differ, and often appreciably, in degree. 'It is,' he writes, 'a good deal more difficult to control variables in observational than in experimental material, so that the experimental method has unravelled and will continue to unravel mysteries before which uncontrolled observation would be powerless. But there is no difference in principle. There are no such categories as first-class evidence and second-class evidence. There are merely associations, whether observational or experimental, that, in a given state of knowledge, can be accounted for in only one way or in several different ways. If the latter, it is our obligation to state what the alternative explanations and variables might be and to see how their effects can be eliminated, while if the former it is equally our obligation to state so. To distinguish between statistical association on the one hand and relationships that are established by experimentation on the other, without any reference to alternative variables that are present in one case but not the other, seems to us to be neither good statistics, good science, nor good philosophy—though it may be good red herring.' (I need hardly say that he was concerned with the question of smoking and cancer of the lung). He adds, with truth, that if we ask for 'proof' in medicine, or in any other empirical science, we may be asking for something that does not exist.

In short, preventive medicine must often proceed by means of carefully designed observation. In admitting that I would nevertheless return to my opening thesis: I would still maintain that the first approach to the solution of any problem must be to ask oneself: 'Is an experiment possible?' In answering the question it will be well to keep in mind that to refuse to experiment on ethical grounds may, in fact, imply the doing of an experiment. In other words *no* experiment can nevertheless be an experiment; it may well denote action which is experimental and, at the same time, uninformative and less ethical than would be a true experiment.

It is in this light that, I think, one might regard, for instance, the wholesale removal of tonsils. The value of the operation on that scale is arguable and argued. On the other hand it is also maintained that it would be unethical to conduct an experiment to find out. Yet the removal of tonsils in a situation of doubt is surely in itself an experiment? It is an in-the-dark hit-or-miss procedure and one in which the darkness is so impenetrable that it provides no effective evidence as to whether the target was hit. That there are undoubted cases in which the operation is called for need not be denied. That fact presents no difficulty. Such cases are obviously not relevant to the argument at all and it should not be beyond the wit of medically-qualified men and women to define them so that they may be put outside the trial. With the remainder is it so ethical to operate upon the lot and pay no further attention, and so unethical to operate upon some representative proportion and make a close follow-up of the results in the operated and not-operated groups? If in the course of the follow-up it becomes clear that a child in the latter group must be operated upon, that also presents no serious impediment to the experiment. It is a part of what we set out to learn. Without going into details I cannot myself see that this particular question, of now such ancient vintage, could not be approached experimentally. Neither ethical nor practical problems would seem to be insuperable. On the other hand merely, as has been suggested, to contrast the tonsillectomized with those for whom it was recommended but not for some special reason carried out, would be unlikely to carry conviction. In such circumstances we should be quite uncertain whether we had effectively 'controlled' subjects and treatments so that the comparison would be valid. We might be wasting our time and energy. One trial, such as I suggest above, has, I believe, now been instituted.

Another subject, on the borderline of preventive medicine and sociology, that I have long thought wide-open to the experimental approach is the handling of the juvenile delinquent and adolescent criminal. Needless to say, it may be necessary to lock certain persons up for the protection of the public. With others, it may be argued that man-made retribution should overtake them for their acts against society—in spite of frequent assertions to the contrary from on high. I am not concerned with either of these situations. The questions—once again arguable and argued—is whether one particular treatment—whether it be flogging, a spell in a Borstal institution or a heart-to-heart talk with the psychiatrist—is more, or less, likely to lead a young man to think better of his ways and not to repeat his offence. Flogging, in particular, has been the subject of controversy, a controversy more emotional than factual in its content. Does it, in fact, prevent the commission or repetition of crimes of violence? I do not, let me hasten to say, envisage the judge with the black cap and Blackstone's commentaries upon one side of the bench and upon the other Bradford Hill's Random Sampling Numbers. But I would believe that a very serious study ought to be made of the possibilities of controlled experimentation in this setting as compared with the present uncontrolled and, largely, uninformative experimentation. For surely that is what it amounts to?

Thus, under the title of 'Penalties to fit the Crime,' Dr. Mannheim points out in an article published in *The Times* of 27 November, 1957, that 'Some quarter sessional courts impose prison sentences in less than a third of their cases, others in over two-thirds. Some have a probation rate of over 50 per cent, others of only 5 per cent. There are magistrates' courts with 5 per cent and others with 45 per cent of prison sentences for men committing indictable offences.' In this situation he rightly stresses the need for factual and scientific knowledge. He suggests that 'remand and classification centres, child guidance clinics, pre-sentence inquiries, follow-up and prediction studies will yield some of the answers', and he cites three recent investigations—a 'prediction' study of Borstal boys, a small-scale investigation of the success of probation and an inquiry into the effects of short prison sentences and the possibility of using more constructive, and cheaper, alternatives. There is clearly no doubt of the problems, and no doubt that they are of the very greatest importance. There *is* doubt, I submit, that they can be adequately solved without deliberate experimentation of which I find no hint in Dr. Mannheim's article. Of course, it will be said that it is impossible —that no two cases before the Courts are alike. So was it said of sick persons in relation to the trial of a new method of treatment. The same retort must surely apply—that if every case is indeed unique then no action of the Court can ever be based upon its previous observations of other cases. We are merely wasting our time in seeking the 'best' approach.

If, on the other hand, there is, as I would believe, a broad equality of characteristics in many cases, then we could learn what *on the average* is likely to be the best—what is likely to confer the most benefit upon the greatest number. Step by step we might learn, as with clinical trials, appropriate adjustments to that treatment and appropriate sub-divisions of the groups to whom the sentences should be applied.

I have strayed dangerously from my own field. In preventive medicine itself, however, there is no dearth of opportunity for experiment. From a very cursory reading of medical journals over a few days I culled the following examples. I put them forward not necessarily as evidence of the worthwhileness of their subject matter but as instances in which the experimental approach would seem to me to be desirable.

The most important single measure for tuberculosis control is, writes Vollner (1959), the early diagnosis and treatment of primary tuberculosis. The tuberculin test is the most reliable and inexpensive means of early discovery of the primary infection but its merely occasional use by the physician is of little value. He therefore suggests that tuberculin patch testing of all children at the age of six months onwards could be done every three months by their mothers. He believes that the mothers could be adequately instructed in the test and would be quick to notify their doctors in any instance of conversion. Thus early treatment would be permitted and the dissemination of infection prevented. In short, 'such a testing program may prove to be a valuable contribution to the conventional methods of tuberculosis control'. Such a 'testing program,' I would add, first demands a programme to test it. Will it indeed fulfil its object by reducing tuberculosis?

In the same field much interest lies in the possibilities of a prophylactic use of isoniazid, 'a cheap, orally administered drug that has been demonstrated during the past four years to be extremely effective in the treatment of patients with tuberculosis and to be practically non-toxic in therapeutic doses. A drug that can reverse the course of far-advanced cavitary disease might, if given at the right time, prevent the appearance of clinical disease, (U.S. Public Health Reports, 1957). In this instance the Public Health Service of the United States has already begun a series of experimental studies with early results of promise (U.S. Public Health Service, 1957).

A campaign of preventive measures to reduce the incidence of accidents in childhood should, says a report of the World Health Organization (1957), 'be based on educational methods and should include publicity material backed by demonstrations not only for parents, children and teachers but also for toy manufacturers, architects, builders and legislators'. Experiment might well play a part and prevent us going too fast and too far in our measures.

And, lastly, I saw some fearsome figures on the incidence of still-births, prematurity and neo-natal mortality in relation to the smoking habits of the mother during pregnancy. This in particular would seem to me to cry aloud for an experiment which should not, I believe, prove impossible nor, indeed, very difficult.

One grave difficulty that does sometimes face the experimenter in the field of preventive medicine is the scale necessary for his operations. For example, in the statistics for the country as a whole, the absolute number of children suffering an accident is great; the number contracting tuberculosis or poliomyelitis is distressingly large. Yet, in relation to the population at risk, and to the would-be experimeter, they are distressingly small. He cannot set up and control his own experiment in his own 'laboratory'. In such instances co-ordinated teamwork spread over a number of areas, and, usually, substantial financial resources are the only solution. Neither is easily come by.

A second difficulty is that in the public at large and in the Press there is with regard to human experimentation, a very great deal of loose thinking—though, perhaps, 'thinking' is too euphemistic a description. The cry of human guinea-pig, particularly where children are concerned, arouses emotions—fears always of dangerous and unpleasant procedures and, no less, of dangerous and equally unpleasant scientists. The general population certainly does not understand the thesis that I adopted previously, that to do no experiment *is* to experiment. Equally certainly (sometimes, very fortunately) it does not realize how ignorant we are.

Let us, for instance, set up a well-controlled trial of an unproven vaccine against, say, poliomyelitis by allocating the volunteers by some random (and, therefore, axiomatically 'inhuman') process to either inoculation or to nothing beyond a murmur of 'God bless you'. We run the gravest risk of being accused of treating children like guinea-pigs. We are making experimental animals of the poor little things. But let us stick this unproven vaccine into *all* the volunteers, and let us compare their experience with that of children whose parents did not volunteer. Then we are almost certainly safe from public criticism. Yet in the second instance we have obviously made an experiment and in the course of it we have put an unproven vaccine into twice as many children, *i.e.*, human guinea-pigs, and we have made a comparison which is of no value whatever. This is bad enough but, furthermore, one bad experiment is likely to beget others or, still worse, to mislead us into action widening in space and time until finally, after many years perhaps, the procedure falls into disrepute. The critics of the clear-cut experiment, including the politicians and their civil servants, scornful of scientific delay and caution, have sometimes no conception of what in fact they are doing.

A true experiment, both practicable and ethical, is likely to give an answer that may justifiably speed up the rejection or acceptance of a measure of prevention. Therein, indeed, lies clearly one of the great assets of the experimental over the observational approach. With the latter there is, as I stressed before, greater scope for uncontrolled variables to have crept in unperceived and to have produced the observed association. There is, therefore, not only greater scope for false deductions honestly made but every opportunity for biased or interested parties to invent ingenious ways of explaining the association and thereby to confuse opinion and delay social action. The experiment is not immune but it allows less latitude. Yet illogically and ignorantly it is so often liable to be attacked as unethical.

This liability, though based upon gross misconception, must make us even more careful than need be in designing experiments which require human beings as subjects—we may, indeed, usefully start by calling them trials instead of experiments. Not only might a thoroughly bad experiment bring the approach into disrepute but, as McCance (1955) has pointed out, one irresponsible experimenter could do irreparable harm to medical science. Personally, I particularly dislike the suggestion, still made occasionally, that in a hazardous type of experiment it would be proper to use persons condemned to capital punishment or volunteers suffering from incurable diseases, physical or mental (with the 'volunteering' sometimes depending upon parents or those in *loco parentis*). To go so far as to hazard life and health in the human subject, however circumstanced, might be, I suggest, to hazard debasing the outlook of the experimenter himself. It might well debase all experimentation in the eyes of the public. That is a danger of which, at all levels, we must in the medical field be constantly conscious. We must also be constantly aware of the importance of not disturbing the doctor-patient relationship, a relationship which may be found in the preventive field as well as in the curative. To take an example, some years ago a very excellent trial was made in the U.S.A. of immunization against whooping cough by means of two doses of an alum-precipitated mixture of diphtheria toxoid and pertussis vaccine (Bell, 1948). Comparison was made between children given this mixture and others given two injections of diphtheria toxoid only. All those born in an odd month received the mixed product and those born in an even month the unmixed product. Except for a code number all the vials were identical in appearance and all were labelled 'A-P diphtheria toxoid'. Inclusion in the trial was stimulated by urging parents to have their children immunized against diphtheria. Neither the local health department personnel administering the products, under appropriate instructions, nor the recipients of the vaccine had any knowledge that pertussis vaccine was involved in the study. Throughout the follow-up no observer knew which product the child had received. I have no doubt that this is, in the words of the author, 'a study arrangement which approaches an epidemiologist's ideal'. I have equally no doubt that it is an arrangement which, at least in this country, is most undesirable. The product may be safe (the reactions were reported as few and negligible); there may be an excellent chance that it will confer protection upon its recipients (as, indeed, it did). The fact remains, that the parents had not been informed that their child might be treated in a certain way, and no opportunity had been offered them to give or withhold their consent. I am convinced that they ought to have that opportunity, however poor their judgement may prove to be. If we deprive them of it we will surely run a grave risk of upsetting their faith in their doctors. However safe or innocuous an *experimental* preventive procedure may be (or appear to be) it is not, I suggest, for the doctor to decide who shall take part in a trial of that procedure. That rests with the recipients or, in children, with those qualified to speak for them. I would add that apart from this criticism I regard this trial as admirable in its design and in its execution.

From a quite different angle a more recent experiment in the field of preventive medicine, also reported from the United States, is instructive (Armijo, 1957). In schools in Puerto Rico there had been numerous outbreaks of acute gastro-enteritis amongst the children participating in school lunches. The principal symptoms were nausea, vomiting, abdominal pain and diarrhoea, without fever, beginning one to five hours after lunch and with virtually complete recovery within 24 hours. A spray-dried milk-powder was suspected as the responsible food and the clinical symptoms and incubation period pointed to a staphylococcal enterotoxin as the responsible agent. The epidemiological evidence was strong but not wholly convincing for it was difficult to extract accurate information from young children. There was available, however, a tin of spray-dried milk which had been partially consumed at a school the previous day when an outbreak had occurred. One of the investigators deliberately consumed a glass of it and two hours later had his curiosity satisfied by the sudden onset of nausea, dizziness, abdominal cramps and profuse diarrhoea. Presumably to make this assurance doubly sure, and because of negative bacteriological results, a more extensive human feeding experiment was then carried out. Reconstituted milk was made from the powder in proportions and volume as used in the schools. It was poured into 13 glasses. Commercially purchased non-fat milk solids were prepared similarly and poured into another 13 glasses. The glasses were 'coded and comingled' and set before 26 adult volunteers who were allowed to make their own 'random selection'. Marked vomiting, diarrhoea, cramps, weakness and dizziness were the lot of five of the unlucky 13 who chose and consumed the suspect milk (and one spent three days in hospital). Milder symptoms were experienced by four others of this group. Among those consuming the 'control' milk two experienced very mild symptoms three and six hours later. In short, the well-designed experiment achieved its object of incriminating the spray-dried milk powder.

There is, I suggest, another lesson to be learnt from it—though one that should not have to be learnt. Of the 13 potential victims only five were really affected, and similarly, of course, amongst the schoolchildren at their lunches only some proportion of the imbibers had been attacked. This is clearly what one would expect. There is, nevertheless, a curiously widespread misconception of scientific evidence of cause and effect that arises in even well-educated minds.

Judging from the correspondence columns of the weekly medical journals and from my personal correspondence, the well-educated minds of doctors are by no means free from it. One might, perhaps, call it the all-or-none syndrome. It lies in the argument that some personally-observed exceptions gravely weaken, or even destroy, the more general and often very extensive, evidence of cause and effect. At the present time this view is peculiarly to the forefront in the rather sillier discussions of smoking and cancer of the lung. But that it is so freely used, it would seem hardly worthy of reference.

One need hardly say that the exceptions to an apparent rule are, or may be, important in all circumstances of experiment and observation. The fact that a non-smoker may contract lung cancer, or one who forswears water succumb to typhoid fever, is both interesting and important. We are by these means informed, whatever we may believe about smoking and polluted water supplies, that there are certainly other means of acquiring these diseases. In other words we have not wholly solved the epidemiological problems involved in their spread. Similarly, the fact that heavy smokers or drinkers of a contaminated water supply do *not* fall sick is also important. We are thereby informed that there must be further undetected constitutional or environmental factors to sway the balance upwards or downwards in the individual case. But clearly that is not incompatible with the observation that *on the average* the drinkers of sewage with their water will have more typhoid fever than those who prefer their water neat, and that those who smoke the most will *on the average* die more frequently of lung cancer. Whether we deal with the *Bacillus typhosus*, a carcinogenic agent or an industrial dust hazard, there are very few things in life that have an all-or-none reaction. The clear-cut milk-drinking experiment that I have quoted, with its apparently precise equality of exposure to 13 potential victims, is a rather more graphic illustration than usual of that glimpse of the obvious.

According to Finney (1952), some people believe that statisticians are persons who deliberately set out to make simple questions appear difficult. That has not been my aim and I hope I shall not be accused of it. I have attempted, however, in this lecture to show that while the questions we seek to answer in preventive medicine are frequently quite simple—and can be kept simple even by statisticians—their solution often does present far greater difficulty than is sometimes recognized, particularly by the non-scientifically trained.

The scientific method, it has been said (Blount, 1955), is nothing more than planned experiment and logical deduction. There is no reason why the exponents of preventive medicine should lack powers of logic. In interpreting nature's rather badly designed experiments they will, indeed, need them to the full. In drawing conclusions, and in basing action upon them, they will constantly be called upon to find a nice balance between Matthew Arnold's 'keen unscrupulous course which knows no doubt, which feels no fear' and its Shakes-perian counterpart which maintains that 'our doubts are traitors and make us lose the good we oft might win by fearing to attempt'. (*Measure for Measure*.) I have in this lecture set out my view that our first step should be to seek that balance through experiment in man. I have shown that we may well fail for ethical reasons or on grounds of practicability, and that we may, therefore, be forced to rely upon carefully made and well-designed observations. I have equally shown, I hope, that we might well succeed—that the experimental approach would often be possible if only its importance, and the true ethical issues involved, were more clearly grasped.

II—CONTROLLED TRIALS OF VACCINES

DURING the years that have elapsed since the end of the second World War some of the most striking and effective experiments in preventive medicine—both in this country and in the U.S.A.—have been the large-scale field trials of different vaccines. Of the absolute necessity for such trials I do not believe there can be any question. With vaccines (or similar prophylactic agents) already commonly in use, or at least peeping round the corner, against smallpox, diphtheria, whooping-cough, tetanus, poliomyelitis, tuberculosis, influenza, the adeno-viruses and some others that I am sure I have forgotten, the dimpled arms and buttocks of the children of Western civilization are fast being reduced to pin-cushions. This clearly has its disadvantages. It is hardly likely that it will go far to promote in the infant and tiny toddler that trust and esteem that is, throughout life, the essence of the doctor/patient relationship. I know of no evidence of any lasting harm, or 'psychological trauma', produced in this way—whether in child or parent. But I doubt whether we should just shrug our shoulders or dismiss it with a smile as unworthy of attention. We certainly cannot do that with those grave, though fortunately rare, sequels of inoculations, such as the encephalopathies and paralytic poliomyelitis. Such ill-effects certainly do sometimes occur and with measurable frequency (Medical Research Council, 1956). The risk to the individual produced thereby must be weighed against the risk of remaining unprotected against a particular disease. Obviously we cannot make that assessment unless we know the protective value of the vaccine with which we are concerned. Before, therefore, we add another one to the list we must make quite sure that it will, in fact, confer protection against the disease in question upon the great majority of its recipients. To make thus sure we have to measure how an inoculated group of persons will respond to the ordinary everyday risks of infection to which the population, or some particular section of it, is exposed in epidemic or endemic times. And this response must be weighed in the balance against the corresponding response in a comparable uninoculated group. In short, we must conduct a

Reprinted from the *Journal of the Royal Institute of Public Health and Hygiene*, 1958, **21**, 185.

strictly controlled experiment in the human herd. The necessity for this strict control and the objections to any material departures from it are, I believe, not fully appreciated even now. It will, perhaps, be salutary to consider the objections.

The greatest source of error usually lies, in my opinion, in the comparison of persons who volunteer, or choose, to be inoculated (or volunteer on behalf of their children) with those who do not volunteer or choose. The volunteers may tend to come from a different age group and thus, on the average, be older or younger; they may tend to include more—or fewer—males than females; they may tend to be drawn from one social class rather than another. Given adequate records these, and similar easily defined characteristics can be identified. The comparisons of the inoculated and uninoculated can then be made within like categories.

But far more subtle and undetectable differences may very well be involved. The volunteers for inoculation may be persons more careful of their health, and more aware of the presence of epidemic disease in the community. They may on such occasions take other steps to avoid infection—keeping themselves, for example, at a safe distance from modern overcrowded transport systems compared with which, my teacher Professor Major Greenwood was fond of saying, the Black Hole of Calcutta was absolute solitude. They may temporarily avoid theatres and cinemas. Again, it may be that the more intelligent mothers bring their children to be inoculated, and the less intelligent do not respond to the offer. Those who have had five children and only buried two know all about their upbringing without these new fangled notions. This superior intelligence of the volunteers may also lead them to other simple precautionary measures in epidemic times, particularly, again, a temporary isolation from the possible focuses of infection, outside or even within the home. Lastly, with diseases that do not have a uniform incidence and do not themselves confer a lasting protection—for example, influenza and the common cold—there may well be in the act of volunteering a grave element of self-selection. Few of us are so altruistic, or masochistic, as to offer ourselves on the altar of the hypodermic syringe for a disease from which we never, or rarely, suffer. In an early trial of an influenza vaccine in the London School of Hygiene and Tropical Medicine, I can vividly remember how one member of my staff said that it would be of no help for her to volunteer since she never caught influenza. To my intense satisfaction she contracted it a week later. But accepting that as a mere fortunate act of retribution it is clear that if (as I believe) there are persons peculiarly susceptible or resistant to influenza or the common cold (even if it be but temporarily), then self-selection may well bring the susceptibles into the volunteer-for-inoculation class and leave the resistants as controls. Those who have suffered continuously from the common cold will naturally seek any form of relief and defence; why should those who have escaped do so? Such differential features must bear upon the act of volunteering and may entirely ruin the comparisons that it is sought to make.

The importance of these various selective factors is not merely the product of the statistician's customary obsessional thinking. They have been demonstrated quite often in carefully documented trials. An excellent example can be found in the report by Levine and Sackett (1946) on results of B.C.G. immunization in New York City. Writing in 1946 they first point out that most previous reports had been optimistic on the value of the B.C.G. but that the vast majority of the studies had been poorly controlled.

In some studies the mortality rate from tuberculosis of the general population was compared with the vaccinated group; in others a different age group served as a control; in some the tuberculosis mortality of vaccinated children was compared with the tuberculosis mortality of previous years; in other studies the controls comprised cases where vaccination was refused; in still others the control group was less carefully followed than the vaccinated group; in one study, only the vaccinated cases were temporarily separated from the tuberculous source. In many observations controls were entirely omitted. In brief, then, conclusions stemming from most of the previous work are open to criticism.

The basis for this assertion is a careful review of as many as 47 earlier studies.

The New York study which they particularly and critically report can be divided into two parts. The children concerned came from tuberculous families and were referred from tuberculosis clinics and hospitals. From 1927 to 1932 a physician was assigned to a number of cases and was told to vaccinate half of the group. The choice for inclusion in that half lay with the physician. Experience showed, as would be expected, that the tendency was to inoculate the children of the more intelligent and co-operative parents and to keep the children of the non-co-operative parents as controls. On 1 January, 1933, the procedure was, accordingly, changed so that alternate children were routinely vaccinated, the remainder serving as controls. The selection was now made centrally, as soon as names were received, and the appropriate instructions were then given to the staff physicians. Very unco-operative families were not included at all and a few others were eliminated subsequently.

A brief comparison of these two parts of the trial is shown in Table **10**, 1.

TABLE **10**, 1

Vaccination with B.C.G. in New York City (constructed from data published by Levine and Sackett)

Period of trial	No. of children	No. of deaths from tuberculosis	Death rate %	Average No. of visits to clinics during 1st year of follow-up	Proportion of parents giving good co-operation as judged by visiting nurses
1927–32 Selection for vaccination made by physician:					
B.C.G. group	445	3	0·68	3·6	43%
Control Group	545	18	3·38	1·7	24%
1933–44 Alternate selection for vaccination carried out centrally:					
B.C.G. group	566	8	1·41	2·8	40%
Control group	528	8	1·51	2·4	34%

In the earlier part of the trial when allocation to B.C.G. was made by the physician, there is a pronounced difference between the death rates from tuberculosis in the contrasted groups. But one's faith in this contrast is somewhat shaken by the correspondingly pronounced differences in the other listed characteristics of the groups. Those given B.C.G. were, on the average, brought to the clinic twice as often as those not vaccinated; almost twice as many of their parents were judged by the visiting nurses as good co-operators. How important are these characteristics? They cannot be lightly dismissed. With the strict alternation to B.C.G. or control of the second part of the inquiry these differences have all but disappeared;

and so has the difference in protection as judged by the tuberculosis mortality. On this evidence Levine and Sackett were, naturally enough, left sceptical of the virtues of B.C.G. They point out, I should add, that this lack of benefit to the vaccinated children may have been due, at least partially, to the fact that the children were not segregated but all remained in contact with the tuberculous case. But I am concerned here to weigh, not the results of the B.C.G., but the effects of selective factors operating in 'real life'.

Another interesting example of their importance can be found in the pioneer studies in immunization against whooping-cough carried out during the years 1939 to 1943 by Dr. Pearl Kendrick and her collaborators (Kendrick and Eldering, 1939; Kendrick and Weiss, 1942; Kendrick, 1943). The vaccinated children in these trials consisted 'of all children of acceptable age and history who presented themselves at the city immunization clinics for pertussis vaccination'. The selection of the controls was made from a file, maintained in the City Department of Health, of all pre-school children believed at a given time to be susceptible to whooping-cough. Children were chosen to match those immunized in respect of age, sex and area of residence in the city of Grand Rapids and its suburbs. Calls by nurses were then made to verify the details of the selected child and 'to assure co-operation in obtaining follow-up information as to exposure to pertussis and attacks of the disease'. Obviously, it might be easier to secure co-operation from those seeking vaccination than from those being sought as controls. However that may be, the exposures to whooping-cough that were recorded in this series of trials were as set out in Table 10, 2.

TABLE 10, 2

Vaccination against Pertussis in Grand Rapids (constructed from data published by Kendrick and Eldering)

	Immunized	Controls
Number of children observed	4,789	5,011
Number of children reported to have been exposed to whooping-cough:		
(a) in their own homes	131	288
(b) elsewhere	303	160
Total	434	448

It will be seen that the total number of exposures recorded was very similar—434 and 448 or 9.1 per cent and 8.9 per cent of the populations at risk. On the other hand this similarity in total is deceptive; it conceals an important difference in the components. General experience shows that exposure to whooping-cough in the home leads to a very high secondary attack rate in the unimmunized —not less than 80–90 per cent. But in this experience it will be seen that the inoculated were exposed to another case in their own homes less than half as frequently as the uninoculated (131 exposures to 288). The explanation seems to be partly that sometimes all the children in a small family were inoculated and, therefore, no within-the-home exposure was possible, and partly that *a higher proportion of the inoculated children compared with the control children were only children* (it was as many as 47 per cent compared with 20 per cent in one of the trials). The method of selecting the controls had not equalized this very important characteristic. It is not equally clear why there should be in the inoculated group so great an excess of exposures outside the home. Possibly it may flow from a greater degree of awareness of the disease and willingness to co-operate in those who originally came forward for vaccination. Possibly, single children go out to play elsewhere more frequently.

These differences between the two groups are consistently present, though in varying magnitude, in all the three trials reported by Dr. Kendrick. It is therefore possible, as she herself stresses in her third report, that 'the lower gross attack rate in the test group is in part due to less exposure as well as to greater resistance, as compared with the control group'. However that may be I am once again only concerned to point a moral and adorn a tale.

As my last tale in this connection I pass to poliomyelitis and California where, in the summer of 1956, a sample survey was conducted by the State Department of Public Health (*California Medicine*, 1957). The sample, consisting of about one household in every 1,200 in the State, included 3,342 children under 15 years of age. For this age group Salk vaccine had been available for about eight months before the survey, from either private physicians or public clinics. In total 42 per cent of the children had received their first vaccination. This proportion varied considerably, however, with the income level of the family, being only 17 per cent where the annual income was under $2,000 and 53 per cent where it was above $8,000. In addition, the children who were vaccinated tended to come more often from white families and to have mothers with 12 or more years of education behind them and fathers in white-collar occupations. Such were the self-selective factors in a country where the light of medical education is hardly hidden under a bushel and new fangled notions are not automatically condemned. It is a sobering thought.

In all such circumstances of personal choice the difficulties of assessing the value of a vaccine are, therefore, very great indeed. When the application of the vaccine is made, and the choice exerted, throughout the rise and fall of an actual epidemic, large in relation to the population at risk, the task of assessment becomes, in my opinion, impossible. In such circumstances persons are continually passing from the unvaccinated to the vaccinated class and an attempt has, therefore, to be made to measure the exposure in each of these two classes. Given adequate records it would, of course, be possible to add up the actual *length of time* that a person first spent in the unvaccinated group and, subsequently, after vaccination in the vaccinated group. But can the mere length of time be always equated to exposure? Clearly not if vaccination took place when the epidemic was almost at its close. In that event exposure in the unvaccinated phase would have been vastly greater. With vaccination continuously taking place during an epidemic this error to some unknown extent is continuously creeping into the comparisons for, by definition, the vaccinated during an epidemic are, on the average, always entering the vaccinated class at a point of time later in the epidemic than that applicable to the unvaccinated class. Further, it is likely that many persons who have passed through the opening weeks of an epidemic without clinical attack will, through exposure, have nevertheless become immunized. Or indeed, their resistance to attack over these opening weeks may indicate the presence of a natural immunity. Their experience *from that point of time* would then be more favourable than that of the unvaccinated *observed over the whole of the epidemic* whether or not they were vaccinated. Their experience from that point of time clearly ought to be compared with the experience of the unvaccinated from the same point of time —although it may be necessary to delay the time until any immunity due to the vaccine has developed. It seems to me that the only strictly valid procedure in these circumstances would be to select randomly at the proper time a comparable control person for each person vaccinated, the former to remain unvaccinated. But this procedure while an epidemic is in progress is out of the question both on ethical and practical grounds. In short, if vaccination administered throughout an epidemic can conceivably do good—physiologically or psychologically—then, I suggest, one should go ahead and vaccinate; but it would be wise to refrain after the event from seeking too far, or too hopefully, for answers as to whether or no it did in fact do good and, still more, as to the extent to which it did good.

The only wholly satisfactory solution, to return to the opening words of this lecture, lies in the designed experiment in which the vaccinated and unvaccinated populations are set up *ab initio* and then subsequently observed equally through the endemic and epidemic occurrences that, in the normal course of life, await them. In following this procedure there are two main problems to be solved.

The first is the scale of the events which it is proposed to enumerate. With almost all diseases (the common cold is, perhaps, the only exception) the annual attack rate to be measured, and influenced by vaccination, is small. Thus in the Medical Research Council's first trial (1951) of a vaccine against pertussis there occurred 687 cases of whooping-cough in nearly 4,000 unvaccinated children observed, on the average, for two and a quarter years. In other words, the average annual attack rate was only 8 per cent. With tuberculosis the rate, of course, is far lower even than this. There were 13,200 tuberculin negative controls in the Medical Research Council's trial (1956) of B.C.G. and vole bacillus vaccines and only 64 of them definitely contracted tuberculosis in the first two and a half years of the inquiry—approximately 2 per 1,000 per year. Still further down the scale with poliomyelitis the paralytic attack rate has to be measured in terms of per *100,000* children at risk (Medical Research Council, 1957). Even with influenza it is, I believe, unusual, outside closed communities, such as schools and colleges, for more than 15 to 25 per cent of the population to be attacked during an epidemic—and one has to take into account, also, how capricious this disease may be in its choice of towns and villages upon which to alight heavily. It is by no means as universal as the daily press would sometimes lead one to suppose.

In short, whatever the disease at issue, the trial of a vaccine almost invariably calls for the observation of very large numbers of persons, usually widely spread in space and observed for months if not years. This in turn usually demands a central organization to plan an appropriate scheme, and to be appropriate it must be simple enough to be set in train and operated without misconception, error, or bias in many places and by many observers. That is not always quite as easy as it sounds. For instance, it is not at all difficult to devise from an armchair half-a-dozen plans for allocating persons at random to the vaccinated and unvaccinated groups. But not one of them might be simple enough to ensure they were applied consistently and without error by 50 different persons in 50 different places. Simplicity must, I submit, be the keystone of the plan in this field as in many others.

The second main problem to be met is in reaching a just compromise between the two proverbs 'ignorance is bliss' and 'honesty's the best policy'. The experimenter wishes, quite rightly, to keep entirely in the dark the participants in his experiment. He does not wish those who were unvaccinated to know that they were merely unprotected 'controls'. In addition, he does not wish the doctors who observe their subsequent illnesses to know the groups to which the victims belonged. With a general distribution of ignorance he feels secure from a differential distribution of bias.

On the other hand, we have to keep in mind that if we use a placebo, e.g., the injection of normal saline, for the controls, then inevitably we must expect a normal attack rate from the disease in question to fall upon those controls. If, however, we have concealed from the population that half of them were given a placebo, there may well be considerable alarm and despondency at the apparent failure of the vaccine in many families. And, since virtue has no news value, the failures will have quite disproportionate publicity. The public health worker may well fear that the cynical views thus engendered on one vaccine may overlap into the other, and proven, vaccination procedures for which he is responsible. As a reader of Sir Alan Herbert's Misleading Cases, he may recall the judge's reference to the thirteenth stroke of a crazy clock, which not only is itself thereby discredited, but casts a shade of doubt over all previous assertions. Despite experimental requirements we must, therefore, be honest with our clients.

I may, perhaps, take as an example the Medical Research Council's first field trials (1953), of an influenza vaccine. Here it was our announced ambition to test in parallel the virtues of two different vaccines. One was the trial vaccine, a polyvalent virus vaccine of

9

modern vintage, the other 'a bacterial "anti-influenza" vaccine of low potency'. This latter, I admit, was a somewhat old-fashioned brew; but who were we to know *in advance* that the modern variety was likely to be any more efficacious? It was proper, therefore, I suggest, to seek volunteers for a trial of *two* influenza vaccines, the value of which we did not know and could not guarantee to their recipients, none of whom would be further informed upon what they were about to receive.

The experimental requirements were met in somewhat similar fashion in the Medical Research Council's first trials (1951) of whooping-cough vaccines. In pamphlets explaining the scheme and inviting mothers to register their children, it was made clear that 'the vaccines were being tested, that it was necessary to inoculate some of the children with a substance which was not whooping-cough vaccine, and that parents and observers would not know until the end of the investigation whether a child was in the vaccinated or unvaccinated group'. The 'substance' was an 'anti-catarrhal' vaccine unlikely, of course, to influence the incidence of whooping-cough but which might, it was hoped, reduce the incidence of colds and coughs.

In this trial, to illustrate my general thesis, the Medical Research Council's Whooping-cough Immunization Committee endeavoured to meet fully the strict experimental demands that I have described. The children for whom the parents requested entry were divided by sex and age and, within each of eight such stratified sub-groups, the whooping-cough vaccine and the anti-catarrhal vaccines were allocated entirely at random by means of previously prepared lists. The vaccine to be given in each case was denoted by a symbol and neither parent nor doctor was informed of the actual nature of the injection. Lest, however, the interpretation of even these symbols became possible—through, for example, a different incidence of inoculation reactions—the follow-up of the children, and the observations of their illnesses, were made without any knowledge of them. The equality of the vaccinated and unvaccinated groups in respects other than vaccination was demonstrated by the collection and analysis of other 'epidemiological' characteristics (see Table **10**, 3). Such equality adds very considerably to the faith we can place in the one substantial difference noted, namely the incidence of pertussis. It is particularly important, therefore, to measure such characteristics whenever we have to deal with groups not randomly

TABLE **10,** 3

Observations of the Participants in a Trial of Vaccination against Whooping-cough (constructed from data published by the Medical Research Council's Whooping-cough Immunization Committee)

Characteristic	Vaccinated with Whooping-cough vaccine	Vaccinated with anti-catarrhal vaccine
Total number of children entered for inoculation	4,515	4,412
Percentage excluded before three injections completed	15·8	14·8
Total number given three injections	3,801	3,757
Percentage excluded during follow-up	11·7	10·8
Males as per cent of total children	48	51
Average age in months	12·2	12·2
Average duration of follow-up in months	27·1	27·2
Average number of children under 14 years of age per household	1·8	1·8
Percentage of inoculated children reported to have been breast fed	80	80
Average duration of breast feeding in months	5·3	5·4
Percentage vaccinated against smallpox	63	62
Percentage attacked during follow-up by measles, chicken pox or broncho-pneumonia	34·3	33·7
Percentage attacked during follow-up by whooping-cough	3·9	18·3

divided *e.g.*, volunteers versus non-volunteers. As I previously emphasized, a difference between such groups merely in the incidence of the specific disease in question cannot command confidence. Other features of the groups, apart from vaccination, may have produced it. But if we can secure a measurement of several other features, and find equality, especially in the incidence of other diseases, we are obviously in a much more favourable position to draw conclusions. Even with the more exactly planned trial we must remember too that randomization does not in itself invariably produce comparable groups. By the play of chance the groups will differ sometimes, and, if small numbers are involved, even considerably. We must then see whether such differences have, indeed, occurred and whether they appear to be relevant to the issue. The recording of other epidemiological characteristics will greatly aid us in this pursuit.

Somewhat different methods had to be used by the Medical Research Council's Tuberculosis Vaccines Clinical Trials Committee in their field experiments with B.C.G. and the vole bacillus vaccine. To begin with, it was on ethical grounds held to be quite impossible to carry out a controlled trial on the infant in contact in the home with a tuberculous parent. To be effective such a procedure would have required immediate separation of the infant from the home for some weeks. The infant would then have been inoculated with B.C.G., or, if a control left uninoculated, and after an interval for the former to become tuberculin positive would have been returned to the tuberculous environment. The belief, however, that B.C.G. conferred some protection was far too strongly held, however weak the evidence might be in detail, to allow a procedure that required an uninoculated child to be returned in the same way and setting to a tuberculous parent.

Attention was, therefore, turned to the adolescent passing from school life to the world of adult work, a time at which the notification rate and mortality from tuberculosis in Great Britain begin to rise from their low levels in childhood. Some 57,000 volunteers, nearly all in their fifteenth year and forming about 60 per cent of the population available, were enrolled shortly before they left secondary-modern schools in or near London, Birmingham and Manchester. At an initial examination each entrant was allotted a number (given in serial order) given a chest radiograph and an intracutaneous test with 3 T.U. (tuberculin units). Any child found to be suffering from tuberculosis, or known to have been in recent contact with a case of pulmonary tuberculosis at home, was immediately excluded. Those with negative reactions to 3 T.U. were tested with 100 T.U. Those negative to this strength also, were allocated to vaccination or control on the basis of the last digit of their serial number. This had been given it will be remembered, *before* it was known whether the child was tuberculin positive, and therefore ineligible for vaccination, or negative and eligible. Schematically we have:

All entrants given a serial number, chest X-ray and a tuberculin test to 3 T.U.

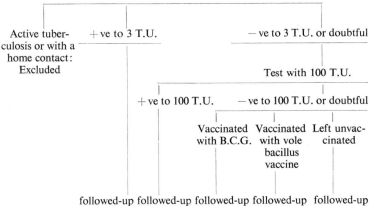

An equally intensive follow-up of all groups was constituted, the aim being an annual X-ray and tuberculin test for not less than seven years. While it will clearly be impossible to fulfil this aim in 100 per cent of the participants, intensive efforts are being made to ensure that *every* clinically active case of tuberculosis that arises is brought to light through one channel or another. The X-rays, and other clinical findings, of all definite and suspected cases are then reviewed and classified by an independent assessor who is kept unaware of the results of any tuberculin tests and vaccination procedures. It will be noted, however, that this trial falls short of the ideal in one respect—no placebo injection was given to the controls. The children who were in this group could hardly know that they were controls since, apart from the tuberculin reaction, they are on a par with the children who had been found positive to 100 T.U. On the other hand it was not possible to conceal from them the fact that they had not been vaccinated and, *a fortiori*, it was likely to be clear to the vaccinated that they had been vaccinated. It is difficult to see, however, how one could effectively simulate the course of B.C.G. inoculation with a dummy injection. According to the Committee's first report on this trial 'many of those who received only tuberculin tests were under the impression that they too had been vaccinated'. It is hard to see, therefore, how this limited knowledge of the participants could influence the observation of, and comparison between the groups, with regard to the incidence of *clinically active tuberculosis*. The cases are being discovered over a period of years following the vaccination, many of them by persons entirely unconnected with the inquiry. They are finally, as I have said, reviewed by one physician who is kept wholly in the dark. In these circumstances I do not myself believe that the omission of a dummy injection, which was foreseen and deliberately made in the plan of the investigation, can materially influence the results recorded.

The same omission was inevitable in the assessment of the protective value of the British vaccine against poliomyelitis. For two reasons it was essential to make this assessment in spite of the fact that a most impressive trial in the United States had already shown that the Salk vaccine (as originally manufactured) conferred considerable protection on children (Poliomyelitis Vaccine Evaluation Centre, 1957). In the first place in the British vaccine the Brunenders strain had been used as the Type I component in place of the more virulent Mahoney strain of the American vaccine. It was important to know whether that substitution had reduced the protective value of the vaccine. Secondly, the American trial had given clear evidence of protection against paralytic attacks at ages six to nine years but dealt with no other age group. It was important to know whether a formolized vaccine would also protect the pre-school children who in the United Kingdom still have the highest paralytic attack rates.

The plan of this study was severly hampered by three factors, namely (1) the shortage of vaccine which was only enough for some 200,000 children all told, (2) the shortage of time in which to inject it, which was limited to two months, May and June, 1956, and (3) the necessity to distribute the available supplies throughout the whole country which meant the experimental procedures had to be very simple and of general applicability. There was no way of meeting difficulties (1) and (2); as usual no more than a pint can be extracted from a pint pot. What is more, the landlord provided very poor measure since the year 1956 proved to be singularly lacking in poliomyelitis. To meet the third problem the scheme of randomization for the selection of children to be vaccinated was based upon their month of birth. Of the 1,900,000 children registered for vaccination the supplies were allocated to those born in a November in 1947 to 1954 and those born in a March in 1951 to 1954. Our hope, I need hardly stress, had been to spread the allocation over a much wider span of the year and thus to include in the vaccinated group, children whose months of birth had coincided with the different phases of the customary poliomyelitis epidemic year, *i.e.*, births that preceded, were during or followed the normal epidemic period. The lack of vaccine made this impossible and we had to be content with one month of births that had taken place either side of the usual epidemic period in this country.

A much graver weakness proved to be the number of registered children who were born in March and November and who ought, therefore, to have been vaccinated, but, for some unknown reasons, were not vaccinated. No such 'absentees' could voluntarily withdraw, or be withdrawn, from the control group of children born in the months not eligible for vaccination. In other words, since no placebo injection was used these children were not called to the clinic and therefore could not default. As a result the comparability of the vaccinated groups is immediately in question and the analysis of the results to meet the point must be more involved. In my opinion the point was met in the Medical Research Council's report and the value of the British vaccine was established though the degree of protection was not measured with precision. In the limited time available for injections it certainly would not have been practicable (even if ethical) to have called up nearly one-and-three-quarter million children for a placebo injection, or, indeed, even a sample of them. Any attempt to do so would have brought the whole scheme of assessment to nought.

On the other hand where, in my opinion, we in this country sadly failed was in not attempting to continue the assessment in the following year, 1956. With the supplies of vaccine then likely to be available it was almost certain that the remaining 1,750,000 children could not all be vaccinated before the 1957 poliomyelitis season had wholly passed. If, therefore, the allocation had been continued on the 'birthday lottery' basis a further valid comparison of the vaccinated and unvaccinated children would have been possible. This comparison would have given information on three important points: (1) we would have measured with much greater precision the benefit actually given by two injections of this British vaccine to children of different ages, (2) whether this benefit, derived from two injections, showed signs of waning after the lapse of 12 months, and (3) whether vaccination influenced the incidence of non-paralytic attacks; our trial in 1956 had given a suggestion that it might do so (particularly in the non-paralytic cases established by the isolation of the virus); the U.S. vaccine in their 1954 trial appeared not to have done so. Answers to these questions could materially influence our national policy with this vaccine.

To continue the trial in this way would not, in my opinion, have raised any ethical problems. If there were insufficient vaccine to vaccinate all the children before the end of the epidemic season of 1957, then some order of priority *had* to be adopted. The problem was therefore one of practicability. The birthday allocation not only offered a method of priority but was a method which would allow further valuable evidence to be collected. On the other hand the policy of letting the Medical Officer of Health of each area adopt whatever scheme best suited him (which was the official policy actually followed) automatically rendered useless any further records of the experience of the vaccinated and unvaccinated. There could no longer be any assurance that these two groups were comparable in other respects, *e.g.*, in their geographical or social class distribution.

Continuation of the birthday scheme would undoubtedly in the long run have thrown rather more work on medical officers of health—even though more than a million children could immediately have been 'released' to them for vaccination. Sooner or later they would have had to return to all their areas to vaccinate the children born in the unselected months. The reason for its continuation would have to have been explained to the parents of the registered children. But in the introduction of a preventive measure of this magnitude and of this importance, affecting the whole nation, I am reluctant to believe that the medical officers of health of Great Britain, when clearly told the issues, would not willingly face an extra burden. I am equally reluctant to believe that the British public, if properly instructed, would not accept an obvious but ethical experiment, just as readily as do our American cousins.

If I am wrong in these beliefs, or if we should allow political expediency to influence our judgements in such matters, then as Sir John Ledingham said nearly 30 years ago, we shall again fall behind other countries in this field, and in similar fields, of preventive medicine.

III—INFLUENZA AND THE COMMON COLD

A S that great novel *Rob Roy* draws to its close the author, in a dramatic passage, admits that neither by his own observation nor through the medical attendants could he ascertain

that Sir Hildebrand Osbaldistone died of any formed complaint, bearing a name in the science of medicine. He seemed to me completely worn out and broken down by fatigue of body and distress of mind, and rather ceased to exist than died of any positive struggle; just as a vessel buffeted and tossed by a succession of tempestuous gales, her timbers overstrained, and her joints loosened, will sometimes spring a leak and founder, when there are no apparent causes for her destruction.

I always advise my students that the Registrar-General is unlikely to look with favour upon a death certificate couched in these terms. On the other hand senile psychosis due to myocardial degeneration will prove wholly acceptable, though quite possibly, and even probably, is no more in keeping with the undetermined underlying pathology.

Much the same doubt must frequently prevail with what we are pleased on clinical grounds to call an attack of influenza. 'Ye can call it influenza if ye like,' said Mrs. Machin irritably in a later and much lesser novel (Bennett, 1911), 'there was no influenza in my young days. We called a cold a cold.' What we may call it today is quite another matter. In *my* young days there were no Coxsackie, no adeno and no ECHO viruses. Knowledge advances and fashions change. With the aid of the laboratory the causative agents of acute respiratory diseases and febrile catarrhs are being slowly disentangled. But there is no reason to suppose that thereby the clinical picture is rendered any more decisive than it ever was. The label 'influenza', is still likely to extend, particularly in non-epidemic periods, over a group of diseases, a number of which have quite other origins than the influenza viruses. It is this lack of accurate discrimination that makes the trial of an influenza vaccine in the general population peculiarly difficult.

In measuring the incidence of influenza in the vaccinated and unvaccinated groups we are bound to be including, to an unknown

Reprinted from the *Journal of the Royal Institute of Public Health and Hygiene*, 1958, **21**, 209.

extent, illnesses due to other causes and against which the vaccine would be expected to be powerless. We are accordingly, by this dilution, weakening the evidence in favour of the vaccine. Instead of comparing the two relative rates of influenza (x_1 versus x_2) we are comparing the relative rates of influenza plus in each group a constant amount of other diseases (($x_1 + y$) versus ($x_2 + y$)). If the other diseases are relatively infrequent, as they may well be when influenza itself is acutely epidemic, then clearly the assessment of the vaccine will not be seriously at fault (y is a small and unimportant component). But if the other diseases are relatively frequent, as they may well be when influenza itself is merely sporadic, then the assessment of the vaccine may be in serious jeopardy (y dominates the comparison).

The solution to the dilemma may, in time, lie with the laboratory. At present one may perhaps doubt the evidence which is given by an antibody rise observed during the illness of an unvaccinated person and which is, perhaps, lacking in a similarly sick vaccinated person. May not the vaccination itself have interfered with the antibody level even though it has failed to protect? In the unvaccinated person the rise can certainly be interpreted as evidence of the presence of influenza. I think we would be overbold to conclude that the lack of rise in the vaccinated person rules out the presence of influenza. We would, however, be on much safer ground with regard to the isolation of the influenza virus from the sick person by means of throat swabs—or, in its absence, by the isolation of some other virus. The difficulty here lies rather in the practicability of obtaining garglings at a sufficiently early stage of the illness in a very large number of cases in the normal working population living in their own homes.

It was these practical difficulties that, in its early experiments, led the Medical Research Council's Committee on Clinical Trials of Influenza Vaccine to seek a compromise. It first ensured that the diagnosing practitioner and his patient would both be kept in complete ignorance of the nature of the vaccine which the latter had received—whether it was the trial vaccine or the control vaccine. Where clinically the nature of the illness can be in serious doubt this is a *sine qua non*. Secondly the practitioner's attention was especially drawn to the alternative diagnosis of febrile sore throat and febrile cold which, endemic in the population during the winter season, might be confused with influenza. To avoid inclusion of the common cold, illnesses which caused an absence from work of less than two days were not recorded. A 'spotting' scheme, parallel to the vaccine trial and organized by the Public Health Laboratory Service, was relied upon to show when and where influenza viruses could be detected in the community. Under these conditions what the doctor said on clinical grounds was accepted as evidence.

The participants in the first trial were volunteers drawn from industry, hospital staff, the fighting services and university students. They were allocated to one or other vaccine—the modern virus variety or the somewhat outmoded bacterial vaccine—by means of random order lists supplied to each centre. The results are shown briefly in Table 10, 4.

TABLE 10, 4

Vaccination against Influenza. Attacks of Illness of Two or more Days' Duration (adapted from a progress report to the Medical Research Council by its Committee on Clinical Trials of Influenza Vaccine, 1953)

Diagnosis	% of persons attacked		Difference and Standard error
	6,340 given Trial Vaccine	6,370 given Control Vaccine	
Influenza	3·0	4·9	1·9 ± 0·34
Febrile Cold	3·4	3·8	0·4 ± 0·33
Febrile Sore Throat	1·4	1·4	0·0 ± 0·20
Other respiratory diseases	2·1	2·3	0·2 ± 0·26
Non-respiratory diseases	4·0	3·3	−0·7 ± 0·33
Total	13·9	15·5	1·6 ± 0·65

It will be seen that the incidence of influenza was significantly lower in the group given the trial vaccine, but the actual reduction was only about 40 per cent. There is, however, no suggestion that the difference is an artefact, that what has been called influenza in the vaccinated group has been called by some other name in the control group. The double-blind procedure was, of course, designed to prevent this possible bias. On the contrary though not differing significantly, the remaining febrile and other respiratory diseases tend also to be slightly lower in the vaccinated group. And this is what one would expect if, as is likely, the detection of true influenza sometimes affects these groups too (for we are then comparing the level of $(y+x_1)$ with the level of $(y+x_2)$ and, if the vaccine does protect, x_1 should be less than x_2 and therefore $(y+x_1)$ less than $(y+x_2)$, the degree varying according to the relative frequency of the x component).

On the other hand there appears to have been some slight excess of the non-respiratory diseases in the group given the trial vaccine. This may have been due to chance (the formal significance test is only borderline) or it may be due to a tendency for persons who have already, through a sickness absence, lost time (and often money) not to lose time again, if they can avoid it, within the few months that the observations covered. The weakness of the experiment lies, if this be so, in the fact that we are then measuring absences from work and not as really required, the true frequency of the occurrence of illness. I have seen the same question arise in other circumstances and, though we cannot necessarily meet it, we do well to bear it in mind in all such inquiries.

The main point at issue, in this particular trial, however, is the degree of protection which was conferred by the vaccine. Was it worth all the bother and fuss for what is likely to be merely a short-time cover? Accepting the figures of Table **10,** 4 it was approximately only 40 per cent (since the attack rate of 3.0 in the vaccinated group is 61 per cent of the rate of 4.9 in the control group). But for the reasons I have already given I am sure one cannot accept the figures at their face value. The 40 per cent is almost certainly a minimum figure—though it has been widely bandied about as the true figure. To examine the situation more closely a further analysis of the data obtained in this trial was made in relation to geographical area, the areas being grouped according to the intensity with which they were attacked by influenza (as measured by mortality in the great towns). Table **10,** 5 gives illustrative results (omitting the areas of medium mortality).

The 'protection' conferred in the areas where influenza was not in fact prevalent (as judged by mortality) was negligible—as one would expect if many of the diagnoses of influenza here are erroneous. It was considerably greater in the areas where influenza was more prevalent and where the true influenza fraction in the rate might therefore be considerably higher. Let us suppose that two-thirds of what was diagnosed as influenza in the control group in the low mortality areas was not, in fact, influenza at all, *i.e.*, 2.40 per

TABLE **10**, 5

Influenza Attack Rates in Two Types of Area (adapted from a progress report to the Medical Research Council by its Committee on Clinical Trials of Influenza Vaccine, 1953)

	Percentage attacked		(1) as % of (2)
	Trial Vaccine Group (1)	Control Vaccine Group (2)	
Areas of low influenza mortality (8·1 per 100,000 or less)	2·92	3·60	*81*
Areas of high influenza mortality (16·2 per 100,000 or more)	3·79	6·61	*57*

cent. Let us further suppose (which is most unlikely) that this attack rate of 2.40 per cent, representing the incidence of non-influenzal diseases diagnosed as influenza, is a constant feature applying to each of the four groups of Table **10**, 5. Then our true comparisons of *influenza* incidence should be not those of the table but 0.52 compared with 1.20 and 1.39 compared with 4.21 giving protection factors of 57 per cent and 67 per cent. These figures, I need hardly stress, are largely imaginative. They do, however, serve to indicate how misplaced must be a faith in the 40 per cent protection figure given by the total crude results. An even more striking example of the difficulty can be culled from the Committee's later trials of which I give an extract in Table **10**, 6.

It is clear that protection was conferred by each of the two virus A vaccines but, if we accept the total line representing the whole period of the inquiry, it was of the order of a miserable 30 per cent only. On the other hand the two divisions of the experience show very clearly that while no protection whatever was apparent during many weeks when influenza was not epidemic it was of the order of 50 per cent in the few weeks when it was prevalent. Once more, this is almost certainly a minimum figure but at the same time the results suggest that we are more likely to reach something more akin to the truth when influenza is sharply epidemic than when it is not.

One of the grave difficulties of all these British trials has been the absence of epidemic influenza from the country. It looks, and I regret it on all but statistical grounds, as if the Asian variety may

TABLE **10,** 6

Number of Illnesses of Two or More Days' Duration Ascribed to Influenza (adapted from the third progress report to the Medical Research Council by its Committee on Clinical Trials of Influenza Vaccine, 1957)

	No. of illnesses ascribed to influenza in three groups of approximately 2,500 persons inoculated with:		
	A monovalent influenza Virus A vaccine	A polyvalent influenza Virus A vaccine	An influenza Virus B vaccine
During six weeks of relatively high incidence of influenza	39	35	76
During 19 weeks of relatively low incidence of influenza	49	49	49
Total	98	84	125

now correct the balance and provide us with a more extensive and profitable experimental field. Early results (Medical Research Council, 1958) already suggest that in this sharply epidemic setting we have been able to reach a protective level of not less than 70 per cent. This success, too, appears to have been achieved with only one injection of a vaccine which according to serological tests produced a relatively poor antigenic response in terms of antibody levels. How much further we can go in this particular field in terms, for example, of developing still more effective vaccines, of measuring the duration of the immunity conferred and deciding upon the optimum number and dosage of injections, must depend very largely, I believe, upon the solution of the diagnostic problem that I have elaborated.

The common cold presents a similar, and hardly less troublesome, problem of definition and diagnosis. It has, however, the advantage to the would-be experimenter of its ubiquity in the population and its frequency in the individual. It follows that an experiment aimed at its prevention demands far fewer human victims. To illustrate this thesis, and the special problems that do arise, I take one example from each side of the North Atlantic.

Twenty years ago Diehl, Baker and Cowan (1948), working in Minnesota, made a trial of vaccines. Their subjects were university students invited to volunteer if they believed themselves to be particularly susceptible to colds. They were allocated at random to the vaccine and control groups. With the mixed vaccine under test the former were inoculated twice a week for three weeks and then every other week throughout the autumn, winter and spring—in all, I suppose, some 20 injections. The control group, *under the impression that they were being vaccinated*, were given injections of normal saline administered in the same way, at the same time intervals and over the same period. All were required to keep a record of each cold of more than 24 hours' duration and to report to the students' health service whenever a cold developed.

So that these observations and reportings shall be unbiased, and equally comprehensive and reliable, I have no doubt whatever that, with this vaguely defined illness, the control group must be given some placebo. I have no doubt whatever that the recipients must not know which brew they actually receive. But whether it is ethical (and in this country, legal) to do that without a warning to the potential volunteers is a matter to which I have already referred at length in my previous lectures. I need, therefore, pay no further attention to it now. I would merely add that the control group's 'unprejudiced attitude towards the study' conceivably took a turn for the worse after publication of the experimental method. A few of the results of this carefully conducted experiment are given in Table **10**, 7.

TABLE **10**, 7

The Results of Vaccination against the Common Cold (adapted from a study by Diehl, Cowan and Baker)

	Vaccine Group	Control Group
Number of recipients who completed study	272	276
Average no. of colds per person in previous year	5·9	5·6
Average no. of colds per person in study year	1·6	2·1
Per cent reduction in current year	73	63
Average no. of days lost from work through colds	1·1	1·0
Percentage of colds with complications (bronchitis, etc.)	2·8	1·7
Percentage of recipients who had no colds at all	20	11

One of the most striking features is the enormous reduction in the colds observed in the current year compared with those of the previous year. Suppose no control group had been incorporated in the trial, should we not have been impressed—or, at the very least, have been invited by the experimenter to be impressed—by a reduction as great as 73 per cent? We have all seen many secular comparisons of this kind. We have all been told that so great a change could not be expected to occur from one year to the next. Have we invariably been uneasy at the absence of a control? Have we invariably returned the canny Scots verdict of not proven? These figures should indeed caution us to step warily in such a situation.

In the present setting the answer may be that the records of the previous year, gathered retrospectively from those who believed themselves unduly susceptible to colds, were the products of unhappy and distorted memories. It may be that the careful definitions of a cold laid down for the current year could not, or would not, be applied by the students to their memories of the past year. It may even be that in the past year the students *did* have all those colds and so in the current year, as a result, they enjoyed a considerable, if temporary, immunity. If that were the case a weakness of the experiment would lie in limiting it to persons who believed themselves unduly susceptible to attack. For the time being they might, so to speak, have worn out their welcome and the invitation to the trial would have been better if extended to all and sundry. But, whatever the explanation, the danger of deducing cause and effect from the secular trend is patent. Alongside the control group, however, it falls into perspective and it appears that the vaccine achieved nothing very remarkable for its recipients. Nevertheless some of them were well satisfied for the authors report that from time to time physicians would write to them saying 'I have a patient who took your cold vaccine and got such splendid results that he wants to continue it. Will you be good enough to tell me what vaccine you are using?' It must have been embarrassing to all parties to reply 'water'. Yet in that simple reply lies all the fallibility of the individual *post hoc ergo propter hoc* judgement.

The British experiment that I have selected as illustrative in this field is somewhat different. It relates to a trial of artificial sunlight treatment in industry (Colebrook, 1946).

It has been claimed, says the introduction to the report upon its results, that exposure to the rays of quartz mercury arc lamps for but a few minutes in each week is equivalent to some hours of natural sunbathing; and from this, and the popular notion of the 'tonic' effects of sunbathing, has arisen the much more far-reaching claim that a course of these exposures should have the effect of reducing absenteeism due to sickness, accidents, the common cold and general ill-health. The administration of the treatment to large numbers of work people is simple, and can be done with a relatively small loss of working time; if, indeed, the treatment were found to have the good general effects sometimes attributed to it, there would be no serious difficulty in extending its use to cover large sections of those employed in industrial and other occupations.

If, indeed—that was the question facing Dr. Dora Colebrook working for the Artificial Irradiation Committee of the Industrial Health Research Board in 1945. To solve it experiments were carried out in three very different working environments—a Government office, a factory and a mine. Within each of these, four groups were set up:

(1) To receive the full range of ultra-violet rays from quartz mercury arc lamps and a capsule of an inert oil at each attendance.

(2) To receive irradiation from identical lamps but fitted with glass screens impermeable to the shorter ultra-violet rays and a similar capsule of an inert oil at each attendance.

(3) The same as group (2) but receiving at each attendance a capsule containing a maintenance dose of vitamin D.

(4) No treatment at all.

The inclusion of group (3) and of the inert capsules in groups (1) and (2) was directed towards determining whether any beneficial result from irradiation that might be found was due merely to the correction of a vitamin D deficiency in the population.

With the appeal for volunteers a brief statement was circulated explaining that 'to gain more exact knowledge of the effect of the rays, the volunteers would be divided by lot into two treatment groups, the one to receive long rays only, the other both long and short rays; and that both groups would be asked to take capsules, some of which would contain a vitamin'. In other words we were, once again, honest with the customer and, though the glass screens could not be concealed from him, there is no sign in the results that they introduced a subjective reaction. Indeed, to cut short a long story, with which I am not primarily concerned here, there was no significant difference between the three irradiated groups in such measurable features as amount of sickness absence, the number of days spent with colds and proportion of persons who thought that their health had been better during the period of attendance at the light clinics.

The features of the experiment with which I am specially concerned were the recording of the occurrence of colds and the construction and observation of the untreated controls of group (4). In Table **10,** 8 I give a brief summary of the available data on the colds reported.

TABLE **10,** 8

The Average Number of Days with Colds per Person per Month (adapted from Industrial Health Research Board Report No. 89)

	Government office (Feb.–April, 1945)	Factory (Feb.–March, 1945)	Mine (Nov., 1944-Feb., 1945)
Group 1 Unscreened lamp	4·8	4·7	? (3·0)*
Group 2 Screened lamp with vitamin	4·9	4·2	? (3·1)*
Group 3 Screened lamp without vitamin	4·8	4·9	? (2·6)*
Group 4 Untreated	3·9	?	? (2·3)*

* Average number per month absent from work through colds expressed as a percentage of the number in the group.

Within the treated groups of both the Government office and the factory there is clearly no important difference whatever. At the mine no such figures could be obtained at all. Though the procedure within the light clinic, it is reported, was always orderly and reasonably quiet, the record room was fully exposed to all the noises of the miners' shower baths 'so that the taking of verbal evidence' was 'virtually impossible'. I suspect this feature of experimentation in the human herd might have been overcome. The sting lies in the next sentence. 'Moreover, in his anxiety not to miss his bus, the miner is accustomed to pass through the baths at speed; it had been made clear to us that good attendance at the clinic would depend on our success in getting him through the solarium with the least possible delay.' In short, to ensure the greater gain on the roundabouts—constant attendance for the treatment—one had to suffer a loss in the swings.

A more serious loss in each experiment lay in the untreated controls. In the Government office where they had a statistically significantly *smaller* mean number of days with colds it is almost certain that the difference has no real significance. The number of days upon which symptoms were noticed was obtained from the irradiated by cross-examination upon each attendance at the clinic. The untreated were instructed to fill in a simple record form distributed weekly. It is probable that as a result of the twice-weekly interviews the treated had become more 'colds conscious' than their untreated form-filling companions.

At the factory matters were still more difficult. Its medical officer having, in his appeal for volunteers and by considerable effort, aroused interest in the treatment amongst the work people, was finally (and not unnaturally) averse to excluding one-quarter therefrom by lot. He, therefore, decided to ask amongst the volunteers for the names of any man willing to stand down. An adequate number did so. But adequacy in numbers is perhaps the least important feature. The factors entering into the construction of such a group are quite unknown; they may be correlated, directly or inversely, with the health variables being studied, and the use of the group at all is clearly most hazardous. Their recorded number of days of colds was, in fact, very low in comparison with the figure for the treated but no meaning can be attached to it.

Similarly, at the mine it was concluded that as many as 250 men could not be excluded from the light clinic when their interest had been deliberately aroused. 'We felt that we should run the risk of having an untreated control group of disappointed men; that the spirit of co-operation among the rest might be threatened by what might appear to them to be a high-handed action; or even that "gate-crashing" might disrupt our organization.' And so, with the *vox populi* rumbling through the clinic no comparable untreated group was ever constituted.

Such are some of the difficulties of the controlled experiment in mankind. In this particular setting the issues were, in my opinion, satisfactorily answered by the three different treatment groups. Their inclusion was, of course, deliberately decided upon in the belief that the experiment would be likely to fail, and fail seriously, if a wholly untreated group were the *only* form of control used. In many situations in scientific work, indeed, one control is, surely, an error. Especially in designing field experiments, or in making similar observations of mankind, we should, I suggest, invariably ask ourselves not what control *group* is required but what control *groups* shall we seek?

In the experiments in man that I have described, and, indeed, in all such experiments, we are, needless to say, dependent upon volunteers. That is clearly as it should be. We have no compulsory powers to give injections or to make persons submit to any other procedures, pleasant or unpleasant. Whether, on the principle of *pro bono publico*, one favours such powers in the *proven* case, there can be no argument whatever for them in the *unproven* experimental setting. How far the results apparent with volunteers, even with the perfect experiment, are applicable to the generality of mankind may, of course, be arguable. We may be faultlessly observing the relative incidence of disease in vaccinated and unvaccinated children and both groups may belong, unduly, to small families with careful mothers. Whether the answer we have reached is equally applicable to large families with scatter-brained mothers we do not know, and cannot know. But as usual we must not make the best the enemy of the good. In the ivory tower we must decide precisely upon the question to which we should seek an answer and then, abandoning the tower, we must consider whether with the modifications demanded by the market-place we can still answer a useful, if not the ideal, question. That is invariably the situation in 'real' life.

Similarly we shall have frequently to consider how far we can afford to forego the ideal in our methodology. Our observations should be so standardized as to apply equally and without bias to the entire study population. What differences in procedure, then, can we allow between the study groups and yet be sure of the validity of our answers? For example, in the trial of vaccines when dare we dispense with a placebo injection to the controls? Some would say never; for myself I would believe one would thereby lose much of high value in the search for perfection. Obviously the issues must be weighed afresh in each set of circumstances; the experimental requirements and the extent to which we can safely relax them will vary with the problem. There can be no simple all-embracing code.

One main difficulty is not only that we are experimenting with man but that frequently, as I have shown, we are having to do so on a very large scale. A handful of conscientious objectors in wartime, the staff of a scientific department, or a class of medical students can be made to understand, without grave difficulties, the exacting demands of an experiment. With understanding they will allow themselves to be moved like pawns to meet these demands.

It is obviously not so easy with the population of the town or village, of the factory or office. But I have no doubt whatever that it frequently can be done and, indeed, the experience of this and other countries in recent years has *shown* that it can be done. Given an honesty of purpose and an honestly declared intention I do not believe that the more general public will be backward in support. They may not invariably grasp our why's and wherefore's. Occasionally they may even take the view of the doctor who, in protest at my insistence upon a particular experimental procedure, wrote that he had always suspected that statisticians were damned fools and now he knew it. However that may be (and I would be the last to deny it), we have to make the attempt to educate the public. We can in preventive medicine no longer subscribe to the philosophy of Monsieur Dupont who, while entertaining the most generous affection for the human race as a whole, regarded the separate entities who composed it with the gloomiest aversion (France, 1899). It would seem today that further advances in the public health will come less from our adjustment of the environment and more from the personal actions of those separate entities. We must inevitably, therefore, bear with their whims and foibles and we must woo their aid both in proving, or disproving, our hypotheses and in applying our established tenets.

Finally, I would lay particular stress on two things. Firstly, and emphatically, the experimental approach in preventive medicine is *not* the prerogative of a medical research council, a university or any similar Gargantuan institution. I have, indeed, in these lectures illustrated my thesis by large-scale inquiries, carried out through such a central organization; I have done so merely because I have myself been closely concerned with these particular experiments and because the problems that they have revealed illustrate effectively the peculiar problems that run through this whole field of experiment in man, which it has been my object to display. But, given an experimental outlook, the public health worker is, I believe, not likely to lack opportunities to exercise his philosophy and his skills over a wide range of scales.

Secondly, the search for knowledge through experiment in man is not a harsh and heartless search.

It is surprising, writes Professor Melville Arnott (1955), how many apparently educated people, including many doctors, regard science as an affair of laboratories, apparatus, and formulae rather than as an attitude of mind which relates hypothesis and plan to controlled observation. It is because of this misconception that some mistakenly hold that the qualities of solicitude and compassion are incompatible with the scientific method. But, in fact, it is as much a crime against science as it is against humanity to neglect those qualities of kindliness which are essential to the care of the sick and the supervision of the health of the individual.

To that I would add but one word. In experiments in curative medicine I have never known the experimentalist, however intense his passion for precision and objectivity, lagging behind his colleagues in compassion for the subjects of his research. I believe that the experimental approach in preventive medicine, to which I have been privileged to devote these lectures, makes no less demands upon our intellectual integrity and upon our sympathies. To the attitude of mind that it comprises, to the problems and controversies that we seek thereby to solve, we must assuredly bring this same blending of passion and compassion.

REFERENCES

LECTURE 1

Armijo, R., Henderson, D. A., Timothée, R., and Robinson, H. B. (1957). *Amer. J. publ. Hlth.* **47**, 1093.
Bell, J. A. (1948). *J. Amer. med. Ass.* **137**, 1276.
Blount, B. K. (1955). *J. R. Soc. Arts*, **104**, 108.
Cohen, Henry (1953). *Pharm. J.* **171**, 331.
Cornfield, J. (1954). *Amer. Statistician*, **8**, No. 5, 19.
Finney, D. J. (1952). *Ann. Soc. Sci. méd. nat. Brux.* **5**, 54.
Hill, A. Bradford (1955). *Principles of Medical Statistics*, 6th ed. London: Lancet.
Ledingham, J. C. G. (1939). *Brit. med. J.* **ii**, 841.
McCance, R. A. (1951). *Proc. R. Soc. Med.* **44**, 189.
Pickering, G. W. (1949). *Proc. R. Soc. Med.* **42**, 229.
United States Public Health Service (1957). *U.S. publ. Hlth Rep.* No. 72, 412.
United States Public Health Service (1957). *Amer. Rev. Tuberc.* **76**, 942.
Vollner, H. (1957). *J. Dis. Child.* **93**, 396.
World Health Organization (1957). *Tech. Rep. Wld. Hlth Org.* No. 118,

LECTURE 2

California Medicine (1957). **86**, 142.
Kendrick, P. (1943). *Amer. J. Hyg.* **38**, 193.
Kendrick, P., and Eldering, G. (1939). *Amer. J. Hyg.* **29**, 133.
Kendrick, P., and Weiss, E. S. (1942). *Amer. J. publ. Hlth.* **32**, 615.
Levine, M. I., and Sackett, M. F. (1946). *Amer. Rev. Tuberc.* **53**, 517.

Medical Research Council Whooping-cough Immunization Committee (1951). *Brit. med. J.* **i**, 1464.

Medical Research Council Committee on Clinical Trials of Influenza Vaccine (1953). *Brit. med. J.* **ii**, 1173.

Medical Research Council Tuberculosis Vaccines Clinical Trials Committee (1956). *Brit. med. J.* **i**, 413.

Medical Research Council Poliomyelitis Vaccines Committee (1957). *Brit. med. J.* **i**, 1271.

Medical Research Council Committee on Inoculation Procedures and Neurological Lesions (1956). *Lancet*, **ii**, 1223.

Francis, T. (1957). *Evaluation of the 1954 Field Trial of Poliomyelitis Vaccine. Final Report.* Ann Arbor: University of Michigan.

LECTURE 3

Arnott, W. Melville (1955). *Lancet*, **ii**, 783.

Bennett, Arnold (1911). *The Card.* London: Methuen.

Colebrook, Dora (1946). *Rep. industr. Hlth. Res. Bd. (Lond.)*, No. 89.

Diehl, H. S., Baker, A. B., and Cowan, D. W. (1938). *J. Amer. med. Ass.* **111**, 1168.

France, Anatole (1899). *Pierre Nozière.* Paris: Lemerre.

Medical Research Council Committee on Clinical Trials of Influenza Vaccine (1953). *Brit. med. J.* **ii**, 1173.

Medical Research Council Committee on Clinical Trials of Influenza Vaccine (1957). *Brit. med. J.* **ii**, 1.

Medical Research Council Committee on Influenza and other Respiratory Virus Vaccines (1958). *Brit. med. J.* **i**, 415.

CHAPTER 11

THE PREVENTION OF WHOOPING-COUGH
BY VACCINATION

SINCE 1942 investigations have been in progress under the direction of the Whooping-cough Immunization Committee of the Medical Research Council to assess the prophylactic value of pertussis vaccines. From 1942 to 1944 controlled trials were made in Oxford City with children attending welfare clinics and day nurseries, and also in Oxfordshire, Berkshire, and Buckinghamshire with children in residential nurseries. A report of this work was published by McFarlan, Topley, and Fisher (1945). No significant difference was observed in the incidence or severity of the disease between the vaccinated and unvaccinated groups. In the Oxford City trial 12.5 per cent of 327 vaccinated and 14.1 per cent of 305 unvaccinated children developed pertussis, while in those residential nurseries in which whooping-cough occurred 55 per cent of 33 vaccinated children and 63 per cent of 30 unvaccinated children were attacked. Similar unfavourable results have been reported by others. Doull and his colleagues (1939) described a trial, comprising 479 vaccinated and 496 unvaccinated children who were the older siblings of the former, in which the numbers of cases of pertussis in the two groups were 74 and 94 respectively. Siegel and Goldberger (1937), in a trial in a tuberculosis sanatorium, reported attack rates in children exposed to the disease of 53 per cent in the vaccinated and 58 per cent in the unvaccinated groups.

On the other hand, the majority of vaccination studies, most of which were made in the United States of America and Canada, indicated that pertussis vaccine produced a significant degree of

A Medical Research Council Investigation. Members of the Whooping-cough Immunization Committee of the Medical Research Council: Professor S. P. Bedson, F.R.S. (chairman), Dr. W. C. Cockburn, Dr. E. T. Conybeare, Professor R. Cruickshank, Professor A. W. Downie, Professor A. Bradford Hill, Dr. P. L. Kendrick, Dr. J. Knowelden, Professor J. W. McLeod, F.R.S., Dr. H. J. Parish, Mr. A. F. B. Standfast, Dr. G. S. Wilson, Dr. D. G. Evans (secretary).

Reprinted from the *British Medical Journal*, 1951, i, 1464.

protection. Many of these studies were reviewed by Felton and Willard (1944) and by Tudor Lewis (1946). The first hopeful results were observed by Zachariassen (Madsen, 1933) in two epidemics in the Faroe Islands. A plain vaccine was used prepared from freshly isolated strains of *Haemophilus pertussis*. In the first epidemic, vaccination was begun during the outbreak and was found to have no effect on incidence, although it was reported to have reduced the severity of the disease. In the second epidemic, vaccination was completed shortly before the outbreak occurred, and of the 1,832 vaccinated children 75 per cent contracted pertussis, compared with 98.2 per cent among the 446 unvaccinated children. Encouraging results were later obtained by Sauer (1937), who used a plain vaccine prepared from strains which fulfilled the criteria for phase I *H. pertussis* described by Leslie and Gardner (1931). In this investigation Sauer vaccinated 1,122 children, and reported that of 128 who were subsequently exposed to pertussis, 94 in their own homes, only six developed the disease. Of the many studies made with plain vaccine the best known are those conducted by Kendrick and Eldering (1939). These studies comprised a total of 4,212 children, divided into vaccinated and unvaccinated groups which were similar in a number of respects. Of children exposed to infection in the home 34.9 per cent in the vaccinated group contracted pertussis compared with 89.4 per cent in the unvaccinated group.

In the majority of studies with plain vaccine the total dosage was relatively large in volume (sometimes 7 ml.) and in numbers of organisms (70 to 120 thousand million), and was given in three to five injections. More recently investigations have been made to determine whether effective protection could be obtained with alum-precipitated pertussis vaccine when given in smaller doses than those used with plain vaccines. Bell (1941, 1948) made two well-controlled trials, the first with alum-precipitated vaccine alone and the second with alum-precipitated combined pertussis vaccine and diphtheria toxoid. In each trial the total dose of vaccine was 20 thousand million organisms, given in two inoculations at an interval of four weeks. The incidence of the disease among the unvaccinated children was three to four times greater than that among the vaccinated. Kendrick (1942, 1943) also obtained good results with an alum-precipitated vaccine which was given in three doses.

In view of these favourable reports the Whooping-cough Immunization Committee concluded that the vaccines used in their trials in 1942–4 differed in some material though unknown way from those vaccines which had been shown to give protection. The Committee therefore decided to carry out a new series of field trials with a number of vaccines prepared in different laboratories and to include vaccines of American origin which in previous studies had been reported to give substantial protection.

The first trial in this new series was in Oxford City. Three batches of Sauer vaccine, prepared by Parke Davis and Co., of Detroit, were tested. In all, 1,530 children between the ages of six months and five years were inoculated, 785 with pertussis vaccine and 745 with 'anticatarrhal' vaccine containing no *H. pertussis*. After inoculation the children were observed for a period of two to three years. The total number of definite cases of pertussis diagnosed in those children who received pertussis vaccine was 113 and in those who received 'anticatarrhal' vaccine 165, giving attack rates per 1,000 child-months of observation of 5.28 and 8.17 respectively. In addition to these definite cases there were 143 doubtful cases—80 in the group which received pertussis vaccine and 63 in the comparative group. This trial was begun during the war, in 1944, when it was impossible to obtain adequate staff to deal with intensive follow-up investigations. Further, the staff necessary and the number of visits required to ensure the standard of accuracy needed in these trials were, at this early stage, underestimated by the Committee. The follow-up studies, therefore, were in many cases incomplete. For this reason the Committee does not propose to draw any firm conclusions from the results of this early trial, though it appears unlikely that the vaccines were highly effective. The trial, however, provided invaluable information regarding the problems associated with organization, and the subsequent trials, reported below, were planned in the light of experience gained in the Oxford investigation.

GENERAL PLAN OF INVESTIGATION

In all trials a uniform plan was followed. Children between the ages of six and 18 months, whose parents agreed that they should be inoculated, were divided by the method of random sampling into two groups of approximately equal size. *The children in one group were inoculated with pertussis vaccine and are referred to subsequently as 'vaccinated'. Those in the other group were given a similar dose of 'anticatarrhal' vaccine which contained no H. pertussis and are re-*

ferred to subsequently as 'unvaccinated'. After inoculation each child was visited at frequent intervals for a period of two to three years by a nurse-investigator. Neither the parents nor the observers knew whether a child was in the vaccinated or the unvaccinated group.

Five batches of pertussis vaccine from three manufacturers—Parke Davis & Co., of Detroit, the Michigan Department of Health, and Glaxo Laboratories Ltd.—were used in 10 separate field trials in Leeds, Manchester, Tottenham and Edmonton, Wembley, and West Ham. Information on the nature and dosage of the vaccines and the areas to which they were allocated is given in Table 11, 1. The 'anticatarrhal' vaccine was prepared specially for the inquiry by Burroughs Wellcome & Co. It contained killed suspensions of *Staphylococcus aureus, Streptococcus pneumoniae, Corynebacterium hofmannii, and Neisseria catarrhalis*, and was similar in turbidity to the plain pertussis vaccines. It was dispensed in the same type of bottle as that used for the pertussis vaccines.

PROCEDURE IN THE FIELD

In each trial area a 'pertussis team' was appointed comprising a full- or part-time medical officer, a nurse-investigator for each group of 400–500 children, and a full- or part-time clerk. The members of the teams in most areas were appointed from the staff of the local health department who had had close associations in their routine work with mothers of young children and experience in the administration and day-to-day work of diphtheria immunization schemes. Where it was not possible to make such arrangements the teams were appointed by the Committee in collaboration with the medical officer of health.

Propaganda

Parents with children aged 6–18 months were given a pamphlet, to which was attached a parent's consent form, explaining the scheme. The pamphlet was either sent by post, distributed at welfare centres, or handed to the mothers by a health visitor on her routine visits. In the pamphlet it was made clear that the vaccines were being tested, that it was necessary to inoculate some of the children with a substance which was not whooping-cough vaccine, and that parents and observers would not know until the end of the investigation whether a child was in the vaccinated or the unvaccinated group.

TABLE **11**, 1   *Trial Areas, Vaccines, and Dosage Schedules*

Trial Area	Vaccine				Dosage Schedule	
	Batch	Manufacturer	Description	Conc. in Millions of Organisms/ml. (Amer. Count)*	Doses at Monthly Intervals (ml.)	Total Dose in Millions of Organisms
Manchester	Sauer 087860	Parke Davis & Co., Detroit	Plain suspension	15,000	1, 2, 3	90,000
Manchester, Tottenham and Edmonton, Wembley	Michigan D231	Michigan Dept. of Health	,,	10,000	1, 2, 3	60,000
Leeds	Glaxo 61	Glaxo Laboratories	Alum precipitated	50,000	0·75, 0·75, 0·75	112,000
Leeds West Ham	Glaxo 174 Glaxo 174	,, ,,	,, ,,	50,000 50,000	0·75, 0·75, 0·75 0·5, 0·5, 1	112,000 100,000
Manchester, Tottenham and Edmonton, Wembley	Michigan A236	Michigan Dept. of Health	Plain suspension	10,000	1, 2, 3	60,000

*Concentrations of all vaccines are given in terms of the American count, as British and American vaccines, with the same labelled concentration, differ considerably in density (MacFarlan, Topley, and Fisher, 1945).

In addition, posters were displayed in welfare centres and nursery schools, and in some areas the medical officers of health publicized the scheme with the help of the Press, the cinema, and the radio. A letter was sent to all general practitioners in the area giving them details of the plan and inviting them to co-operate by giving advice on the scheme to parents and by informing the health department of suspected cases of pertussis among trial children under their care.

Allocation of Children to the Vaccinated and Unvaccinated Groups

On receipt of signed consent forms from the parents, children with no previous history of pertussis or of previous inoculation with pertussis vaccine were classified by sex and placed in one of the following age groups: 6–8, 9–11, 12–14, and 15–17 months; a few children were accepted just after they had reached the age of 18 months. For each age and sex group, sheets were previously drawn up on which vaccine letters A, B, C, and D in random order were repeated a sufficient number of times to deal with all expected volunteers in the appropriate age and sex group. As each child's name was received it was written in the first vacant space on the appropriate sheet, and the vaccine letter opposite the child's name determined what it should receive and was inserted on the child's record card.

Although four vaccine letters were used, two of them in fact indicated the pertussis vaccine being tested in the trial and the other two the 'anticatarrhal' vaccine. It was thought that by employing this method field-workers would be less likely to distinguish the pertussis vaccine from the 'anticatarrhal' vaccine. As the early trials progressed it became evident that more cases of pertussis were occurring in children inoculated with vaccines A and C—the 'anticatarrhal' vaccines—than in children with vaccines B and D—the pertussis vaccines. There was also some difference in the incidence of slight inoculation reactions between the pertussis and 'anticatarrhal' vaccines. To ensure, therefore, that follow-up observations remained unbiased, the vaccine letter on each record card was covered by a thick label until the end of the investigation or until the duration and severity of an attack of pertussis had been recorded on the card.

Inoculation of Children

When sufficient names had been obtained, clinic sessions were arranged on an appointment system. On arrival at the clinic the children were inoculated with vaccine from the bottle labelled with the appropriate vaccine letter. Three inoculations were given at monthly intervals. In general the inoculations were given intra-muscularly, although in some areas at the beginning of the trials they were given subcutaneously. One child in every five was visited 24–72 hours after each inoculation to determine the severity of the reaction.

If a child failed to attend for the first inoculation, a second and, if necessary, a third appointment was arranged, and if these were not kept, no further steps were taken and the child was excluded from the trial. Further appointments were also made for those children who failed to attend for the second or third inoculation, and if they still failed to attend they were visited to ascertain the reason. In most cases a satisfactory reason was obtained.

When each child received the last inoculation the mother was given a report slip in a stamped envelope addressed to the health depart-ment and was instructed to post this slip if the child had been in contact with whooping-cough or had developed suspicious symp-toms.

Follow-up Observations

When the course of inoculations was completed each child was visited monthly by a nurse-investigator until the end of the in-vestigation or until he was excluded from the trial. On the first visit the information already entered on the record card was checked and notes were made of the duration of breast-feeding and of the number of other children under 14 years of age living in the house. On subsequent monthly visits information was obtained on exposures to pertussis, the incidence of upper respiratory-tract infections, the history of diphtheria immunization and smallpox vaccination, and the incidence of measles, chicken-pox, bronchopneumonia, and diphtheria.

When it was found, either on a routine visit or by receipt of the report slip from the parent, that a child had been exposed to pertussis or had developed suspicious symptoms, repeated visits were made to determine the diagnosis and to assess the severity of the attack if it proved to be pertussis. So far as possible these special visits were made by the senior nurse-investigator or by the medical member of the pertussis team. During the special visits a detailed history of the intimacy and duration of exposure was obtained and, where possible, nasopharyngeal swabs were taken. Sometimes swabs were also taken from the presumed infecting case. The mother was asked to make notes of the number of paroxysms during each 24 hours at the height of the disease. Notes were also made by the observers of the nature and severity of complications. At the end of the illness the degree of severity of the attack (see footnote to Table **11,** 7) and the duration of the cough were recorded.

Once children who had developed pertussis were considered to have made a complete recovery, nurse-investigators were not required to visit them more often than every three months, although in fact in most areas it was found convenient to continue the monthly visits. These visits were necessary to obtain information on diphtheria immunization, on smallpox vaccination, and on the incidence of other infectious diseases.

NUMBER OF CHILDREN AND DURATION OF TRIALS

The number of children whose parents agreed to take part in the investigation was 8,927, of whom 4,515 were allocated to the vaccinated and 4,412 to the unvaccinated group (Table **11,** 2). Of these, 7,558 completed the course of inoculations—3,801 in the vaccinated and 3,757 in the unvaccinated group. Most of the remainder, 1,369 in all, were children whose parents repeatedly failed to keep appointments for the first inoculation. After the first inoculation few parents defaulted, and those that did had good reasons, such as prolonged illness in the child or removal from the trial area. The period for observation began as soon as each child received its third inoculation. After the completion of inoculations, 848 children were lost from observation at varying intervals, in most cases because they left the area. Other reasons for withdrawal are given in the footnote to Table **11,** 2. Observations on these children, up to the time when they were lost from the investigation, were included in the analysis. At the end of the investigation 6,710 children remained; 3,358 were in the vaccinated and 3,352 in the unvaccinated group.

Trials were begun between November, 1946, and April, 1948, and were completed during 1950. In all trials, except that in West Ham, the inoculations were given within a period of three to six months; in West Ham most of the children were inoculated during the first

TABLE 11, 2 *Numbers of Children in All 10 Trials*

	Vaccinated (Inoculated with Pertussis Vaccine)			Unvaccinated (Inoculated with 'Anticatarrhal' Vaccine)			Total
	Male	Female	Both Sexes	Male	Female	Both Sexes	
Total children entered for inoculation	2,182	2,333	4,515	2,273	2,139	4,412	8,927
Excluded before completion of inoculations*	359	355	714	341	314	655	1,369
Total number given 3 inoculations	1,823	1,978	3,801	1,932	1,825	3,757	7,558
Excluded during follow-up period†	218	225	443	213	192	405	848
Total number remaining at end of follow-up period	1,605	1,753	3,358	1,719	1,633	3,352	6,710

* Persistent defaulters; developed or were in contact with pertussis; moved from area; illness or death not associated with pertussis or inoculation.

† Moved from area; reinoculated by private doctor; death not associated with pertussis or inoculation; unco-operative parents. Observations on these children, up to the time when they were lost from the investigation, were included in the analysis.

year of the investigation. On the average, each child was observed for 27 months after his third inoculation; the average period varied from 23 to 30 months in the separate trials. The period of each trial in relation to the incidence of notified cases of pertussis in the general population is shown in Fig. **11,** 1.

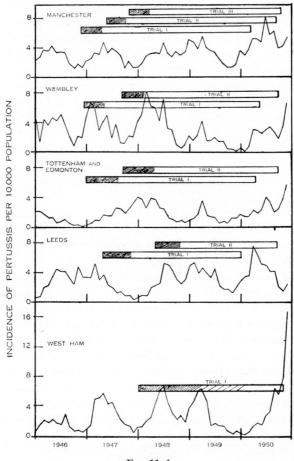

FIG. **11,** 1

Chart showing notified incidence of pertussis per 10,000 population (all ages), from 1946 to 1950, in the trial areas. The horizontal blocks indicate the period of the trials and the shaded areas the period during which the inoculations were given. In the West Ham trial the densely shaded area indicates the period during which the majority of children were inoculated.

10   S.M.M.

SIMILARITY OF VACCINATED AND UNVACCINATED GROUPS

The method of allocation of the children to vaccinated and un-vaccinated groups was found, by examining certain relevant attributes of the children, to give two groups of closely similar character. It is clear from Table **11,** 3, which relates to all 10 trials, that the two groups were similar in the number of children, their average age, the average number of children (including the trial child) under 14 years of age in the families, and the average duration of the period over which they were observed. Furthermore, the similarity of the two groups was evident from the information relating to breast-feeding, infectious diseases other than pertussis, immunization against diphtheria, and vaccination against smallpox. In each separate trial also, the two groups were similar in character.

REACTIONS TO INOCULATIONS

One child in every five in the vaccinated and unvaccinated groups was visited 24–72 hours after each inoculation. With the plain vaccines no severe local or general reactions were observed, although a number of children developed a rise in temperature within 24 hours of inoculation, and in some the site of inoculation was red and swollen for one to two days. In only a few instances were the reactions such that the mother refused to co-operate further. There was no apparent increase in the incidence of reactions after the second and third inoculations. In trial areas where alum-precipitated vaccines were used, six children developed sterile abscesses.

Byers and Moll (1948), Toomey (1949), and others, in the United States of America, and Anderson and Morris (1950), in this country, reported the occurrence of convulsions and encephalopathies as rare complications of pertussis vaccination. Martin (1950), McCloskey (1950), Geffen (1950), and Bradford Hill and Knowelden (1950) drew attention to the occurrence of poliomyelitis in which the paralysis affected with undue frequency the limb which had recently been injected with diphtheria or pertussis or with the combined prophylactic. These reports were made while the present studies were in progress, and the records of all children who had completed the course of inoculations were carefully scrutinized and most of the

TABLE 11, 3 *Similarity of Vaccinated and Unvaccinated Groups in All 10 Trials*

	Vaccinated			Unvaccinated			Grand Total
	Male	Female	Total	Male	Female	Total	
Total No. of children given 3 inoculations	1,823	1,978	*3,801*	1,932	1,825	*3,757*	7,558
Average age (months)	*12.1*	*12.3*	*12.2*	*12.2*	*12.2*	*12.2*	*12.2*
Average duration of observation per child (months)	*26.9*	*27.2*	*27.1*	*27.2*	*27.2*	*27.2*	*27.1*
Average No. of children under 14 years per household	*1.8*	*1.8*	*1.8*	*1.8*	*1.8*	*1.8*	*1.8*
Breast-feeding:							
No. breast-fed	1,457	1,575	*3,032*	1,540	1,471	*3,011*	6,043
Average duration of breast-feeding (months)	*5.4*	*5.3*	*5.3*	*5.3*	*5.4*	*5.4*	*5.4*
No. not breast-fed	321	350	*671*	344	308	*652*	1,323
No. where history not known	45	53	*98*	48	46	*94*	192
No. of cases of certain other infectious diseases in children during the trial:							
Measles	440	480	*920*	471	420	*891*	1,811
Chicken-pox	138	151	*289*	139	141	*280*	569
Bronchopneumonia	50	45	*95*	53	41	*94*	189
Diphtheria	0	1	*1*	1	0	*1*	2
Total	628	677	*1,305*	664	602	*1,266*	2,751
No. known to be:							
Immunized against diphtheria	1,592	1,736	*3,328*	1,716	1,609	*3,325*	6,653
Vaccinated against smallpox	1,151	1,240	*2,391*	1,205	1,141	*2,346*	4,737

children who had not completed the course were revisited. None of the children had a history of convulsions, and in none did poliomyelitis develop withing the arbitrarily chosen period of two months after inoculation. In only two trials—Manchester II and Leeds I—were the children inoculated during periods of high incidence of poliomyelitis, and as the numbers of children were relatively small the risk of any one child developing poliomyelitis was remote.

INCIDENCE AND SEVERITY OF PERTUSSIS

Attack Rates per 1,000 Child-months of Observation

In all ten trials the total number of cases of pertussis diagnosed in the vaccinated groups was 149 and in the unvaccinated groups 687 (Table **11,** 4). The corresponding attack rates per 1,000 child-months of observation were 1.45 and 6.72—a ratio of 1:4.6 This difference in attack rates is clearly significant. In both vaccinated and unvaccinated groups the attack rates in females were higher than in males, an observation in agreement with previous epidemiological studies.

It is also evident (Table **11,** 5) that in each separate trial the attack rate in the vaccinated was substantially less than in the unvaccinated group, but the ratio of the attack rates was not the same for all trials. These differences in ratios are taken into account when comparing the potency of vaccines (Table **11,** 14).

Attack Rates in Children Known to have been Exposed to Pertussis

Analysis of information on the exposure of the children to pertussis showed that such occurrences could be conveniently divided into two categories: (1) 'Home exposures'—children exposed in their own homes to infection in one or more siblings; (2) 'other exposures'—children exposed to infection in day nurseries, in nursery schools, at parties, in cinemas, in buses, and while playing outside the home with other children. The figures for each of these categories are given for each trial and also for all 10 trials (Table **11,** 6). In the table the number of exposures to pertussis is recorded, not the number of children exposed, as some children were exposed on more than one occasion. Exposure to infection could also occur *after* a child in the trial had developed pertussis, but such exposures were not recorded.

TABLE **11**, 4 *Number of Cases of Pertussis and Attack Rates per 1,000 Child-months of Observation in Vaccinated and Unvaccinated Groups in All 10 Trials*

	Vaccinated				Unvaccinated			
	No. of Children given 3 Inoculations	Duration of Observation* (Child-months)	Cases of Pertussis	Attack Rate per 1,000 Child-months	No. of Children given 3 Inoculations	Duration of Observation* (Child-months)	Cases of Pertussis	Attack Rate per 1,000 Child-months
Males	1,823	49,105	68	1·38	1,932	52,472	327	6·23
Females	1,978	53,856	81	1·50	1,825	49,708	360	7·24
Both sexes	3,801	102,961	149	1·45	3,757	102,180	687	6·72

* Observation began from the date of the third inoculation

TABLE **11**, 5 *Number of Cases of Pertussis and Attack Rates per 1,000 Child-months of Observation in Vaccinated and Unvaccinated Groups in Each Trial*

Trial Area	Area-trial No.	Vaccine	Vaccinated				Unvaccinated			
			No. of Children given 3 Inoculations	Duration of Observation (Child-months)	Cases of Pertussis	Attack Rate per 1,000 Child-months	No. of Children given 3 Inoculations	Duration of Observation (Child-months)	Cases of Pertussis	Attack Rate per 1,000 Child-months
Manchester	I	Sauer 087860	415	12,125	32	2·64	449	13,241	89	6·72
Tottenham and Edmonton	I	Michigan D231	167	4,394	3	0·68	183	4,726	33	6·98
Wembley	I	Michigan D231	142	3,680	2	0·54	144	3,828	33	8·62
Manchester	II	Michigan D231	321	9,522	12	1·26	328	9,762	63	6·45
Leeds	I	Glaxo 61	489	13,392	27	2·02	464	12,864	85	6·61
Leeds	II	Glaxo 174	484	11,488	25	2·18	425	10,215	97	9·50
West Ham	I	Glaxo 174	727	16,768	29	1·73	771	17,464	92	5·27
Manchester	III	Michigan A236	460	13,445	11	0·82	458	13,828	94	6·80
Tottenham and Edmonton	II	Michigan A236	306	9,307	5	0·54	257	7,471	49	6·56
Wembley	II	Michigan A236	290	8,840	3	0·34	278	8,781	52	5·92
Totals			3,801	102,961	149	1·45	3,757	102,180	687	6·72

TABLE **11**, 6

Number of Cases of Pertussis and Percentage Attack Rates by Type of Exposure in Vaccinated and Unvaccinated Groups in Each Trial

Trial Area	Area-trial No.	Vaccine	'Home Exposures'						'Other Exposures'						No. of Cases with no History of Exposure	
			Vaccinated			Unvaccinated			Vaccinated			Unvaccinated				
			No. of Exposures	No. of Cases	% Cases/Exposures	No. of Exposures	No. of Cases	% Cases/Exposures	No. of Exposures	No. of Cases	% Cases/Exposures	No. of Exposures	No. of Cases	% Cases/Exposures	Vaccinated	Unvaccinated
Manchester	I	Sauer 087860	36	8	22·2	20	17	85·0	100	15	15·0	73	24	32·9	9	48
Tottenham and Edmonton	I	Michigan D231	12	0	0	15	14	93·3	20	1	5·0	21	9	42·9	2	10
Wembley	II	Michigan D231	9	1	11·1	12	8	66·7	33	0	0	42	12	28·6	1	13
Manchester	I	Michigan D231	20	2	10·0	12	9	75·0	78	5	6·4	65	26	40·0	5	28
Leeds	I	Glaxo 61	23	7	30·4	21	19	90·5	69	6	8·7	71	29	40·8	14	37
Leeds	II	Glaxo 174	29	7	24·1	24	21	87·5	60	9	15·0	72	28	38·9	9	48
West Ham	I	Glaxo 174	18	7	38·9	19	18	94·7	23	4	17·4	36	22	61·1	18	52
Manchester	III	Michigan A 236	26	3	11·5	21	19	90·5	112	6	5·4	90	35	38·9	2	40
Tottenham and Edmonton	II	Michigan A236	14	2	14·3	16	15	93·8	26	1	3·8	22	12	54·5	2	22
Wembley	II	Michigan A236	16	0	0	13	11	84·6	45	0	0	69	16	23·2	3	25
Totals			203	37	18·2	173	151	87·3	566	47	8·3	561	213	38·0	65	323

The average attack rate in the 'home exposures' for all 10 trials was 18.2 per cent in the vaccinated and 87.3 per cent in the unvaccinated groups. A high incidence of pertussis occurred in the unvaccinated group of each trial; in only one trial was the attack rate less than 75 per cent. The attack rates in the vaccinated groups varied considerably with the different trials, and this variation is considered when comparing the potency of the vaccines (Table 11, 14).

With the 'other exposures', the average attack rate for all 10 trials was 8.3 per cent in the vaccinated and 38.0 per cent in the unvaccinated groups. In this category the attack rates in both groups varied, but the variation was not as great in the unvaccinated as in the vaccinated groups.

A history of exposure was not obtained for every case, and 65 children in the vaccinated and 323 in the unvaccinated groups developed pertussis without the source of infection being known.

It is of interest that in the 'home exposures', the 'other exposures', and in children with no history of exposure the ratio of the incidence of pertussis in the vaccinated to that in the unvaccinated children was almost identical—namely, 1:4.8, 1:4.6, and 1:5.0.

Severity and Duration of Attack

The assessment of the degree of severity of attack was based, in general, on the parent's record of the number of paroxysms in 24 hours during the height of the disease (see footnote to Table 11, 7). Parents varied in their ability to keep accurate records of the number of paroxysms and, in any event, no record could be made of the severity of each paroxysm. As a general guide to severity of attack, however, the method was valuable, particularly as neither parents nor members of the team knew whether any one child suffering from the disease was in the vaccinated or the unvaccinated group.

The severity of attack for cases in both the vaccinated and the unvaccinated groups for all 10 trials is given in Table 11, 7. Degrees of severity of 1 and 2 may be considered as mild, and 3, 4, and 5 as moderate, severe, and complicated attacks. In the vaccinated 73.2 per cent of cases were mild compared with 24.1 per cent in the unvaccinated groups. Two complicated cases occurred in the vaccinated, compared with 28 in the unvaccinated. There were no deaths in either group.

TABLE **11**, 7

Degree of Severity of Attack in Diagnosed Cases of Pertussis in All 10 Trials

	Vaccinated (149 Cases)					Unvaccinated (687 Cases)					
	Degree of Severity*					Degree of Severity*					
	1	2	3	4	5	1	2	3	4	5	Not Stated
No. of cases	32	77	29	9	2	17	148	281	212	28	1
Percentage	21·5	51·7	19·5	6·0	1·3	2·5	21·6	40·9	30·9	4·1	
	73·2		26·8			24·1		75·9			

* 1 = An abortive attack, with or without occasional paroxysms confirmed bacteriologically. 2 = Fewer than 10 paroxysms in 24 hours at height of disease. 3 = 10–20 paroxysms in 24 hours at height of disease. 4 = More than 20 paroxysms in 24 hours at height of disease. 5 = Attack complicated by bronchopneumonia, atelectasis, etc.

TABLE **11**, 8

Duration of Cough in Diagnosed Cases of Pertussis in All 10 Trials

	Vaccinated (149 Cases)					Unvaccinated (687 Cases)					
	Duration (Weeks)					Duration (Weeks)					
	Under 4	4–	6–	8–	10+	Under 4	4–	6–	8–	10+	Not Stated
No. of cases	20	46	47	15	21	15	82	178	159	240	13
Percentage	13·4	30·9	31·5	10·1	14·1	2·2	12·2	26·4	23·6	35·6	
	44·3		55·7			14·4		85·6			

An additional indication of severity was obtained by recording the duration of the cough (Table **11,** 8). By this method also, a difference between the two groups was observed: 44.3 per cent of cases in the vaccinated had a cough for less than six weeks, compared with 14.4 per cent in the unvaccinated groups.

Similar differences in severity and duration of attack between vaccinated and unvaccinated children were observed when each trial was considered separately.

Duration of Immunity

An analysis was made which indicated that during the period of observation there was no waning in the degree of protection afforded by the pertussis vaccines. Attack rates at intervals after inoculation are given in Table **11,** 9 for those vaccinated and unvaccinated

TABLE **11,** 9

Percentage Attack Rates in 'Home Exposures' at Intervals after Inoculation in Vaccinated and Unvaccinated Children in All 10 Trials

Period after Third Inoculation (Months)	Vaccinated			Unvaccinated		
	No. of Exposures	No. of Cases	% Cases/ Exposures	No. of Exposures	No. of Cases	% Cases/ Exposures
0–5	54	8	15	49	44	90
6–11	50	10	20	45	38	84
12–17	36	6	17	41	39	95
18–23	36	8	22	22	18	82
24 and over	27	5	19	16	12	75
Totals	203	37	18	173	151	87

children who were exposed to infection in their own homes. It is evident that the attack rate in the unvaccinated children was almost constant during the whole period of observation, and it is therefore justifiable to compare the corresponding attack rate in the vaccinated children. Throughout the period of observation the attack rate in the vaccinated children remained at approximately 20 per cent and showed no evidence of increasing even two years after inoculation.

A further analysis was made for each of the five vaccines separately, and for none of them, within the limits of the small numbers of cases involved, was there evidence of waning immunity during the period of observation.

Occurrence of Coughs not Diagnosed as Pertussis After Exposure to Infection

After reported exposure to pertussis particular attention was paid to all children for a period of 42 days. During this period a number of children developed a cough which was not paroxysmal in character. Most of those in whom the cough lasted for more than a week were swabbed. The average number of swabs taken from each child was 1.5. From some of these cases *H. pertussis* was isolated, and they were recorded as cases of pertussis with a degree of severity of 1, but in the majority no bacteriological evidence of pertussis infection was obtained.

The duration of the cough in these cases is given in Table **11,** 10. It is evident that in 90 per cent of the children the cough was of short

TABLE **11,** 10

Duration of Cough in Children who Did not Develop Pertussis but who had a Cough which began Between 7 and 42 Days After Known Exposure to Pertussis

	Vaccinated (231 Children)					Unvaccinated (129 Children)				
	Duration (Weeks)					Duration (Weeks)				
	Under 2	2–	3–	4–	5+	Under 2	2–	3–	4–	5+
No. of cases	111	61	29	20	10	45	46	27	5	6
Percentage	48·0	26·4	12·6	8·7	4·3	34·9	35·6	20·9	3·9	4·7
	87·0			13·0		91·4			8·6	

duration, lasting for less than four weeks, and that there was no pronounced difference between the vaccinated and unvaccinated

TABLE **11**, 11

Incidence of Cough in Children who Did not Develop Pertussis After Exposure

	Vaccinated	Unvaccinated
Total No. of 'home' and 'other' exposures	769	734
No. of exposures followed by pertussis	84	364
No. of exposures not followed by pertussis	685	370
No. of cases of cough not diagnosed as pertussis	231	129
Percentage of cases of cough in exposures not followed by pertussis	34	35

groups in its average duration. Further, from Table **11**, 11 it is evident that the incidence of this type of cough in those who were exposed to pertussis but did not develop it was similar in both groups. For these reasons it was considered that most of these cases were not due to infection with *H. pertussis.*

BACTERIOLOGICAL OBSERVATIONS

Swabs were taken from 806 (96.4 per cent) of the 836 clinically diagnosed cases (Table **11**, 12). Postnasal swabs were used in the early stages of the investigation, but later it was found that pernasal swabs gave better results (Cockburn and Holt, 1948) and these were then used in all areas. So far as possible the swabs were obtained in the first two weeks of the disease and the average number of swabs per child was 1.85 for all trials; the figures for the separate trials are also given in Table **11**, 12. *H. pertussis* was isolated from 59.8 per cent of the cases which were swabbed and from 57.7 per cent of all cases diagnosed. The proportion of clinical cases confirmed bacteriologically varied from area to area, but the percentage in the vaccinated was similar to that in the unvaccinated group for each trial and for all trials together (Table **11**, 13).

Haemophilus parapertussis was isolated from 24 children with clinical symptoms of pertussis. None of these cases occurred in Tottenham and Edmonton, nine were in West Ham, and the remainder were distributed in the other trial areas. There were 10 cases in the vaccinated and 14 in the unvaccinated group. Nearly all were mild; in 21 the degree of severity was 3, and in 18 the cough lasted

TABLE **11,** 12 *Number and Percentage of Cases from which H. pertussis was Isolated by Swab Culture in Both Vaccinated and Unvaccinated Groups in Each Trial*

Trial Area	Area-trial No.	Vaccine	Cases of Pertussis	No. of Cases Swabbed	Average No. of Swabs per Swabbed Child	No. of Cases giving Pos. Swab	Percentage of Total Cases giving Pos. Swab	Percentage of Swabbed Cases giving Pos. Swab
Manchester	I	Sauer 087860	121	119	2·26	76	62·8	63·9
Tottenham and Edmonton	I	Michigan D231	36	36	1·67	18	50·0	50·0
Wembley	I	Michigan D231	35	35	2·03	24	68·6	68·6
Manchester	II	Michigan D231	75	72	2·14	43	57·3	59·7
Leeds	I	Glaxo 61	112	104	1·63	67	59·8	64·4
Leeds	II	Glaxo 174	122	113	1·37	79	64·8	69·9
West Ham	I	Glaxo 174	121	121	1·94	44	36·4	36·4
Manchester	III	Michigan A236	105	104	2·00	75	71·4	72·1
Tottenham and Edmonton	II	Michigan A236	54	48	1·52	23	42·6	47·9
Wembley	II	Michigan A236	55	54	1·85	33	60·0	61·1
Totals			836	806	1·85	482	57·7	59·8

TABLE **11**, 13

Number and Percentage of Bacteriologically Confirmed Cases in
Vaccinated and Unvaccinated Groups in All 10 Trials

Vaccinated			Unvaccinated		
Cases of Pertussis	Confirmed Bacteriologically		Cases of Pertussis	Confirmed Bacteriologically	
	No.	%		No.	%
149	83	55·7	687	399	58·1

less than six weeks. *Haemophilus bronchisepticus* was isolated from one case with clinical symptoms of pertussis which occurred in Leeds. The child had a cough for six weeks and the degree of severity was estimated as 3. There have been previous reports of the isolation of *H. parapertussis* from cases clinically diagnosed as pertussis (Bradford and Slavin, 1937; Eldering and Kendrick, 1938; Miller, Saito and Silverberg, 1941; Cruickshank and Knox, 1946; Sohier and Fauchet, 1949), and a case, with symptoms of pertussis, from which *H. bronchisepticus* was isolated has also been described (Brown, 1926).

COMPARISON OF THE PROPHYLACTIC POTENCY OF THE VACCINES

It is not possible from the results of these trials to make a direct comparison of the prophylactic potency of the vaccines, as they were not tested in the same area and at the same time. In Table **11**, 14, however, the attack rates in children have been compiled for each vaccine and the corresponding attack rates in the unvaccinated children are also given. It is evident that the attack rate per 1,000 child-months of observation in the unvaccinated children for each of these vaccine groups was almost constant, varying only from 6.48 to 7.04. This was no doubt due to the fact that the incidence of pertussis in the general population, over the whole period of the investigation, was alike in each trial area and that no large epidemic occurred (Table **11**, 1). There was only slight variation also in the attack rate in the unvaccinated children exposed in the home—from 79.5 per cent to 90.7 per cent—and considerable uniformity was evident in the

TABLE **11,** 14

Attack Rates in Vaccinated and Unvaccinated Groups for Each Batch of Vaccine Tested

Vaccine	Attack Rate per 1,000 Child-months		% Attack Rate in 'Home Exposures'		% Attack Rate in 'Other Exposures'	
	Vac-cinated	Unvac-cinated	Vac-cinated	Unvac-cinated	Vac-cinated	Unvac-cinated
Sauer 087860	2·64	6·72	22·2	85·0	15·0	32·9
Michigan D231	0·97	7·04	7·3	79·5	4·6	36·7
Michigan A236	0·60	6·48	8·9	90·0	3·8	34·8
Glaxo 61	2·02	6·61	30·4	90·5	8·7	40·8
Glaxo 174	1·91	6·83	29·8	90·7	15.7	46·3

attack rate in the unvaccinated children in the 'other exposures' category—from 32.9 per cent to 46.3 per cent.

It is justifiable, because of these similarities in the incidence of pertussis in the unvaccinated groups, to compare the prophylactic value of the different vaccines. Each vaccine gave substantial protection. It is evident that for the trial with the Sauer vaccine the ratio of the attack rate per 1,000 child-months of observation in the vaccinated to that in the unvaccinated group was 1:2.5. There was a slightly greater degree of protection with each of the two Glaxo vaccines, where the corresponding ratios were 1:3.3 and 1:3.6. The two Michigan vaccines, however, gave a considerably greater degree of protection than any of the others; the ratios with these were 1:7.3 and 1:10.8. Similar differences in the degree of protection are revealed by the rates of attack in 'home exposures' and 'other exposures'.

FURTHER STUDIES

It is evident from the results of these field trials that pertussis vaccines may vary considerably in their protective property. This variation in potency is possibly related to the many variables concerned in the preparation of vaccines, such as the selection of strains, the composition of the medium on which the organisms are grown, the method of harvesting the growth, and the nature of the killing and preservative agents. In these trials the vaccines prepared by the

Michigan Department of Health proved to be more potent in the field than any of the others tested, and full details of the method of preparation have been made available to the Committee. Vaccines prepared in this country by the Michigan method are now being tested in the field in comparison with a new batch of Michigan vaccine with the object of ascertaining whether the method, in the hands of British manufacturers, gives vaccines of high potency. Some of the field trials with these new vaccines have already been begun in Manchester, Oxford, Cardiff, Poole, Leeds, Tottenham, and Wembley.

Although the Michigan method of preparation may, in the hands of others, prove to give vaccine of high prophylactic potency, it would not be advisable to adopt the method as a standard procedure, as other methods may be equally satisfactory or even better. The ideal method of controlling the prophylactic activity of pertussis vaccine would be to adopt a reference vaccine which has been shown to give substantial protection in the field and in terms of which the potency of other vaccines could be assayed by means of comparative tests made in the laboratory. Such a procedure is being investigated in the United States of America by the Biologics Control Laboratory of the National Institutes of Health and the Michigan Department of Health (Pittman and Lieberman, 1948; Kendrick, Updyke, and Eldering, 1947, 1949), and a provisional reference pertussis vaccine has been adopted (United States Biologics Control Laboratory, 1948).

The method of comparative testing employed by these workers necessitates the immunization of mice with pertussis vaccine and the determination of the level of immunity by the intracerebral challenge injection of virulent *H. pertussis*. It is, however, not yet known whether there is a correlation between this laboratory test and the ability of vaccines to induce immunity in children. It was therefore decided to investigate this problem by testing the prophylactic property of a number of vaccines in children and comparing the results with those obtained by laboratory tests. With this aim in view, trials were begun in Manchester, Oxford, Cardiff, Poole, Walthamstow, and Leyton, and have now been in progress for two years. The results will be reported later.

SUMMARY AND CONCLUSIONS

Controlled trials were made to assess the prophylactic value of pertussis vaccine in children. Those between the ages of 6 and 18 months whose parents consented to take part in the study were divided by the method of random sampling into two groups of equal size. The groups proved to be strikingly similar in the average age of the trial children, the average number of children in the families, and the average duration of observation. The close similarity of the groups was also evident from a comparative history of breast-feeding, infectious diseases other than pertussis, immunization against diphtheria, and vaccination against smallpox.

The children in one group (referred to as the vaccinated group) were inoculated with pertussis vaccine and those in the other (referred to as the unvaccinated group) with 'anti-catarrhal' vaccine containing no *H. pertussis*. Each child was visited at frequent intervals for a period of two to three years by a nurse-investigator. Neither parents nor observers knew to which group a child had been allocated.

Five batches of pertussis vaccine from three manufacturers— Parke Davis & Co., of Detroit, the Michigan Department of Health and Glaxo Laboratories, Ltd.—were tested. Ten separate field trials were made in five different areas. In all, 7,558 children were inoculated and followed up—3,801 in the vaccinated and 3,757 in the unvaccinated group. With only a few exceptions there were no severe local or general reactions after inoculation. None of the children had convulsions and in none did poliomyelitis develop within two months of inoculation.

In all the trials, 149 vaccinated and 687 unvaccinated children developed pertussis. The corresponding attack rates per 1,000 child-months of observation were 1.45 and 6.72, giving a reduction in the incidence of the disease of 78 per cent. Among children exposed to pertussis in their own homes the attack rates were 18.2 per cent in the vaccinated and 87.3 per cent in the unvaccinated groups. The cases that occurred in the vaccinated were on the average less severe and of shorter duration than those in the unvaccinated children. During the two- to three-year periods of observation there was no evidence of a waning in the degree of protection afforded by the pertussis vaccines.

Swabs were taken from 96.4 per cent of all clinical cases, and in 59.8 per cent a bacteriological confirmation was obtained.

Each batch of vaccine gave substantial protection, but the two batches supplied by the Michigan Department of Health gave a considerably greater degree of protection than the others.

Vaccines prepared in this country according to the method used by the Michigan Department of Health are now being tested in similar field trials. An investigation is also being made in which the immunizing properties of vaccines as indicated by laboratory tests are being compared with their prophylactic value in the field.

REFERENCES

Anderson, I. M., and Morris, D. (1950). *Lancet*, **1**, 537.

Bell, J. A. (1941). *Publ. Hlth Ref., Wash.*, **56**, 1535.

Bell, J. A. (1948). *J. Amer. med. Ass.*, **137**, 1276.

Bradford, W. L., and Slavin, B. (1937). *Amer. J. publ. Hlth.*, **27**, 1277.

Brown, J. H. (1926). *Bull. Johns Hopk. Hosp.* **38**, 147.

Byers, R. K., and Moll, F. C. (1948). *Pediatrics*, **1**, 437.

Cockburn, W. C., and Holt, H. D. (1948). *Mon. Bull. Minist. Hlth. Lab. Serv.* **7**, 156.

Cruickshank, R., and Knox, R. (1946). *Mon. Bull. Minist. Hlth. Lab. Serv.* **5**, 233.

Doull, J. A., Shibley, G. S., Haskin, G. E., Bancroft, H., McClelland, J. E., and Hoelscher, H. (1939). *Amer. J. Dis. Child.* **58**, 691.

Eldering, G., and Kendrick, P. (1938). *J. Bact.* **35**, 561.

Felton, H. M., and Willard, C. Y. (1944). *J. Amer. med. Ass.* **126**, 294.

Geffen, D. H. (1950). *Med. Offr.* **83**, 137.

Hill, A. Bradford, and Knowelden, J. (1950). *Brit. med. J.* **ii**, 1.

Kendrick, P. L. (1942). *Amer. J. publ. Hlth*, **32**, 615.

Kendrick, P. L. (1943). *Amer. J. Hyg.* **38**, 193.

Kendrick, P. L., and Eldering, G. (1939). *Amer. J. Hyg.* (Sect. B), **29**, 133.

Kendrick, P. L. Eldering, G., Dixon, M. K., and Misner, J. (1947). *Amer. J. publ. Hlth.* **37**, 803.

Kendrick, P. L. Updyke, E. L., and Eldering, G. (1949). *Amer. J. publ. Hlth.* **39**, 179.

Leslie, P. H., and Gardner, A. D. (1931). *J. Hyg. Camb.* **31**, 423.

Lewis, J. Tudor (1946). *Med. Offr.* **76**, 5.

McCloskey, B. P. (1950). *Lancet*, **i**, 659.

McFarlan, A. M., Topley, E., and Fisher, M. (1945). *Brit. med. J.* **ii**, 205.

Madsen, T. (1933). *J. Amer. med. Ass.* **101**, 187.

Martin, J. K. (1950). *Arch. Dis. Childh.* **25**, 1.

Miller, J. J., Saito, T. M., and Silverberg, R. J. (1941). *J. Pediat.* **19**, 229.

Pittman, M., and Lieberman, J. E. (1948). *Amer. J. publ. Hlth.* **38**, 15.

Sauer, L. (1937) *J. Amer. med. Ass.* **109**, 487.

Siegel, M., and Goldberger, E. W. (1937). *J. Amer. med. Ass.* **109**, 1088.

Sohier, R., and Fauchet, S. (1949). *Bull. Acad. nat. Méd. Paris*, **133**, 202.

Toomey, J. A. (1949). *J. Amer. med. Ass.* **139**, 488.

United States Biologics Control Laboratory, National Institutes of Health (1948). Minimum requirements for pertussis vaccine.

CHAPTER 12

B.C.G. AND VOLE BACILLUS VACCINES IN THE PREVENTION OF TUBERCULOSIS IN ADOLESCENTS

FIRST REPORT

IT is now more than 30 years since a live vaccine containing B.C.G. (bacille Calmette-Guérin) was first used in man. In the interval B.C.G. vaccination has come to be accepted in many countries as an effective method of preventing progressive tuberculosis, and it has been particularly widely used since 1945. It has, however, been adopted to only a limited extent in Great Britain. Despite the many millions of vaccinations which have been undertaken, there is still disagreement on the value of the vaccine as a preventive measure. In particular, there has been no adequate study of the contribution which it might make to the control of tuberculosis in an industrial community, such as that in Great Britain, with well-developed health services and with relatively low tuberculosis incidence and mortality.

In 1937 Wells discovered the mycobacterium of vole tuberculosis, and later explored the use of a live vaccine containing it. Vole bacillus vaccine has since been used in a few countries, but on a very small scale compared with B.C.G. vaccine. Its value as a preventive measure has also not been fully assessed.

In July, 1949, the Medical Research Council, aware that a clinical trial of these two vaccines was needed to provide essential information, appointed a Tuberculosis Vaccines Clinical Trials Committee to plan and direct an appropriate investigation. The following is the first report of this trial, which is still in progress. It presents pre-

First (Progress) Report to the Medical Research Council by their Tuberculosis Vaccines Clinical Trials Committee. Members of the Committee: Dr. P. D'Arcy Hart (chairman), Sir John Charles, Professor R. Cruickshank, Dr. Marc Daniels (secretary until his death in 1953), Dr. W. Pointon Dick (resigned in 1951), Dr. J. E. Geddes, Professor A. Bradford Hill, Sir Wilson Jameson, Dr. V. H. Springett, Dr. Ian Sutherland, Dr. A. Q. Wells, Dr. G. S. Wilson, Dr. T. M. Pollock (secretary).

Reprinted from the *British Medical Journal*, 1956, i, 413

liminary findings up to the time at which each participant had been in the trial for two and a half years, with some supplementary incomplete information up to four years.

The work described was carried out by the Council's Tuberculosis Research Unit, with the assistance of many other statutory and voluntary organizations, whose help is acknowledged at the end of the report. The team operating in the London area was directed first by Dr. W. Pointon Dick and later by Dr. T. M. Pollock, that in the Birmingham area by Dr. J. P. W. Hughes and later by Dr. D. N. Mitchell, and that in the Manchester area by Dr. G. G. Lindsay and later by Dr. S. Keidan. The trial was co-ordinated by the late Dr. Marc Daniels and then by Dr. Pollock. Throughout the planning and execution of the trial there has been close co-operation with the Council's Statistical Research Unit, and Dr. Ian Sutherland of that unit has taken a major part in it. Dr. Pollock and Dr. Sutherland have analysed the results and prepared the present report. Assessments of the cases of tuberculosis were made by Dr. V. H. Springett; a few supplementary assessments of non-pulmonary disease were made by Mr. J. A. Cholmeley.

Examinations of cultures from cases of tuberculosis in B.C.G.-vaccinated children were undertaken by Colonel H. J. Bensted and Dr. H. D. Holt, and in vole-bacillus-vaccinated children by Dr. A. Q. Wells. Histological specimens were assessed by Dr. R. J. W. Rees. Part-time assistance to the physicians directing the teams was given by Dr. Christine Miller, and also by Dr. E. C. Fear, Dr. W. L. Gordon, and Dr. Phyllis A. Lavelle. Advice on radiological procedures was given by Dr. A. J. Eley, who also, with Dr. L. A. McDowell and Dr. J. Rimington, made independent duplicate readings of the routine chest radiographs taken by the teams. Advice on the classification of primary tuberculosis in adolescents was given by Dr. Margaret MacPherson. The planning of the trial was assisted by preliminary data assembled by Dr. Pointon Dick, and by the findings of the National Tuberculin Survey, 1949–50 (Medical Research Council, 1952).

PLAN AND CONDUCT OF THE TRIAL

To assess the contribution of each of the two vaccines to the control of tuberculosis in the community, it was desirable to study their effects under ordinary conditions of life, and not in groups with a special risk of exposure to the disease. The Committee decided that it was of importance to investigate the degree and the duration of protection afforded by each vaccine in adolescence, since the notification rate and mortality from tuberculosis in Great Britain begin to rise at about the age of 15 years from their low levels in childhood. For the same reason any benefit from vaccination would be most readily detected in adolescence. It was also recognized that the incidence of tuberculosis in the vaccinated groups must be compared with that in a similar but unvaccinated group, and that this comparison would not be valid unless those suitable for vaccination were assigned at random to the vaccinated and unvaccinated groups. Moreover, the adolescents would have to be followed up intensively for a period of several years at least, and a variety of methods, including regular radiographic examinations, would be required to ensure that few, if any, of the cases of tuberculosis which arose would escape detection. Finally, large numbers of young people had to be included in the trial, partly because a substantial proportion would give a positive reaction to tuberculin and so be ineligible for vaccination, and partly because the total incidence of tuberculosis would not be large, and it was important to be able to detect even minor degrees of protection due to the vaccines.

Arising out of these considerations, the general plan of the trial was to include more than 50,000 boys and girls during their final year at secondary modern schools, when nearly all of them were aged between $14\frac{1}{2}$ and 15 years. (A description of these schools was given by the Ministry of Education in 1947; in 1953 they were attended by half the child population of England and Wales aged between 14 and 15 years—Ministry of Education, 1954.) Children giving a negative reaction to tuberculin were divided by an effectively random process into three groups; those in one group were not vaccinated, those in another received B.C.G. vaccine, and those in the third group received vole bacillus vaccine. The children with a positive reaction to tuberculin, as well as those in the unvaccinated and the two vaccinated groups, have been questioned and examined at intervals since they left school, with the aim of discovering all the cases of tuberculosis which occurred. A more detailed account of the organization of the trial follows.

The Intake

To obtain the large number of volunteers required, and to facilitate their periodic re-examination, it was necessary to carry out the investigation in large and densely populated areas. Suitable districts were therefore selected in or near North London, Birmingham, and Manchester. The conduct of the trial in each of these three areas has been the responsibility of a special team of the Tuberculosis Research Unit, headed by a physician, and equipped with a mobile van for miniature radiography (lent by the Ministry of Health). The trial has been co-ordinated centrally at the unit's headquarters, Hampstead, London; techniques were standardized and frequent staff meetings have been held. In each area the support and assistance of the county borough, county and local medical officers of health, and the school medical officers, were enlisted, and approaches were made, through the education authorities, to the head teachers of the secondary modern schools in the chosen districts.

The intake of volunteers in the London area lasted from the autumn term, 1950, to the spring term, 1952, and in the Birmingham and Manchester areas from the spring term, 1951, to the autumn term, 1952. During the intake the team visited each of the chosen districts once in each school term. Before the visit a leaflet was distributed to all the children who were in their penultimate term at school, explaining the scheme and inviting them to participate, subject to the written consent of their parents. Approximately 60 per cent of those approached agreed to take part and attended for a first examination. Nearly all the children were aged between $14\frac{1}{2}$ and 15 years and were born in 1936, 1937, or 1938 (all were between 14 and $15\frac{1}{2}$ years).

First Examination of Participants

The first examination took place at a convenient centre, which was usually one of the schools. In addition to personal information, details (supplied by the parents) of any history of tuberculosis in the immediate family, and of any recent contact with the disease, were noted on a record card bearing a printed serial number. Children known to have been in recent contact with a case of pulmonary tuberculosis at home were excluded from the trial because they were already eligible for B.C.G. vaccination under a scheme introduced by the Ministry of Health in 1949.

Each child was given the following standard examination:

(*a*) A 35-mm. radiograph of the chest was taken. Any child whose film was considered by the physician in charge of the team to show unusual radiographic appearances was recalled for a full-plate chest radiograph. Children found or suspected to have any form of tuberculosis (apart from calcification of primary type) at this first examination were excluded from the trial and referred to their local chest clinic.

(*b*) An intracutaneous tuberculin (Mantoux) test was made on the forearm with 3.3 tuberculin units (3 T.U.), using 0.1 ml. of 1/3,000 Old Tuberculin (international standard strength; a single batch of heat-concentrated synthetic medium tuberculin, prepared in June, 1950, by the Ministry of Agriculture, Fisheries and Food, Veterinary Laboratory, Weybridge, Surrey); the greatest diameter of palpable infiltration at the end of 72 hours was recorded in millimetres.

(*c*) If there was no infiltration, or if its diameter was less than 5 mm., the reaction to 3 T.U. was regarded as negative, and another intracutaneous test was made on the same forearm with 100 T.U., using 0.1 ml. of 1/100 Old Tuberculin; the greatest diameter of infiltration at the end of 72 hours was again recorded.

Children with no infiltration, or with a diameter of infiltration of less than 5 mm., at the second tuberculin test, were regarded as negative reactors to 100 T.U. and were eligible for vaccination.

Those who completed this first examination (and who were not excluded on other grounds) were regarded as having entered the trial on the date of the first radiographic examination and tuberculin test.

Vaccination Procedures

In the London area, vole bacillus vaccine was not used, and the children eligible for vaccination were allocated equally, according to the final digit of the serial number appearing on their record card, to an unvaccinated or a B.C.G.-vaccinated group. (The serial number had been given, it will be recalled, before it was known whether the child was eligible for vaccination.) A similar procedure applied for a short period early in 1952 in the Birmingham and Manchester areas, when no vole bacillus vaccine was being prepared. Apart from this short period, the children eligible for vaccination in the Birmingham and Manchester areas were divided equally into three groups: those due to receive no vaccine, B.C.G. vaccine, or vole bacillus vaccine. The division was again made according to the final digit of the serial number on the record card; it had been arranged that in these areas the numbers did not end in 0. There were, however, several temporary failures in the supply of vole bacillus vaccine, and in these circumstances the children due to receive vole bacillus vaccine were given B.C.G. vaccine instead. There were also very occasional temporary failures in the supply of B.C.G. vaccine to the Birmingham and Manchester teams, and vole bacillus vaccine was then used instead.

The B.C.G. vaccine (0.75 mg. of semi-dried weight bacilli per ml.) was freshly prepared in liquid form by the State Serum Institute, Copenhagen, and was supplied through the Central Public Health Laboratory, Colindale, London. Each batch was stored in a refrigerator and used within eight days of its receipt, and within 14 days of the harvesting of the cultures. The dose was 0.1 ml., injected intracutaneously in the left deltoid region in the boys, and in the upper and outer part of the left thigh in the girls.

The vole bacillus vaccine (2 mg. of wet weight bacilli per ml.) was freshly prepared in liquid form by Mr. A. F. B. Standfast and Miss D. Card at the Lister Institute, Elstree, Herts; the strains were provided by Dr. A. Q. Wells. Each batch was stored in a refrigerator and used within eight days of its receipt, and within 14 days of the harvesting of the cultures. Unfortunately neither the concentration of bacilli nor the strain used was satisfactory in the earlier batches (see below). The vaccine was introduced into the skin by a multiple-puncture instrument with 40 needles, projecting 2 mm. on release. The sites used were as for B.C.G. vaccination.

Those due to be vaccinated were given the appropriate vaccine immediately after the result of the test with 100 T.U. had been read.

Second Examination of Participants

The children who entered the trial in 1950 and in 1951 in their penultimate term at school were re-examined in their final term, after an interval usually of three to five months, when the team again visited the district. The purpose of this examination was to observe the immediate effects of vaccination and to obtain a further chest radiograph. The examination consisted of (a) a 35-mm. chest radiograph for every child, and, if indicated, a full-plate radiograph;

(b) tuberculin tests, as at the first examination, for all children except those who had given strongly positive reactions at the previous test—that is, except those who either had given positive reactions to 3 T.U. or had shown a diameter of infiltration of at last 10mm. to 100 T.U.; (c) the measurement of each B.C.G. vaccination reaction, and the classification of each vole bacillus vaccination reaction; (d) the recording of local complications of vaccination.

No participant was vaccinated or revaccinated at this or any subsequent examination by the teams.

Some children entered the trial only when they were in their final term, and so could not be examined for a second time at school. In addition, none of the children who entered the trial in 1952 was given a full second examination at school because the mobile radiography vans were already required for the follow-up examinations of the children who had entered at the begining of the intake. In the Birmingham and Manchester areas, however, it was possible to perform tuberculin tests on, and examine the vaccination reactions for, a sample of the children given each batch of vaccine during 1952.

Follow-up of Participants

Each participant was approached directly three times in the period of approximately 14 months after leaving school.

(1) Approximately four months after the child had left school an inquiry form was sent by post, asking for details of any intercurrent illnesses, hospital or clinic visits, and of any contact with tuberculosis. Those who did not reply were sent a second, and sometimes a third, form.

(2) Approximately 10 months after leaving school the participant was visited at home by a health visitor on the staff of the local medical officer of health. She made the same inquiries as those on the postal form, reminded the participants that the team would shortly be in the district again, and urged them to attend for examination.

(3) Approximately 14 months, and usually between 10 and 18 months, after the participant had left school the team revisited the district and set up the mobile radiography van at a suitable centre. The participants, now nearly all in employment, were invited to an examination which consisted of (a) a 35-mm. chest radiograph, and, if indicated, a full-plate radiograph; since June, 1954, all the radio-

graphs have been read separately by the team physician and by an independent observer; (b) tuberculin tests, as at the first examination; every participant, whatever the results of the tuberculin tests at the first examination, was expected to have these tests, but some who attended for the radiograph failed to complete them; the results of the tuberculin tests were read by the team physician before looking at the record card, so that he was unaware of the results of the previous tuberculin tests and of whether any vaccination had been performed; (c) the inspection and measurement of each B.C.G. vaccination reaction, and the inspection and classification of each vole bacillus vaccination reaction. Participants who did not attend this examination were invited to an extra and similar examination when the team next visited the district seven months later. As stated above, none of the participants was vaccinated or revaccinated at any follow-up examination.

The same cycle of inquiry and examination has been repeated in each subsequent 14-month period, starting with a postal inquiry four months after the team had visited the district. Small but increasing numbers of the entrants, however, have moved to other parts of the country as the trial has proceeded, and a few have emigrated. They have been sent postal inquiry forms annually and arrangements have been made, through local or national health authorities, for an annual home visit and an annual radiographic examination, including, if possible, tuberculin tests.

Unsparing efforts have thus been made to keep in frequent touch with every volunteer, and these approaches have been the principal means for the discovery of the cases of tuberculosis occurring among them. Information has also been continually made available to the teams from the tuberculosis notification lists of the local medical officers of health, and from the records of the chest clinics in the districts concerned. Cases of tuberculosis have thus been discovered both by the unit's periodic radiographic examinations and by the normal methods of the National Health Service.

The physicians in charge of the three teams were not responsible for the further investigation or treatment of any participant who had an abnormal radiograph; those who were found to have an abnormal radiograph at an examination by one of the teams were referred to their local chest clinic. With very few exceptions, however, every case of definite or suspected tuberculosis, whether discovered by the teams or by the National Health Service, was also examined in due course by one of the unit physicians; further details of the progress of the case was thenceforward obtained at six-monthly intervals.

To ensure that cases of tuberculosis were not missed, full records were kept not only for the definite cases but also for those in which tuberculosis was either suspected or considered to be even a possible diagnosis. The records were kept centrally so that the cases could eventually be assessed and classified by an independent assessor. Details were also obtained of all deaths, from whatever cause.

The records available for each case thus consisted of periodic radiographs, the results of the clinical examination by one of the unit physicians, the results of clinical examinations by other physicians, and the results of any bacteriological or pathological examinations. If bacteriological or pathological confirmation of the diagnosis had not been otherwise obtained, further examinations were arranged by the unit physicians. Histological specimens were assessed at the National Institute for Medical Research.

In cases of definite or suspected tuberculosis arising in B.C.G.-vaccinated participants, any cultures growing acid-fast bacilli were examined as a routine at the Central Public Health Laboratory, Colindale, London, where the type, pathogenicity, and, if necessary, drug sensitivity of the bacilli were determined. Particular attention was paid to the possibility that the infecting organism was B.C.G. itself. Similarly, cultures growing acid-fast bacilli from vole-bacillus-vaccinated participants were examined at the Sir William Dunn School of Pathology, Oxford.

PROGRESS OF THE TRIAL

Sample Analysis of the Records

Since the trial is still in progress, the record cards with the results of the periodic examinations of each participant are in continual use. An exact enumeration of the participants, and a full analysis of the extent to which contact with them has been maintained, is thus at present impracticable. For this first report representative samples of the record cards held by each team have been used to estimate the numbers of participants in each area and in each follow-up group, the numbers excluded from the trial, the results of the tuberculin test at the second examination at school, and the extent of contact with the participants after they left school. The cases of tuberculosis among the participants, on the other hand, have been completely enumerated, and not estimated from the samples.

For these samples, all the record cards with serial numbers ending in certain pairs of digits were located in the files and information was transcribed from them on to a specially designed analysis card. The choice of pairs of digits was effectively random, while at the same time they were approximately equally spaced in each cycle of 100 numbers and were chosen so as to ensure the correct representation of the tuberculin-negative unvaccinated group and of the two vaccinated groups (which, as already described, were determined by the final digit of the serial number). A 4 per cent sample of the London area records and 3 per cent samples of the Birmingham and Manchester area records were drawn.

Number of Participants in the Trial

A total of approximately 61,400 children presented themselves for the first examination at school. The following groups of children were excluded both from participation in the trial and from the analysis of the results: (*a*) Those who were suffering from any form of definite or suspected tuberculosis (apart from calcification of primary type) at the time of the first examination, whether diagnosed on entry to the trial or not until later. (*b*) Those who were in known contact with a case of pulmonary tuberculosis at home, either at the time of the first examination or within the previous two years whether this was discovered on entry to the trial or not until later.

Approximately 1,800 children were excluded on one or other of these grounds. In addition, some 2,500 children failed to complete the initial radiographic examination and tuberculin tests, and so could not participate.

A small number of children, about 400 in all, were excluded from the analysis for various reasons, such as having been given the wrong vaccine, having incorrectly been left unvaccinated, or having received an anti-tuberculosis vaccination prior to entering the trial. After these exclusions there remained approximately 56,700 participants in the analysis.

As a result of the tuberculin tests and vaccinations at the first examination, the children were automatically classified on entry to the trial into the following five groups, in which they remain for the purpose of the ensuing analysis, whatever the results of subsequent tuberculin tests:

Negative unvaccinated.—Negative to 100 T.U. on entry and left unvaccinated.

B.C.G. vaccinated.—Negative to 100 T.U. on entry and then given B.C.G. vaccine.

Vole bacillus vaccinated.—Negative to 100 T.U. on entry and then given vole bacillus vaccine.

Positive to 3 T.U.—Positive to 3 T.U. on entry and left unvaccinated.

Positive only to 100 T.U.—Negative to 3 T.U. and positive to 100 T.U. on entry, and left unvaccinated.

The numbers of participants from each area, according to their skin-test and vaccination group, are shown in Table **12,** 1. The largest intake was in the Birmingham area, where 23,400 adolescents

TABLE **12,** 1

Total Number of Participants in the Trial (*Estimates Based on Representative Samples*)

Skin-test and Vaccination Group*	Area			All Areas	
	London	Bir-mingham	Man-chester	No. of Partici-pants	Percen-tage of Total
Tuberculin negative, left un-vaccinated	4,400	5,200	3,700	13,300	*23*
Tuberculin negative, B.C.G. vaccinated	4,400	5,600	4,100	14,100	*25*
Tuberculin negative, vole bacillus vaccinated	—	3,900	2,800	6,700	*12*
Tuberculin positive to 3 T.U.	3,800	6,100	6,100	16,000	*28*
Tuberculin positive to 100 T.U., but not to 3 T.U.	1,900	2,600	2,100	6,600	*12*
All groups	14,500	23,400	18,800	56,700	*100*

* The group was determined for each participant on entry to the trial. For full definitions of the groups, applicable to this and to all the other tables, see text.

took part, followed by the Manchester area with 18,800 and the London area with 14,500. In the three areas combined, 22,600 of the children (40 per cent) gave a positive tuberculin reaction on entry,

16,000 (28 per cent) reacting to the weaker concentration of tuberculin (3 T.U.). Of the 34,100 children who were negative reactors to
tuberculin, 13,300 were left unvaccinated, 14,100 were given B.C.G.
vaccine, and 6,700 were given vole bacillus vaccine.

Plan of the Present Report

It will be recalled that some children in the Birmingham and
Manchester areas entered the trial when both B.C.G. and vole
bacillus vaccines were being given, that others (including all those
in the London area) entered when B.C.G. vaccine only was being
given, and that a small number (approximately 700) entered when
vole bacillus vaccine only was available. Throughout the trial, however, and whatever vaccines were being given, the children with
negative reactions to tuberculin on entry were allocated at random
to the unvaccinated and vaccinated groups.

A valid assessment of the value of B.C.G. vaccination must be
based upon those children who were admitted *concurrently* to the
negative unvaccinated, the B.C.G. vaccinated, and the two tuberculin-positive groups. The data are presented in this way in Section A
of Tables 12, 2 to 12, 4. (The comparison includes all the children
admitted to the trial in these four groups, except the small number
who entered when vole bacillus vaccine only was available.)

Some, but not all, of the children included in this assessment of
B.C.G. vaccine entered the trial concurrently with children given
vole bacillus vaccine. The results for these children, concurrently
admitted to the negative unvaccinated, the two vaccinated, and the
two tuberculin-positive groups, permit both an assessment of the
value of vole bacillus vaccination and a valid comparison of it with
B.C.G. vaccination. The data are presented in this way in Section B
of Tables 12, 2 to 12, 4. (Apart from those given vole bacillus
vaccine, all the participants in Section B also appear in Section A.)

The children who entered when vole bacillus vaccine only was
being given appear in neither of these comparisons. Because of their
small numbers they add very little to the assessment of vole bacillus
vaccination and are not considered further in the present report.

Contact with the Participants After They Left School

At the time when the representative samples of the records were
drawn some participants had not been in the trial for more than 18
months. The sample information on the effectiveness of the follow-

TABLE **12**, 2. *Percentages of Participants who Returned a Postal Inquiry Form, who were Visited by a Health Visitor or who had a Chest Radiograph taken after Leaving School (Estimates Based on Representative Samples)*

| Section | Skin-test and Vaccination Group | No. of Participants | Within 18 Months of Entry to the Trial | | | | Between 18 Months and 2 Years after Entry to the Trial |
			Percentage Returned a Postal Inquiry Form	Percentage Visited by a Health Visitor	Percentage who had a Chest Radiograph Taken	Percentage Brought in Contact with the Teams by at Least One of These Means	Minimum Additional Percentage who had a Chest Radiograph Taken
A — Children admitted concurrently with those given B.C.G. vaccine	Negative unvaccinated	13,200	83	77	51	96	26
	Negative, B.C.G. vaccinated	14,100	79	80	50	94	24
	Positive to 3 T.U.	15,800	75	73	57	94	17
	Positive only to 100 T.U.	6,500	77	77	50	95	25
B — Children admitted concurrently with those given vole bacillus vaccine	Negative unvaccinated	6,400	78	72	51	95	21
	Negative, B.C.G. vaccinated	6,400	73	76	48	92	21
	Negative, vole bacillus vaccinated	6,400	71	69	53	92	17
	Positive to 3 T.U.	8,600	70	69	59	94	16
	Positive only to 100 T.U.	3,500	70	73	44	93	25
C	All participants included in the above comparisons*	56,000	77	76	52	94	22

* That is, all participants in Section A plus the vole-bacillus-vaccinated group in Section B.

up of the participants after they had left school is therefore complete for only 18 months after entry, although there is some incomplete information for a further six months; the position is shown in Table **12**, 2.

Section C of Table **12**, 2 summarizes the follow-up of the participants included in Sections A and B of the tables—that is, all those in Section A plus the vole-bacillus-vaccinated group in Section B. In all, 77 per cent of the entrants had returned at least one postal inquiry form, 76 per cent had been visited at home at least once, and 52 per cent had had a chest radiograph taken after leaving school. During the period only 6 per cent of the entrants were not in contact with the teams by any of these means.

The figures for the radiographic examinations do not give a true indication of the actual response of the participants to the invitations to attend. They were not invited to a follow-up examination until between 10 and 18 months after leaving school; however, most had entered the trial three to five months *before* leaving school. As a result, approximately one-third had no opportunity to attend for a radiograph after leaving and within 18 months of entering the trial. Indeed, the incomplete information from the sample analysis beyond 18 months (Table **12**, 2) shows that at least a further 22 per cent of the participants had a chest radiograph taken in the following six months, and this includes many of the 6 per cent not previously brought in contact with the teams by the postal inquiry or the health visitor.

It is important to note from Sections A and B of Table **12**, 2 that the success of the follow-up was similar in all the skin-test and vaccination groups in each section. Thus any differences which may be observed in the incidence of tuberculosis between the groups are unlikely to be due to differences in the intensity of case-finding procedures.

Deaths in the First Two and a Half Years

The total number of participants known to have died within two and a half years of entering the trial was 38. None of the deaths was due to any form of tuberculosis. The principal causes of death were accidents (13), malignant disease (seven), and pneumonia (three). There appear to be no more than chance differences between the mortalities in the five skin-test and vaccination groups.

THE IMMEDIATE EFFECTS OF VACCINATION

Complications of Vaccination

Leaflets describing the normal course of the vaccination reaction were given to the vaccinated children, and they were instructed to report any abnormality to the school medical officer. By these measures a few cases of regional adenitis with cold abscess formation, following both B.C.G. and vole bacillus vaccination, were brought to the notice of the teams, but there was no evidence that such complications were common. At the second examination at school very few complications, either of B.C.G. or of vole bacillus vaccination, were observed. Those that were found consisted of delayed healing of the vaccination lesion, with shallow ulceration; the regional glands were not routinely examined. Certain other complications of vaccination were not discovered until later, and these are described below.

Conversion to Tuberculin Positivity Following Vaccination

A positive reaction to tuberculin following either B.C.G. or vole bacillus vaccination is generally regarded as a sign of satisfactory vaccination. Table 12, 3 gives the results of the tests at the second examination at school, based on the representative samples of the participants. The findings in the negative unvaccinated group illustrate the effects of natural infection with tubercle bacilli in the period of three to five months between the two examinations at school, coupled with variations inherent in the performance of the tuberculin test. At the second examination, only 0.4 per cent of these children were positive to 3 T.U. and a further 5.3 per cent were positive to 100 T.U. only (Section A). In contrast, 85.8 per cent of the B.C.G.-vaccinated group were positive to 3 T.U. and a further 13.8 per cent to 100 T.U. only, representing a total of 99.6 per cent. From Section B of Table 12, 3 it will be seen that 59.8 per cent of the children in the vole-bacillus-vaccinated group were positive to 3 T.U. and a further 34.6 per cent to 100 T.U. only, giving a total of 94.4 per cent converted. Compared with the figures for the children concurrently given B.C.G. vaccine, the total percentage converted with vole bacillus vaccine was slightly smaller, and the percentage positive to 3 T.U. was considerably smaller.

TABLE **12**, 3. *Percentages of Participants, in the Negative Unvaccinated and in the Two Vaccinated Groups, who had Positive Tuberculin Reactions at the Second Examination at School (Estimates Based on Representative Samples of Participants)*

Section	Skin-test and Vaccination Group (On Entry to the Trial)	At the Second Examination at School			
		No. who Completed the skin Test	Percentages with Positive Tuberculin Reactions		
			Positive to 3 T.U.	Positive Only to 100 T.U.	Total Positive
A	Children admitted concurrently with those given B.C.G. vaccine Negative unvaccinated Negative, B.C.G. vaccinated	5,700 7,300	0·4 85·8	5·3 13·8	5·7 99·6
B	Children admitted concurrently with those given vole bacillus vaccine Negative unvaccinated Negative, B.C.G. vaccinated Negative, vole bacillus vaccinated	2,600 3,400 3,600	0·0 84·5 59·8	5·2 14·5 34·6	5·2 99·0 94·4
C	*Period of vaccination* Vole bacillus vaccinated Jan., 1951–July, 1951 Sept., 1951–Dec., 1952	1,700 1,900	29·4 87·5	58·8 12·5	88·2 100·0

The percentage converted was studied for each batch of vaccine as the trial proceeded, as a check both of the vaccination techniques and of the potency of the vaccines. It was found that the earlier batches of vole bacillus vaccine, given to approximately 2,300 participants (one-third of the total receiving this vaccine), produced low conversion, particularly to 3 T.U., compared with B.C.G. vaccine. On examination it was discovered that these batches were weaker than the standard originally intended. In September, 1951, the vaccine was brought up to standard, and thereafter, as illustrated in Section C of Table **12,** 3, the percentages converted were almost identical with those for B.C.G. vaccine. The possible consequences of this variation in the strength of the vole bacillus vaccine will be studied in a later report.

Size of B.C.G Vaccination Reactions

The average diameters of the B.C.G. vaccination reactions measured at the second examination at school (estimated from the samples) were 8.1 mm. for boys, vaccinated on the arm, and 9.9 mm. for girls, vaccinated on the thigh.

THE CASES OF TUBERCULOSIS

Assessment of the Cases of Tuberculosis

All the definite and suspected cases of tuberculosis were reviewed by an independent assessor. To avoid bias this assessor was kept unaware of the results of any tuberculin tests and of whether any vaccination had been performed. A few cases of suspected tuberculosis of bones or joints, without bacteriological or histological confirmation, were referred to a second assessor, under the same conditions

The assessor first decided from the series of radiographs and the findings of the clinical and other examinations whether the case was one of active tuberculosis. For some cases he decided that the disease was not tuberculosis; for a few others the evidence in favour of or against tuberculosis was inadequate, and these were classed as 'possible' cases. For the cases of definite tuberculosis the assessor described the form of the disease, and the character, course, and maximal extent of any lesions apparent on the series of radiographs.

It was also important for the assessor to distinguish between cases of tuberculosis present at the time of entry to the trial and those arising after entry. Many of the cases which were present on entry had been detected at that time and the children excluded from the trial, but some children who were accepted into the trial were discovered only during the follow-up to have had tuberculosis on entry.

Finally, the assessor noted the date by which the disease first became manifest—that is, for pulmonary lesions, when the first abnormal radiograph was taken, and, for other lesions, when the first definite symptoms or signs were observed (irrespective of when the diagnosis of tuberculosis had been made). This date has been regarded as the starting-point of the illness. It will be appreciated that for some cases the starting-point may be a considerable time after the true, but unknown, date of onset of the disease.

Cases of Tuberculosis Present on Entry to the Trial

As stated above, children found by the teams to be suffering from definite or suspected tuberculosis at the first examination at school were excluded from participation in the trial, and those not already under the care of a clinic were referred for investigation. A recent review of these previously unsuspected cases has shown that 70 were considered by the chest clinic physicians to be of definite tuberculosis.

In addition, a total of 85 cases, discovered after the 56,700 participants had completed the first examination and had entered the trial, were judged by the independent assessor to have started before entry. Of these, 64 were previously unsuspected cases of definite tuberculosis, seven were definite cases under the care of a clinic (unknown to the teams at the time of the first examination), and 14 were cases of possible tuberculosis. These 85 children should have been excluded from the trial and have therefore been excluded from all the tables which follow.

In 67 of the 85 cases the radiograph taken on entry showed, on re-scrutiny, abnormal appearances indicative of tuberculosis; in one case with a normal 35-mm. radiograph on entry there had been a pleural effusion two months earlier, and in 13 cases of non-pulmonary disease symptoms had been present before the participant entered the trial. There remain four cases of definite tuberculosis where the assessor decided that the disease must have been present at the time of entry, although the symptoms or lesions were not apparent until later. In one of them, symptoms of non-pulmonary disease appeared only three months after the child had entered the trial. In the other three, pulmonary lesions were first seen on radiographs taken at the second examination at school; the 35-mm. radiograph on entry in one case was considered not to be of sufficiently high quality to exclude the presence of the lesion, and in another the film had been lost; in the third case the assessor considered that the lesion was probably present on entry but was obscured by bony shadow. These four children had (unknown to the assessor) all given a positive reaction to tuberculin on entry to the trial.

Tuberculous Lesions Attributed to Vaccination

In five participants, lesions which developed subsequent to B.C.G. or vole bacillus vaccination were brought to the attention of the teams as cases of tuberculosis and submitted to the assessor, but were regarded by him as complications of vaccination, to be classed with the complications referred to above. These were two cases of erythema nodosum, one case of tuberculous cervical adenitis, and two cases of tuberculous axillary adenitis, occurring one, one, three, six, and eight months respectively after entry to the trial. In the course of his assessment, the assessor suggested that if the participant had been vaccinated the lesions could have been due to the vaccinating organism. For these cases, and for no others, the assessor was then informed that the participant had been vaccinated. As a result, he attributed all five cases to the vaccinating organism. The two cases of erythema nodosum occurred in B.C.G.-vaccinated participants, and the three cases of tuberculous adenitis in vole-bacillus-vaccinated participants.

In addition, examinations of the vole-bacillus-vaccination sites during the follow-up revealed occasional lesions indistinguishable from lupus vulgaris, at or around the site of vaccination. These ranged from a few discrete pin-point lesions, corresponding to the original puncture marks, to a confluent lesion occupying the entire vaccination area or extending beyond it. Up to the end of June, 1955, a total of 22 cases severe enough to require treatment had been observed. These cases all occurred among the 4,100 participants given the vaccine after it had been brought up to standard (see above); 10 of the lesions were on the arm (among 2,100 boys), and 12 on the thigh (among 2,000 girls). Further information on all these lesions will be given in a later report. The B.C.G. vaccination sites were also examined, but no similar lesions were found.

All these lesions have been regarded as complications of vaccination, and none of the cases has been included in the tables which follow. It should be emphasized that there was no evidence that any of the other cases of tuberculosis in vaccinated participants were due to the vaccinating organism (see below).

Incidence of Tuberculosis in the First Two and a Half Years

By the end of June, 1955, every participant had been in the trial for at least two and a half years. The great majority of the cases of tuberculosis starting within two and a half years of entry may be presumed to have come by now (January, 1956) to the notice of the teams, and it is thus possible in the present report to compare the incidence of tuberculosis in the various skin-test and vaccination groups during this 30-month follow-up.

A total of 165 cases of definite tuberculosis started within 30 months of entry to the trial, and a further nine were assessed as possible tuberculosis. Of the definite cases 75 were first discovered by the teams through their radiographic examinations, and 90 came to the notice of the teams after discovery by the National Health Service. As stated above, there were no deaths from tuberculosis during this period.

The numbers of cases in the various skin-test and vaccination groups are given in Table 12, 4. Section A, which contains the findings for all the children given B.C.G. vaccine, and for those admitted concurrently in the other skin-test and vaccination groups, shows that there were 64 cases in the tuberculin-negative unvaccinated group, giving an annual incidence of 1.94 cases per 1,000 participants. With 13 cases, the annual incidence in the B.C.G.-vaccinated group was much lower, being 0.37 per 1,000, approximately one-fifth of the rate in the negative unvaccinated group. The possibility of this difference having occurred by chance is very remote (less than one in a million). The annual incidence in the first 30 months after entry among those initially positive to 3 T.U. was rather less than that in the negative unvaccinated group— namely, 1.75 per 1,000; among those positive only to 100 T.U. the annual incidence was 0.74 per 1,000. This difference in incidence between the two positive groups is statistically significant $(0.01 > P > 0.001)$, and so is that between the negative unvaccinated group and those positive only to 100 T.U. $(0.01 > P > 0.001)$. The incidence in the B.C.G.-vaccinated group is also substantially and significantly

TABLE **12**, 4.   *Cases of Tuberculosis Starting within Two and Half Years of Entry to the Trial* *

Section	Skin-test and Vaccination Group	Estimated No. of Participants	Definite Cases of Tuberculosis		Possible Cases of Tuberculosis Starting within 30 Months
			No. Starting within 30 Months	Annual Incidence per 1,000 Participants	
A	Children admitted concurrently with those given B.C.G. vaccine				
	Negative unvaccinated	13,200	64	1·94	2
	Negative, B.C.G. vaccinated	14,100	13	0·37	2
	Positive to 3 T.U.	15,800	69	1·75	3
	Positive only to 100 T.U.	6,500	12	0·74	1
B	Children admitted concurrently with those given vole bacillus vaccine				
	Negative unvaccinated	6,400	33	2·06	2
	Negative, B.C.G. vaccinated	6,400	5	0·31	1
	Negative, vole bacillus vaccinated	6,400	7	0·44	1
	Positive to 3 T.U.	8,600	37	1·72	2
	Positive only to 100 T.U.	3,500	6	0·69	0
C	All participants included in the above comparisons†	56,000	165	—	9

* For the definition of the starting-point of the illness, see text.

† That is, all participants in Section A plus the vole-bacillus-vaccinated group in Section B.

lower than that in the group initially positive to 3 T.U. (0.001 > P), but, while rather less, does not differ significantly from that in the group positive only to 100 T.U. (0.2 > P > 0.1).

Section B of Table **12,** 4 contains the findings for children given vole bacillus vaccine and those for the children (already included in Section A) who were admitted concurrently in the other skin-test and vaccination groups. Compared with the negative unvaccinated group there was a low incidence of tuberculosis in the vole-bacillus-vaccinated group, the annual rates being respectively 2.06 and 0.44 per 1,000 participants; the possibility of this difference having occurred by chance is small (less than 1 in 10,000) the difference between the annual rates for the vole-bacillus-vaccinated group (0.44) and for the concurrent group of B.C.G.-vaccinated children (0.31) does not attain statistical significance.

Within the group initially positive to 3 T.U. there was an association (not shown in Table **12,** 4) between the diameter of induration recorded at the tuberculin test on entry and the subsequent incidence of tuberculosis. Among the 7,100 entrants giving reactions of 15 mm. induration or more to 3 T.U., 52 definite cases of tuberculosis started within 30 months, representing an annual incidence of 2.93 per 1,000, compared with 17 cases among the 8,700 entrants giving reactions of 5 to 14 mm. induration to 3 T.U., or an annual incidence of 0.78 per 1,000. The difference is statistically significant (0.001 > P). The subsequent incidence of tuberculosis among those with the smaller reactions to 3 T.U. was almost the same as that in the group positive only to 100 T.U. In this latter group the number of cases is small, and no association was apparent between size of reaction to tuberculin and subsequent incidence of tuberculosis.

Table **12,** 4 also shows that there were only nine cases where the assessor was in doubt over the diagnosis. The above comparisons would have remained practically unaltered if these possible cases had been included with the definite cases.

Vaccination Reactions and Tuberculin Tests in Cases of Tuberculosis Occuring in Vaccinated Participants

The results of examinations subsequent to entry for the 20 definite cases of tuberculosis in the two vaccinated groups are summarized in Tables **12,** 5 and **12,** 6. Nine cases (B.C.G. 1, 3, 4, 5, 6, 7, 8, and Vole 1, 5) were observed to have a positive reaction to tuberculin in conjunction with a normal chest radiograph between two and six

TABLE 12, 5

Summary of Results of Examinations of B.C.G.-vaccinated Participants who Developed Definite Tuberculosis within Two and a Half Years of Entry to the Trial

B.C.G. Case No.	Date of Vaccination	Results of Examinations Subsequent to Vaccination				Interval Between Vaccination and Starting-point of Illness, in Months*
		Interval Between Vaccination and Examination in Months*	Chest Radiograph	Vaccination Reaction	Tuberculin Test	
1	18/1/51	3	Normal	9 mm.	+ 3 T.U.	29
		15	Normal	...	+ 3 T.U.	
		29	Pulmonary tuberculosis	...	+ 3 T.U.	
2	22/2/51	31	Pleural thickening from previous effusion	5 mm.	+ 3 T.U.	30 (Pleurisy)
3	1/3/51	4	Normal	Present but not measured	+ 3 T.U.	15
		15	Pulmonary tuberculosis	...	...	
4	5/3/51	3½	Normal	...	+ 3 T.U.	27
		15	Normal	...	...	
		27	Pulmonary tuberculosis	5 mm.	+ 3 T.U.	
5	21/6/51	4½	Normal	8 mm.	+ 3 T.U.	29
		29	Pleural effusion	...	...	

Case	Date		Diagnosis		+T.U.	
6	28/6/51	2	Normal	8 mm.	+ 3 T.U.	27
		20	Normal	...	...	
		27	Pulmonary tuberculosis	...	...	
7	28/6/51	2	Normal	9 mm.	+ 3 T.U.	16 (Erythema nodosum)
		16	Hilar gland enlargement	...	+ 10 T.U. (at hospital)	
8	9/7/51	3	Normal	9 mm.	+ 3 T.U.	28
		12	Normal	...	...	
		28	Pulmonary tuberculosis	9 mm.	+ 3 T.U.	
9	15/10/51	3	Pulmonary tuberculosis	7 mm.	+ 3 T.U.	3
10	18/2/52	13	Normal	6 mm.	...	28
		28	Pulmonary tuberculosis	...	+ 3 T.U.	
11	10/3/52	13	Normal	...	+ 3 T.U.	29
		29	Pulmonary tuberculosis	8 mm.	+ 3 T.U.	
12	15/9/52	13	Pulmonary tuberculosis	...	+ 3 T.U.	13
		23	Pulmonary tuberculosis	10 mm.	...	
13	11/12/52	14	Pulmonary tuberculosis	7 mm.	+ 3 T.U.	14

* To the nearest half month up to six months, and to the nearest month thereafter.

TABLE 12, 6. *Summary of Results of Examinations of Vole-Bacillus-Vaccinated Participants who Developed Definite Tuberculosis within Two and a Half Years of Entry to the Trial*

Vole Case No.	Date of Vaccination	Interval Between Vaccination and Examination, in Months*	Results of Examination Subsequent to Vaccination			Interval Between Vaccination and Starting-point of Illness, in Months*
			Chest Radiograph	Vaccination Reaction	Tuberculin Test	
1	16/2/51	2½	Normal	Weak	+ 100 T.U.	22
		16	Normal	...	...	
		22	Pulmonary tuberculosis	...	...	
2	8/3/51	20	Pleural effusion	...	...	19 (Pleurisy)
		24	Pleural thickening from previous effusion	None	+ 10 T.U. (at hospital)	
3	31/5/51	4	Normal	None	+ 100 T.U.	15 (Pleurisy)
		17	Pleural effusion	...	...	
4	9/7/51	4½	Normal	None	+ 3 T.U.	26
		26	Pulmonary tuberculosis	...	...	
5	18/10/51	5½	Normal	Weak	+ 100 T.U.	21
		20	Normal	None	+ 3 T.U.	
		21	Pulmonary tuberculosis	...	+ 10 T.U. (at chest clinic)	
6	11/2/52	3½	...	Strong	+ 3 T.U.	29 (Pleurisy)
		31	Pleural effusion	None	+ 3 T.U.	
7	20/10/52	15	Normal	Strong	...	20 (Symptomatic onset of non-pulmonary tuberculosis)
		21	Normal	...	+ 10 T.U. (at hospital)	

* To the nearest half month up to six months, and to the nearest month thereafter.

months after vaccination, and a healed vaccination reaction was also observed either then or later. One more case (B.C.G. 11) had no second examination at school, but similar observations were made 13 months after vaccination. One case (Vole 6) had a positive reaction to tuberculin and a healed vaccination reaction three months after vaccination, but no radiograph was taken. In two cases (Vole 3 and 4) no vaccination reaction was seen on examination, but each was positive to tuberculin and had a normal chest radiograph four months after vaccination. Six cases (B.C.G. 2, 9, 10, 12, 13, and Vole 7) had no tuberculin test after entry and before the disease had developed, but in all six a healed vaccination reaction was observed at some time. Thus, in all 13 B.C.G.-vaccinated cases and in six of the seven vole-bacillus-vaccinated cases, there is evidence that the participants had been satisfactorily vaccinated, as judged by the usual criteria, although for case B.C.G. 9, the only one known to have developed within six months of vaccination, the disease could well have arisen before any protection had been conferred.

For the remaining case (Vole 2) the vaccination site was not examined, nor was a tuberculin test given, until five months after the tuberculous pleural effusion. At this time (two years after entry to the trial), no vaccination reaction was seen, and so it is possible that this case had not been satisfactorily vaccinated. It has, however, been observed in the course of the trial that, with the multiple-puncture technique for vole bacillus vaccination, the vaccination reactions frequently become less obvious and may disappear (as, for example, in cases Vole 5 and 6). Cases Vole 1, 2, 3, and 4 were all admitted to the trial during the period when the vole bacillus vaccine was producing a low percentage conversion (see above).

The Forms of Tuberculosis

The forms of tuberculosis which occurred in the various skin-test and vaccination groups are shown in Table **12,** 7. If two or more were present the case was assigned to the major form; for example, tuberculous meningitis took precedence over any other form, and pulmonary tuberculosis took precedence over a pleural effusion. A division of the cases of pulmonary tuberculosis into those showing primary and other pulmonary lesions was considered, but, in view of the difficulties inherent in classifying tuberculosis radiographically in adolescents on these lines, no such grouping is used in the present

TABLE **12,** 7. *Definite Cases of Tuberculosis Starting Within Two and a Half Years of Entry to the Trial, According to the Form of the Disease*

Skin-test and Vaccination Group	Total Cases	Form of Tuberculosis						
		Pulmonary Tuberculosis	Tuberculous Pleural Effusion*	Hilar Gland Enlargement†	Tuberculous Meningitis	Bone or Joint Tuberculosis	Tuberculous Cervical Adenitis	Other Forms
Negative unvaccinated	64	39	17	1	3	0	3	1‡
Negative, B.C.G. vaccinated	13	10	2	0	0	0	0	1§
Negative, vole bacillus vaccinated	7	3	3	0	0	1	0	0
Positive to 3 T.U.	69	45	10	0	0	3	8	3‖
Positive only to 100 T.U.	12	7	4	0	0	0	0	1¶
All groups	165	104	36	1	3	4	11	6

* Without evidence of pulmonary tuberculosis. † Without other evidence of tuberculosis. ‡ Tuberculous peritonitis with small associated pulmonary lesion. § Erythema nodosum with associated hilar gland enlargement. ‖ 1 tuberculous peritonitis; 1 tuberculous epididymitis; 1 lupus vulgaris. ¶ Tuberculous axillary adenitis.

report. The occurrence of hilar gland enlargement, indicative of a primary lesion, is studied below.

Pulmonary tuberculosis was observed in 104 of the 165 cases (63 per cent), and occurred in all the skin-test and vaccination groups. Although the numbers of cases in the two vaccinated groups are small, there is no evidence of important differences between the five groups in the ratio of the number of pulmonary to the total cases.

Tuberculous pleural effusion, without evidence of pulmonary tuberculosis, was the next most numerous form, with 36 cases (22 per cent). In addition, a pleural effusion preceded, or was discovered at the same time as, the pulmonary lesions in eight more cases. The ratio of the number of pleural effusions to the total cases was greater among those initially positive only to 100 T.U. (5 of 12) than among those positive to 3 T.U. (12 of 69), but the difference is not statistically significant. The negative unvaccinated group (22 of 64) and the vaccinated groups combined (5 of 20) occupied an intermediate position in this respect.

Hilar gland enlargement, with no other lesion, was noted in only one case, which was in the negative unvaccinated group. It was also found, however, in association with other lesions (mainly pulmonary lesions, pleural effusions, or both) in 17 more cases. In all, hilar gland enlargement was observed in a larger proportion of the cases in the negative unvaccinated group than in the vaccinated groups (14 to 64 compared with one of 20), although on these numbers the difference is not statistically significant; hilar gland enlargement was noted in one of the 69 cases in those initially positive to 3 T.U. and in two of the 12 in those initially positive only to 100 T.U.

There were three cases of tuberculous meningitis, all in the negative unvaccinated group, one of which was associated with miliary pulmonary tuberculosis, and one both with miliary pulmonary tuberculosis and with a pleural effusion. In addition, three of the pulmonary lesions, also in the negative unvaccinated group, were of miliary type. Thus tuberculous meningitis, miliary pulmonary tuberculosis, or both, occurred in six of the 64 cases in the negative unvaccinated group. None occurred in any of the other groups.

Nature and Maximal Extent of the Pulmonary Lesions

The pulmonary lesions were classified by the independent assessor according to their maximal radiographic extent up to the time when the assessment was made, as shown in Table **12,** 8. Of the 104 pul-

TABLE **12,** 8. *Definite Cases of Pulmonary Tuberculosis Starting within Two and a Half Years of Entry to the Trial, According to the Nature and Maximal Extent of the Pulmonary Lesions*

Skin-test and Vaccination Group	Total Pulmonary Cases	Miliary Type of Lesions	Lesions with Cavitation		Lesions without Cavitation		
			Lesions Involving More than 2 Rib Interspaces	Lesions Involving Up to 2 Rib Interspaces	Involving More than 2 Rib Interspaces	More than 6 sq. cm. in Extent, Involving Up to 2 Rib Interspaces	Up to 6 sq. cm. in Extent
Negative unvaccinated	39	3	9	4	3	15	5
Negative, B.C.G. vaccinated	10	0	4	1	1	1	3
Negative, vole bacillus vaccinated	3	0	1	0	0	2	0
Positive to 3 T.U.	45	0	10	3	3	22	7
Positive only to 100 T.U.	7	0	1	2	0	3	1
All groups	104	3	25	10	7	43	16

274

monary cases in all groups, three, just referred to, showed lesions of miliary type. Of the cases with other pulmonary lesions, 35 showed cavitation on radiographic examination; in 25 of these the entire lesion involved more than two rib interspaces. The remaining 66 cases had pulmonary lesions without cavitation; in seven the total extent of the lesions involved more than two rib interspaces, in 43 their extent was greater than 6 sq. cm. but did not involve more than two interspaces, and in only 16 was their extent 6 sq. cm. or less (on a full-size chest radiograph).

Cases with cavitation were observed in all the groups, being found in 13 of the 39 cases in the negative unvaccinated groups, in six of the 13 cases in the vaccinated groups combined, and in 16 of the 52 cases in the tuberculin-positive groups combined. Although the total number of pulmonary cases in some of the groups is small, the distribution offers no evidence of important differences in the nature or extent of the pulmonary lesions between the groups. The protection afforded by the vaccines thus does not appear to be limited to the prevention of lesions of a particular nature or extent.

Action taken by the Physician in Charge of the Patient

Further evidence of the serious nature of many of the cases of tuberculosis which occurred is provided by Table 12, 9. Of the 165

TABLE 12, 9

Definite Cases of Tuberculosis Starting within Two and a Half Years of Entry to the Trial, According to the Action Taken by the Clinician

Skin-test and Vaccination Group	Total Cases	Taken Off Work and Treated		Remaining at Work under Observation
		For 3 Months or More	For Less than 3 Months	
Negative unvaccinated	64	45	4	15
Negative, B.C.G. vaccinated	13	8	0	5
Negative, vole, bacillus vaccinated	7	6	0	1
Positive to 3 T.U.	69	44	7	18
Positive only to 100 T.U.	12	10	2	0
All groups	165	113	13	39

patients, 113 (68 per cent) were taken off work for a period of at least three months. Of these 113 patients, 88 received chemotherapy, collapse therapy, or surgery, in addition to rest in bed; 16 of the remaining 25 were cases of pleural effusion. At the other extreme, 39 patients (24 per cent) remained at work and were kept under observation; one of these patients also received some chemotherapy.

Of the 64 patients in the negative unvaccinated group, 45 were taken off work for three months or more; similarly, 14 of the 20 patients in the vaccinated groups combined, 44 of the 69 in the group positive to 3 T.U., and 10 of the 12 in the group positive only to 100 T.U. were taken off work for three months or more. Bearing in mind the small numbers of cases in some groups, there is again no evidence of important differences between the groups in regard to the severity of the lesions, as judged by the action taken by the physician responsible for the care of the patient.

Bacteriological and Pathological Investigations

Of the 104 cases of pulmonary tuberculosis, eight had no bacteriological examinations at any time. Positive bacteriological results were obtained in 41 of the remaining 96 cases. In five of the 55 cases with negative bacteriological results the examinations were made only after the start of chemotherapy, but the other 50 all had negative results at a time when no chemotherapy had been given. Since the investigation and treatment of all cases were carried out at local chest clinics and were not the responsibility of the unit physicians, there was no opportunity for the unit to carry out intensive bacteriological examinations, and in many instances no special emphasis was laid upon these tests in the routine management of the cases. The proportion of cases confirmed bacteriologically is therefore relatively low.

In all, tubercle bacilli were isolated from 16 of the 39 cases of pulmonary tuberculosis in the tuberculin-negative unvaccinated group, from five of the 10 cases in the B.C.G.-vaccinated group, from two of the three in the vole-bacillus-vaccinated group, from 14 of the 45 in those positive to 3 T.U., and from four of the seven in those positive only to 100 T.U. The organisms isolated from the five cases in the B.C.G.-vaccinated group and from the two in the vole-bacillus-vaccinated group were found to be virulent and of human type.

A specimen of the fluid was examined in only 18 of the 36 cases of pleural effusion classified as tuberculous: in 15 the fluid was sterile, and in 10 of these a high proportion of lymphocytes was recorded; in the other three cases (none vaccinated) tubercle bacilli were cultured from the fluid. In all four cases of tuberculosis of bones or joints, and in seven of the 11 cases of cervical adenitis, the diagnosis was established by histological examination; in one of the remaining four cases of cervical adenitis the diagnosis was confirmed bacteriologically. The three cases of tuberculous meningitis were all confirmed by bacteriological examination of the cerebrospinal fluid.

Reliability of the Independent Assessments

It is conceivable that the withholding of information on the results of skin tests, essential though it is for an unbiased comparison between the various groups, might have resulted in some cases being incorrectly diagnosed by the assessor. It is therefore of interest to compare his diagnosis with that of the chest clinic or other physician taking charge of the case. For 157 of the 165 definite cases of tuberculosis arising after entry and accepted for this report there was agreement on diagnosis between assessor and physician in charge; five of the eight disagreements concerned pleural effusions regarded by the assessor as due to tuberculosis, but by the physician in charge as due to non-tuberculous conditions. Of the other three cases, two were regarded as possible pulmonary tuberculosis, and one as not pulmonary tuberculosis, by the physician in charge. Four of these eight disagreements were in the negative unvaccinated group and four in the group positive to 3 T.U. In addition to the 165, seven cases were regarded by the physician in charge, but not by the assessor, as tuberculous; three of these were considered by the assessor to be possible cases; in the other four he decided that there was no evidence of tuberculosis. Three of these seven cases were in the negative unvaccinated group, two were in the B.C.G.-vaccinated group, and two were in the group positive to 3 T.U.

Further confirmation of the reliability of the independent assessments is provided by the results of tuberculin tests, subsequent to entry, for the cases in the originally tuberculin-negative unvaccinated group classed as definite tuberculosis by the assessor. Of the 64 cases, 57 became tuberculin positive between entry to the trial and the development of the disease; six cases had no tuberculin tests during this period, but the diagnosis of tuberculosis was confirmed in five bacteriologically and in one histologically; the remaining case (one of the disagreements of diagnosis referred to above) had a negative reaction to 10 T.U. in hospital at the time of the pleural effusion.

Supplementary evidence on the same point is provided by the results of the initial tuberculin tests for the cases classed by the assessor as definite tuberculosis present on entry. Of the 71 cases, 64 were positive to 3 T.U. and four were positive only to 100 T.U. The remaining three were in the negative unvaccinated group. In two, pleurisy followed by pulmonary tuberculosis was discovered after entry to the trial, but the assessor classed them as having had tuberculosis on entry because he noted hilar gland enlargement on one of the initial 35-mm. radiographs, and pleural thickening on the other; in both cases sensitivity to tuberculin developed after entry. The third case was regarded as tuberculous cervical adenitis both by the assessor and by the surgeon who treated the case two months before entry to the trial.

Starting-point to the Illness

As already described, the assessor decided retrospectively, from the detailed records of each case of tuberculosis, the date of the earliest radiographic or clinical manifestation of the disease, which has been regarded as the starting-point of the illness. The intervals between entry to the trial and the starting-point of the illness are given in Table **12,** 10. Of the 165 definite cases, 21 had a starting-point within six months of entry, 13 between six months and one year, 42 between one year and 18 months, 41 between 18 months and two years, and 48 between two years and 30 months. These figures incidentally demonstrate the defects of the starting-point (as here defined) as a measure of the time of onset of the disease; the number of cases with starting-points between six months and one year is less than that before and after, probably because relatively few participants had a radiographic examination by the teams during this period, and not because of a low incidence of the disease. However, this disadvantage applies equally in all the skin-test and vaccination groups, and so does not invalidate comparisons between them.

Only one case in a vaccinated participant had a starting-point within six months of entry, whereas, from the experience in the negative unvaccinated group, 6.3 cases would have been expected in the two vaccinated groups combined. This indicates that the vaccines confer protection soon after being given. Between six and

24 months the actual and expected numbers of cases in vaccinated participants in the successive six-month periods were 0 and 5.4, 5 and 22.8, and 4 and 33.3. There were 10 cases in vaccinated participants with starting-points between 24 and 30 months after entry, whereas from the experience in the negative unvaccinated group 33.3 cases would have been expected. Thus the vaccines still confer substantial protection between 24 and 30 months.

Table **12,** 10 shows a change during the first two years in the relative incidence of tuberculosis in the negative unvaccinated group and in the group positive to 3 T.U. In the first six months, only four cases started in the negative unvaccinated group, compared with 14 in those positive to 3 T.U.; between six months and one year the numbers were four and nine; between one year and 18 months 14 and 17; and between 18 months and two years 21 in the negative unvaccinated group but only 15 in those positive to 3 T.U. These trends indicate that the importance of the negative un-vaccinated group as a source of cases of tuberculosis, relative to the group positive to 3 T.U., was increasing during the two years. However, it is not possible to determine whether the incidence of tuberculosis was really increasing in the negative unvaccinated group during the two years, and remaining uniform in the group positive to 3 T.U., because the starting-points depend to some extent upon the frequency of radiographic examinations, which varied from period to period; full information on these variations and their effects is not yet available.

Supplementary Information on Cases of Tuberculosis Starting After the First Two and a Half Years

There is some preliminary information on the continuance, beyond the first two and a half years, of the protection afforded by the vaccines. All the participants have now (January, 1956) been in the trial for three years, some have been in for as long as four years, and a small proportion, who entered at the beginning of the intake, have completed five years. All definite cases of tuberculosis with starting-points more than 30 months after entry are being assessed as they come to the notice of the teams, in exactly the same way as those with starting-points within 30 months, and the present totals up to four years are shown in Table **12,** 10, according to the interval since entry. Although the numbers of cases become progressively less complete as the interval since entry increases, this does not

TABLE **12,** 10   *Definite Cases of Tuberculosis, According to the Interval Between Entry and the Earliest Radiographic or Clinical Manifestation (the Starting-point) of the Illness*

Skin-test and Vaccination Group	Total Cases Starting within 30 Months of Entry	Months between Entry to the Trial and the Starting-point of the Illness								Cases Starting between 30 Months and 4 Years after Entry
		0–	6–	12–	18–	24	30– (Incomplete)	36– (Incomplete)	42–48 (Incomplete)	
Negative unvaccinated	64	4	4	14	21	21	15	13	10	38
Negative, B.C.G. vaccinated	13	1	0	4	0	8	5	0	0	5
Negative, vole bacillus vaccinated	7	0	0	1	4	2	0	0	0	0
Positive to 3 T.U.	69	14	9	17	15	14	11	5	8	24
Positive only to 100 T.U.	12	2	0	6	1	3	3	3	2	8
All groups	165	21	13	42	41	48	34	21	20	75

invalidate comparisons between the various skin-test and vaccination groups.

Of the definite cases with starting-points between two and a half and four years after entry, 38 were in the negative unvaccinated group and only five in the B.C.G.-vaccinated group. A comparison with the corresponding totals of 64 and 13 for the first 30 months shows no evidence of any diminution in the efficacy of B.C.G. vaccine up to four years. In particular, the sudden rise in the number of cases starting in the B.C.G.-vaccinated group, from 0 between 18 and 24 months, to eight in the following six months, which, in the absence of later information, might have indicated a waning in the efficacy of B.C.G. vaccine, appears to be no more than an unusually large fluctuation in the emergence of cases in this group.

Of the 38 cases starting between two and a half and four years after entry in the negative unvaccinated group, 21 (not shown separately in Table 12, 10) occurred among participants admitted concurrently with those given vole bacillus vaccine, compared with none in the vole-bacillus-vaccinated group. The corresponding numbers of cases in the first 30 months were 33 and seven. Thus there is also no evidence of any diminution in the efficacy of vole bacillus vaccine up to four years.

DISCUSSION

Although it is now more than 30 years since B.C.G. vaccine was first used in man, the investigation described in this progress report is the first controlled trial of the vaccine to be undertaken in Great Britain, and one of the few so far undertaken in any part of the world. The early results of the present trial provide clear evidence, for a period of two and a half years, of the efficacy of B.C.G. vaccination, and also of vole bacillus vaccination, in the prevention of tuberculosis in the particular group of adolescents studied, and in the present circumstances in this country.

Features of the Trial

In addition to the inclusion of a comparative assessment of vole bacillus vaccine, the trial embodies a number of other important features. First, the effects of the two vaccines are being studied in adolescence under the ordinary conditions of urban and suburban life prevailing in an industrial community with well-developed health services and with relatively low tuberculosis incidence and mortality. The findings are therefore of special relevance to the control of tuberculosis in such a community.

Secondly, entry to the trial was confined to a narrow and susceptible age group—namely, to children who volunteered with parental consent in their final year at secondary modern schools in or near North London, Birmingham, and Manchester, when nearly all of them were aged between $14\frac{1}{2}$ and 15 years. Moreover, those found, as a result of an examination which included a chest radiograph, to be suffering from any form of tuberculosis, and those found to be in contact at home with a case of pulmonary tuberculosis at the time of entry, were excluded from the trial. The 56,700 participants thus come from a wide range of social and economic backgrounds, they represent a clearly defined section of the population, and they were initially free both from active tuberculosis and from known contact with the disease at home.

A third feature in the design of the trial, which is of fundamental importance in the interpretation of the results, is that the children with negative reactions to tuberculin on entry were allocated by a random process to three groups; those in one group were left unvaccinated, those in another received B.C.G. vaccine, and those in the third group received vole bacillus vaccine. These three groups of participants can therefore be regarded as alike on entry to the trial, apart from their vaccination state, and they have been observed and examined subsequently to a similar extent. In addition, the children with positive reactions to tuberculin on entry have been followed in the same way as those with negative reactions. A knowledge of the relative incidence of tuberculosis in all these groups is necessary for an assessment of the reduction to be expected in the total incidence of tuberculosis as a result of vaccination.

Fourthly, special efforts have been made to keep in close and frequent touch with all the participants through postal inquiries and home visits, and to use every available source of information to discover the cases of tuberculosis which have developed among them. A most important aspect of the follow-up has been that, in addition to access to chest clinic and other routine records of the National Health Service, there has been a scheme for the regular radiographic examination of the participants. As a result it is probable that few cases of tuberculosis have escaped detection; it is an indication of the success of the various approaches that many cases have independently come to the notice of the investigating teams through more than one channel.

Fifthly, when the trial was planned, emphasis was laid upon the need to detect and study the cases of tuberculosis rather than the deaths; in the event 165 of the participants are known to have contracted tuberculosis within two and a half years of entering the trial, but there was no death from the disease during this period.

It must be emphasized that, for a full evaluation of the two vaccines, a much longer period of observation than two and a half years will be necessary, but the early results of the trial are of sufficient importance to be considered in this progress report. The scope of the report is also limited because the numbers of participant (though not the numbers of cases of tuberculosis) had to be estimated from representative samples of the records, so that the first results should be available rapidly.

All cases in which tuberculosis was considered to be even a possible diagnosis were assessed by an independent assessor who, to avoid bias, was kept unaware of the results of any tuberculin tests and of whether the participant had or had not been vaccinated. There was a close correspondence between his diagnoses and those of the chest clinic or other physicians responsible for the investigation and treatment of the cases. The assessor decided that there was a total of 165 definite cases of tuberculosis in which the illness had begun after, but within 30 months of, entry to the trial.

Protection Afforded by Vaccination

As a consequence of the random allocation process, and because of the absence of bias, both in the intensity of the follow-up and in the assessment of the cases, any differences in the incidence of tuberculosis between the tuberculin-negative unvaccinated and the two vaccinated groups may be attributed directly to the vaccination. Although those who were vaccinated were told the expected course of the vaccination reaction, and therefore knew that they had been vaccinated, it is hard to see how this knowledge could have influenced the comparison. Indeed, despite the explanations given, many of those who received only tuberculin tests were under the impression that they too had been vaccinated.

In the first 30 months of observation, the number of definite cases of tuberculosis among 13,200 participants who were tuberculin negative on entry and were left unvaccinated was 64, giving an annual incidence of 1.94 per 1,000. In contrast, there were only 13 cases among the 14,100 participants, also tuberculin negative on entry, who received B.C.G. vaccine, giving an annual incidence of 0.37 per 1,000, or approximately one-fifth of the rate in the negative unvaccinated group. Between the ages of 15 and 17 years, and during the transition from school life to early employment, in an urban or suburban environment, B.C.G. vaccine therefore confers a substantial degree of protection against tuberculosis.

The number of cases of tuberculosis among 6,400 vole-bacillus-vaccinated participants during the 30 months following vaccination was seven, representing an annual incidence of 0.44 per 1,000, or approximately one-fifth of the incidence of 2.06 per 1,000 among those admitted concurrently to the tuberculin-negative unvaccinated group. The benefit to those given vole bacillus vaccine is thus substantial. Its efficacy appears to be very similar to that of B.C.G. vaccine; the difference in incidence between the two vaccinated groups could well have arisen by chance. Moreover, the earlier batches of vole bacillus vaccine, which gave unexpectedly low percentages of subsequent positive reactions to tuberculin, were found to have been weaker than the standard originally intended; the strength of the subsequent batches of vaccine was adjusted to this standard. Four cases of tuberculosis occurred among 2,300 participants given vole bacillus vaccine during the earlier period, and three among 4,100 given the vaccine in the later period.

There have been a few other trials of B.C.G. vaccine, in general population groups, in which the subjects found to be tuberculin negative were selected by a random process either for vaccination or to be left unvaccinated. In most of these trials the populations had low standards of living and high tuberculosis rates. Outstanding is the trial in North America Indians, which started in 1936 (Aronson, 1948; Aronson and Aronson, 1952; Stein and Aronson, 1953). About 1,500 tuberculin-negative subjects from infancy up to the age of 20 years were given B.C.G. vaccine, and a similar number were left unvaccinated; those initially tuberculin positive were not followed up. The morbidity from tuberculosis, as judged by annual radiography and tuberculin tests, was studied for 11 years, and the mortality has been reported for 15 years. A substantial degree of protection was demonstrated which was sustained for 10 years; there was a suggestion that it might wane thereafter. In 1949–50 the U.S. Public Health Service began studies on American Indian and on Puerto Rican schoolchildren, but Palmer and Shaw reported in 1953 that there were still too few cases to provide any definite evidence of the effectiveness of B.C.G. vaccine, though some protection was suggested. Sergent, Cantanei, and Ducros-Rougebief (1954) reported a clear effect of B.C.G. vaccine, given orally at birth, and again at one and three years, upon the mortality from all causes up to the age of five years, among Muslim children in Algiers.

The investigation of B.C.G. vaccine in a population group most closely approximating to that of the present trial is that in progress under the U.S. Public Health Service among all the 10,000 who were schoolchildren in Muscogee County, Georgia, in 1947. There were 4,800 negative reactors to tuberculin, 2,500 of whom, chosen at random, were given B.C.G. vaccine. No cases of tuberculosis have been reported in six years among either the vaccinated or the tuberculin-negative unvaccinated children, and only five among the 5,200 who were initially tuberculin positive (Palmer and Shaw, 1953). This investigation covers a wider and generally less vulnerable age group than that of the present trial, and for case-finding relies solely upon the established system of notification of cases of tuberculosis.

In a retrospective investigation of Swedish conscripts, who were offered B.C.G. vaccination on entry to the army, Dahlström and Difs (1951) and Dahlström (1953) found that the vaccine did not appear to confer protection against primary tuberculosis until two months had elapsed since vaccination, nor against other forms of tuberculosis until six months had elapsed. In the present trial, both vaccines appeared to confer protection within six months, and protection was still substantial between two and two and a half years after vaccination. Supplementary incomplete information suggests that the protection is maintained up to four years. As already stated, Aronson and Aronson (1952) reported that in North American Indians the substantial degree of protection was sustained for at least 10 years.

When the forms of tuberculosis and their severity (as judged by several criteria) were studied for the 64 cases in the negative unvaccinated group, it was clear that most would be regarded as clinically important. A comparison with the corresponding information for the 20 cases in the two vaccinated groups combined suggests that the disease took similar forms, and that the lesions were as extensive and severe, in the vaccinated participants. However, there were three cases of tuberculous meningitis and three of miliary pulmonary tuberculosis in the negative unvaccinated group, and none in either of the vaccinated groups. Again, hilar gland enlargement, indicative of primary tuberculosis, was noted in 14 of the 64 cases in the negative unvaccinated group, and in only one of the 20 cases among those vaccinated. In view of the difficulty found in distinguishing radiographically between primary and other pulmonary lesions in adolescents, no such classification has been used in the present report.

Complications of Vaccination

Complications attributable to vaccination have to be set against the efficacy of the vaccines in preventing tuberculosis. With each vaccine, regional adenitis and delayed healing of the vaccination lesion were occasionally recorded. In addition, among the 14,100 participants given B.C.G. vaccine, two cases of erythema nodosum developed after four weeks, and were attributed to the vaccine. The findings of Wylie, Bennet, and Swithinbank (1954) and Frew Davidson, and Reid (1955) have also been confirmed, *i.e.*, that lesions at the site of vaccination, indistinguishable from lupus vulgaris, develop in a number of those given vole bacillus vaccine. In 22 of 4,100 participants given the standard strength of vaccine in the present trial, these lesions have been sufficiently severe to require treatment; no lesions requiring treatment were found among 2,300 participants given the substandard vaccine, but the conversion rates to tuberculin positivity were not so high for this group as for those given the standard vaccine. It should be noted, further, that the vole bacillus vaccine was administered by multiple puncture, and it is possible that the intracutaneous method, which is in use in Czechoslovakia (Sula, 1955) and is being explored in this country (Wells and Wylie, 1955), will not produce this complication.

Incidence of Tuberculosis in Those Initially Tuberculin Positive

Whereas the tuberculin-negative unvaccinated, and the two vaccinated, groups are alike, apart from the vaccination (by virtue of the random allocation process), the two initially tuberculin-positive groups are not. These groups differed on entry not only from those initially tuberculin negative, in the fact of sensitivity to tuberculin, but also from each other, in the degree of this sensitivity. Moreover, the interpretation of any differences in the incidence of tuberculosis between these groups must take into account the differing backgrounds which have led up to the specific differences in sensitivity. Among 15,800 participants with a positive reaction to 3 T.U. (tuberculin units) on entry, the annual incidence of tuberculosis during the first two and a half years was 1.75 per 1,000 participants. Among the 6,500 participants initially negative to 3 T.U. and positive to 100 T.U. who were admitted concurrently with them, the annual incidence was much lower, being 0.74 per 1,000. Thus, as a group, those initially positive only to 100 T.U. were less likely to contract tuberculosis than those positive to 3 T.U. Positive tuberculin reactions at the two levels clearly have different implications. Moreover, the incidence of tuberculosis within the group positive to 3 T.U. was associated with the intensity of the initial reaction to tuberculin. For those with reactions of 5–14 mm. induration to 3 T.U. initially the annual incidence was 0.78 per 1,000, almost the same as for those initially positive only to 100 T.U. but for those with larger reactions to 3 T.U. the incidence was 2.93 per 1,000 (which is higher even than in the negative unvaccinated group).

It has been suggested (Edwards and Palmer, 1935; Palmer, 1953; World Health Organization Tuberculosis Research Office, 1955) that nearly all the reactions which occur only to a high concentration of tuberculin indicate a non-tuberculous allergy. If, in the present trial, they were *all* non-specific, the incidence of tuberculosis among those positive only to 100 T.U. and that in the negative unvaccinated group might be expected to be similar (unless the non-tuberculous allergy is associated with some protection against tuberculosis). Actually the annual rates differ considerably, being 0.74 per 1,000 for those initially positive only to 100 T.U. and 1.94 per 1,000 for those in the negative unvaccinated group. Indeed, the experience of the group positive only to 100 T.U. is closer to that of the vaccinated groups than to that of the negative unvaccinated group. The interpretation of tuberculin reactions, in relation both to the subsequent development of tuberculosis and to resistance to the disease, requires much more investigation; it is hoped that further information from the present trial may become available for a later report.

Assessment of the Benefits of Vaccination

According to the present results, if *none* of the tuberculin-negative entrants had been vaccinated, 165 cases of tuberculosis would have been expected among them within 30 months of entry. If *all* of them had received B.C.G. vaccine, 30 cases would have been expected.

The difference of 135 cases represents a reduction of 82 per cent in the incidence of tuberculosis *in the tuberculin-negative group.*

However, many of the children entering the trial were already tuberculin positive and were thus ineligible for vaccination; the incidence of tuberculosis in this group would not be directly affected by vaccination. It follows that the reduction to be expected in the incidence of tuberculosis in a population group similar to that of the present trial, as a result of vaccinating all the negative reactors to tuberculin, would be substantially less than the 82 per cent expected in the tuberculin-negative group only. In the present trial, taking the 81 cases among the tuberculin-positive entrants into consideration, the expected reduction in the total number of cases within 30 months of entry would have been from 246 (165 plus 81) to 111 (30 plus 81). The difference of 135 cases thus represents an expected reduction of 55 per cent in the incidence of tuberculosis in the tuberculin-negative and tuberculin-positive groups combined.

This estimate, however, has been calculated after the exclusion of 134 previously unsuspected cases of definite tuberculosis which were present on entry to the trial and were nearly all detected as a result of the initial radiographic examination at school (70 excluded at the time of entry, plus 64 subsequently excluded by the assessor; see above). If the preliminary radiograph had not been taken, many of these 134 cases would apparently have arisen after, and within 30 months of, entry to the trial, and would have increased the total cases among those initially tuberculin positive from 81 to a figure of the order of 200. The apparent reduction in the incidence of tuberculosis in the 30 months, as a result of giving B.C.G. vaccine to all those initially tuberculin negative, would in the absence of an initial radiograph have been of the order of 35 per cent (that is, from 165 plus 200 to 30 plus 200), considerably less than the 55 per cent estimated above. As a corollary, in any scheme of vaccination in adolescence, the radiographic examination and follow-up of those found at the outset to be tuberculin positive, particularly those with strong reactions, should be considered.

The benefit to be expected from B.C.G. vaccination may also be expressed in terms of the administrative action required. The expected reduction of 135 cases in the first 30 months would have resulted from the tuberculin testing of 56,000 schoolchildren and the B.C.G. vaccination of the 33,700 with negative reactions to tuberculin. This corresponds to the prevention of 1.6 cases annually (for a period of two and a half years) among every 1,000 children given B.C.G. vaccine, or the prevention of 1.0 cases of tuberculosis annually (for two and a half years) for every 1,000 children given tuberculin tests preparatory to vaccination. The expected effects of using vole bacillus vaccine in place of B.C.G. vaccine would be very similar.

In considering the implications of these findings it should be borne in mind that in the present trial the participants were vaccinated towards the end of their fifteenth year, by which time 40 per cent were tuberculin positive. The substantial number of previously un-suspected cases of tuberculosis which were present on entry, coupled with the subsequent incidence among the entrants with positive reactions to tuberculin, indicate that it might be desirable to vac-cinate schoolchildren before so large a proportion of them had been infected naturally. Until there has been a longer period of follow-up, however, it will not be possible to know whether the protection afforded by the vaccines persists throughout the period of risk in adolescence, although the supplementary results suggest that the substantial protection during the first two and a half years is main-tained up to four years after vaccination. In November, 1953, the Ministry of Health introduced an adoptive scheme for the B.C.G. vaccination of tuberculin-negative schoolchildren approaching their fourteenth birthday. In the light of present results, this is a valuable measure. However, not until further information becomes available on the duration of protection afforded by vaccination, and this is considered in relation to the proportions of schoolchildren who are tuberculin positive at different ages, will it be possible to judge the optimum age at which to institute a scheme for a single vaccination of adolescents.

Finally, it should be borne in mind that the cases discovered in the group tuberculin negative on entry and remaining unvaccinated are manifestations of tuberculosis appearing within a few years of a natural first infection with the tubercle bacillus, and that the pro-tection shown to have been afforded by the vaccines concerns these manifestations. The investigation provides no information about the development of tuberculosis in the vaccinated participants during later life.

The trial is still in progress, and the present report is an interim communication. Later reports will contain more detailed analysis over longer periods of time.

VI. SUMMARY

A controlled clinical trial of B.C.G. and vole bacillus vaccines in the prevention of tuberculosis in adolescent boys and girls started in September, 1950. By December, 1952, approximately 56,700 volunteers, all in their final year at secondary modern schools in or near North London, Birmingham, and Manchester, had been included; nearly all were aged between 14½ and 15 years. Those found at an initial radiographic examination to be suffering from tuberculosis, and those known to have been in recent contact with a case of pulmonary tuberculosis at home, were excluded from the trial. This first report presents preliminary results after each participant had been in the trial for two and a half years, with supplementary incomplete information up to four years.

At the initial examination, each entrant had a chest radiograph and an intracutaneous test with 3 T.U. (tuberculin units); those with negative reactions to 3 T.U. were tested with 100 T.U. Those negative to both strengths were allocated by a random process to an unvaccinated, a B.C.G.-vaccinated, or a vole-bacillus-vaccinated group. The participants were thus automatically classified on entry into the following five groups: tuberculin negative, left unvaccinated (13,300 entrants); tuberculin negative, B.C.G. vaccinated (14,100); tuberculin negative, vole bacillus vaccinated (6,700); tuberculin positive to 3 T.U. (16,000); and tuberculin positive to 100 T.U. but not to 3 T.U. (6,600). Vole bacillus vaccine was not used in the London area, and was not available for all of the time in the Birmingham and Manchester areas. Many of the volunteers had a second examination (similar to the first) three to five months after entry, while they were still at school. No participant was vaccinated or revaccinated by the investigating teams subsequent to the examination on entry.

After leaving school, participants in each of the five groups have been followed with similar intensity by means of a 14-month cycle of inquiry and examination, each cycle consisting of a postal inquiry, a home visit by a health visitor, and an examination which, as before, included a chest radiograph and tuberculin tests. As a result, contact was made with 94 per cent of the participants by at least one of these three means within 18 months of entry; information has since been obtained from many of the remaining 6 per cent. In addition to these methods of discovering the cases of tuberculosis which arose, information from notification lists of medical officers of health and from chest clinic records was also made available.

All definite and suspected cases of tuberculosis have been reviewed and classified by an independent assessor, who, to avoid bias, was kept unaware both of the results of all the tuberculin tests and of whether any vaccination had been performed. A total of 165 definite cases began within two and a half years of entry to the trial. Of these, 63 per cent were of pulmonary tuberculosis and 22 per cent of pleural effusion without evidence of pulmonary tuberculosis; 68 per cent of the cases were severe enough for the patients to be taken off work for at least three months. There was no death from the disease during the two and a half years.

The annual incidence of tuberculosis in the tuberculin-negative unvaccinated group was 1.94 per 1,000; in the B.C.G.-vaccinated group it was only 0.37 per 1,000; and in the vole-bacillus-vaccinated group only 0.44 per 1,000. (Strictly this last figure should be compared with the incidence among those participants in the Birmingham and Manchester areas who were admitted concurrently with those given vole bacillus vaccine—namely, with 2.06 per 1,000 in the negative unvaccinated group and 0.31 per 1,000 in the B.C.G.-vaccinated group.) Each vaccine therefore conferred a substantial and similar degree of protection against tuberculosis over a period of two and a half years in adolescence. The strength of the earlier batches of vole bacillus vaccine was below the standard intended.

The protection conferred by each vaccine was evident soon after it had been given, and was still substantial between two and two and a half years after entry. Supplementary incomplete information up to four years suggests that the protection is maintained for this period. Although the numbers of cases in the vaccinated groups were small, the evidence does not indicate that protection was limited to tuberculosis in particular sites, nor that the pulmonary lesions were less extensive or severe in those who had been vaccinated but developed the disease.

Complications of vaccination consisted of occasional regional adenitis and delayed healing of the local lesion. Two cases of erythema nodosum were also attributed to B.C.G. vaccine. In addition, a number of those given vole bacillus vaccine developed lesions, indistinguishable from lupus vulgaris, at the site of vaccination; up to the end of June, 1955, 22 of these had required treatment.

Among the entrants with a positive reaction to 3 T.U. the annual incidence of tuberculosis was 1.75 per 1,000, compared with 0.74 per 1,000 among those positive only to 100 T.U. The annual incidence was particularly high among those with strong reactions to 3 T.U. on entry (15 mm. induration or more)—namely, 2.93 per 1,000, compared with 0.78 per 1,000 among those with 5–14 mm. induration. Thus, in this age group those highly sensitive to tuberculin appear to have a special risk of developing tuberculosis.

The annual incidence of 0.74 per 1,000 among those positive only to 100 T.U. compares with 1.94 per 1,000 in the concurrent negative unvaccinated group. These results are not those which would be expected if positive reactions to 100 T.U. only were non-specific for tuberculous infection. The interpretation of weak reactions to tuberculin requires further investigation.

If no participant in the present trial had been vaccinated, a total of 246 cases of tuberculosis would have been expected within two and a half years of entry; if all the tuberculin-negative entrants had received B.C.G. vaccine a total of 111 would have been expected. This represents an expected reduction of 55 per cent in the total incidence of tuberculosis for the two and a half years. However, 134 cases of previously unsuspected definite tuberculosis which were present on entry were excluded from the trial, nearly all as a result of the initial radiographic examination. In the absence of this radiograph, many of these cases would apparently have arisen after entry, and the apparent reduction in the total incidence of tuberculosis would have been only of the order of 35 per cent.

The implications of these interim findings for the use of vaccination in the control of tuberculosis in adolescents are discussed. The trial is still in progress, and later reports will contain more detailed analyses over longer periods of time.

REFERENCES

Aronson, J. D. (1948). *Amer. Rev. Tuberc.* **58**, 255.
Aronson, J. D., and Aronson, C. F. (1952). *J. Amer. med. Ass.* **149**, 334.
Dahlström, G. (1953). *Acta tuberc. scand.* Suppl. **32**.
Dahlström, G., and Difs, H. (1951). *Acta tuberc. scand.* Suppl. **27**.
Edwards, L. B., and Palmer, C. E. (1953). *Lancet*, **i**, 53.
Frew, H. W. O., Davidson, J. R., and Reid, J. T. W. (1953). *Brit. med. J.* **i**, 133.
Medical Research Council (1952). *Lancet*, **i**, 775.

Ministry of Education (1947). *The New Secondary Education*. London: H.M.S.O.
Ministry of Education (1954). *Education in 1953*. Report of the Ministry of Education Cmd. 9155. London: H.M.S.O.
Ministry of Health (1949). Circular 72/49.
Ministry of Health (1953). Circular 22/53.
Palmer, C. E. (1953). *Amer. Rev. Tuberc.* **68,** 678.
Palmer, C. E., and Shaw, L. W. (1935). *Amer. Rev. Tuberc.* **68,** 462.
Sergent, E., Cantanei, A., and Ducros-Rougebief, H. (1954). *Arch. Inst. Pasteur Algér.* **32,** 1.
Stein, S. C., and Aronson, J. D. (1953). *Amer. Rev. Tuberc.* **68,** 695.
Sula, L. (1955). In *Vaccination against Tuberculosis: Collection of Communications presented at the International Congress of the Pneumological and Phthisiological Society, 1953*, p. 252. Prague: State Health Publishing House.
Wells, A. Q. (1937). *Lancet*, **i,** 1221.
Wells, A. Q., and Wylie, J. A. H. (1955). Personal communication.
World Health Organization Tuberculosis Research Office (1955). *Bull. Wld. Hlth Org.* **12,** 63.
Wylie, J. A. H., Bennett, D. H., and Swithinbank, J. (1954). *Thorax*, **9,** 190.

CHAPTER 13

B.C.G. AND VOLE BACILLUS VACCINES IN THE PREVENTION OF TUBERCULOSIS IN ADOLESCENTS

SECOND REPORT

A CLINICAL trial of B.C.G. and vole bacillus vaccines, directed by the Tuberculosis Vaccines Clinical Trials Committee of the Medical Research Council (M.R.C.), was begun in England in 1950, and is still in progress. The effect of the vaccines is being studied during adolescence and early adult life in groups with no special risk of exposure to tuberculous infection, and initially free both from active tuberculosis and from known contact with the disease at home. There are more than 50,000 participants of both sexes in the investigation, all aged 14 to $15\frac{1}{2}$ years on entry, and now aged between 21 and 23 years. Those with negative reactions to tuberculin on entry were vaccinated with B.C.G. or vole bacillus vaccine or left unvaccinated, according to a method of random allocation. All the participants, including those with a positive reaction to tuberculin initially, have now (January, 1959) been followed intensively for more than six years.

The first report of this investigation (Medical Research Council, 1956; see also Hart, Pollock, and Sutherland, 1957) presented complete results after each participant had been in the trial for two and a half years. The present report gives corresponding results for the period of five years since entry to the trial, together with preliminary incomplete information for the period between five and seven and a half years after entry.

Second Report to the Medical Research Council by their Tuberculosis Vaccines Clinical Trials Committee. Members of the Committee: Dr. P. D'Arcy Hart (chairman), Dr. C. Metcalfe Brown, Sir John Charles, Professor R. Cruickshank, Dr. Marc Daniels (secretary until his death in 1953), Dr. W. Pointon Dick (resigned in 1951), Dr. J. E. Geddes, Professor A. Bradford Hill, Sir Wilson Jameson, Dr. V. H. Springett, Dr. Ian Sutherland, Dr. A. Q. Wells (died in 1956), Dr. G. S. Wilson, Dr. T. M. Pollock (secretary).

Reprinted from the *British Medical Journal*, 1959, ii, 379.

The work described was carried out by the Council's Tuberculosis Research Unit, with the assistance of many statutory and voluntary organizations.

PLAN AND CONDUCT OF THE TRIAL

A detailed description of the plan and conduct of the trail was given in the first report (Medical Research Council, 1956). The following are the main features.

The Intake

The participants in the trial volunteered with their parents' consent between September, 1950, and December, 1952; they were all aged between 14 and $15\frac{1}{2}$ years, and most (82 per cent) were between $14\frac{1}{2}$ and 15 years. All were in their final year at secondary modern schools in densely populated districts in or near North London, Birmingham, and Manchester. A record card bearing a printed serial number was prepared for each volunteer, who was then given the following standard examination by one of three special teams of the Tuberculosis Research Unit, each operating in one of the main areas: (a) A 35-mm. radiograph of the chest; and, if indicated, a full-plate radiograph. (b) An intracutaneous tuberculin (Mantoux) test with 3 T.U. (tuberculin units) of Old Tuberculin (human). (c) If there was no palpable infiltration, or if its greatest diameter was less than 5mm. at the end of 72 hours, the reaction to 3 T.U. was regarded as negative and another test was made with 100 T.U.

Participants with no infiltration, or with a diameter of infiltration of less than 5mm., in response to the second test, at the end of 72 hours, were regarded as negative reactors to 100 T.U. and were eligible for vaccination.

Vaccination Procedures

The children eligible for vaccination were allocated, according to the final digit of the serial number on their record card, to the unvaccinated group, or to one of the two vaccinated groups. B.C.G. vaccine was given in all three areas, but vole bacillus vaccine was not given in the London area. On a few occasions in the Birmingham and Manchester areas, when there was a temporary failure in the supply of one of the vaccines, the other was used instead. Because of these local differences the numbers of participants in the un-vaccinated groups and in the two vaccinated groups were unequal. Throughout the trial, however, and whatever vaccines were being given, the allocation was always strictly in accordance with the final digit of the serial number, and so was effectively random.

The B.C.G. vaccine used was the fresh liquid preparation from the State Serum Institute, Copenhagen, and was given by intra-cutaneous injection. In the course of the trial 75 of the Institute's routine batches were used. The viable units/mg. for each batch (Tolderlund, 1952, 1955) ranged from 7.8 to 53.4 m., and 74 per cent of the participants given B.C.G. were vaccinated with batches which had counts between 20 and 40 m. viable units/mg. The vole bacillus vaccine was a fresh liquid preparation from the Lister Institute, Elstree, Herts, and was given by multiple puncture. The earlier batches of this vaccine were below the strength originally intended. Further details of both vaccines, and of the vaccination procedures, are given in the first report (Medical Research Council, 1956); the tuberculin conversion rates are given below in Table **13,** 2.

The appropriate vaccine was given immediately after the reading of the test with 100 T.U.

Number of Participants in the Trial

In this report the numbers of participants in the trial have been estimated from the same representative samples of the record cards as were used in the first report. The cases of tuberculosis and other diseases, however, have, as before, been completely enumerated. (In the final report the analysis will be based on a complete enumeration of the participants also; in the meantime, however, checks have shown that any inaccuracies in the numbers of participants, as estimated from the samples, will not affect the final rates appreciably.)

The following groups of children were excluded from participation: (*a*) Those found or suspected to have any form of tuberculosis (apart from calcification of primary type) at the time of the first examination. (*b*) Those, who, at the time of the first examination, had been in recent contact at home with a case of pulmonary tuberculosis. (*c*) Those who failed to complete the first examination.

In addition, a small number (about 400) have been excluded from the analysis of the results for such reasons as having been given the wrong vaccine, incorrectly left unvaccinated, or given a tuberculosis vaccine prior to entering the trial. After these exclusions there remain 56,700 participants in the analysis.

As a result of the tuberculin tests and vaccinations at the first examination, the children were automatically classified on entry into the following five trial groups, in which they remain for the purpose of the ensuing analysis, whatever the results of subsequent tuberculin tests:

Negative unvaccinated.—Negative to 100 T.U. on entry and left unvaccinated: 13,300 participants.

Negative, B.C.G.-vaccinated.—Negative to 100 T.U. on entry and then given B.C.G. vaccine: 14,100 participants.

Negative, vole-bacillus-vaccinated.—Negative to 100 T.U. on entry and then given vole bacillus vaccine: 6,700 participants.

Positive to 3 T.U.—Positive to 3 T.U. on entry and left unvaccinated: 16,000 participants.

Positive only to 100 T.U.—Negative to 3 T.U. but positive to 100 T.U. on entry, and left unvaccinated: 6,600 participants.

Second Examination of Participants

In 1950 and 1951, the children in the trial had another chest radiograph before leaving school, usually three to five months after the first examination; those with negative reactions to 100 T.U. at the first examination, whether vaccinated or not, were retested as before. At the same time the B.C.G.- and vole-bacillus-vaccination reactions were examined. In 1952, to check the potency of the vaccines, a sample of the children given each batch had tuberculin tests performed, and vaccination reactions examined, three to five months after vaccination.

Follow-up of Participants

Since leaving school the participants in each of the five trial groups have had the following cycle of inquiry and examination, repeated at intervals of about 14 months: (a) An inquiry form by post about four months after leaving school (or after the previous chest radiograph). (b) A home visit by a trained nurse about six months after the postal inquiry. (c) The three teams have visited each district in turn about four months after the home visit, to take chest radiographs and make tuberculin tests, exactly as at the first examination at school (except that some of the tuberculin tests were read at 48 instead of 72 hours); participants who failed to attend this examination were invited again to a special examination about seven months later. Since June, 1954, all the radiographs have been read separately by a physician unconnected with the conduct of the trial as well as by the team physician.

The great majority of the participants have continued to live in their original areas, and only about 6 per cent have moved to a district (either in this country or abroad) not visited by the teams' mobile radiography units. For these participants the home visits and the radiographic examinations were arranged by the local health authority.

Arrangements were made with the medical services of the Royal Navy, the Army, and the Royal Air Force for the close follow-up of participants during their two-year period of military service. This has involved about two-thirds of the young men, mostly between the ages of 18 and 20 years. The Army and the Royal Air Force introduced a special scheme for the prompt notification to the M.R.C. teams of any case of tuberculosis which developed in a trial participant, and arranged, where practicable, for chest radiographs and (in the Royal Air Force) tuberculin tests on demobilization. The Royal Navy made available a nominal roll of those invalided with tuberculosis. During this period of military service the M.R.C. teams also made a single postal inquiry to the participant's home.

In addition, where it was known that a participant had attended one of the mass miniature radiography units of the National Health Service, or had had any other routine chest radiograph (for example, at an antenatal clinic), efforts were made to ascertain the result.

Recent analysis of a sample of the records (for all whose surnames began with A or D, representing 6.5 per cent of the total) has shown that contact was made by one or more of these means with 89 per cent of the participants during the two-year period 1957–8, compared with 94 per cent within the first 18 months after entry to the trial (Medical Research Council, 1956). Sixty per cent of the participants had at least one chest radiograph taken in 1957–8, compared with at least 74 per cent within the first two years after entry.

Information has also been continually made available to the teams from the tuberculosis notification registers of the medical officers of health and from the records of attendances at the chest clinics and mass radiography units of the National Health Service, in the districts concerned. Cases of tuberculosis have therefore come to the notice of the M.R.C. teams through the usual channels of the National Health Service (56 per cent of the cases within five years of entry) as well as by their own radiographic examinations (44 per cent). Throughout this report, the small number of cases arising among participants during their period of service in the Armed Forces have been included with the National Health Service cases.

Vaccination of Trial Participants from Outside Sources

No participant was vaccinated or revaccinated by the M.R.C. teams subsequent to the initial examination, and there was little opportunity for participants to receive B.C.G. vaccine from outside sources during the course of the trial. Those known to be in contact at home with pulmonary tuberculosis at the time of entry were excluded from participation, and the current national scheme for the vaccination of 13-year-old schoolchildren (Ministry of Health, 1953) did not begin until all the participants were aged at least 16 years. Some participants, however, have come into contact with tuberculosis at home since entry, and some have had an opportunity for vaccination in their occupation (for example, nursing) or in other ways.

Information on such vaccination has been made available to the teams at frequent intervals from the vaccination records of the chest physicians and medical officers of health in the districts concerned. In addition, any participant in the negative unvaccinated group who has become tuberculin-positive since September, 1955, has been routinely questioned about possible vaccination from outside sources, and the arm has been examined for a vaccination reaction. As a result of these inquiries and other information, it has been found that very few participants have been given B.C.G. vaccine from outside sources. A recent survey of a sample of the records has shown only four instances of non-trial B.C.G. vaccination in a total of about 2,500 participants from all trial groups (1.6 per 1,000). Two were initially in the tuberculin-negative unvaccinated group and one was in each of the two vaccinated groups. It is evident that the present extent of non-trial vaccination of participants can have had only a negligible influence on the results.

Records of Cases

The physicians in charge of the M.R.C. teams were not responsible for the further investigation or treatment of any participant who had an abnormal radiograph; those found to have an abnormal radiograph at an examination by one of the teams were referred to their local chest clinics. However, almost every case of definite or suspected tuberculosis brought to the notice of the teams was also examined by one of the team physicians, and further details of progress were obtained at regular intervals. To ensure that cases of tuberculosis were not missed, full records were kept, not only for the definite cases, but also for those in which tuberculosis was either suspected or considered to be even a possible diagnosis. Similar records were kept for all non-tuberculous pulmonary lesions which came to the notice of the teams. As a precaution, it was decided in November, 1953 (with retrospective application), that any pulmonary radiographic abnormality, whatever its apparent cause, which persisted for longer than 14 days without complete clearing must be investigated. Details were obtained of all deaths, from whatever cause.

In cases of definite or suspected tuberculosis arising in B.C.G.-vaccinated or vole-bacillus-vaccinated participants, routine examinations of cultures growing acid-fast bacilli were made to investigate whether the organisms were B.C.G. or vole bacilli.

Assessment of Cases

All definite, suspected, and possible cases of tuberculosis, and all other pulmonary radiographic abnormalities persisting for longer than 14 days, which came to the notice of the teams were reviewed by an independent assessor who was kept unaware of the results of any tuberculin tests and whether any vaccination had been performed. The great majority of the cases were reviewed by one assessor, but a second was used for a small number of cases which happened to be under the routine clinical care of the first; and a few cases of suspected tuberculosis of bones or joints, without bacteriological or histological confirmation, were referred to a third.

The assessor decided, from the periodic radiographs, from the results of the clinical examination by one of the team physicians, from the results of clinical examinations by other physicians, and from the results of any bacteriological or pathological examinations: (a) whether the disease was definite (and active) tuberculosis, possible tuberculosis, or not tuberculosis; for a few cases he decided that there was no evidence of any disease, tuberculous or non-tuberculous; (b) for cases of definite or possible tuberculosis, the form of the disease and the character, course, initial, and maximal extent of any lesions apparent on the series of radiographs; (c) for pulmonary lesions, the date of the first abnormal radiograph, or, for other lesions, the date when the first definite symptoms or signs were observed (irrespective of when the diagnosis of tuberculosis had been made); this date has been regarded as the starting-point of the illness, though it will be appreciated that for some cases the starting-point, thus defined, may be a considerable time after the true, but unknown, date of onset of the disease.

THE CASES OF TUBERCULOSIS

Cases of Tuberculosis Present on Entry to the Trial

As described in the first report (Medical Research Council, 1956), 70 cases of previously unsuspected definite tuberculosis were discovered at the first examination at school, and so were excluded from the trial. In addition (up to the end of January, 1959) 111 cases, discovered after the 56,700 participants had completed the first examination and had entered the trial, were judged by the assessor to have started before entry (all except seven were, unknown to the assessor, tuberculin positive on entry). Of these, 80 were cases of definite but previously unsuspected tuberculosis, 18 were definite cases with a history of tuberculosis prior to entry to the trial (unknown to the teams at the time of the first examination), and 13 were cases of possible tuberculosis. These 111 children should also have been excluded from the trial, and have therefore been excluded from the analysis.

In 86 of the 111 cases the radiograph taken on entry showed, on rescrutiny, abnormal appearances indicative of tuberculosis; in one case with a normal 35-mm. radiograph on entry there had been a pleural effusion two months earlier, and in 19 cases of non-pulmonary disease symptoms had been present before the participant entered the trial. There remain five cases of definite tuberculosis where the assessor decided that the disease must have been present at the time of entry, although the symptoms or lesions were not apparent until later. In one of the five, symptoms of non-pulmonary disease appeared only three months after the child had entered the trial. In the other four, pulmonary lesions were first seen on radiographs taken at the second examination at school; the 35-mm.

radiograph on entry in one case was considered not to be of sufficiently high quality to exclude the presence of the lesion, and in two others the film had been lost; in the fourth case the assessor considered that the lesion was probably present on entry but was obscured by bony shadow. These five children had (unknown to the assessor) all given a positive reaction to tuberculin on entry to the trial.

Tuberculous Lesions Attributed to Vaccination

In seven participants, lesions which developed subsequent to B.C.G. or vole-bacillus-vaccination were brought to the attention of the teams as cases of tuberculosis and submitted to the assessor, but were regarded by him as complications of vaccination. There were three cases of erythema nodosum, all observed one month after entry to the trial. There were also four cases of regional tuberculous adenitis (one cervical, two axillary, and one inguinal) observed three, six, eight, and 22 months respectively after entry to the trial. In the course of his assessment, the assessor suggested that if the participant had been vaccinated the lesions could have been due to the vaccinating organism. For these cases, and for no others, the assessor was then informed that the participant had been vaccinated. As a result, he attributed all seven cases to the vaccinating organism. The three cases of erythema nodosum occurred in B.C.G.-vaccinated participants, and the four cases of tuberculous adenitis in vole-bacillus-vaccinated participants (all of whom were given the vaccine after it had been brought up to standard—see Vaccination Procedures, above).

In addition, as described in the first report (Medical Research Council, 1956), examinations of the vole-bacillus-vaccination sites during the follow-up revealed occasional lesions indistinguishable from lupus vulgaris, at or around the site of vaccination. All occurred among the 4,200 participants given the vaccine after it had been brought up to standard. Of these cases, 23 severe enough to require treatment were found up to the end of January, 1959; all had been referred for treatment before July, 1955. A recent inquiry has shown that in 17 of these 23 cases the lesions had healed; three cases had made a satisfactory early response to treatment, but have not been seen recently; and three failed to attend for treatment or subsequent observation. The B.C.G.-vaccination sites were also examined as a routine, but no similar lesions were found.

All these lesions have been regarded as complications of vaccination, and none of the cases has been included in the tables which follow (but see Discussion, p. 332). It should be emphasized that there was no evidence that any of the other cases of tuberculosis in vaccinated participants were due to the vaccinating organisms (see Bacteriological and Pathological Investigations, p. 317).

Death from Tuberculosis in the First Five Years

Only one participant is known to have died of tuberculosis within five years of entry to the trial. The participant was in the tuberculin-negative unvaccinated group, and died from acute tuberculous meningitis 39 months after entry.

Incidence of Tuberculosis in the First Five Years

By the end of June, 1958, every participant had been in the trial for five years, and some for as long as seven and a half years. The great majority of the cases of tuberculosis starting within five years of entry are therefore presumed to have come by now (January, 1959) to the notice of the teams. A total of 349 cases of definite tuberculosis started within five years of entry (including the above fatal case) and a further 23 were assessed as possible tuberculosis. Of the definite cases, 153 occurred in the negative unvaccinated group, 27 in the B.C.G.-vaccinated group, 11 in the vole-bacillus-vaccinated group, 128 among those initially positive to 3 T.U., and 30 among those initially positive only to 100 T.U.

A valid assessment of the value of B.C.G. vaccination must be based upon those children who were admitted *concurrently* to the negative unvaccinated, the B.C.G.-vaccinated, and the two tuberculin-positive groups. The data are presented in this way in Section A of Table **13**, 1. (The comparison includes all the children admitted to the trial in these four groups, except for the small number who entered when vole bacillus vaccine only was available.) In this comparison there were 151 cases of tuberculosis in the tuberculin-negative unvaccinated group, giving an annual incidence of 2.29 cases per 1,000 participants. With its 27 cases, the annual incidence in the B.C.G.-vaccinated group was much lower, being 0.38 per 1,000, or approximately one-sixth of the rate in the negative unvaccinated group. The possibility of this difference having occurred by chance is remote (less than one in a million). Among those initially positive to 3 T.U. the annual incidence was 1.61 per 1,000,

TABLE 13, 1

Cases of Tuberculosis Starting Within Five Years of Entry to the Trial

Section*	Trial Group	Estimated No. of Participants	Definite Cases of Tuberculosis		Possible Cases of Tuberculosis Starting Within 5 Years
			No. Starting Within 5 Years	Annual Incidence per 1,000 Participants	
A	Children admitted con-currently with those given B.C.G. vaccine				
	Negative unvaccinated	13,200	151	2·29	9
	Negative, B.C.G. vaccinated	14,100	27	0·38	3
	Positive to 3 T.U.	15,800	127	1·61	6
	Positive only to 100 T.U.	6,500	30	0·92	3
B	Children admitted con-currently with those given vole bacillus vaccine				
	Negative unvaccinated	6,500	85	2·62	7
	Negative, vole bacillus vaccinated	6,700	11	0·33	2
	Positive to 3 T.U.	8,800	76	1·73	3
	Positive only to 100 T.U.	3,600	17	0·94	2
C	Children admitted con-currently with those given B.C.G. and those given vole bacillus vaccine				
	Negative, B.C.G. vaccinated	6,400	10	0·31	2
	Negative, vole bacillus vaccinated	6,400	8	0·25	2

* Many participants and cases of tuberculosis appear in more than one of the three separate sections of this table (see text), and the figures from different sections can therefore not be totalled. The total number of participants and cases of tuberculosis in each trial group are shown in Table 13, 8.

304

rather less than that in the negative unvaccinated group, while in the group positive only to 100 T.U. it was much less, namely 0.92 per 1,000; the latter rate was, however, higher than the rate in the B.C.G.-vaccinated group. These four rates all differ significantly from each other at the 1 per cent level. The variations in incidence *within* the group initially positive to 3 T.U., noted in the first report (Medical Research Council, 1956), are considered in detail below (see Incidence of Tuberculosis in Different Periods, p. 318).

Similarly, a valid assessment of the value of vole bacillus vaccination must be based upon those children admitted *concurrently* to the negative unvaccinated, the vole-bacillus-vaccinated, and the two tuberculin-positive groups, as shown in Section B of Table **13,** 1. (This comparison therefore includes some but not all of the children considered in Section A above, together with the small number who entered the trial at a time when vole bacillus vaccine only was available.) In this comparison there were 85 cases of tuberculosis in the negative unvaccinated group, giving an annual incidence of 2.62 per 1,000; in the vole-bacillus-vaccinated group there were 11 cases, giving a rate of 0.33 per 1,000, or approximately one-eighth of the rate in the negative unvaccinated group. The possibility of this difference having occurred by chance is remote (less than one in a million). Among those initially positive to 3 T.U. the annual incidence was 1.73 per 1,000, rather less than that in the negative unvaccinated group, while in the group positive only to 100 T.U. it was much less, namely 0.94 per 1,000; the latter rate was, however, higher than that in the vole-bacillus-vaccinated group. These four rates all differ significantly from each other at the 1 per cent level (apart from rates in the two initially positive groups, which differ from each other at the 5 per cent level).

Finally, a valid comparison between the value of B.C.G. and vole bacillus vaccination must also be based on concurrent admissions to these two groups; the date for this comparison are shown in Section C of Table **13,** 1. (These participants are all included either in Section A or in Section B.) The difference between the annual rates for the B.C.G.-vaccinated group (0.31 per 1,000) and for the concurrent group of vole-bacillus-vaccinated children (0.25 per 1,000) does not attain statistical significance.

The 23 cases judged by the assessor to be possibly but not definitely due to tuberculosis are also shown in Table **13,** 1; their distribution among the five trial groups is similar to that of the definite cases.

The above comparisons would not have been appreciably affected if these possible cases had been included with the definite cases.

Although it is essential for valid comparisons between the trial groups to base them upon concurrent admissions, it is also evident from Table **13,** 1 that the incidence of tuberculosis in each trial group is closely similar in the different sections of the table. In fact, when allowance is made for the overlap between the sections, none of these differences in incidence attains statistical significance. Because of this homogeneity of the findings, it is unnecessary to set out all the results on a strictly concurrent basis. For most of this report, therefore, the findings are presented for the *whole* of each trial group.

Incidence of Tuberculosis in Participants Given Different Batches of B.C.G. Vaccine

Counts of viable bacilli were made as a routine on each weekly batch of B.C.G. vaccine at the State Serum Institute. Copenhagen, prior to dispatch to Britain. These counts were available for all except one of the 75 batches used in the trial (Tolderlund, 1952, 1955). It was thus possible to investigate whether the tuberculin conversion rate, or the incidence of tuberculosis, following vaccination, was associated with routine fluctuation in the strength of the vaccine. The batches were divided into four groups, according to viable count (Table, **13,** 2).

The total proportion converted (based on representative samples) was practically 100 per cent for each group of batches; but there was a definite trend in the proportion converted to 3 T.U. with increasing viable count, from 76 per cent for the batches with a count of less than 20 m. per cent viable units/mg. to 97 per cent for those with a count of 40 m. per cent or more.

Despite the trend in percentage converted to 3 T.U., there was no obvious trend in the incidence of tuberculosis following vaccination with the different groups of batches. In particular, it is of value to note that the weakest batches in the range used conferred substantial protection against the disease. Of the 12 batches with counts of less than 20 m. viable units/mg., 11 had counts between 19.2 and 11.4 m., and one had a count of 7.8 m. Four cases of tuberculosis started within five years of entry among the 1,900 participants vaccinated with these 12 batches, giving an annual incidence of 0.42 per 1,000. This was considerably less than the annual rate of 2.00 per 1,000

TABLE 13, 2

Conversion Rates and Incidence of Tuberculosis in Participants Given Different Batches of the B.C.G. and the Vole Bacillus Vaccines

Classification of Vaccine Batches			Conversion Rates (Estimated from Sample)				Incidence of Tuberculosis		
			No. Who Completed Skin Tests 3 to 5 Months After Vaccination	Percentages with Positive Tuberculin Reactions			Total Participants Given These Batches (Estimated from Sample)	Definite Cases of Tuberculosis Starting Within 5 Years	Annual Incidence per 1,000 Participants
				Positive to 3 T.U.	Positive Only to 100 T.U.	Total Positive			
B.C.G. Vaccine	Viable Units (million) per mg.	Under 20	1,200	76	24	100	1,900	4	0·42
		20–	2,200	82	17	99	4,300	12	0·56
		30–	3,000	89	11	100	6,200	7	0·23
		40 or more	800	97	3	100	1,500	4	0·53
		All batches*	7,200	86	14	100	13,900	27	0·39
Vole Bacillus Vaccine	Concentration of Bacilli and Strain	Substandard† (Jan., 1951/July, 1951)	1,800	31	56	87	2,500	5	0·40
		Standard (Sept., 1951/Dec., 1952)	2,000	88	12	100	4,200	6	0·29
		All batches	3,800	61	33	94	6,700	11	0·33

* Excluding one batch of B.C.G. vaccine, given to about 200 participants, for which no viable count was available.
† That is, below the standard originally intended.

for the 18 cases occurring in the 1,800 concurrent admissions to the negative unvaccinated group (not shown in Table **13**, 2); the difference is significant at the 1 per cent level.

Incidence of Tuberculosis in Participants Given Certain Batches of Vole Bacillus Vaccine

As described in the first report, the early batches of vole bacillus vaccine, used from January to July, 1951, were weaker than the standard originally intended, and the strength of the subsequent batches was adjusted to the intended standard. The findings on tuberculin conversion and subsequent incidence of tuberculosis in participants given these two groups of batches are shown in the lower part of Table **13**, 2.

For the early batches the proportion converted to 3 T.U. was 31 per cent, and the total proportion converted was 87 per cent; for the later batches the corresponding proportions were 88 per cent and 100 per cent.

Despite this considerable difference in the degree of sensitivity produced by the two groups of batches, the incidence of tuberculosis in the participants given the early vaccine was not substantially different from that in the participants given the late vaccine. These early batches, despite the low conversion rate, thus afforded considerable protection against the disease. Five cases of tuberculosis started within five years of entry among the 2,500 participants vaccinated with the early batches, giving an annual incidence of 0.40 per 1,000, compared with 35 cases among the 2,300 concurrent admissions to the negative unvaccinated group, an annual incidence of 3.04 per 1,000 (not shown in Table **13**, 2). The difference between the rates is significant at the 0.1 per cent level.

Evidence of Vaccination in Cases of Tuberculosis Occurring in Vaccinated Participants

Evidence that the vaccination was technically satisfactory for the 38 definite cases of tuberculosis in the two vaccinated groups is summarized in Table **13**, 3. Within six months of vaccination 21 were found to be tuberculin positive (18 to 3 T.U.), and 19 of these (not shown separately in the table) had a normal radiograph either then or subsequently (two had no radiograph before the disease started.) A further five cases were tuberculin positive (four to 3 T.U.) when first tested more than six months after vaccination, and all

TABLE **13,** 3

Evidence of Technically Satisfactory Vaccination in the 38 Vaccinated Participants who Developed Definite Tuberculosis within Five Years of Entry to the Trial

Results of First Skin Test After Vaccination and Before Starting-point of Disease		Vaccination Reaction			
		Total	Present	Absent	Not Examined
Tests within 6 months of vaccination*	Positive to 3 T.U.	18	14	2	2
	Positive only to 100 T.U.	3	2	1	0
	Negative to 100 T.U.	0	0	0	0
Tests 6 months or more after vaccination*	Positive to 3 T.U.	4	4	0	0
	Positive only to 100 T.U.	1	0	1	0
	Negative to 100 T.U.	0	0	0	0
	No test	12	10	1	1
	All cases	38	30	5	3

* Of the total of 26 vaccinated participants known to have become tuberculin positive, 24 had a normal chest radiograph at the same time or subsequently; two had no chest radiographs taken after vaccination and before the starting-point of the disease.

five had a normal chest radiograph at the same time or subsequently. Of these 26 cases, 20 were found to have in addition a healed vaccination reaction, in two the vaccination site was not examined, and in four (all vole-vacillus-vaccinated) the vaccination reaction was looked for but not found (four, six, six, and 12 months after vaccination respectively.)

In 12 cases there were no tuberculin tests after entry and before the disease developed, and therefore no information on whether vaccination produced tuberculin conversion, but 10 had a healed vaccination reaction. In one of the remaining two cases it has not been possible to examine the B.C.G.-vaccination site, and, in the other, the vole-bacillus-vaccination site was examined only 24 months after entry to the trial, when no reaction was observed; a reaction may nevertheless have occurred and subsequently disappeared (Medical Research Council, 1956).

In summary, these last two cases of the 38 may not have been satisfactorily vaccinated, as judged by the usual criteria. It should be added that one B.C.G.-vaccinated case had a starting-point three months after vaccination; for this, the only case in a vaccinated participant within 12 months of vaccination, the disease could well have arisen before any protection had been conferred.

The Forms of Tuberculosis

The forms of tuberculosis which occurred in the various trial groups are shown in Table **13,** 4. If two or more were present, the case was assigned to the major form—for example, tuberculous meningitis took precedence over any other form, and pulmonary tuberculosis took precedence over a pleural effusion.

Seventy per cent of the cases (245 of 349) were of pulmonary tuberculosis. There is no evidence of any important differences between the five trial groups in this percentage.

Tuberculous pleural effusion, without pulmonary tuberculosis, was the next most numerous form, with 59 cases (17 per cent). In addition, a pleural effusion preceded, or was discovered at the same time as, the pulmonary lesions in 13 more cases (not identified separately in the table). The ratio of pleural effusions to total cases was greatest in the negative unvaccinated group (44 of 153, or 29 per cent) and least among those initially positive to 3 T.U. (12 of 128, or 9 per cent), this difference being significant at the 0.1 per cent level. There were eight pleural effusions among the 38 cases in the vaccinated groups combined, and eight among the 30 cases initially positive only to 100 T.U. There was no significant difference in the ratio of pleural effusions to total cases between the vaccinated and the negative unvaccinated groups.

There were two cases of hilar gland enlargement, with no other lesion, both in the negative unvaccinated group. Hilar gland enlargement was also found, however, in association with other lesions (mainly pulmonary lesions, pleural effusions, or both) in 34 more cases (not identified separately in the table). In all, hilar gland enlargement was noted most frequently among the cases in the negative unvaccinated group (27 of 153, or 18 per cent) and least frequently among those initially positive to 3 T.U. (two of 128, or 2 per cent), this difference being significant at the 0.1 per cent level. Hilar gland enlargement was noted in three of the 38 cases in the vaccinated groups combined and in four of the 30 cases initially positive only to 100 T.U. There was no significant difference in the ratio of hilar

TABLE 13, 4

Definite Cases of Tuberculosis Starting Within Five Years of Entry to the Trial, According to Form of Disease

Trial Group	Total Cases	Pulmonary Tuberculosis		Tuberculous Pleural Effusion*	Hilar Gland Enlargement†	Tuberculous Meningitis	Bone or Joint Tuberculosis	Tuberculous Cervical Adenitis	Tuberculous Peritonitis	Erythema Nodosum	Other Forms
		No.	%								
Negative unvaccinated	153	100	65	36§	2	4	2‡	3	2‖	3	1¶
Negative, B.C.G. vaccinated	27	20	74	5	0	0	0	0	1	1	0
Negative, vole bacillus vaccinated	11	7	64	3	0	0	1	0	0	0	0
Positive to 3 T.U.	128	97	76	9	0	1	3	11	1	0	6**
Positive only to 100 T.U.	30	21	70	6	0	0	2	0	0	0	1††
All groups	349	245	70	59	2	5	8	14	4	4	8

* Without evidence of pulmonary tuberculosis. † Without other evidence of tuberculosis. ‡ One with erythema nodosum. § Three with erythema nodosum. ‖ One with small associated pulmonary lesion. ¶ Tuberculous bronchiectasis. ** One tuberculous endobronchitis; one tuberculous tonsils and cervical glands; three genito-urinary tuberculosis. †† Tuberculous axillary adenitis.

gland enlargements to total cases between the vaccinated and the negative unvaccinated groups.

Twelve cases of tuberculous cervical adenitis (one associated with tuberculous tonsils) occurred in the group initially positve to 3 T.U. and three in the negative unvaccinated group; none occurred in any of the other groups.

There were five cases of tuberculous meningitis—four in the negative unvaccinated group and one (41 months after entry) in the group initially positive to 3 T.U. In addition, five of the pulmonary lesions were of miliary type; four of these were in the negative un-vaccinated group and one (with a starting-point 57 months after entry) in the group initially positive to 3 T.U. Thus, tuberculous meningitis or miliary tuberculosis occurred in eight of the 153 cases in the negative unvaccinated group and in two of the 128 cases in the group initially positive to 3 T.U. None occurred in the vaccinated groups, or in the group initially positive to 100 T.U.

Nature, Initial and Maximal Extent of the Pulmonary Lesions

The assessor classified the pulmonary lesions according to both their initial and their maximal extent. The *initial* extent was that seen on the first abnormal chest radiograph, a substantial pro-portion of these being 35-mm. radiographs. If a full-size chest radiograph had been taken within six weeks after the abnormal 35-mm. radiograph, the assessments of cavitation and extent were made instead from the full-size radiographs, because of the difficulty of making an accurate classification from a miniature film. (In a few instances a '5-in. by 4-in.' (12.5-cm. by 10-cm.) film was used similarly for the assessments, if no suitable full-size radiograph was available.) In all, 54 (22 per cent) of the assessments of initial extent were made only from a 35-mm. radiograph; these included 12 cases which subsequently developed cavitation, no cavitation having been seen on the abnormal 35-mm. radiograph.

The nature and *initial* radiographic extent of the pulmonary lesions are shown in Table 13, 5. Of the total of 245 pulmonary cases, five, just referred to, were of miliary type, and 51 (21 per cent) showed cavitation on the first abnormal radiograph. Lesions with cavitation were observed in 25 per cent of the 100 cases in the negative unvaccinated group; in 22 per cent of the 27 cases in the vaccinated groups combined; and in 17 per cent of the 117 cases in the groups initially positive to 3 T.U. or 100 T.U. There is thus no

TABLE 13, 5

Definite Cases of Pulmonary Tuberculosis Starting Within Five Years of Entry to the Trial, According to the Nature and Extent of the Pulmonary Lesions Seen on the First Abnormal Chest Radiograph

Trial Group	Total Pulmonary Cases	Miliary Type of Lesions	Lesions with Cavitation			Lesions without Cavitation		
			Lesions Involving More than 2 Rib Interspaces	Lesions More than 6 sq. cm. in Extent Involving Up to 2 Rib Interspaces	Lesions Up to 6 sq. cm. in Extent	Involving More than 2 Rib Interspaces	More than 6 sq. cm. in Extent, Involving Up to 2 Rib Interspaces	Up to 6 sq. cm. in Extent
Negative unvaccinated	100	4	18	6	1	4	36	31
Negative, B.C.G. vaccinated	20	0	2	2	1	0	6	9
Negative, vole bacillus vaccinated	7	0	1	0	0	0	3	3
Positive to 3 T.U.	96*	1	8	7	1	8	37	34
Positive only to 100 T.U.	21	0	1	3	0	1	11	5
All groups	244*	5	30	18	3	13	93	82

* Excluding one patient for whom the extent of the lesions was not classified because the first abnormal radiograph, taken before a thoracoplasty was performed, could not be found; the diagnosis was confirmed bacteriologically.

evidence of important differences in the presence of cavitation between cases in the different groups.

Lesions involving more than two rib interspaces (with or without cavitation, and including the miliary cases) were observed on the first abnormal film in 26 (26 per cent) of the 100 cases in the negative unvaccinated group, compared with 3 (11 per cent) of the 27 cases in the vaccinated groups combined; at the other extreme, lesions up to 6 sq. cm. in extent (on a full-size chest radiograph) were observed in 32 (32 per cent) of the cases in the negative unvaccinated group, compared with 13 (48 per cent) of those in the vaccinated groups combined. There is thus a suggestion (which does not attain statistical significance) that in the vaccinated cases the lesions, when first detected, were on average not as extensive as those in the negative unvaccinated group.

The nature and the *maximal* radiographic extent of the pulmonary lesions are shown in Table **13,** 6. Comparison with Table **13,** 5 shows that cases with cavitation (on one or more postero-anterior radiographs) had increased from 51 to 79 since the first abnormal radiograph. (Tomograms were not taken as a routine: to avoid bias in comparing the severity of the lesions in the different groups, evidence of cavitation obtained only from tomograms has therefore been disregarded.) Many of the lesions had also increased in extent since the first abnormal radiograph; lesions which involved more than two rib interspaces (with or without cavitation) had increased from 43 to 64, and lesions with an extent of 6 sq. cm. or less had decreased from 85 to 55.

Lesions with cavitation were now observed in 33 per cent of the 100 cases in the negative unvaccinated group, in 33 per cent of the 27 cases in the vaccinated groups combined and in 32 per cent of the 117 cases in the tuberculin-positive groups combined. There is again no evidence of important differences in the presence of cavitation between cases in the different groups.

On the other hand, lesions involving more than two rib interspaces (with or without cavitation, and including the miliary cases) were now observed in 36 (36 per cent) of the cases in the negative unvaccinated group, in six (22 per cent) of the cases in the vaccinated groups combined, and in 27 (23 per cent) of the cases in the tuberculin-positive groups combined; at the other extreme, lesions up to 6 sq. cm. in extent were observed in 23 (23 per cent) of the cases in the negative unvaccinated group, in 11 (41 per cent) of those in the

TABLE 13, 6

Definite Cases of Pulmonary Tuberculosis Starting Within Five Years of Entry to the Trial, According to the Nature and Maximal Extent of the Pulmonary Lesions

Trial Group	Total Pulmonary Cases	Miliary Type of Lesions	Lesions with Cavitation			Lesions without Cavitation		
			Lesions Involving More than 2 Rib Interspaces	Lesions More than 6 sq. cm. in Extent Involving Up to 2 Rib Interspaces	Lesions Up to 6 sq. cm. in Extent	Involving More than 2 Rib Interspaces	More than 6 sq. cm. in Extent, Involving Up to 2 Rib Interspaces	Up to 6 sq. cm. in Extent
Negative unvaccinated	100	4	22	10	1	10	31	22
Negative, B.C.G. vaccinated	20	0	5	0	1	0	6	8
Negative, vole bacillus vaccinated	7	0	1	2	0	0	2	2
Positive to 3 T.U.	96*	1	19	12	0	4	44	16
Positive only to 100 T.U.	21	0	1	5	0	2	8	5
All Groups	244*	5	48	29	2	16	91	53

* See footnote to Table **13**, 5

315

vaccinated groups, and in 21 (18 per cent) of those in the tuberculin-positive groups. There is again a suggestion (which does not attain statistical significance) that pulmonary tuberculosis was on average rather less extensive in the vaccinated than in the unvaccinated cases. In other words, the degree of protection from vaccination for the extensive lesions was at least as great as, and may have been greater than, that for the less extensive lesions.

Action Taken by the National Health Service Physician Assuming Charge of the Patient

Further evidence of the serious nature of many of the cases of tuberculosis which occurred is provided by Table **13,** 7. Of the 349 patients, 243 (70 per cent) were taken off work for at least three

TABLE **13,** 7

Definite Cases of Tuberculosis Starting Within Five Years of Entry to the Trial, According to the Action Taken by the Clinician

Trial Group	Total Cases	Taken Off Work		Remaining at Work Under Observation
		For 3 Months or More	For Less Than 3 Months	
Negative unvaccinated	153	112	7	34*
Negative, B.C.G. vaccinated	27	15	1	11*
Negative, vole bacillus vaccinated	11	7	0	4
Positive to 3 T.U.	128	86	12	30*
Positive only to 100 T.U.	30	23	2	5
All groups	349	243	22	84

* Including one patient who failed to attend the clinic for complete investigation.

months by the physician assuming charge of the patient. Of these 243 patients 222 received chemotherapy, collapse therapy, or surgical treatment, in addition to rest in bed; 14 of the remaining 21 were cases of pleural effusion. At the other extreme, 84 patients (24 per cent) remained at work and were kept under observation; 18 of these patients also received some chemotherapy.

Of the 153 patients in the negative unvaccinated group, 73 per cent were taken off work for three months or more, compared with

58 per cent of the 38 patients in the vaccinated groups combined, and 69 per cent of the 158 in the tuberculin-positive groups combined. There is thus again a suggestion (not statistically significant) that the cases were less severe in the vaccinated than in the unvaccinated. In other words, the degree of protection from vaccination for the severe lesions was at least as great as, and may have been greater than, that for the less severe lesions.

Bacteriological and Pathological Investigations

Of the 245 cases of pulmonary tuberculosis, 18 had no bacteriological examination at any time. Positive bacteriological results were obtained in 92 of the remaining 227 cases—67 on culture and in 25 only on direct microscopic examination. In 10 of the 135 with negative results the examinations were made only after the start of chemotherapy, but all the other 125 had negative results (76 from culture of laryngeal swab or gastric lavage, 18 on direct examination, and 31 on culture of sputum) at a time when no chemotherapy had been given. Since the investigation and treatment of all cases were carried out at local chest clinics and were not the responsibility of the M.R.C. team physicians, there was no opportunity for the latter to initiate intensive bacteriological examinations, and in many instances no special emphasis was laid upon these tests in the routine management of the cases. As a consequence, the proportion of cases confirmed bacteriologically is low.

In all, tubercle bacilli were isolated from 39 of the 100 cases of pulmonary tuberculosis in the tuberculin-negative unvaccinated group, from nine of the 20 cases in the B.C.G.-vaccinated group, from three of the seven in the vole-bacillus-vaccinated group, from 31 of the 97 in those positive to 3 T.U., and from 10 of the 21 in those positive only to 100 T.U. The organisms isolated from the nine cases in the B.C.G.-vaccinated group and from the three in the vole-bacillus-vaccinated group were found to be virulent and of human type.

A specimen of the fluid was examined in only 36 of the 59 cases of pleural effusion classified as tuberculous; in 32 the fluid was sterile, and in 23 of these a high proportion of lymphocytes was recorded; in the other four cases (none vaccinated) tubercle bacilli were cultured from the fluid. In six of the eight cases of tuberculosis of bones or joints, and in 10 of the 14 cases of cervical adenitis, the diagnosis was established by histological examination; in one of the remaining four cases of cervical adenitis the diagnosis was confirmed bacteriologically. Of the five cases of tuberculous meningitis, four were confirmed by bacteriological examination of the cerebrospinal fluid, and one at the post-mortem examination (see Death from Tuberculosis, p. 303).

Reliability of the Independent Assessments

It is conceivable that the withholding of the information on the results of skin tests, essential though it is for an unbiased comparison between the various groups, might have resulted in some cases being incorrectly diagnosed by the assessor. As in the previous report, therefore, his diagnosis is compared with that of the chest clinic or other physician taking charge of the case. For 332 (95 per cent) of the 349 definite cases of tuberculosis arising after entry and accepted for this report, there was agreement on diagnosis between assessor and physician in charge. In addition to the 349 cases, however, a further 13 were regarded by the physician in charge, but not by the assessor, as definite tuberculosis.

Incidence of Tuberculosis in Different Periods Since Entry to the Trial

As already described, the assessor decided retrospectively, from the detailed records of each case of tuberculosis, the date of the earliest radiographic or clinical manifestation of the disease. This has been regarded as the starting-point of the illness. Because the starting-point does not necessarily represent the true (and unknown) date of onset of the disease, the number of cases with starting-points in a given period will depend partly upon the intensity of radiographic examination of participants during that period. Since this intensity has not differed from group to group, the incidence rates in different trial groups *in a particular period of time* may validly be compared. However, the intensity of radiographic examination has shown some decline in the course of the trial, and caution must therefore be exercised when comparing the incidence rates in a particular trial group *from one period to another*.

Table 13, 8 gives the numbers of definite cases of tuberculosis with starting-points in the first and second periods of two and a half years since entry to the trial, with corresponding incidence rates (also illustrated in Figs 13, 1 and 13, 2). The table and the figures also contain some preliminary information for a third period, from five to seven and a half years after entry. Although the information

TABLE 13, 8

Definite Cases of Tuberculosis, According to the Interval Between Entry and the Earliest Radiographic or Clinical Manifestation (the Starting-point) of the Illness

Trial Group	Estimated No. of Participants	Total Cases			Annual Incidence per 1,000 Participants		
		Starting Within 2½ Years of Entry*	Starting Between 2½ and 5 Years After Entry	Starting Between 5 and 7½ Years After Entry (Incomplete)	0–2½ Years	2½–5 Years	5–7½ Years
Negative unvaccinated	13,300	66	87	30	1·98	2·62	1·38
Negative, B.C.G.	14,100	15	12	8	0·43	0·34	0·34
Negative, vole bacillus vaccinated	6,700	7	4	3	0·42	0·24	0·29
Positive to 3 T.U.							
Induration 15 mm. or more in diameter	7,200	63	30	10	3·50	1·67	0·88
Induration 5–14 mm. in diameter	8,800	17	18	6	0·77	0·82	0·44
Positive only to 100 T.U.	6,600	12	18	8	0·73	1·09	0·76
All groups	56,700	180	169	65	—	—	—

* These figures are slightly greater than those for the first two and a half years given in the first report (M.R.C., 1956) as a result of more recent information.

is incomplete for this period, the annual incidence rates have been calculated by taking into account the varying periods of observation for participants beyond the first five years.

During the first two and a half years the annual incidence in the negative unvaccinated group was 1.98 per 1,000, in the B.C.G.-vaccinated group 0.43 per 1,000, and in the vole-bacillus-vaccinated group 0.42 per 1,000 (Fig. **13,** 1). The incidence in the two vaccinated groups combined was 21 per cent of that in the negative unvaccinated

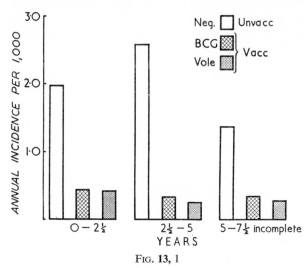

FIG. **13,** 1

Annual incidence of tuberculosis in the negative unvaccinated and
the two vaccinated groups

group. During the second two and a half years the corresponding rates were 2.62, 0.34, and 0.24 per 1,000; the incidence in the two vaccinated groups combined was 12 per cent of that in the negative unvaccinated group. There is clearly no evidence of any waning in the protection afforded by either of the vaccines up to five years after vaccination. The incomplete figures for the period between five and seven and a half years also show no evidence of any serious decline in protection, the incidence in the two vaccinated groups combined being 24 per cent of that in the negative unvaccinated group. The average duration of observation of the participants so far is six and a half years. Protection from both vaccines has therefore remained at a high level for at least this length of time.

Turning to the groups with positive reactions to tuberculin initially, those with the largest reactions (15 mm. induration or more to 3 T.U.) have been separated in Table **13,** 8 and Fig **13,** 2 from those with smaller reactions to 3 T.U., because they were found in the first report (Medical Research Council, 1956) to have a particularly high incidence of tuberculosis in the first two and a half years. During this period the annual incidence in this sub-group was 3.50

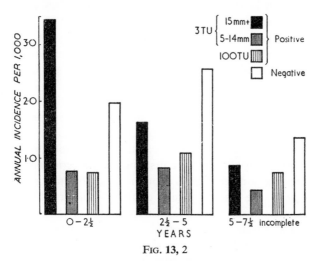

FIG. **13,** 2

Annual incidence of tuberculosis in initially positive and negative
unvaccinated groups

per 1,000, substantially greater than that in the negative unvaccinated group (1.98 per 1,000). It was very much greater than the rates among those with smaller reactions to 3 T.U. (0.77 per 1,000), as well as among those positive only to 100 T.U. (0.73 per 1,000). During the second two and a half years the incidence in the group with the larger initial reactions to 3 T.U. (1.67 per 1,000) was now substantially *less* than that in the negative unvaccinated group (2.62 per 1,000); the rate still was greater than the rates of 0.82 and 1.09 per 1,000 among the two groups with weaker positive reactions. On the basis of the incomplete information for the period between five and seven and a half years, the incidence in the group with the larger initial reactions to 3 T.U. was still rather greater than the rates in the two groups with weaker positive reactions; as in the preceding period, it was less than that in the negative unvaccinated group. It will be noted that in each of the three periods the lowest rates were those among the vaccinated participants.

In interpreting the trends in incidence from period to period, a number of points must be considered. First, there is the steep increase in the total incidence of tuberculosis between the ages of 15 and 20 years, and one might therefore expect an increase in at least some of the trial groups. On the other hand, there has been in England a fall in the risk of exposure to tuberculosis in this age group (as indicated by notification data) from about 1952 onwards. Finally, the general slight decline in the intensity of follow-up during the course of the trial (see Follow-up of Participants, p. 297) may have enhanced any decline, and detracted from any increase, in the incidence rates.

Considering first the group with the larger reactions to 3 T.U. initially, and taking these points into account, there seems no doubt of the steep decline in incidence from the high initial rate. (The different forms of tuberculosis appear to have declined to a similar extent in this group; between the first and second periods of two and a half years, the number of cases of pulmonary tuberculosis decreased from 47 to 23, the cases of pleural effusion from three to two, and the other cases from 13 to five). In contrast, the rates in the two groups with weaker positive reactions initially have remained at much the same level during the whole period of seven and a half years, with the result that the rates in all three initially tuberculin-positive groups are now not markedly different.

In the negative unvaccinated group, an increase between the first and second periods of two and a half years, and a larger decrease between the second and the third period, have been apparent. Parallel with this there has been little change in the rates in the two vaccinated groups. It is difficult to decide the relative contributions of the factors referred to above in explaining these trends.

MORTALITY AND MORBIDITY FROM CAUSES OTHER THAN TUBERCULOSIS

Deaths from Causes Other than Tuberculosis

The number of participants known to have died within five years of entry to the trial is 126: one from tuberculosis (p. 303), 70 from other diseases, and 55 from accidental causes or on active military service. Of the 70 deaths from non-tuberculous diseases, 22 were due to malignant disease; no other individually classified cause was responsible for as many as 10 deaths.

Table **13, 9** shows that the mortality from non-tuberculous diseases was less in each of the vaccinated groups than in the corresponding negative unvaccinated group, but the numbers are small and the differences are not statistically significant. The mortality among those who were tuberculin positive (to either 3 or 100 T.U.) was rather greater than among those who were tuberculin negative on entry (whether vaccinated or not); for Section A of the table the difference is significant at the 5 per cent level.

Table **13, 9** also shows that the mortality from accidental causes (including deaths on active military service) was similar in each of the vaccinated groups and in the corresponding unvaccinated group. There was no great difference in the mortality between those who were tuberculin positive (to either 3 or 100 T.U.) and those who were tuberculin negative on entry (whether vaccinated or not).

Cases of Non-tuberculous Diseases

A total of 152 cases, when submitted to the assessor, were classified by him as not due to tuberculosis. These consisted mainly of chest diseases such as pneumonia, bronchiectasis, and pleurisy, submitted because the radiographic abnormality persisted for more than 14 days (see Records of Cases, p. 299), but they included also a few non-pulmonary lesions where tuberculosis, although a possible diagnosis, was not accepted by the assessor.

Table **13, 9** shows that there are no more than chance differences between the rates in the various trial groups, and indicates that there is no protective effect of B.C.G. or vole bacillus vaccine against these non-tuberculous diseases, when taken as a group. The principal categories were pneumonitis and other non-specified pulmonary lesions (62 cases), pneumothorax (22 cases), non-tuberculous pleural effusions (as judged by duration, resolution with non-tuberculous chemotherapy, etc.—18 cases), bronchiectasis and allied lesions(16 cases), and definite or possible sarcoidosis (seven cases). Analysis of the figures for each of these categories separately suggests that vaccination does not influence the incidence of disease in any of them. For example, three of the pleural effusions were in the negative unvaccinated group and five in the two vaccinated groups

TABLE 13, 9

Deaths from Causes Other than Tuberculosis and Cases Assessed as Diseases Other than Tuberculosis Within Five Years of Entry of the Trial; also Cases Assessed as Having No Evidence of Any Disease

Section*	Trial Group	Estimated No. of Participants	Deaths from Diseases Other Than Tuberculosis†		Deaths From Accidental Causes		Cases Assessed as Diseases Other Than Tuberculosis		Cases Assessed as No Disease
			No. Occurring Within 5 Years	Annual Mortality per 1,000 Participants	No. Occurring Within 5 Years	Annual Mortality per 1,000 Participants	No. Starting Within 5 Years	Annual Incidence per 1,000 Participants	
A — Children admitted concurrently with those given B.C.G. vaccine	Negative unvaccinated	13,200	16	0·24	12	0·18	35	0·53	9
	Negative, B.C.G. vaccinated	14,100	8	0·11	16	0·23	42	0·60	7
	Positive to 3 T.U.	15,800	25	0·32	15	0·19	49	0·62	12
	Positive only to 100 T.U.	6,500	12	0·37	10	0·31	17	0·52	3
B — Children admitted concurrently with those given vole bacillus vaccine	Negative unvaccinated	6,500	10	0·31	4	0·12	18	0·55	2
	Negative, vole bacillus vaccinated	6,700	7	0·21	3	0·09	9	0·27	3
	Positive to 3 T.U.	8,800	19	0·43	9	0·20	19	0·43	7
	Positive only to 100 T.U.	3,600	5	0·28	4	0·22	7	0·39	1

* Many participants, deaths, cases of diseases other than tuberculosis, and cases with no evidence of disease appear in both sections of this table (see text), and the figures from the two sections can therefore not be totalled.

† There was one death from tuberculosis within five years of entry (see text).

combined; nine occurred among those initially positive to 3 T.U., and one among those positive only to 100 T.U.

The final column of Table **13, 9** shows the distribution of the 34 cases, submitted to the assessor as suspected or possible cases of tuberculosis, for which he decided that there was no evidence of any disease, tuberculous or non-tuberculous; the number in each trial group is roughly proportionate to the number of participants in that group.

CRITICAL APPRAISAL OF THE DESIGN OF THE TRIAL

The present investigation was designed to give reliable estimates of the degree of protection afforded by B.C.G. and vole bacillus vaccination, and embodied three main safeguards against bias. These were, first, the random allocation of the tuberculin-negative participants to the unvaccinated and vaccinated groups on entry to the trial; second, the comprehensive scheme for the follow-up of the participants and the detection of cases of tuberculosis and other chest diseases among them, these methods being designed to be equally intensive and comprehensive in all the trial groups; and third, the system for the independent assessment of all the cases discovered, without any knowledge of skin-test results or of vaccination. It is desirable to examine critically the possibility of any deficiencies in the practical working-out of these safeguards before reliance is placed on the degree of protection revealed.

Before doing so, a general point concerning the background of the investigation will be considered. The trial took place among volunteers, initially not in known contact with tuberculosis at home, approximately 60 per cent of those approached agreeing to participate. It is possible that the effect of vaccination in this selected community may differ from its effect in the whole adolescent and young adult population of Britain. This point cannot be tested directly; but there is indirect evidence that the trial population is not grossly unrepresentative—namely, that when allowance is made for the effects of vaccination, the total of 349 cases of tuberculosis within five years of entry to the trial is of the order of magnitude that would have been expected from the national notification figures (Sutherland, 1959).

Allocation to the Tuberculin-negative Unvaccinated and Vaccinated Groups on Entry to the Trial

The reason for allocating the tuberculin-negative participants to the unvaccinated or to one of the vaccinated groups, according to the final digit of the serial number on the record card, was to ensure that the allocations were not determined either by any of the team members personally or by the participants themselves, but by an independent process. Care was taken to exclude from the analysis all of the few participants who were allocated to the incorrect group, in case any personal choice might have entered into these allocations. This effectively random allocation process should therefore have resulted in the concurrent admission of similar groups of participants to the negative unvaccinated and the two vaccinated groups, with no more than chance differences between them. Direct checks made on representative samples of the records show that the unvaccinated and vaccinated groups were closely similar on entry in their distributions by age, sex, and numbers of brothers and sisters.

Intensity of Follow-up and Case-finding Procedures

It was shown in the first report (Medical Research Council, 1956), that the success of the follow-up during the first 18 to 24 months after entry was similar in those concurrently admitted to the negative unvaccinated and the two vaccinated groups. Recent analysis of a further random sample of the records has also shown no appreciable differences between the negative unvaccinated and the two vaccinated groups in the proportions of the participants brought in contact with the teams, or given chest radiographs, in the period 1957–8. It may be concluded that the co-operation of the participants has been similar in these groups throughout the trial; there is thus no reason to believe that the numbers of cases reported have been affected by any differences in the intensity of the case-finding procedures from group to group.

Participant's Knowledge of the Skin-test and Vaccination State

As described in the first report (Medical Research Council, 1956), leaflets explaining the scheme were distributed to the children before it started. In addition, those vaccinated were given other leaflets describing the normal course of the vaccination reaction, and the vaccination sites were later examined. It is conceivable that this knowledge could have influenced the comparisons between the groups. For example, believing themselves to be protected, those vaccinated might have taken less care to avoid exposure to infection; this would tend to reduce the apparent degree of protection. In the same belief, they might alternatively have been less ready to attend for radiographic examination, or to report any symptoms; this would tend to exaggerate the degree of protection.

The data provide some evidence on the latter possibility. First, as stated above, the amount of co-operation, and in particular the proportions who had routine chest radiographs taken by the M.R.C. teams, were similar in the vaccinated and the unvaccinated groups. Secondly, the first section of Table **13,** 10 shows the total of 191 cases of definite tuberculosis starting within five years of entry in the negative unvaccinated and the two vaccinated groups, sub-divided into the cases which were discovered because the participants sought medical attention from the National Health Service for symptoms— that is, where the participants knew they were ill—and into those which were discovered only as a result of a routine chest radiograph (whether taken by the M.R.C. teams or elsewhere)—that is, where the participants were unaware that they were ill. The final line of Table **13,** 10 shows the percentage reduction in the incidence of tuberculosis, attributable to vaccination, for each method of discovery. The degree of protection for participants who were aware of their illness was closely similar to that for participants who were unaware of it; this does not suggest that the vaccinated participants ignored their illnesses.

Further, if there was any suppression of illnesses by vaccinated participants, this would presumably occur mainly with the less extensive and less severe lesions; the degree of protection would thus appear to be greater for these than for the other lesions. It has already been found, on the contrary, that the degree of protection is *not* greater for the less extensive and severe lesions, as judged by their radiographic extent and the action taken by the physician in charge (see Extent of the Pulmonary Lesions, p. 312, and Action Taken by the Physician, p. 316.)

TABLE 13, 10

Definite Cases of Tuberculosis in the Negative Unvaccinated and the Two Vaccinated Groups within Five Years of Entry, Subdivided (a) According to the Method of Discovery of the Disease, (b) According to the Physician First Diagnosing the Case, and (c) According to the Trial Area

Trial Group	Total Cases of Definite Tuberculosis	Method of Discovery of Disease		Physician First Diagnosing Case		Area		
		Medical Attention Sought for Symptoms	Routine Chest Radiograph	National Health Service	Medical Research Council	London	Birmingham	Manchester
Negative unvaccinated	153	71	82	103	50	37	67	49
Negative, B.C.G. vaccinated	27	11	16	14	13	7	7	13
Negative, vole bacillus vaccinated	11	4	7	7	4	—	4	7
Total	191	86	105	124	67	44	78	69
Percentage reduction in incidence of tuberculosis attributable to vaccination	84	86	82	87	78	81	91	78

Physician's Knowledge of the Skin-test and Vaccination State of the Participant

Physicians in the National Health Service

For those cases which were first discovered by the usual methods of the National Health Service, it is possible that the physician might have been influenced in making the diagnosis by knowledge of the patient's participation in the trial, and of the skin-test and vaccination state. However, the follow-up scheme through the chest clinics ensured that both tuberculous and non-tuberculous diagnoses would have come to the notice of the M.R.C. teams for review of the case by the assessor. The diagnoses of the National Health Service physician can therefore validly be compared with those of the independent assessor. Of the total of 124 National Health Service cases accepted as definite tuberculosis by the assessor, two were regarded by the National Health Service physician as only possibly due, and three as not due, to tuberculosis, and in a further case no diagnosis was made; three of these six disagreements occurred among the 21 cases in the two vaccinated groups combined. On the other hand, three cases (not included in the 124) were regarded by the National Health Service physician as definite tuberculosis; the assessor regarded two of these as possibly due to tuberculosis, and one as inactive tuberculosis, present on entry, with no evidence of subsequent activity; two of these three disagreements occurred in vaccinated participants. Thus any knowledge of skin-test results or of vaccination on the part of the National Health Service physicians has not influenced the results appreciably.

M.R.C. Team Physicians

It has been suggested (Palmer, Shaw, and Comstock, 1958) that knowledge of the skin-test and vaccination state by the M.R.C. team physicians may have led them to select which cases were to be submitted to the independent assessor, and thereby to introduce a bias between the tuberculin-negative unvaccinated and the vaccinated groups.

Knowledge of the skin-test and vaccination state of the participants was indeed readily available to the teams. If this had influenced the diagnoses of the team physicians—and had thereby affected which of their cases were submitted to the assessor—a different degree of protection might be expected for cases first discovered by the team physicians and for those first discovered by the National Health Service. The relevant sub-division of the total cases of definite tuberculosis is made in the second section of Table 13, 10. The final line shows a similar degree of protection for the cases discovered in the two ways.

Supplementary evidence on this point is provided by the third section of Table 13, 10, in which the cases of definite tuberculosis are sub-divided according to the three main areas of the study; the degree of protection afforded by vaccination is of the same high order in all three. The conduct of the trial in each area was the responsibility of a different M.R.C. team physician, and the findings thus do not indicate that there was any differential bias between these physicians.

Finally, as has been emphasized (see Records of Cases, p. 299), *all* cases with a pulmonary radiographic abnormality persisting for more than 14 days were submitted to the assessor. Moreover, all 35-mm. as well as full-size chest radiographs of the participants have been read separately by a physician unconnected with the trial and unaware of the skin-test or vaccination state of any participant, as well as by the team physician (see Follow-up of Participants, p. 297). A persistent abnormality found by either reader qualified the case for submission to the assessor. With this comprehensive system, any unconscious suppression of cases of tuberculosis by the team physician is highly improbable.

The Independent Assessor

There remains the possibility that the independent assessment was itself in some way biased. However, the assessor was rigorously kept unaware of the results of any tuberculin tests and of whether any vaccination had been performed. Moreover, as already stated, these 'blind' assessments showed a very substantial difference in the incidence of definite tuberculosis between the negative unvaccinated and the vaccinated groups (Table 13, 1), but no important differences in the incidence of cases and deaths from non-tuberculous causes (Table 13, 9).

ESTIMATED BENEFITS OF VACCINATION

From the foregoing critical appraisal it appears justifiable to conclude that no serious bias has entered into the comparison between the unvaccinated and vaccinated groups, and that their difference in incidence of tuberculosis may be confidently attributed to the vaccination.

On the basis of this conclusion it is permissible to assign limits of chance fluctuation to the observed degree of protection afforded by each of the two vaccines. The percentage reduction in the incidence of tuberculosis in the B.C.G.-vaccinated group, compared with the incidence in those concurrently admitted to the negative unvaccinated group, was 83 per cent for the five-year period following vaccination. Making allowances for chance fluctuations in the numbers of cases observed, it is possible to say with a high degree of confidence (99 per cent) that the protection afforded by B.C.G. vaccination in the tuberculin-negative section of the population studied lay between 71 per cent and 90 per cent.

The corresponding estimate for the degree of protection afforded by vole bacillus vaccination was 87 per cent. Allowing for chance fluctuations, it is very likely (99 per cent) that the protection lay between 73 per cent and 96 per cent.

In any mass-vaccination scheme this protection would apply only to the tuberculin-negative section of the population. There would be no direct effect on the number of cases among those who were already tuberculin positive at the pre-vaccination test (and therefore ineligible for vaccination); in assessing the total contribution of vaccination to the reduction in incidence of tuberculosis these cases must be taken into account. In the present trial 158 cases of tuberculosis were found in such tuberculin-positive participants within five years of entry; this represents 29 per cent of the total of 550 cases expected in the trial population if no vaccination had been given.

According to the present results, if *none* of the tuberculin-negative entrants had been vaccinated, 392 cases would have been expected among them within five years. If *all* of them had received B.C.G. vaccine, 65 cases would have been expected among them, or, if all had received vole bacillus vaccine, 56 cases. Including the 158 cases observed among the tuberculin-positive entrants within five years of entry with each of these estimates, the reduction in the total number of cases within five years of entry would have been from 550 (392 plus 158) to 223 (65 plus 158) with B.C.G. vaccination, or to 214 (56 plus 158) with vole bacillus vaccination. This represents a reduction of 59 per cent with B.C.G. vaccine, or of 61 per cent with vole bacillus vaccine, in the incidence of tuberculosis in the entire trial population—that is, in the tuberculin-negative and tuberculin-positive groups combined—for the five-year period. The figure of 59 per cent corresponds to that of 55 per cent for B.C.G. vaccine for the first two and a half years, given in the first report (Medical Research Council, 1956).

The above estimate has been calculated after the exclusion of 150 previously unsuspected cases of definite tuberculosis which were present on entry to the trial, this being discovered in the great majority because there was an initial radiographic examination (70 excluded at the time of entry plus 80 excluded subsequently by the assessor—see Cases of Tuberculosis Present on Entry, p. 301). If the preliminary radiograph had not been taken, many of these cases would apparently have arisen after entry, and would have increased the total cases among those tuberculin positive from 158 to a figure of the order of 300, The apparent reduction in the incidence of tuberculosis, as a result of vaccinating all those who were initially tuberculin negative, would in these circumstances have been of the order of 50 per cent with each vaccine, instead of the 60 per cent estimated above.

DISCUSSION

In this second report of the Medical Research Council's Tuberculosis Vaccines Clinical Trials Committee, the period of observation of the participants is extended from two and a half years (Medical Research Council, 1956) to five years after entry to the trial. The results show that the two vaccines conferred substantial protection against tuberculosis for this period in a large group of adolescents living under the ordinary urban and suburban conditions prevailing in industrial communities in Britain; the reduction in incidence in the vaccinated group, compared with the tuberculin-negative unvaccinated group, was 83 per cent for B.C.G. vaccine and 87 per cent for vole bacillus vaccine. Preliminary incomplete information beyond five years has shown that the protective efficacy of the vaccines has been maintained at a similar high level for at least six and a half years.

Most of the 349 definite cases of tuberculosis known to have started within five years of entry were clinically important, as judged by the form of the disease, its extent, and the treatment given; and the pulmonary lesions in the negative unvaccinated group were clinically as important as those in the initially tuberculin-positive groups. Moreover, the degree of protection from vaccination for the clinically important lesions was certainly as great as (and may even have been greater than) that for the less important lesions. These findings should be set against the doubts expressed by Myers (1957) and again by Anderson, Dickey, Durfee, Farber, Jordan, L. S., Jordan, K. B., Kupka, Lees, Levine, McKinlay, Marshal, Meyerding, Myers, Ornstein, Slater, Stoesser and Sweany (1959) that in this trial the protection might apply only to 'primary pulmonary infiltrates' and not to clinical tuberculosis.

Seven cases (three of erythema nodosum closely following B.C.G. vaccination, and four of regional adenitis following the vole bacillus vaccination) were regarded as complications of vaccination and were not included in the total of 349 cases. It is possible that some or all of these may nevertheless have resulted from infection with virulent tubercle bacilli. If, as an extreme, all seven cases had been regarded instead as cases of tuberculosis in vaccinated participants, the apparent protection against tuberculosis within five years of entry would only have been reduced from 83 per cent to 82 per cent for B.C.G. vaccine and from 87 per cent to 81 per cent for vole bacillus vaccine.

The incidence of non-tuberculous deaths and diseases in the different trial groups has been compared in this report as for tuberculosis. Taken as a whole, such deaths and diseases were found to have a similar incidence in the vaccinated and the tuberculin-negative unvaccinated groups; the mortality was, however, slightly greater in the two tuberculin-positive groups. When the more frequent diagnoses were considered separately, no evidence of protection by B.C.G. or vole bacillus vaccination was revealed against any specific cause of death, nor against any chest disease other than tuberculosis.

The batches of B.C.G. vaccine maintained a satisfactory protective potency, despite routine fluctuations in viable count and corresponding slight variations in the degree of post-vaccination tuberculin sensitivity. The data provide no information in the level of viable count at which protective efficacy would show a decline. It is of particular interest that the early batches of vole bacillus vaccine, which were unintentionally weaker than the later batches, also conferred a high degree of protection against tuberculosis. Thus these 'substandard' batches, or possibly even weaker batches still, could have been used throughout the trial, and would have provided substantial protection, despite the low level of tuberculin sensitivity which they produced. This finding has important practical implications for the assessment of vole bacillus vaccine. The routine use of this vaccine seemed to be contraindicated (Medical Research Council, 1956) because of the occurrence of lupus vulgaris at the site of vaccination in a number of cases. Such complications, however, occurred only among the participants receiving the later, stronger vaccine, none being observed among those receiving the earlier, weaker vaccine. This weaker vole bacillus vaccine has therefore proved both safe and effective, in agreement with the experience of Sula (1958), using an attenuated strain of the vole bacillus.

From the data just discussed it also appears that the protective efficacy of vole bacillus vaccine cannot necessarily be gauged by the degree of post-vaccination tuberculin sensitivity, at least to human tuberculin. The same conclusion is not justified for B.C.G. vaccine, since even the weakest batches produced an acceptably high degree of post-vaccination sensitivity (76 per cent to 3 T.U. and 100 per cent to 100 T.U.); a high conversion rate should therefore remain the aim of any B.C.G. vaccination scheme.

Although the vaccinated and the tuberculin-negative unvaccinated groups were alike, except for the fact of vaccination, the groups tuberculin positive on entry differed not only by virtue of their sensitivity but also by the (unknown) previous circumstances which produced that sensitivity. A notable feature of the first report was the high incidence of tuberculosis occurring during the first two and a half years among those participants who entered the trial with high degrees of tuberculin sensitivity (induration of 15mm. or more to 3 T.U.), which was much greater than among those with weaker positive reactions (5–14mm. induration to 3 T.U., or positive reactions only to 100 T.U.). A similar contrast was previously noted among African mining recruits (Tuberculosis Research Committee, 1932), and among young nurses in England (Daniels, Ridehalgh, and Springett, 1948), and has since been reported for other population groups (Frimodt-Moller, 1957; Palmer, 1957; Palmer, Jablon, and Edwards, 1957; Groth-Petersen, 1959). It has now been found that this high incidence of tuberculosis among the highly tuberculin-sensitive entrants has after a few years become markedly reduced, although it is still rather higher than the rates in the groups with lesser sensitivity. This suggests that in any programme for the periodic radiography of adolescents found to be highly sensitive to tuberculin in connexion with the national vaccination scheme for 13-year-old schoolchildren, the highest yield of cases of tuberculosis is likely to be in the first few years of observation.

The initial high incidence of tuberculosis among the participants with high tuberculin sensitivity may well reflect active infections acquired before entry, but not visible on the initial radiograph, a proportion of these giving radiographic manifestations of disease soon after entry. It seems unlikely that many of the active cases in these participants have arisen from a fresh infection sustained after entry, since there is evidence from other studies that the tuberculosis incidence in groups with high levels of initial tuberculin positivity is largely independent of subsequent exposure to tuberculosis. Thus, a substantial incidence has been found in environments where the rate among initially tuberculin-negative persons observed in parallel was relatively low (Frimodt-Moller, 1957; Palmer, 1957; Palmer, Jablon and Edwards, 1957), as well as in environments where it was relatively high (Daniels, Ridehalgh and Springett, 1948). It should be noted that the decline in incidence in the highly tuberculin-sensitive group in the present trial was associated not only with a lengthening interval from the time of the original infection but also with an increase in age from 15–17 years to 20–22 years, and so perhaps with a change in susceptibility.

The comparatively stable low incidence of tuberculosis among those with initial low-grade sensitivity (weak positive reactions to 3 T.U. or positive reactions only to 100 T.U.) may reflect, in the main, old or subsiding infections, or more recent infections of a minor character. However, whether these or some other explanations apply, it should be noted that these tuberculosis rates were considerably lower throughout the whole period of observation than those in the tuberculin-negative unvaccinated group. This finding suggests that low-grade sensitivity is associated with a naturally acquired specific immunity against fresh exogenous tuberculous infections, of a degree not possessed by those who were tuberculin negative on entry.

It has been suggested (World Health Organization Tuberculosis Research Office, 1955; Palmer, 1957; Edwards and Palmer, 1958) that low-grade tuberculin sensitivity in man is mainly due to previous infection with organisms other than mammalian tubercle bacilli, but closely related antigenically. Latterly it has been further suggested that these 'non-specific' infections may confer some degree of anti-tuberculous immunity (Palmer, 1957). This is not the place to enter deeply into this matter, but it should be stated that none of the conclusions from the present trial is inconsistent *either* with the hypothesis that all grades of tuberculin sensitivity concerned are caused by the tubercle bacillus, *or* with the extreme hypothesis that positive reactions of 15 mm. or more to 3 T.U. are tuberculous in origin, while positive reactions of 5–14 mm. to 3 T.U., as well as positive reactions to 100 T.U. but not to 3 T.U., are caused by other organisms (provided that these organisms also confer protection against tuberculosis).

The benefit to be expected from mass-vaccination of a given population—that is, the reduction in the total incidence of tuberculosis—will depend in general upon four main factors, which may vary with circumstances: (1) the basic degree of protection afforded by vaccination to those who are tuberculin negative; (2) the risks run by the latter (if not vaccinated) of acquiring natural tuberculous infection and disease during the ensuing years; (3) the incidence of disease during the ensuing years in those already tuberculin positive at the age at which vaccination is offered; and (4) the relative proportions of individuals tuberculin positive and negative at this age. These factors are to some extent interrelated.

In the present trial, the benefit that would have accrued to the entire population, tuberculin positive and negative combined, during the first five years, had *all* the tuberculin-negative entrants been vaccinated, was estimated as 59 per cent for B.C.G. vaccine and 61 per cent for vole bacillus vaccine. This assessment relates to a large section of the urban population of Britain, whose observation began in 1950–2. Since then there has been a decrease in the exposure to tuberculous infection in the young adult age group, which, by decreasing the cases to be expected in the tuberculin-negative group, and leaving those in the positive groups largely unaffected, would tend to decrease the benefit. But there has also been a notable decline in the prevalence of tuberculin sensitivity to 3 T.U. in those aged 13–15 years (compare Medical Research Council, 1958, with Medical Research Council, 1956), which, by increasing the proportion of the population group eligible for vaccination, would tend to increase the benefit. Because of these opposing tendencies, the percentage reduction in total incidence of tuberculosis, as a result of vaccination of a similar group of schoolchildren at the present time, is unlikely to differ substantially from the above figure of about 60 per cent (Sutherland, 1959). As a corollary, however, vaccination at a rather earlier age than 14 years, when a smaller proportion would have been infected naturally, would tend to increase the benefit of vaccination. Since the publication of our first report, other controlled trials of B.C.G. vaccination have progressed further. That in North American Indians by the late J. D. Aronson and his wife concerned about 1,500 tuberculin-negative subjects from infancy to 20 years old who were given B.C.G. vaccine; a similar number were left unvaccinated. The tuberculosis morbidity, judged by annual radiography, was studied for 11 years and the mortality for 20 years (Aronson, Aronson, and Taylor, 1958). The protection against pulmonary tuberculosis was 75 per cent and against death from tuberculosis 82 per cent; since very few deaths had occurred in the latter part of the 20-year observation period, it was difficult to be sure that the protection was maintained beyond the first 10 years. The incidence of non-tuberculous pulmonary lesions was somewhat greater in the control group than among the vaccinated; the non-tuberculous death rate was similar in the two groups.

The follow-up of Muslim children in Algiers, after oral vaccination of half of them at birth and again at the ages of one and three years, has continued to show an advantage to the vaccinated in mortality from all causes up to the age of seven years (Sergent, Catanei, and Ducros-Rougebief, 1956). Rosenthal (1955, 1956) has followed 5,737 vaccinated and 4,378 unvaccinated newborn infants in Chicago (of whom 311 and 250 respectively were born into tuberculous households) for periods of up to 18 years; he found a 77 per cent reduction in morbidity and an 81 per cent reduction in mortality in the vaccinated as compared with the control group. To these planned trials, all with results of a similar order to those in the Medical Research Council trial, must be added the unique study by Hyge (1947) of an epidemic in a school which had been partly subjected to prior B.C.G. vaccination; the follow-up has now been extended to 12 years (Hyge, 1956) and is of particular interest in providing some evidence of protection against 'post-primary' tuberculosis appearing after a considerable interval.

The preliminary stages of two large trials under the U.S. Public Health Service—in Puerto Rico and in Georgia and Alabama—were mentioned in the first report (Medical Research Council, 1956). A progress report, summarizing the results during a follow-up period of six to seven years, has now been published (Palmer, Shaw, and Comstock, 1958). In Puerto Rico nearly 200,000 volunteers aged 1–18 years were included; in Georgia and Alabama the 64,000 volunteers were aged five and upwards. The results differ from those of the present trial in two principal respects over a similar observation period. First, the proportion of the total cases which arose among the initially tuberculin-positive participants was much greater in the American trials; second, B.C.G. vaccination was found to have a much lower protective efficacy—namely, 31 per cent in Puerto Rico and 36 per cent in Georgia and Alabama, compared with 83 per cent in Britain.

There are many obvious differences between the U.S. Public Health Service trials and the British trial, in the populations studied, the criteria for vaccination, the vaccines used, and the methods of follow-up. Because of these numerous differences in approach, it is difficult to discuss profitably the reasons for the differences in the results until further information on all three trials has been published. In this connexion, however, an important epidemiological point deserves mention. This is the inclusion, both in the vaccinated and in the control groups in the American trials, of some persons who, while negative to the tuberculin tests used as criteria for vaccination, still had some low-grade tuberculin sensitivity (to 100 T.U.), and possibly a certain degree of specific antituberculous immunity. According to Palmer (1957) the prevalence of such low-grade sensitivity is much greater in the areas covered by the two American trials than in the British investigation. If this factor has contributed to the differing results it follows that in the areas of the U.S.A. where, like Northern Europe, low-grade sensitivity is relatively uncommon (World Health Organization Tuberculosis Research Office, 1955), a similar efficacy to that found in the British trial might have been discovered, had the American investigations taken place there instead of in the southern states and in Puerto Rico.

The main objective of the present trial is to define the extent and duration of the protective efficacy of B.C.G. and vole bacillus vaccination among those who were tuberculin negative on entry. The official national mass-vaccination scheme (Ministry of Health, 1953) for tuberculin-negative schoolchildren aged 13, which in 1958 was responsible for the B.C.G. vaccination of 241,434 children in England and Wales (Ministry of Health, 1959) out of a total of

658,000 of this age, is designed to cover the susceptible years of adolescence; and the duration of protection is thus crucial if revaccination is to be avoided. Duration of protection is also important in relation to the suggestion (Barns, 1955; Griffiths and Gaisford, 1956; Pollock, 1957) that the age for vaccination should be earlier in childhood, in order to anticipate some of the naturally acquired infections already present at age 13. It is therefore our intention to continue this trial in its present form until 1960, in order to provide information on the duration of protection up to eight to 10 years after vaccination.

Tuberculosis is still a major problem in young adults in England and Wales. In 1958, 2,501 new cases were notified among those aged 15–19 years, and 3,414 at ages 20–24 years. These figures underline the scope which still exists for the vaccination of adolescents in Britain.

SUMMARY

A controlled clinical trial of B.C.G. and vole bacillus vaccines in the prevention of tuberculosis in England started in 1950 and is still in progress. The 56,700 participants were initially free both from active tuberculosis and from known contact with the disease at home. On entry they were children, all aged 14 to $15\frac{1}{2}$ years, and about to leave school; they are now (1959) young men and women aged between 21 and 23 years. The great majority have continued to live in their original urban areas, in or near North London, Birmingham, and Manchester, apart from the two-year period of military service, which has involved about two-thirds of the young men. This second report presents results after each participant had been in the trial for five years, with preliminary incomplete information up to seven and a half years.

As a result of an initial examination at school by M.R.C. teams, the participants were automatically classified into five trial groups: tuberculin negative (to 100 tuberculin units—T.U.) and left unvaccinated (13,300 participants); tuberculin negative, B.C.G. vaccinated (14,100); tuberculin negative, vole bacillus vaccinated (6,700); tuberculin positive to 3 T.U. (16,000); and tuberculin positive to 100 T.U. but not to 3 T.U. (6,600). Those tuberculin negative, and thus eligible for vaccination, were allocated to the unvaccinated or to one of the two vaccinated groups by a random process.

The participants in all five trial groups have been followed intensively by means of routine periodic radiographic examinations and tuberculin tests by the M.R.C. teams, individual contact also being maintained by postal inquiries and visits to the home. Cases of tuberculosis and other chest diseases have also been discovered by chest clinic and other National Health Service physicians and by the medical services of the Armed Forces, and have been brought to the notice of the teams by routine inquiries.

All definite and suspected cases of tuberculosis, and all cases of pulmonary radiographic abnormality persisting for more than 14 days, were submitted to an independent assessor for a final diagnosis; to avoid bias, he was kept unaware of the results of all tuberculin tests, and of whether any vaccination had been performed. As an integral part of the present report, a detailed appraisal was made of these and other essential safeguards against bias incorporated into the trial; this showed that no serious bias had entered into the comparisons between the unvaccinated and vaccinated groups, and that their difference in incidence of tuberculosis could be confidently attributed to the vaccination.

A total of 349 definite cases of tuberculosis started within five years of entry to the trial; of these, 70 per cent were of pulmonary tuberculosis and 17 per cent of tuberculous pleural effusion without evidence of pulmonary tuberculosis; 70 per cent of the total cases (73 per cent in the negative unvaccinated group) were severe enough to be taken off work for at least three months; 32 per cent of the pulmonary cases (33 per cent in the negative unvaccinated group) showed cavitation radiographically, and 28 per cent (36 per cent in the negative unvaccinated group) involved more than two rib interspaces. There was one death from tuberculosis in the five-year period.

During the five-year period the annual incidence of tuberculosis in the B.C.G.-vaccinated group was 0.38 per 1,000, compared with 2.29 per 1,000 among those in the tuberculin-negative unvaccinated group who were admitted concurrently; this represents a reduction, attributable to vaccination, of 83 per cent. Over the same period, the annual incidence of tuberculosis in the vole-bacillus-vaccinated group was 0.33 per 1,000, compared with 2.62 per 1,000 among those admitted concurrently to the tuberculin-negative unvaccinated group; this represents a protection of 87 per cent. (The difference in incidence between the two vaccinated groups, when based also on concurrent admissions, could well have arisen by chance.) The protective efficacy of each vaccine was thus substantial and was closely similar to that found for the first two and a half years in the earlier report (Medical Research Council, 1956). Moreover, the incomplete information beyond five years shows that similar high levels of protection have continued up to at least six and a half years after entry.

The degree of protection was similar for pulmonary tuberculosis, for tuberculous pleural effusion, and for hilar gland enlargement (in association with other lesions). On the other hand, since four cases of tuberculous meningitis and four of miliary tuberculosis were found among the negative unvaccinated participants, but none among those who were vaccinated, the degree of protection may have been greater for these forms. There is now a suggestion also that the lesions in the vaccinated cases were less extensive (both on the first abnormal radiograph and at their maximal extent) and less severe (as judged by the action taken by the clinician) than those in the negative unvaccinated cases. In other words, the degree of protection for the more extensive and severe lesions was certainly as great as, and may even have been greater than, that for the less extensive and severe lesions.

The proportion of participants reacting to 3 T.U. after B.C.G. vaccination varied slightly with the routine fluctuations in the viable count of the batches used, though virtually all participant converted to 100 T.U. Even the batches with the lowest counts gave substantial protection.

The strength of the early batches of vole bacillus vaccine was below the standard intended, and the conversion rates, both to 3 T.U. and to 100 T.U., were considerably less for these batches than for the later batches. The early batches, nevertheless, conferred substantial protection against tuberculosis, and lupus vulgaris at the site of vaccination (noted in the first report) did not occur with these batches.

Among those with strong positive reactions to 3 T.U. on entry (15mm. induration or more) the annual incidence of tuberculosis was 3.50 per 1,000 in the first two and a half years, 1.67 in the second two and a half years, and 0.88 in the (incomplete) five to seven-and-a-half year period. In contrast, the annual incidences among those with weaker positive reactions to 3 T.U., and among those positive only to 100 T.U., were respectively 0.77 and 0.73 per 1,000 in the first two and a half years, and remained at much the same level thereafter. Thus, in this age group, those highly sensitive to tuberculin had a special risk of developing tuberculosis during the following few years. Those with lesser sensitivity to tuberculin on entry had consistently lower rates than those in the negative unvaccinated group, suggesting that they had some degree of protection against fresh infection, though not as great as that in the vaccinated groups.

In assessing the benefit that would have accrued to the entire trial population from the use of vaccine for *all* those tuberculin negative on entry, the contribution to the total tuberculosis morbidity made by those initially tuberculin positive (and therefore ineligible for vaccination) had to be included. This benefit—that is, the percentage reduction in incidence of tuberculosis during the five-year period—was 59 per cent for B.C.G. vaccine and 61 per cent for vole bacillus vaccine.

In all, 125 participants died from causes other than tuberculosis within five years of entry to the trial. In addition 151 cases, when submitted to the assessor, were classified by him as not due to tuberculosis, these consisting mainly of other chest diseases submitted because the radiographic abnormality persisted for more than 14 days. The incidence of these non-tuberculous deaths and diseases in the five trial groups reveals no significant evidence of protection by B.C.G. or vole bacillus vaccination against any specific cause of death, nor against any chest disease other than tuberculosis.

The trial is still in progress, and later reports will contain more detailed analyses over longer periods of time.

REFERENCES

Anderson, A. S., Dickey, L. B., Durfee, M. L., Farber, S. M., Jordan, L. S., Jordan, K. B., Kupka, E., Lees, H. D., Levine, E. R., McKinlay, C. A., Marshall, M. S., Meyerding, E. A., Myers, J. A., Ornstein, G. G., Slater, S. A., Stoesser, A. V., and Sweaney, H. C. (1959). *Brit. med. J.* i, 1423.

Aronson, J. D., Aronson, C. F., and Taylor, H. C. (1958). *Arch. intern. Med.* 101, 881.

Barns, T. (1955). *J. Obstet. Gynaec. Brit. Emp.* 62, 162.

Daniels, M., Ridehalgh, F., and Springett, V. H. (1948). *Tuberculosis in Young Adults.* London: Lewis.

Edwards, L. B., and Palmer, C. E. (1958). *Amer. J. Hyg.* 68, 213.

Frimodt-Moller, J. (1957). *Bull. int. Un. Tuberc.* 27, 111.

Griffiths, M. I., and Gaisford, W. (1956). *Brit. med. J.* ii, 565.

Groth-Petersen, E. (1959). *Acta tuberc. scand.* Suppl. 47, 132.

Hart, P. D'Arcy, Pollock, T. M., and Sutherland, I. (1957). *Advanc. Tuberc. Res.* 8, 171.

Hyge, T. V. (1947). *Acta tuberc. scand.* **21**, 1.

Hyge, T. V. (1956). *Acta tuberc. scand.* **32**, 89.

Medical Research Council (1956). *Brit. med. J.* **i**, 413.

Medical Research Council (1958). *Brit. med. J.* **i**, 79.

Ministry of Health (1953). Circular 22/53.

Ministry of Health (1959). Personal communication.

Myers, J. A. (1957). *Advance. Tuberc. Res.* **8**, 272.

Palmer, C. E. (1957). *Bull. int. Un. Tuberc.* **27**, 106.

Palmer, C. E., Jablon, S., and Edwards, P. Q. (1957). *Amer. Rev. Tuberc.* **76**, 517.

Palmer, C. E., Shaw, L. W., and Comstock, G. W. (1958). *Amer. Rev. Tuberc.* **77**, 877.

Pollock, T. M. (1957). *Brit. med. J.* **ii**, 20.

Rosenthal, S. R. (1955). *J. Amer. med. Ass.* **157**, 801.

Rosenthal, S. R. (1956). *Amer. Rev. Tuberc.* **74**, No. 2. Part 2. (Suppl.), 313.

Sergent, E., Catanei, A., and Ducros-Rougebief, H. (1956). *Bull. Acad. nat. Méd. Paris*, **140**, 562.

Sula, L. (1958). *Tubercle (Lond.)* **39**, 10.

Sutherland, I. (1959). *Tubercle (Lond.)* **40**, 413.

Tolderlund, K. (1952). *Acta path. microbiol. scand.* Suppl. **93**. 299.

Tolderbund, K. (1955). Personal communication.

Tuberculosis Research Committee (1932). *Publ. S. Afr. Inst. med. Res.* **5**, No. 30.

World Health Organization Tuberculosis Research Office (1955). *Bull. Wld. Hlth Org.* **12**, 63.

CHAPTER 14

TRIALS OF AN ASIAN INFLUENZA VACCINE

EARLY in May, 1957, reports were received in this country of the occurrence of epidemic influenza in Japan, Hong Kong, and Singapore. It was subsequently ascertained that the epidemic had made its first appearance in South-Western China in February. Laboratory investigations at the World Influenza Centre, Mill Hill, London, the International Influenza Centre for the Americas, Montgomery, Alabama, the Walter Reed Army Institute of Research, U.S.A., and the Walter and Eliza Hall Institute, Melbourne, quickly showed that the causal virus was a new variant of virus A unrelated to all previously isolated strains. In these circumstances it was almost certain that this 'Asian' influenza would spread from the Far East to this country. An opportunity was thereby presented to carry out serological and clinical trials of a vaccine made from the virus of this new type.

I. THE SEROLOGICAL TRIAL

The Vaccines

With the object of establishing the minimum strength of haemagglutinating units necessary to give an adequate antibody response, four saline vaccines were prepared by Dr. F. Himmelweit of the Wright-Fleming Institute of Microbiology. The methods of preparation were similar to those described in previous reports (Medical

Fourth Progress Report to the Medical Research Council by its Committee on Influenza and Other Respiratory Virus Vaccines. Members of the Committee: Professor C. H. Stuart-Harris (chairman), Dr. C. H. Andrewes, F.R.S., Dr. B. E. Andrews, Brigadier G. T. L. Archer, Dr. W. H. Bradley, Brigadier P. J. L. Capon, Surgeon Captain T. L. Cleave, Professor R. Cruickshank, Dr. J. J. O'Dwyer, Professor A. Bradford Hill, F.R.S., Dr. F. Himmelweit, Dr. A. Isaacs, Dr. F. O. MacCallum, Dr. J. C. McDonald, Dr. W. J. Martin, Dr. A. T. Roden, Dr. I. N. Sutherland, Professor Wilson Smith, F.R.S., Air Commodore J. S. Wilson, Brigadier A. E. Richmond (secretary).

Reprinted from the *British Medical Journal*, 1958, i, 415.

Research Council, 1953, 1955, 1957), the vaccines being made from the egg-adapted line of the Asian strain A/Singapore/1/57. Concentration from the original allantoic fluids provided a vaccine A of 20,000 haemagglutinating units* per dose. This was then diluted to give three vaccines of lesser strength. Thus the four vaccines employed were:

Vaccine A: 20,000 H.U. per dose
Vaccine B: Two-thirds of A, about 14,000 H.U. per dose
Vaccine C: One-third of A, about 7,000 H.U. per dose
Vaccine D: One-sixth of A, about 3,500 H.U. per dose

The haemagglutinating units of virus were in each vaccine adsorbed on to 10 mg. of aluminium phosphate per dose, and the dose in each was 1 ml., inoculated deep subcutaneously into the upper arm.

Organization of the Trial

The trial was carried out in two groups: (*a*) Army personnel at the R.A.M.C. Field Training Centre at Mytchett, Hants, and (*b*) Royal Air Force personnel at Lindholme, Finningley, and Bawtry. In each group about 60 volunteers were obtained, mostly young men. They were divided into four sub-groups, each to receive one of the four vaccines. Two serum samples were collected from each volunteer, the first just before inoculation and the second three weeks later. In view, however, of the comparatively small antibody responses which were observed after one dose, it was decided to ascertain the effect of a second dose given three to four weeks after the first. This was done in all the volunteers remaining in the sub-groups originally given vaccines A and C. The sera were examined at the Wright-Fleming Institute, and the results confirmed at the World Influenza Centre, Mill Hill, and the Virus Laboratory at Lodge Moor, Sheffield.

* The equivalence between haemagglutinating units and the C.C.A. units used in American reports is at present being investigated. Based on preliminary inquiries by means of direct comparisons of the two methods and comparison of stock vaccines with American standard preparations kindly supplied by Dr. Roderick Murray, National Institutes of Health, Bethesda, U.S.A., 1 C.C.A unit seems to be equivalent to between 25 and 40 haemagglutinating units. Further investigations are being carried out to enable a more precise figure of equivalence to be reached.

RESULTS

Table **14,** 1 shows the responses, by the haemagglutination-inhibition test, three weeks after one dose of the various vaccines. The most marked feature is the low antibody rises obtained with all four—although, except with the lowest strength of vaccine D, there were a few individuals who gave surprisingly good responses. These

TABLE **14,** 1

Haemagglutination-inhibition Titres Observed Three Weeks After Primary Inoculation with Asian Influenza Vaccine of Different Strengths*

Titre	VaccineA 20,000 H.U. per Dose	Vaccine B 14,000 H.U. per Dose	Vaccine C 7,000 H.U. per Dose	Vaccine D 3,500 H.U. per Dose
10 or under	9	15	13	11
12·5–17·5	9	8	6	6
20–50	13	3	6	8
60–120	3	2	4	—
Total	34	28	29	25
Geometric mean titre	14·9	7·6	9·8	7·2

* The H.I. titres prior to inoculation were in all cases less than 5.

generally low antibody rises are not necessarily attributable to the virus being a poor antigen. They may be due to lack of any previous experience of the virus in the population or be associated with certain biological characteristics of the new strain predominantly due to its high sensitivity to non-specific inhibiting factors in the sera. This sensitivity necessitated treatment of the sera with cholera enzyme, which may reduce the antibody level to some degree.

The geometric mean titres do not differ significantly between vaccines B, C, and D, while the difference between vaccine A and vaccines B, C, and D combined is just significant (t = 2.32 with 114 d.f., $0.02 < p < 0.05$).

The complement-fixation test on 34 paired samples (carried out at the Central P.H. Laboratory, Colindale) demonstrated a better response than the H.I. test.

The results of a second dose of vaccines A and C, given three to four weeks subsequent to the first dose, are shown in Table **14**, 2. It will be seen that the boosting effects of the second dose were considerable and that there was little to choose between the two vaccines in this repect.

TABLE **14**, 2

Haemagglutination-inhibition Titres Observed About Three Weeks After First and Second Doses of Asian Influenza Vaccines, the Second Dose Given Three to Four Weeks After the First

Titre	Vaccine A 20,000 H.U. per Dose		Vaccine C 7,000 H.U. per Dose	
	After First Dose	After Second Dose	After First Dose	After Second Dose
Under 20	13	—	16	1
20–50	7	5	3	8
60–120	—	13	2	11
121–240	—	2	—	1
Total	20	20	21	21
Geometric mean titre	8·8	77·7	4·2	56·5

II. FIELD TRIALS

It was impossible to complete these serological trials and, consequently, to decide upon the vaccines, doses, etc., to be employed in the field trials until the end of August, 1957. Meanwhile it was known that cases of the Asian type of influenza had been imported and there had been a few localized outbreaks. The first evidence of the epidemic spread of the disease was in schools in Colne (Lancs) in the week ending 24 August and at the same time in Sheffield (Yorks). From then onwards the epidemic spread rapidly, reaching its peak earlier in the north of the country than in the south. Maximum incidence in the East and West Ridings of Yorkshire was in the week ending 24 September and in the Northern and North-Western regions and Wales in the week ending 1 October. In the Midland regions the peak was reached in the week ending 8 October, and in the Eastern, London, and more southerly regions in the week ending 15 October. The recession subsequent to these weeks of maxima was gradual, but by mid-November the prevalence was low compared with that of the peak period. In view of this early arrival of the epidemic the field trials, originally planned for the late autumn, had to be expedited to the utmost extent. However, while it was possible to hasten the start in some of the centres, little could be done with regard to the public schools and teachers training colleges, which did not reopen for the Michaelmas term until after mid-September. Furthermore, in a number of these centres the epidemic began so early in the term that no trial was possible.

The Centres.—Ultimately the centres in four main groups which took part were as follows:

A. *Public Schools.*—Canford School, Durham School, Epsom College, Haileybury and Imperial Service College, St. Lawrence College, Marlborough College, Stonyhurst School, Trent College.

B. *Teachers Training Colleges.*—Bedford College of Physical Education, Dartford College of Physical Education, the City of Leeds, Didsbury, Trent Park, and Westminster Training Colleges.

C. *Miscellaneous Centres.*—Ministry of Health (London), Ministry of Pensions and National Insurance (Newcastle), London County Council Ambulance Service, London Transport Executive (Chiswick), H.M. Dockyard Portsmouth, Sheffield University, Messrs. Boots Pure Drug Company Limited, Nottingham.

D. *Chronic Bronchitics.*—Approximately 2,500 volunteers from chest clinics in England, Wales, and Scotland in a special trial organized in association with the Research Committee of the British Tuberculosis Association.

The trials in all these centres were planned to continue until the spring of 1958. This present report deals only with the period from their start until the end of November, and is limited to those centres from which sufficient information is already available for study. Thus two schools, one teachers training college, and the whole of group D are excluded.

Procedure.—As in the previous trials (Medical Research Council, 1953, 1957), volunteers for vaccination were allotted in random order to the different vaccines under trial, and they, as well as the medical practitioners subsequently diagnosing their illnesses, were kept in ignorance of the particular vaccine that had been given to any recipient. In the diagnosis of influenza reliance had to be placed mainly upon clinical assessment. On the other hand, the Public Health Laboratory Service, and certain other laboratories, were active in laboratory diagnosis and confirmed the presence of the Asian strain in a proportion of the cases occurring in some trial centres, particularly in the public schools.

The Vaccines

The vaccines against the Asian virus were based on the results of the serological trials, and the aim of the field trial was to study the relative values of the following procedures:

(1) Two doses, each of about 7,000 haemagglutinating units
(2) One dose of about 7,000 haemagglutinating units
(3) One dose of 20,000 haemagglutinating units

In addition a polyvalent vaccine from the older strains was used to find out whether a vaccine containing these strains had any preventive effect. A vaccine of the influenza B type was used as a control.

The following gives in detail the vaccines made at the Wright-Fleming Institute of Microbiology, and employed in the different groups.

A. *Public Schools.*—(1) An Asian type saline vaccine from the strain A/Singapore/1/57, with 20,000 H.U. per dose of 1 ml. and 10 mg. of aluminium phosphate, to be given in one dose. (2) A polyvalent saline influenza A vaccine containing equal proportions of Swine PR.8 and FM.1 with 20,000 H.U. per dose of 1 ml. and 10 mg. of aluminium phosphate, to be given in one dose. (3) An influenza B vaccine (1954) with 20,000 H.U. per dose of 1 ml. and 10 mg. of aluminium phosphate, to be given in one dose.

B. *Teachers Training Colleges*, and C. *Miscellaneous Centres.*—(1) An Asian type saline vaccine from the strain A/Singapore/1/57 with approximately 7,000 H.U. per dose of 1 ml. and 10 mg. of aluminium phosphate, to be given in two such doses, the second to be given 28 days after the first. (2) The same as (1) but limited to one dose only. (3) An influenza B vaccine as in A (3) above.

These vaccines have been given to 3,093 persons in the trials here described. Soreness of the arm and a slight malaise for 24–36 hours have not been unusual, but no serious reactions have so far been noted.

Influenza Prevalence in Relation to Inoculation Dates in the Areas and Communities Concerned in the Trials

Before examining the results it is necesssry to consider periods in which Asian influenza was prevalent in relation to dates of inoculation.

For the public schools comprising group A detailed information is given in the note accompanying Table **14**, 3.

In the teachers training colleges of group B the inoculation dates varied from 16 to 30 September, with the large majority between 23 and 25 September. In every centre save one in this group the influenza epidemic started shortly before the inoculations were given, while in the one exception it began the day after.

It should be added that volunteers who before inoculation had succumbed to an attack of Asian influenza were automatically excluded from the trial.

In the miscellaneous centres comprising group C most of the inoculations were given between 10 and 19 September. In the Ministry of Health some inoculations were delayed till late September and early October, while in the London Transport Executive establishment at Chiswick none were given until the second week in October. At Sheffield University, while volunteers amongst the resident staff were inoculated in the last fortnight of September, inoculation of the students was not done until between 1 and 18 October.

In the London area influenza was particularly prevalent from about 23 September to 2 November, and in Portsmouth the situation was much the same. In Sheffield, Newcastle, and Nottingham, the epidemic had begun two to three weeks earlier. In Sheffield University students, as distinct from resident staff, the epidemic began after the students had rejoined, and the peak of the epidemic in them was reached by 15 October, a month later than in the resident staff.

In general it may be stated that in these centres influenza was definitely prevalent for some time subsequent to the inoculations. On the other hand, as a result of this overlap between inoculations and epidemicity in various centres, it has been impossible to measure the effect of two doses as compared with one. Many of these second doses were given within or subsequent to the recession of the epidemics. Under these circumstances the two-dose and single-dose vaccines were to all intents and purposes the same vaccine, and they have therefore been combined in presenting the results.

RESULTS

To take account of the fact that the inoculations were not complete before the epidemics began, the results in each centre have been analysed for different intervals of time following the inoculations. Thus Tables **14,** 3, **14,** 4, and **14,** 5 show the attack rates falling upon the different vaccinated groups within the first eight days of their vaccination and at later intervals.

TABLE 14,3 *Public Schools. Influenza Cases in Inoculated Boys According to the Length of Time Elapsing after Inoculation*

Vaccine	School	No. of Boys Inoculated	No. of Cases Occurring Days after Inoculation			Cases Expressed as a Percentage of those Inoculated in Each Vaccine Group Days after Inoculation		
			1–8	9–15	16 and Over	1–8	9–15	16 and Over
Asian	Canford School	75	2	7	—	2·7%	9·3%	—
	Epsom College	51	15	2	—	29·4%	3·9%	—
	Haileybury and I.S. College	139	23	10	2	16·5%	7·2%	1·4%
	Marlborough College	97	51	10	3	52·6%	10·3%	—
	St. Lawrence College	42	4	4	—	9·5%	9·5%	—
	Trent College	64	36	—	3	56·3%	—	7·1%
	Total (excluding Trent College)	404	95	33	5	23·4%	8·2%	1·2%
Polyvalent Virus A (Non-Asian)	Canford School	70	3	19	5	4·3%	27·1%	7·1%
	Epsom College	62	16	17	1	25·8%	27·4%	1·6%
	Haileybury and I.S. College	140	27	33	5	19·3%	23·6%	3·6%
	Marlborough College	103	48	25	—	46·6%	24·3%	—
	St. Lawrence College	62	7	13	3	11·3%	21·0%	4·8%
	Trent College	71	52	2	—	73·2%	2·8%	—
	Total (excluding Trent College)	437	101	107	14	23·1%	24·5%	3·2%
Control Virus B	Canford School	73	4	23	4	5·5%	31·5%	5·5%
	Epsom College	56	14	7	5	25·0%	12·5%	3·5%
	Haileybury and I.S. College	143	18	43	—	12·6%	30·1%	—
	Marlborough College	100	55	21	5	55·0%	21·0%	12·3%
	St. Lawrence College	57	3	12	7	5·3%	21·1%	—
	Trent College	62	43	—	—	69·4%	—	—
	Total (excluding Trent College)	429	93	106	16	21·7%	24·7%	3·7%

Canford School: Epidemic began 5 October, ended 19 October; whole school attack rate about 46%. Inoculations 27 and 28 September with one or two boys a few days later.
Epsom College: Epidemic began 27 September, ended 13 October; whole school attack rate about 61%. Inoculations 28 September.
Haileybury and I.S.C.: Epidemic began about 21 September, ended about 16 October; whole school attack rate about 44%. Inoculations 23, 24, 26, 27 September.
Marlborough: Epidemic began 22 September, ended 4 October; whole school attack rate about 80%. Inoculations 27 September.
St. Lawrence College (senior school): Epidemic began 1 October, ended 23 October; whole school attack rate about 42%. Inoculations mainly 29 September and 1 October, but some 13 October. Through a clerical error, not affecting the random allocation, rather fewer boys were given the Asian vaccine.
Trent College: Epidemic began 25 September, ended 6 October; whole school attack rate about 79%. Inoculations 27 and 28 September. Excluded from the total, since the epidemic was over within the eight days after inoculations.

A. Public Schools (Table 14, 3)

The figures for all schools combined show very clearly that in the first eight days after inoculation there was practically no difference at all between the three vaccinated groups in the proportions contracting influenza, the attack rates being 23.4 per cent, 23.1 per cent, and 21.7 per cent. On the other hand, within 9 to 15 days after inoculation there is one pronounced difference between the three groups, since the attack rate was only 8.2 per cent of those given the Asian vaccine compared with 24.5 per cent and 24.7 per cent in the other two groups given non-Asian vaccine. This advantage was maintained in the 16 days and over period, though by then the actual number of cases occurring was small.

Within the individual schools the same trend was consistently apparent (with the exception of Trent College, in which the epidemic came to an end within eight days). During days 9–15 the boys in the non-Asian vaccine groups in Epsom College, Haileybury and Imperial Service College, and Canford School had attack rates from influenza three times or more greater than the boys in the Asian vaccine group. In Marlborough and St. Lawrence Colleges the attack rate in the non-Asian vaccine group was approximately twice that of the Asian vaccine group. There was no evidence that the polyvalent non-Asian virus A vaccine exerted any preventive effect, since the attack rates with it and the virus B vaccine are remarkably similar.

If the figures are looked at in a slightly different way there were 309 boys who were inoculated with the Asian vaccine, 336 inoculated with the polyvalent virus A vaccine, and 336 inoculated with the virus B vaccine who had not been attacked by influenza within the first eight days after their inoculation. The numbers who succumbed after eight days were 38, 121, and 122, or only 12 per cent, in those given the Asian vaccine, compared with 36 per cent in each of the other two groups. In other words, the protection given appears to have been of the order of 67 per cent.

B. Teachers Training Colleges (Table 14, 4)

The numbers of volunteers inoculated in these centres was only 318, and the centres have therefore been amalgamated. Of the 62 cases of influenza reported, 44 occurred within the first eight days after inoculation. In this period the attack rates of those inoculated with Asian vaccine and the control vaccine were very similar—namely, 14.8 per cent and 11. 8 per cent respectively. On the other hand, subsequent to the eighth day the attack rates were 2.8 per cent in those who received the Asian vaccine and 11.7 per cent in those given the virus B vaccine. The advantage to the former group is significant, and gives (on these small figures) a protective ratio of 75 per cent.

TABLE **14,** 4

Teachers Training Colleges. Influenza Cases in Inoculated Students in Five Centres According to the Length of Time Elapsing After Inoculation

Vaccine	No. of Students Inoc- ulated	No. of Cases Occurring			Cases Expressed as a Percentage of those Inoculated in Each Vaccine Group		
		Days after Inoculation			Days after Inoculation		
		1–8	9–15	16 and Over	1–8	9–15	16 and Over
Asian	216	32	4	2	14·8%	1·9%	0·9%
Control virus B	102	12	8	4	11·8%	7·8%	3·9%

C. Miscellaneous Centres (Table 14, 5)

Up to 15 days after inoculation cases of influenza and of other respiratory infections were few in number and did not differ significantly between the two vaccinated groups. On the other hand, from 16 days or more after inoculation, when the number of cases sharply increased under both diagnoses, 10.3 per cent of those given the control virus B vaccine contracted influenza compared with 4.9 per cent of those inoculated with the Asian type, the difference being statistically significant. As regards other respiratory infections there was no significant difference, the figures being 4.8 per cent and 6.0 per cent respectively. The protective ratio when influenza appears to have become prevalent is 52 per cent.

TABLE **14,** 5

Miscellaneous Centres. Absences from Work Reported as Due to (a) Influenza; (b) Other Respiratory Infections in Seven Centres According to the Length of Time Elapsing After Inoculation

Vaccine	No. Inoculated	No. of Cases Occurring within Specified Intervals after Inoculation					
		1–8 Days		9–15 Days		16 Days and Over	
		No.	Rate	No.	Rate	No.	Rate
(a) Influenza							
Asian	861	10	1·2%	9	1·0%	42	4·9%
Control virus B	447	2	0·4%	4	0·9%	46	10·3%
(b) Other Respiratory Infections							
Asian	861	9	1·0%	5	0·6%	41	4·8%
Control virus B	447	2	0·4%	2	0·4%	27	6·0%

DISCUSSION

The results obtained in these trials suggest that a very substantial protective effect was afforded by the Asian vaccine subsequent to the eighth day after its inoculation. The evidence from the public schools is particularly impressive, since the total number of volunteers was relatively large and the boys were under close observation. Laboratory investigations were carried out in a few individuals at most of them and confirmation of the cause of the epidemics was obtained. Particular attention may perhaps be given to Canford School, in which the epidemic did not begin until some days after the completion of inoculation. The attack rates during days 9–15 are very similar in the two non-Asian vaccine groups, 27.1 per cent and 31.5 per cent, whereas in the Asian vaccine group only 9.3 per cent were attacked. The situation was similar in the 16-day-and-over period, though the actual number of cases was smaller. From these figures it seems legitimate to estimate a protection rate of not less than 66 per cent. If the total figures for the schools are taken, there is a very similar picture.

The Asian vaccine on trial in the miscellaneous centres and teachers training colleges was only one-third the strength in haemagglutinating units of the vaccine employed in the public schools. It is however, difficult to make any precise comparison between these strengths, since extensive epidemics of Asian influenza comparable to those in the schools did not materialize in these two groups, and the numbers of absences reported as due to influenza were comparatively small. The results obtained from these two groups, however, support those obtained from the public schools.

SUMMARY

Serological trials were carried out in some 120 volunteers in Army and Royal Air Force units in July and August, 1957, to establish the optimum dosage and strength in haemagglutinating units to be recommended in a vaccine made from the Asian strain A/Singapore/1/57. Four vaccines were prepared with 20,000 and about 14,000, 7,000, and 3,500 H.U. per dose respectively. The antibody response to a single dose was low with each strength, though there was a somewhat greater response to the strongest. A second dose given three to four weeks later gave much greater antibody responses.

In field trials carried out in public schools, teachers training colleges, and other miscellaneous centres volunteers were allocated at random to an Asian influenza vaccine, a polyvalent virus A vaccine, or a virus B vaccine. Severe epidemics took place in the public schools, and, subsequent to eight days after inoculation with one dose, a very definite preventive effect was apparent in the Asian vaccine group. After that interval of time its attack rate fell to one-third of the rate observed in the other two groups. The equality in these other two groups suggests that no protection was conferred by the polyvalent virus A vaccine (though the young ages of the boys concerned may have been a factor in this). At a much lower epidemic level a similar protective effect was observed in the training colleges and other centres.

REFERENCES

Medical Research Council Committee on Clinical Trials of Influenza Vaccine (1953). *Brit. med. J.* **ii,** 1173.
Medical Research Council Committee on Clinical Trials of Influenza Vaccine (1955). *Brit. med. J.* **ii,** 1229.
Medical Research Council Committee on Clinical Trials of Influenza Vaccine (1957). *Brit. med. J.* **ii,** 1.

PART III

THE EPIDEMIOLOGICAL APPROACH

CHAPTER 15

SCIENTIFIC METHOD IN FIELD SURVEYS

GENERAL PRINCIPLES OF FIELD SURVEYS

IN opening this discussion of scientific method in field surveys I had thought of adopting the more flippant title of Twenty Questions. I should have done so to emphasize two points. The first is the, admittedly, somewhat obvious one that in any survey of a human population we are involved in asking questions. We may ask them by means of questionnaires, we may prefer to use third-degree methods of cross-examination applied by ourselves or through social workers, we may make clinical examinations, or we may merely extract existing records. But all the time, whatever the means, we are asking questions. We are not making an experiment to see what happens; we are asking questions to see what exists and also, usually, to determine what relationships may prevail in the population between one of its characteristics and the incidence of a disease. The second point I had in mind in considering the title Twenty Questions is less obvious but very much more important. It is this: that, broadly speaking, of any 20 questions asked in a field survey, not more than five should be put to the surveyed, and not less than 15 should be put to the surveyor by himself before he enters the field or, indeed, ventures to look over the gate.

QUESTIONS AND ANSWERS

When shall the survey be made? Is one time preferable to another? By what means shall it be made? And why? (Sometimes indeed, looking at published reports, one wonders.) Those are the broad basic queries that must be posed. Accompanying them must be a detailed consideration of every question that is to be propounded in the field. That approach, if a survey is to have any hope of success, is fundamental.

Merely to draw up when you have half an hour to spare—or still

Reprinted from *The Application of Scientific Methods to Industrial and Service Medicine*, 1951, London: H.M.S.O.

worse, to instruct a junior to draw up—a long and rambling set of questions is to invite disaster. Yet how often do we see it done in this lighthearted way. Not so long ago I had submitted to me the plan for a proposed inquiry into the causes of prematurity. It ran to a trifle of 180 questions, which covered a catholic range. For instance, it seemed that the author was confident that some person or persons —undefined in the draft I saw—could accurately inform her for each of the woman's previous confinements of the time interval between birth of the child and the placenta; the incidence of congenital malformations in her blood relations; whether she wore high- or low-heeled shoes; how often she took a hot bath; the state of health of the father at the time of conception; and the frequency of sexual intercourse, which was engagingly included under the sub-heading 'social amenities'. This, in my view, is not the scientific method; it is mere wishful thinking, mere hoping that *some* rabbit may come out if only the hat be made big enough. I am myself equally unimpressed by questions (again from real life) which either involve a hypothetical situation—'would you enjoy chasing bandits in a sheriff's posse?'—or touch upon the character of the questioned— 'do you win confidence and loyalty from those around you?' (In this particular inquiry 84 per cent of gentlemen of mature age were able to say 'yes'.) Heaven knows, without entering such fields as these, how difficult it is to frame adequately the simplest question so that an accurate and intelligible answer will be obtained. The country visitor to London surveying one of the larger Ministries in Whitehall asked a policeman, 'How many persons work in there?'. to which the policeman cynically replied, 'About half.' Or take that largest of field surveys, the census of England and Wales. Since 1891 we have asked the inhabitants of Wales and Monmouthshire what languages they speak. The instruction is perfectly clear: 'If only English, write English; if only Welsh, write Welsh; if English and Welsh, write both.' Yet in 1891 the report on the census says that abundant evidence was received that either the question was misunderstood or the value of the reply set at naught by a large number of those Welshmen who could speak both languages but entered Welsh only, probably on the grounds that this was the language spoken habitually or preferentially. 'Indeed,' the report adds, 'so desirous do many householders appear to have been to add to the number of monoglot Welshmen, that they not only returned themselves as speaking only Welsh but made similar returns as to infants who were only a few months or even only a few days old.' The same report emphasizes that 'those who are conversant with forms and schedules scarcely realize the difficulty which persons, not so conversant, find in filling them up correctly'.

That was years ago. Today we are perhaps better educated, certainly more conversant with forms. But the problem is still fundamental to the field survey. Can we frame questions that will— so far as is humanly possible—be read alike and understood by many different persons? Can we frame questions that can be put verbally by, say, social workers, so that a different emphasis on the questions or on the answers may not be introduced by the varying workers? Can we arrange that measurements taken by different persons will be of the same standard of accuracy or even be comparable at all? Can we see that *every* question—particularly in a clinical examination—has *some* answer, so that we are not faced finally with a number of blanks and unable to determine whether the person was in fact negative in some respect or merely not examined for it? That is not so difficult and should be almost a *sine qua non* for every inquiry—some answer must be given to every question. The other requirements are difficult, but, I repeat, they are fundamental.

One of the first and most decisive steps in a field survey is, therefore, to construct the form of record. This must be given the closest thought, each question in turn, to see whether it is clear and definite; what the possible answers are; whether the answers can be adequately if not wholly accurately obtained, and how they can be put into a statistical table at the end of the survey. In short, remember that if your questions are ill-conceived no statistical black magic can make up for it at the end and produce the answer you had hoped to get. And the time to remember that is at the beginning of the survey, not at its end.

POPULATIONS AND SAMPLES

The second fundamental step in a field survey, which does not necessarily follow the first chronologically, is to determine the population to be surveyed: is it to be the whole population in which our interest lies or some cross-section of it? The answer will be partly determined, of course, by practical considerations—the size of the population involved and of the facilities at our disposal (and sometimes, even in these days, money). If we can deal with the whole population—for example, that of a factory in relation to the number of minor injuries occurring at work—then we clearly have none of those nice problems that arise when we embark upon sampling to consider. Or have we? Indeed we may have, and the air of superiority sometimes worn by those who adopt the principle of the population, the whole population and nothing but the whole population, can be more than a trifle misplaced. These people are, or course, on firm and indeed uncontestable ground so long as the whole population *is* surveyed. But if they o'er-reach themselves in the attempt to record the 'universe' involved in the inquiry, if there shall occur refusals and no answers, the unknown and the untraced, then instantly there arises the problem of a sample and indeed the problem at its very worst. For we do not know whether those who choose to answer the questions, who choose to keep records or respond to the clarion call to a clinical examination, are representative of the population concerned—whether the refusals, the unknowns, the untraced have characteristics that differentiate them from those who are incorporated in the survey. Sometimes they may well differ and differ seriously. The neurotic may be over-anxious to attend for clinical examination, the physically unfit in some circumstances may be anxious *not* to attend. The stupid may have more accidents and also be more prone not to keep records. Those who do not return the questionnaire may include an unduly high proportion of negatives who conclude that they have nothing of interest to report, while the positives may include those who more freely respond. We record the successes but not the failures. And so on.

I would therefore myself infinitely sooner have, say, a one in four sample of the population, of a size thereby which enabled me to pursue relentlessly, and complete the records for, all or nearly all the persons in it, than have to interpret figures derived from survey of the 'whole' population from which finally a quarter was missing. From the well-constructed sample we can at least infer the values that exist in the population, or, rather, the limits between which they are most likely to lie. With the incomplete 'whole' population we are merely left with a spate of doubts and conclusions that should be, but too frequently are not, excessively tentative. Do not, therefore, think that the scientific aim is *necessarily* more likely to be achieved by approaching the population rather than a sample.

If we do decide to sample, then the fundamental question is how to do it in such a way as to ensure that we deal with a cross-section of the population concerned. The general principles were laid down by the Ancient Mariner who 'stoppeth one in three', but the techniques will vary in detail somewhat with the problem and I should not embark, I think, upon such matters of detail now. The statistical principles of sampling are not very difficult to follow and a close attention to logic will take one a long way, In essence, everybody in the 'universe' must have an equal chance of appearing in the sample —there must be no greater chance of, say, a male appearing than a female, a tall man than a short one, a sick person than a well one, an obsessional than one who couldn't care less. We may draw them randomly by some device and our first consideration must then be the 'randomness' of our procedure. To take but one example: in recent inquiry into the frequency of certain congenital defects in infants it was proposed to survey a sample of mothers-about-to-be, who were to be selected from those whose surnames began with certain letters. Is that a random group? It is not easy to say, but I would myself be most reluctant to accept it as such. Suppose we take the letters M, J and O; then our sample of pregnant women will most certainly be composed of unduly large numbers of the Scotch, the Welsh and the Irish. Whether they have more, or fewer, congenitally defective babies than the English, far be it from me to say—we simply don't know, and therefore must distrust a survey based upon such a sample. On the other hand if we chose mothers-to-be who had themselves been born on the seventh and fifteenth days of any month of the year I can see no catch—why should they have more or fewer defective babies than someone born on any other date? It is from these aspects that we must examine our sampling procedure.

We must also remember that even if we do survey the whole population, that too can be only a sample, for it is a sample in time. And sometimes time is of the greatest importance. Clearly, if you wish to show the Ministry of Health the amount of work the general practitioner does, you do not, I hope, base your survey wholly upon the month of January and an influenza epidemic, even if you have an eye on the capitation fee. You must make your sample in time cover the whole seasonal rise and fall of sickness. Similarly, in determining the incidence of accidents in factories we may have to take into account variations by days of the week, variations by hour of the day. We must plan our survey to cover such changes or we shall over- or under-estimate the true incidence.

Finally, one can sometimes most effectively combine a survey of the whole population for one factor with a survey of a sample, or samples, of it for some other factors. This can be particularly worth while if many questions are involved. Too many questions may well kill the goose that is to lay the golden egg or so increase the refusal-to-lay rate that, as I have already pointed out, the survey becomes open to grave doubts. Far too often, and particularly in committees, I have seen a cheerful piling up of questions without any thought whatever to the questioned. But we might effectively ask everyone surveyed, say, five basic questions and at the same time divide the population into half a dozen randomly constructed samples and ask the members of each another two questions, which are different for each sample. Thus in a survey I made before the war a random sample of 500 general practitioners kept in each month of the year a record of the attendances of and their visits to their panel patients. At the same time a random 100 drawn from these 500 recorded night visits, another 100 recorded the amount of form-filling they had to do, another 100 recorded minor operations and so on. Each, therefore, was limited in what he had to do, yet information was obtained on half a dozen different items. That kind of sampling is, I am sure, not sufficiently appreciated. Earlier this month I had an interesting example. A particular treatment had been given to a large number of ambulant patients in a very short space of time. It was quite impossible in the circumstances to follow them up to check the results and it had to be inferred that if the patient did not come back in 24 hours for more drugs he was cured. No one can say whether that inference is valid. But I think it might well have been possible to follow up a random sample of the patients—one in five, say—and this procedure would have unequivocally shown whether the inference was in fact reasonable or seriously at fault. So little can sometimes save, or redeem, so much.

CONTROLS

The third point to consider in the field survey—and again not necessarily in chronological order—is that of controls. Control is a much abused word with often an ill-conceived notion lying beneath its use. Do we need controls? To answer that we must switch back to my original queries regarding the survey—why and what for? If our object is to measure the frequency of a certain event, to see, for instance, whether measures to prevent it should be taken, then clearly we need no so-called controls. If, on the other hand, we wish to deduce cause and effect, to determine *what* measures of prevention should be taken, then almost invariably we do need controls. To be specific, if we survey the deaths of infants in the first month of life and find that so many are caused by dropping the baby on its head on the kitchen floor I am not myself convinced that we need controls to satisfy us that that is a bad habit. If, on the other hand, so many of the deaths are found to be of infants whose mothers had influenza during pregnancy then I should shriek for controls before I was satisfied that the two events were related. To repeat, in the first example we merely want to know how often something occurs and no control group whatever will make any difference to the result. In the second example we want to know not merely how often two things occur together but whether they are causally related. And we cannot answer that question unless we know the relative death rates of infants whose mothers did and did not suffer from influenza during pregnancy or using the approach I made previously, we want to show that of the mothers of dead babies more had had influenza than was the case with mothers of surviving babies. In other words we must have a control group of living babies to contrast with the dying babies.

To change the example—my colleague, Dr. Doll, and I have been making a survey of persons with cancer of the lung. When such persons have entered certain London hospitals we have been notified, and with the aid of highly skilled social workers we have endeavoured to record particulars about them—their occupations, their previous illnesses, and specifically, of course, their habits with regard to smoking. Here controls are an essential feature of the inquiry. We are not interested in the *absolute* frequency of smoking in patients with cancer of the lung; we are acutely interested in its *relative* frequency. In other words, we might find that half these patients had previously smoked like chimneys. What then? If we had bent our minds to it we might have found that half of them had had a red-headed aunt. There is no more reason, taking that information alone, why we should deduce cause and effect in the one case more than in the other. We *must* in this situation have a comparative group—a cross-section of hospital patients or of the population who have not got cancer of the lung. That is, I fear, dreadfully obvious, but I equally much fear that within the next 12 months many of us will accept without demur some conclusion that is drawn from uncontrolled observations and—if we stayed to think—in an equally obvious situation.

One last point on this matter. Often in experimental medicine but also in field surveys many of the contrasts we wish to make are dependent upon subjective judgements rather than on objective evidence. The evidence, too, may sometimes be coloured by our own preconceptions. The statistician therefore, believe me, means no harm, he offers no veiled insult, when with customary humility he suggests that the observer might profitably make his judgements without being allowed to know whether he is dealing with a 'marked' or a 'control' case. This blind assessment not only nullifies any bias that may creep in with the observer but also saves the observer obsessed with the feeling that he may be biased from over-correcting or correcting for something that may not exist. For instance, Dr. Doll and I endeavoured, though in view of practical difficulties not wholly successfully, to have the cancer of the lung and other patients cross-examined about smoking and other habits of their lives without the social worker knowing with which type of patient she was then dealing. My own belief is that my twenty questions should always include, 'Can these observations be influenced by the way in which they are made? Can they be influenced by the observer, and, if there *is* any such danger, can they be made blindly so that they *cannot* be influenced by the observer?'

REPORTS

Lastly, logically and chronologically this time, I come to the presentation of the results. For we have now decided precisely what we hoped to achieve by a survey; after long and anxious thought we have framed our questions (and of course I use the verb in its more usually accepted sense); we have, to save time and unnecessary expense, sampled the population in our particular field; and we have provided a control group (if such was, in fact, needed). We have totted up the answers—and in my discussion I have passed over and propose to pass over this particular operation: adding up is a painful procedure to some, so let us have done with it. At long last we have to present the answers to others, often to lay them before the lacklustre eye of a superior officer or even an editor. In this connexion it is my custom to put two quotations to those to whom I lecture in this School. On this occasion I shall venture to add a third.

'It is the essence of Science to disclose both the data upon which a conclusion is based and the methods by which the conclusion is attained.'

'Care should be taken not that the reader may understand if he will, but that he must understand, whether he will or no.'

And lastly from a discussion by that great American thinker, James Thurber, on oversimplification.

' "In so far as men assert and counter-assert, you draw an assertion from the comparison of their assertions." As it stands that is not oversimplified, because no one can point to any exact or absolute meaning it has. Now I will oversimplify it. A says "Babe Ruth is dead" (assertion). B says "Babe Ruth is alive" (counter-assertion). C says "You guys seem to disagree" (assertion drawn from comparison of assertions).'

The essence of this advice, then, is that in your report on a field survey you should say, and say clearly, exactly what you have done; and you cannot (I speak from experience) oversimplify. If you drew a sample you should state categorically how you drew it—give the nature of your sampling procedure. If you failed to get data from all persons in your sample, or in the population if you used the whole of it, you should state just how many were missing and consider closely how far they may affect the conclusions you draw —whether the absentees are of a particular kind or likely to be the ordinary run of the mill. If you do not believe some of the observations or do not fancy the look of them you should never leave them out without informing the reader and giving your reasons. If you have a control group, it needs just as precise a definition as the specially observed—you must state how it was chosen, if there were any lapses, and so on. It seems to me that it is quite often overlooked that in any comparison both groups are of equal and fundamental importance; there can be no glossing over the nature of the controls.

In short the scientific method in the field survey demands precision of aim, accuracy of recording, intellectual honesty in approval and interpretation and, at its end, if possible, clarity of exposition.

I have not stressed mathematical statistical methods. They have their place, and a most important place it is, but there is still, fortunately for the lesser of us, much to be done, much to be learnt from quite simple numerical methods within the compass of us all. In support of that belief I take for my conclusion a sentence from Fifty Years of Medicine (*British Medical Journal*, 1950). An anonymous author contributed a leading article on statistics in medicine and I have good reason to believe that he would have no objection to my purloining his quotation. 'Mathematical analysis is an excellent machine for threshing out the facts, but the facts have first to be harvested and there is a place for even the humblest gleaner.'

REFERENCE

British Medical Journal (1950), **i**, 68.

CHAPTER 16

OBSERVATION AND EXPERIMENT

TWO years ago, in his Cutter Lecture, one of my predecessors pointed out that the object of any science is 'the accumulation of systematized verifiable knowledge', and that this is to be achieved through 'observation, experiment and thought'—the last including both criticism and imagination. He then added, 'the use of the experimental method has brilliant discoveries to its credit, whereas the method of observation has achieved little' (Sinclair, 1951). This dictum must surely prove, at least at first sight, more than a little disconcerting to the exponent of preventive medicine. In dealing with the characteristics of human populations, in sorting out the features of the environment that are detrimental from those that are beneficial, he does not often find it easy to experiment. The method of observation frequently plays a large part in the particular study of mankind that is his prerogative. Is it, then, quite so useless? Must he give it up as merely a time-wasting hobby?

Looking farther back in time I found that these questions had been considered, as indeed I had expected, by my statistical forebears and teachers in Great Britain. They did not perhaps have quite so pessimistic an outlook as the one I have quoted above, but they certainly did not underrate the difficulties of the observational approach or overlook the value of the experimental method. Thus, in 1924, Yule's (1924) view was that the student of social facts could not experiment but had to deal with circumstances operating entirely beyond his control; he must accept records simply of what has happened. He wrote:

The expert in public health, for example, must take the records of deaths as they occur, and endeavour as best he can to interpret, say, the varying incidence of death on different districts. Clearly this is a very difficult matter . . . The purpose of *experiment* is to replace these highly complex tangles of causation, [and] the more perfect the experiment—the more nearly the experimental ideal is attained—the less is the influence of disturbing causes, and the less necessary the use of statistical methods.

The Cutter Lecture on Preventive Medicine, delivered at the Harvard School of Public Health, 25 March, 1953.

Reprinted from the *New England Journal of Medicine*, 1953, **248**, 995.

Greenwood (1924) has a characteristic passage, which I quote in full since I believe that the part of it that has no close bearing on my present thesis will nevertheless more than bear repetition today:

My conception of the statistical method in medicine has changed in the last 20 years; this is especially so with regard to the bearing of statistical method upon experiment. I used to see in the statistician the critic of the laboratory worker: it is a rôle which is gratifying to youthful vanity, for it is so easy to cheat oneself into the belief that the critic has some intellectual superiority over the criticised. I do not think even now that statistical criticism of laboratory investigations is useless, but I attach enormously more value to direct collaboration, the making of statistical experiments, and the permeation of statistical research with the experimental spirit.

The last words—written nearly 30 years ago—are, I suggest, the operative clause in the present setting—the permeation of statistical research with the experimental spirit. Although, as Yule said, facts must often, inevitably, be accepted as they occur, one does not have merely to accept facts as they are reported. One need not accept as final what some third party can give, or chooses to give—for example, a registrar-general or a census bureau. Such reported observations may, of course, prove to be a most valuable indicator of a problem; they may be, thereby, the starting-point of research. But when the pattern of cause and effect is complicated they are often not likely to provide a solution. The methods of partial correlation, enthusiastically accepted a quarter of a century ago, no longer seem to have an 'unlimited power to penetrate the secrets of nature' (Tippett, 1943). One must go seek more facts, paying less attention to technique of handling the data and far more to the development and perfection of methods of obtaining them. In so doing one must have the experimental approach firmly in mind. In other words, can observations be made in such a way as to fulfil, as far as possible, experimental requirements?

ANCIENT OBSERVATION (THE CHOLERA)

It was in this way, nearly a hundred years ago, that John Snow approached his problem, not only as an incomparable master of logical deduction from observations but also, it should be noted, as the constructor of observations. To recapitulate briefly, his opening arguments are based on vital statistics of the different areas of

London. Using the deaths given in the first report of the Metropolitan Sanitary Commission (1847), he first shows the excessive mortality from cholera that in the epidemic of 1832 befell the districts supplied by the Southwark Water Works, a company that drew its water from the Thames at London Bridge and provided worse water, according to Snow, than any other in the metropolis. Even the order of precedence between a flea and a louse is sometimes, it appears, of importance. A death rate from cholera of 11 per 1,000 inhabitants stands out starkly amidst the rates of two, three and four for other districts of the city, but clearly that unenviable record might be explicable in terms of some quite different local characteristic. The evidence gives a lead but no more. The case is somewhat, but not at all convincingly, strengthened by the events of 1849. The highest mortality rates from cholera were again consistently to be found in the districts supplied by the Southwark Company (now combined with the South London Water Company to form the Southwark and Vauxhall) and also in those served by the Lambeth Company; both companies drew their water from the Thames in its most contaminated reaches. In 1853 there begins to appear reason to sit up and even to take notice. The Lambeth Company had removed its works from central London to Thames Ditton, where the river was wholly free from the sewage of the metropolis; the Southwark and Vauxhall Company continued to prescribe for its customers the mixture as before. In the 12 sub-districts served by the latter 192 persons died of cholera in the epidemic of 1853—with 168,000 persons living the crude rate is thus 114 per 100,000. In 16 sub-districts served by both companies 182 persons died; among 301,000 living, that is a rate of 60 per 100,000. In three sub-districts of 15,000 persons served only by the Lambeth Company no deaths from cholera were reported.

So far do the statistical observations run; so far but not far enough. On that showing alone one might even hesitate to accept Snow's 'very strong evidence' against the water supply. He himself was indeed of that mind, for 'the question', he observed, 'does not end here' (he had no intention of letting it end there). It was not said without reason that wherever cholera was visitant there was he in the midst. He noted that the Southwark and Vauxhall and Lambeth companies were competitors so that in some sub-districts the pipes of each went down all the streets and into nearly all the courts and alleys:

Each Company supplies both rich and poor, both large houses and small . . . No fewer than 300,000 people of both sexes, of every age and occupation, and of every rank and station, from gentlefolk down to the very poor, were divided into two groups without their choice, and, in most cases, without their knowledge; one group being supplied with water containing the sewage of London, and, amongst it, whatever might have come from the cholera patients, the other group having water quite free from such impurity.

Here, then, was an unwitting experiment on the grandest scale, and Snow set himself to learn its results.

In 1854, with one medical man to assist him, up and down the streets, courts and alleys of South London he tramped in the summer's sun, learning for every cholera death the water supply of the household. Thus, by personal, persistent and accurate field work were the basic vital statistics infinitely strengthened. In 40,000 houses served by the Southwark and Vauxhall Company 286 fatal attacks were found in the first four weeks of the epidemic of 1854— 71 deaths per 10,000 households; in 26,000 houses served by the Lambeth Company 14 fatal attacks were found—only five deaths per 10,000 households. In such a way was observation successfully added to observation to form a coherent and convincing whole.

It might be argued that Snow was lucky in having at hand a natural 'experiment'. Perhaps he was. But such 'experiments' or, at least, effective 'controls' would not, I believe, really prove to be so rare if one invariably cast one's eyes round for them after vital statistics, or similar observations, had given an appropriate lead.

Certainly, in the famous Broad Street Pump outbreak of cholera no experiment offered. Its story is too well known to need any detailed reference here, but having brought Snow into my picture, I could not bear to pass it by wholly unsung. It is not so much for persuading the local board of guardians to remove the handle of the pump that Snow here deserves credit—though for this alone it is often paid to him. In fact either through the flight of the terrified population from the stricken area (and Snow himself says that 'in less than six days the most afflicted streets were deserted by more than three-quarters of their inhabitants') or through natural epidemiologic causes, the outbreak had been steeply declining for five or six days before the well was thus put out of action. That 'experiment' provides no useful evidence.

It is again in the field work that his strength lies: the map showing the concentration of deaths around the pump with their number diminishing greatly, or ceasing altogether, at each point where it became decidedly nearer to send to another pump; the demonstration of the escape of the inmates of the workhouse, which had its own well, and, similarly, of the 70 workmen in the brewery who knew better than to drink water—or if somehow driven to do so drew from a well within the brewery. And the striking individual histories, the most conclusive of which Sherlock Holmes might well have called 'the curious case of the Hampstead widow'. In the weekly return of births and deaths of 9 September published by the Registrar-General of England and Wales there appeared the following entry: 'At West End [Hampstead], on 2nd September, the widow of a percussion-cap maker, aged 59 years, diarrhoea two hours, cholera epidemica sixteen hours.' (The times refer to the duration of the fatal illness, then—and again now—entered by the medical practitioner upon the certificate of cause of death.) One of the factories in Broad Street made percussion caps, but on inquiry Snow found that the widow had not been in the neighbourhood for many months. However, she still preferred the water from the pump to that of the more salubrious neighbourhood to which she had retired, and she commissioned a carter who drove daily between the two points to bring her a large bottle. The bottle was duly delivered on 31 August. She drank of it and died two days later. A niece on a visit to her likewise drank of it. She then returned to her home in Islington, where she died of cholera. There was no cholera extant in either neighbourhood.

To digress for a moment, there was at least one other person who drank of that bottle. The story here is, perhaps, less well known. The first medical officer of health for Hampstead (now one of the metropolitan boroughs of London) dictated as an old man in 1889 some recollections under the title of *The Sanitary Experiences of Charles F. J. Lord, M.R.C.S.* It is now held in manuscript in the Hampstead Public Library but was privately printed for circulation among the old man's friends. There is a copy in the library of the Surgeon General in Washington under the title, *Jottings: Some experience with reflections derived through life and work in Hampstead from 1827 to 1877* (Pamphlet Vol. 3807). Lord himself died before making final corrections of the proofs. On pages 36 and 37 of the printed version the following passage is included:

A memorable case of what we may consider an imported cause of disease happened at West End; Mrs. Eley Mother of the renowned firm "Eley

Brothers" had lived in Broad Street Soho, and had drunk with glorification from a deep well there situated. On leaving London, she had a big stone bottle brought daily for the use of herself at West End. Summoned hastily to see the old lady I found her in the early stage of Cholera—remedies were unavailing, though solicitously applied in every way by a daughter and one of her sons. A consultation with the highly esteemed Dr. Farre ensued, the Patient never rallied, died that night. The cause of the disease at that time was never suspected; it was proved afterwards by the untiring investigations of Dr. Snow, that the water from the Broad Street well was contaminated and produced the disease; a sort of practical joke arose among the Teetotalers of the Broad Street district; those who stuck to the Porter especially those of the Brewery were rarely victims to the disease while those who drank the water fell fast around. I myself while attending closely on the old lady, as also was her daughter, was much troubled with Diarrhoea having unsuspiciously sipped some of the imported water. This insipient [sic] stage of Cholera soon passed away, in the absence of full or renewed doses.

Here, then, to return to my thesis, is a masterpiece—many persons would say *the* masterpiece—of observation and logical inference, made many years before the discovery of the vibrio of cholera. It shows—as many other examples have shown—that the highest returns can be reaped by imagination in combination with a logical and critical mind, a spice of ingenuity coupled with an eye for the simple and humdrum, and a width of vision in the pursuit of facts that is allied with an attention to detail that is almost nauseating.

MODERN OBSERVATION (RUBELLA)

A modern example of acute observation lies in the story of rubella in pregnancy unfolded, almost a hundred years later, in Australia. Again, the story is too well known to need retelling, but it has a facet perhaps less familiar and yet of great interest to the student of public health—in other words, to the observer of group phenomena. It might well be that the congenital defects observed in Australia in the years 1938 to 1941 were something new in medicine, that the rubella epidemic was of a particular virulence, or that the virus had acquired some unusual characteristic at that time. Indeed, there is so much folklore attached to events in pregnancy that if the effects of German measles were an old phenomenon one might possibly have expected to find some old-wives' tale concerning it. I know of none in Britain. That the story was not, however, new in Australia is strongly indicated by the statistical observations marshalled by Lancaster (1951). In each of the reports on the Australian censuses of 1911, 1921 and 1933 there is a section that deals with the enumerated prevalence of blindness and deaf-mutism. The incidence of the latter is revealing; it shows a maximum in each census corresponding to persons born in the years 1896–1900.

At the census of 1911 the peak lay in the age group from 10 to 14, and the statistician, writes Lancaster, 'was inclined to ascribe the maximum to the more complete enumeration of the deaf at the school ages'; most observers would, I suspect, have taken that view. When, however, in 1921, the peak shifted to the age group 20 to 24 the statistician considered epidemic disease as a possible cause. He suggested that the increased incidence of deafness at certain ages might synchronize with the occurrence of such illnesses as 'scarlet fever, diphtheria, measles, and whooping cough'. In the report on the census of 1933 infective disease was again discussed. But the lead given by the somewhat crude vital statistics was not, it appears, followed up at the time. Lancaster himself has followed it up—in 1951 and therefore, of course, after the clinical observations of 1938–41—by examining the dates of birth of children admitted to institutions for the deaf and dumb. He finds, to take a single example, that of those admitted in New South Wales 15 were born in 1898 and 16 in 1900. For the intermediate year 1899 the figure soared to 70. Furthermore, these 70 are not evenly spread throughout the year but are concentrated in the months of April to September. On such evidence, marshalled in detail and with skill, Lancaster concludes that 'deafness has appeared in epidemic form in Australia in the past, notably among children born in 1899, 1916, 1924, 1925 and in 1938–41' and that 'there is some presumptive evidence that all these epidemics, with the exception of that in 1916, were caused by antecedent epidemics of rubella'. It seems so easy *now*, he rightly observes, to suggest a causal relation; it is always easy to be wise after the event. Nevertheless, there was at least a legible scrawl on the wall—additional and accurate data were there for the seeking and, once sought, offered a clear case for a carefully designed field inquiry. The combined observational and statistical approach could have won the day; it could have won it quite a long time ago.

CANCER OF THE LUNG

This approach seems to me to be the only one possible in another matter of community concern today—the etiology of carcinoma of the lung. The starting-point is as usual the national registration system. 'It is sometimes asked,' says Stocks (1949), 'how statistics can cure disease,' and he suggests that one may counter the question by another question: 'how many researches which have led to real advances in Medicine would ever have been started had there not first been some statistics to suggest that here was a problem to be investigated?' In this particular instance it is, of course, admitted that skill in, and modern adjuncts to, diagnosis make more than dubious the whole gamut of changes that the system of vital statistics reveals. But there is, in my opinion, more than enough evidence to regard some of that change as real and to justify a search for a cause of a truly rising mortality in England and Wales. Aided and abetted by the Medical Research Council, Doll and I set about that search in 1947. Our aim was to make the field observations mirror an experimental design as nearly as possible. For each patient with cancer of the lung we sought a 'control' patient with some other disease—a patient of the same sex, of the same age group, in the same hospital at or about the same time, but otherwise chosen at random. In other words, we sought, as in an experiment, to limit the variables. We limited them, too, not only in this way but also by employing, in history taking, only a few skilled interviewers, each armed with a prescribed set of questions. We made, of course, no frontal attack upon smoking, which in our original questionnaire formed but one section out of nine—11 questions out of nearly 50.

Having admitted to a questionnaire of that magnitude I shall take this opportunity to defend myself. For I have been reported as having advocated, before a conference on the application of scientific methods to industrial and service medicine, 'that nobody should be subjected to more than five questions' (Himsworth, 1924). I am, indeed, in favour of shorter and brighter forms but not always to that extent. What I said on that occasion about the problems of making observations of any value, was this: 'broadly speaking, of any 20 questions asked in a field survey not more than five should be put to the surveyed, and not less than 15 should be put to the surveyor by himself before he enters the field or, indeed, ventures to look over the gate' (Hill, 1951). In other words, I maintained, though doubtless somewhat clumsily, that one may ask as many questions as one believes useful—so long as the ratio one to the surveyed and three to the surveyor is maintained throughout. A basic query in the latter group will be, in every case, 'is this question really necessary?' It is surprising how often that will effectively keep down the number incorporated.

On the other hand the observational approach has perhaps been somewhat discredited by a too frequent failure to keep down that number, a pathetically notable lack of the critical and imaginative thought that, as Sinclair noted, must be an integral part of the scientific method, in other words, and more briefly, too few ideas chasing too many forms. That evil is, of course, no prerogative of the United States of America, but I cannot refrain from citing from Eric Linklater's delectable book (1931) (that is, to an Englishman) *Juan in America*. Even 22 years ago he was moved to write that

the issuing of questionnaires had become a national habit, and work was provided for many people, who might otherwise never have found employment, in dealing with such returns: that is in docketing them, tabulating, copying, indexing, cross-indexing, re-arranging them, according to ethnic, religious, social, geographic and other factors, and eventually composing a monograph on them for the Library of Congress.

Perhaps Americans were quicker off the mark. I would, however, warn them that we on the other side of the Atlantic are not being backward and may even overtake them in these national vices and devices.

Returning to my theme it is, of course, possible that the relative absence of non-smokers and the relative frequency of heavy smokers that Doll and I found in our patients with cancer of the lung (and that other workers have also noted) is really a function of some other difference between the two groups. We do not ourselves, for several reasons, believe that to be so, and it is certainly worth noting that patients with pulmonary cancer and controls are remarkably alike in other characteristics that we have recorded. Nevertheless, here lies, I admit, the weakness of the observational as compared with the experimental approach. With the former we can determine the most probable explanation of a contrast in our data; given the provision that we have taken sufficient care to remove disturbing causes, that probability can be very high. But with a well-designed experiment it should be possible to eliminate (or allow for) nearly all disturbing causes and thus to render the interpretation of the contrast even more certain.

Yet in this particular problem what experiment can one make? We may subject mice, or other laboratory animals, to such an atmosphere of tobacco smoke that they can—like the old man in the fairy story—neither sleep nor slumber; they can neither breed nor eat. And lung cancers may or may not develop to a significant degree. What then? We may have thus strengthened the evidence, we may even have narrowed the search, but we must, I believe, invariably return to man for the final proof or proofs.

In this instance one other method of inquiry is now being applied both in the United States and the United Kingdom: a 'looking-forward' investigation. Up till now investigators have taken already marked subjects—together with a control series—and have inquired into their antecedents. That has been the method not only, of course, in this particular inquiry but in many others. It is a natural approach and one likely to yield quick returns. Adult patients with peptic ulcers are questioned concerning whether they came from broken homes; those with rheumatoid arthritis are questioned on their previous shocks and ills; and the views of the victims of neurosis upon the habits of their fathers are sought. The resulting picture, the contrast between marked and unmarked, may be clear cut, and yet it may be difficult to distinguish between effects and causes, between horse and cart. Memories may well be more profound and more retentive in the 'marked', and they may indeed be more highly coloured—what the adult neurotic thinks of his father may not always be the truth. Even with the method at its best one can rarely hope to make a prognosis by these means, to measure the probabilities of events. But that is what is usually needed: first to observe the broken, and unbroken, home and then to record the subsequent history of its youthful inmates. That is clearly difficult to do and calls for a considerable degree of patience, which most investigators do not possess. But if the forward approach can be employed, it is, I believe, almost always the right way to go to work; in any observational inquiry its possibility should invariably be considered.

In the particular investigation that Doll and I now have under way—broadly into the deaths in the next few years of men and women on the British medical register whose smoking habits are already characterized at a defined point of time (late 1951)—it again, of course, would not follow that any association we might find between death from carcinoma of the lung (or other causes of death) and smoking habits must be a direct association. The heavy smokers may be differentiated from the light smokers in some other way, which might have some bearing on the risks of a bronchial carcinoma. We are still faced with the most probable explanation. But we may, I submit, have further narrowed the field of possible variables, of errors of omission or commission.

THE FIELD EXPERIMENT

There is today an increasing resort to the field experiment, a district, a town, a school or a factory being used as the laboratory. It is a striking development of the present age and, if the requirements of an efficient experiment can be met, a most valuable one. But those requirements *must* be met; a poor experiment serves no purpose. Yet it seems that the very magic in its name may serve to mislead those who worship at the experimental shrine.

As an example, in a recently reported study of vaccination against influenza, the subjects for inoculation were chosen on a voluntary basis and 'without any great propaganda 32.8 per cent of the total employees involved in the Survey voluntarily requested the inoculations'. This one-third, self-selected group is compared with the remaining two-thirds, who, like Gallio, 'cared for none of those things'. Of the 1,148 inoculated persons 10.80 per cent were attacked by influenza, and of the 2,349 remaining population 15.02 per cent. The difference is 'statistically significant' with a 'P of 0.00567'. And yet does this ritual and do all these decimal places mean anything at all? Admittedly, the technical test says that the two groups had experiences that differed by more than one would expect to occur by chance; equally, it tells nothing else. As it stands I do not myself believe that it gives any support whatever for the author's conclusion that here is evidence 'strongly in favour of the immunization of large groups in industry'. Yet I have no doubt that it will be cited in the literature under the caption 'it has been shown by experiment'.

In my view this is not an experiment at all. Some observations have been made of the recorded incidence of 'influenza' in two groups. The investigator knew (and so incidentally did the two groups) that they differed in one respect—inoculation; they may well have differed in a score of others—even, for all one is told, in such simple respects as age and sex. None of the other possible variables of importance were controlled, and it is well known that in trials of vaccines a self-selected group is most unlikely to be a representative sample of the total. Field experiments are not, unfortunately, as easy to design and carry out as all that. In this particular field—vaccination against influenza—I speak with conviction, for the Medical Research Council has during the last winter carried out some experiments in industry, trials of methodology, I should say, as much as of vaccines. We too, of course, have had to rely upon volunteers for our basic material. There is (fortunately) no other way of setting up a trial. But the volunteers were divided at random into two groups—an inoculated group given the influenza vaccine and an inoculated group given a dummy vaccine. We had their general consent to that procedure, but in the individual case it was unknown. It was also unknown to the medical practitioner diagnosing such illnesses as occurred—influenza, possibly influenza and other diseases. In such ways we have endeavoured to equalize our groups *de novo*—to eliminate bias from the subsequent observations. Whether, having to cast our epidemic net wide, we have succeeded in obtaining accurate and comparable records from a score of factories and still more doctors remains to be seen. Such experiments involving human beings are, I repeat, not easy to carry out; they are, as a rule, costly. Yet in relation to the returns rendered they are relatively cheap. A well-designed plan may in a few months, or years, forestall years or decades of indeterminate, unplanned observation.

CONCLUSION

There is one thread that runs—or it might be more accurate to say wanders—through this lecture. I have been unable—even if I would—to conceal my preference in preventive medicine for the experimental approach. At the same time that preference does not lead me to repudiate or even, I hope, to underrate the claims of accurate and designed observations. But I would place all the emphasis at my command upon those adjectives. In this field of preventive medicine I share, on the whole, the view regarding the curative aspects recently expressed by Platt (1952), professor of medicine in the University of Manchester. Records in clinical research are likely, he suggests, to be disappointing:

Unless they have been kept with an end in view, as part of a planned experiment . . . Clinical experiment need not mean the subjection of patients to uncomfortable procedures of doubtful value or benefit. It means the planning of a line of action and the recording of observations designed to withstand critical analysis and give the answer to a clinical problem. It is an attitude of mind.

In appropriately exploiting that attitude of mind one may well need, in this age of technicalities, close and constant collaboration. Today, as Joseph Garland (1952) pointed out in this city of Boston, 'the mathematics of research has expressed itself in a multiplicity of graphs, charts and tables with the aid of which the average reader at a quick glance can often learn next to nothing'. The biostatistician must therefore acquire a taste for lying down with the epidemiologist, and the bacteriologist with the medical officer of health (I speak in fables).

There are, of course, no grounds for antagonism between experiment and observation. The former, indeed, depends on observation but of a type that has the good fortune to be controlled at the experimenter's will. In the world of public health and preventive medicine each will—or should—constantly react beneficially upon the other. Observation in the field suggests experiment; the experiment leads back to more, and better defined, observations. However that may be, it is difficult to see how one can wholly, or ever, escape from Alexander Pope's epigram. How else but by observation upon man himself being born, living and dying, can one set about the solution of such problems as prematurity and still birth at one end of life and cancer and coronary thrombosis at the other? However tangled the skein of causation one must, at least at first, try to un-ravel it *in vivo*. As Pickering (1952) has said: 'Any work which seeks to elucidate the cause of disease, the mechanism of disease, the cure of disease, or the prevention of disease, must begin and end with observations on man, whatever the intermediate steps may be.'

The observer may well have to be more patient than the experi-menter—awaiting the occurrence of the natural succession of events he desires to study; he may well have to be more imaginative—sensing the correlations that lie below the surface of his observa-tions; and he may well have to be more logical and less dogmatic—avoiding as the evil eye the fallacy of *post hoc ergo propter hoc*, the mistaking of correlation for causation.

Lastly, I quote the words of Professor William Topley (1940), a British worker for whom I had a profound admiration and from whose wisdom I endeavoured to learn:

A great part of clinical medicine, and of epidemiology, must still be observation. Nature makes the experiments, and we watch and understand them if we can. No one will deny that we should always aim at planned intervention and closer control. Here, as elsewhere, technique—the way we make our observations and check them—is half the battle; but to force experiment and observation into sharply separated categories is almost as dangerous a heresy as the science and art [of medicine] antithesis. It tends to make the clinician in the ward, the epidemiologist in the field, and the laboratory worker at his bench, think of themselves as doing different things, and bound by different rules. Actually they are all making experiments, some good, some bad. It is more difficult to make a good experiment in the ward than in the laboratory, because conditions are more difficult to control; but there is no other way of gaining knowledge . . . Controlled observation in the ward or in the field is an essential part of medical science, shading through almost imperceptible stages of increasing intervention into the fully developed experimental technique of the laboratory.

Mr. Winston Churchill, revisiting the Niagara Falls after more than 40 years, was asked by a reporter 'Do they look the same?' 'Well,' he is said to have replied, 'the principle seems the same.' General principles are obstinate things; they do tend to remain the same generation after generation. Yet one element of that sameness —their fundamental importance—perhaps justifies their being brought out into the light of day from time to time and, if one cannot weave fresh clothes, at least in a newly dyed costume. In accepting the honour of delivering this Cutter Lecture I indeed trusted that that was so. If I was wrong I must comfort myself like that charming character described by Anatole France: like Monsieur Bonnard, I have the satisfaction of believing that, in following my distinguished predecessors, I have at least 'utilized to their fullest extent those mediocre faculties with which Nature endowed me'.

REFERENCES

Garland, J. (1952). *New Engl. J. Med.* **246,** 801.
Greenwood, M. (1924). *Lancet*, **ii,** 153.
Hill, A. Bradford (1951). *The Application of Scientific Methods to Industrial and Service Medicine*, p. 7. London: H.M.S.O.
Himsworth, H. P. (1951). *The Application of Scientific Methods to Industrial and Service Medicine*, p. 109. London: H.M.S.O.
Lancaster, H. O. (1951). *Brit. med. J.* **ii,** 1429.
Linklater, E. (1931). *Juan in America*. London: Cape.
Pickering, G. W. (1952). *Lancet*, **ii,** 895.

Platt, R. (1952). *Lancet*, **ii,** 977.

Sinclair, H. M. (1951). *New Engl. J. Med.* **245,** 39.

Stocks, P. (1949). In *Modern Trends in Public Health*, chapter xix, ed. Massey, A. London: Butterworth.

Tippett, L. H. C. (1943). *Statistics*. London: Oxford University Press.

Topley, W. W. C. (1940). *Authority, Observation and Experiment in Medicine* p. 40. London: Cambridge University Press.

Yule, G. (1924). *Rep. industr. Hlth. Res. Bd. (Lond.),* No. 28.

CHAPTER 17

SMOKING AND CARCINOMA OF THE LUNG

IN England and Wales the phenomenal increase in the number of deaths attributed to cancer of the lung provides one of the most striking changes in the pattern of mortality recorded by the Registrar-General. For example, in the quarter of a century between 1922 and 1947 the annual number of deaths recorded increased from 612 to 9,287, or roughly fifteenfold. This remarkable increase is, of course, out of all proportion to the increase of population—both in total and, particularly, in its older age groups. Stocks (1947), using standardized death rates to allow for these population changes, shows the following trend: rate per 100,000 in 1901–20, males 1.1, females 0.7; rate per 100,000 in 1936–9, males 10.6, females 2.5. The rise seems to have been particularly rapid since the end of the first world war; between 1921–30 and 1940–4 the death rate of men at ages 45 and over increased sixfold and of women of the same ages approximately threefold. This increase is still continuing. It has occurred, too, in Switzerland, Denmark, the U.S.A., Canada, and Australia, and has been reported from Turkey and Japan.

Many writers have studied these changes, considering whether they denote a real increase in the incidence of the disease or are due merely to improved standards of diagnosis. Some believe that the latter factor can be regarded as wholly, or at least mainly, responsible—for example, Willis (1948), Clemmesen and Busk (1947), and Steiner (1944). On the other hand, Kennaway and Kennaway (1947) and Stocks (1947) have given good reasons for believing that the rise is at least partly real. The latter, for instance, has pointed out that 'the increase of certified respiratory cancer mortality during the past 20 years has been as rapid in country districts as in the cities with the best diagnostic facilities, a fact which does not support the view that such increase merely reflects improved diagnosis of cases previously certified as bronchitis or other respiratory affections'. He also draws attention to differences in mortality between

(With Richard Doll.) Reprinted from the *British Medical Journal*, 1950, **ii**, 739.

some of the large cities of England and Wales, differences which it is difficult to explain in terms of diagnostic standards.

The large and continued increase in the recorded deaths even within the last five years, both in the national figures and in those from teaching hospitals, also makes it hard to believe that improved diagnosis is entirely responsible. In short, there is sufficient reason to reject that factor as the whole explanation, although no one would deny that it may well have been contributory. As a corollary, it is right and proper to seek for other causes.

Possible Causes of the Increase

Two main causes have from time to time been put forward: (1) a general atmospheric pollution from the exhaust fumes of cars, from the surface dust of tarred roads, and from gas-works, industrial plants, and coal fires; and (2) the smoking of tobacco. Some characteristics of the former have certainly become more prevalent in the last 50 years, and there is also no doubt that the smoking of cigarettes has greatly increased. Such associated changes in time can, however, be no more than suggestive, and until recently there has been singularly little more direct evidence. That evidence, based upon clinical experience and records, relates mainly to the use of tobacco. For instance, in Germany, Müller (1939) found that only three out of 86 male patients with cancer of the lung were non-smokers, while 56 were heavy smokers, and, in contrast, among 86 'healthy men of the same age groups' there were 14 non-smokers and only 31 heavy smokers. Similarly, in America, Schrek and his co-workers (1950) reported that 14.6 per cent of 82 male patients with cancer of the lung were non-smokers, against 23.9 per cent of 522 male patients admitted with cancer of sites other than the upper respiratory and digestive tracts. In this country, Thelwall Jones (Personal communication, 1949) found eight non-smokers in 82 patients with proved carcinoma of the lung, compared with 11 in a corresponding group of patients with diseases other than cancer; this difference is slight, but it is more striking that there were 28 heavy smokers in the cancer group, against 14 in the comparative group.

Clearly none of these small-scale inquiries can be accepted as conclusive, but they all point in the same direction. Their evidence has now been borne out by the results of a large-scale inquiry undertaken in the U.S.A. by Wynder and Graham (1950).

Wynder and Graham found that of 605 men with epidermoid, undifferentiated, or histologically unclassified types of bronchial carcinoma only 1.3 per cent were 'non-smokers'—that is, had averaged less than one cigarette a day for the last 20 years—whereas 51.2 per cent of them had smoked more than 20 cigarettes a day over the same period. In contrast, they estimated from the experience of 882 other male patients that 14.6 per cent of general hospital patients of the same age composition as the bronchial carcinoma cases are 'non-smokers' and only 19.1 per cent smoke more than 20 cigarettes a day. They found a similar contrast between the 25 women with epidermoid and undifferentiated bronchial carcinoma and the other female patients, but no such association with smoking could be found in the small group of patients with adenocarcinoma.

Present Investigation

The present investigation was planned in 1947, to be carried out on a sufficiently large scale to determine whether patients with carcinoma of the lung differed materially from other persons in respect of their smoking habits or in some other way which might be related to the atmospheric pollution theory. Patients with carcinoma of the stomach, colon, or rectum were also incorporated in the inquiry, as one of the contrasting groups, and special attention was therefore given at the same time to factors which might bear upon the aetiology of these forms of malignant disease. A separate report will be made upon these inquiries. The present study is confined to the question of smoking in relation to carcinoma of the lung.

The method of the investigation was as follows: Twenty London hospitals were asked to co-operate by notifying all patients admitted to them with carcinoma of the lung, stomach, colon, or rectum. For the most part these hospitals were initially confined to one region of London (the north-west), to allow ease of travelling, but others were subsequently added to increase the scope of the inquiry.

The method of notification varied; in some it was made by the admitting clerk on the basis of the admission diagnosis, in others by the house-physician when a reasonably confident clinical diagnosis had been made, and in yet others by the cancer registrar or the radio therapy department. None of these methods is likely to have resulted in complete notification, but there is no reason to suppose that those who escaped notification were a selected group—that is, selected in such a way as to bias the inquiry—as the points of interest in the investigation were either not known or known only in broad outline by those responsible for notifying.

On receipt of the notification an almoner, engaged wholly on research, visited the hospital to interview the patient, using a set questionnaire. During the inquiry four almoners were employed and all the patients were interviewed by one or other of them. As well, however, as interviewing the notified patients with cancer of one of the four specified sites, the almoners were required to make similar inquiries of a group of 'non-cancer control' patients. These patients were not notified, but for each lung-carcinoma patient visited at a hospital the almoners were instructed to interview a patient of the same sex, within the same five-year age group, and in the same hospital at or about the same time. (Where more than one suitable patient was available the choice fell upon the first one in the ward lists considered by the ward sister to be fit for interview.)

At two specialized hospitals (Brompton Hospital and Harefield Hospital) it was not always possible to secure a control patient by this method, and in such cases a control patient was taken from one of the two neighbouring hospitals, the Royal Cancer and Mount Vernon Hospitals. Even with this relaxation of the rule control cases were deficient at the Brompton Hospital and the numbers had to be made up by using the records of patients who had been interviewed as cancer patients, either there or at the Royal Cancer Hospital, but in whom cancer was finally excluded. Because of these differences in technique the records obtained from these hospitals were analysed separately. As, however, the results were in accordance with those found at the other hospitals, all the records are presented here as a single series.

In view of the method of notification used it could not be expected that the diagnosis then given would invariably be accurate. The diagnosis of each patient was checked, therefore, after discharge from or death in hospital, and this check was made in all but nine instances (0.4 per cent of the total). In these few cases (three of carcinoma of the lung, two of carcinoma of the stomach, two of carcinoma of the rectum, and two non-cancer) no records of any sort could be traced, and they have had to be classified according to the information available at the time of their interview. As a general rule the hospital diagnosis on discharge was accepted as the final diagnosis, but occasionally later evidence became available—for example, by histological examination at necropsy—which contradicted that diagnosis. In these instances a change was made and the diagnosis based upon the best evidence.

The Data

Between April, 1948, and October, 1949, the notifications of cancer cases numbered 2,370. It was not, however, possible to interview all these patients. To begin with, it had been decided beforehand that no one of 75 years of age or more should be included in the inquiry, since it was unlikely that reliable histories could be obtained from the very old. There were 150 such patients. In a further 80 cases the diagnosis was incorrect and had been changed before the almoner paid her visit. Deducting these two groups leaves 2,140 patients who should have been interviewed. Of these, 408 could not be interviewed for the following reasons: already discharged 189, too ill 116, dead 67, too deaf 24, unable to speak English clearly 11, while in one case the almoner abandoned the interview as the patient's replies appeared wholly unreliable. No patient refused to be interviewed.

The proportion not seen is high, but there is no apparent reason why it should bias the results. It was in the main due to the time that inevitably elapsed between the date of notification and the date of the almoner's visit. The remaining 1,732 patients, presumed at the interview to be suffering from carcinoma of the lung, stomach, or large bowel, and the 743 general medical and surgical patients originally interviewed as controls, constitute the subjects of the investigation. The numbers falling in each disease group—that is, after consulting the hospital discharge diagnoses—are shown in Table **17,** 1. The carcinoma cases are here divided into two groups: Group A consisting of cases in which the diagnoses were confirmed by necropsy, biopsy, or exploratory operation, and Group B of the remainder.

The 81 patients classified in Table **17,** 1 as having 'other malignant diseases' were interviewed as cases of carcinoma of the lung, stomach, or large bowel, or as non-cancer controls. On the subsequent checking of the diagnosis either they were found to have primary carcinoma in some site other than one of those under special investigation or histological examination showed that the growth was not, in fact, carcinoma—for example, sarcoma, reticulo-endothelioma, etc. The 335 'other cases' either were interviewed as cases of carcinoma of the

TABLE **17**, 1

Number of Patients Interviewed in Each Disease Group Sub-divided According to Certainty of Diagnosis

Disease Group	No. of Cases		
	Group A. Diagnosis Confirmed at Necropsy, etc.	Group B. Other Criteria of Diagnosis	Total
Carcinoma of lung	489	220	709
Carcinoma of stomach	178	28	206
Carcinoma of colon and rectum	412	19	431
Other malignant diseases	—	—	81
Diseases other than cancer (controls)	—	—	709
Other cases	—	—	335
Excluded	—	—	4
All cases	—	—	2,475

lung, stomach, or large bowel and were subsequently found not to be cases of malignant disease or, having been interviewed as non-cancer controls, they became redundant when the cases of carcinoma of the lung with which they were paired were found not to be carcinoma of the lung. The four 'excluded' cases were excluded on grounds of doubt about their true category. Two were diagnosed at hospital as primary carcinoma of the lung, but there was reason to suppose that the growths might have been secondary to carcinoma of the breast and to carcinoma of the cervix uteri respectively; the other two showed evidence of primary carcinoma in two of the sites under special investigation—that is, lung and colon, and stomach and colon.

The 709 control patients with diseases other than cancer form a group which was, as previously stated, deliberately selected to be closely comparable in age and sex with the carcinoma of the lung patients. Comparisons between these two groups are shown in Table **17**, 2.

It will be seen that the lung-carcinoma patients and the control group of non-cancer patients are exactly comparable with regard to sex and age, but that there are some differences with regard to social class and place of residence. The difference in social class distribution is small and is no more than might easily be due to chance

TABLE **17**, 2

Comparison Between Lung-carcinoma Patients and Non-cancer Patients Selected as Controls, with Regard to Sex, Age, Social Class, and Place of Residence

Age	No. of Lung-carcinoma Patients		No. of Non-cancer Control Patients		Social Class (Registrar-General's Categories. Men Only)	No. of Lung-carcinoma Patients	No. of Non-cancer Patients
	M	F	M	F			
25–	2	1	2	1	I and II	77	87
30–	6	0	6	0	III	388	396
35–	18	3	18	3	IV and V	184	166
40–	36	4	36	4			
45–	87	10	87	10	All classes	649	649
50–	130	11	130	11			
55–	145	9	145	9	*Place of residence*		
60–	109	9	109	9	County of London	330	377
65–	88	9	89*	9	Outer London	203	231
70–74	28	4	27*	4	Other county		
					borough	23	16
					Urban district	95	54
					Rural district	43	27
					Abroad or in		
					Services	15	4
All ages	649	60	649	60	Total (M + F)	709	709

* One control patient was selected, in error, from the wrong age group.

($\chi^2 = 1.61$; n = 2; $0.30 < P < 0.50$). The difference in place of residence is, however, large ($\chi^2 = 31.49$; n = 5; $P < 0.001$), and Table **17**, 2 shows that a higher proportion of the lung patients were resident outside London at the time of their admission to hospital. This difference can be explained on the grounds that people with cancer came to London from other parts of the country for treatment at special centres. When a comparison is made between the 98 lung-carcinoma patients and the 98 controls who were seen at district hospitals in London—that is, those regional board hospitals which do not have special surgical thoracic or radiotherapeutic centres—the difference disappears. Of these 98 patients with carcinoma of the lung, 56 lived in the County of London, 42 in outer London, and none elsewhere; of their non-cancer controls the corresponding numbers were 60, 38, and 0, clearly an insignificant difference.

It is evident, therefore, that the control group of patients with diseases other than cancer is strictly comparable with the group of lung-carcinoma patients in important respects but differs slightly with regard to the parts of England from which the patients were drawn. It is unlikely that this difference will invalidate comparisons, but it must be kept in mind; fortunately, it can be eliminated, if necessary, by confining comparisons to the smaller group of patients seen in the district hospitals.

Assessment of Smoking Habits

The assessment of the relation between tobacco-smoking and disease is complicated by the fact that smoking habits change. A man who has been a light smoker for years may become a heavy smoker; a heavy smoker may cut down his consumption or give up smoking—and, indeed, may do so repeatedly. An acute respiratory disease may force the sufferer to stop smoking, or he may be advised to stop for one of many pathological conditions. In 1947 a further complication was introduced by the Chancellor of the Exchequer, the duty on tobacco being raised to such an extent that many people made large cuts in the amount of tobacco they smoked—often to restore them partially or completely in the succeeding months. Fortunately the interviewing of patients was not begun till a year after the last major change was made in the tobacco duty; in any case the effect was minimized by interviewing the control patients *pari passu* with the lung-carcinoma patients, so that the change in price is likely to have affected all groups similarly.

The difficulties of a varying consumption can be largely overcome if a more detailed smoking history is taken than is customary in the course of an ordinary medical examination—for example, one man who was described in the hospital notes as being a non-smoker admitted to the almoner that he had been a very heavy smoker until a few years previously. In this investigation, therefore, the patients were closely questioned and asked (*a*) if they had smoked at any period of their lives; (*b*) the ages at which they had started and stopped; (*c*) the amount they were in the habit of smoking before the onset of the illness which had brought them into hospital; (*d*) the main changes in their smoking history and the maximum they had ever been in the habit of smoking; (*e*) the varying proportions smoked in pipes and cigarettes; and (*f*) whether or not they inhaled.

To record and subsequently to tabulate these details it was necessary to define what was meant by a smoker. Did the term, for example, include the woman who took one cigarette annually after her Christmas dinner, or the man of 50 who as a youth smoked a couple of cigarettes to see whether he liked it and decided he did not? If so, it is doubtful whether anyone at all could be described as a non-smoker. A smoker was therefore defined in this inquiry as a person who had smoked as much as one cigarette a day for as long as one year, and any less consistent amount was ignored. The histories obtained were, of course, a function of the patient's memory and veracity. To assess their reliability 50 unselected control patients with diseases other than cancer were interviewed a second time six months or more after their initial interview. Table **17,** 3 shows the

TABLE **17,** 3

Amount of Tobacco Smoked Daily Before Present Illness as Recorded at Two Interviews with the Same Patients at an Interval of Six Months or More

First Interview No. of Persons Smoking	Second Interview. No. of Persons Smoking						
	0	1 cig.–	5 cigs.–	15 cigs.–	25 cigs.–	50 cigs.+	Total
0	8	1					9
1 cig.–		4	1				5
5 cigs.–		1	13	3			17
15 cigs.–			4	9	1		14
25 cigs.–				1	3	0	4
50 cigs.+					1	0	1
Total	8	6	18	13	5	0	50

comparison between the two answers obtained to the question 'How much did you smoke before the onset of your present illness?'

The answers to the other questions on smoking habits showed a variability comparable to that shown in Table **17,** 3. It may be concluded, therefore, that, while the detailed smoking histories obtained by this investigation are not, as would be expected, strictly accurate, they are reliable enough to indicate general trends and to substantiate material differences between groups.

Smokers and Non-Smokers

The simplest comparison that can be made to show whether there is any association at all between smoking and carcinoma of the lung is that between the proportion of lung-carcinoma patients who have been smokers and the proportion of smokers in the comparable group of subjects without carcinoma of the lung. Such a comparison is shown in Table 17, 4.

TABLE 17, 4

Proportion of Smokers and Non-smokers in Lung-carcinoma Patients and in Control Patients with Diseases Other than Cancer

Disease Group	No. of Non-smokers	No. of Smokers	Probability Test
Males: Lung-carcinoma patients (649)	2 (0·3%)	647	P (exact method) = 0·00000064
Control patients with diseases other than cancer (649)	27 (4·2%)	622	
Females: Lung-carcinoma patients (60)	19 (31·7%)	41	$\chi^2 = 5·76$; n = 1 0·01 < P < 0·02
Control patients with diseases other than cancer (60)	32 (53·3%)	28	

It will be seen that the vast majority of men have been smokers at some period of their lives, but also that the very small proportion of those with carcinoma of the lung who have been non-smokers (0.3 per cent) is most significantly less than the corresponding proportion in the control group of other patients (4.2 per cent). As was to be expected, smoking is shown to be a much less common habit among women; but here again the habit was significantly more frequent among those with carcinoma of the lung. Only 31.7 per cent of the lung-carcinoma group were non-smokers, compared with 53.3 per cent in the control group.

Amount of Smoking

In the simple comparison of Table 17, 4 all smokers have been classified together, irrespective of the amount they smoked. In Table 17, 5 they have been sub-divided according to the amount they smoked immediately before the onset of the illness which brought them into hospital. (If they had given up smoking before then, they have been classified according to the amount smoked immediately prior to giving it up.) This classification is described subsequently as 'the most recent amount smoked'.

TABLE **17,** 5

Most Recent Amount of Tobacco* Consumed Regularly by Smokers Before the Onset of Present Illness; Lung-carcinoma Patients and Control Patients with Diseases Other Than Cancer

Disease Group	No. Smoking Daily					Probability Test
	1 Cig.–*	5 Cigs.–	15 Cigs.–	25 Cigs.–	50 Cigs.+	
Males: Lung-carcinoma patients (647)	33 (5·1%)	250 (38·6%)	196 (30·3%)	136 (21·0%)	32 (5·0%)	$\chi^2 = 36.95$; n = 4; P < 0·001
Control patients with diseases other than cancer (622)	55 (8·8%)	293 (47·1%)	190 (30·5%)	71 (11·4%)	13 (2·1%)	
Females: Lung-carcinoma patients (41)	7 (17·1%)	19 (46·3%)	9 (22·0%)	6 (14·6%)	0 (0·0%)	$\chi^2 = 5.72$; n = 2; 0·05 < P < 0·10 (Women smoking 15 or more cig-arettes a day grouped to-gether)
Control patients with diseases other than cancer (28)	12 (42·9%)	10 (35·7%)	6 (21·4%)	0 (0·0%)	0 (0·0%)	

* Ounces of tobacco have been expressed as being equivalent to so many cigarettes. There is 1 oz. of tobacco in 26·5 normal-size cigarettes, so that the conversion factor has been taken as: 1 oz. of tobacco a week = 4 cigarettes a day.

From Table **17,** 5 it will be seen that, apart from the general excess of smokers found (in Table **17,** 4) in lung-carcinoma patients, there is in this group a significantly higher proportion of heavier smokers and a correspondingly lower proportion of lighter smokers than in the comparative group of other patients. For instance, in the lung-carcinoma group 26.0 per cent of the male patients fall in the two groups of highest consumption (25 cigarettes a day or more), while in the control group of other male patients only 13.5 per cent are found there. The same trend is observable for women, but the numbers involved are small and the difference here between the carcinoma group and their control patients is not quite technically significant. If, however, the female lung-carcinoma patients are compared with the total number of women interviewed—that is, bringing in the other cancer groups interviewed and making appropriate allowance for age differences between them—then the significance of the trend in their case also is established ($\chi^2 = 13.23$; n = 2; P approximately 0.001).

The results given in Tables **17,** 4 and **17,** 5 are shown together graphically in Fig. **17,** 1. (The percentages in the figure are not all

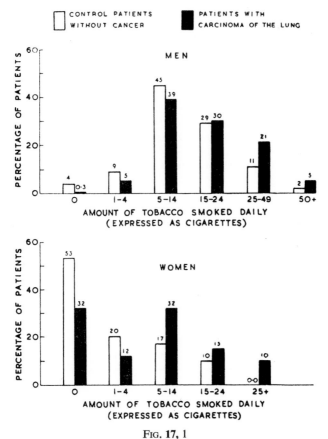

FIG. **17,** 1

Percentage of patients smoking different amounts of tobacco daily

exactly the same as those in the tables. In the figure the percentages are based on the total number of patients in each disease group, smokers and non-smokers alike; in Table **17, 5** they are percentages of smokers alone.)

Smoking History

Going one stage further, it has been noted earlier that the amount smoked daily at any one period does not, of course, necessarily give a fair representation of the individual's smoking history. This has been overcome to some extent in the previous tables by classifying a patient as a non-smoker only if he has never smoked regularly, by classifying him according to the amount he last smoked regularly if he had given up smoking, and by ignoring changes in smoking habits which had taken place subsequent to the illness which brought the patient into hospital. Other methods of analysis have also been adopted. Thus Table **17, 6** shows the results in the two main groups

TABLE **17, 6**

Maximum Amount of Tobacco Ever Consumed Regularly by Smokers; Lung-carcinoma Patients and Control Patients with Diseases Other Than Cancer

Disease Group	No. Smoking as a Daily Maximum					Probability Test
	1 Cig.–	5 Cigs.–	15 Cigs.–	25 Cigs.–	50 Cigs.+	
Males: Lung-carcinoma patients (647)	24 (3·7%)	208 (32·1%)	196 (30·3%)	174 (26·9%)	45 (7·0%)	$\chi^2 = 23\cdot16$; n = 4; P < 0·001
Control patients with diseases other than cancer (622)	38 (6·1%)	242 (38·9%)	201 (32·3%)	118 (19·0%)	23 (3·7%)	
Females: Lung-carcinoma patients (41)	6 (14·6%)	15 (36·6%)	12 (29·3%)	8 (19·5%)	0 (0·0%)	$\chi^2 = 7\cdot58$; n = 2; 0·02 < P < 0·05 (Women smoking 15 or more cigarettes a day grouped together)
Control patients with diseases other then cancer (28)	12 (42·9%)	9 (32·1%)	6 (21·4%)	0 (0·0%)	1 (3·6%)	

when a comparison is made between the maximum amounts ever smoked regularly, and Table **17**, 7 shows a comparison between the estimated total amounts of tobacco smoked throughout the patients' whole lives. The estimates of the total amount smoked (expressed as

TABLE **17**, 7

Estimate of Total Amount of Tobacco Ever Consumed by Smokers; Lung-carcinoma Patients and Control Patients with Diseases Other Than Cancer

Disease Group	No. Who have Smoked Altogether					Probability Test
	365 Cigs.–	50,000 Cigs.–	150,000 Cigs.–	250,000 Cigs.–	500,000 Cigs.+	
Males: Lung-carcinoma patients (647)	19 (2·9%)	145 (22·4%)	183 (28·3%)	225 (34·8%)	75 (11·6%)	$\chi^2 = 30\cdot60$; $n = 4$; $P < 0\cdot001$
Control patients with diseases other than cancer (622)	36 (5·8%)	190 (30·5%)	182 (29·3%)	179 (28·9%)	35 (5·6%)	
Females: Lung-carcinoma patients (41)	10 (24·4%)	19 (46·3%)	5 (12·2%)	7 (17·1%)	0 (0·0%)	$\chi^2 = 12\cdot97$; $n = 2$; $0\cdot001 < P < 0\cdot01$ (Women smoking 15 or more cig-
Control patients with diseases other than cancer (28)	19 (67·9%)	5 (17·9%)	3 (10·7%)	1 (3·6%)	0 (0·0%)	arettes a day grouped to- gether)

cigarettes) have been made by multiplying the daily amount of tobacco smoked by the number of days that the patient has been in the habit of smoking and making allowance for the major recorded changes in the smoking history. Such estimates may, needless to say, be only very rough approximations to the truth, but they are, it is thought, accurate enough to reveal broad differences between the groups.

The results in Tables **17**, 5, **17**, 6, and **17**, 7, are, it will be seen, closely similar. Whichever measure of smoking is taken, the same result is obtained—namely, a significant and clear relationship between smoking and carcinoma of the lung. It might perhaps have been expected that the more refined concepts—the maximum amount ever smoked and the total amount ever smoked—would have shown a closer relationship than the most recent amount smoked before the onset of the present illness. It must be supposed, however, that any greater efficiency that might be introduced by the use of these measures is counterbalanced by the inaccuracy which results from requiring the patient to remember habits of many years past. It seems, therefore, that we may reasonably adopt 'the most recent amount smoked' in subsequent tables as the simplest characteristic to describe a patient's smoking experience.

Comparisons of the age at which patients began to smoke, the number of years they have smoked, and the number of years they have given up smoking are shown in Table **17**, 8.

It will be seen that the lung-carcinoma patients showed a slight tendency to start smoking earlier in life, to continue longer, and to be less inclined to stop, but the differentiation is certainly not sharp and the difference is technically significant only with respect to length of time stopped.

Cigarettes and Pipes

So far no distinction has been made between cigarette and pipe smokers, and it is natural to ask whether both methods of smoking tobacco are equally related to a carcinoma of the lung. Again the difficulty arises that a man who describes himself as a pipe smoker may have smoked cigarettes until shortly before interrogation, or, alternatively, he may have had his teeth extracted and substituted cigarettes for his pipe. To overcome this, we have excluded all the men who gave a history of having ever consistently smoked both pipes and cigarettes and have compared the proportions of 'pure pipe' and 'pure cigarette' smokers among the lung-carcinoma and non-cancer control patients. The results are as follows: of the 525 lung-carcinoma patients who had smoked either pipes or cigarettes but not both 5.7 per cent were pipe smokers and 94.3 per cent were cigarette smokers; of 507 control patients with other diseases 9.7 per cent were pipe smokers and 90.3 per cent were cigarette smokers. The lower proportion of pipe smokers, and the corresponding excess of cigarette smokers, in the lung-carcinoma group is unlikely to be due to chance ($\chi^2 = 5.70$; n = 1; $0.01 < P < 0.02$).

It therefore seems that pipe smoking is less closely related to

TABLE 17, 8

Age of Starting to Smoke, Number of Years Smoked, and Number of Years Stopped Smoking in Lung-carcinoma Patients and Control Patients with Diseases Other Than Cancer (Male and Female)

Age at Starting	Lung-carcinoma Patients		Control Patients	
	No.	%	No.	%
Under 20	541	78·6	488	75·1
20–	118	17·2	129	19·8
30–	17 }	4·2	22 }	5·1
40+	12 }		11 }	
All ages	688		650	

$\chi^2 = 2\cdot40$; n = 2; $0\cdot30 < P < 0\cdot50$

No. of Years Smoking	Lung-carcinoma Patients		Control Patients	
	No.	%	No.	%
1–	14 }	5·1	18 }	7·7
10–	21 }		32 }	
20–	351	51·0	338	52·0
40+	302	43·9	262	40·3
Total	688		650	

$\chi^2 = 4\cdot65$; n = 2; $0\cdot05 < P < 0\cdot10$

No. of Years Stopped	Lung-carcinoma Patients		Control Patients	
	No.	%	No.	%
0	649	94·3	590	90·8
1–	30	4·4	37	5·7
10–	4 }	1·3	14 }	3·5
20+	5 }		9 }	
Total	688		650	

$\chi^2 = 8\cdot59$; n = 2; $0\cdot01 < P < 0\cdot02$

carcinoma of the lung than cigarette smoking. On the other hand, it has been shown in Table **17,** 5 that light smoking is less closely related to carcinoma of the lung than heavy smoking, so that the result might be explained merely on the grounds that pipe smokers tend to smoke less tobacco.

In fact, pipe smokers do consume, on the average, less tobacco than cigarette smokers, but this is unlikely to be the whole explanation of the relative deficiency of pipe smokers observed in the carcinoma group. We find a higher proportion of cigarette smokers and a lower proportion of pipe smokers among the lung-carcinoma patients than among the control group of non-cancer patients at each level of consumption of tobacco—that is, at 1–4, 5–14, 15–24, and 25+ cigarettes or their equivalent a day. On the other hand, if we consider the 'pure pipe' smokers by themselves and sub-divide them according to the amount smoked, then we find a higher proportion of the carcinoma patients than of the control group in the higher smoking categories—that is, smoking more than 6 oz. of tobacco a week. In short, the results of this sub-division are similar to those shown in Table **17,** 5 for all smokers. It seems that the method by which the tobacco is smoked is of importance and that smoking a pipe, though also related to carcinoma of the lung, carries a smaller risk than smoking cigarettes. With the data at our disposal we are unable to determine how great the difference in risk may be.

Inhaling

Another difference between smokers is that some inhale and others do not. All patients who smoked were asked whether or not they inhaled, and the answers given by the lung-carcinoma and non-cancer control patients were as follows: of the 688 lung-carcinoma patients who smoked (men and women) 61.6 per cent said they inhaled and 38.4 per cent said they did not; the corresponding figures for the 650 patients with other diseases were 67.2 per cent inhalers and 32.8 per cent non-inhalers. It would appear that lung-carcinoma patients inhale slightly less often than other patients ($\chi^2 = 4.58$; n = 1; $0.02 < P < 0.05$). However, the difference is not large, and if the lung-carcinoma patients are compared with all the other patients interviewed, and the necessary allowance is made for sex and age, the difference becomes insignificant ($\chi^2 = 0.19$; n = 1; $0.50 < P < 0.70$).

Interpretation of Results

Though from the previous tables there seems to be no doubt that there is a direct association between smoking and carcinoma of the lung it is necessary to consider alternative explanations of the results. Could they be due to an unrepresentative sample of patients with carcinoma of the lung or to a choice of a control series which was not truly comparable? Could they have been produced by an exaggeration of their smoking habits by patients who thought they had an illness which could be attributed to smoking? Could they be produced by bias on the part of the interviewers in taking and interpreting the histories?

Selection of Patients for Interview

The method by which the patients with carcinoma of the lung were obtained has been discussed earlier; there is no reason to suppose that they were anything other than a representative sample of the lung-carcinoma patients attending the selected London hospitals. The control patients, as was shown in Table **17,** 2, were exactly comparable so far as sex and age were concerned and they were sufficiently comparable with regard to social class for the difference between the two series to be ignored. They were not wholly comparable from the point of view of place of residence. The difference in this respect, however, was that more of the lung-carcinoma patients came from small towns and rural districts, and the figures in this inquiry show that consumption of tobacco per head in these areas is less than in London. Clearly this feature cannot have accounted for the observation that the lung-carcinoma patients smoked more: Further, if the comparison is confined to patients seen in district hospitals—and all of these resided in Greater London —the results are the same (Table **17,** 9).

It might possibly be argued that the choice of a control group of patients with various medical and surgical conditions has, of itself, resulted in the selection of subjects with a smoking history less than the average. This would seem very unlikely, as we know of no evidence to suggest that less than average smoking is a characteristic of persons with any one group of diseases, and it certainly could not be held that it is equally a characteristic of persons suffering from all diseases other than carcinoma of the lung. Yet in Table **17,** 10 the smoking habits of the patients in five main groups of diseases are

TABLE **17**, 9

Most Recent Amount Smoked by Lung-carcinoma and Control Patients Seen in District Hospitals (Male and Female)

Disease Group	No. Smoking Daily				
	0	1 Cig.–	5 Cigs.–	15 Cigs.–	25 Cigs.+
Lung-carcinoma patients (98)	2	12	36	27	21
Control patients with diseases other than cancer (98)	9	9	50	19	11

$\chi^2 = 11\cdot68$; n = 4; $0\cdot01 < P < 0\cdot02$

TABLE **17**, 10

Most Recent Amount Smoked by all Patients Other Than Those with Carcinoma of Lung, Divided According to Type of Disease (Male and Female)

Disease Group	No. Smoking Daily				
	0	1 Cig.–	5 Cigs.–	15 Cigs.–	25 Cigs.+
Cancer, other than carcinoma of lung (718)	236*	78	237	110	57
	220·0	*85·3*	*236·9*	*122·8*	*53·0*
Respiratory disease, other than cancer (335)	42	33	128	98	34
	47·0	*29·7*	*136·1*	*84·1*	*38·1*
Cardiovascular disease (166)	22	19	64	38	23
	17·7	*16·7*	*73·8*	*39·5*	*18·3*
Gastro-intestinal disease (328)	39	31	143	81	34
	55·7	*32·3*	*130·2*	*75·8*	*34·5*
Other diseases (215)	38	24	91	44	18
	36·6	*21·1*	*86·0*	*48·9*	*22·1*
	$\chi^2 = 20\cdot14$; n = 16; $0\cdot20 < P < 0\cdot30$				

* The roman figures show the actual numbers observed, those in italics are the numbers that would have occurred if the disease group in question had had in each sex and at each age exactly the same smoking habits as all the patients included in the table.

compared, allowing for their sex and age composition, and no significant difference can be demonstrated between them. (We have brought into this table all the patients with diseases other than carcinoma of the lung.)

As in other tables where sex and age differences between groups have had to be taken into account, the 'expected' numbers have been obtained by taking the actual numbers of patients with each type of disease in each age and sex sub-group, and calculating what proportion of them would fall in each smoking category if they had had exactly the same habits as all the patients included in the table. In other words, we have computed what ought to be the smoking habits of each disease group if it behaved in each sex and at each age like the total population of patients, and compared them with what, in fact, they were. The relatively large numbers of non-smokers in some of the groups are due to the fact that these disease groups included many old women.

There remains the possibility that the interviewers, in selecting the control patients, took for interview from among the patients available for selection a disproportionate number of light smokers. It is difficult to see how they could have done so, but the point can be tested indirectly by comparing the smoking habits of the patients whom they did select for interview with the habits of the other patients, other than those with carcinoma of the lung, whose names were notified by the hospitals. The comparison is made in Table 17, 11 and reveals no appreciable difference between the two groups.

It can therefore be concluded that there is no evidence of any special bias in favour of light smokers in the selection of the control series of patients. In other words, the group of patients interviewed forms, we believe, a satisfactory control series for the lung-carcinoma patients from the point of view of comparison of smoking habits.

Patient's Smoking History

Another possibility to consider is that the lung-carcinoma patients tended to exaggerate their smoking habits. Most of these patients cannot have known that they were suffering from cancer, but they would have known that they had respiratory symptoms, and such knowledge might have influenced their replies to questions about the amount they smoked. However, Table 17, 10 has already shown that patients with the other respiratory diseases did not give smoking histories appreciably different from those given by the patients with

TABLE **17,** 11

Most Recent Amount Smoked by All Patients Other Than Those with Carcinoma of Lung, Divided According to Whether They Were Notified or Selected for Interview (*Male and Female*)

Method of Selection of Patient	No. Smoking Daily				
	0	1 Cig.–	5 Cigs.–	15 Cigs.–	25 Cigs.+
Notified by hospital (1,032)	307*	114	354	179	78
	301·8	*119·0*	*345·2*	*186·1*	*80·0*
Selected by interviewer (730)	70	71	309	192	88
	75·2	*66·0*	*317·8*	*184·9*	*86·0*
$\chi^2 = 2\cdot14$; n = 4; $0\cdot70 < P < 0\cdot80$.					

* See footnote to Table **17,** 10

non-respiratory illnesses. There is no reason, therefore, to suppose that exaggeration on the part of the lung-carcinoma patients has been responsible for the results.

The Interviewers

When the investigation was planned it was hoped that the interviewers would know only that they were interviewing patients with cancer of one of several sites (lung, stomach, or large bowel) but not, at the time, the actual site. This, unfortunately, was impracticable; the site would be written on the notification form, or the nurse would refer to the diagnosis in pointing out the patient, or it would become known that only patients with cancer of one of the sites under investigation would be found in one particular ward. Out of 1,732 patients notified and interviewed as cases of cancer, the site of the growth was known to the interviewer at the time of interview in all but 61. Serious consideration must therefore be given to the possibility of interviewers' bias affecting the results (by the interviewers tending to scale up the smoking habits of the lung-carcinoma cases).

Fortunately the material provides a simple method of testing this point. A number of patients were interviewed who, at that time, were thought to have carcinoma of the lung but in whom the diagnosis was subsequently disproved. The smoking habits of these patients, believed by the interviewers to have carcinoma of the lung, can be compared with the habits of the patients who in fact had carcinoma of the lung and also with the habits of all the other patients. The result of making these comparisons is shown in Tables **17,** 12 and

TABLE **17,** 12

Most Recent Amount Smoked by Patients with Carcinoma of Lung and by Patients Thought Incorrectly by the Interviewer to be Suffering from Carcinoma of Lung (Male and Female)

Disease Group	No. Smoking Daily				
	0	1 Cig.–	5 Cigs.–	15 Cigs.–	25 Cigs.+
Patients with carcinoma of lung (709)	21* *31·7*	40 *48·0*	269 *276·0*	205 *201·0*	174 *152·7*
Patients incorrectly thought to have carcinoma of lung (209)†	35 *24·3*	25 *17·0*	83 *76·0*	50 *54·0*	16 *37·3*
	$\chi^2 = 29\cdot76$; n = 4; P < 0·001.				

* See footnote to Table **17,** 10.

† There is a large number of cases in this group because one hospital notified all cases admitted for bronchoscopy; 147 out of the 209 incorrectly thought to have carcinoma of the lung were interviewed at this hospital.

17, 13, and it will be seen that the smoking habits of the patients who were incorrectly thought to have carcinoma of the lung at the time of interview are sharply distinguished from the habits of those patients who did in fact have carcinoma of the lung (Table **17,** 12), but they do not differ significantly from the habits of the other patients interviewed (Table **17,** 13).

It is therefore clearly not possible to attribute the results of this inquiry to bias on the part of the interviewers, as, had there been any appreciable bias, the smoking habits of the patients thought incorrectly to have carcinoma of the lung would have been recorded as being like those of the true lung-carcinoma subjects and not the same as those without carcinoma of the lung.

We may add that the results cannot be due to different workers

TABLE **17**, 13

*Most Recent Amount Smoked by Patients Incorrectly Thought by
the Interviewers to be Suffering from Carcinoma of Lung and All
Other Patients Not Suffering from Carcinoma of Lung (Male and
Female)*

Disease Group	No. Smoking Daily				
	0	1 Cig.–	5 Cigs.–	15 Cigs.–	25 Cigs.+
Patients incorrectly thought to have carcinoma of lung (209)†	35*	25	83	50	16
	36·8	*20·4*	*82·0*	*48·8*	*20·8*
All other patients not suffering from carcinoma of lung (1,553)	342	160	580	321	150
	340·2	*164·6*	*581·0*	*322·2*	*145·2*
	$\chi^2 = 2{\cdot}58$; n = 4; $0{\cdot}50 < P < 0{\cdot}70$.				

* See footnote to Table **17**, 10.   † See footnote to Table **17**, 12.

interviewing different numbers of patients in the cancer and control
groups, for, while the four interviewers did not see exactly the same
proportions of patients in all the groups, the proportions were very
close. Moreover, if the patients seen by each of the interviewers are
treated as four separate investigations, highly significant differences
are found between the lung-carcinoma patients and the other
patients interviewed in three instances. In the fourth the difference
is in the same direction, but, owing to the small number of patients
seen, the results are not technically significant (P lies between 0.10
and 0.05; in this instance the almoner had to stop work because of
illness, having seen only 46 patients with carcinoma of the lung).

DISCUSSION

To summarize, it is not reasonable, in our view, to attribute the
results to any special selection of cases or to bias in recording. In
other words, it must be concluded that there is a real association
between carcinoma of the lung and smoking. Further, the comparison of the smoking habits of patients in different disease groups,
shown in Table **17**, 10, revealed no association between smoking and
other respiratory diseases or between smoking and cancer of the

other sites (mainly stomach and large bowel). The association therefore seems to be specific to carcinoma of the lung. This is not necessarily to say that smoking causes carcinoma of the lung. The association would occur if carcinoma of the lung caused people to smoke or if both attributes were end-effects of a common cause. The habit of smoking was, however, invariably formed before the onset of the disease (as revealed by the production of symptoms), so that the disease cannot be held to have caused the habit; nor can we ourselves envisage any common cause likely to lead both to the development of the habit and to the development of the disease 20 to 50 years later. We therefore conclude that smoking is a factor, and an important factor, in the production of carcinoma of the lung.

The effect of smoking varies, as would be expected, with the amount smoked. The extent of the variation could be estimated by comparing the numbers of patients interviewed who had carcinoma of the lung with the corresponding numbers of people in the population, in the same age groups, who smoke the same amounts of tobacco. Our figures, however, are not representative of the whole country, and this may be of some importance, as countrymen smoke, on the average, less than city dwellers. Moreover, as was shown earlier, the carcinoma and the control patients were not comparable with regard to their places of residence. The difficulty can be overcome by confining the comparison to the inhabitants of Greater London.

If it be assumed that the patients without carcinoma of the lung who lived in Greater London at the time of their interview are typical of the inhabitants of Greater London with regard to their smoking habits, then the number of people in London smoking different amounts of tobacco can be estimated. Ratios can then be obtained between the numbers of patients seen with carcinoma of the lung and the estimated populations at risk who have smoked comparable amounts of tobacco. This has been done for each age group, and the results are shown in Table 17, 14. It must be stressed that the ratios shown in this table are not measures of the actual risks of developing carcinoma of the lung, but are put forward very tentatively as proportional to these risks.

Thus Table 17, 14 shows clearly, and for each age-group, the conclusion previously reached—that the risk of developing carcinoma of the lung increases steadily as the amount smoked increases.

If the risk among non-smokers is taken as unity and the resulting ratios in the three age groups in which a large number of patients were interviewed (ages 45 to 74) are averaged, the relative risks become 6, 19, 26, 49, and 65 when the number of cigarettes smoked a day are 3, 10, 20, 35, and, say, 60—that is, the mid-points of each smoking group. In other words, on the admittedly speculative assumptions we have made, the risk seems to vary in approximately simple proportion with the amount smoked.

TABLE 17, 14

Ratios of Patients Interviewed with Carcinoma of Lung and with a Given Daily Consumption of Tobacco to the Estimated Populations in Greater London Smoking the Same Amounts (Male and Female Combined; Ratios per Million)

Age	Daily Consumption of Tobacco						Total
	0	1–4 Cigs.	5–14 Cigs.	15–24 Cigs.	25–49 Cigs.	50 Cigs.+	
25–	0*	11	2	6	· 28	—	4
35–	2	9	43	41	67	77	29
45–	12	34	178	241	429	667	147
55–	14	133	380	463	844	600	244
65–74	21	110	300	510	1,063	2,000	186

* Ratios based on less than 5 cases of carcinoma of the lung are given in italics.

One anomalous result of our inquiry appears to relate to inhaling. It would be natural to suppose that if smoking were harmful it would be more harmful if the smoke were inhaled. In fact, whether the patient inhaled or not did not seem to make any difference. It is possible that the patients were not fully aware of the meaning of the term and answered incorrectly, but the interviewers were not of that opinion. In the present state of knowledge it is more reasonable to accept the finding and wait until the size of the smoke particle which carries the carcinogen is determined. Until this is known nothing can be stated about the effect which any alteration in the rate and depth of respiration may have on the extent and site of deposition of the carcinogen (Davies, 1949).

How, in conclusion, do these results fit in with other known facts about smoking and carcinoma of the lung? Both the consumption of tobacco and the number of deaths attributed to cancer of the lung are known to have increased, and to have increased largely, in many countries this century. The trends in this country are given in Fig. **17, 2**, and show that over the last 25 years the increase in deaths attributed to cancer of the lung has been much greater than the increase in tobacco consumption. This might well be because the

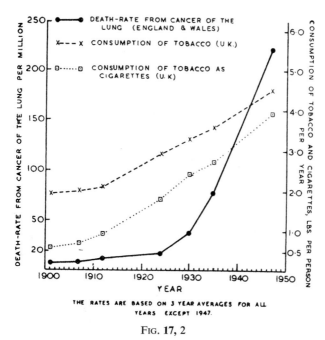

THE RATES ARE BASED ON 3 YEAR AVERAGES FOR ALL YEARS EXCEPT 1947.

FIG. 17, 2

Death rate from cancer of the lung and rate of consumption of tobacco and cigarettes

increased number of deaths in the latter years is partly an apparent increase, due to improved diagnosis; in other words, it is not wholly a reflection of increased prevalence of cancer of the lung. On the other hand, it is possible that the carcinogenic agent is introduced during the cultivation or preparation of tobacco for consumption and that changes in the methods of cultivation and preparation have occurred as well as changes in consumption. However that may be, it is clearly not possible to deduce a simple time relationship in this country between the consumption of tobacco and the number of deaths attributed to cancer of the lung.

The greater prevalence of carcinoma of the lung in men compared with women leads naturally to the suggestion that smoking may be a cause, since smoking is predominantly a male habit. Although increasing numbers of women are beginning to smoke, the great majority of women now of the cancer age have either never smoked or have only recently started to do so. It is therefore tempting to ascribe the high sex ratio to the greater consumption of tobacco by men. If this were true it would be expected that the incidence of carcinoma of the lung would be the same among non-smokers in both sexes. In this series, two out of 649 men and 19 out of 60 women with carcinoma of the lung were non-smokers.

To calculate the incidence rates among non-smokers of either sex it is necessary to estimate the number of non-smokers in the population from which the patients were drawn. For reasons given earlier this cannot be done, but an estimate can be obtained of the expected sex ratio of cases occurring among non-smokers in the Greater London area. From the experience of the patients without carcinoma of the lung who lived in Greater London at the time of their interview it can be calculated that there were, in 1948, 175,000 men and 1,582,000 women in London between the ages of 25 and 75 who had never been smokers according to our definition of the term. Taking these figures, sub-divided by age, in association with the age distribution of the 16 cases of carcinoma of the lung observed among non-smokers living in Greater London, it can be calculated that, if the incidence of the disease were equal among non-smokers of both sexes, one case should have occurred in a man and 15 in women. In fact, the observed ratio was 0 to 16.

This finding is consistent with the theory that the risk of developing carcinoma of the lung is the same in both men and women, apart from the influence of smoking. It is not, however, possible to demonstrate with the data at our disposal that different amounts of smoking are sufficient to account for the overall sex ratio.

As to the nature of the carcinogen we have no evidence. The only carcinogenic substance which has been found in tobacco smoke is arsenic (Daff and Kennaway, 1950), but the evidence that arsenic can produce carcinoma of the lung is suggestive rather than conclusive (Hill and Faning, 1948). Should arsenic prove to be the carcinogen, the possibility arises that it is not the tobacco itself which is dangerous. Insecticides containing arsenic have been used for the protection of the growing crop since the end of the last century and might conceivably be the source of the responsible factor. This, too, might account for the observation that deaths from cancer of the lung have increased more rapidly than the consumption of tobacco.

SUMMARY

The great increase in the number of deaths attributed to cancer of the lung in the last 25 years justifies the search for a cause in the environment. An investigation was therefore carried out into the possible association of carcinoma of the lung with smoking, exposure to car and fuel fumes, occupation, etc. The preliminary findings with regard to smoking are reported.

The material for the investigation was obtained from 20 hospitals in the London region which notified patients with cancer of the lung, stomach, and large bowel. Almoners then visited and interviewed each patient. The patients with carcinoma of the stomach and large bowel served for comparison and, in addition, the almoners interviewed a non-cancer control group of general hospital patients, chosen so as to be of the same sex and age as the lung-carcinoma patients.

Altogether 649 men and 60 women with carcinoma of the lung were interviewed. Of the men 0.3 per cent and of the women 31.7 per cent were non-smokers (as defined in the text). The corresponding figures for the non-cancer control groups were: men 4.2 per cent, women 53.3 per cent.

Among the smokers a relatively high proportion of the patients with carcinoma of the lung fell in the heavier smoking categories. For example, 26.0 per cent of the male and 14.6 per cent of the female lung-carcinoma patients who smoked gave as their most recent smoking habits prior to their illness the equivalent of 25 or more cigarettes a day, while only 13.5 per cent of the male and none of the female non-cancer control patients smoked as much. Similar differences were found when comparisons were made between the maximum amounts ever smoked and the estimated total amounts ever smoked.

Cigarette smoking was more closely related to carcinoma of the lung than pipe smoking. No distinct association was found with inhaling.

Taken as a whole, the lung-carcinoma patients had begun to smoke earlier and had continued for longer than the controls, but the differences were very small and not statistically significant. Rather fewer lung-carcinoma patients had given up smoking.

Consideration has been given to the possibility that the results could have been produced by the selection of an unsuitable group of control patients, by patients with respiratory disease exaggerating their smoking habits, or by bias on the part of the interviewers. Reasons are given for excluding all these possibilities, and it is concluded that smoking is an important factor in the cause of carcinoma of the lung.

From consideration of the smoking histories given by the patients without cancer of the lung a tentative estimate was made of the number of people who smoked different amounts of tobacco in Greater London, and hence the relative risks of developing the disease among different grades of smokers were calculated. The figures obtained are admittedly speculative, but suggest that, above the age of 45, the risk of developing the disease increases in simple proportion with the amount smoked, and that it may be approximately 50 times as great among those who smoke 25 or more cigarettes a day as among non-smokers.

The observed sex ratio among non-smokers (based, it must be stressed, on very few cases) can be readily accounted for if the true incidence among non-smokers is equal in both sexes.

It is not possible to deduce a simple time relationship between the increased consumption of tobacco and the increased number of deaths attributed to cancer of the lung. This may be because part of the increase is apparent—that is, due to improved diagnosis—but it may also be because the carcinogen in tobacco smoke is introduced into the tobacco during its cultivation or preparation. Greater changes may have taken place in the methods involved in these processes than in the actual amount of tobacco consumed.

REFERENCES

Clemmesen, J., and Busk, T. (1947). *Brit. J. Cancer*, **1**, 253.
Daff, M., and Kennaway, E. L. (1950). *Brit. J. Cancer*, **4**, 173.
Davies, C. N. (1949). *Brit. J. industr. Med.* **6**, 245.
Hill, A. Bradford, and Faning, E. L. (1948). *Brit. J. industr. Med.* **5**, 1.
Kennaway, E. L., and Kennaway, N. M. (1947). *Brit. J. Cancer*, **1**, 260.
Müller, F. H. (1939). *Z. Krebsforsch.* **49**, 57.
Schrek, R., Baker, L. A., Ballard, G. P., and Dolgoff, S. (1950). *Cancer Res.* **10**, 49.
Steiner, P. E. (1944). *Arch. Path.* **37**, 185.
Stocks, P. (1947). *Studies on Medical and Population Subjects*, No. 1. London: H.M.S.O.
Willis, R. A. (1948). *Pathology of Tumours*. London: Butterworth.
Wynder, E. L., and Graham, E. A. (1950). *J. Amer. med. Ass.* **143**, 329.

CHAPTER 18

A STUDY OF THE AETIOLOGY OF CARCINOMA OF THE LUNG

IN a previous paper (Doll and Hill, 1950) we reported the first results of a large-scale investigation undertaken to determine whether patients with carcinoma of the lung differed materially from other persons, either in their smoking habits or in some way which might be related to the theory that atmospheric pollution is responsible for the development of the disease. We concluded that smoking is a factor in the production of carcinoma of the lung, and this conclusion was in conformity with the results of some other investigations. Our first observations were, however, limited to patients drawn mainly from London and the adjacent counties. We have now extended the investigation to other parts of the country and have made more detailed inquiries into smoking habits. Many further patients have been interviewed (during January, 1950, to February, 1952) in hospitals in Bristol, Cambridge, Leeds, and Newcastle-upon-Tyne, and also in eight of the 20 London hospitals which co-operated in the first part of the inquiry.

METHOD OF THE INVESTIGATION

The method of inquiry was described in detail in the previous paper. In brief, we obtained notifications of patients admitted with cancer of the lung, stomach, or large bowel to each co-operating hospital, and these patients were interviewed by almoners, engaged wholly on our research, who recorded the answers to a prearranged questionary. The patients with carcinoma of the stomach or large bowel provided one 'control' group, but another, and more important, 'control' was obtained by interviewing patients with diseases other than cancer. Each of these latter patients was chosen so as to match a lung-carcinoma patient—namely, of the same sex, within the same five-year age group, and in the same hospital as nearly as possible at the same time.

(With Richard Doll.) Reprinted from the *British Medical Journal*, 1952, **ii,** 1271.

In the extension of the inquiry this same method has been used, but with modifications. First, notifications were made of patients with lung cancer but no longer of those with cancer of the stomach or large bowel. Secondly, the interviewers could not visit hospitals outside London whenever a suitable patient was admitted; they therefore visited the provincial centres at intervals and interviewed those patients suspected of having lung cancer who were then in the hospitals. At Bristol, Cambridge, and Leeds they also interviewed a few who were attending the out-patient departments.

An important modification was in the choice of the matched control patients. It was impossible to obtain at the provincial centres a group confined, as before, to patients with diseases other than cancer. Our previous analysis, however, had shown that patients with cancer other than lung carcinoma (mainly patients with carcinoma of the stomach or large bowel) gave smoking histories indistinguishable from those given by non-cancer patients; we therefore widened the matched control group to include, with certain exceptions, other forms of cancer. The exceptions which we continued to exclude were cancer of the lip, tongue, mouth, pharynx, nose, larynx, and oesophagus, since it has at times been suggested that cancer of these sites may also bear some relationship to tobacco consumption. We also excluded all other cancers arising inside the chest.

Even then it was still difficult in the provincial centres to find an adequately 'matched' control for each lung-carcinoma patient. The provincial hospitals had been chosen so that a large number of lung-cancer patients could be interviewed at each visit. They were therefore thoracic or radiotherapeutic centres serving regions—that is, town and country. We could not seek control patients in the adjacent general hospitals, since these mainly serve the towns they are situated in, and smoking habits vary between town and country-side. On consideration the field of choice was finally extended to other hospitals or units in the same area, but *only* to those serving as regional centres—that is, like the thoracic or radiotherapeutic centres. Thus the cases and their controls should be drawn from equally wide areas of town and country. We have also included in the control series some patients interviewed as having lung cancer but in whom the condition was finally excluded (as at the Brompton and Harefield hospitals in the first part of the investigation). It will be shown that this procedure does not influence the results.

The classification of each patient was, as a general rule, based upon the hospital discharge diagnosis, obtained from a study of the hospital records after the patient's discharge or death. Where that record was indefinite information was obtained from the practitioner or hospital to whose care the patient had been transferred. Occasionally evidence contradicting the hospital discharge diagnosis became available—for example, by histological examination at necropsy—and in these cases the diagnosis was based upon the best evidence. Five cases with no record of any final diagnosis have been excluded.

THE DATA

Between April, 1948, and February, 1952 (the whole period of this investigation), 3,446 cancer patients were notified (lung, stomach, and large bowel). Of these, 156 were aged 75 years or more and were not interviewed, since we limited the inquiry to young patients who could give more reliable histories of smoking and other personal characteristics. In 82 cases the diagnosis was changed before the almoner paid her visit. Of the remaining 3,208 patients, 85 per cent were interviewed and 498 (15 per cent) were not. The reasons why patients were not interviewed were: already discharged from hospital, 213; too ill, 165; dead, 72; too deaf, 33; unable to speak English clearly, 14; while in one case the interview was abandoned because the patient's replies appeared wholly unreliable. No patient refused to be interviewed. With the lung-cancer group alone the proportion not interviewed was also 15 per cent. We can see no reason why failure to interview all the patients should have biased the results, since it was mainly due to the time that had to elapse between the date of notification and the date of the almoner's visit. Such losses were, of course, few in the provincial centres, since here the almoner was required to interview only those in the hospital at the time of her visit.

The remaining 2,710 patients initially presumed to be suffering from cancer of the lung, stomach, or large bowel and the 1,632 general medical and surgical patients interviewed as matched controls to the lung-carcinoma patients form the subjects of this analysis. Table **18,** 1 gives the numbers in each disease group (final classifications based on the hospital discharge diagnosis, etc., as described above). The 1,488 cases of carcinoma of the lung include

23 for which matched controls had not been interviewed when the investigation ended. Most of our results therefore relate to the 1,465 cases paired with the 1,465 matched controls ('other diseases, A').

Cases diagnosed as carcinoma, or cancer, of the lung or bronchus, pleural endothelioma, and alveolar-cell carcinoma of the lung have been included in the 'carcinoma of the lung' group. Classification of the diagnoses according to the recommendation of the International Symposium on the Endemiology of Cancer of the Lung (Council for the International Organization of Medical Sciences, 1952) gave 70 per cent of the first order of reliability (evidence from biopsy of the primary tumour, from operative, bronchoscopic, or radiographic examination of the primary tumour together with cytological examination of the sputum or biopsy of a secondary tumour, or from necropsy), 29 per cent of the second order of reliability (cytological examination of the sputum alone or operative, bronchoscopic, or radiographic examination without biopsy), and only 1 per cent of the third order of reliability (case history and physical examination alone or death certificate).

The 70 cases classified in Table **18,** 1 as 'carcinoma of other special sites' are all other cancers arising inside the chest (for example,

TABLE **18,** 1

Numbers of Patients Interviewed in Each Disease Group

Disease Group	No. of Patients Interviewed
Carcinoma of lung	1,488
Carcinoma of other special sites	70
Carcinoma of uncertain primary site	36
Other diseases, A (matched controls)	1,465
Other diseases, B (other controls)	1,278
Uncertain diagnosis (records untraced)	5
All groups*	4,342

* A further 531 patients were interviewed in rural hospitals, with regard to smoking habits in country areas—see section on estimated risks in town and country.

sarcoma of lung and cancer of the mediastinum and of the trachea) and those other cancers of the respiratory passages, buccal cavity, and oesophagus for which a possible relationship with smoking has at times been postulated. The 36 cases of 'carcinoma of uncertain primary site' include patients with carcinomatosis and some in whom there was doubt whether the lung growth was primary or secondary.

The 1,278 'other diseases, B' include: (1) patients with carcinoma of the stomach or large bowel interviewed in the earlier part of the investigation as a second control group; (2) patients initially interviewed as having carcinoma of the lung, stomach, or large bowel, but later found to have other diseases; and (3) others interviewed as matched controls and not required when the patients with whom they were paired were found not to have carcinoma of the lung.

In Table **18,** 2 the matched patients in the lung-carcinoma and

TABLE **18,** 2

Comparison Between Lung-carcinoma Patients and Matched Control Patients with Other Diseases

Attribute for Com- parison	No. of Lung- carcinoma Patients		No. of Control Patients		Attribute for Com- parison	No. of Lung- carcinoma Patients, M and F	No. of Control Patients, M and F
	M	F	M	F			
Age:					Place of inter- view:		
25–	17	3	17	3	Greater London	1,035	1,035
35–	116	15	116	15	Bristol	73	73
45–	493	38	493	38	Cambridge	36	36
55–	545	34	545	34	Leeds	58	58
65–74	186	18	186	18	Newcastle	263	263
All ages	1,357	108	1,357	108	All places	1,465	1,465
Social class (Registrar- General's categories):					Place of resi- dence:		
I	39	—	53	—	Greater London	791	900
II	165	—	172	—	Other county boroughs	225	181
III	750	—	720	—	Other urban districts	275	213
IV	172	—	198	—	Rural districts	155	164
V	231	—	214	—	Abroad	19	7
All social classes	1,357	—	1,357	—	All places	1,465	1,465

control groups are compared for sex and age distribution, places of interview, places of residence, and, for males, social status. The method of selecting control patients leads automatically to an exact correspondence in sex, age, and places of interview. Differences in social status show no regular trend and are no greater than might be due to chance ($\chi^2 = 5.28$, n = 4, $0.20 < P < 0.30$). On the other hand, the places of residence reveal considerable differences: fewer of the lung-carcinoma group were residents of Greater London ($\chi^2 = 17.22$, n = 4, P < 0.01). The meaning of this inequality is considered later (section on Place of Residence). Since our observations show that the consumption of tobacco tends to be greatest in London the inequality will, if anything, have somewhat reduced the contrasts we find between the groups in their smoking habits. In our previous report, however, we showed that the inequality was unlikely to be of importance.

ASSESSMENT OF SMOKING HABITS

The difficulties of acquiring and assessing accurately a smoking history and the measures taken to overcome them were discussed by Doll and Hill (1950). It will be sufficient to repeat here that the patients were asked (a) if they had smoked at any period of their lives; (b) the ages at which they had started and stopped; (c) the amount they were in the habit of smoking before the onset of the illness which had brought them into hospital; (d) the main changes in their smoking history and the maximum they had ever been in the habit of smoking; (e) the proportions smoked in pipes and cigarettes; and (f) whether they inhaled. A test was made of the accuracy of the answers by cross-examining 50 patients again, six months or more after their first interview. While there was, as expected, some variability of reply, we concluded that the data were reliable enough *to indicate general trends and to substantiate material differences between groups.*

Fortunately the difficulties of inquiry have been reduced through the level of taxation remaining almost constant throughout the investigation. National figures show that the total home consumption remained fairly steady—namely, 213.7, 211.5, 213.8, 221.2 million lb. in the four years ending 31 March, 1951 (Board of Trade, 1952). (The last major change in the standard rate of duty payable on tobacco was on 16 April, 1947, when it rose from 35s. 6d. to 54s. 10d. a lb.; on 7 April, 1948, it became 58s. 2d.)

In the latter stages of the inquiry somewhat fuller smoking histories were sought, and the last 557 lung-carcinoma patients (523 men, 34 women) and their matched controls were asked questions on their use of (a) different types and brands of tobacco; (b) filter-tipped cigarettes; (c) cigarette-holders; and (d) petrol lighters.

THE AMOUNT SMOKED

The results of the inquiry provide a number of ways in which the smoking habits of the patients can be categorized and compared. The simplest is the amount smoked immediately before the onset of the illness which brought the patient into hospital. This, however, can be very misleading, since some persons—including heavy smokers—give up smoking periodically, and it would be wrong to classify them as non-smokers merely because they were interviewed during a period of abstention. In Table **18,** 3, therefore, the comparison is made in a modified form: non-smokers are defined, as in our previous study, as persons who have never consistently smoked as much as one cigarette a day for as long as one year; the smokers are sub-divided either according to the amount they were smoking immediately before the onset of their illness or, if they had previously stopped smoking, according to the amount they were smoking before they last gave up. This is described as 'the most recent amount smoked'.

Table **18,** 3 shows that in both men and women there were fewer non-smokers and considerably more of the heavier smokers among the lung-carcinoma patients than among the control patients. Amongst 1,357 men with carcinoma of the lung, only seven, or 0.5 per cent, were non-smokers; there were 61, or 4.5 per cent, among the same number of men with other diseases. At the other end of the scale, 25 per cent of the men with lung carcinoma had smoked 25 or more cigarettes a day (or the equivalent in pipe tobacco); the proportion in the control patients was only 13.4 per cent. Similarly, amongst the 108 women with carcinoma of the lung, 37.0 per cent were non-smokers against 54.6 per cent of the women with other diseases. Among women with carcinoma 11.1 per cent had smoked 25 or more cigarettes a day; among those with other diseases this proportion was 0.9 per cent.

TABLE **18**, 3

Most Recent Amount of Tobacco Smoked Regularly Before the Onset of the Present Illness: Lung-carcinoma Patients and Matched Control Patients with Other Diseases

Disease Group	No. of Non-smokers	No. Smoking Daily*					
		1 Cig.-	5 Cigs.-	15 Cigs.-	25 Cigs.-	50 Cigs.+	
Men:							
1,357 lung-carcinoma patients (99·9%)	7 (0·5%)	49 (3·6%)	516 (38·0%)	445 (32·8%)	299 (22·0%)	41 (3·0%)	
1,357 control patients with other diseases (100%)	61 (4·5%)	91 (6·7%)	615 (45·3%)	408 (30·1%)	162 (11·9%)	20 (1·5%)	
Women:							
108 lung-carcinoma patients (100%)	40 (37·0%)	14 (13·0%)	30 (27·8%)	12 (11·1%)	12 (11·1%)	0	
108 control patients with other diseases (100%)	59 (54·6%)	18 (16·7%)	22 (20·4%)	8 (7·4%)	1 (0·9%)	0	

Difference between proportions of non-smokers and smokers—Men: $\chi^2 = 43\cdot99$, n = 1, P < 0·000001.

Women: $\chi^2 = 6\cdot73$, n = 1, P < 0·01.

Difference between proportions of smokers smoking different amounts—Men: $\chi^2 = 69\cdot74$, n = 4, P < 0·000001.

Women: $\chi^2 = 8\cdot99$, n = 3, 0·02 < P < 0·05.

* Ounces of tobacco have been expressed as being equivalent to so many cigarettes. There is 1 oz. of tobacco in 26·5 normal-size cigarettes, so that the conversion factor has been taken as: 1 oz. of tobacco a week = 4 cigarettes a day.

These results are essentially the same as those recorded in our preliminary report. In Greater London, indeed, the results for the two periods 1948–9 and 1950–1 are remarkably alike (see Table **18, 4**, where they are set out separately and alongside figures from the provincial centres). Table **18,** 4 also shows that the contrast between the smoking habits of the men in the two disease groups was observed quite consistently at the provincial centres. In each case the proportions of non-smokers and of men smoking less than five cigarettes a day were *lower*, and the proportion smoking 25 or more cigarettes a day was substantially *higher*, among the lung-carcinoma patients. In women similar results were obtained during the two periods of inquiry in Greater London, while at Bristol, Cambridge, and Leeds the numbers are too small to warrant attention. At Newcastle, however, the smoking habits of the female lung-carcinoma patients did not differ appreciably from those of their matched controls—in fact, the proportion of non-smokers was slightly higher in the lung-carcinoma group. Though the number interviewed was small (19 cases), the divergence from the experience of the lung-cancer groups elsewhere is sufficient to be statistically significant. Adding the provincial centres together gives the following figures for women:

	Non-smokers	Smoking 1–14 Cigs.	Smoking 15 + Cigs.	Total
Lung-carcinoma group	16	11	1	28
Control group	16	12	–	28

The presence of only one woman with lung carcinoma who had smoked 15 or more cigarettes a day is not, perhaps, surprising; it seems that very few women in the provinces smoke so much. Of all the 58 women interviewed at provincial centres, and who suffered from 'other diseases' (other than lung carcinoma, carcinoma of other sites possibly related to tobacco, and carcinoma of uncertain primary site) none gave a history of smoking 15 or more cigarettes a day. In contrast, this amount was smoked by nearly 8 per cent of 553 similar women with all other diseases interviewed in Greater London. There is, however, an absence in the provinces of any difference between the two groups in the numbers of non-smokers and of women smoking fewer than 15 cigarettes a day.

TABLE **18**, 4 *Most Recent Amount of Tobacco Smoked Regularly Before the Onset of the Present Illness: Lung-carcinoma Patients and Matched Control Patients with Other Diseases, Subdivided by Place and Date of Interview*

Disease Group	Place and Date of Interview	Percentage Non-smokers	Percentage Smoking Daily*				No. Interviewed
			1 Cig.–	5 Cigs.–	15 Cigs.–	25 Cigs. +	
Carcinoma of lung (men)	Greater London, 1948–9	0·3	5·1	38·5	30·2	25·9	649
	Greater London, 1950–1	1·0	3·3	38·2	31·4	26·1	306
	Bristol, 1950–1	2·8	0·0	22·5	40·8	33·8	71
	Cambridge, 1951	0·0	0·0	50·0	29·4	20·6	34
	Leeds, 1950–1	0·0	1·9	47·2	34·0	17·0	53
	Newcastle, 1950–1	0·0	2·1	37·3	39·3	21·3	244
	Whole investigation	0·5	3·6	38·0	32·8	25·0	1,357
Control patients with other diseases (men)	Greater London, 1948–9	4·2	8·5	45·1	29·3	12·9	649
	Greater London, 1950–1	4·2	4·9	46·1	28·4	16·3	306
	Bristol, 1950–1	4·2	2·8	49·3	28·2	15·5	71
	Cambridge, 1951	2·9	8·8	52·9	29·4	5·9	34
	Leeds, 1950–1	5·7	7·5	39·6	35·8	11·3	53
	Newcastle, 1950–1	5·3	4·9	43·9	34·0	11·9	244
	Whole investigation	4·5	6·7	45·3	30·1	13·4	1,357
Carcinoma of lung (women)	Greater London, 1948–9	31·7	11·7	31·7	15·0	10·0	60
	Greater London, 1950–1	25·0	15·0	20·0	10·0	30·0	20
	Bristol, 1950–1	(50·0)†	—	(50·0)	—	—	2
	Cambridge, 1951	(50·0)	—	—	(50·0)	—	2
	Leeds, 1950–1	(20·0)	(20·0)	(60·0)	—	—	5
	Newcastle, 1950–1	68·4	15·8	15·8	—	—	19
	Whole investigation	37·0	13·0	27·8	11·1	11·1	108
Control patients with other diseases (women)	Greater London, 1948–9	53·3	20·0	16·7	10·0	0·0	60
	Greater London, 1950–1	55·0	10·0	20·0	10·0	5·0	20
	Bristol, 1950–1	(50·0)	(50·0)	(50·0)	—	—	2
	Cambridge, 1951	(50·0)	—	(50·0)	—	—	2
	Leeds, 1950–1	(60·0)	—	(40·0)	—	—	5
	Newcastle, 1950–1	57·9	15·8	26·3	—	—	19
	Whole investigation	54·6	16·7	20·4	7·4	0·9	108

* See footnote to Table 18, 3.   † The percentages in parentheses are based upon very small numbers and have no reliability.

The 'most recent amount smoked' will not necessarily give the best representation of a smoking history, even though defined, as here, to include the amount smoked by ex-smokers at the time they last gave up. Its advantage as a criterion is that the information is easily obtained and likely to be reasonably accurate. Its disadvantage is that smoking habits vary over a lifetime, sometimes considerably, and previous habits, which may be relevant, are being ignored. We have therefore calculated other quantitative estimates of the amount smoked as revealed in the patient's history. These are (a) the amount smoked immediately before the patient's illness, (b) the maximum amount ever smoked regularly, (c) the total amount smoked since smoking was begun, and (d) the average amount smoked daily over the 10 years preceding the patient's illness, over the penultimate 10 years, and over the whole of the patient's life since the age of 15, taking into account recorded changes during these periods.

Qualitatively similar results are obtained whichever of these estimates is used. The sharpest differentiation between the lung-carcinoma and control patients, for both men and women, appears to be given by the average daily amount smoked over the 10 years preceding the patient's illness. The results of this calculation are shown in Table **18**, 5 and differences between the groups of patients—particularly in the women—are more pronounced than those in Table **18**, 3.

For men, the amount smoked immediately before the patient's illness is equally good, but the estimates of the total amount consumed throughout life, the average daily amount since the age of 15, and the average daily amount over the penultimate 10 years give differences only of the same order as those shown by 'the most recent amount smoked'; the maximum daily amount ever smoked differentiates the groups less clearly. For women, all the estimates except the amount smoked immediately before the patient's illness are more discriminating than 'the most recent amount smoked', though the maximum daily amount ever smoked gives only a slightly increased divergence between the two groups.

In view of these results with varying measures of the smoking history we have used in subsequent tables *the average amount smoked daily over the 10 years preceding the patient's illness* as the most appropriate criterion. A whole life history should perhaps be a truer measure of the 'exposure to risk', but, as we pointed out in our previous paper, too much inaccuracy may result from requiring the patient to remember habits of many years past.

THE DURATION OF SMOKING

Comparisons of the ages at which the patients reported that they began to smoke, the number of years they had smoked, and, when

TABLE **18**, 5

Average Amount of Tobacco Smoked Daily Over the 10 Years Preceding the Onset of the Present Illness; Lung-carcinoma Patients and Matched Control Patients with Other Diseases

Disease Group	No. of Non-smokers	No. Smoking Daily Average* of					
		Less than 5 Cigs.	5 Cigs.–	15 Cigs.–	25 Cigs.–	50 Cigs. +
Men:						
1,357 lung-carcinoma patients (99·9%)	7 (0·5%)	55 (4·0%)	489 (36·0%)	475 (35·0%)	293 (21·6%)	38 (2·8%)
1,357 control patients with other diseases (100%)	61 (4·5%)	129 (9·5%)	570 (42·0%)	431 (31·8%)	154 (11·3%)	12 (0·9%)
Women:						
108 lung-carcinoma patients (100%)	40 (37·0%)	16 (14·8%)	24 (22·2%)	14 (13·0%)	14 (13·0%)	0
108 control patients with other diseases (100%)	59 (54·6%)	25 (23·1%)	18 (16·7%)	6 (5·6%)	0 (0·0%)	0

Difference between proportions of smokers smoking different amounts—Men: $\chi^2 = 93·77$, n = 4, P < 0·000001.
Women: $\chi^2 = 17·41$, n = 3, P < 0·001.

* Ounces of tobacco have been expressed as being equivalent to so many cigarettes. There is 1 oz. of tobacco in 26·5 normal-size cigarettes, so that the conversion factor has been taken as: 1 oz. of tobacco a week = 4 cigarettes a day.

appropriate, the number of years since they last gave up are shown in Table **18**, 6.

The lung-carcinoma patients are seen, on the average, to have begun smoking rather earlier, to have continued longer, and to have been rather less inclined to stop. In men, these differences are all statistically significant. In women they are not significant, but they are in the same direction, and no less distinct, so that it is reasonable to accept them as real.

The most pronounced difference appears in the number of years since smoking had last been given up. Since the control group contained more light smokers (Table **18**, 3) the higher proportion of ex-smokers in it here seen might, it was thought, be due to the fact that it is light smokers who more readily give up. In fact, the opposite appeared to be true. Of the 124 male control patients who had given up smoking nearly one-third (31.5 per cent) were smoking 25 or more cigarettes a day when they gave up; of those who continued to smoke, only 12.2 per cent consumed as much.

THE METHOD OF SMOKING

So far the only distinction we have drawn between smokers is in the *quantity* of tobacco consumed. There are, however, qualitative differences which might be important—namely, whether the smoker inhales, smokes a pipe, uses a cigarette holder, smokes filter-tipped cigarettes, rolls his own cigarettes, or lights his tobacco with matches or a petrol lighter.

Inhaling

All the smokers and ex-smokers were asked whether they inhaled (with the exception of three lung-carcinoma and two control patients, in whom the question was inadvertently omitted). Of 1,415 lung carcinoma patients (men and women), 64.6 per cent said yes and 35.4 per cent said no; of the 1,343 control patients with other diseases, 66.6 per cent said yes and 33.4 per cent said no. The differences are negligible. Similar results were obtained for men and women considered separately. (Further consideration is paid to inhaling in the section dealing with site of tumour.)

Cigarettes and Pipes

Some persons usually smoke cigarettes, others usually smoke a pipe. Habits, however, do not remain constant, and it has been

TABLE 18, 6

Age at Starting to Smoke, Number of Years Smoked, and Number of Years Since Smoking was Given Up, Lung-carcinoma Patients and Matched Control Patients

Sex	Age at Starting	Lung-carcinoma Patients No.	%	Control Patients No.	%	No. of Years Smoking	Lung-carcinoma Patients No.	%	Control Patients No.	%	No. of Years Given Up	Lung-carcinoma Patients No.	%	Control Patients No.	%
Men	Under 20	1,077	79·8	992	76·5	1–	12 }	3·4	15 }	6·2	0–	1,280	94·8	1,172	90·4
	20–	251	18·6	264	20·4	10–	34 }		65 }		1–	56	4·1	75	5·8
	30–	18 }	1·6	33 }	3·1	20–	746	55·3	725	55·9	10–	6 }	1·0	26 }	3·8
	40+	4 }		7 }		40+	558	41·3	491	37·9	20+	8 }		23 }	
	All ages	1,350	100·0	1,296	100·0	All periods	1,350	100·0	1,296	100·0	All periods	1,350	99·9	1,296	100·0

$\chi^2 = 7 \cdot 95$; n = 2; $0 \cdot 01 < P < 0 \cdot 02$ $\chi^2 = 12 \cdot 66$; n = 2; $P < 0 \cdot 01$ $\chi^2 = 25 \cdot 87$; n = 2; $P < 0 \cdot 001$

Sex	Age at Starting	Lung-carcinoma Patients No.	%	Control Patients No.	%	No. of Years Smoking	Lung-carcinoma Patients No.	%	Control Patients No.	%	No. of Years Given Up	Lung-carcinoma Patients No.	%	Control Patients No.	%
Women	Under 20	20	29·4	12	24·5	1–	14 }	38·2	18 }	53·1	0–	58	85·3	41	83·7
	20–	23	33·8	15	30·6	10–	12 }		8 }		1–	9	13·2	6	12·2
	30–	10 }	36·8	7 }	44·9	20–	36	52·9	20	40·8	10–	0 }	1·5	0 }	4·1
	40+	15 }		15 }		40+	6	8·8	3	6·1	20+	1 }		2 }	
	All ages	68	100·0	49	100·0	All periods	68	99·9	49	100·0	All periods	68	100·0	49	100·0

427

necessary to divide male smokers into three broad categories: (*a*) those who have never smoked a pipe regularly for as long as one year ('pure cigarette-smokers'); (*b*) those who have smoked cigarettes and a pipe; and (*c*) those who have never smoked cigarettes regularly for as long as one year ('pure pipe-smokers'). Among the 1,350 male lung-carcinoma patients who smoked, 3.9 per cent were pure pipe-smokers and 74.4 per cent were pure cigarette-smokers; among the 1,296 male control patients who smoked the corresponding proportions were 6.9 per cent and 69.4 per cent. The differences, though not striking, are statistically highly significant (χ^2 for the three groups, pure pipe, mixed, pure cigarette = 15.85; n = 2, P < 0.001). It would appear that pipe-smoking is less closely associated with the development of lung carcinoma than cigarette-smoking. Pipe-smokers, however, consume, on the average, less tobacco than cigarette-smokers, and this must account for some of the relative deficiency of pipe-smokers in the lung-carcinoma group. It does not seem that it can account for the whole difference, since the proportion of pure pipe-smokers is somewhat lower at each level of tobacco consumption. The relevant figures are as follows:

	Percentage of Pure Pipe-smokers among all Smokers at Each Average Daily Consumption Level (Measured in Terms of Cigarettes)			
	Less than 5 Cigs.	5 Cigs.–	15 Cigs.–	25 Cigs.+
Male lung-carcinoma patients	9·1%	7·2%	1·3%	2·1%
Male control patients with other diseases	10·9%	10·5%	3·5%	2·4%

On the other hand, studying the pure pipe-smokers alone we find that 9.4 per cent of those with lung-carcinoma smoked the equivalent of less than five cigarettes a day and 13.2 per cent smoked the equivalent of 25 or more a day; in the control group the proportions were 15.1 per cent and 4.3 per cent. In other words, a higher proportion of the pure pipe-smokers with carcinoma of the lung fall into the higher smoking categories—as with the cigarette-smokers.

We conclude, as in our earlier report, that the method of smoking is of importance and that smoking a pipe, though also related to carcinoma of the lung, appears to carry a smaller risk than smoking cigarettes (see also section on Estimated Risks).

Cigarette-holders

A possible explanation of this lower risk of pipe-smoking is that the pipe-stem acts as a partial filter of a carcinogenic agent. If that were so, we might expect that fewer of the patients with carcinoma of the lung had used cigarette-holders. We sought information on this point in the latter stages of the inquiry—from the last 523 pairs of male lung-carcinoma and control patients to be interviewed. Judged by the proportions of non-smokers and pure pipe-smokers in the two groups, these last patients seem to be a representative sample of the total. Table **18,** 7 shows results obtained from them.

TABLE **18,** 7

Use of Cigarette-holders: Male Lung-carcinoma and Matched Control Patients. (Information Obtained During the Last Part of the Investigation Only)

Disease Group	Non-smokers	Never Smoked Cigar-ettes	Cigarette-smokers Holders Used			Total Cigarette-smokers
			Never	Occa-sionally	Regu-larly	
523 lung-carcinoma patients	4	15	479	15	10	504
523 control patients	26	30	413	27	27	467

Few patients had ever used holders, but the proportion of cigarette-smokers who had done so was significantly smaller in the group with carcinoma of the lung (5 per cent) than in the control patients (12 per cent) ($\chi^2 = 14.74$, n = 2, P < 0.001).

This difference might merely be due to an association between using a holder and light smoking, but the available evidence suggests not. Among the 54 cigarette-smokers in the control group who had used holders five (9 per cent) smoked an average of fewer than 15 cigarettes a day and six (11 per cent) smoked an average of 25 or more; the corresponding figures for the 413 cigarette-smokers who had not used holders were 32 (8 per cent) and 55 (13 per cent). Further evidence that an association with light smoking cannot account for the relative deficiency of users of cigarette-holders in the lung-carcinoma group is the finding that the proportion who had used holders was lower at each level of tobacco consumption— namely:

	Percentage of Cigarette-smokers who had ever used Holders at Each Average Daily Consumption Level			
	Less than 5 Cigs.	5 Cigs.–	15 Cigs.–	25 Cigs. +
Male lung-carcinoma patients who smoked cigarettes	5·9%	4·0%	6·0%	4·5%
Male control patients with other diseases who smoked cigarettes	13·5%	12·6%	10·4%	9·8%

Types of Cigarettes

Cigarette-smokers were asked whether they bought manufactured cigarettes or bought tobacco and rolled their own. Of the 1,297 male lung-carcinoma patients who had ever smoked cigarettes 20.7 per cent smoked mostly hand-rolled cigarettes; of the 1,203 similar control patients the proportion was 19.1 per cent. Evidently there is no specific association of manufactured, as opposed to hand-rolled, cigarettes and carcinoma of the lung. It can also be concluded that the different risks associated with cigarette- and pipe-smoking are unlikely to be the result of the different types of tobacco consumed, as a number of men who roll their cigarettes use pipe tobacco.

In view of the presence of arsenic in American tobacco and its almost complete absence from Oriental tobacco (Daff and Kennaway, 1950) it was clearly of interest to determine whether there was any difference in the proportions of American and 'Turkish' tobacco smokers in the lung-carcinoma and control groups. The results of such inquiry were inconclusive because nearly all smokers had habitually smoked 'Virginian'. In fact, only one smoker was found who had never regularly smoked it (a man of 70, under treatment for an enlarged prostate). Of the 504 male lung-carcinoma patients who had smoked cigarettes only 3.8 per cent said that they had at some period, regularly smoked Turkish tobacco; among the 467 control patients the figure was 4.5 per cent. The difference is statistically insignificant.

During the last part of the investigation inquiries were also made about the brands of cigarettes smoked and the use of filter-tipped cigarettes. The results (Table **18,** 8) show that none of the four

TABLE **18,** 8

Brands of Cigarettes Smoked and Use of Filter-tipped Cigarettes: Male Lung-carcinoma and Matched Control Patients. (Information Obtained During the Last Part of the Investigation Only)

Type of Smoker	Lung-carcinoma Patients	Control Patients
Cigarette-smokers, smoking manufactured cigarettes— Brand mainly smoked:		
Brand A	72 (18·2%)	70 (19·4%)
Brand B	11 (2·8%)	14 (3·9%)
Brand C	123 (31·1%)	107 (29·6%)
Brand D	21 (5·3%)	15 (4·2%)
Other brands	36 (9·0%)	39 (10·8%)
Mixed brands	133 (33·6%)	116 (32·1%)
All brands	396 (100·0%)	361 (100·0%)
Brand not stated (present smokers of hand-rolled cigarettes or pipes)	108	106
All cigarette-smokers	504	467
Cigarette-smokers, filter-tipped cigarettes:		
Ever smoked regularly*	3	15
Never smoked regularly	501	452
All cigarette-smokers	504	467

* For one or more years

main brands recorded was more closely associated with carcinoma of the lung than another. The proportions are remarkably similar in the two groups of patients. On the other hand, very few of the men with lung carcinoma had ever regularly used filter-tipped cigarettes —three in 504 compared with 15 in the 467 controls. The difference is significant ($\chi^2 = 7.74$, n = 1, P < 0.01), but with so few observations the conclusions to be drawn must be highly speculative. The explanation may be that filter-tipped cigarettes are smoked predominantly by light smokers, but we have insufficient data to test that possibility.

Use of Petrol Lighters

In the two groups of 523 male patients last interviewed inquiry was made into the use of petrol lighters. Of the 504 male patients with carcinoma of the lung who smoked cigarettes, 42.9 per cent reported that at some period they had regularly used petrol lighters; of the 468 similar control patients, the proportion was 41.3 per cent. The difference is negligible, and the evidence is against the hypothesis—often put forward—that petrol lighters are the responsible carcinogenic agent.

Use of Tobacco for Chewing and as Snuff

Although extraneous substances will be brought into contact with the bronchial mucosa more readily by smoking than by chewing or by snuff, it is possible that particles of tobacco are inspired into the bronchial tree by these latter means and that these uncombusted particles are carcinogenic. The possibility is suggested by the frequent occurrence of cancer of the buccal cavity in Eastern countries where the inhabitants have the habit of chewing quids of tobacco mixed with flavouring agents.

Questions about chewing tobacco and the use of snuff were asked of 1,209 male patients with lung carcinoma and of the 1,209 corresponding control patients.* The results show (Table **18**, 9) that fewer patients with lung carcinoma had chewed tobacco (40, or 3.3 per cent against 64, or 5.3 per cent) and slightly fewer had ever taken snuff (33, or 2.7 per cent, against 43, or 3.6 per cent); the differences are small though statistically significant for chewing. That this latter difference is likely to be real is borne out by the fact that it is more marked for those who had chewed regularly (28 to 49) than for those who had done so occasionally (12 to 15), and most marked for those who had chewed regularly for more than 10 years (17 to 32). The number of patients who were still in the habit of chewing was too small for it to be possible to assess the amount they smoked in comparison with others. It may be that there were fewer lung-carcinoma patients who had chewed tobacco because men who chew will smoke less.

* After the completion of the first part of the investigation these questions were temporarily omitted from the questionary, and 148 male patients with lung carcinoma interviewed outside London and their corresponding control patients were not asked whether they chewed tobacco or used snuff.

TABLE **18,** 9

Use of Tobacco for Chewing and as Snuff: Male Lung-carcinoma and Matched Control Patients. (Information Obtained During Part of the Investigation Only)

Disease Group	Tobacco Never Chewed	Tobacco Chewed				Total who had Chewed Tobacco
		Occasionally		Regularly		
		Less than 10 Yrs.	10 Yrs.+	Less than 10 Yrs.	10 Yrs.+	
1,209 lung-carci- noma patients	1,169	8	4	11	17	40
1,209 control patients	1,145	6	9	17	32	64
	Tobacco Never Taken as Snuff	Tobacco Taken as Snuff				Total who had Taken Tobacco as Snuff
1,209 lung-carci- noma patients	1,176	8	7	10	8	33
1,209 control patients	1,166	11	5	16	11	43

Significance tests of differences between lung-carcinoma and control patients:

Chewing: $\chi^2 = 5\cdot79$, n = 1, $0\cdot01 < P < 0\cdot02$.
Snuff-taking: $\chi^2 = 1\cdot36$, n = 1, $0\cdot20 < P < 0\cdot30$.

NATURE OF THE CARCINOMA IN RELATION TO SMOKING

Histological Type

According to Wynder and Graham (1950), adenocarcinoma of the lung is less closely related to smoking than the other histological types of lung carcinoma. Primary adenocarcinoma of the lung is an uncommon condition, but of particular interest, in relation to smoking, in that it has invariably been reported as being relatively commoner in women than in men. In the present series, all patients with a histologically confirmed diagnosis (approximately 70 per cent in each sex) have been divided according to type, with the following results:

	Histological Type				
	Epidermoid	Oat-cell or Anaplastic	Adeno-carcinoma	Unclassi-fied	No Histological Confirmation
1,357 men	475 (52%)	303 (33%)	33 (4%)	105 (11%)	441
108 women	18 (23%)	38 (48%)	10 (13%)	13 (16%)	29

In Table **18,** 10 the numbers of men and women smoking different amounts of tobacco are shown separately for each histological type of growth and are compared with the numbers expected from the experience of all male and all female patients in whom the diagnosis was confirmed histologically. There is no statistically significant difference between the amounts smoked by patients in the different histological groups in either sex. The number of proved cases of adenocarcinoma is, however, too small (43) to conclude that no difference exists. There were, in fact, relatively more non-smokers and very light smokers (average consumption less than five cigarettes a day) among the patients with adenocarcinoma in both sexes, and it is possible that larger numbers would have supported Wynder and Graham's findings.

Table **18,** 10 also shows that it is not possible to detect any difference, in amount smoked, between the cases diagnosed clinically and those in whom the diagnoses were histologically confirmed. This result suggests that the 'clinical' diagnoses were generally accurate—which is not surprising, since they were based on findings at thoracotomy or at necropsy in 93 (19.8 per cent), on direct observation of the tumour broncho-scopically in a further 96 (20.4 per cent), while in many of the remainder bronchoscopic examinations suggested the presence of a carcinoma though no tumour was seen.

Site of Tumour

The site of origin of a tumour within the lung may be of interest, since it is possible that aetiological agents might reach the main bronchi but not the bronchioles and alveoli. In the present series 1,154 (90.4 per cent) were considered to have arisen centrally and 122 (9.6 per cent) peripherally (in 189 it was not possible to decide).

Analysis of the smoking habits of the patients in these two groups reveals no difference between them in the amounts smoked but a

TABLE **18**, 10.—*Average Amount of Tobacco Smoked Daily Over the 10 Years Preceding the Onset of the Present Illness, Divided According to Histological Type: Lung-carcinoma Patients*

Histological Type	No. of Non-smokers	Average Amount Smoked Daily over 10 Years Number Smoking:			
		Less than 5 Cigs.	5 Cigs.–	15 Cigs.–	25 Cigs. +
A			*Men*		
Epidermoid carcinoma (475)	1 (2·4)*	14 (19·3)	169 (166·9)	175 (172·4)	116 (114·1)
Oat-cell or anaplastic carcinoma (303)	2 (1·8)	12 (11·2)	110 (106·7)	105 (111·4)	74 (72·0)
Adenocarcinoma (33)	2 (0·2)	2 (0·9)	7 (11·5)	16 (12·3)	6 (8·2)
Type unclassified (105)	0 (0·6)	8 (4·7)	36 (37·0)	38 (38·0)	23 (24·8)
B					
Histological evidence obtained (916)	5 (4·9)	36 (34·5)	322 (328·5)	334 (322·4)	219 (225·8)
No histological evidence (441)	2 (2·1)	19 (20·5)	167 (160·5)	141 (152·6)	112 (105·2)
C			*Women*		
Epidermoid carcinoma (18)	11 (8·6)	1 (1·9)	4 (4·3)	1 (1·6)	1 (1·6)
Oat-cell or anaplastic carcinoma (38)	12 (11·2)	6 (5·1)	9 (10·0)	7 (7·4)	4 (4·3)
Adenocarcinoma (10)	5 (3·8)	2 (1·2)	1 (2·7)	0 (1·4)	2 (1·0)
Type unclassified (13)	1 (5·5)	2 (1·8)	5 (3·0)	4 (1·6)	1 (1·1)
D					
Histological evidence obtained (79)	29 (28·7)	10 (11·1)	20 (18·4)	12 (10·9)	8 (10·1)
No histological evidence (29)	11 (11·3)	5 (3·9)	5 (6·6)	2 (3·2)	6 (4·0)

* The figures in parentheses are the numbers that would have occurred if the patients in the histological group in question had had, at each age, exactly the same smoking habits as all the patients with which the group is being compared. That is, in part A of the table, all male patients with histological evidence of the growth; in part B, all male patients; in part C, all female patients with histological evidence of the growth; in part D, all female patients.

slight difference in the prevalence of inhaling. (See Table **18,** 11. The comparison here does not allow for differences in age distribution of the patients with central and peripheral growths, but these differences are small and do not materially affect the results.) It will be seen that a slightly higher proportion of the males with peripheral growths inhaled regularly (62.6 per cent) compared with the men with central growths (52.4 per cent)—a statistically significant difference (0.05 level). The patients in each group can also be compared with their own matched controls. It is then found that the males with central growths include rather fewer regular inhalers than their controls 52.4 per cent to 57.1 per cent), while the group with peripheral growths contain rather more (62.6 per cent to 53.3 per cent). The difference is statistically significant in the former case but not in the latter, where the observations are too few to eliminate chance as an explanation. With the women the numbers are too small to warrant consideration.

ESTIMATED RISKS

Amount of Smoking

To measure approximately the relative risks associated with different levels of smoking we need to know (*a*) the number of people smoking different amounts of tobacco in each age group— that is, the numbers 'at risk'—and (*b*) the number of people smoking different amounts in each age group who died from carcinoma of the lung. It would then be possible, because of the very high fatality of the disease, to equate the calculated death rates to the risks of developing it.

The present investigation cannot provide estimates of these figures for the whole country, since the patients interviewed were drawn mainly from Greater London, and smoking habits and the lung-cancer death rate both vary between countryside and town. For example, in 1949 the report of the Registrar-General shows that the recorded death rates from lung cancer in men were 597, 521, 398, and 292 per million in, respectively, Greater London, county boroughs outside Greater London, other urban districts, and rural districts.

For the Greater London area alone we may, however, proceed on three assumptions—namely, (*a*) that the smoking habits reported by the control patients without carcinoma of the lung who lived in

TABLE 18, 11

Prevalence of Inhaling: Patients with Carcinoma of the Lung Arising Centrally and Peripherally and Corresponding Matched Control Patients

Disease Group	No. of Smokers Inhaling			Total No. of Smokers	No. of Non-smokers
	Regularly	Occasionally	Never		
Male lung-carcinoma patients with:					
1,070 central growths	558 (52·4%)	126 (11·8%)	380 (35·7%)	1,064 (99·9%)	6
116 peripheral growths	72 (62·6%)	13 (11·3%)	30 (26·1%)	115 (100%)	1
Male control patients corresponding to lung-carcinoma patients with:					
1,070 central growths	583 (57·1%)	116 (11·4%)	322 (31·5%)	1,021 (100%)	49
116 peripheral growths	63 (53·3%)	12 (10·5%)	39 (34·2%)	114 (100%)	2
Female lung-carcinoma patients with:					
84 central growths	24	6	17	47	37
6 peripheral growths	1	1	3	5	1
Female control patients corresponding to lung-carcinoma patients with:					
84 central growths	14	5	20	39	45
6 peripheral growths	0	0	1	1	5

Significance tests. Prevalence of inhaling (regular plus occasional):
Male lung-carcinoma patients, central compared with peripheral growths: $\chi^2 = 4·24$, n = 1, $0·02 < P < 0·05$.
Male patients, patients with central growths compared with corresponding controls: $\chi^2 = 4·07$, n = 1, $0·02 < P < 0·05$.
Male patients, patients with peripheral growths compared with corresponding controls: $\chi^2 = 1·79$, n = 1, $0·10 < P < 0·20$.

Greater London at the time of their interview are, at each age and in each sex, typical of the inhabitants of Greater London generally; (b) that the smoking habits reported by the patients with carcinoma of the lung, also living in Greater London at the time of their interview, are typical of the inhabitants who died of the disease during the period of the survey; and (c) that the deaths attributed by the Registrar-General to lung cancer both in men and in women provide a reasonable estimate of the actual numbers of deaths due to carcinoma of the lung. On these assumptions, which are bold but, we think, not wholly unreasonable, we can calculate, for the one region, death rates for each level of tobacco consumption.

The population of Greater London given by the Registrar-General for 30 June, 1950, has been taken as the population at risk. The numbers of persons within this population smoking different amounts of tobacco have been estimated from the data for each sex and for each of the age groups 25–44, 45–64, and 65–74.

TABLE **18,** 12

Estimated Annual Death Rates from Lung Cancer per 1,000 Men and per 1,000 Women Living in Greater London; by Age Group and Average Amount of Tobacco Smoked Daily in Preceding 10 Years*

Sex and Age	Annual Death Rate per 1,000 Persons						No. of Lung-carcinoma Patients Inter-viewed
	Non-smokers	Average Amount Smoked Daily in Preceding Ten Years					
		Less than 5 Cigs.	5 Cigs.–	15 Cigs.–	25 Cigs.–	50 Cigs.+	
Men							
25–	0·00†	0·03	0·13	0·12	0·17	0·52	61
45–	0·14	0·59	1·35	1·67	2·95	4·74	539
65–74	0·00	2·38	2·66	3·88	6·95	10·24	130
Women							
25–	0·006	0·04	0·03	0·13		—	9
65–	0·09	0·06	0·34	1·19		—	39
45–74	0·32	0·70	0·59	2·37		—	13

* The reasons for the adoption of this measure of smoking habits is explained in the text (see section on Amount Smoked).

† Rates based on observation of fewer than five cases of carcinoma of the lung are given in italics.

Thus at ages 45–64 we had 932 male patients resident in Greater London with diseases other than lung carcinoma; 4.1 per cent were non-smokers, 9.3 per cent had smoked an average over the preceding 10 years of fewer than five cigarettes (or their equivalent) a day, 42.6 per cent an average of 5–14 a day, 29.9 per cent an average of 15–24 a day, 12.8 per cent an average of 25–49 a day, and 1.3 per cent an average of 50 or more a day. The male population of Greater London at ages 45–64 was 937,000, and this population has been given the above proportions of non-smokers and smokers of different amounts. (In making these estimates we ignore the lung-carcinoma patients in the total population, but their proportion is too small to make any material difference.) In the same way the numbers of persons of each sex and age dying from lung cancers in Greater London in 1950 have been divided up on the basis of the smoking habits of the lung-carcinoma patients who were interviewed.

The death rates thus obtained (Table **18**, 12) increase with both age and amount smoked. They pass from a negligible figure for male non-smokers aged 25–44 to a level of the order of one in 100 per year among men aged 65–74 who have smoked an average of 25 cigarettes or more a day for the preceding 10 years. The greatest number of our subjects were aged 45–64, and the rates for this group should therefore be the most reliable. In Fig. **18**, 1 these are shown

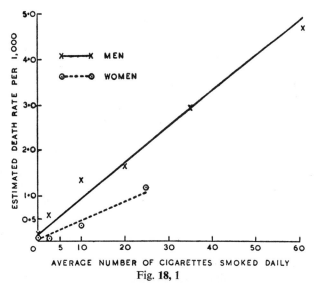

Fig. 18, 1

Estimated annual death rates from lung cancer in Greater London for men and for women aged 45–64, in relation to the average amount of tobacco smoked daily (measured in terms of cigarettes) in the preceding 10 years.

graphically against the amounts smoked. It appears, on the assumptions made, that the death rate increases in approximately simple proportion with the amount smoked. Among women the death rate seems to rise more slowly, but the numbers are smaller and considerably less reliable.

Cigarettes or Pipe

On the same assumptions, that our data are representative of Greater London, it is also possible to estimate mortality rates for each type of smoker—that is, cigarettes only, cigarettes and pipe, pipe only. As previously shown, the pure pipe-smokers are few and we can therefore calculate rates only for the one broad age group 45–74. The results are:

	Estimated Annual Mortality Rates from Lung Cancer per 1,000 Men Aged 45–74. Average Amount Smoked Daily for Preceding 10 Years in Terms of Cigarettes*				
	Less than 5 Cigs.	5 Cigs.–	15 Cigs.–	25 Cigs.–	50 Cigs.+
Pure cigarette-smokers	1·11	1·71	2·16	3·50	7·37
Smokers of cigarettes and pipe	0·87	1·67	1·98	3·35	2·24†
Pure pipe-smokers	0·95†	1·35	0·79†	2·08†	—
All smokers	1·04	1·66	2·05	3·42	5·42

* See footnote to Table **18**, 3.   † Based on fewer than five cases.

At each smoking level the estimated death rate of pipe-smokers is less than that of cigarette-smokers, and the difference increases with heavier smoking. In three of the four groups the death rate of those smoking cigarettes and pipe is intermediate. With the amount of data at our disposal and the assumptions made in calculating these rates we would be reluctant to draw any precise conclusion on the relative level of the risks. But it certainly appears that the risks are less in pipe-smokers than in cigarette-smokers, and perhaps to the greatest extent in the heavier-smoking categories.

Town and Country

There seem to be differences in smoking habits between townsmen and countrymen (briefly referred to above), and our data may be used to see whether they can wholly, or partially, account for the reported different mortality rates from carcinoma of the lung—though they are insufficient to give more than an approximate answer. The patients interviewed in this inquiry lived in different parts of the country. Grouping them according to place of residence, we can roughly estimate the smoking habits of persons living in Greater London, county boroughs, urban districts, and rural districts. There were, however, relatively few patients living in the country, and a special survey was therefore made (in February, 1950) of the smoking habits of 531 other patients, aged 25–74, admitted to hospitals in rural areas of Dorset and Wiltshire.

To facilitate comparisons the male inhabitants of England and Wales between the ages of 25 and 74 have been taken as a standard population, and the smoking habits in this population have been estimated from the incidence rates of smoking actually observed in the age groups in each of the four areas (Table **18,** 13). It appears that as the place of residence becomes more highly urbanized the proportion of non-smokers and of pure pipe-smokers decreases and the proportion of heavier smokers and pure cigarette-smokers increases. Thus the changes are in the direction which would lead to a higher death rate from carcinoma of the lung in the towns. Whether they can account for the observed differences in mortality is difficult to say. On the assumption that the estimated death rates of Table **18,** 12 should prevail equally in all areas, it would seem that the recorded differences in mortality between town and country are greater than could be attributed wholly to the differences in smoking habits. In other words, the differences in smoking habits shown in Table **18,** 13 are not sufficient to lead to a rural mortality rate which is only about half that of the large towns.

OTHER AETIOLOGICAL FACTORS

The inquiry here reported was designed to throw light on any aetiological agent in carcinoma of the lung—for example, on substances which pollute the atmosphere. The questions on smoking were merely one facet of the investigation. We now turn to other aspects.

Occupation and Social Class

Occupational histories were taken from all patients, but these reveal no gross association between any type of occupation and lung

TABLE **18**, 13

Smoking Habits of Male Patients Living in Different Parts of the Country; Divided According to Density of Population. (Standardized to age distribution of population of England and Wales, aged 25–74)

Area of Residence	Percentage of Non-smokers	Percentage Smoking Daily Average of					Percentage of			No. of Patients Interviewed
		Less than 5 Cigs.	5 Cigs.–	15 Cigs.–	25 Cigs. +	Pure Cigarette -smokers	Cigarette and Pipe-smokers	Pure Pipe-smokers		
Greater London	5·1	8·3	38·3	33·7	14·6	74·2	16·0	4·8	1,393
County borough	6·8	6·6	42·7	34·0	9·9	66·3	22·8	4·1	240
Other urban district	8·4	13·3	37·1	32·3	8·9	59·9	23·9	7·8	439
Rural district	10·4	13·7	40·8	27·6	7·7	58·4	21·5	9·8	327

carcinoma which might indicate an aetiological agent of general significance—for example, persons occupationally exposed to motor fumes or road dust do not appear more frequently in the lung-carcinoma group. The results will be published in full later.

Social class has already been considered (Table **18,** 2); it showed no significant difference between the male patients with lung carcinoma and their controls. This observation is in keeping with the Registrar-General's 1930–2 decennial supplement on occupational mortality, though in the present inquiry the lack of association may be over-emphasized from the fact that our control patients were usually, and deliberately, taken from the same hospitals as the patients with carcinoma of the lung. This designed equality in some respects may give an over-estimated equality in social class.

Place of Residence

The Registrar-General's evidence that cancer of the lung is more frequent in the large towns than in the smaller towns and countryside suggests that a higher proportion of our lung-carcinoma patients would be expected to have been living in Greater London and the county boroughs. In fact, as shown in Table **18, 2**, this was not the case. If, however, the patients' places of residence are analysed separately, for those interviewed in Greater London and those interviewed in the provinces, a different picture is obtained (Table **18,** 14).

Of patients interviewed in Greater London, fewer with lung carcinoma lived there (76 per cent) compared with the controls (87 per cent); more lived in each of the other types of area. Of patients interviewed in the provinces, more with lung carcinoma lived in the county boroughs (45 per cent against 38 per cent) and fewer lived in rural districts (22 per cent against 28 per cent).

The differences in Greater London can reasonably be explained on the ground that patients with cancer living outside London tend, more than patients with other diseases, to come to London for treatment. In the provinces, however, the control patients with other diseases were interviewed in hospitals which were deliberately chosen because, like the thoracic units, they also served as regional centres. Consequently there should not be on demographic grounds any deficiency among them of patients living in the smaller towns or in the countryside. It would be reasonable to suspect that any difference between the places of residence of patients in the lung-

TABLE **18**, 14

Place of Residence: Lung-carcinoma and Matched Control Patients, Subdivided by Place of Interview

Place of Residence	Place of Interview			
	Greater London		Provinces	
	Lung-carcinoma Patients	Control Patients	Lung-carcinoma Patients	Control Patients
Greater London	791	900	0	0
Other county boroughs	31	16	194	165
Other urban districts	133	71	142	142
Rural districts	62	42	93	122
Abroad	18	6	1	1
All places	1,035	1,035	430	430

Difference between places of residence:
  Patients interviewed in Greater London: $\chi^2 = 40 \cdot 50$, n = 4, P $< 0 \cdot 001$.
  Patients interviewed in provinces (excluding patients residing abroad):
    $\chi^2 = 6 \cdot 25$, n = 2, $0 \cdot 02 < P < 0 \cdot 05$.

carcinoma and control groups would reflect differences in the relative incidence of the conditions in the different areas. The observation in the provinces that a smaller proportion of the lung-carcinoma than of the control patients lived in the country supports, therefore, the contention that lung carcinoma is less common in rural than in urban areas.

Evidence can also be obtained by comparing, for patients living in a given type of area at the time of interview, the proportion who had previously lived for any long time in the countryside (see Table **18**, 15). Among the lung-carcinoma patients living in Greater London at the time of interview, 4.3 per cent had previously lived for 10 or more years in a rural district; among control patients living in Greater London the proportion was 6.9 per cent. For each type of area this proportion is lower among the lung-carcinoma patients. The differences, though slight, are consistent and in conformity with the previous conclusion. They are not, however, statistically significant ($\chi^2 = 6.45$, n = 4, $0.10 < P < 0.20$).

TABLE **18**, 15

Residence for 10 *or More Years in the Countryside: Lung-carcinoma and Matched Control Patients, Subdivided by Place of Residence at the Time of Interview*

Residence at Time of Interview	Lung-carcinoma Patients			Control Patients		
	No. Inter-viewed	Lived for 10 or More Years in a Rural District		No. Inter-viewed	Lived for 10 or More Years in a Rural District	
		No.	%		No.	%
Greater London	791	34	4·3	900	62	6·9
Other county boroughs	225	13	5·8	181	12	6·6
Other urban districts	275	37	13·5	213	32	15·0
Rural districts	155	136	87·7	164	149	90·9
Abroad	19	1	—	7	0	—
All places	1,465	221	(15·1)	1,465	255	(17·4)

Residence Near a Gasworks

Gasworkers have been reported as specially liable to carcinoma of the lung (Kennaway and Kennaway, 1947; Doll, 1952), and it was therefore thought possible that residence near a gasworks with inhalation of its fumes might conduce to the disease. All the patients were asked whether they had ever lived near a gasworks and, if so, for how long. The results revealed no difference: 23.0 per cent (337/1,465) of the lung-carcinoma patients and 21.5 per cent (315/1,465) of the control patients had lived near a gasworks for a year or more ($\chi^2 = 0.95$, n = 1, $0.30 < P < 0.50$). This result agrees with that obtained by McConnell, Gordon, and Jones (1952).

Exposure to Different Forms of Heating

Further information on the possible effects of exposure to coal-gas was sought by asking the form of heating used in the houses in which the patients had lived. This question also related to the possibility that exposure to benzpyrene in the soot of domestic fires might be conducive to the development of carcinoma. Analysis was made of the kinds of heating used in the living-rooms of all the houses in which the patients had resided for three or more years,

TABLE **18**, 16

Exposure to Different Forms of Heating: Lung-carcinoma and Matched Control Patients.
(Information obtained during part of the investigation only)

Type of Heating in Living-room of Patients' Residence	Disease Group	No. of Patients Exposed for Different Durations of Time				Total No. of Patients	Test of Significance of Difference
		Never	1 Yr.-	30 Yrs.-	50 Yrs.+		
Coal fire	Lung carcinoma	9	93	434	735	1,271	$\chi^2 = 1{\cdot}01$, n = 3, $0{\cdot}70 < P < 0{\cdot}80$
	Other diseases	11	105	429	726	1,271	
Anthracite stove	Lung carcinoma	1,261	6	3	1	1,271	Combining all over 1 yr.:
	Other diseases	1,258	12	1	0	1,271	$\chi^2 = 0{\cdot}39$, n = 1, $0{\cdot}50 < P < 0{\cdot}70$
Gas fire	Lung carcinoma	1,192	59	13	7	1,271	Combining all over 30 yrs.:
	Other diseases	1,169	74	21	7	1,271	$\chi^2 = 3{\cdot}25$, n = 2, $0{\cdot}10 < P < 0{\cdot}20$
Electric fire	Lung carcinoma	1,184	62	14	11	1,271	Combining all over 30 yrs.:
	Other diseases	1,172	71	21	7	1,271	$\chi^2 = 0{\cdot}84$, n = 2, $0{\cdot}50 < P < 0{\cdot}70$
Radiator	Lung carcinoma	1,191	66	8	6	1,271	Combining all over 30 yrs.:
	Other diseases	1,169	85	12	5	1,271	$\chi^2 = 2{\cdot}89$, n = 2, $0{\cdot}20 < P < 0{\cdot}30$
Other heating	Lung carcinoma	1,192	55	14	10	1,271	Combining all over 30 yrs.:
	Other diseases	1,189	59	16	7	1,271	$\chi^2 = 0{\cdot}17$, n = 2, $0{\cdot}90 < P < 0{\cdot}95$

and the numbers of years were calculated that each patient had been exposed, in his living-room, to a coal fire, a gas fire, an electric fire, an anthracite stove, a radiator, or other form of heating. The results (Table **18,** 16) reveal very little difference in the histories given by the two groups of patients.

Previous Respiratory Illnesses

A large number of the control patients had some respiratory disease, and we clearly cannot assume that the history of previous respiratory illnesses given by these patients would be characteristic of other patients generally. It would not, therefore, be proper to compare the lung-carcinoma patients with the general control groups of patients to determine whether previous respiratory illnesses play any part in the aetiology of carcinoma of the lung. We have accordingly compared lung-carcinoma patients with patients with other forms of cancer (mainly stomach and large bowel, and excluding those in whom the site of origin of the growth was in no doubt and also those with growths elsewhere in the chest, upper respiratory passages, and mouth).

The general cancer group was not selected to be of the same sex and age distribution as the lung-carcinoma group, and it is therefore necessary to allow for sex and age differences between them. For this purpose we have first calculated for *all* the cancer patients put together—lung, stomach, large bowel, etc.—the reported incidence of previous respiratory illness in each sex and 10-year age sub-group. These rates we have then applied to the numbers of patients of corresponding sex and age with (*a*) carcinoma of the lung, and (*b*) other forms of cancer, to calculate how many cases of previous respiratory illness would have occurred in each sub-group if both types of patients had had these same rates of attack. The total number expected for each illness was then readily obtained by summing the numbers in each sub-group. The numbers, 'expected' on the basis of equality, can be compared with the histories actually recorded. To avoid bias due to any confusion between an earlier independent respiratory illness (in which our interest lay) and an illness induced by the presence of the tumour, we included in the analysis only such illnesses as had occurred at least five years before the interview. Occasionally illnesses occurring more than five years previously may have been due to a slow-growing tumour, but the number is unlikely, we think, to be important.

Questions were asked about the past occurrence of pneumonia, pulmonary tuberculosis, pleural effusion, chronic bronchitis, asthma, and chronic nasal catarrh. The results (Table **18,** 17) show that the lung-carcinoma patients more frequently had a history of

TABLE **18**, 17

Frequency of Occurrence of Respiratory Illnesses in the Past History; Lung-carcinoma and Other Cancer Patients*

Type of Respiratory Illness	Lung-carcinoma Patients				Other Cancer Patients				Test of Significance of Difference
	No. of Patients	History of Illness 5 or More Years Previously			No. of Patients	History of Illness 5 or More Years Previously			
		Observed		Expected		Observed		Expected	
		No.	%	No.		No.	%	No.	
Asthma	1,465	19	1·3	19·5	853	13	1·5	12·5	$\chi^2=0.033$, n=1, $0.80 < P < 0.90$
Chronic bronchitis	1,465	254	17·3	222·9	853	94	11·3	125·1	$\chi^2=14.13$, n=1, $P < 0.001$
Chronic nasal catarrh	1,465	198	13·5	189·2	853	90	11·0	98·8	$\chi^2=1.35$, n=1, $0.20 < P < 0.30$
Pleural effusion	1,465	25	1·7	25·7	853	14	1·7	13·3	$\chi^2=0.057$, n=1, $0.80 < P < 0.90$
Pneumonia	1,465	250	17·1	224·8	853	83	10·1	108·2	$\chi^2=10.03$, n=1, $P < 0.01$
Pulmonary tuberculosis	1,465	11	0·8	13·1	853	8	1·1	5·9	$\chi^2=1.09$, n=1, $0.20 < P < 0.30$

* Excluding cancer patients notified incorrectly as having lung carcinoma (see Table **18**, 19)

TABLE 18, 18

Frequency of Occurrence of Previous Pneumonia and Chronic Bronchitis: Lung-carcinoma and Other Cancer Patients,* Sub-divided by Age and Sex

	Men										Women										
	Lung-carcinoma Patients					Other Cancer Patients*					Lung-carcinoma Patients					Other Cancer Patients*				
	No. of Patients	History of Illness 5 or More Years Previously				No. of Patients	History of Illness 5 or More Years Previously				No. of Patients	History of Illness 5 or More Years Previously				No. of Patients	History of Illness 5 or More Years Previously			
		Pneumonia		Chronic Bronchitis			Pneumonia		Chronic Bronchitis			Pneumonia		Chronic Bronchitis			Pneumonia		Chronic Bronchitis	
Age		No.	%	No.	%		No.	%	No.	%		No.	%	No.	%		No.	%	No.	%
25–	17	5 } 18		3 } 16		7	0 } 15		0 } 4		3	1 } 22		0 } 17		7	2 } 12		0 } 0	
35–	116	19		18		46	8		2		15	3		3		26	2		0	
45–	493	83	17	72	15	109	15	14	11	10	38	4	11	10	26	81	4	5	5	6
55–	545	103	19	107	20	213	20	9	27	13	34	3	9	7	21	101	5	5	13	13
65–74	186	26	14	30	16	151	18	12	22	15	18	3	17	4	22	112	9	8	14	13
Total	1,357	236	—	230	—	526	61	—	62	—	108	14	—	24	—	327	22	—	32	—

* See footnote to table 18, 17.

449

preceding pneumonia or chronic bronchitis, while other respiratory illnesses were referred to with approximately equal frequency by the two groups. The differences in the incidence of pneumonia and chronic bronchitis are statistically significant (particularly the latter), though the actual proportion of lung-carcinoma patients with positive histories is not large (with each disease 17 per cent). Detailed figures for the previous occurrence of these two diseases are given in Table **18,** 18. The lung-carcinoma patients show a uniformly higher incidence of each disease in both sexes and in all age groups, though in men many of the differences are quite small. In neither group, however, does the frequency of a past history of pneumonia increase with age as would naturally be expected. It is not unlikely that some older patients forgot their earlier attacks of pneumonia. This being so, the differences found between the lung-carcinoma and the other cancer patients may merely have arisen because patients with a respiratory disease recall more completely their previous respiratory infections—that is, for the very reason which led us to exclude other respiratory illnesses from the control group.   This possibility can, however, be tested by comparing the histories given by patients thought to have carcinoma of the lung when they were interviewed but in whom the diagnosis turned out to be erroneous (Table **18,** 19) with the histories given by the lung-carcinoma patients and by the other cancer patients (Table **18,** 18).

The incorrectly notified patients gave, in nearly every sex and age group, a history of previous pneumonia and chronic bronchitis of similar frequency to that given by the patients with lung carcinoma and of greater frequency than that of the patients with other forms of cancer. For all sex and age groups taken together the proportions with a positive history were:—pneumonia: incorrectly notified patients 20 per cent, lung-carcinoma patients 17 per cent, other cancer patients 10 per cent; chronic bronchitis: incorrectly notified patients 21 per cent, lung-carcinoma patients 17 per cent, other cancer patients 11 per cent.

When age and sex differences are allowed for (Table **18,** 19) the incorrectly notified patients and the lung-carcinoma patients do not differ significantly, while the differences between the incorrectly notified patients and the group of other cancers are highly significant. It would seem, therefore, that the more frequent history of a pre-ceding attack of pneumonia or of frequent attacks of chronic bronchitis in the lung-carcinoma group may well result from

TABLE **18**, 19

Frequency of Occurrence of Previous Pneumonia and Chronic Bronchitis: Patients Incorrectly Thought to have Lung Carcinoma, Subdivided by Age and Sex

Age	Patients Incorrectly Thought to have Lung Carcinoma							
	Men				Women			
	No. of Patients	History of Illness 5 or More Years Previously:				No. of Patients	History of Illness 5 or More Years Previously:		
		Pneumonia		Chronic Bronchitis			Pneumonia		Chronic Bronchitis
		No.	%	No.	%		No.	%	No.	%
25–	17	5 ⎫		2 ⎫		14	1 ⎫		5 ⎫	
35–	48	11 ⎭ 25		7 ⎭ 14		9	4 ⎭ 22		2 ⎭ 30	
45–	79	11	14	10	13	25	4	16	5	20
55–	98	25	26	25	26	15	3 ⎫		3 ⎫	
65–74	25	3	12	9	36	5	1 ⎭ 20		1 ⎭ 20	
All ages	267	55	—	53	—	68	13	—	16	—

Comparison with patients proved to have lung carcinoma

Patients incorrectly thought to have lung carcinoma:

No. giving a history of previous pneumonia 68
No. expected to give such a history .. .. 59·9

$$\chi^2 = 1·64, \ n = 1, \ P = 0·20$$

No. giving a history of previous chronic bronchitis 69
No. expected to give such a history .. .. 61·99

$$\chi^2 = 1·20, \ n = 1, \ 0·20 < P < 0·30$$

Comparison with other cancer patients

Patients incorrectly thought to have lung carcinoma:

No. giving a history of previous pneumonia 68
No. expected to give such a history .. .. 48·22

$$\chi^2 = 13·84, \ n = 1, \ P < 0·001$$

No. giving a history of previous chronic bronchitis 69
No. expected to give such a history .. .. 44·5

$$\chi^2 = 21·43, \ n = 1, \ P < 0·001$$

patients with respiratory symptoms recalling their previous attacks of certain common respiratory illnesses more readily than other patients (though it is possible that the lung-cancer and the incorrectly diagnosed groups both have suffered a greater frequency of such attacks in the past). On the present evidence we feel unable to deduce any aetiological relationship between lung carcinoma and previous respiratory illness.

VALIDITY OF THE RESULTS

The larger and more detailed data that we have presented here confirm those in our preliminary report, and support our conclusion that there is an association between smoking and carcinoma of the lung. Other explanations of the figures might, however, be possible, and we carefully considered several alternatives in our earlier paper—namely, (a) that our group with carcinoma of the lung was unrepresentative of patients with that disease; (b) that the patients in the control group were not truly comparable with the lung-carcinoma patients; (c) that the method of selection of the control patients had led to the choice of patients who smoked less than the average; (d) that the lung-carcinoma patients tended, because of their disease, to exaggerate their smoking habits; (e) that the inter-viewers tended to scale up the smoking habits of the lung-carcinoma patients; and (f) that the individual interviewers might have obtained different results and have interviewed different proportions of the patients in the various disease groups.

The main points of the arguments that we put forward against these alternative explanations are illustrated in Table **18,** 20, which, utilizing the various groups of control patients, shows the pro-portions who smoked different amounts of tobacco, standardized according to the age distribution of the population of England and Wales, between the ages of 45 and 74.

In this standardization the incidence rate of smoking in a given age group in a given sample of patients was applied to the number of men— or women—in that age group in England and Wales to give the numbers of smokers in the general population. The summation of the figures thus derived from each separate sex/age group gave the total distribution in the standard population of smokers of different amounts—which were then converted into a percentage distribution as shown in Table **18,** 20. The two age groups under 45 years were omitted from the calculations because there were few such patients in some disease groups, and these unreliable figures would have been given undue weight in the process of standardiza-tion.

Table **18,** 20 shows (a) that the lung-carcinoma group contains a smaller proportion of non-smokers and light smokers and a higher proportion of heavy smokers than *any* of the other disease groups,

TABLE **18,** 20

The Smoking Habits of Patients in Different Disease Groups,
Standardized According to the Age Distribution of the Population
of England and Wales Aged 45–74, at 30 June, 1950

Disease Group	Percent-age of Non-smokers	Percentage Smoking Daily Average of				No. of Patients Inter-viewed Aged 45–74
		Less than 5 Cigs.	5 Cigs.–	15 Cigs.–	25 Cigs.+	
Men						
Carcinoma of lung	0·3	4·6	35·9	35·0	24·3	1,224
Patients incorrectly thought to have carcinoma of lung	5·3	9·9	35·5	37·8	11·4	202
Other respiratory diseases	1·9	9·9	38·3	38·7	11·2	301
Other cancers	4·6	9·4	47·2	26·0	12·8	473
Other diseases	5·6	9·0	44·8	26·9	13·7	875
Women						
Carcinoma of lung	40·6	13·7	22·0	9·5	14·2	90
Patients incorrectly thought to have carcinoma of lung	66·9	16·4	12·7	4·2	0·0	45
Other respiratory diseases	66·5	22·4	0·0	11·1	0·0	25
Other cancers	68·4	14·3	11·0	5·0	1·3	294
Other diseases	55·9	22·1	17·5	3·6	0·9	157

and (*b*) that the proportions in the group of patients incorrectly
thought to have carcinoma of the lung and in the groups with other
respiratory diseases, with cancer in other sites, and with other
diseases, are similar. We would, as before, lay special stress upon
the group of patients believed by the interviewers to have carcinoma
of the lung at the time of interview, but who proved finally not to
have that disease. This group reveals a distribution of smoking
habits very similar to that shown by the other groups, but very
different from that of the lung-carcinoma patients.

These observations make it unreasonable, we suggest, (*a*) to
attribute the results to exaggeration by the lung-carcinoma patients,
since patients with other respiratory diseases would presumably be
equally inclined to exaggerate their smoking histories; (*b*) to attribute
the results to bias on the part of the interviewers, since patients who
were believed by them to have lung carcinoma but who were finally
proved not to would have been recorded, had there been bias, as

having smoking habits similar to the patients proved to have lung carcinoma; (c) to attribute the results to some special selection of control patients who were, on the average, light smokers, since there is no important difference between patients without carcinoma of the lung who were *notified* to us—that is, the incorrectly diagnosed group and the greater part of the other cancer group—and patients who were *selected* as controls by the interviewers on the basis laid down (that is, the respiratory disease group and the great majority of the 'other diseases' group).

The further extensive data collected since the publication of our first report have proved to be essentially similar to the earlier data, and we have obtained no subsequent information to throw doubt on the validity of the conclusion that there is a real association between smoking and carcinoma of the lung.

Some figures for the smoking habits of the general population of Great Britain in 1951 have been obtained, for other purposes, by the Social Survey of the Central Office of Information, and it is of interest to see how these compare with the habits recorded by our hospital patients. The survey of the general population was made in May, 1951, and was based upon interviews made by trained investigators with a representative random sample of the civilian population of Great Britain aged 21 years and over. The names of persons to be interviewed were selected at random from local records in a representative sample of about 100 urban and rural local authority areas of different types throughout Great Britain. The sample thus adequately represented the population in respect of sex, age, and all other relevant factors. The questions about smoking were part of an extensive investigation concerned mainly with other subjects; they were, however, drawn up in such a way as to permit the replies to be compared with those of our inquiry.

To avoid difficulties of geographical variations in smoking habits we have limited the comparison to patients and individuals in the Social Survey sample who were resident in Greater London—from which the greater part of our data came. To eliminate differences due to variation in smoking habits with age we have taken the age distribution of the Social Survey sample as a standard and adjusted the patients to that age distribution before calculating the percentage distribution of the different grades of smokers (by, as usual, applying the incidence rates of smoking in the patients at each given age to the Social Survey population of that age and summing for the age groups). Persons of 75 and over were excluded. Table **18,** 21 shows that the percentages of non-smokers and light smokers

TABLE **18,** 21

Comparison Between Smoking Habits of Patients Without Carcinoma of the Lung, Interviewed in the Investigation, and of the General Public, Interviewed by the Social Survey Investigators; Residents in Greater London Only

Subjects	Percentage of Non-smokers	Most recent amount smoked. Percentage Smoking:				No. Interviewed
		1 Cig. −	5 Cigs. −	15 Cigs. −	25 Cigs. +	
Men Patients with diseases other than lung carcinoma	7·0	4·2	43·3	32·1	13·4	1,390*
Sample of general public (Social Survey)	12·1	7·0	44·2	28·1	8·5	199
Women Patients with diseases other than lung carcinoma	54·7	13·0	21·6	8·2	2·5	456
Sample of general public (Social Survey)	52·9	16·9	24·3	4·7	1·2	255

*This number is three less than that shown in Table **18,** 13, because the patients interviewed in the special investigation in rural hospitals are not included.

among women agree closely, but it appears on the whole that somewhat heavier smoking habits have been recorded amongst the patients than in the sample of the general public.

Differences in the dates of the interviews (April, 1949, to February, 1952, in the one case, May, 1951, in the other) are unlikely to have influenced the results appreciably, as the national consumption of tobacco varied very little over that period. It may be argued that the differences indicate an association between smoking and many separate diseases; they may, on the other hand, result from the different methods of interviewing and from the different groups of interviewers employed. The comparison certainly provides no evidence that the association we have observed between smoking and carcinoma of the lung can be attributed to a selective choice, for comparison with the lung-carcinoma patients, of other patients who tended to be light smokers.

DISCUSSION

In discussing the data of our preliminary report we concluded that there is a real association between carcinoma of the lung and smoking, but pointed out that this is not necessarily to say that smoking causes carcinoma of the lung.

The association would occur if carcinoma of the lung caused people to smoke or if both attributes were end-effects of a common cause. The habit of smoking was, however, invariably formed before the onset of the disease (as revealed by the production of symptoms), so that the disease cannot be held to have caused the habit; nor can we ourselves envisage any common cause likely to lead both to the development of the habit and to the development of the disease 20 to 50 years later. We therefore conclude that smoking is a factor, and an important factor, in the production of carcinoma of the lung.

Investigations in Germany (Müller, 1939; Schairer and Schöniger, 1943) and in the U.S.A. (Schrek, Baker, Ballard, and Dolgoff, 1950; Wynder and Graham, 1950; Levin, Goldstein, and Gerhardt, 1950; Mills and Porter, 1950) have led to very similar conclusions. In Britain, McConnell, Gordon, and Jones (1952) found no difference between the proportions of 'non-smokers' in 100 lung-carcinoma patients and in 200 control patients (collected at a later date). On the other hand, they showed a considerable difference among cigarette-smokers between the proportions smoking the larger quantities: 44.1 per cent of the lung-carcinoma group had smoked more than 20 cigarettes a day against 23.2 per cent of the controls.

The present analysis of nearly 1,500 cases, or more than double the number dealt with in our preliminary report, supports the conclusion then reached and has revealed no alternative explanation—for example, in the use of petrol lighters.

It has been suggested that subjects with a particular physical constitution may be prone to develop (a) the habit of smoking and (b) carcinoma of the lung, and that the association might therefore be indirect rather than causal (Parnell, 1951). We know of no evidence of such a physical constitution characteristic of patients with lung carcinoma. If it does exist we should still have to find some environmental factor to account for the increased incidence of the disease in recent years.

To say that smoking is a factor in the production of carcinoma of the lung is not, of course, to say that it contributes to the development of *all* cases of the disease. All observers agree that the disease occurs in non-smokers, and in the present series there were 34 such cases confidently diagnosed and histologically proved. These five men and 29 women said that they had never smoked at all or had smoked so little as never to have consumed as much as one cigarette a day for as long as one year. Such patients in the ordinary course of their lives must have inspired air containing tobacco smoke, and it is not possible to say whether the disease would occur in its complete absence. The reasonable presumption is that it would. Experience of cancer in other sites (for example, cancer of the skin) indicates that it is unlikely for one environmental agent to be the effective cause in all cases.

Whether smoking is the sole cause of the *increase* in the disease in recent years is another matter. There is no evidence to show whether there has been an increased incidence among non-smokers. It is certain, we think, that some, if not much, of the increase is spurious and merely the result of improved diagnosis. Rigdon and Kirchoff (1952) have pointed out that in the U.S.A. the death rate attributed to lung cancer in the different States is positively correlated with the number of physicians per 1,000 inhabitants, and it can be shown, from their figures, that this is true independently of the correlation with cigarette consumption—which is also related to the number of physicians per 1,000 inhabitants. The extent to which the increase is real does not, however, affect the present evidence from which the association between smoking and lung carcinoma is deduced. It would be material if it were proved that there had, in fact, been *no* true increase of the disease following a great increase in the consumption of tobacco; but that, in our opinion, is as far from having been proved as that the recorded increase is all real. The position, then, as we see it, is (*a*) that an association has been demonstrated—here and elsewhere—between tobacco-smoking and carcinoma of the lung; (*b*) that, independently of this evidence, there has been a recorded increase over the years in the number of deaths attributed to the disease and an increase has also occurred in the consumption of tobacco, and particularly of cigarettes; (*c*) that the increase in the number of deaths recorded is relatively greater than the increase in the consumption of tobacco, but the actual relation between the real increase in the number of deaths and the increase in the consumption of tobacco is entirely a matter of conjecture.

Needless to say, environmental factors other than tobacco may be responsible for part of the presumed increase. The part played by any such factors cannot, however, be deduced merely from a contemporaneous increase in their incidence and in the death rate from lung cancer—that is, on the basis of a correlation in time: a direct association between the disease and exposure to them must be demonstrated. In the present investigation some additional, but not very strong, evidence was obtained that lung carcinoma is commoner in urban than in rural areas, but otherwise we found no major or clear association apart from that with the consumption of tobacco.

We should perhaps point out that we made no inquiries which would throw light upon a relationship between the development of lung carcinoma and an attack of influenza during the pandemic of 1918–19—a relationship from time to time suggested in the literature (*Lancet*, 1951). It would be difficult to gather sufficiently accurate information on such a disease after the passage of so many years. We may note (*a*) that no appreciable increase in lung cancer has occurred in Iceland (Dungal, 1950), though the influenza pandemic was severe there, and (*b*) that, in Britain, influenza in 1918–19 affected both sexes almost equally (as judged by mortality), while deaths from lung cancer occur predominantly in men.

Year	Influenza (Death Rate per Million)		Year	Lung Cancer (Death Rate per Million)	
	M	F		M	F
1918	3,360	2,967	1948	422	83
1919	1,350	1,101	1949	453	86

All methods of smoking tobacco do not, according to our results, carry equal risks. As in our previous report, smoking a pipe appears to be less closely associated with the disease than smoking cigarettes. In the present observations we have found that, contrasted with other patients, rather fewer of the patients with carcinoma of the lung have used a cigarette-holder or smoked filter-tipped cigarettes. These observations are of interest, though it is impossible to draw any firm conclusions from them since so few people have limited themselves throughout their lives to one method of smoking. It must also be remembered that any smoking technique which is differentially associated with a tendency to light smoking will necessarily, according to our figures, appear to be less closely related to lung carcinoma. Nevertheless, it seems possible, from these results, that pipes, cigarette-holders, and filter tips may, to some unknown extent, each partly separate out an active agent before it reaches the respiratory tract.

On the other hand, the observation that patients who recognize that they inhale are found no more frequently in the lung-carcinoma group than in the control group appears somewhat paradoxical. We pointed out, however, in our preliminary report that until the size of the particles carrying the carcinogen is determined nothing can be stated about the effect which differences in depth of respiration may have on the extent and site of deposition of the carcinogen. From the present extended observations it seems that patients with growths of central origin inhale less frequently than normal (though the difference is very small), while patients with peripheral growths may inhale rather more frequently. Such a finding could be expected if smoke when not 'inhaled' were to penetrate mainly to the large bronchi while inhaling spread the deposition of smoke particles more evenly throughout the bronchial tree.

From the evidence collected about each patient's smoking habits it has been possible to compute some estimates of the risks of dying from carcinoma of the lung in different age groups at different levels of tobacco consumption. These estimates, we would emphasize, are speculative and dependent on the validity of three assumptions: namely, first, that the smoking habits of the lung-carcinoma patients interviewed in this inquiry and resident in Greater London are representative of the habits of all persons dying of the disease in Greater London in 1950; secondly, that the smoking habits of the patients with other diseases interviewed in this inquiry and residents of Greater London are representative of the habits of the general population of Greater London in 1950; and, thirdly, that the actual numbers of deaths from carcinoma of the lung in each sex in Greater London were close to the numbers recorded by the Registrar-General. The only one of these assumptions upon which we have a check is the second. Observations on smoking habits made by the Social Survey upon a cross-section of inhabitants of Greater London do not differ radically from the observations based upon our patients, though they reveal rather fewer heavy smokers than we have found. Keeping these assumptions in mind, our estimates indicate that the risk of dying of lung carcinoma increases with age, as is of course known, and in approximately simple arithmetical proportion with the amount smoked.

A test of the truth of this conclusion is to see whether it accords with the observed incidences of lung carcinoma and of tobacco consumption in different sections of the community and in different parts of the world. In this country there is a pronounced difference in the smoking habits of men and women; it appears inadequate to account for the whole excess of cases which occur in men, as is shown by the different death rates estimated for each sex at each level of tobacco consumption (Table **18,** 12 and Fig. **18,** 1, based upon it). On the other hand, the sex ratio of the relatively few cases observed in non-smokers is not incompatible with a similar incidence in men and women in the absence of smoking—it could not be identical because of risks associated with certain industrial occupations. There is also an appreciable difference in smoking habits between men living in town and country, which should lead to a higher death rate in the towns, but not to the extent that is actually observed.

It may be that other factors also operate to produce these different death rates in men and in women, in towns and in the countryside. On the other hand, the relationship between smoking and lung carcinoma is quite likely to be more complex than that depicted in Table **18,** 12. For example, common observation would suggest that some women—especially the light smokers among them—tend to hold their cigarettes in their mouths less continuously than men and not to smoke them to the end. An equal number of cigarettes a day may not therefore be the same thing, from the point of view of cancer risk when smoked by men and by women. Again, differences in consumption of cigarettes in town and country may have been more pronounced 10 or 20 years ago than they are today. We have no information to guide us.

Stocks (1952) has, however, shown a distinct relation between the size of a town—assessed by the number of occupied dwellings—and the mortality from lung cancer. It would seem likely that some agent other than tobacco (present perhaps in domestic chimney smoke or in the exhaust fumes of cars) is at least partly responsible for the excess mortality in towns.

Comparisons between the recorded death rates at different epochs and in different countries present many difficulties in interpretation. Varying standards of diagnosis of the cause of death, differences in methods of preparation and consumption of tobacco, changes in consumption over the last 50 years, may all introduce gross errors. Nevertheless, some correlation between national figures for cigarette consumption and the death rate from lung cancer would be expected, though in view of the uncertainties of the data the correlation is unlikely to be high. Studying the incidence of lung cancer in some European countries, Daff, Doll, and Kennaway (1951) conclude:

'The consumption of tobacco per head has been for the last ten years rather higher in Switzerland than in the United Kingdom, and in Norway has been about one-half that in the other two countries, while the crude death rates at the beginning and end of the period were roughly in the proportion of ten (England and Wales) to five (Switzerland) and two (Norway). Cigarette consumption was approximately in the proportion of four (England and Wales) to two (Switzerland) and one (Norway), and was more in accord with the relative death rates. The increase in the number of deaths has been about the same (twofold) in all three countries, but the increase in consumption of tobacco and cigarettes has been less. The differences in the incidence of cancer of the lung are therefore quite different in extent from those in the quantity of tobacco consumed; they are more like (though still different from) those in the quantity of cigarettes consumed. The study of the relation between the national consumption of tobacco and the national incidence of cancer of the lung has scarcely begun.'

No responsible agent in tobacco smoke has been detected. The suggestion that arsenic, introduced by insecticides sprayed on the growing crop, might be a factor would seem to be discountenanced by the absence of arsenic from Turkish tobacco and the high proportion of lung carcinoma found at necropsy in Istanbul (Daff, Doll, and Kennaway, 1951; Saglam, 1944). Benzpyrene has not been detected in cigarette smoke (Waller, 1952). Long-continued exposure of mice to atmospheres containing tobacco smoke has failed to produce lung cancer (Campbell, 1936; Lorenz, Stewart, Daniel, and Nelson, 1943), but it may be of significance, in view of our findings, that the smoke was brought to the mice through long tubes. In contrast, tumours of the skin of mice can be produced by the application of tars obtained from tobacco burnt at temperatures which occur in normal smoking (Lamb and Sanders, 1932; Flory, 1941). Goulden, Kennaway, and Urquhart (1952) have pointed out that carcinogenic agents in tobacco smoke and in town dust might supplement one another, and have summarized the available data about the additive effects of two carcinogens. An agent in tobacco

462 STATISTICAL METHODS IN MEDICINE

smoke might be by itself only weakly, if at all, carcinogenic, but might act as a co-carcinogen in the presence of, for example, the benzpyrene in urban atmospheres.

SUMMARY

In an investigation designed to throw light on the aetiology of carcinoma of the lung nearly 5,000 hospital patients have been interviewed by four specially appointed almoners. The interviews took place in the years 1948 to 1952 in hospitals in London, Bristol, Cambridge, Leeds, Newcastle-upon-Tyne, and (for a limited purpose) in the rural areas of Dorset and Wiltshire. The questions asked covered a very wide range, including the occupational histories of the patients, where they had lived and the forms of domestic heating in their homes, their previous attacks of respiratory illnesses, their habits with regard to smoking, and, for other purposes, some particulars of their dietary habits and use of purgatives.

Preliminary figures on tobacco-smoking were published in a previous paper (Doll and Hill, 1950). The present paper gives corresponding data for the whole of the material collected as well as the analysis of other questions included in the inquiry. The main comparisons are between 1,465 patients with carcinoma of the lung and an equal number of 'matched control' patients with other diseases, each of these being carefully chosen so as to be of the same age, the same sex, and, so far as possible, in the same hospital at the same time as a lung-carcinoma patient.

There is no appreciable difference between the two groups in the number of persons belonging to the Registrar-General's five social classes, and no association has been found between any type of occupation and lung carcinoma which would suggest the presence of an aetiological agent likely to be of general significance.

With regard to the possible effects of fumes in the atmosphere, both within and without the home, there is no significant difference between the groups. Of the lung-carcinoma patients 23.0 per cent, and of the control patients 21.5 per cent, had lived near a gasworks for a year or more. Their use of coal, gas, or electric fires or other forms of heating in the living-rooms of their homes did not differ appreciably.

In conformity with the national death rates rather fewer of the lung-carcinoma patients lived, or had lived, in the countryside and more, correspondingly, in the towns.

The lung-carcinoma group in comparison with patients with other forms of cancer more often gave a history of a previous attack of pneumonia and of chronic bronchitis. Detailed analysis of the data suggests, however, that this difference may be due merely to the lung-carcinoma patients, with their respiratory symptoms, recalling more readily than other persons their previous attacks of respiratory illness. The data are not accurate enough for an aetiological relationship to be postulated.

Of the 1,357 men with carcinoma of the lung seven, or 0.5 per cent, were non-smokers (as defined in the text); of the 108 women there were 40, or 37.0 per cent. The corresponding figures for their paired controls were 61 men (4.5 per cent) and 59 women (54.6 per cent). Of the men with lung carcinoma 25.0 per cent reported that they had been smoking, before the onset of their illness, an average of 25 or more cigarettes a day (or the equivalent in pipe tobacco). The corresponding figure for the male control patients was only 13.4 per cent. For women these proportions were 11.1 per cent for the carcinoma group and 0.9 per cent for the controls.

For men these differences are present consistently in each of the five areas of inquiry. For women they are present in London but not in the 28 patients observed in the provincial towns, where only one woman with the heavier smoking habits was found.

Estimated death rates for Greater London (on assumptions stated in the text) indicate that the mortality from carcinoma of the lung may increase in approximately simple proportion with the amount smoked. Amongst men of ages 45–64 the death rate in non-smokers is negligible, while in the heavier-smoking categories it is estimated to reach three to five deaths per annum per 1,000 living.

Regular users of petrol lighters were found with equal frequency in patients with lung carcinoma and in the control patients with other diseases (42.9 per cent and 41.3 per cent): the proportions who said they inhaled were similar (64.6 per cent and 66.6 per cent); and so were the proportions of cigarette-smokers who had smoked mainly hand-rolled cigarettes (20.7 per cent and 19.1 per cent). On the other hand, rather fewer of the cigarette-smoking patients with lung carcinoma had ever used a cigarette-holder, regularly (5 per cent against 12 per cent of the controls), and only three out of 504 had smoked filter-tipped cigarettes, compared with 15 out of 467 controls. The observations in these respects are too few for a definite conclusion, but conceivably they may have a bearing on the appreciably lower risks reported here for pipe-smokers compared with cigarette-smokers. Each of these methods of smoking might partly separate out an active agent before it reached the respiratory tract.

The validity of these various results is studied, and it is concluded that the association between smoking and carcinoma of the lung is real. It is not argued that tobacco smoke contributes to the development of all cases of the disease—a most unlikely event. It is not argued that it is the sole cause of the increased death rate of recent years nor that it can wholly explain the different mortality rates between town and country.

REFERENCES

Board of Trade (1952). *Accounts relating to Trade and Navigation of the United Kingdom, January 1951 and January 1952.* London: H.M.S.O.

Campbell, J. A. (1936). *Brit. J. exp. Path.* **17,** 146.

Council for the International Organization of Medical Sciences, Paris (1953). *Cancer of the Lung (Endemiology.)*

Daff, M. E., Doll, R., and Kennaway, E. L. (1951). *Brit. J. Cancer,* **5,** 1.

Daff, M. E., and Kennaway, E. L. (1950). *Brit. J. Cancer,* **4,** 173.

Doll, R. (1952). *Brit. J. industr. Med.* **9,** 180.

Doll, R., and Hill, A. Bradford (1950). *Brit. med. J.* **ii,** 739.

Dungal, N. (1950). *Lancet,* **ii,** 245.

Flory, C. M. (1941). *Cancer Res.* **1,** 262.

Goulden, F., Kennaway, E. L., and Urquhart, M. E. (1952). *Brit. J. Cancer,* **6,** 1.

Kennaway, E. L., and Kennaway, N. M. (1947). *Brit. J. Cancer,* **1,** 260.

Lamb, F. W. M., and Sanders, E. (1932). *J. Hyg. Lond.* **32,** 298.

Lancet (1951), **ii,** 737.

Levin, M. L., Goldstein, H., and Gerhardt, P. R. (1950). *J. Amer. med. Ass.* **143,** 336.

Lorenz, E., Stewart, H. L., Daniel, J. H., and Nelson, C. V. (1943). *Cancer Res.* **3,** 123.

McConnell, R. B., Gordon, K. C. T., and Jones, T. (1952). *Lancet,* **ii,** 651.

Mills, C. A., and Porter, M. M. (1950). *Cancer Res.* **10,** 539.

Müller, F. H. (1939). *Z. Krebsforsch.* **49,** 57.

Parnell, R. W. (1951). *Lancet,* **i,** 963.

Rigdon, R. H., and Kirchoff, H. (1952). *Tex. Rep. Biol. Med.* **10,** 76.

Saglam, T. (1944). *Bull. Fac. Med. Istanbul.* **7,** pt. 2, 3793.

Schairer, E., and Schöniger, E. (1943). *Z. Krebsforsch.* **54,** 261.

Schrek, R., Baker, L. A., Ballard, G. P., and Dolgoff, S. (1950). *Cancer Res.* **10,** 49.

Stocks, P. (1952). *Brit. J. Cancer,* **6,** 99.

Waller, R. E. (1952). *Brit. J. Cancer,* **6,** 8.

Wynder, E. L., and Graham, E. A. (1950). *J. Amer. med. Ass.* **143,** 329.

CHAPTER 19

LUNG CANCER AND OTHER CAUSES OF DEATH IN RELATION TO SMOKING

ON 31 October, 1951, we sent a simple questionary to all members of the medical profession in the United Kingdom. In addition to giving their name, address, and age, they were asked to classify themselves into one of three groups—namely, (*a*) whether they were, at that time, smokers of tobacco; (*b*) whether they had smoked but had given up; or (*c*) whether they had never smoked regularly (which we defined as having never smoked as much as one cigarette a day, or its equivalent in pipe tobacco or cigars, for as long as one year). All smokers and ex-smokers were asked additional questions. The smokers were asked the ages at which they had started smoking and the amount of tobacco that they were smoking, and the method of smoking it, at the time of replying to the questionary. The ex-smokers were asked similar questions but relating to the time at which they had last given up smoking.

On the basis of their replies to the questionary, we classified the doctors in a few broad groups according to their sex and age, the amount of tobacco they smoked, their method of smoking, and whether smoking had been continued or abandoned. Subsequently we have recorded the deaths occurring in each of these groups. To ensure a high proportion of replies we intentionally made the questionary extremely short and simple. In particular, we did not ask for a life-history of smoking habits, though in studying the incidence of lung cancer, with a long induction period, we realized that the habits of early adult life might be more relevant than the most recent habits. In addition, we have made no further inquiry into any change of habits that may have taken place since October, 1951. In short, we have related the deaths of doctors that have occurred since October, 1951, to the non-smoking, present smoking, and ex-smoking groups as constituted at that date.

It follows that, while we can make an accurate comparison between life-long non-smokers and all smokers *past or present*, any

(With Richard Doll.) Reprinted from the *British Medical Journal*, 1956, **ii,** 1071.

gradient of mortality that we may observe in relation to the amount of smoking will be an *understatement* of the true relationship. We shall, for instance, have included in the group of 'light' smokers persons who had previously smoked 'heavily' but at 1 November, 1951, had reduced their consumption. Similarly, a 'heavy' smoker at 1 November, 1951, may previously have been a light smoker or may since then have given up smoking altogether; we shall have continued to count him, or her, as a heavy smoker. If there is a differential death rate with smoking, we must by such errors tend to inflate the mortality among the light smokers and to reduce the mortality among the heavy smokers. In other words, the gradients we present in this paper may be understatements but (apart from sampling errors due to the play of chance) cannot be overstatements.

In 1954 we published a preliminary report on the results of this inquiry (Doll and Hill, 1954a). The number of deaths from lung cancer was then small (36) and standing alone they would not have justified a firm conclusion. In showing a steadily rising mortality from lung cancer as the amount of smoking increased, they were, however, in close conformity with the figures we had previously found in our extensive retrospective inquiries into the smoking histories of patients with cancer of the lung and other diseases. With the passage of another two years we are now able to present from this prospective inquiry a considerably increased body of data, and, in consequence, a more exhaustive analysis. The four main questions to which we have sought answers are: (1) What are the relative risks of lung cancer associated with the smoking of different amounts of tobacco by different methods? (2) Is there a reduction in the risk if smoking is given up? (3) What is the most likely explanation of the observed association? (4) Is there a relationship between smoking and any other cause of death?

THE EXPOSED TO RISK

The questionary was sent out to 59,600 men and women on the *Medical Register*. Of the 41,024 replies received 40,701 were sufficiently complete to be utilized; 34,494 of these were received from men and 6,207 from women.* For the purposes of the present report

---

* These numbers are slightly different from those given in our preliminary report, as a re-examination of the forms enabled an additional 137 to be utilized, while in a few cases it was found that the age group had been allocated incorrectly.

the doctors concerned have been followed until 31 March, 1956—
that is, for four years and five months. No new additions have been
made to the population and the total number of survivors exposed
to risk at the beginning of each new period of 12 months has therefore steadily diminished. At the same time each of the survivors has
grown older and mortality has, of course, fallen more heavily on
the older age groups; as a result, the age distribution of the population has altered. These changes are shown for men in Table **19,** 1

TABLE **19,** 1

*Number of Men Living in Each Age Group at the Beginning of
Each Year of the Study and the Total Number of Years of
Exposure*

Age in Years	No. of Men Living at:						Total No. of Years of Exposure
	1/11/51	1/11/52	1/11/53	1/11/54	1/11/55	1/4/56	
Under 35	10,140	9,145	8,232	7,389	6,281	5,779	35,489
35–44	8,886	9,149	9,287	9,414	9,710	9,796	41,211
45–54	7,117	7,257	7,381	7,351	7,215	7,191	32,156
55–64	4,094	4,212	4,375	4,601	5,057	5,243	19,909
65–74	2,694	2,754	2,823	2,873	2,902	2,928	12,462
75–84	1,382	1,433	1,457	1,485	1,483	1,513	6,431
85 and over	181	200	223	256	278	296	1,028
All ages	34,494	34,150	33,778	33,369	32,926	32,746	148,686

as well as the total numbers of years of exposure in each age group
during the course of the study. The total number of years for all age
groups is 148,686 for men and 27,187 for women. (These figures
have been obtained by taking the average of the numbers of survivors at the beginning and at the end of each year and summing for
the four years and five months of the study. For example, the
number of male doctors aged 45–54 was 7,117 on 1 November, 1951,
and 7,257 on 1 November, 1952; on average, therefore, there were
7,187 male doctors alive in that age group throughout that year.
Similarly there were 7,319 male doctors alive in the same age group

throughout the second year, 7,366 throughout the third year, 7,283 throughout the fourth year, and 7,203 throughout the first five months of the fifth year. The total number of years lived by male doctors in that age group is therefore calculated to be 7,187 + 7,319 + 7,366 + 7,283 + 5/12 of 7,203, or 32,156 years.)

Figures for the number of years of exposure of men and women with different smoking habits have been obtained in the same way. Table **19,** 2 shows the figures for men, divided according to the daily

TABLE **19,** 2

Total Number of Man-Years of Exposure by Non-smokers and Smokers of Different Amounts of Tobacco: Men Only, Divided by Age

Age in Years	Non-Smokers*	All Smokers	Men Smoking a Daily Average of:		
			1–14 g.†	15–24 g.	25g. or More
Under 35	10,143	25,346	12,548	10,002	2,796
35–44	7,130	34,081	13,625	13,380	7,076
45–54	4,136	28,020	9,477	10,371	8,172
55–64	1,907	18,002	6,333	6,514	5,155
65–74	1,078	11,384	5,201	3,893	2,290
75–84	720	5,711	3,334	1,701	676
85 and over	136	892	616	230	46
All ages	25,250	123,436	51,134	46,091	26,211

* A non-smoker is defined as a person who has never consistently smoked as much as 1 g. of tobacco a day for as long as one year.

† 1 cigarette is equivalent to 1 g. of tobacco.

amount of tobacco stated to have been smoked at the time of the inquiry in 1951, or immediately before smoking had last been given up. It will be seen that the distribution of smoking habits varies considerably from one age group to another, and it will therefore be necessary to use death rates at specific ages, or a rate standardized for age, in comparing the mortality experiences of men in the different smoking categories.

THE DEATHS

Through the courtesy of the Registrars-General in the United Kingdom a form showing particulars of the cause of death has been provided, since the questionary was sent out, for every death identified as referring to a medically qualified person. Lists of the deaths of doctors notified to them since 31 October, 1951, have also been obtained from the General Medical Council and the British Medical Association. These extra sources of information have proved necessary since it is not always possible for the Registrars-General to determine at registration of death that the deceased person was, in fact, a doctor. For example, occasionally the occupation of a doctor who had served in the Army, or who had held a university appointment, may be described at the time of death merely as 'Colonel (retired)' or 'University teacher'. Similarly with a married woman who has ceased to practise medicine there may well be no reference at registration of death to the fact that she possessed a medical qualification. It must also be noted that the deaths of civilians occurring abroad do not form part of the records of the Registrars-General. It has therefore been necessary to seek information about them, and their cause of death, from other sources—from the records of the Service departments, from the Registrars' offices of Commonwealth countries, and, in a few instances, from relatives. For all deaths occurring in the United Kingdom, irrespective of the source of our information, we have ascertained the certified cause of death.

In the 53 months covered by the present study (November, 1951, to March, 1956) 1,854 deaths have been reported. Table **19,** 3, in which they are set out by age and sex, shows that their numbers are small for women and for men under 35 years of age. Our principal analyses in this paper have therefore been confined to the mortality experience of men aged 35 years and above, involving, 1,714 deaths from all causes.

We first classified these 1,714 deaths according to the underlying cause as certified. The eight cases in which we obtained the cause of death only from the other sources mentioned above we classified according to the reported cause; in a further 12 cases we have not yet obtained any statement of cause. Of the total 1,714 deaths among men aged 35 years or more, 82 were certified as due to lung cancer, while in three others lung cancer was mentioned as having contributed to death without being the primary cause. No deaths from lung cancer were reported in men under the age of 35 years and only three such deaths at all ages have been reported among women.

For every one of these 88 deaths we sought confirmation of the diagnosis by writing to the doctor who certified the death and also, when necessary, to the hospital or consultant to whom the patient

TABLE **19**, 3

Number of Deaths of Doctors Reported as Occurring Between 1 November, 1951, and 31 March, 1956, Inclusive

Age in Years	Males	Females
Under 35	34	3
35–44	68	10
45–54	189	8
55–64	311	26
65–74	417	24
75–84	543	23
85 and over	186	12
All ages	1,748	106

had been referred. Additional information on the nature of the evidence was thus obtained in every case and is summarized in Table **19**, 4. In two cases, one male and one female, we have not accepted the cause of death as established. With the man, histological examination of the operation specimen had failed to confirm the presence of a carcinoma. With the woman, the histological report was 'sarcoma of lung'. In seven of the remaining 86 cases the site of the primary growth had been diagnosed by clinical examination only. In 79 the site of the primary growth had been confirmed at necropsy or by operation, bronchoscopy, or radiological examination. Clearly the diagnosis may have been incorrect in some of the cases, but the evidence suggests that it is not likely to have been wrong in more than a small proportion. In making comparisons between the mortality of different groups within the investigation, we have therefore used the 84 male cases in which the additional information did not throw doubt upon the diagnosis of lung cancer.

TABLE **19,** 4

Criteria on Which Diagnosis of Primary Lung Cancer was Based

Diagnostic Criteria	Male Cases		Female Cases
	No.	% of Total	No.
I. Necropsy evidence, with or without histological examination; or histological evidence plus evidence of the site of the primary tumour from operation, bronchoscopy, or radiological examination	39*	46	1†
II. Evidence of the site of the primary tumour from operation and/or bronchoscopy and/or radiological examination, but without histological evidence	38	45	1
III. Evidence from clinical examination only	7	8	0
All cases, diagnosis accepted	84	99	2
Diagnosis not regarded as established	1	—	1

* 16 squamous-cell carcinoma, 16 oat-cell or anaplastic carcinoma, 3 adenocarcinoma, 3 cell-type undetermined, and 1 not examined histologically.
† Squamous-cell carcinoma.

RESULTS

The Amount Smoked

The complete data for the present 53 months of the follow-up have been used, and the death rates per annum from all causes of death and from five groups of diseases have been calculated for four categories of men—namely, non-smokers and smokers of small, moderate, or large amounts of tobacco. These rates have been standardized for age (by the direct method), using the total male population of the United Kingdom aged 35 years or above on

TABLE **19,** 5

Standardized Death Rates Per Year Per 1,000 Men Aged 35 Years or More, in Relation to the Most Recent Amount Smoked*

Cause of Death	No. of Deaths	Death Rate Among:					
		All Men	Non-smokers	All smokers	Men Smoking a Daily Average of		
					1 — 14 g.	15 — 24 g.	25 g. or More
Lung cancer	84†	0·81	0·07	0·90	0·47	0·86	1·66
Other cancer	220	2·02	2·04	2·02	2·01	1·56	2·63
Other respiratory diseases	126	1·10	0·81	1·13	1·00	1·11	1·41
Coronary thrombosis	508	4·78	4·22	4·87	4·64	4·60	5·99
Other causes	779	6·79	6·11	6·89	6·82	6·38	7·19
All causes	1,714	15·48	13·25	15·78	14·92	14·49	18·84

* That is, at 1 November 1951, for those smoking at that time and at the date of giving up for those who had given up at 1 November 1951.

† The three cases in which lung cancer was recorded as a contributory but not a direct cause of death are included under both lung cancer and the cause to which death was assigned by the Rigistrar-General.

31 December, 1951, as the standard population.‡ The results are shown in Table **19,** 5 and in Fig. **19,** 1.

If all causes of death are taken first, it will be seen that the mortality is highest among men who smoked 25 g. or more of tobacco a day (18.84 per 1,000), and that the rates for light smokers (14.92 per 1,000) and moderate smokers (14.49 per 1,000) are 10 to 13 per cent above the rate for non-smokers (13.25 per 1,000). Of the five groups of diseases separately considered, lung cancer is the only one to show a marked and steady increase with the amount smoked. Its death rate rises from 0.07 per 1,000 among non-smokers to 1.66 per

‡ Thus death rates for each cause of death were calculated separately for each age group for each of the smoking categories shown in Table **19,** 2. These age rates for a smoking category were then applied to the corresponding U.K. populations in 1951 to obtain the death rate at all ages that would have prevailed in the U.K. population if it had experienced the rates at specific ages of the particular smoking group.

1,000 among heavy smokers—that is, an increase of approximately twentyfold. Other respiratory diseases and coronary thrombosis also show some increase with rising tobacco consumption, particularly the former. But in both instances the difference between the extreme rates is, compared with lung cancer, relatively small. For other respiratory diseases the rate for heavy smokers (1.41) is 74 per cent above the rate of non-smokers (0.81), while for coronary throm-

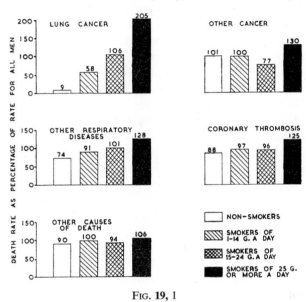

FIG. **19,** 1

Relationship between death rate, expressed as a percentage of the rate for all men, and the amount smoked, for five disease groups.

bosis the corresponding figure is 42 per cent (5.99 to 4.22). The equality of non-smokers and smokers in cancer of other sites is striking and no trend with the amount of smoking is apparent. (These death rates from diseases other than cancer of the lung are considered in more detail in a later section.)

The statistical significance of the differences in the death rates is best assessed from the actual numbers of deaths recorded—that is, by comparing them with the numbers which would have been expected to occur in each smoking category if smoking were un-related to the cause of death under inquiry. For example, 31 men aged 65–74 died with lung cancer. The man-years of exposure in this age group of men who had always been non-smokers (at the time the questionary was completed) formed 8.65 per cent of the total exposure of all men (Table **19,** 2). If the mortality from lung cancer is quite unrelated to smoking, then the proportion of non-smokers among the 31 lung cancer deaths should also be 8.65 per cent. A similar calculation has been made for the numbers of men dying with lung cancer in the other age groups—namely, one at ages 35–44, nine at ages 45–54, 24 at ages 55–64, 16 at ages 75–84, and three at ages 85 and above. The total number of deaths expected among non-smokers of all ages was then obtained by adding the numbers for the separate age groups. Corresponding calculations were made to obtain the number of deaths which would be expected to have occurred in men who smoked small, moderate, or large amounts, and likewise for the other principal disease groups of Table **19,** 5. The results are shown in Table **19,** 6.

If non-smokers are compared with smokers it is found that for all causes of death the observed difference is not quite statistically significant (P = 0.06). Division by cause shows that it is highly significant for lung cancer (P < 0.01) but not significant for any of the other four diseases or groups of diseases. (The numbers of deaths of non-smokers are still small in some of these groups and it is quite possible that significant differences may be obtained with more extensive data.)

When comparisons are made between the different grades of smokers, it is proper to take account not only of the actual extent of the differences but also of the order in which they occur. The statistical test which has been applied to the results is therefore a test of the significance of the trend of the differences between the observed and expected numbers of deaths as the amount smoked increases (Armitage, 1955). It is thus found that there is a significant trend, with an excess of deaths among heavy smokers, for all causes of death (P < 0.01) and a highly significant trend for cancer of the lung (P < 0.001). Other forms of cancer and other diseases reveal no significant change with smoking, and the observed rise in other respiratory diseases and in coronary thrombosis is not, on present numbers, more than might quite easily be due to chance. (With the latter the rise is significant if the non-smokers are brought into the test of gradient along with the smokers of different amounts.)

We may also note, at this point, that a finer analysis of the lung cancer data has shown a marked gradient at each stage of life. The

Observed Deaths From All Causes, and From Particular Causes, in Non-smokers and Smokers Compared With the Number of Deaths that Would Have Been Expected to Occur in Each Such Group if There Were no Association Whatever Between Smoking and Mortality

	Non-smokers	All Smokers	Test of Significance* P	Men Smoking a Daily Average of			Test of Significance† P
				1–14g.	15–24g.	25g. or More	
All causes: Observed deaths	163	1,551	0·06	727	468	356	Less than 0·01
Expected deaths	187·4	1,526·6		751·2	510·2	289·6	
Lung cancer: Observed deaths	1	83	Less than 0·01	22	27	34	Less than 0·001
Expected deaths	8·5	75·5		36·9	28·3	17·9	
Other cancer: Observed deaths	25	195	Between 0·8 and 0·9	95	51	49	Between 0·3 and 0·5
Expected deaths	23·9	196·1		92·8	64·9	37·3	
Other re-spiratory diseases: Observed deaths	11	115	Between 0·3 and 0·5	55	36	24	Between 0·2 and 0·3
Expected deaths	13·8	112·2		59·8	36·5	18·7	
Coronary thrombosis: Observed deaths	44	464	Between 0·1 and 0·2	200	148	116	0·06
Expected deaths	53·9	454·1		211·2	156·7	96·1	
Other diseases: Observed deaths	82	697	Between 0·5 and 0·7	356	207	134	Between 0·7 and 0·8
Expected deaths	87·6	691·4		351·9	224·9	120·2	

* Based on χ^2 test with n = 1.

† Based on χ^2 test applied to the trend with n = 1.

mortality rates for four age groups above 35 years are shown in Table **19,** 7.

Mortality From Lung Cancer in Relation to the Amount Smoked at Different Ages Above 35 Years: Annual Rates Per 1,000 Men

Age in Years	No. of Deaths	Death Rate Among:			
		Non-smokers	Men Smoking a Daily Average of:		
			1–14g.	15–24g.	25g. or More
35–54	10	0·00	0·09	0·17	0·26
55–64	24	0·00	0·32	0·52	3·10
65–74	31	0·00	1·35	3·34	4·81
75 and over	19	0·70	2·78	2·07	4·16
All ages	84	0·07	0·47	0·86	1·66

Method of Smoking

For classifying our population into cigarette smokers, pipe smokers, or smokers by both methods our data are certainly faulty. As pointed out above, the questionary asked for smoking habits at a particular point of time (1 November, 1951) and not for a life-history. In a covering letter we invited doctors to add any information on their smoking habits or histories which they thought might be of interest to us, and a number of them did so. In those instances we have, of course, used all the information given. For example, if a man stated that in November, 1951, he was smoking two ounces of tobacco weekly in a pipe but added in a footnote that previously he had, in addition, smoked 20 cigarettes a day, we classified him as a 'mixed' smoker. But we can be sure that some, and perhaps many, men who had changed their habits did not volunteer this extra information. It follows that some whom we have classified as 'pure' cigarette smokers or as 'pure' pipe smokers really belong to the mixed class. The rates we give in Table **19,** 8 cannot therefore indicate the full extent of the difference in risk associated with the two methods of smoking; the difference must be blurred by this inclusion in each 'pure' group of men who belong to the 'mixed' group. (In the mixed group we have included the few men who smoked cigars.)

TABLE **19**, 8

*Standardized Death Rates Per Year Per 1,000 Men Aged 35
Years or More, in Relation to the Method of Smoking*

Cause of Death	No. of Deaths Among Smokers	Death Rate Among Men Smoking:			Test of Signifi-cance † P
		Pipes	Pipes and Cigarettes*	Cigarettes	
Lung cancer	83‡	0·38	0·68	1·25	Less than 0·001
Other cancer	195	2·37	1·57	2·15	Over 0·95
Other respiratory diseases	115	0·79	0·62	1·52	Less than 0·01
Coronary thrombosis	464	4·22	4·37	5·17	Between 0·1 and 0·2
Other causes	697	5·75	5·79	7·70	0·02
All causes	1,551	13·52	13·03	17·71	Less than 0·001

* Including men who smoked cigars.
† Based on χ^2 test applied to the trend from pipes to cigarettes; $n = 1$.
‡ See second footnote to Table **19**, 5.

However, in spite of this blurring of the picture, we find an excess
mortality among cigarette smokers compared with pipe smokers for
all causes of death and for three of the specific groups. For all causes
of death the trend of the differences is highly significant ($P < 0.001$)
though the mortality of the 'mixed' group is not in step. For lung
cancer the trend is continuous and also highly significant ($P < 0.001$);
the death rate among the cigarette smokers is over three times as
great as the rate among the pipe smokers, The death rate among
cigarette smokers is also higher than that among pipe smokers for
other respiratory diseases, coronary thrombosis, and the miscellaneous group of other diseases. The excess is less marked than for
lung cancer, but it is sufficiently great for the trend to be statistically
significant for other respiratory diseases and for the miscellaneous
group. The mortality from these diseases among mixed cigarette and
pipe smokers is, however, either lower or inappreciably higher than
that among pipe smokers. For cancer of other sites no relationship is
apparent.

The pronounced differences of Table **19,** 8 for persons dying of lung cancer can be explained, to some extent, by the fact that pipe smokers use, on the average, less tobacco than cigarette smokers (in the present study the average was 12g. a day for pipe smokers against 20g. a day for cigarette smokers). This difference in consumption can be allowed for by calculating at each different level the distribution of the observed deaths that would have been expected to occur if the method of smoking bore no relationship at all to the rate of mortality. The resulting figures still show a significant difference between the categories (P < 0.01). The same conclusion can also be reached by calculating separately, for each level of smoking, the standardized death rate for pipe smokers and cigarette smokers. It is then found that the death rate of pipe smokers is less than that of cigarette smokers at each level. We may repeat, too, that the contrasts obtained must almost certainly be an understatement of the true difference.

Effects of Giving up Smoking

To measure any effects that might follow the giving up of smoking, we divided the doctors into three groups: (1) those who, on replying to the questionary, reported that they had given up smoking for at least 10 years; (2) those who reported that they had given up within the previous 10 years; and (3) those who, at 1 November, 1951, reported that they were then smokers. We know nothing of any subsequent changes in habits, so again any contrasts we find between these groups will be minimal. The mortality rates for the three groups are shown in Table **19,** 9. It will be seen that only for cancer of the lung is there a progressive and statistically significant reduction in mortality with the increase in the length of time over which smoking has been given up. Cancer of all other sites shows the same trend, but the observed differences are relatively small, and, with the numbers involved, might be due to chance. On the other hand, for cancer of the lung the mortality among the present smokers at 1 November, 1951, has been three times as great as that among men who at that date had stopped smoking for 10 years or more, and 76 per cent greater than the rate for men who had given up within the previous 10 years.

These differences cannot be accounted for by differences between the three groups in the amount smoked or in the method of smoking. The average amount smoked (at 1 November, 1951, for the smokers

TABLE **19,** 9

Standardized Death Rates Per Year Per 1,000 Men Aged 35 Years or More, in Relation to Giving Up of Smoking

Cause of Death	Total No. of Deaths Among Smokers and Ex-smokers	Death Rate Among:			Test of Signifi-cance* P
		Ex-smokers, who had given up 10 Years or More at 1/11/51	Ex-smokers, who had given up Less than 10 Years at 1/11/51	Smokers at 1/11/51	
Lung cancer	83†	0·35	0·59	1·03	0·02
Other cancer	195	1·31	1·79	2·15	Between 0·1 and 0·2
Other respira-tory diseases	115	1·17	1·28	1·11	Between 0·9 and 0·95
Coronary thrombosis	464	3·98	5·23	4·88	Between 0·3 and 0·5
Other causes	697	7·24	7·22	6·71	Between 0·2 and 0·3
All causes	1,551	14·04	16·11	15·84	Between 0·5 and 0·7

* Based on χ^2 test applied to the trend, n = 1.
† See second footnote to Table **19,** 5.

and at the date of giving up for the ex-smokers) was practically the same—namely, men who had given up for 10 years or more, 18 g. a day; men who had given up within the previous 10 years, 19 g. a day; men who were still smoking, 18 g. a day. In regard to method, the proportion of 'pure' cigarette smokers was also almost the same amongst those who had given up and amongst the continuing smokers—88 per cent in men who had given up for 10 years or more; 87 per cent in men who had given up within the previous 10 years; 84 per cent in men who were still smoking.

We may also note at this point that the average age at which men had given up smoking was 44 years for those who had given up within the last 10 years and 42 years for those who had given up for 10 years or longer.

In spite of these equalities the three groups are, of course, self-selected, and it seems not unlikely that selective factors may play some part in the contrasts of mortality between continuing smokers and ex-smokers of different durations. Thus, amongst those who have more recently given up smoking there are likely to be some who have given up on grounds of ill-health. Such persons are likely to have a higher-than-average mortality in the ensuing years. There is in the figures for all causes of death given in Table **19,** 9 a slight suggestion of such an effect—the death rate is 16.11 per 1,000, compared with 15.84 per 1,000 for those who were continuing to smoke. On the other hand, we would not expect such a selective influence to be very pronounced in our data, since many seriously ill persons would not have returned our questionary at all. In the course of time those with a higher-than-average mortality will have been eliminated and the death rate among the group of persons who gave up smoking many years ago may be expected to fall—the actual figure is 14.04.

While such selective factors might, we think, contribute to the observed trend of mortality from all causes (and from coronary thrombosis in particular), they will not explain the continuous trend of the lung cancer mortality to its highest point in those who were continuing to smoke.

Mortality Among Present Cigarette Smokers

Since the mortality from lung cancer has been shown to be greater (*a*) among cigarette smokers than among pipe smokers, and (*b*) among present smokers than among past smokers, it is clear that the highest rates of mortality must have been recorded among those doctors who were continuing to smoke cigarettes at the time of the inquiry (1 November, 1951). In fact, the mortalities among men in this group are substantially higher than the corresponding mortalities among all smokers—past and present, pipe, cigarette, and mixed (as shown in Table **19,** 5). Thus, for men aged 35 years and over who at 1 November, 1951, smoked 1–14g. a day in cigarettes the subsequent annual mortality from lung cancer has been 0.95 per 1,000; for those similarly smoking 15–24g. a day it has been 1.67 per 1,000; and for those similarly smoking 25g. or more a day it has been 2.76 per 1,000. The corresponding rates for all smokers are 0.47, 0.86, and 1.66. In other words, the rates for the continuing cigarette smokers have been 102 per cent, 94 per cent, and 66 per cent higher than the corresponding rates for all smokers, past or present. While remembering that the numbers involved are small, we may note that the rate for men who were continuing to smoke 25 or more cigarettes a day at the time of the inquiry (2.76 per 1,000) was almost 40 times the rate observed among non-smokers (0.07 per 1,000).

Histological Type

There is now evidence to suggest that the relationship holds only for epidermoid and anaplastic cancers (including oat-cell cancer) and that it apples to a less marked degree (if it applies at all) to adenocarcinoma (Wynder and Graham, 1950; Wynder, 1954; Kreyberg, 1955). In the present study only three of the histologically proved cases were diagnosed as adenocarcinoma. This is too few for rates to be calculated for different smoking categories, but it may, perhaps, be noted that the amount smoked by the three patients (three cigarettes a day, 20 cigarettes a day, and 14 g. daily in a pipe) was, on average, somewhat less than the amount smoked by men of the same ages (12.3 against 16.3 g. a day). whereas the average amount smoked by men dying of epidermoid or anaplastic cancer was substantially greater (23.6 against 16.4 g. a day).

Mortality Among Women

The total number of deaths recorded among women (106) is still too small for reliable estimates to be made of the mortality from different causes among different categories of smokers. Two deaths were attributed to carcinoma of the lung—one a woman of 66 years who smoked 15 cigarettes a day at 1 November, 1951, and the other of a woman of 55 years who smoked 30 cigarettes a day. A third woman, aged 44, was certified as having died of sarcoma of the lung; she had started smoking at the age of 27 years, and smoked 30 cigarettes daily.

The total mortality from all causes of death recorded among women aged 35 years and over has been much less than that recorded among men. Thus their standardized death rate is 7.82 per 1,000 for non-smokers, 7.87 per 1,000 for all smokers, and 16.90 per 1,000 for smokers of 25 or more cigarettes a day (a small group). The corresponding figures for men are 13.25, 15.78, and 18.84 per 1,000. It is very probable that these lower rates for women are not wholly due to a lower actual mortality but partly to a less complete recording.

Deaths in women are likely to be certified according to the married name, whereas a number of the women are recorded in our series only under the name that they used professionally and which they entered upon our questionary. This has created considerable difficulty in identifying the women doctors who replied to the questionary and who have subsequently died. A number of deaths have certainly been missed. A more complete identification is in progress and the further analysis of female mortality in relation to smoking habits is therefore postponed to a subsequent report.

QUESTIONS OF BIAS

Diagnosis of Cause of Death

It might perhaps be argued that doctors have more readily diagnosed lung cancer in heavy smokers than in light smokers or in non-smokers, and have thus produced the gradient of mortality recorded here. As one means of investigating this possibility we wrote in the last two years of the inquiry to all the doctors who signed the death certificates referring to cancer of the lung. We asked them whether they knew the patient's smoking habits when they diagnosed the cause of death, and, if so, whether they thought their diagnosis was influenced by that knowledge. Of the 47 doctors involved, 40 replied that they had some knowledge of their patients' smoking habits and seven that they were ignorant of them. Of the 40 with some knowledge, 36 did not believe that it had in any way influenced their judgement, one thought that it had (the patient was a man of 68 years who smoked 18 cigarettes a day), another that it might have done so subconsciously (the patient was a man of 68 years who smoked 15 cigarettes a day), and two did not express an opinion.

A second, and perhaps more convincing, test of this possible bias can be made by comparing the mortality gradient with smoking for those cases in which the diagnosis was firmly established (category I in Table **19,** 4) with that observed for the cases in which the diagnosis contains a greater element of doubt (categories II and III in Table **19,** 4). The figures are given in Table **19,** 10, from which it will be seen that with the firmly established cases the trend of mortality with smoking is certainly no less steep, and possibly steeper, than that shown by the remaining deaths.

In view of these results it seems to us most improbable that the

TABLE 19, 10

Standardized Death Rates From Lung Cancer in Relation to the Amount Smoked, Divided According to the Basis of the Diagnosis

Basis of Diagnosis		Standardized Death Rate per 1,000 Men Aged 35 Years and Above per Year			
		Non-smokers	Men Smoking a Daily Average of:		
			1–14g.	15–24g.	25g. or More
Category I.* Firm diagnosis based on necropsy, histological evidence, etc. (39 cases)	Rate	0·00	0·22	0·31	0·94
	Rate as % of rate for all men	0	58	80	244
Categories II and III.* Less well established diagnosis lacking histological confirmation (45 cases)	Rate	0·07	0·24	0·55	0·71
	Rate as % of rate for all men	18	56	129	166

* For full definitions see Table 19, 4.

relationship we have observed between smoking and lung cancer can be attributed merely to a biased attitude among the medical profession.

The Population at Risk

In our preliminary report on this inquiry (Doll and Hill, 1954a) we pointed out that the mortality we had recorded amongst doctors in the 29 months of follow-up was considerably less than that which we would have expected to occur at the death rates of the general population. We suggested that the main reason for this—and one which would apply to all causes of death and not only to lung cancer—was that doctors who were already ill of a disease, likely to prove fatal within a foreseeable space of time, would have been disinclined, or indeed unable, to answer our questionary. In other words, we should learn of their deaths but we would have no corresponding completed questionary on our files. The question we had to consider was whether such a bias in the population at risk would differentially affect the mortality of the non-smoking and smoking groups. Could it have artificially produced the gradient with smoking that we had observed with cancer of the lung whilst not producing any such gradient with other causes of death (excepting, possibly, coronary thrombosis)? Not only did that seem to us very unlikely on general grounds, but we noted two specific pieces of evidence in support of our view: (a) although the number of deaths from cancer of the lung was small we had not seen any obvious change in its gradient with smoking over the 29 months of inquiry; (b) the gradient we had observed in this prospective inquiry closely resembled that which we had already obtained in our earlier retrospective inquiry.

The preliminary results of the large-scale inquiry conducted by the American Cancer Society (Hammond and Horn, 1954) showed the same characteristic—namely, a low death rate from all causes in the subjects of the inquiry compared with that of the general population. Further, contrary to our own observations, Hammond and Horn reported an appreciably heavier mortality in smokers than in non-smokers for every disease group examined—for cancer of other sites, for coronary thrombosis, and for other diseases—though the gradient with lung cancer, we may note, was very much sharper than that shown by the other causes.

These results led Berkson (1955) to suggest that not only is the total population in these studies biased, by the absence of the seriously ill at the time of initial inquiry into smoking habits, but that the component smoking and non-smoking groups may be *differentially* biased to the advantage of the latter in the subsequent mortality experience. He points out that this would be the effect if non-smokers in good health came more readily into the study than smokers in good health—for example, because answering the questionary is a simpler task for the non-smoker—whereas the chances of inclusion in the study were low for men seriously ill and *unrelated to the smoking habits*. In such circumstances the already seriously ill component would be artificially low, but still representative of the parent population; the component in good health would be large but unrepresentative. It would contain proportionately too many healthy non-smokers. It follows that the total mortality would be lower than that anticipated from general population rates, and the mortality among non-smokers would be less than that amongst smokers—and for all causes of death.

The final test of Berkson's thesis lies with the passage of time. For as time passes it becomes progressively less likely that the shadow of death could have been foreseen at the start of the inquiry, less likely that such pre-knowledge could have influenced response to our questionary. As stated in our preliminary report, and quoted above, we had seen over the first 29 months no signs of a change in the gradient of lung cancer mortality to suggest an initial selective bias. We are now able to analyse the observations over four complete years. The figures are given in Table **19,** 11 and show, as expected,

TABLE **19,** 11

Standardized Death Rates From Lung Cancer in Each Year of the Inquiry by Amount Smoked

Year of Inquiry (and No. of Deaths)	Standard Death Rate per 1,000 Men Aged 35 Years and Above per Year				
	Non-smokers	Men Smoking a Daily Average of:			All Men
		1–14 g.	15–24 g.	25 g. or More	
1st (12)	0·00	0·29	0·60	0·86	0·53
2nd (14)	0·00	0·26	0·43	1·80	0·57
3rd (31)	0·33	0·82	1·51	2·44	1·31
4th (21)	0·00	0·54	0·98	1·67	0·92
As percentages of rate for all men					
1st	0	54	112	161	100
2nd	0	45	75	315	100
3rd	25	62	115	187	100
4th	0	59	107	182	100

death rates in the third and fourth years of the inquiry substantially greater than those of the first and second years. (With the relatively small population at risk we think the steep rise in the third year and the fall in the fourth year are no more than chance fluctuations.) On the other hand, the *gradient* of mortality in relation to amount smoked has been remarkably constant in the first, third, and fourth years—that is, irrespective of the absolute levels of mortality. The second year shows a much steeper gradient, but with only 14 deaths involved we think no emphasis can be placed upon this. In short, it would seem that the association between death rate and amount smoked has shown very little change between the beginning of the inquiry and the later years. It certainly has not become any less

18

pronounced with more representative death rates. The observations do not seem to us to support Berkson's thesis.

As regards the total mortality of our population of doctors we can also make a check as to how far it has been unrepresentative of the rate for all doctors. For this purpose we have accumulated details of the mortality that has occurred year by year amongst a 10 per cent sample (randomly drawn) of all the doctors who did *not* reply to our questionary. This population of 'non-answerers' was not obtained until several months after the start of the inquiry, when the names of doctors who had died in the first few months had already been erased. We cannot, therefore, reconstruct the total population nor measure the first year's mortality among those who did not reply. In the subsequent years, however, we can estimate the mortality rate of *all* doctors by combining the figures for those who *did* reply to the questionary with the figures for those who did *not* reply (multiplying the sample by 10). In the second year of the inquiry we thus reach a standardized death rate at all ages of 20.4 per 1,000 for all doctors, compared with a rate of 14.7 for those who replied to us. The latter is only 72 per cent of the former, revealing, as we previously recognized, the initial effects of selection through the absence of the seriously ill. In the third year of observation the rate for all doctors is calculated to be 18.6 per 1,000; for those who replied it was 16.1; the ratio is 87 per cent. In the fourth year the rates are respectively 18.4 and 17.0 per 1,000, and the ratio is 92 per cent.

We see, therefore, that though the effect of self-selection initially present may still not have entirely worn off, it is certainly no longer large. Conceivably it may be rather larger than 92 per cent suggests, since it is possible that we are able to trace the deaths of those who replied to us more fully than the deaths of those who did not reply. But we have no evidence to that effect. On the other hand, the difference may never wholly vanish. If non-smokers answered us proportionally more frequently than did smokers, then our population will always contain a higher proportion of the persons who suffer a relatively low mortality rate. In other words, we should *always* have a population which—in total—has a relatively favourable mortality experience. But it does not follow that its components (smokers and non-smokers) cannot be validly contrasted. That very marked contrast is not, as we have shown above, diminishing with the passage of years.

In this analysis we have compared the mortality observed amongst the doctors who answered us with our estimate of the mortality of all doctors whether they answered us or not. This latter figure is, in our view, the proper standard of comparison, to reveal how far our group is representative of the total. If, however, we compare our rate for all doctors with the corresponding figure for the general population of the whole country, we find that the doctors' rate in the last two years of the inquiry has been 83 per cent of the national mortality. We cannot from this result deduce that the deaths of doctors have been incompletely recorded in our inquiry. It may well be that in these years the medical profession was experiencing lower death rates than the general population of all social classes. Unfortunately, in the absence of the national occupational mortality analysis since 1930–2 there is no evidence available.

ASSOCIATION, DIRECT OR INDIRECT

Site of Growth

In relation to the observed association between lung cancer and smoking it has been suggested that smoking does not produce cancer in a person in whom cancer would not otherwise have occurred at all, but merely determines the primary site of a growth that is destined to appear in some part of the body (Fairweather, 1954; Goodheart, 1956). In short, a man predestined to have cancer increases his chance of having it in the lung if he smokes and increases his chances of having it elsewhere in the body if he does not smoke. If he is not predestined to have cancer, smoking and other environmental factors obviously have no relevance. This hypothesis is in line with the general theory discussed by Cramer (1934) that cancer susceptibility is predetermined by heredity, that the effect of environmental stimuli is merely to elicit the response in particular tissues, and that, as a result, the total cancer incidence in a given population is a fixed sum uninfluenced by changes in the stimulus. The primary sites may change, the total does not. The final test of the theory will require accurate observations of cancer morbidity, but several recent studies of cancer mortality seem to us to provide strong evidence that the theory is untrue.

Thus Case (1954) has shown that among certain chemical workers exposed to β-naphthylamine mortality from bladder cancer has been almost double that expected for cancer of *all* sites; the excess in the particular site is certainly not balanced by a reduction in other sites. Similarly Doll (1952, 1955) has shown that the raised death rate from lung cancer among gas workers and asbestos workers is not compensated for by a reduction in mortality from other types of cancer, and Brinton, Frasier, and Koven (1952) have made a similar observation among chromate workers. Case and Lea (1955) have obtained a similar result in another field. They studied 1914–18 war pensioners with chronic bronchitis and found a substantial excess of cancer of the lung, while the mortality from cancer of other sites was normal and unreduced.

Specific to the present issue, Doll and Hill (1954b), in their retrospective study of patients' smoking habits, found no evidence that tobacco produced an effect by the mechanism postulated. While a large excess of heavy smokers was a feature of their lung-cancer group there was no deficit of heavy smokers in patients with cancer in other sites—that is, in comparison with patients with other diseases. The data from the present investigation are also inconsistent with the theory. If tobacco merely determines the site of the cancer without affecting the total incidence of the disease, then the mortality from *all* forms of cancer should be similar among non-smokers and smokers and among the different grades of smokers. In fact it is seen from Table **19,** 5 that the annual death rate from all cancer rose from 2.11 per 1,000 among non-smokers to 2.91 per 1,000 among smokers.* The rise in lung cancer from 0.07 to 0.90 is not balanced by a reduction in cancer of other sites, the rates for which are almost identical—2.04 and 2.02 per 1,000 in non-smokers and smokers respectively. In the smoking grades the total cancer rates are almost the same in the 1–14 g. and 15–24 g. groups—namely, 2.48 and 2.42—but the substantial rise in lung cancer in the heavy smoking group (1.66) is certainly not balanced by any fall in cancer of other sites. The total incidence of 4.25 per 1,000 is significantly higher than that of the other two groups of smokers and of the non-smokers.* In short, our data, both retrospective and prospective,

---

* The death rates for all cancer shown for smokers (2.91 per 1,000) and for heavy smokers (4.25 per 1,000) are slightly lower than the sum of the rates for lung cancer and for other cancer, since one doctor suffered from primary cancer in both lung and larynx and his death was included in both categories in Table **19,** 5.

indicate a total incidence of cancer in the smoking groups in excess of the incidence that would have prevailed in the absence of smoking.

Constitutional Type

The observed association between the mortality from lung cancer and the amount of smoking could conceivably be explained in terms of some common factor which produced lung cancer and was also associated (directly or indirectly) with cigarette smoking. For example, it has been suggested that constitutional and psychological factors might have such an effect—that is, that persons of a certain 'make-up' are peculiarly liable to lung cancer and to smoke. We know of no published evidence to this effect. It is difficult, too, to see how such indirect association could explain the rise in lung cancer mortality of recent years.

Atmospheric Pollution

It has been argued that, since cigarette smoking is, in general, more prevalent in towns than in country districts, the comparison of different smoking groups is, in part, merely a comparison of urban and rural residents, the former being exposed to an atmospheric pollution which the latter escape. On the other hand, if the difference between the smoking habits of town and country were somewhat greater 20 to 30 years ago than it is today, there may be no reason at all to invoke atmospheric pollution as the explanation of the higher mortality from lung cancer in urban areas. Cigarette smoking could, in that event, be the answer. However that may be, atmospheric pollution could not account for the pronounced gradient in mortality that we record here. For example, the national figures record that the lung-cancer death rate among men in Greater London is about twice that among men in rural districts. Our data, prospective and retrospective (Doll and Hill, 1952) give a mortality among the heavy smokers more than twenty times the mortality among non-smokers. Further, the association with smoking has been shown to persist when the observations are limited to men living within a particular type of area. We ourselves found it for male patients resident in Greater London (Doll and Hill, 1952); Stock and Campbell (1955) have reported a most marked gradient within two wholly rural counties of North Wales and a slighter gradient in the City of Liverpool; Hammond and Horn (1955) have found consistently higher death rates for smokers compared with non-smokers within specific types of areas in the U.S.A.

Finally, in this present study we have analysed the smoking habits of doctors resident in different types of areas (using a 10 per cent sample randomly drawn from the questionaries returned by doctors aged 35 years and over). The results show (Table **19**, 12) that within this

TABLE **19**, 12

Numbers of Doctors Aged 35 Years or Over Smoking Different Amounts of Tobacco (Most Recent Amount Smoked) According to Place of Residence at 1 November, 1951

Amount Smoked Daily	Percentage Smoking given Amount in:			
	Greater London (525 Doctors)	Large Towns in the U.K.* (716 Doctors)	Elsewhere in the U.K. (1,147 Doctors)	Abroad or Unspecified Place (46 Doctors)
Nil	16	13	11	13
1–14 g.	31	32	35	35
15–24 g.	34	38	31	33
25 g. or more	19	17	23	19
Total	100	100	100	100

* County boroughs in England and Wales together with Belfast, Edinburgh, and Glasgow.

occupationally relatively homogeneous population there is remarkably little difference between the smoking habits of the residents in the specified areas. The tendency is for more non-smokers and fewer heavy smokers to be found in the large urban communities. It follows that the contrasts in lung cancer mortality that we have observed between smokers and non-smokers, and between light, medium, and heavy smokers, cannot be explained in terms of a differential exposure to atmospheric pollution which happens to be associated with smoking habits.

SMOKING IN RELATION TO DISEASES OTHER THAN LUNG CANCER

For the large number of deaths attributed to other causes further information was not specially sought from the certifying doctors, and these deaths have therefore been classified according to the cause of death as certified (or by the informant in the few cases where no such information was available). In the main the Registrar-General's rules for the classification of causes of death have been followed, but occasionally some other classification seemed more appropriate and was adopted. The observed death rates for individual diseases other than lung cancer are not, therefore, strictly comparable with the national rates.

Cancer of Other Sites

Deaths attributed to cancer of sites other than the lung are shown in Table **19,** 13. In none of the groups is the difference between

TABLE **19,** 13

Standardized Death Rate Per 1,000 Men Aged 35 Years and Over Per Year, for Cancer of Sites Other than the Lung

Site of Primary Cancer	No. of Deaths	Death Rate Among:					
		All Men	Non-smokers	All Smokers	Men Smoking a Daily Average of:		
					1–14 g.	15–24 g.	25 g. or More
Upper respiratory and upper digestive tracts	13	0·12	0·00	0·14	0·13	0·09	0·21
Stomach	32	0·29	0·41	0·28	0·36	0·10	0·31
Colon and rectum	57	0·52	0·44	0·53	0·54	0·37	0·74
Prostate	30	0·28	0·55	0·25	0·26	0·22	0·34
Other sites (excluding lung)*	88	0·81	0·64	0·83	0·72	0·76	1·02
All cancer, other than cancer of the lung	220	2·02	2·04	2·02	2·01	1·56	2·63

* Including seven of unspecified primary site.

smokers and non-smokers significant, and in none is there a steady —or significant—increase in death rate with the amount smoked. One group consists of deaths attributed to cancer of the upper respiratory or upper digestive tracts, types of cancer which, it has been suggested, may also be related to smoking. It will be seen that no death occurred among non-smokers and the highest death rate occurred among heavy smokers, but the total number of cases is at present too small to give reliable results. The 13 deaths include one from cancer of the buccal cavity, eight from cancer of the oeso-phagus, and four from cancer of the larynx; the average amount smoked by these men was 17.3 g. a day, against an average of 15.1 g. for all men of corresponding ages in the inquiry.

Coronary Thrombosis

The data for deaths from coronary thrombosis have already been given in Tables **19,** 5, **19,** 6, **19,** 8, and **19,** 9, and in Fig. **19,** 1. The increase in mortality with the amount smoked (from 4.22 per 1,000 non-smokers to 4.64 for men smoking 1–14 g., 4.60 for men smoking 15–24 g. a day, and to 5.99 per 1,000 men smoking 25 or more g. a day) is consistent with the existence of a slight relationship,

TABLE **19,** 14

Death Rates From Coronary Thrombosis in Relation to the Amount Smoked, Recorded During the Earlier and Later Parts of the Inquiry

| Period | | Standardized Death Rate per 1,000 Men Aged 35 Years and Above per Year | | | |
| | | Non-smokers | Men Smoking a Daily Average of: | | |
			1–14 g.	15–24 g.	25 g. or More
First 30 months (278 cases)	Rate	4·20	4·46	4·83	5·59
	Rate as % of rate for all men	89	95	103	119
Subsequent 23 months (230 cases)	Rate	4·32	4·85	4·33	6·37
	Rate as % of rate for all men	89	100	89	131

and this, as noted previously, is not very likely to be due to chance (P = 0.02). To test whether this result might, however, be due to a selective bias on the part of the doctors replying to the questionary (as previously discussed) the data obtained in the first two and a half years of the inquiry have been compared with those obtained in the subsequent 23 months. Table **19,** 14 shows that in the second period the increase in mortality is certainly less regular than that observed in the first period, though in both periods the highest rate falls on heavy smokers. It does not seem likely that the trend is entirely due to bias arising from the method of investigation.

Our findings agree broadly with those of Hammond and Horn (1954), in that both sets of data show an increase in mortality with smoking. But in our experience the increase is distinctly less marked. These different results might, we thought, be due to the difference in the age of the subjects, our population of doctors being of all ages over 35 and Hammond and Horn's men being limited to 50–69

TABLE **19,** 15

Relationship at Different Ages Between Mortality From Coronary Thrombosis and Most Recent Amount Smoked: Standardized Death Rates Per Year Per 1,000 Men Aged 35 Years or More

Age in Years	No. of Deaths	Death Rate Among:			
		Non-smokers	Men Smoking a Daily Average of:		
			1–14g.	15–24g.	25g. or More
35–54	90	0·44	0·95	1·47	1·84
55–64	122	7·34	6·79	4·45	6·98
65–74	143	11·13	10·77	10·53	14·85
75 and over	153	15·18	20·00	22·27	24·95
All ages 35 and over	508	4·22	4·64	4·60	5·99

years. Analysis of our death rates from coronary thrombosis by age, however, reveals an even greater discrepancy. We find a distinct gradient of mortality with amount of smoking at ages under 55 and a rather less distinct gradient at ages 75 and above. We observe none at ages 55–74 (Table **19,** 15). A possible explanation of this paradox may lie in the fact that we have classified men as dying of coronary thrombosis solely on the basis of the certified cause. It is, perhaps, reasonable to suppose that, for this group of deaths, the diagnosis is most likely to be accurate at the youngest ages.

Other Causes of Death

The results for other causes of death are shown in Table **19**, 16. They reveal a steady increase in mortality from non-smokers to

TABLE **19**, 16

Standardized Death Rates Per Year Per 1,000 Men Aged 35 Years or More, in Relation to the Most Recent Amount Smoked: Diseases Other than Cancer and Coronary Thrombosis

Cause of Death	No. of Deaths	Death Rate Among:					
		All Men	Non-smokers	All Smokers	Men Smoking a Daily Average of:		
					1–14g.	15–24g.	25g. or More
Pulmonary tuberculosis	19	0·18	0·00	0·20	0·16	0·18	0·29
Chronic bronchitis	42	0·37	0·12	0·39	0·29	0·39	0·72
Other respiratory diseases	65	0·56	0·69	0·54	0·55	0·54	0·40
Cardiovascular diseases other than coronary thrombosis	279	2·36	2·23	2·37	2·15	2·47	2·25
Cerebral haemorrhage or thrombosis	227	2·03	2·01	2·02	1·94	1·86	2·33
Peptic ulcer	18*	0·17	0·00	0·19	0·14	0·16	0·22
Violence	77	0·68	0·42	0·73	0·82	0·45	0·90
Other diseases (including 12 of unspecified nature)	183	1·60	1·45	1·63	1·81	1·47	1·57

* Including five cases in which peptic ulcer was referred to as a contributory cause, but not the direct cause of death.

heavy smokers in three instances—pulmonary tuberculosis, chronic bronchitis, and peptic ulcer. For chronic bronchitis the increase is sixfold (from 0.12 per 1,000 among non-smokers to 0.72 per 1,000 among smokers of 25g. or more a day) and the trend is statistically significant (P < 0.01). Further analysis shows that the death rate is higher among cigarette smokers (0.61 per 1,000) than among mixed pipe and cigarette smokers (0.21 per 1,000) or pure pipe smokers (0.21 per 1,000), and these differences are significant (P < 0.01). With such a chronic disease it is obvious that the disease itself may influence the amount smoked and thus obscure any relationship. It may also be that the presence of a 'smoker's cough' may influence the physician to attribute death to chronic bronchitis when, in its absence, he would have diagnosed some other respiratory (or cardiovascular) condition. Table **19,** 16 does, in fact, show some fall in the mortality from 'other respiratory diseases' as smoking increases, suggesting a transference from one label to another. But this fall does not wholly compensate for the rise in chronic bronchitis mortality.

The differences observed between the various categories of smokers dying with pulmonary tuberculosis or peptic ulcer are not statistically significant; but the numbers of deaths are so small that strong relationships with smoking might exist, without significant results being obtained. The average amount smoked by the 19 men who died of pulmonary tuberculosis was 19.5 g. a day, against an average of 15.2 g. for all men in the inquiry of corresponding ages; for the 18 men who died with a peptic ulcer the average was 18.8 g. a day, against an expected average of 15.3 g.

Possible Related and Unrelated Causes

In the causes of death that we have analysed there are six which have from time to time been regarded as possibly related to smoking —namely, cancer of the lung, cancer of the upper respiratory and upper digestive tract, coronary thrombosis, chronic bronchitis, peptic ulcer, and, recently (Lowe, 1956), pulmonary tuberculosis. In the present study 676 doctors died of these causes—nearly 40 per cent of all the deaths in the doctors aged 35 years and over. We have set out the death rates from these causes in Table **19,** 17. Alongside them we give the rates derived from all other causes of death. The relative stability of these other rates (based upon over 1,000 deaths) is, we think, striking. They provide, we suggest, a further answer to the question of selective bias. If the association suggested by the upper part of the table were due merely to a bias in our method of investigation, we would expect to see that bias operating to some extent in all, or nearly all, causes of death. It does

TABLE **19**, 17

*Standardized Death Rates Per Year Per 1,000 Men Aged 35
Years or More in Relation to Amount Smoked; a Summation of
Groups of Causes of Death*

Causes of Death	No. of Deaths	Death Rate Among:			
		Non-smokers	Men Smoking a Daily Average of:		
			1–14 g.	15–24 g.	25 g. or More
Lung cancer Cancer of upper respiratory and upper digestive tracts Pulmonary tuberculosis Chronic bronchitis Peptic ulcer } *	168	0·19	1·13	1·62	2·99
Coronary thrombosis	508	4·22	4·64	4·60	5·99
Diseases possibly related to smoking	676	4·41	5·77	6·22	8·98
All other diseases	1,038	8·84	9·15	8·26	9·87

* The figures given are lower than those obtained by summing the figures for the five individual groups of diseases, because eight deaths included in Tables **19**, 5 and **19**, 16 under lung cancer and peptic ulcer have been excluded. For these deaths, lung cancer and peptic ulcer were certified only as associated causes; they are included here in the disease group to which death was primarily attributed.

not appear to do so. Secondly, if the effect of smoking were merely to influence the apparent cause of death, without in any way determining the occurrence of death, the second group of diseases should show a negative association complementary to the positive association of the first group. They do not do so.

SUMMARY AND CONCLUSIONS

1. In reply to a questionary sent out at the end of 1951, over 40,000 men and women on the British *Medical Register* informed us of their smoking habits at that time or, in the case of ex-smokers, when they previously gave up smoking. On the basis of these answers we classified them into a few broad groups—namely, non-

smokers and smokers (or ex-smokers) of three different amounts by cigarette, pipe, or both (Tables **19,** 1 and **19,** 2). The subsequent mortality of each of these groups has now been recorded for nearly four and a half years (Table **19,** 3). The present study relates to men aged 35 years and above, amongst whom there were 1,714 deaths, including 81 from lung cancer (in three others lung cancer was mentioned as a contributory cause).

2. The analysis shows that in this population there has been a marked and steady increase in the death rate from lung cancer as the amount smoked increases. Its death rate per year rises from 0.07 per 1,000 in non-smokers (based upon the observations of one death only) to 0.47 per 1,000 in 'light' smokers of 1 to 14g. a day, to 0.86 per 1,000 in 'medium' smokers of 15 to 24g. a day, and finally to 1.66 per 1,000 in smokers of 25g. or more a day (1g. is almost equal to one cigarette). The death rate of the heavy smokers is approximately twenty times the death rate of the non-smokers (Tables **19,** 5 and **19,** 6).

3. This rising mortality from lung cancer in smokers compared with non-smokers, and in heavy smokers compared with lighter smokers, has been a feature of each stage of life, 35–54 years, 65–74, and 75 years and over (Table **19,** 7).

4. The mortality from lung cancer has been substantially and significantly greater in cigarette smokers than in pipe smokers, with smokers by both methods falling in between (Table **19,** 8). This difference between pipe and cigarette smokers is to be observed for each of the smoking categories, light, medium, and heavy, and therefore appears to be a function of the method of smoking irrespective of the amount.

5. Those who reported themselves as smokers at 1 November, 1951, have been compared with those who had given up smoking at that time within the previous 10 years or for more than 10 years. The comparison reveals a progressive and significant reduction in mortality with the increase in the length of time over which smoking has been given up (Table **19,** 9).

6. From conclusions 4 and 5 it follows that the highest mortalities have occurred amongst those who reported themselves as continuing to smoke cigarettes at 1 November, 1951. Among them the annual death rate rose from 0.95 per 1,000 for smokers of one to 14 cigarettes a day, to 1.67 per 1,000 for smokers of 15 to 24 cigarettes a day, and to 2.76 per 1,000 for smokers of 25 cigarettes or more a

day—that is, to approximately forty times the death rate of the non-smokers.

7. For every death attributed to cancer of the lung confirmation of the diagnosis was sought from the certifying doctor and, when necessary, from hospital or consultant. Additional information was obtained in every case. The deaths can thus be divided into those quite firmly established by necropsy, histological evidence, and the like, and those less well established and lacking histological evidence (Table **19**, 4). The increased death rate associated with the increase in smoking is found to be just as great with the firmly established cases as it is with the remainder (Table **19**, 10). The relationship cannot therefore be attributed to a biased attitude in the medical profession in certifying cancer of the lung as the cause of death.

8. Analysis of the deaths from lung cancer separately in each of the first four years of the inquiry shows that the increase in mortality associated with increase in smoking has been a feature of each year. On the whole there has been a remarkably constant gradient which has become no less marked with the passage of time (Table **19**, 11). We also estimate that in the fourth year of the inquiry the mortality of the doctors who answered the questionary was as much as 92 per cent of the mortality of all doctors, whether they answered us or not. On these grounds we do not believe that the gradient of mortality with smoking can be regarded as merely an artifact due to bias in those who chose to reply to the questionary.

9. An analysis of a random sample of the questionaries shows that there was remarkably little difference between the smoking habits of doctors resident (at 1 November, 1951) in Greater London, in large towns, or in other districts (Table **19**, 12). The contrasts in lung cancer mortality between smokers and non-smokers, and between light, medium, and heavy smokers, cannot therefore be attributed to a differential exposure to atmospheric pollution which happens to be associated with smoking habits. This observation supports those of previous investigations.

10. Study of the deaths from cancer in sites other than the lung reveals, with one possible exception, no association between mortality and smoking. The exception is cancer of the upper respiratory and upper digestive tracts, from which the number of deaths is at present insufficient to substantiate a possible trend. In total, cancer of sites other than the lung shows a mortality of 2.04 per 1,000 in non-smokers and 2.02 per 1,000 in smokers. It reveals no gradient

by amount smoked (Table **19**, 13). In other words, the marked and steadily increasing mortality from lung cancer in association with smoking is not compensated for by a decrease in cancer of other sites. The result indicates a total mortality from cancer in the smoking groups in excess of the mortality that would have prevailed in the absence of smoking.

11. If the causes of death as certified are accepted at their face value, mortality from coronary thrombosis reveals a slight but significant relationship with smoking (Table **19**, 5). Division by age, however, shows that the trend is distinct only at the youngest ages, 35–54 years (Table **19**, 15).

12. Three other causes of death show a steady increase in mortality from non-smokers to heavy smokers—chronic bronchitis, peptic ulcer, and pulmonary tuberculosis (Table **19**, 16). Only with chronic bronchitis is the gradient statistically significant. The remaining causes of mortality reveal no trend (Table **19**, 17).

13. From our retrospective studies of the smoking habits of nearly 1,500 patients with lung cancer and over 3,000 patients with other illnesses we concluded that if large groups of persons of different smoking habits were observed for a number of years they would reveal distinct differences in their rates of mortality from lung cancer. They would show, we believed, (1) a higher mortality in smokers than in non-smokers, (2) a higher mortality in heavy smokers than in light smokers, (3) a higher mortality in cigarette smokers than in pipe smokers, and (4) a higher mortality in those who continued to smoke than in those who gave it up. In each case the expected result has appeared in the prospective inquiry here reported. These results are evident in spite of the fact that our method of inquiry is such as constantly to *underestimate* the mortality differences. The reason for the underestimate is that our classifications are based, for the most part, upon a statement of the smoking habits at one point of time. We have seldom been able to take previous habits into account, and any subsequent changes have been unknown to us. As a result we shall sometimes have included in the light smoking group persons who had previously smoked heavily for a long time; we shall sometimes have included as 'pure' pipe smokers persons who had previously smoked cigarettes and vice versa; we shall sometimes have continued to class as smokers persons who have given up. All such errors in classification must inevitably have reduced the, neverthe-

less, clear associations between the mortality from lung cancer and the smoking of cigarettes which we have observed in these British doctors.

REFERENCES

Armitage, P. (1955). *Biometrics*, **11,** 375.
Berkson, J. (1955). *Proc. Mayo Clin.* **30,** 319.
Brinton, H. P., Frasier, E. S., and Koven, A. L. (1952). *Publ. Hlth. Rep. Wash.* **67,** 835.
Case, R. A. M. (1954). *Brit. med. J.* **ii,** 987.
Case, R. A. M., and Lea, A. J. (1955). *Brit. J. prev. soc. Med.* **9,** 62.
Cramer, W. (1934). *Lancet,* **i,** 1.
Doll, R. (1952). *Brit. J. industr. Med.* **9,** 180.
Doll, R. (1955). *Brit. J. industr. Med.* **12,** 81.
Doll, R., and Hill, A. Bradford (1952). *Brit. med. J.* **ii,** 1271.
Doll, R., and Hill, A. Bradford (1954a). *Brit. med. J.* **i,** 1451.
Doll, R., and Hill, A. Bradford (1954b). *Brit. med. J.* **ii,** 240.
Fairweather, R. F. (1954). *Brit. med. J.* **ii,** 100.
Goodhart, C. B. (1956). *Brit. med. J.* **i,** 1296.
Hammond, E. C., and Horn, D. (1954). *J. Amer. med. Ass.* **155,** 1316.
Hammond, E. C., and Horn, D. (1958). *J. Amer. med. Ass.* **166,** 1159.
Kreyberg, L. (1955). *Brit. J. Cancer*, **9,** 495.
Lowe, C. R. (1956). *Brit. med. J.* **ii,** 1081.
Stocks, P., and Campbell, J. M. (1955). *Brit. med. J.* **ii,** 923.
Wynder, E. L. (1954). *Penn. med. J.* **57,** 1073.
Wynder, E. L., and Graham, E. A. (1950). *J. Amer. med. Ass.* **143,** 329.

CHAPTER 20

POLIOMYELITIS IN ENGLAND AND WALES
BETWEEN THE WARS

THE starting-point of the study here reported was a Press reference in the early summer of 1953 to poliomyelitis being
epidemic in the County of Essex. I could recall at least three previous
epidemics in that same county. But, remembering that Essex is a
large county, was there anything odd about that? Was it merely
due to chance or were there localities in this country which poliomyelitis specially tended to visit or in which it particularly cared to
linger? In an attempt to answer those questions I set about extracting
the relevant information, based upon the notifications published in
the weekly and annual reports of the Registrar General of England
and Wales.

THE NOTIFICATIONS OF POLIOMYELITIS

Poliomyelitis first became notifiable in this country in 1912 but,
avoiding the years of the first World War as possibly atypical, I took
the year 1919 as my starting-point. Whilst I was delving into the
records of these early years Benjamin and Logan (1953) published
an article on the Geographical and Social Variations in the incidence
of Notified Poliomyelitis. Their field of study was directed, however, to the large-scale epidemics of recent years, 1947–50. This
enabled me to bring my own observations to an end in the year 1946
and yet to be in a position to compare past with present. What I
have called 'between the Wars', is, therefore, roughly the period
between their two conclusions, namely 1919 to 1946.

There will, of course, be much error in the original uncorrected
notifications. The hospital survey of 1947 made by Bradley and
Gale (1949) showed that among 6,762 patients admitted to hospital
with a diagnosis of poliomyelitis, or polio-encephalitis, the diagnosis
was subsequently confirmed in only about 70 per cent. On the other
hand, in earlier years the error might lie rather in omission than

Presidential Address to the Section of Epidemiology and Preventive Medicine.
Reprinted from the *Proceedings of the Royal Society of Medicine*, 1954, **47**, 795.

addition—that, in particular, the non-paralytic case would go unreported. For example Bruce Low in his report to the Local Government Board in 1915–16 wrote that

'there is evidence that in some towns poliomyelitis is endemic though attracting little attention. For example, in the borough of Sunderland, which had, in 1911, a population of 165,295, paralysed children are brought year after year to the Sick Children's Hospital where the true nature of the ailment is recognized. In 1912 the hospital books show that 8 such cases were treated; 10 in 1913, 9 in 1914, 12 in 1915. On the other hand, the Medical Officer of Health for the borough only received six notifications of poliomyelitis between September 1912 and March 1916'

(Low, 1916). His reference is to the early years of notification (and of war) which I deliberately excluded from my account. But, clearly, such errors will have continued throughout all years, on some unknown scale and with, quite possibly, changes taking place with the passage of time. They must inevitably blur the picture I put forward, they may even so distort it as to make it worthless. That we must consider.

THE CALCULATION OF EXPECTED CASES

In their study of the large-scale epidemics of 1947–50 Benjamin and Logan compared the recorded notifications in each administrative county and county borough with those that would have occurred in each such area or town if it had suffered the average attack rate that had prevailed in all England and Wales. I have followed the same procedure for the earlier years. In each year 1919–46 I first calculated the attack rate in all England and Wales (notifications/total population), and then in each year separately I applied the attack rate to the mid-year population of each administrative county and each county borough. The observed and 'expected' cases in each area I then summed into three periods— 1919–28, 1929–38, 1939–46. Taking the ratio of the observed to the expected cases I can compare these results with those found by Benjamin and Logan. For this purpose I grouped the counties and county boroughs into four groups on the basis of their observed/ expected ratios in 1947–50 (regardless of the standard errors and statistical significance of the ratios). The four groups I took are:

(1) Areas with observed cases less than 66 per cent of those expected in 1947–50.

(2) Areas with observed cases 66–99 per cent of those expected in 1947–50.

(3) Areas with observed cases 100–133 per cent of those expected in 1947–50.

(4) Areas with observed cases 134 per cent or more of those expected in 1947–50.

The observed/expected ratios for these same groups in earlier years are set out in Tables **20, 1** and **20, 2**.

THE CONTRAST OF 1947–50 WITH EARLIER PERIODS

It is clear that with the administrative counties (Table **20, 1**) the four groups have tended to occupy the same position in each of the four periods of time. Those with relatively low attack rates in the wide-scale epidemics of 1947–50 experienced also, on the average, a relatively low attack rate during the years of 1919–46 when the incidence of the disease in this country was small. To counties with relatively high rates in 1947–50, high rates were no new phenomenon. The same type of picture is revealed by the county boroughs (Table **20, 2**) but it is certainly less distinct. In terms of correlation coefficients these associations are shown in Table **20, 3**.

TABLE **20,** 1

The Ratio of Observed (O) to Expected (E) Cases in Groups of Administrative Counties

Groups of Administrative Counties		Period of Years				
		1947–50	1939–46	1929–38	1919–28	1919–46
Group I. 8 A.C.s with observed	O	520	175	202	203	580
cases less than 66% of the expected	E	990	224	246	230	701
in 1947–50	%	53	78	82	88	83
Group II. 24 A.C.s with observed	O	7,340	1,714	1,958	1,476	5,148
cases 66–99% of the expected in	E	8,330	1,776	1,912	1,620	5,307
1947–50	%	88	97	102	91	97
Group III. 21 A.C.s with observed	O	7,445	1,843	1,665	1,351	4,859
cases 100–133% of the expected	E	6,710	1,454	1,523	1,285	4,261
in 1947–50	%	111	127	109	105	114
Group IV. 8 A.C.s with observed	O	906	168	181	152	501
cases 134% or more of the ex-	E	508	112	121	110	343
pected in 1947–50	%	178	151	149	138	146
Group V. London A.C.	O	2,743	339	745	745	1,829
	E	2,147	417	700	701	1,818
	%	128	81	106	106	101

TABLE **20,** 2

The Ratio of Observed (O) to Expected (E) Cases in Groups of County Boroughs

Groups of County Boroughs		Period of Years				
		1947–50	1939–46	1929–38	1919–28	1919–46
Group I. 32 C.B.s with observed	O	1,120	314	500	454	1,268
cases less than 66% of the ex-	E	2,288	489	617	573	1,678
pected in 1947–50	%	*49*	*64*	*81*	*79*	*76*
Group II. 28 C.B.s with observed	O	2,373	448	616	648	1,712
cases 66–99% of the expected in	E	2,767	581	700	600	1,879
1947–50	%	*86*	*77*	*88*	*108**	*91*
Group III. 15 C.B.s with observed	O	2,313	520	561	532	1,613
cases 100–133% of the expected	E	2,083	490	585	527	1,602
in 1947–50	%	*111*	*106*	*96*	*101*	*101*
Group IV. C.B.s with observed	O	2,549	301	348	440	1,089
cases 134% or more of the ex-	E	1,486	317	366	323	1,006
pected in 1947–50	%	*172*	*95*	*95*	*136*	*108*

* If the exceptional epidemic in Kingston-upon-Hull be excluded this percentage falls to 93.

TABLE **20,** 3

The Degree of Correlation Between the Ratios of Observed to Expected Cases in (a) 1947–50, (b) Each Earlier Specified Period

	1919–28	1929–38	1939–46
Administrative Counties (62)	0·26	0·45	0·33
County Boroughs (83)	0·10	0·19	0·23

THE GEOGRAPHICAL VARIATIONS IN 1919–46

For the years 1919–46 as a whole the geographical vagaries under-lying these associations are shown in Fig. **20,** 1 (in which the county boroughs have been included in the administrative counties—they usually, but not always, behave in the same fashion). The most striking characteristics of the distribution are the significantly low ratios of the northern and most of the Welsh counties, and the significantly high ratios of, perhaps, three distinct groups of counties, (*a*) the East Riding of Yorkshire, Lincolnshire (Parts of Lindsey and Kesteven), Leicestershire and Rutland, (*b*) Herefordshire and Shropshire on the Welsh borders and extending into Radnor and, probably, Montgomery, and (*c*) a long southern belt of counties stretching across the country from Devon, and probably Cornwall,

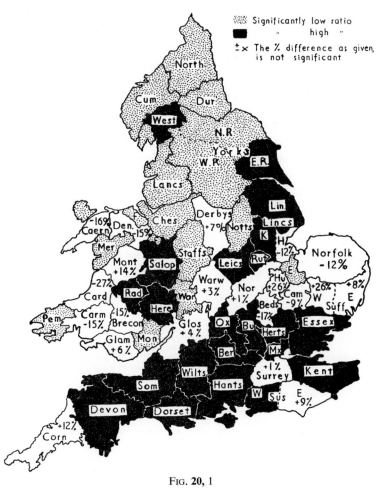

Significantly low ratio
          "   high "
±× The % difference as given,
     is not significant

FIG. **20**, 1

Counties of England and Wales. Observed/Expected Cases in 1919–46
A.C's. together with Associated C.B's.

to Essex and Kent. Correlating these ratios for 1919–46 with the
corresponding ratios for 1947–50 gives a coefficient of 0.43. In
other words there was quite an appreciable degree of similarity in
the geographical scatter of poliomyelitis in its day of low incidence
in 1919–46 and in its widespread epidemicity in 1947–50.

Can this similarity, these geographical differences, be explained
wholly in terms of inaccurate diagnosis or of notification? I would

have thought not. For instance, most of the Welsh counties have low rates; yet where they touch the borders of Hereford and Salop cases do not go undetected; the counties of Radnor and Montgomery have distinctly unfavourable experiences. The year-after-year deficiency in the northern and north-western counties does not prevent repeated, though small, epidemic outbreaks being detected and reported in Westmorland. The little group of counties (Parts of Holland (Lincolnshire), Cambridge, Ely, Peterborough, Northamptonshire, Bedfordshire and Huntingdon) is hemmed in by areas of relatively high incidence to north and south. Yet their observed cases in 1919–46 (366 in total) were 13 per cent below expectation.

Further contrasts are given numerically in Table **20,** 4. That the observations and habits of so many doctors can vary so considerably

TABLE **20,** 4

Some Selected Examples of Observed and Expected Cases

Counties with associated County Boroughs	1919–28			1929–38			1939–46		
	Obs.	Exp.	Ratio	Obs.	Exp.	Ratio	Obs.	Exp.	Ratio
Westmorland	29	9	*322*	17	10	*170*	36	10	*360*
Cheshire and Lancashire	633	937	*68*	741	1,024	*72*	665	876	*76*
Lincolnshire, Kesteven and Lindsey	102	79	*129*	217	89	*244*	143	79	*181*
Nottinghamshire	93	102	*91*	78	121	*64*	91	112	*81*
Herefordshire and Salop	74	55	*135*	71	58	*122*	85	57	*149*
Staffordshire	204	216	*94*	152	242	*63*	218	217	*100*
Oxfordshire	58	29	*200*	101	36	*281*	76	38	*200*
Bedfordshire	24	32	*75*	25	39	*63*	46	43	*107*

over so long a span of years in these closely contiguous areas would not seem to be very likely. To seek some other explanation would, therefore, seem justifiable and, possibly, profitable.

THE GEOGRAPHICAL VARIATIONS IN DETAIL

A. Towns

In promoting the search a more detailed picture of the main areas of epidemicity must first be constructed. In so doing I studied the year-by-year variations in recorded incidence in each individual city and county both in relation to their annual movements, up or down, between 1919 and 1946, and also with regard to the number of cases actually observed in any given year as compared with those that might have been expected at the average rate of that year (*i.e.* the rate for all England and Wales). With these criteria I endeavoured to pick out all the most striking epidemic events of these 28 years. In the process many small foci—a dozen cases in a town when two or three would have been expected—were, or course, omitted. Even those selected will very often have had quite low attack rates in relation to the populations at risk but they *were* distinct epidemics, *i.e.* in terms of those pre-1947 days of, in this country, low polio-myelitis incidence.

The relevant figures for the county boroughs are given in Table 20, 5. It may be noted that of the total 83 boroughs only 20 appear

TABLE **20,** 5

County Boroughs Experiencing Epidemics in Given Years
(in Brackets Observed and Expected Cases)

Bristol	1919 (17, 6)	1921/22 (40, 9)	1929 (18, 5)	1938 (24, 15)
Oxford	1919 (18, 1)	1932/34 (15, 3)	1938 (34, 3)	1941 (29, 3)
Sheffield	1922 (19, 5)	1924 (53, 10)	1931 (45, 4)	1932 (24, 8)
Plymouth	1919 (18, 3)	1921 (18, 3)	1928 (13, 2)	
Kingston-upon-Hull	1927 (109, 6)	1933 (36, 6)	1938 (25, 4)	
Cardiff	1923 (46, 3)	1924 (22, 4)	1940 (43, 6)	
Portsmouth	1934 (27, 4)	1938 (19, 9)	1944 (10, 2)	
Manchester	1936 (30, 10)	1939 (31, 12)	1941 (31, 15)	
Birmingham	1923/24 (74, 33)	1935 (26, 16)	1940 (55, 28)	
Leicester	1926 (80, 7)	1938 (26, 9)		
Grimsby	1930 (36, 1)	1938 (17, 3)		
Wolverhampton	1940 (25, 4)	1945 (16, 3)		
Liverpool	1923 (37, 13)			
Merthyr Tydfil	1923 (21, 1)			
Nottingham	1926 (31, 8)			
Leeds	1940 (26, 13)			
West Ham	1937 (18, 5)			
Reading	1938 (17, 4)			
Swansea	1938 (40, 6)			
Lincoln	1941 (17, 2)			

here as having shown a substantial epidemic spread during the 28 years and only 12 have had more than one distinct outbreak. On the other hand there are nine large towns in which poliomyelitis was epidemic three or four times in this quarter of a century, *viz.* Bristol, Oxford, Sheffield, Plymouth, Kingston-upon-Hull, Cardiff, Portsmouth, Manchester and Birmingham. Is this mere chance or has any special environmental characteristic tended to bring these cities to the forefront? It seems idle to seek the answer in general socio-economic conditions as measured by the proportions of un-skilled workers, infant mortality, housing density and so on. Various workers have already failed to discover any such associations (Benjamin and Logan, 1953; Daley and Benjamin, 1948; Hill and Martin, 1949). There is, however, one possibly relevant feature, namely the large number of ports which appear in the list. Of the total 20 towns, half are ports (including West Ham under the port of London) while of the leading nine towns with several epidemic experiences six are ports (the exceptions are Oxford, Sheffield and Birmingham). It would seem possible, therefore, that in these years of low prevalence in England and Wales quite frequent introductions of the disease were being made from abroad but that these intro-ductions did not succeed in spreading seriously or very far afield. To take two examples: In 1927 there was a particularly severe epidemic in Kingston-upon-Hull—109 cases in a population of 297,000 or a rate of 37 per 100,000 persons. There was some spread to immediately adjacent areas for a rise is shown in the East and West Ridings, in Leeds C.B. and in the Parts of Lindsey in Lincoln-shire. The rest of the country appears quite unaffected. Three years later, in 1930, there was an outbreak of the same relative magnitude in Grimsby, 36 cases in a population of 92,000 or a rate of 39 per 100,000. The Parts of Lindsey, Lincolnshire, were also heavily affected but almost entirely on the eastern side of the county and particularly in Cleethorpes U.D. and Grimsby R.D. There was a slight spread in Northamptonshire. The rest of the country appears free.

B. Counties

Table **20,** 6 gives similar figures for the Administrative Counties. Of the total 62 areas 19 appear to have had at least one distinct epidemic, 14 have had two or more outbreaks, and seven have had three, four or five outbreaks during the 28 years under review, *viz.* Essex, Hampshire, Cornwall, Westmorland, Parts of Lindsey (Lincolnshire), Kent and Somerset. In some of these counties with repeated epidemics it would appear likely that the spread may well have been from the ports referred to in the previous table. Thus in relation to the Parts of Lindsey in Lincolnshire it may be noted that its epidemics took place in the same years as those occurring in Kingston-upon-Hull (1927), in Grimsby (1930) and in both these

TABLE **20**, 6

Administrative Counties Experiencing Epidemics in Given Years
(in Brackets Observed and Expected Cases)

Essex	1926 (90, 30)	1936 (72, 17)	1937 (62, 25)	1938 (181, 50)	1945 (44, 28)
Hampshire	1928 (21, 5)	1934 (37, 7)	1938 (34, 19)	1941 (26, 13)	1944 (22, 7)
Cornwall	1919 (29, 5)	1921 (24, 4)	1941 (19, 9)	1945 (29, 7)	
Westmorland	1922 (15, 1)	1924 (9, 1)	1937 (9, 1)	1940 (17, 2)	
Lincs. Lindsey	1927 (17, 5)	1930 (61, 3)	1938 (37, 10)	1942 (21, 4)	
Kent	1926 (86, 33)	1937 (55, 25)	1939 (80, 25)	1942 (36, 19)	
Somerset	1934 (18, 6)	1940 (23, 13)	1942 (20, 8)	1944/46 (59, 22)	
Hertfordshire	1937 (23, 9)	1941 (34, 14)	1945/46 (63, 20)		
Derbyshire	1920 (23, 5)	1932 (20, 10)	1935 (27, 10)		
Leicestershire	1926 (69, 8)	1935 (37, 5)	1938 (20, 7)		
Wiltshire	1929 (19, 4)	1934 (19, 4)	1946 (18, 5)		
Berkshire	1934 (20, 3)	1938 (23, 8)	1941 (56, 7)		
Devonshire	1937 (33, 8)	1944 (23, 6)			
Sussex E and W.	1938 (73, 20)	1944 (24, 7)			
Yorks.					
East Riding	1927 (37, 3)				
Dorset	1945 (21, 5)				
Buckinghamshire	1941 (63, 10)				
Gloucestershire	1935 (31, 5)				
Carmarthenshire	1938 (40, 6)				

ports (1938). Only in 1942 does it appear alone with no obvious origin. Similarly, in 1919 and 1921 Plymouth appears in the epidemic list and it is possible that the epidemics in Cornwall emanated from here. The years 1934, 1938 and 1944 were epidemic years in Hampshire and there were also epidemics in Portsmouth (a very slight one in 1944). These associations in space and time between ports and hinterland are obviously suggestive though unfortunately it must be admitted that no clear distinction can be drawn between cart and horse. In other of these counties, however, there is a further suggestion of introductions from abroad. Thus in 1926 the main brunt of the Essex epidemic fell upon Grays Thurrock, situated upon the Thames. The notifications suggest a subsequent spread to Tilbury U.D. and the adjacent Orsett R.D. Concentrated mainly within a couple of months (17 July to 25 September) Grays Thurrock had some 40 cases in a population of 18,000, or an incidence of 220 per 100,000. In the October of the same year, 1926, the famous Broadstairs epidemic took place in the County of Kent. It had been preceded in August by small though sharp outbreaks in the urban districts of Sheerness and Queenborough at the mouth of the Thames.

One other point of interest may be noted in Table **20**, 6. In spite of the generally low notification rate in the Welsh counties, including Carmarthenshire, this county appears in the list with a pronounced outbreak in 1938. This would suggest again that it is not for lack of recognition of the disease and notification of cases that certain areas normally have favourable low rates of attack.

GEOGRAPHICAL VARIATIONS WITHIN COUNTIES

Administrative Counties are, of course, very large areas. In discussing the apparent localization of the disease in epidemic form, it will, therefore, be necessary to look within the county boundaries. This has already been done by Gale and Hargreaves (1953) in a most interesting study of poliomyelitis in the Counties of Devon and Cornwall over the years 1911 to 1952. They could find no direct evidence of the introduction of infection from other parts of England into these two holiday counties but they did observe a tendency for outbreaks to recur in the same rather ill-defined areas, sometimes at intervals of many years. These areas revealed no common social characteristics to which these recurrences could be attributed. I do not possess the data to allow me to study in similar close and interesting detail the events that have taken place in other counties. I have, however, considered the distribution of notifications in space and time in a few of the counties given in Table **20,** 6 and I offer these as illustrative. Whenever possible I have also consulted the relevant annual reports of the Medical Officers of Health. With changing local authority boundaries it is not easy to compute and compare the incidence over so long a period of time. The available statistics, too, often differ, though usually slightly, between weekly reports, annual reports and reports of the M.O.H. Often I must offer epidemiological impressions rather than completely accurate statistics.

A. Westmorland

The County of Westmorland is particularly interesting for its small but very clear epidemic recurrences set mainly in an area notable for its relative absence of notifications. Here, there was an extremely sharp epidemic prior to the period with which I am concerned. In the report of the County Medical Officer of Health for 1922 it is said that there were outbreaks in 1910 to the seaward of the County—in Barrow-in-Furness in Lancashire, Workington,

Maryport and Carlisle in Cumberland. Once again we have a possible importation by sea. In the summer and autumn of the following year, 1911, 51 cases were reported in Westmorland. They fell almost wholly in two areas, the Borough of Kendal with 22 cases and the Rural District of South Westmorland with 27 cases. Eleven years later, 1922, the same strip of South Westmorland Rural District was affected, with 10 cases; of the remaining five notifications in that outbreak the Borough of Kendal claimed four. The Medical Officer of Health reports that there were three cases in the village of Staveley and that in that same village the 1911 outbreak began with five cases (Fig. **20**, 2).

In 1924 there were three notifications very early in the year (mid-February) from Westmorland; in the more usual autumn epidemic period five cases came from Kendal. In 1937 the localization was wholly different. All nine notifications came from North Westmorland and there was an associated rise in Penrith over the Cumberland border. On the other hand the epidemic of 1940 returns to the more usual haunts with two cases in Kendal and 14 in South Westmorland. Eleven of these were notified in one week and were, it is reported, from a privately evacuated school.

In this brief history there are two points of interest. There does appear to have been a very distinct tendency for the disease to be unduly localized in the southern rural district of the county and in the Borough of Kendal—remembering, at the same time, that these areas contain some half of the population of the county. The second point of interest is the period of these epidemics. In 1922 most of the notifications lay in the weeks ending 14 October to 18 November, in 1924 27 September to 1 November, in 1937 18 September to 27 November and mostly after mid-October, while in 1940 11 of the 14 cases in South Westmorland were reported in the week ending 9 November. We do not, of course, know the dates of onset and often notifications are long delayed. But these outbreaks do seem to show, for this country, an unduly late period of the year.

B. Leicestershire

Turning to the Midland areas I took for closer study the County of Leicestershire. Here there have been three epidemics—a major outbreak in 1926 and minor outbreaks in 1935 and 1938. All three reveal a quite distinct and similar localization of cases. They have a concentration in mid-county and in its eastern parts, and an almost entire absence in the west. Thus in 1926 the areas principally affected were the Borough of Loughborough (seven cases), Barrow Rural District (17 cases), Billesdon Rural District (13), Melton Mowbray Urban District and Rural District (five cases), Wigston Magna Urban District and Blaby Rural District (eight cases). This epidemic spread as far west as Hinckley Urban District and Rural District (13 cases) but as stated in the report of the Medical Officer of Health 'a relative immunity was shown by the coal mining districts of the western part of the county' (Fig. **20**, 3). In the smaller epidemics of 1935 and 1938 it is the same areas that appear prominently— Loughborough M.B. (four and one case), Barrow R.D. (four and three cases), Melton U.D. (four and two cases), Billesdon R.D. (two and two cases), Blaby R.D. (one and three cases), Melton and Belvoir R.D. (17 and three cases). Except for Shepshed U.D. (one and four cases) the western areas do not appear at all in these epidemic years and, indeed, over all the years 1931 to 1946 (for which figures are readily available) they have reported but a handful of cases—*e.g.*, the Urban Districts of Coalville, Ashby de la Zouche, Ashby Woulds and Oadby. The Medical Officer of Health in his report for 1938 himself notes that these three epidemics 'had a very similar distribution, most of the cases occurring in the Melton Mowbray area in each instance'. Possibly, as he suggested in 1926, the disease 'selects sparsely populated areas, in which acquired immunity is low, rather than populous areas, where the threshold of resistance to common infections is relatively high'.

C. Berkshire

On the other hand the third county whose figures I examined in more detail—Berkshire—hardly fits that hypothesis. It suffered two small outbreaks in 1934 and 1938 and a relatively severe one in 1941. The epidemic of 1934 struck the Newbury and Hungerford area (some 13 cases) and to a lesser extent Cookham, Windsor and Wokingham (nine cases). Both in 1938 and 1941 it was this more urban side of the county that was affected. There were eight cases in Wokingham R.D. and 12 in Easthampstead R.D. in 1938. In 1941 there were 50 notifications revealing small foci in the Rural Districts of Wokingham (three), Cookham (six), Easthampstead (three), and Windsor (two), and relatively large outbreaks in New Windsor M.B. (14 cases) and Maidenhead M.B. (22 cases). Totalling the three epidemics gives 79 notifications in a population (at 1938) of about

Fig. **20, 3**

Diagram of Leicestershire

FIG. **20**, 2

Diagram of Westmorland

115,000 persons in this relatively small eastern and more urbanized section of the county (Boroughs of Maidenhead, New Windsor and Wokingham; Rural Districts of Cookham, Easthampstead, Windsor and Wokingham). On the other hand there were only 28 notifications in a population of almost identical size in the whole of the remainder of the county (Boroughs of Abingdon, Newbury and Wallingford, Urban District of Wantage, Rural Districts of Abingdon, Bradfield, Faringdon, Hungerford, Newbury, Wallingford and Wantage) Fig. **20,** 4.

The tendency to recurrences in the same localities is not as striking in Berkshire as in Westmorland and Leicestershire but there are some signs that it is there. On the other hand, examination of two further counties, Wiltshire and Hampshire, gave no such suggestion. In both counties the small outbreaks appeared to be widespread and the foci that arose, such as Swindon and Aldershot, did not recur.

THE ABSENCE OF EPIDEMICS IN CERTAIN TOWNS AND AREAS

Equally striking is the complete lack of epidemics, or even a ripple on the yearly level, in certain large towns and other areas. Examples are given in Fig. **20,** 5 which relates to four selected county boroughs in the Counties of Durham, Lancashire, Cheshire and the West Riding. Between 1919 and 1946 none of these towns shows any epidemic fluctuation. Annually they report no cases at all or only two or three. Yet when the widespread epidemic of 1947–51 appeared they still remained but little affected. In these years each had, as Benjamin and Logan show, a level substantially and significantly below the average for the whole country. Their relative absence of cases, between 1919 and 1946 would have rendered, them particularly vulnerable, one might have expected, to the widespread infection of 1947. If, on the other hand, the absence of overt cases in the mid-war years implies subclinical infections and the maintenance of a high level of immunization, continuing into the post-period, then the question again arises, why this should be a feature of these towns and not of many other equally densely populated towns in England and Wales? What are the characteristics that differentiate them?

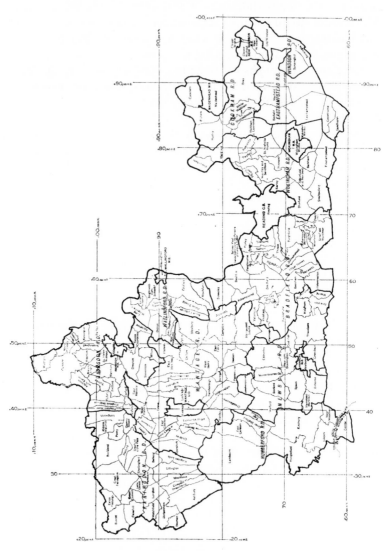

Fig. 20, 4

Diagram of Berkshire

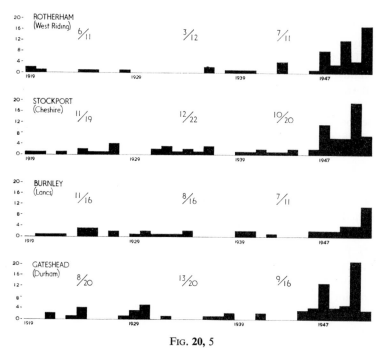

Annual notifications of Poliomyelitis in four County Boroughs

FIG. 20, 5

Annual notifications of poliomyelitis in four County Boroughs with observed and expected cases for specified periods

THE AGE INCIDENCE OF ATTACK

At a loss to answer these questions I pass to other aspects of my subject. The changing age distribution of attack during the present century has naturally attracted much attention. There is no doubt that, in this country at least, more older persons are attacked then heretofore. Figures given by Benjamin and Gale (1949) show the following proportional distribution for reported cases in England and Wales:

Period	0–4 years	5–14 years	15 and over
1912–19	65%	28%	7%
1944–48	32%	36%	32%

The figures for 1944–48 are almost identical with those published by Logan (1952) for 1947–50 (34 per cent, 35 per cent and 31 per cent). These changes are clearly far beyond what might be due merely to the changing age constitution of the population at risk (as may be shown by converting the absolute figures into rates of attack).

The figures for 1912–19 Benjamin and Gale extracted from the Annual Reports of the Medical Officer of the Local Government Board and the first report of the Chief Medical Officer of the Ministry of Health. They lament that 'unfortunately there is a long period, from 1920 to 1943, for which comprehensive figures for the whole country are not available'. While that statement is undoubtedly true I believe that much information, and possibly representative information, on the age distribution in these years could be gleaned from a study of the reports of Medical Officers of Health. I have not made any such general study but I have consulted the local reports for all the areas in which in any given year there has been some epidemic spread. Most of these reports give age particulars of the notifications. Clearly epidemic areas may not be representative and might well have an unusual age incidence; but in fact the figures I have compiled for such county boroughs are not very dissimilar from those given for the whole country in 1912–19 by Benjamin and Gale (Table **20**, 7). Their figures were 65, 28 and 7 per cent; for half a dozen county boroughs in 1919–23 I have 70, 24 and 6 per cent. The interesting point of the table is the relative lack of change between 1919–23 and 1931–37—possibly a slight increase in the proportion of older persons attacked but certainly very slight. In 1938, when England and Wales experienced its sharpest epidemic up to that time, there was, however, a decided break. A much greater proportion of the notifications fell at school ages and beyond. This change persisted in 1939–46 and in the widespread epidemics of 1947 and subsequently it has become still more marked. Again age changes in the population at risk can play but a small part. Conceivably, however, it might be due merely to the fact that I am considering different groups of county boroughs in these years. I have, therefore, limited the comparisons to four towns which experienced epidemics both in earlier years and in 1938 (Table **20**, 8). The same picture still emerges. On the other hand some few figures available from county records reveal a much higher age distribution than that of the towns from 1919 onwards; and they show no such change in 1938 (Table **20**, 7).

TABLE **20**, 7

The Age Distribution of Notified Cases in Different Periods of Time

Age in Years	County Boroughs												Administrative Counties					
	1919–23		1924–26		1927–30		1931–37		1938		1919–28		1929–37		1938	
	No.	%	No.	%	No.	%	No.	%	No.	%	No.	%	No.	%	No.	%
0–4	140	70	147	74	136	67	145	66	85	39	41	40	64	39	21	37
5–14	49	24	39	19	52	25	58	26	92	42	48	46	74	45	25	45
15+	13	6	15	7	16	8	17	8	41	19	15	14	26	16	10	18
Total	202	100	201	100	204	100	220	100	218	100	104	100	164	100	56	100

The areas involved are:

County Boroughs:

1919–23	Bristol, Oxford, Plymouth, Birmingham, Liverpool, Cardiff.
1924–26	Sheffield, Walsall, Cardiff, Nottingham, Leicester.
1927–30	Leeds, Kingston-upon-Hull, Liverpool, Bristol, Grimsby.
1931–37	Sheffield, Liverpool, Kingston-upon-Hull, Wigan, St. Helens, Portsmouth, Exeter, Manchester, Gt. Yarmouth, West Ham.
1938	Ipswich, Swansea, Reading, Grimsby, Bristol, Portsmouth, Kingston-upon-Hull, Cardiff, Oxford.

Administrative Counties:

1919–28	Westmorland, Rutland, Leicester.
1929–37	Lancashire, Devon, Leicester.
1938	Carmarthen, Leicester.

TABLE **20**, 8

The Age Distribution of Notified Cases in Four County Boroughs*

Age in Years	1919–33		1938	
	No.	%	No.	%
0–4	198	66	49	46
5–14	77	26	35	32
15+	25	8	26	22
Total	300	100	110	100

* The County Boroughs and the years involved are:
Bristol, 1919, 1921, 1929, 1938.
Oxford, 1919, 1938.
Cardiff, 1923, 1924, 1938.
Kingston-upon-Hull, 1927, 1933, 1938.

19

A similar time study was made by Benjamin and Gale for the County of London and revealed a significant rise in the average age of attack 'after the middle of the 1930s'. The change appears to have started there in 1933–5 but to have become much more pronounced in 1936–8. I would agree with them that it is unlikely that such a movement can be accounted for by increased reporting of abortive cases. In the county boroughs studied here it seems to have been remarkably abrupt. Perhaps the 1938 epidemic was due to a new strain of virus against which the city populations had acquired no immunity in early life.

SITES OF PARALYSIS

For a few of these epidemics it is also possible to extract the sites of paralysis from the reports of the local Medical Officers of Health. From Cardiff (1923), Birmingham (1923), Kingston-upon-Hull (1933) and Manchester (1936) there are 150 such cases of which 74 per cent were children under the age of five. Between them they had 223 recorded sites of paralysis in upper and lower limbs and a ratio of 1 upper limb to 3.2 lower limbs. In the children under five reported upon by Bradford Hill and Knowelden (1950)—excluding those who had been inoculated within a month of their illness—the ratio in 424 sites was 1 upper limb to 2.3 lower limbs. The difference between the two ratios might well be due to chance (P is approximately 0.10). In other words there is no significant evidence of a general change in the arm/leg ratio with the greatly increased incidence of inoculations that has occurred since 1942. The effect of inoculations again appears to be limited to those recently carried out.

SUMMARY AND CONCLUSION

Finally, for all these major and minor epidemics in England and Wales between the wars I studied the reports of the Medical Officers of Health (I am indebted to many who sent or lent me these early reports). It seemed just possible that seen *en masse* and in retrospect at this later date some epidemiological feature might stand out. There was none that I could detect. Many give fascinating accounts of these outbreaks but they are, perhaps, more striking in their variety than in their resemblance. Thus I am left with wholly unresolved questions.

If it be true that fresh introductions of poliomyelitis were quite frequently taking place through the ports why was the spread so limited at this time? Some of these epidemics were on no mean scale—for example those in Grimsby and Kingston-upon-Hull. Yet they did not seem to travel far or wide in epidemic form but on the whole to stay in the town and closely adjacent counties. Similarly a county epidemic would often appear to be limited to that county or contiguous areas. This would seem to conform rather to the present conception of the disease as following relatively narrow channels of dissemination through immediate contacts than to the more generally held view of a widely dispersed virus infecting nearly all the people of an area. It might, perhaps, be argued that dissemination was widespread but in a subclinical form. The fact then that the disease appeared clinically and epidemically over a circumscribed area but no less widely but yet subclinically over a more distant area would clearly call for explanation.

Secondly there is the question of the changes in age of incidence. It has long been noted that 'infantile paralysis' has ceased to be predominantly infantile (or indeed paralytic). There has been, it has been maintained, a gradual shift to an older age distribution in countries with improving standards of hygiene. The explanation put forward is lack of immunization in childhood with the subsequent exposure to risk of non-immunes at school ages and in adult life. Yet, however that may be, in the towns of England and Wales for which I have been able to offer figures there may also, it seems, have been quite an abrupt change in, or near to, the widespread epidemic of 1938. Did a new strain of virus find lodgment about that date, and are we suffering from yet another in the epidemics since 1947?

Lastly there is the main question from which I set out. Why do certain cities experience repeated outbreaks whereas others report none though they would appear to be no more or no less vulnerable in terms of overcrowding and hygienic standards? Why does the disease tend to reappear in certain localities? If the phenomena of 1947 were due to a new strain of virus one might at least expect it to strike equally at cities whose past experience had been good or ill. Yet in the main it seems to have fallen more heavily upon those areas of England and Wales which had had a similar unfavourable experience of poliomyelitis in 1919–46, less heavily upon those with a favourable history. What are the barriers and facilities in these respective areas? The records of the General Register Office can, I suspect, take us no farther and there would seem to be scope for field studies.

REFERENCES

Benjamin, B., and Gale, A. H. (1949). *Mon. Bull. Minist. Hlth. Lab. Serv.* **8**, 208.

Benjamin, B., and Logan, W. P. D. (1953). *Brit. J. prev. soc. Med.* **7**, 131.

Bradley, W. H., and Gale, A. H. (1949). *Proc. R. Soc. Med.* **42**, 47.

Daley, A., and Benjamin, B. (1948). *Med. Offr.* **80**, 171.

Gale, A. H., and Hargreaves, E. P. (1953). *Brit. J. prev. soc. Med.* **7**, 180.

Hill, A. Bradford, and Knowelden, J. (1950). *Brit. med. J.* **ii**, 1.

Hill, A. Bradford, and Martin, W. J. (1949). *Brit. med. J.* **ii**, 357.

Logan, W. P. D. (1952). *Mon. Bull. Minist. Hlth. Lab. Serv.* **11**, 147.

Low, R. B. (1915–16). 45th Annual Report of the Local Government Board, 1915–16. Supplement containing Report of the Medical Officer for 1915–16. Comd. 8423. London: H.M.S.O.

CHAPTER 21

INOCULATION AND POLIOMYELITIS

THE immunization campaign which began in 1942 has led, it is well known, to a dramatic reduction in the incidence of and mortality from diphtheria in this country. During its progress, however, there have been reported occasional and sporadic cases of paralysis following the injection of an antigen. This paralysis has sometimes been limited to the limb in which the injection was made; sometimes it has involved other limbs as well. In most cases a diagnosis of poliomyelitis has been made. It is, however, clear that when inoculations are being given to hundreds of thousands of children and when, at the same time, poliomyelitis is endemic or epidemic, then the disease must *inevitably* follow injections in some children without there being any causal relationship whatever between the two events. In other words, children receiving injections might have no more risk of acquiring paralytic poliomyelitis than any other children.

There was in those earlier years no evidence to suggest that they had a greater risk—and, indeed, we do not now know for certain that the danger then existed, though we may well suspect that it did. In the autumn of 1949, on the other hand, it was known that much more incriminating evidence was accumulating in several quarters, evidence which has since been published. J. K. Martin (1950) had collected 17 cases in which paralysis of a single limb had occurred within 28 days of an injection being given. The diagnosis in almost all was poliomyelitis. No statistical proof of the relationship was available, but it appeared very unlikely that the association was wholly fortuitous.

At the same time it was known that observations of the association had been made, and statistical evidence of cause and effect collected, by B. P. McCloskey (1950) working in Melbourne, Australia. Of 340 cases of poliomyelitis investigated by him 31 had received an injection of diphtheria toxoid or pertussis vaccine, alone or in combination, within three months of the onset of their symptoms. In these 31 patients paralysis was distinctly more frequent in their inoculated than in their uninoculated limbs. Likewise in the 17 of them who were under three years of age and had received an inoculation within the preceding 35 days, the severity of the paralysis was much greater in the last inoculated limbs than in a comparable group of children not recently inoculated.

Concurrently, D. H. Geffen (1950) had become aware of the occurrence of poliomyelitis in recently inoculated children in the Metropolitan Borough of St. Pancras, an observation which he subsequently extended by the collection of records from other parts of London. Once more the frequency of the occurrence and the tendency for the paralysis to be localized to the limb of injection made it somewhat unlikely that the association was fortuitous.

These reports, at that time incomplete and unpublished, made it essential that a wide-scale statistical inquiry be immediately undertaken, one which could reveal as speedily as possible whether indeed in this country there was a case for believing that paralytic poliomyelitis could be justly attributed to a preceding inoculation.

MODE OF INQUIRY

For a full answer to the statistical problem the requirements are the numbers of children of given ages injected with defined antigens at given points of time and in specified areas, and then the number of these who develop poliomyelitis within subsequent periods. In relation to the general incidence of poliomyelitis, these figures will accurately measure the probability that an inoculated child will develop poliomyelitis and, likewise, they will show the relative risks at different ages and with different antigens. Such a method is the *only* means by which those risks can be satisfactorily and effectively measured. It is an inquiry, however, that would take a very long time to carry out, since there are no readily available data which give, in the required detail, the numbers of children inoculated. In the circumstances it was essential to use a speedier, even if less comprehensive, approach.

AREAS OF INQUIRY

The method we adopted was to choose deliberately all those administrative areas of the country in which a large number of cases of poliomyelitis had been notified during the three months July, August, and September, 1949 (the number we laid down was 20 of all ages). We then sought the inoculation histories of all the cases of poliomyelitis in which the patient was less than five years of age. This procedure led us to seek for returns from 25 areas. It soon, however, became apparent that these areas were unlikely to provide sufficient data for all the sub-divisions we wished to make. At the same time, the epidemic of 1949 was unexpectedly prolonged beyond the usual season of poliomyelitis. We therefore sought data from another 14 areas in each of which at least 20 cases of all ages had been notified in the five months July to November inclusive.

From these 39 areas we subsequently eliminated the following: three areas (involving 21 records) which could not provide the detailed data that we essentially needed—the inoculation histories of the children were not known or the site of inoculation or of paralysis was lacking; one area which had had only abortive and doubtful cases (nine records); one area in which the recorded incidence of 20 cases, upon which it was selected, related mainly to cases brought into the town's hospitals from rural areas outside it and which itself had had only a single case in a child under five years of age (one record); and one area in which the records of paralysis available related not to the early stages of the disease but to the residual paralysis some weeks later (eight records).*

Excluding these 39 records we were left with 410 records derived from 33 widespread areas (the Metropolitan Boroughs of Battersea, Hackney, Hammersmith, Islington, Kensington, Lewisham, Paddington, St. Pancras, and Wandsworth; the County Boroughs of Birmingham, Bournemouth, Brighton, Bristol, Dewsbury, Hull, Leeds, Leicester, Liverpool, Manchester, Nottingham, Portsmouth, Reading, Salford, Sheffield, Southampton, and York; the Municipal Boroughs of Finchley, Hendon, Hornsey, and Willesden; the Urban Districts of Camborne and Redruth, and Hoyland Nether; and the Rural District of New Forest).

* We also excluded from the present analysis four records sent to us from Belfast through the kindness of Dr. James Boyd and Dr. F. F. Kane, to whom we express our thanks.

THE PROTOCOLS

The Medical Officer of Health of each of these areas was asked to provide two series of data, the one relating to the confirmed poliomyelitis cases, limited to children under five since inoculation at older ages is less frequent, and the other to a series of 'controls'. For the former we sought sex; date of birth; date of notification of poliomyelitis and date of onset of symptoms; whether there was paralysis and, if so, which limbs or other sites were affected and whether the attack was fatal; and then the child's full history of inoculations (excluding vaccination) from the time of his or her birth up to 30 September, 1949, in the first series of areas and to 30 November, 1949, in the second series. Under this history we sought the date of each injection, the dose, site, whether subcutaneous or intramuscular, the nature of the vaccine and its origin.

From these particulars we could see how frequently the site of paralysis coincided with the site of injection at given intervals of time after that injection, and also whether the incidence of paralysis on the various limbs, upper and lower, differed in its distribution between those children (of the same age) who had been recently inoculated and those who had not.

THE CONTROLS

As a further standard of comparison we sought a control group of children under five years of age—one which would be representative of all such children in the area concerned. By such means we might see whether the poliomyelitis patients had been recently inoculated more often than the general run of children—that is, whether inoculation appeared to be bringing them into the paralytic class. A method of choosing these controls in so many areas and yet by some random process was not easy. We finally determined to ask the medical officer of health to take for each of his poliomyelitis cases a child of the same sex as that case and of closely similar age, but one who was notified at approximately the same date as the poliomyelitis case as suffering from measles. Failing this we asked him to take for each poliomyelitis case a child of the same sex who was born at the same time as the poliomyelitis case, the name to be drawn from the notification of births register.

To the 'measles control' there might be objection in that we have to presume that children suffering from measles at ages under five are, in relation to the incidence of inoculation, a cross-section of all children of those ages. The 'birthday control' presented some difficulty in that the child chosen had to be known to be still living in the area concerned. Difficulty also arose through the dearth of cases of measles at that time of year in 1949. Many such cases we subsequently had to discard since they did not match closely enough in age and date of notification the poliomyelitis case they were supposed to control. We were thus left finally with only 164 controls derived from one or other of the above methods, each of which had been closely 'paired' with a corresponding poliomyelitis case.

In obtaining these various data we asked the Medical Officer of Health to take the following precautions:

(*a*) to ensure that the evidence may be wholly objective, and therefore not open to criticism, it is most important that, whenever possible, *the details of the attack of poliomyelitis should be entered before the inoculation history of the child has been determined;* (*b*) the 'control' case of measles to a poliomyelitis case should be chosen to give, as near as can be, equality in sex, age, and date of notification, but otherwise be picked at random and *particularly, if possible, without any* prior knowledge of the child's inoculation history.

THE RESULTS

The basic data relating to the 410 cases of poliomyelitis are set out in Table **21,** 1. They relate, it will be seen, to 248 boys and 162

TABLE **21,** 1

Number of Children with Poliomyelitis, the Number of Sites of Paralysis, and the Inoculation Histories

Age at Onset of Polio-myelitis (Months)	No. of Children			No. of Sites of Paralysis and (Mean No. per Child)	Inoculation History		
	M	F	Total		Inoculated at Some Time	Not Inoculated	Not Known
0–	32	24	56	103 (1·8)	18	37	1
12–	75	44	119	204 (1·7)	82	27	10
24–	70	33	103	166 (1·6)	65	27	11
36–	45	39	84	123 (1·5)	61	17	6
48–59	26	22	48	49 (1·0)	23	12	13
Total	248	162	410	645 (1·6)	249	120	41

girls, with the maximum incidence falling in the second and third years of life. It may also be observed that the number of sites of paralysis in these young children declines steadily with advancing age. This is due, at least in part, to an increasing frequency of non-paralytic cases as age rises—whether as a real phenomenon or through a greater frequency of missed cases very early in life. The incidence of such non-paralytic attacks was 5.4 per cent of all cases in the first year of life, 6.7 per cent in the second year, 11.7 per cent in the third, 15.5 per cent in the fourth, and 25 per cent in the fifth. In total, it will be seen, these 410 children were paralysed in 645 sites.

Site of Paralysis and Previous Inoculation

In Tables **21,** 2 and **21,** 3 we turn to the main issue, our first comparison being between the sites of paralysis revealed by recently inoculated children and by others not so recently inoculated. Table **21,** 2 gives the figures for children under two years and Table **21,** 3 those for children aged 2–5. Looking first at the younger children (Table **21,** 2) and at those without any history of previous inoculations, the percentage distribution of paralysis shows (column 4) that the two arms are almost equally affected—11 per cent and 12 per cent—and that the two legs also do not differ greatly—31 per cent and 26 per cent. On the other hand, the legs are paralysed about two and a half times as often as the arms—57 per cent to 23 per cent. Turning next to column 3, it will be seen that children who had been inoculated at least three months before the onset of their attack of poliomyelitis give remarkably similar figures—arms 10 per cent and 13 per cent, legs 25 per cent and 30 per cent, ratio of legs to arms 55 per cent to 23 per cent. There is clearly no indication whatever that an injection three or more months previous to the illness affects the distribution of paralysis.

Turning, however, to column 1 we see a material change. Of the 82 sites of paralysis recorded for these 35 recently injected children the right arm was involved in 18 per cent, the left arm in 28 per cent. Both these proportions are distinctly greater than those shown by the uninoculated or not recently inoculated children (of columns 3 and 4), and together they give to the arms 46 per cent of the paralysis against the 23 per cent in the arms of the latter groups. Also the left arm in these children is affected more often than the right, and the left arm is, it is known, the more usual site of inoculation in this

TABLE **21**, 2

Sites of Paralysis and Previous Inoculation History in Children
Under 2 Years of Age

Site of Paralysis	Interval Between Last Injection and Onset of Poliomyelitis			No Previous Inoculations	Inoculation History Not Known	Total
	Less than a Month*	Between 1 and 3 Months	3 or More Months Previous			
Right arm	15	1	8	12	2	38
Left arm	23	6	10	14	3	56
Right leg	17	9	20	35	1	82
Left leg	15	5	24	29	1	74
Trunk	9	2	12	10	1	34
Cranial nerves	3	0	6	13	1	23
Total No. of						
(a) Sites	82	23	80	113	9	307
(b) Children	35	16	49	64	11	175
Percentages						
	(1)	(2)	(3)	(4)	(5)	(6)
Right arm	*18*	*4*	*10*	*11*	—	*12*
Left arm	*28*	*26*	*13*	*12*	—	*18*
Right leg	*21*	*39*	*25*	*31*	—	*27*
Left leg	*18*	*22*	*30*	*26*	—	*24*
Trunk	*11*	*9*	*15*	*9*	—	*11*
Cranial nerves	*4*	*0*	*7*	*11*	—	*8*
Total sites	*100*	*100*	*100*	*100*	—	*100*

* Here and in all tables less than a month means 0–28 days inclusive, between one and three months is 29 to 91 days inclusive, and three or more months is 92 days and onwards.

country. (Taking, in fact, these 100 children aged 0–2 as one group we find 85 per cent had been inoculated in an arm against 9 per cent in the leg and 4 per cent in the buttocks (2 per cent unknown site), and the ratio of left arm to right arm is $4\frac{1}{2}$ to 1. The figures for the older children are very similar.) As a corollary of the excess incidence of paralysis in the arms in the recently inoculated group, the legs are proportionately less often affected. In place of the customary ratio of $2\frac{1}{2}$ to 1 for leg paralysis to arm paralysis, we have here a ratio rather less than 1 to 1 (39 per cent legs to 46 per cent arms).

TABLE **21,** 3

Sites of Paralysis and Previous Inoculation History in Children
Between 2 and 5 Years of Age

Site of Paralysis	Interval Between Last Injection and Onset of Poliomyelitis			No Previous Inoculations	Inoculation History Not Known	Total
	Less than a Month	Between 1 and 3 Months	3 or More Months Previous			
Right arm	0	1	20	9	5	35
Left arm	2	0	21	9	6	38
Right leg	3	0	52	16	11	82
Left leg	4	2	59	23	10	98
Trunk	1	0	27	14	6	48
Cranial nerves	0	0	28	6	3	37
Total No. of						
(*a*) Sites	10	3	207	77	41	338
(*b*) Children	7	4	138	56	30	235
Percentages						
	(1)	(2)	(3)	(4)	(5)	(6)
Right arm	—	—	*10*	*12*	*12*	*10*
Left arm	—	—	*10*	*12*	*15*	*11*
Right leg	—	—	*25*	*21*	*27*	*24*
Left leg	—	—	*29*	*30*	*24*	*29*
Trunk	—	—	*13*	*18*	*15*	*14*
Cranial nerves	—	—	*13*	*8*	*7*	*11*
Total sites	—	—	*100*	*101*	*100*	*99*

Turning finally to the children injected more than one month but
less than three months before the onset of their illness, we have but
16 of these, with 23 sites of paralysis. The number is too small to
be convincing. There is perhaps a suggestion of an absence of
paralysis in the right arm and in excess on the left, but the arms
show 30 per cent in total to the 61 per cent in the legs, a ratio very
similar to that found in the uninoculated children.

Turning next to the older children (Table **21,** 3), we may note
once again that those who had been inoculated at least three months
before the onset of poliomyelitis reveal almost precisely the same
distribution of sites of paralysis as the children who had never been

inoculated—arms 20 per cent and legs 54 per cent (column 3), against arms 24 per cent and legs 51 per cent (column 4). The similarity is striking, and confirms the previous conclusion that distant injections produce no changes in the distribution of paralysis.

Of recently inoculated children there were at these ages only seven. This is, of course, due to the fact that inoculations are much less frequently performed at these ages, and the few figures we have are clearly of little value.

Sites of Paralysis and Site of Injection

A closer picture of the association between the site of paralysis and the site of recent injection (whether in arm, leg, or buttock) is given in Tables **21**, 4 and **21**, 5. Including here only those children who had at some time or other been inoculated, we show how often the site of paralysis coincided with the site of injection. Table **21**, 4 shows that, of the children who had been inoculated in the month

TABLE **21**, 4

Sites of Paralysis in Relation to Site of Last Inoculation. Children Under 2 Years of Age

Site of Paralysis in Relation to Site of Inoculation	Interval from Last Inoculation to Onset of Poliomyelitis (Months)				
	0–	1–	3–	6+	Total
Same site*	11	3	1	1	16
Included site*	18	1	3	4	26
Different site	3	8	10	24	45
No paralysis	1	2	1	1	5
No record	3	2	1	3	9
Total No. of children	36†	16	16	33	101†
% of total falling in same and included categories	*81*	*25*	*25*	*15*	*42*

* 'Same site' denotes that the site of inoculation was the *only* site of paralysis 'included site' that the site of inoculation was *one* of the sites of paralysis but not the only site in which paralysis occurred.

† The total number of children was 100, and the extra one here is due to the fact that one child was given two antigens on the same day, one into the left arm and the other into the right, and developed paralysis in the right arm 10 days later. We have had, here and elsewhere, to include this child twice.

TABLE **21,** 5

Site of Paralysis in Relation to Site of Last Inoculation. Children Between 2 and 5 Years of Age

Site of Paralysis in Relation to Site of Inoculation	Interval from Last Inoculation to Onset of Poliomyelitis (Months)				
	0–	1–	3–	6+	Total
Same site*	1	0	0	4	5
Included site*	3	0	0	10	13
Different site	0	2	4	88	94
No paralysis	2	1	0	17	20
No record	1	1	1	14	17
Total No. of children	7	4	5	133	149
% of total falling in same and included categories	*57*	*0*	*0*	*10*	*12*

* 'Same site' denotes that the site of inoculation was the *only* site of paralysis, 'included site' that the site of inoculation was *one* of the sites of paralysis but not the only site in which paralysis occurred.

preceding their illness, four-fifths (81 per cent) had paralysis in the limb of injection (though not necessary confined to that limb). This proportion is greatly in excess of the figure shown by children whose last injection was more than a month distant. In these groups the limb of injection was involved in 25 per cent when an injection was one to three months before, 25 per cent when it was three to six months before, and 15 per cent when it was six or more months before (proportions which between themselves differ insignificantly).

The older children of Table **21,** 5 reveal a similar excess in the very small number who had been recently inoculated. Four of these seven children (57 per cent) had paralysis in the limb of injection, whereas of the large group whose inoculation lay more than six months distant only 10 per cent showed an association of these sites of injection and paralysis (a difference which is technically significant; the 'exact' probability test gives $P = 0.005$).

Comparison of Antigens

Analysis of the figures according to the antigen last injected gives the results set out in Tables **21,** 6 and **21,** 7. Our numbers are small

TABLE **21**, 6

Sites of Paralysis in Relation to Site of Last Inoculation with Specified Antigens. Children Under 2 Years of Age†

Site of Paralysis in Relation to Site of Inoculation	A.P.T.			Combined A.P.T. and Pertussis			Pertussis		
	Interval in Months			Interval in Months			Interval in Months		
	0–	1–	3+	0–	1–	3+	0–	1–	3+
Same site*	2	2	2	8	1	–	1	–	–
Included site*	4	–	3	14	1	3	–	–	–
Different site	1	5	24	1	3	7	1	–	2
No paralysis	1	1	1	–	1	–	–	–	1
No record	–	1	3	3	1	1	–	–	–
Total No. of children	8	9	33	26	7	11	2	–	3
% of total falling in same and included categories	75	22	15	85	29	27	–	–	–

* 'Same site' denotes that the site of inoculation was the *only* site of paralysis, 'included site' that the site of inoculation was *one* of the sites of paralysis but not the only site in which paralysis occurred.

† Two children not included here had had other antigens more than three months previously.

even at the younger ages (Table **21**, 6) but there is, we think, a clear association here between site of recent injection and site of paralysis with A.P.T. and with the combined vaccine (A.P.T. and pertussis). With the former antigen six out of eight children (75 per cent) had paralysis in the limb of injection; of the more distantly inoculated the numbers were two out of nine children inoculated between one and three months before (22 per cent), and five out of 33 children inoculated three or more months before (15 per cent). The difference between the recently and not recently inoculated groups (one month or over) is more than would be likely to occur by chance (by 'exact' probability test $P = 0.002$).

Similarly with the combined vaccine 22 out of 26 recently inoculated children (85 per cent) show paralysis in the limb of injection, while with more distant inoculations the proportion falls to just

TABLE **21,** 7

Sites of Paralysis in Relation to Site of Last Inoculation with
Specified Antigens. Children Between 2 and 5 Years of Age†

Site of Paralysis in Relation to Site of Inoculation	A.P.T.			Combined A.P.T. and Pertussis			Pertussis		
	Interval in Months			Interval in Months			Interval in Months		
	0–	1–	3+	0–	1–	3+	0–	1–	3+
Same site*	1	–	4	–	–	–	–	–	–
Included site*	2	–	9	1	–	–	–	–	1
Different site	–	2	76	–	–	6	–	–	5
No paralysis	–	1	14	–	–	1	2	–	2
No record	–	–	12	–	–	1	1	–	1
Total No. of children	3	3	115	1	–	8	3	–	9

* 'Same site' denotes that the site of inoculation was the *only* site of paralysis, 'included site' that the site of inoculation was *one* of the sites of paralysis but not the only site in which paralysis occurred.

† Seven children not included here had had other antigens—six of whom were injected more than three months previously and one between one and three months previously.

under 30 per cent (two in seven and three in 11 children). Again the difference would be unlikely to arise by chance (P less than 0.001). For the pertussis vaccine alone we have no figures of any value. It was clearly not being extensively used in these areas.

At the older ages (Table **21,** 7) our data are very few and the most we can say is that the figures for A.P.T. are in conformity with those for younger children. Of the 115 children who had been inoculated with this antigen three or more months before the onset of their poliomyelitis, approximately one in 10 had paralysis in the limb of injection. Of the three children who had been injected within the preceding month all had paralysis in the limb of injection.

To allow comparisons to be made we have in Table **21,** 8 put our data on the different antigens into the form adopted by McCloskey which contrasts inoculated with uninoculated limbs in relation to the frequency of paralysis. In this form we observe again a clear association between the site of paralysis and recent injection with A.P.T. and with the combined vaccine. Our four cases of inoculation with pertussis vaccine give no evidence of association.

TABLE **21**, 8

Contrast of Inoculated and Uninoculated Limbs in Children Having an Injection within 30 Days of Onset of Poliomyelitis*

Agent	Site	Inoculated Limbs		Uninoculated Limbs		Total Limbs
		Paralysed	Not Paralysed	Paralysed	Not Paralysed	
A.P.T. (11 cases)	Legs	2	—	10	10	22
	Arms	7	2	2	11	22
Combined vaccine (24 cases)	Legs	4	1	20	23	48
	Arms	19	—	10	19	48
Pertussis vaccine (4 cases)	Legs	—	1	—	7	8
	Arms	1	2	1	4	8

* This table excludes four children in whom the exact site of inoculation was unknown.

Comparison of Poliomyelitis Cases and Their Controls

In Table **21**, 9 we turn to our control group and contrast the inoculation histories of the children with poliomyelitis with the corresponding histories of their controls. To be sure of this contrast

TABLE **21**, 9

Interval from Last Inoculation to Onset of Poliomyelitis in Cases and in their Matched Controls

	Interval from Last Inoculation to Onset of Poliomyelitis Case (Months)						Not Inoculated	Not Known
	0—	1—	3—	6—	12+	All Intervals		
0–23 months of age:								
71 Poliomyelitis cases	11	7	7	13	3	41	26	4
71 Controls	1	9	7	18	1	36	32	3
24 months of age and over:								
93 Poliomyelitis cases	5	1	2	9	38	55	24	14
93 Controls	—	1	3	9	34	47	35	11
All ages:								
164 Poliomyelitis cases	16	8	9	22	41	96	50	18
164 Controls	1	10	10	27	35	83	67	14

we can take only 164 out of the toal 410 poliomyelitis cases, since it was only in these that we had been able to obtain a satisfactorily 'paired' control. This 'pairing' was made closely for age and sex, while measles cases were accepted only if their date of notification lay *after* the onset of the corresponding case of poliomyelitis. The previous inoculation history was then measured in each such pair from the date of onset in the poliomyelitis case. Eighty-eight of these controls were 'measles' controls and 76 were 'birthday' controls. This pairing, therefore, seriously reduces the numbers at our disposal, but any less rigorous procedure is in our opinion open to grave objection, since the incidence of inoculation is closely associated with age. Table 21, 9 shows that in each of our age groups rather more of the children with poliomyelitis had had some

TABLE **21**, 10

Interval from Last Inoculation to Date of Onset of Poliomyelitis in Children who had been Inoculated within 28 Days of Onset

Interval from Last Inoculation to Onset of Poliomyelitis (Days)	No. of Children*	
	Under 2 Years	Between 2 and 5 Years
1	(*1*)	
7	(*1*)	
8	4	
9	2	
10	1 (*1*)	1
11	3	1
12	1	(*1*)
13	1	1
14	3	(*1*)
15	3	
16	1	(*1*)
17	4	
18	1 (*1*)	
19	1	1
20	1	
21	1	
22	1 (*1*)	
25	(*1*)	
28	1	
All intervals	29 (*6*)	4 (*3*)

* The italicized figures in parentheses are of children who were not paralysed in the limb of injection.

previous inoculations—41 to 36 and 55 to 47. Division of these figures into the intervals of time that had elapsed between the last injection and the onset of poliomyelitis (in a specified child and its pair) shows a striking result. There is no marked difference in the numbers of distant inoculations, and the excess of inoculations in the poliomyelitis group lies in injections which took place within a month of the onset of the illness.

Time Interval Between Inoculation and Poliomyelitis

Finally, in Table 21, 10 we set out the intervals of time that had elapsed between the last inoculation and the recorded onset of the illness. In the great majority (26) of the 33 children who had paralysis within 28 days in the limb of injection, the recorded date of onset of symptoms lay in the 10-day interval 8–17 days subsequent to that injection. None fell below eight days, though there were two such cases in which the site of injection was not a site of paralysis. These two cases and others at the upper end of the scale may well have been fortuitous occurrences which must inevitably take place (as Tables 21, 4 and 21, 5 show).

DISCUSSION

Whichever way we choose to set out the statistics collected in this inquiry they reveal clearly an association between recent injections and paralysis. For instance, Tables 21, 2 and 21, 3 show that in those inoculated within a month of the onset of their attack of poliomyelitis the distribution of the bodily sites of paralysis is quite abnormal. There is in these cases a high incidence of paralysis in the arms instead of the normal concentration upon the legs, there is an excess in the left arm compared with the right. We know that inoculations are given predominantly in the arms and mainly in the left arm (and the figures of the present inquiry confirm that general knowledge).

Alternatively we may bring the site of inoculation (whatever it may have been) into a more exact comparison with the site, or sites, of paralysis. We then see (Tables 21, 4 and 21, 5) that the two sites frequently coincide when the inoculation is of very recent date (that is, within the previous month) and come together significantly less frequently when the inoculation is an event of the more distant past.

Lastly, following McCloskey's analysis, we may consider how

often, in the same children, their inoculated limbs are paralysed compared with their uninoculated limbs. We find an excess of paralysis in the former.

We must conclude, therefore, that in the 1949 epidemic of poliomyelitis in this country cases of paralysis were occurring which were associated with inoculation procedures carried out within the month preceding the recorded date of onset of the illness. On the other hand, we find no evidence whatever that any inoculations carried out three months or more before the onset of illness have had any such effect. There is not the slightest indication in our figures that such distant injections have localized the paralysis (Tables **21,** 2 and **21,** 3) or that they have produced paralysis which would not otherwise have occurred (Table **21,** 9). On inoculations within one to three months of the onset of poliomyelitis we have very little evidence—what little there is suggests no evil effects—though obviously at the lower end of that period there might be some slight risk. On the other hand, the great majority of the intervals between last inoculation and onset of symptoms that were less than a month lay between eight and 17 days. Taking a narrower interval, McCloskey reported that 63 per cent of his cases had an interval of 7–14 days. Confining attention to cases with paralysis in the limb of injection, we show a closely similar figure—55 per cent.

With the figures made available by this mode of inquiry we cannot satisfactorily measure the *relative* risks of poliomyelitis following an inoculation, either at different ages or with different antigens. The data do, however, show that the occurrence can (and does) take place in both the age groups we have used—namely, under two years and between two and five years (Tables **21,** 4, **21,** 5, **21,** 6, **21,** 7, and **21,** 9). The smaller number of positive cases in the higher age group is not necessarily due to any lowering of the risk as age advances, for it must be, in part if not wholly, a function of the frequency with which inoculations are carried out. That frequency is, we know, lower in the higher age group.

Similarly, our figures show that paralysis has certainly followed the injection both of A.P.T. and of the combined A.P.T. and pertussis vaccine; for the pertussis vaccine alone we have no convincing data, and presumably it was not being extensively used (Tables **21,** 6, **21,** 7, and **21,** 8). As stated, we cannot with figures of this kind determine whether one vaccine is more prone to produce paralysis than another. On the present published evidence we can see little support for the belief that the pertussis and the combined antigens are more prone to do this than A.P.T.

It has naturally been suggested that the effect of a recent inoculation is merely to localize the paralysis in the limb of injection in a child already incubating poliomyelitis. In the absence of inoculation the paralysis would not have occurred necessarily in that limb, but it would have occurred in some limb. The comparison of our cases with their paired controls (Table 21, 9) suggests that this argument may not be well founded. The excess of recently inoculated children in the poliomyelitis group—and the equality in other intervals—does, we think, indicate that the group includes cases which would not have been diagnosed as poliomyelitis at all if there had been no previous and recent inoculation. Such children may already have been cases of non-clinically recognizable poliomyelitis, but the data suggest that they have been brought by inoculation into the paralytic class.

SUMMARY AND CONCLUSIONS

An investigation has been made to determine speedily whether, in the epidemic of 1949 in England and Wales, cases of paralysis diagnosed as and indistinguishable from poliomyelitis were occurring in association with inoculation procedures.

Records of 410 patients aged under five years were collected from 33 administrative areas, and in 164 of these cases a record was obtained for a closely paired control child.

The distribution of the bodily sites of paralysis was quite abnormal in children who had been inoculated within the month preceding the onset of their illness. In this group paralysis in the arms was just as frequent as paralysis in the legs, and the left arm showed paralysis more often than the right; in children without recent injections the two arms were equally affected and the legs were affected two to three times as often as the arms. The distribution in the recently inoculated is in accordance with the customary inoculation procedure in this country—that is, use of the arms more than the legs, and predominantly the left arm.

In the recently inoculated children the limb of injection (arm or leg) was a site of paralysis much more frequently than was the case with children not recently inoculated.

There is no evidence whatever that inoculations carried out in the

more distant past have any effect at all upon the incidence or localization of paralysis. These effects appear to be confined to injections
given within about a month of the onset of poliomyelitis, and after
that interval from inoculation has elapsed no risk need be envisaged.

It has been suggested elsewhere that the recent injection of an
antigen merely localizes an already developing paralysis in that
particular limb of the child. The contrast of the present poliomyelitis cases with their specially collected and paired control
children indicates, however, that there may be present in the poliomyelitis group cases which would not have been clinically diagnosed
as poliomyelitis at all if their inoculation had not brought them into
the paralytic group.

Paralysis in the limb of recent injection was observed to follow
both inoculations with A.P.T. and inoculations with the combined
A.P.T. and pertussis antigens. Few figures were available for pertussis vaccine, but one case of paralysis following a recent injection
was recorded.

The intervals of time less than 28 days that elapsed between the
last injection of an antigen and the recorded onset of symptoms of
poliomyelitis lay mainly between eight and 17 days.

The mode of inquiry was such as to give a rapid and sufficiently
accurate answer to the problem at issue—were such cases, in fact,
occurring more frequently than could be attributed to chance?
From the data thus collected it is not possible to determine the
relative risks of injections either at different ages or with different
antigens. For that purpose another, and a very laborious, statistical
investigation is required.

REFERENCES

Geffen, D. H. (1950). *Med. Offr.* **83**, 137.
McCloskey, B. P. (1950). *Lancet*, **i**, 659.
Martin, J. K. (1950). *Arch. Dis. Childh.* **25**, 1.

CHAPTER 22

VIRUS DISEASES IN PREGNANCY AND CONGENITAL DEFECTS

TO determine the probability that an illness of the mother during her pregnancy will give rise to a congenital malformation in the infant, essentially demands a prospective method of inquiry. In other words, the attack of illness in the pregnant woman must first be observed and medically diagnosed, and the condition of the child born to her must subsequently be noted. The retrospective approach, *i.e.* noting first the congenital deformity in the new-born child and then obtaining the history of the mother during pregnancy, inevitably omits the normal children whose mothers were affected, and is thus bound to give a highly exaggerated picture of the risks involved. The prospective inquiry is, however, extremely difficult to carry out on an adequate scale. The attack rates from infectious diseases are relatively low in adult life and very large numbers of women must be observed. It is specially important, too, that the occurrence of disease in the mother be recognized and recorded at a time when she may not even know that she is pregnant, *i.e.* during the first month of pregnancy.

One way of securing such records in Great Britain has been described in an earlier paper (Hill and Galloway, 1949). The data there used were automatically collected by the approved societies operating up to 5 July, 1948, under the National Health Insurance Acts. Under these Acts, if an employed and insured married woman drew benefit for a sickness which caused her to be absent from work, she had to present a sickness certificate giving the dates of her illness and the general practitioner's diagnosis of its cause. If she subsequently gave birth to a child (live or still) she would be entitled to draw maternity benefit and the date of birth would therefore also be recorded by the approved society. Thus the dates of the two events would be available in records automatically maintained. By these means information was collected on 22 cases over the space of some

(With Richard Doll, T. McL. Galloway, and J. P. W. Hughes.) Reprinted from the *British Journal of Preventive and Social Medicine*, 1958, **12**, 1.

two years; they included 10 cases of rubella and six of measles. The infants were specially examined not long after birth and one case of congenital heart disease following rubella in the first month of pregnancy was observed. The authors concluded their report with the hope that it might 'be possible to extend these observations through the records of the new health and social services' (which came into being on 5 July, 1948). This hope has been fulfilled. With the aid of the Ministry of Pensions and National Insurance we have been able to collect similar records for 100 women reported to have suffered from rubella, measles, mumps, or chickenpox during, or shortly before, pregnancy. A further seven cases were brought to our notice privately but prospectively (*i.e.* before the birth of the child). It is with this total of 129 'double-events' that the present paper is concerned.

NOTIFICATION OF CASES

The identification of relevant cases followed the system described above. In local offices of the Ministry of Pensions and National Insurance a special note was made on the file of any married woman who returned a sickness certificate signed, as required, by a medical practitioner and bearing a diagnosis of rubella (German measles), morbilli (measles), varicella (chickenpox), or epidemic parotitis (mumps). A form was set up showing the identification particulars of the insured woman and the nature and dates of her illness. If the same woman claimed maternity benefit for the birth of a child within 12 months of the end-date of that illness, then the date of confinement and the name of the doctor or midwife in attendance were added to the form, and notification of the 'double event' was made to the Ministry.

In setting up this notification system, steps were specially taken to avoid any breach of medical confidence. As each case was notified to the Ministry of Pensions and National Insurance a letter from the Chief Medical Officer to the Ministry (or his deputy) was sent to the doctor who had signed the original sickness certificate. This letter enclosed a copy of the completed form relating to his patient and told him that the case was of interest in an inquiry into congenital defects being made by one of us (B. H.) from whom he would be hearing. At the same time the Ministry sent to the Statistical Research Unit similar particulars of the case—dates of illness, etc.—

and including the certifying doctor's name but omitting that of the patient.

On receipt of these particulars we immediately communicated with the doctor asking for his help and for permission to visit the mother and baby, known by name to him but not to us. Very few difficulties arose and the mothers were seen and the babies examined by one of us in nearly all instances.

The scheme was operated in London and the home counties from November, 1949, and in a group of midland and north-midland counties* from January, 1951, until the end of March, 1953.

It will be noted that the method of inquiry is limited to the observation of stillbirths and to the condition of liveborn infants; it automatically excludes miscarriages and abortions. If virus diseases in pregnancy contribute to early foetal loss this inquiry cannot reveal it.

DATA

In analysing the data we have calculated the stage of the pregnancy from the first day of the last preceding menstrual period. This is open to criticism in that the first two weeks of 'pregnancy' may consequently represent a period which actually preceded conception. We have, however, followed this technique, because it is the normal obstetric procedure, which most other investigators have followed, and furthermore, because several instances have been recorded in which rubella manifested itself in the mother during the two weeks following the menstrual period and the infant showed the characteristic rubella defects. On the other hand, no instances have been recorded in which the infection appeared before the last menstrual period. In those cases which followed infection in the first two weeks, the infection may have persisted until after conception or the wrong date may have been given for the last menstrual period. In the present series, we determined the date of onset of the last menstrual period whenever possible according to the mother's statement. In 44 cases (37 per cent), however, no such statement was recorded, and, in these, we calculated the date by subtracting 40 weeks from the date of delivery.

Our method of inquiry was based, for administrative convenience,

* Staffordshire, Warwickshire, Derbyshire, Leicestershire, Northamptonshire, and Nottinghamshire.

upon a date of delivery that lay within 12 months of the end of the specified illness. It thus automatically produced a number of cases of disease that must have preceded conception by any time up to three months. It is, however, of interest to see whether there is any evidence of congenital defects related to an illness *shortly* preceding conception and we have, therefore, examined such babies and included them in the study.

Of the total 129 cases notified to us we subsequently omitted 10 from the analysis. In four cases the diagnosis of the illness that occurred during pregnancy was not substantiated when we visited the mother and certifying practitioner (three cases of 'measles' in the series reported by Hill and Galloway and one of 'mumps' in the later series). Three cases of measles had occurred too long before conception to be of interest, and one of mumps occurred too close to delivery (four days). These eight exclusions are obviously called for and are of no importance, but two other cases were lost for different reasons. In one case of chickenpox in the fourth week, the mother refused to allow the child to be examined and no report could be obtained from the family doctor. In one case of mumps in the eleventh week, no early examination of the infant was made and the case was subsequently lost to sight.†

The remaining 119 cases are included in the analyses that follow. They concern 44 cases of rubella (six preceding and 38 during pregnancy), 35 cases of mumps (six preceding and 29 during pregnancy), 30 cases of chickenpox (six preceding and 24 during pregnancy), and 10 cases of measles (four preceding and six during pregnancy). One of the women who had chickenpox gave birth to twins so that altogether 120 babies were available for study of whom 110 were personally examined by one of us shortly after birth. In the remaining 10 we had information from a hospital or private doctor. Further information was obtained after the child had reached at least three years of age. In most cases we again made personal contact, usually with a special examination, and in the remainder we had reports from private doctors, except in two cases in which the family had emigrated and we had to rely upon a report of normality from the mother.

† This child (birth weight 10lb. 4oz.; 4·7kg.) was traced after this paper had gone to press; at age 4½ years it had no physical defects.

RESULTS

Rubella

The observations on rubella are set out in Table **22,** 1 and in the following brief case histories:

(1) Start of last menstrual period (mother's statement) 13.4.52, (calculated date) 13.3.52; onset of rubella 24.4.52; delivery 18.12.52. Birth weight 4 lb. 9 oz. (2.1 kg.). Bilateral cataract, harsh systolic murmur all over praecordium. Hospital report 'murmur suggestive of ventricular septal defect.' Died aged three months; certified cause congenital heart disease; no autopsy.

(2) Start of last menstrual period (mother's statement) 9.4.52, (calculated date) 8.4.52; onset of rubella 29.4.52; delivery 13.1.53. Birth weight 6 lb. 2 oz. (2.8 kg.). Bilateral cataract, microphthalmos.

(3) Start of last menstrual period (calculated date) 19.2.47; onset of rubella 17.3.47; delivery 26.11.47. Birth weight 5 lb. 8 oz. (2.5 kg.). Patent interventricular septum, severe bilateral deafness. Deafness not detected at first examination (Hill and Galloway, Case 1).

(4) Start of last menstrual period (calculated date) 7.5.47; onset of rubella 13.6.47; delivery 11.2.48. Birth weight not known. Died aged five weeks; certified cause pneumonia. Not examined personally (Hill and Galloway, Case 2).

(5) Start of last menstrual period (mother's statement) mid-January, 1947, (calculated date) 23.1.47; onset of rubella 15.4.47; delivery 30.10.47. Birth weight 6 lb. 7 oz. (2.9 kg.). Partial bilateral deafness, requiring education in a special school for deaf children. Deafness not detected at first examination (Hill and Galloway, Case 5). A test on the mother four years after the child's birth suggested that she might also have had a subclinical infection with toxoplasma.

(6) Start of last menstrual period (mother's statement) 31.1.52, (calculated date) 25.1.52; onset of rubella 5.5.52; delivery 1.11.52. Birth weight 5 lb. 6 oz. (2.4 kg.). Mongol.

(7) Start of last menstrual period (mother's statement) 13.12.51, (calculated date) 29.12.51; onset of rubella 28.3.52; delivery 5.10.52. Stillbirth, weight 4 lb. 4 oz. (1.9 kg.). No specific cause found at autopsy. The mother also had an attack of herpes zoster during the pregnancy, starting on 17.3.52.

(8) Start of last menstrual period (calculated date) 5.2.46; onset of rubella 1.7.46; delivery 12.11.46. Birth weight not known. Died aged one week; certified cause pneumonia (Hill and Galloway, Case 8).

It will be seen that, of the seven infants whose mothers had rubella in the first four weeks of pregnancy, three had major and characteristic abnormalities. There were 11 cases of rubella occurring in the next 9 weeks, *i.e.* up to the end of the first trimester, and amongst these was one baby who died aged five weeks unexamined and one child who was deaf. As regards the first trimester, therefore, there were certainly four and possibly five affected babies in a total of 18 Of the 15 infants whose mothers were infected in the second trimester,

TABLE **22,** 1

Observations on Rubella (German Measles)

Stage at which Rubella Commenced		No. of Cases	No. of Babies Stillborn or who Died before Examination	No. of Liveborn Babies in whom Abnormalities were Detected	No. of Babies Born weighing 5½ lb. or Less
Before last menstrual period		6	0	0	0
Week of Pregnancy	1st	2	0	0	0
	2nd	1	0	1	1
	3rd	2	0	1	0
	4th	2	0	1	1
	5th	2	0	0	0*
	6th	2	1	0	0*
	7th	1	0	0	1
	8th	1	0	0	0
	9th	0	—	—	—
	10th	0	—	—	—
	11th	2	0	0	0
	12th	0	—	—	—
	13th	3	0	1	0
	14th	3	0	1	1
	15th	0	—	—	—
	16th	1	1	0	1
	17th	2	0	0	0
	18th	1	0	0	0
	19th	0	—	—	—
	20th	0	—	—	—
	21st	3	1	0	0*
	22nd	0	—	—	—
	23rd	3	0	0	0
	24th	0	—	—	—
	25th	0	—	—	—
	26th	2	0	0	0
	27th or Later	5	0	0	0
Total		44	3	5	5

* Birth weight not available for one child.

one was stillborn, one was a mongol, and one died at the age of one week, unexamined. A fourth child was found at the second examination, at the age of $4\frac{1}{2}$ years, to have a moderately loud systolic murmur at the left sternal edge, varying in intensity with the position of the child; in the absence of any other signs, this has been regarded as physiological. The mother had had rubella in the twenty-fourth week of her pregnancy and the child's birth weight was 7 lb. 10 oz. (3.4 kg.). Of the five infants whose mothers were infected in the third trimester, none showed any defect. This was also the case with the six infants whose mothers had had rubella before the last menstrual period.

Of the eight children known to be defective or who died before examination, the birth weight was available in six; four weighed 5 lb. 8 oz. (2.5 kg.) or under, and none weighed as much as 7 lb. (3.2 kg.).

Of the 36 normal children, 33 were known to be alive and well when aged three years or more; one was certified as having died at five months from 'asphyxia due to overlaying' (maternal rubella one month before the last menstrual period, birth weight 8 lb. (3.6 kg.)) and two were not traced after the initial examination. The birth weight was available in 35; one baby weighed 4 lb. 9 oz. (1.8 kg.), eight weighed over $5\frac{1}{2}$ and less than 7 lb. (2.5 to 3.2 kg.), and 26 weighed 7 lb. (3.2 kg.) or over.

Mumps

The observations on mumps are set out in Table **22,** 2 and in the accompanying footnotes. One congenital defect (bilateral talipes equino-varus) was noted in the 29 instances in which the disease occurred during pregnancy. One child died of 'white asphyxia' at the age of three days and the autopsy revealed no other specific defect. All the six infants whose mothers were infected before the last preceding menstrual period survived and no defects were observed.

Of the 33 normal children, 31 were known to be alive and well when aged three years or more, one had suffered from Still's disease and had died when aged $3\frac{1}{2}$ years, and one was not traced after the initial examination. At birth, one of the normal children weighed 5 lb. 1 oz. (2.3 kg.), five weighed over $5\frac{1}{2}$ and less than 7 lb. (2.5 to 3.2 kg.), and 26 weighed 7 lb. (3.2 kg.) or more; the weight of one child was not known.

TABLE **22,** 2

Observations on Mumps (Epidemic Parotitis)

Stage at which Mumps Commenced		No. of Cases	No. of Babies Stillborn or who Died before Examination	No. of Liveborn Babies in whom Ab-normalities were Detected	No. of Babies Born weighing 5½ lb. or Less
Before last menstrual period		6	0	0	0
Weeks of Pregnancy	1st– 4th	1	0	0	0
	5th– 8th	10	0	0	0
	9th–12th	5	0	1(*a*)	0
	13th–16th	2	1(*b*)	0	0
	17th–20th	1	0	0	0
	21st–24th	3	0	0	1
	25th or Later	7	0	0	0*
Total		35	1	1	1

* Birthweight not available for one child.

(*a*) Start of last menstrual period (mother's statement and calculated date) 1.8.51; onset of mumps 2.10.51; delivery 8.5.52. Birth weight 7 lb. 12 oz. (3.5 kg.). Bilateral talipes equino-varus.

(*b*) Start of last menstrual period (mother's statement) 21.7.50 (calculated date) 8.8.50; onset of mumps 21.10.50; delivery 15.5.51. Birth weight 6 lb. 11 oz. (3.0 kg.). Died on third day with 'white asphyxia'; no abnormalities detected at autopsy.

Chickenpox

The observations on chickenpox are set out in Table **22,** 3. The only congenital defect noted was an isolated defect of pancreatic secretion, and in this case the mother's infection had occurred four weeks before the start of the last menstrual period. Two babies were stillborn. Autopsy in one case showed atelectasis and suprarenal haemorrhage, with no specific congenital abnormality. The second foetus was five weeks premature and was macerated and a large clot was found behind the placenta. It may be recalled that another stillbirth followed an attack of herpes zoster in the fourteenth week of pregnancy, when the mother had also suffered from rubella in the fifteenth week (Case 7).

TABLE **22**, 3

Observations on Chickenpox (Varicella)

Stage at which Chickenpox Commenced		No. of Cases	No. of Babies Stillborn or who Died before Examination	No. of Liveborn Babies in whom Abnormalities were Detected	No. of Babies Born weighing $5\frac{1}{2}$ lb. or Less
Before last menstrual period		6	0	1(*a*)	0
Weeks of Pregnancy	1st– 4th	1	0	0	0
	5th– 8th	3	0	0	0*
	9th–12th	3	1(*b*)	0	0
	13th–16th	5	0	0	0
	17th–20th	2	1(*c*)	0	1
	21st–24th	3	0	0	0
	25th or Later	8	0	0	1
Total		31†	2	1	2

* Birthweight not available for two children.

† Including one pair of twins (chickenpox in the fifth week); excluding one normal child whose mother had chickenpox in the seventeenth week following rubella in the fifth week, and one stillborn child whose mother had herpes zoster in the fourteenth week and rubella in the fifteenth week (Rubella, Case 7).

(*a*) Start of last menstrual period (mother's statement and calculated date) 22.6.49; onset of chickenpox 24.5.49; delivery 29.3.50. Birthweight 7 lb. 11 oz. (3.5 kg.). Isolated defect of pancreatin secretion.

(*b*) Start of last menstrual period (mother's statement) 25.4.50, (calculated date) 29.4.50; onset of chickenpox 10.7.50; delivery 3.2.51. Birthweight 9 lb. 3 oz. (4.2 kg.). Stillborn; atelectasis and suprarenal haemorrhage found at autopsy; no other abnormality.

(*c*) Start of last menstrual period (mother's statement) 15.11.51, (calculated date) 12.10.51; onset of chickenpox 24.3.52; delivery 19.7.52. Birthweight 4 lb. 6 ox. (2.0 kg.). Stillborn; macerated foetus with large clot behind the placenta.

Of the 28 normal children, 24 were known to be alive and well when aged three years or more, and four were not traced after the initial examination. Birthweights were available for 26 of the children; one weighed 5 lb. 6 oz. (2.4 kg.), 12 weighed over $5\frac{1}{2}$ and less than 7 lb. (2.5 and 3.2 kg.) and 13 weighed 7 lb (3.2 kg.) or over.

Measles

As nearly all children in Great Britain have measles, an attack is relatively rare in adult life, and Table 22 4 gives data for only ten

TABLE 22, 4

Observations on Measles (Morbilli)

Stage at which Measles Commenced		No. of Cases	No. of Babies Stillborn or who Died before Examination	No. of Liveborn Babies in whom Ab-normalities were Detected	No. of Babies Born weighing $5\frac{1}{2}$lb. or Less
Before last menstrual period		4	0	1(a)	0
Weeks of Pregnancy	1st– 4th	1	0	0	0
	5th– 8th	0	—	—	—
	9th–12th	0	—	—	—
	13th–16th	1	0	0	0*
	17th–20th	2	0	0	0
	21st–24th	0	—	—	—
	25th or Later	2	0	1(b)	0*
Total		10	0	2	0

* Birthweight not available for one child.

(a) Start of last menstrual period (mother's statement) 15.4.49, (calculated date) 26.4.49; onset of measles 14.4.49; delivery 31.1.50. Birthweight 6lb. 3oz. (2.8kg.). Right talipes equino-varus.

(b) Start of last menstrual period (calculated date) 28.9.46; onset of measles 27.3.47; delivery 5.7.47. Birthweight 7lb. 9oz. (3.4kg.). Cerebral diplegia. The mother also had mild toxaemia one month before delivery.

cases. In four of these, the attack of measles began before the menstrual period which preceded the pregnancy. Two congenital defects were observed—a right talipes equino-varus following measles that occurred one day before the start of the last menstrual period, and a cerebral diplegia following measles in about the twenty-fifth week of pregnancy. In the latter case, the mother had also shown signs of toxaemia one month before delivery. Of the eight normal children, six were known to be alive and well when aged three years or more, and two were not traced after the initial examination. Birthweights were available for six of the children; one weighed 4lb. 5oz. (2.0kg.) and the others all weighed 7lb. (3.2kg.) or over.

DISCUSSION

The present investigation is clearly not extensive enough to provide an accurate estimate of the risk of malformation following an attack of rubella at different stages during pregnancy. Reports have, however, been published of several other investigations in which a prospective method of inquiry has been strictly applied, and the results of these studies may be combined. The combined results of four such studies, reported by Brown and Nathan (1954), Brawner (1955), Pitt (1957), and the present authors, are shown in Table **22,** 5. They comprise—with one exception—all the studies available to us which satisfy the following criteria:

(1) the occurrence of the attack of rubella was in every case recorded *before* the child was born;

(2) the children born to nearly all the affected mothers were subsequently examined;

(3) the data was published in sufficient detail for a separate estimate to be made of the risk for each *month* of pregnancy.

One other inquiry which satisfies these criteria was reported by Lamy and Seror (1956). Their results, however, are so different that it is preferable to consider them separately.

Table **22,** 5 shows that the risk of abnormality may be as high as 50 per cent when the infection occurs in the first month of 'pregnancy' (that is, in the four weeks following the start of the last preceding menstrual period). Subsequently, as the length of time between the last menstrual period and the appearance of the disease increases, the risk of abnormality steadily decreases. Of the 19 mothers showing the disease in or after the twenty-fifth week, none gave birth to a defective child. Not all the defects included, however, can be attributed with certainty to the maternal disease. Of the 11 infants with major defects with whom the maternal disease had occurred within the first two months of pregnancy, all showed a congenital heart disease, cataract, or deafness. It may be presumed, therefore, that all these defects were the result of the infection. Of the three infants with defects whose mothers were reported to have been ill in the third month, two died of a congenital heart lesion and one had a hare lip and cleft palate. Of the three infants whose mothers were reported to have been ill in the fourth, fifth, and sixth

TABLE **22,** 5

Risk of Defect in the Infant Following Maternal Rubella During Pregnancy (*Summation of data from four series*)

Stage of Pregnancy at which Rubella Commenced		Number of Cases	Infants with Major Defects	
			Number	Per cent
Weeks of Pregnancy	1st– 4th	12	6	50
	5th– 8th	20	5	25
	9th–12th	18	3	17
	13th–16th	18	2	11
	17th–24th	17	1	6
	25th or Later	19	0	0
	Total	104*	17	—

* Excluding two cases which terminated in abortion (rubella in the fifth and twelfth weeks respectively) and three cases in which the children could not be traced. One pair of fraternal twins (rubella in the twenty-first week) is included as two cases.

months, one showed bilateral deafness (the mother's illness occurred in the thirteenth week of pregnancy), and the other two were respectively a mongol (maternal illness, fourteenth week) and an anencephalic (maternal illness, twenty-first week). It is possible that the last two defects were not related to the preceding rubella, and that therefore no defects were due to the maternal illness when it occurred after the thirteenth week of pregnancy (some 50 cases in all). On the other hand, a number of lesions attributable to the disease may have been omitted from the various inquiries represented in Table **22,** 5. One foetus was stillborn and macerated following rubella in the sixth week, and another was stillborn, without any specific lesion being found at autopsy, following rubella in the fifteenth week. Two children died within six weeks of birth without being specially examined (following rubella in the sixth and twenty-first week), and one child was thought to have a 'possible mild grade of pulmonary stenosis' following rubella in the fourteenth week (Pitt, 1957). Moreover, some of the children were examined on only one occasion and at a relatively early age (one year or less) and cases of deafness may thus have been missed.

The results of the inquiry of Lamy and Seror (1956), which were excluded from Table **22,** 5, are summarized in Table **22,** 6. In this study, a questionnaire was sent to over 100,000 insured women who

TABLE **22,** 6

Observations of Lamy and Seror (1956) on Effects of Maternal Rubella During Pregnancy

Stage of Pregnancy at which Rubella Commenced		Number of Cases	Number ending in Abortion	Infants with Major Defects	
				Number	No. as per cent of Cases not ending in Abortion
Weeks of Pregnancy	1st– 4th	7	0	6	86
	5th– 8th	21	5	13	81
	9th–12th	12	0	3	25
	13th–20th	8	1	3	43
	Total	48	6	25*	—

* One other child was stillborn (rubella in the eighth week) and one died at the age of 15 days, cause unknown (rubella in the eleventh week).

stated they were pregnant between 1.3.53 and 31.3.54. The questionnaires were sent out in the fifth month of the pregnancies. Nearly half the women replied: 50 stated that they had had rubella in the first four months of the pregnancy and 48 of these could be followed up. The results suggest that the risk to the foetus may be substantially greater than was observed in the four studies summarized in Table **22,** 5.

Other studies, however, have suggested that the risk may be lower. Greenberg, Pellitteri, and Barton (1957), for example, have summarized the data from seven series not included in Table 22, 5. Among 96 infants born to mothers affected by rubella during the first trimester of pregnancy, six were stillborn (6.3 per cent). and only seven showed any major congenital defect (7.3 per cent). In most of the series it is not possible to distinguish between the risks in the various months of the first trimester, and, since rubella in the early months has been regarded as an indication for abortion, it is possible that the data are disproportionately weighted with cases occurring towards the end of that trimester. This, however, cannot account for the low incidence of defects reported by Lundström (1952). An epidemic of rubella occurred in Sweden in the spring of 1951 and the staffs of all the Swedish maternity hospitals were requested to question all women who were delivered in them or who were treated for a spontaneous abortion during the following year. Altogether, 1,067 women reported that they had had rubella during pregnancy. The proportion of stillbirths, neonatal deaths, and congenital abnormalities rose from 10 per cent when the disease was contracted in the first month, to 14 per cent for the second month; it fell again to 10 per cent for the third month and finally to about 3 per cent for the last four months of pregnancy. The corresponding figure for a control group of 2,452 children born in the same hospital at the same period was approximately 4 per cent.

The great differences in the results obtained by different groups of workers may be explained, in part, by the operations of chance and, in part, by differences in the methods used to investigate the problems and in the presentation of the results. It seems unlikely, however, that all the differences can be thus explained, and it is possible that the effect of a maternal attack of rubella may vary in space and time.

The results obtained in the present study from the follow-up of mothers who were infected during their pregnancy with mumps, chickenpox, or measles, provide no clear evidence of any deleterious effect of these diseases on the foetus. The only possible exception was chickenpox. Half the mothers who suffered from this disease gave birth to children weighing less than 7lb., compared with 22 per cent of the normal infants born to mothers who had one of the other diseases. The mean birth weights were not, however, significantly different (7.09lb. for chickenpox and 7.43 for the other diseases: 't' = 1.48; P greater than 0.1). Other workers (for example, Grönvall and Selander, 1948) failed to observe any characteristic effect from these infections and it seems very unlikely that they carry any important risk to the foetus.

SUMMARY

By a special recording system the occurrence of certain infectious diseases was noted in women whose illness, medically observed and diagnosed, fell during, or shortly before, a pregnancy. Information was subsequently sought regarding the infants born to them (live or still but excluding abortions or miscarriages), shortly after birth and again at an age of not less than three years. Data were thus acquired on 44 cases of German measles (rubella), 35 of mumps (epidemic parotitis), 30 of chickenpox (varicella), and 10 of measles (morbilli). There was no evidence that mumps or measles had had any deleterious effect upon the foetus. With chickenpox there was also no evidence of the production of congenital defects, but the proportion of liveborn children with low birth weights was relatively high (though the difference was not statistically significant). With rubella occurring early in pregnancy, the well-known congenital defects of heart, vision, and hearing were observed.

By the addition of these present cases to similar published records, some estimates are reached of the risks involved with rubella in different stages of pregnancy. An incidence of six affected children out of 12 with rubella in the mother in the first month of pregnancy (50 per cent) declines to five out of 20 for the second month (25 per cent) and to three out of 18 for the third month (17 per cent). With 54 women in whom the attack of rubella occurred in the second and third trimesters, 51 infants were unaffected, and only one of the three affected cases seemed likely to be attributable to the preceding rubella.

Other published data have shown both considerably higher and considerably lower incidence rates of congenital defects following rubella in early pregnancy. It may be therefore that the risk varies in space or time.

REFERENCES

Blawner, D. L. (1955). *J. med. Ass. Ga*, **44**, 451.
Brown, C. M., and Nathan, B. J. (1954). *Lancet*, **i**, 975.
Greenberg, M., Pellitteri, O., and Barton, J. (1957). *J. Amer. med. Ass.* **165**, 675.
Grönvall, H., and Selander, P. (1948). *Nord. Med.* **37**, 409.
Hill, A. Bradford, and Galloway, T. M. (1949). *Lancet*, **i**, 299.
Lamy, M., and Seror, M. E. (1956). *Sem. méd. prof. méd.-soc.* **32**, 1085.
Lundström, R. (1952). *Acta paediat.* (*Uppsala*), **41**, 583.
Pitt, D. B. (1957). *Med. J. Aust.* **1**, 233.

CHAPTER 23

ASIAN INFLUENZA IN PREGNANCY AND CONGENITAL DEFECTS

INFLUENZA caused by the Asian strain of virus A first became epidemic in Great Britain in the latter half of the year 1957. Available statistics show that it spread rapidly and widely, affecting the southern parts of the country rather later than the northern. Most of the strains isolated from patients throughout the country were shown to be of the Asian variety (McDonald, 1958; Ministry of Health, 1960).

In a detailed inquiry into its incidence in a general practice situated on the south-eastern outskirts of London (Woodall, Rowson, and McDonald, 1958), it was shown that the epidemic in that area lasted about eight weeks, that the main incidence lay between mid-September and late October, and that the peak was reached in the week ending 13 October. About one-third of persons of all ages, children as well as adults were recorded as attacked, and it was concluded, from a comparison with national insurance statistics, that this prevalence was not unlike that for the country as a whole. In particular we may note from this local investigation that of 253 women in the childbearing age group of 15–39 years, influenza was diagnosed in as many as 28 per cent. Under such conditions as these the opportunity was taken to investigate the possible effects of this new (or renewed) influenza virus upon the foetus when the illness concerned a woman in pregnancy.

ASCERTAINMENT OF CASES

To identify such women, who during their pregnancy suffered an attack of influenza, all those who attended the antenatal clinic at the Central Middlesex Hospital (North-west London) for the first time between 29 November, 1957, and 7 March, 1958, were specially interrogated by an almoner wholly employed and experienced in

(With Richard Doll and J. Sakula.) Reprinted from the *British Journal of Preventive and Social Medicine*, 1960, **14**, 167.

medical research. The date of her last menstrual period having been recorded, each woman was asked whether since the summer of 1957 she had been ill with influenza, and if so, the dates of the attack. If she said she had had influenza, three further questions were asked:

(a) Whether she had had a temperature.

(b) Whether she stayed in bed.

(c) Whether she consulted a doctor.

If she had consulted a doctor, a letter was sent to him asking whether in his opinion the illness referred to appeared likely to have been influenza. There could, of course, be no evidence that any such illness was due to the Asian strain of virus but it is known, as already stated, that the epidemic at this time was in general due to it.

Of 661 women interviewed in this way, 240 (36.3 per cent) said that they had had influenza. Of these 240 cases relevant to the investigation, 65 were excluded from further observation for the following reasons:

(a) Three subsequently proved not to be pregnant.

(b) Twelve aborted (naturally or induced).

(c) Fifty were referred elsewhere for the supervision of their confinement and passed outside our observation.

We have, therefore, particulars of the infants born to 175 women delivered in the Central Middlesex Hospital. (Two bore twins so that the number of babies involved is 177.)

Not all these 175 women, however, were regarded as having suffered an attack of influenza. In accordance with the criteria mentioned above, they may be divided as in Table **23**,1, which shows that 128 were accepted as having had influenza (though it is likely that some did not) and 47 were not accepted (though it is possible that some did have influenza). The attack rate of 128 in 606 women (21 per cent) is of the same order as the 28 per cent reported by Woodall, Rowson and McDonald (1958) in S.E. London.

The 177 infants subsequently born to these women were all specially examined for congenital defects by one of us (J.S.). The inquiry thus meets the requirements of a prospective investigation.

In analysing the results we have followed the normal obstetric procedure of calculating the stage of pregnancy at which the illness took place from the first day of the last preceding menstrual period.

TABLE **23,** 1

Ascertainment of 175 *Possible Cases of Influenza During Pregnancy*

Nature of Evidence regarding Influenza	No. of Cases
(*a*) Diagnosis confirmed by doctor who saw the patient during the illness	49
(*b*) Doctor called in during illness but kept no record of the case (22 cases) or did not reply to letter of inquiry (27 cases)	49
(*c*) Mother's statement that she had a temperature or stayed in bed	30
Total accepted as influenza	128
(*d*) Diagnosis not confirmed by doctor who saw the patient during the illness	40
(*e*) Mother had not had a temperature nor stayed in bed	7
Total not accepted as influenza	47
Total	175

RESULTS

The results of the inquiry are set out in Tables **23,** 2 to **23,** 5.

Of the 50 infants born to women whose attack of influenza had been medically confirmed two showed abnormalities (Table **23,**2), in one case a hare lip and extensive naevus of the face, and in the other an extra digit attached to a finger. In both instances, however, the influenza attack had *preceded* the pregnancy—by as much as two months in one instance and by 2–3 weeks in the other (Table **23,**4). Of the 22 infants whose mothers had had influenza during the first trimester of their pregnancy, none had defects and none was stillborn.

Turning attention to the group of women whose attack had not been medically confirmed, there were, it will be seen, 41 whose illness took place in the first trimester. Of the babies subsequently born to them one was stillborn and two had defects: *viz.* one case of hypospadias following influenza in the first week or two of pregnancy and one infant who died soon after delivery with a diagnosis of congenital heart lesion and ? cerebral haemorrhage following influenza at about the eleventh to twelfth week of pregnancy. There was also one woman with a stillborn child whose attack preceded the start of pregnancy by about two weeks (Tables **23,**2 and **23,**4).

TABLE **23**, 2

Observations on Cases Accepted as Influenza

| Stage of Pregnancy at which Influenza Commenced | Nature of Evidence of Influenza in Mother | | | | | |
| | Confirmed by Doctor | | | Mother's Statement | | |
	No. of Children	No. Stillborn	No. Liveborn with Abnormality	No. of Children	No. Stillborn	No. Liveborn with Abnormality
Before Last Menstrual Period	17	0	2 (a, b)	23	1 (c)	0
Weeks of Pregnancy — 1st– 4th	10	0	0	13	0	1 (d)
5th– 8th	5	0	0	14	0	0
9th–12th	7	0	0	14	1 (e)	1 (f)
13th–16th	6	0	0	10	0	0
17th or Later	5*	0	0	5	0	0
Total	50*	0	2	79	2	2

* Including one pair of fraternal twins.   For *a*, *b*, *c*, *d*, *e*, *f*, see Table **23**, 4

Looking finally at the group of 48 infants born to women whose illness was not accepted as influenza, there was one who had a stillborn child and whose illness preceded the pregnancy. Of the 30 women in this group whose illness took place during the first trimester none had a stillborn and none a defective child (Tables 23, 3 and 23, 4).

TABLE 23, 3

*Observations on Cases Not Accepted as Influenza**

Stage of Pregnancy at which Influenza Commenced		No. of Children	No. Stillborn	No. Liveborn with Abnormality
Before last menstrual period		7†	1(g)	0
Weeks of Pregnancy	1st– 4th	10	0	0
	5th– 8th	9	0	0
	9th–12th	11	0	0
	13th–16th	7	0	0
	17th or Later	4	0	0
Total		48†	1	0

* The seven cases where the mother's statement was not accepted (see Table 23, 1) lie as follows: one at first to fourth, one at ninth to twelfth, two at thirteenth to sixteenth, three at seventeenth or later.

† Including one pair of fraternal twins.

(g) See Table 23, 4.

In short, there is no clear evidence in these data of congenital defects following the Asian influenza during pregnancy. Taken at its worst there were 63 women who had 'accepted' influenza during the first trimester and two of their infants had defects. On the other hand, there were 66 women who had 'accepted' influenza either before their pregnancy commenced or in the second or third trimester and again two of their infants had defects (both of which occurred in the 'preceding pregnancy' group). An alternative comparison we can make is between (a) the two defective babies in 89 born to mothers whose influenzal attack took place during pregnancy, an incidence of 2.2 per cent, and (b) a general figure for congenital malformations (excluding minor blemishes) found in all infants born alive in the same hospital from a special count made some years earlier (in 1953), namely 27 in 1,996 livebirths or 1.35 per cent.

In Table 23, 5 we have examined the data from the point of view

Details of Stillbirth and Congenital Defects

Reference* (and Stage of Pregnancy)	Start of Last Menstrual Period	Onset of Influenza	Date of Delivery	Child		
				Sex	Birth Weight lb. oz.	Condition
a (Before)	10.11.57	Mid-sep., 1957	26.8.58	F	5 6	Hare lip and extensive naevus left side of face.
b (Before)	3.10.57	15.9.57	6.7.58	M	6 9	Extra digit attached to right fifth finger.
c (Before)	10.11.57	End Oct., 1957	3.9.58	M	8 2	Stillborn, difficult delivery, cord round neck
d (1–4) week	13.11.57	23.11.57	9.9.58	M	8 15	Hypospadias.
e (9–12) week	24.8.57	End Oct., 1957	31.5.58	?	?	Macerated foetus, died in utero.
f (9–12) week	9.9.57	Near end of Nov., 1957	8.4.58	M	3 8	Died after eight hours, *post mortem* refused. Diagnosis, congenital heart-lesion, ? cerebral haemorrhage.
g (Before)	15.9.57	August, 1957	15.6.58	M	?	Stillborn, Caesarean section after failed forceps, birth injuries.

* In references (a) to (f) the illness in the mother was accepted as influenza; in (g) it was not.

TABLE **23**, 5

Mean Birth Weights of Liveborn Children

Stage of Pregnancy at which Influenza Commenced		Cases with Diagnosis Confirmed by Doctor		Cases Based on Mother's Statement		All Cases Accepted as Influenza		Cases not Accepted as Influenza
		lb.	oz.	lb.	oz.	lb.	oz.	lb.	oz.
Before Last Menstrual Period		7	4* (1)	6	14 (2)	7	0 (3)	7	4* (1)
	1st–4th	7	2	7	7 (1)	7	5 (1)	7	9
Weeks	5th–8th	7	6	6	6 (3)	6	11 (3)	7	14
of	9th–12th	6	6 (1)	7	5 (2)	7	0 (3)	7	3
Pregnancy	13th–16th	6	8 (1)	7	4	6	15 (1)	7	7
	17th or Later	6	13*	7	1	6	15*	6	8 (1)
All Periods		7	0* (3)	7	0 (8)	7	0* (11)	7	6* (2)

* Including one pair of fraternal twins. Figures in brackets indicate number of infants weighing 5½ lb. or less at birth.

of birth weight. The only contrast of interest within these data appears to be between the 89 women with 'accepted' influenza during pregnancy, amongst whom there were eight infants weighing $5\frac{1}{2}$lb. or less (9 per cent) and the 41 women with 'not accepted' influenza during pregnancy, who had only one such baby (2.5 per cent). The difference is not, however, statistically significant and it may also be noted that amongst the 47 women whose illnesses *preceded* pregnancy there were four babies of $5\frac{1}{2}$lb. or less (8.5 per cent). The mean birth weight of the babies born to mothers who had influenza during pregnancy was 7lb. compared with 7lb. 6oz. for those whose illness was not accepted as influenza and 7lb. 3oz. for 60 babies born to mothers who had either chickenpox, mumps, or measles during pregnancy (Hill, Doll, Galloway, and Hughes, 1958). The differences are clearly slight.

DISCUSSION

The negative findings of this present small inquiry are in contrast to those reported by Coffey and Jessop (1959) who studied women exposed to this same epidemic of Asian influenza in Dublin. Of 663 births to women who, in reply to questioning at antenatal clinics, said that they had had influenza, 3.6 per cent were malformed compared with only 1.5 per cent in 663 paired controls without influenza. The excess malformations were serious, for almost all affected the central nervous system, anencephaly being the most frequent. In addition, their incidence was clearly related to the trimester in which the influenza occurred, the percentage rates being 7.4, 4.3, and 2.0. As in the present inquiry, there was no evidence of an increase in the frequency of births of low birth weight.

Some slight support to these observations in Dublin is given by a study reported by Pleydell (1960) from the County of Northamptonshire. From a questionnaire sent to all midwives practising in the county, 43 pregnant women were identified as suffering from Asian influenza (the mothers 'suffered from a febrile illness with symptoms and signs similar to influenza during the time when the Asian influenza reached epidemic proportions in the country'). After the baby was born the midwives' ante-natal records and Health Visitors' birth inquiry cards were checked for abnormalities, and where an abnormality was recorded its nature was obtained from the records of the general practitioner concerned, from death certification, or from hospital records. By these means three abnormalities were found compared with 14 in the 1,040 births to mothers who were pregnant while the Asian influenza was prevalent but who were not reported as having been attacked. The three abnormalities were a case of hydrocephalus amongst 12 births following influenza in the first trimester, a case of congenital heart disease amongst 18 births following influenza in the second trimester, and a case of spina bifida and hydrocephalus amongst 13 births following influenza in the third trimester. These figures show no trend in relation to the time of attack though taking also into account two abortions and an infant death attributed to bronchopneumonia the author himself concludes that 'as with rubella, the risk of foetal damage appears to be greater when the illness has occurred in the early months of pregnancy'.

Two studies have been reported from the U.S.A. Wilson, Heins, Imagawa and Adams (1959) measured the haemagglutination-inhibition titre against pooled Asian influenza antigen in the serum of 738 women who attended Los Angeles County Hospital for antenatal examination between March and May, 1958. The women included in the inquiry were those in whom conception was believed to have taken place between the previous October and December, 1957, the period when an epidemic of Asian influenza first occurred in Los Angeles. Of these women, 126 were subsequently interviewed and their babies were examined. Four abnormalities were found: *viz.* two cases of anencephaly among 75 women whose sera gave positive titres, and one cleft palate and one possible amyotoria among 51 women whose sera were negative. Each of the mothers of the anencephalic babies gave a history of a cold in the third month of pregnancy, associated with a three-day fever in one case and unassociated with general symptoms in the other; the mothers of the other two abnormal children reported no illness in the first trimester. In the opinion of the authors no significant effect of Asian influenza was demonstrated.

Walker and McKee (1959) also used the haemagglutination-inhibiting titre to indicate whether the mothers had contracted Asian influenza. They, however, used several different viral antigens obtained from strains isolated from cases which occurred in Iowa City, and obtained a much higher incidence of positive results. Of 297 women who were delivered at the State University Hospital of Iowa and who were interviewed in the puerperium, 158 (53 per cent) gave a clinical history of influenza; among these positive sera were obtained in 154 (97.5 per cent). Positive results were, however, obtained in the whole of a further series of 101 mothers who were examined irrespective of their clinical history. Asian influenza was prevalent in Iowa from September to November, 1957, and it is presumed that all the 398 women in both series had been in contact with influenza during the first and second trimester of their pregnancy. Altogether 13 congenital anomalies were found, including two cases in stillborn children; one of these children was anencephalic. The incidence of anomalies was slightly lower for women who had had symptomatic influenza (6/214 or 2.8 per cent) than for women who did not report symptoms (7/184 or 3.8 per cent). Both figures being lower than the standard incidence of 4.2 per cent reported by Davis and Potter (1957), the authors concluded that there was no apparent alteration in incidence which could be attributed to the epidemic of influenza.

An earlier study reported by Campbell (1953) precedes the development of the Asian strain and relates to the sharp epidemic of Virus A influenza that struck a number of places in 1950–51. All expectant mothers attending certain antenatal clinics in Belfast (Northern Ireland), and whose last menstrual period lay between 1 September, 1950, and 31 January, 1951, were asked whether they had suffered from influenza (defined as 'a febrile illness with a sharp onset, characterized by pains in the legs, back, or head, and sufficiently severe to require that the patient went to bed, the first day of the illness falling between 15 December and 31 January inclusive'). Following influenza there were 164 births, and as controls, with no reported influenza, there were 825 births. The stillbirth rates were 2.4 and 1.5 per cent respectively, and of the livebirths four and seven (2.5 and 0.9 per cent) had abnormalities. In relation to the month of pregnancy in which influenza occurred, the numbers of livebirths and deformities were as follows:

    1st month   35   No deformities;
    2nd month   39   One clubfoot, one hydrocephalic;
    3rd month   45   One absence of kidney;
    4th month   41   One clubfoot.

The numbers are small but again there is no evidence of a trend. Amongst the stillbirths there was one with anencephaly following influenza, but in the non-infected mothers there were also three such cases, together with one of spina bifida and one described as 'I.V.D.'.

In all these inquiries (including our own) there is, it will be noted, no laboratory evidence to confirm the clinical diagnosis of influenza. We ourselves endeavoured to check the accuracy of the mothers' history by reference to the medical attendant and as a result of the replies we removed a quarter of our cases from the influenza category.

In the studies from the U.S.A. the diagnosis was based on the discovery of a positive serum reaction some time after the infection was presumed to have occurred, and it is clear from one of these that a positive reaction was common in the absence of a clinical history of any illness. It is evident, therefore, that no series provides a clear-cut comparison between mothers infected at an early period of pregnancy and mothers who were not infected or were infected only at a different period. Any difference observed between the defined groups is likely to be less than the real one as a result of the inclusion of cases not due to the influenza virus in the influenza series and of true influenzal infections in the control series. Nevertheless, if the influenza virus is capable of bringing about a congenital malformation in the foetus, it should be possible to detect this by showing that the malformation rate among children of infected mothers is higher than that normally encountered in the same area. One can, moreover, rely on there being a high probability that the majority of reported cases will in fact be influenza *when the disease is sharply epidemic*, and a comparison between mothers who report infections at different periods of pregnancy at that time should reveal a difference in the effect on the children. Judged by these criteria, our own data certainly do not suggest any appreciable hazard, since the 63 attacks occurring in the first trimester of pregnancy and the 66 attacks in a later stage of pregnancy or before the last preceding menstrual period were both followed by one stillbirth and two cases of congenital abnormality. In total, these figures are not unlike those that we reported as following mumps, chickenpox, or measles, where 60 cases of such illnesses during pregnancy were succeeded by three stillbirths and two defective infants.

If, however, the hazard was small, it would be difficult to detect by this method unless very large numbers of children were examined. In these circumstances, an indication might be obtained from national vital statistics, by seeing if there was any temporal relation between the occurrence of an epidemic and the recorded incidence of malformations. Data for the number of stillbirths due to congenital malformations are published separately for each month by the Registrar-General for Scotland, and his figures for the 10 years 1950–59 (Table **23,** 6) show that the numbers of stillbirths attributed to anencephaly in 1958 and in 1959 were above the average for the preceding eight years; in fact, the stillbirth rate due to anencephaly was greater in both these years than at any other time since 1939, when these data began to be published. In contrast, there was no increase in 1958 and 1959 in the stillbirth rate due to other malformations. It may be noted that this latter rate was below average in both these years; but it is hardly reasonable to suppose that the recorded increase in anencephaly is an artefact due to changes in the standards of diagnosis. The increase in the number of stillbirths due to anencephaly in 1958 occurred principally in the eight months May to December, when the number was 39 per cent above average; in the first four months of the year the increase was only 3 per cent above average. Figures for the total numbers of births are not available by month, but the quarterly figures for 1958 show that the total numbers of births in Scotland were 6 per cent, 2 per cent, 1 per cent, and 11 per cent above the average for the first, second, third, and fourth quarters in 1950–7, respectively. According to Grist (1959), serological tests showed evidence of influenza infection in Glasgow between August, 1957, and April, 1958, with peaks in September to October and January to March. The 1958 stillbirth data may, therefore, be regarded as fitting in with the concept that there is a small risk of producing anencephaly in the foetus, if the mother contracts Asian influenza during the first two months of pregnancy. In 1959, the excess number of stillbirths due to anencephaly was practically limited to the four months April to July; in this period the number was 48 per cent above average, whereas in the remaining eight months it was only 5 per cent above average. Data are not at present available to us to show whether there was any serological evidence of fresh infection in Scotland during this period.

In the light of all the evidence, the most reasonable conclusion would appear to be that anencephaly may be produced if the mother contracts Asian influenza during the first few months of pregnancy. The extent of the hazard is, however, clearly small, and it is possible that it may be produced only when other circumstances are suitable (for example, in an area where the incidence of anencephaly is normally high).

TABLE 23, 6

Stillbirths Due to Anencephaly and Other Congenital Malformations of the Foetus in Scotland, 1950–9

Cause of Stillbirth	Period	No. of Stillbirths													Rate per 1,000 Total Births
		Jan.	Feb.	Mar.	April	May	June	July	Aug.	Sept.	Oct.	Nov.	Dec.	Whole Year	
Anencephalus	Average 1950–7	27·0	21·0	21·9	22·0	17·5	19·4	19·5	20·3	19·8	22·4	22·9	27·1	260·6	2·74
	1958	31	27	18	19	30	32	21	33	24	34	26	35	330	3·24
	1959	31	31	18	30	27	27	32	16	17	25	29	24	307	3·02
Other Congenital Malformations	Average 1950–7	22·8	19·3	19·5	19·1	24·0	16·8	17·5	18·6	17·9	16·5	19·1	20·3	231·3	2·43
	1958	28	15	25	5	8	18	21	14	12	16	22	24	208	2·04
	1959	15	21	19	19	12	12	18	8	14	15	19	16	188	1·85

SUMMARY

Following the introduction into Great Britain of the Asian strain of influenza virus A, and the epidemic that it caused in the latter half of the year 1957, steps were taken to identify women who had suffered an attack during their pregnancy. Special observations were then made of 177 infants subsequently born to (*a*) 88 women whose influenzal attack took place during their pregnancy, (*b*) 40 women whose influenzal attack preceded their pregnancy, and (*c*) 47 women whose attack was not regarded as one of influenza.

No hazard to the foetus was detected in those cases in which the illness fell within pregnancy, or, in particular, in its early stages. A positive effect has been reported in some other studies and an increase in the stillbirth rate due to anencephaly has been recorded in Scotland in 1958 and (to a lesser extent) in 1959. It seems probable that infection of the mother with Asian influenza during the early months of pregnancy can increase the risks of anencephaly, but that the extent of the hazard is normally small.

REFERENCES

Campbell, W. A. B. (1953). *Lancet*, **i**, 173.
Coffey, V. P., and Jessop, W. J. E. (1959). *Lancet*, **ii**, 935.
Davis, M. E., and Potter, E. L. (1957). *Pediatrics*, **19**, 719.
Grist, N. R. (1959). *Scot. med. J.* **4**, 446.
Hill, A. Bradford, Doll, R., Galloway, T. McL., and Hughes, J. P. W. (1958). *Brit. J. prev. soc. Med.* **12**, 1.
McDonald, J. C. (1958), *Proc. R. Soc. Med.* **51**, 1016.
Ministry of Health (1960). *Rep. publ. Hlth. med. Subj. Lond.* No. 100.
Pleydell, M. J. (1960). *Brit. med. J.* **i**, 309.
Walker, W. M., and McKee, A. P. (1959). *Obstet. Gynec.* **13**, 394.
Wilson, M. G., Heins, H. L., Imagawa, D. T., and Adams, J. M. (1959). *J. Amer. med. Ass.* **171**, 638.
Woodall, J., Rowson, K. E. K., and McDonald, J. C. (1958). *Brit. med. J.* **ii**, 1316.

CHAPTER 24

INCIDENCE OF LEUKAEMIA AFTER EXPOSURE
TO DIAGNOSTIC RADIATION IN UTERO

INTEREST in the effects of small doses of ionizing radiations has focused attention on the possibility that doses of X rays such as are used in medical diagnostic radiology may on occasion be carcinogenic. Little direct evidence is available, since the effect (if it exists) is small, and to detect it very large numbers of subjects need to be studied. Mostly the evidence relates to the special cases of the foetus irradiated during examination of the mother's abdomen or pelvis, and it has been obtained by retrospective inquiry into the history of her pregnancy after the child's death was known to have occurred.

The most extensive data are those published by Stewart and her colleagues at Oxford (Stewart, Webb, Giles, and Hewitt, 1956; Stewart, Webb, and Hewitt, 1958). In their study, histories were obtained from mothers whose children had died of malignant disease throughout England and Wales during the period 1953–6, and the results were compared with those obtained from a control group of mothers whose children were still alive. It was concluded that children who were exposed *in utero* to pelvimetry, or to another similar procedure, had approximately double the normal risk of dying from cancer before the age of 10 years.

In the present study, data have been obtained by a different technique. Women who were irradiated during pregnancy have been identified in the records of the radiological departments of selected hospitals and the subsequent deaths from leukaemia of the children of these pregnancies have then been discovered. The observed mortality from leukaemia has been compared with that expected on the basis of the national mortality rates. With the technique

(With W. M. Court Brown and Richard Doll, and the co-operation of Drs. D. H. Cummack, Margaret S. King, Eric Samuel, and W. N. Thomson (Edinburgh), and R. E. Lawrence, F. Pygott, R. E. Steiner, and E. Rohan Williams (London).)

Reprinted from the *British Medical Journal*, 1960, **ii**, 1539.

employed it was possible to study only leukaemia, and no evidence has been obtained about other types of cancer.

The Children Studied

Eight hospitals were selected, four of which served most of Edinburgh and four a compact area in North-West London. With the co-operation of the radiological departments, lists were compiled of all those women known to have been exposed, between 1945 and 1956, to diagnostic X-ray examination of the pelvis or abdomen during pregnancy. The great majority of these women were delivered in the same hospital, and information was obtained from the maternity department about the mother's address, the date of birth and sex of the child, and whether the child was born alive or dead. It was possible to obtain the same information for a small number of these women who (1) were found to have been delivered at another of the hospitals participating in the inquiry (or at another associated hospital), or (2) were delivered at home, but for whom out-patient records of delivery were readily available. Women whose maternity records were not thus available were excluded from the study. The great majority of these women were under the care of general practitioners or were private patients. The numbers in the various categories are shown in Table **24,** 1.

In nearly all cases the information provided by the hospital enabled the registration of the child's birth to be identified in either

TABLE **24,** 1

Number of Women who Received Abdominal or Pelvic Irradiation During Pregnancy and Proportion for whom Maternity Records were Available

Maternity Records	Irradiated Women	
	No.	%
Available:		
Delivered in same hospital	38,114	87·1
Delivered in other hospital	351	0·8
Delivered at home	1,122	2·6
Not available	4,155	9·5
Total	43,742	100·0

the local or the central Register of Births. These registers then provided information about the first names of the child and the first names and the occupation of the father. The numbers of children for whom full records were obtained in this way are shown in Table **24,** 2. No attempt was made to trace the registration entries

TABLE **24,** 2

Number of Children Known to have been Irradiated in utero and Proportion for Whom Adequate Records were Obtained

Records of Child	No. of Children			Total Children	
	Male	Female	Sex not Recorded	No.	%
Adequate records:					
Aborted	75	89	349	513	1·2
Stillborn	979	930	90	1,999	4·8
Liveborn	20,982	18,174	10	39,166	93·6
Inadequate records:					
Liveborn	76	70	2	148	0·4
Total	22,112	19,263	451	41,826	100·0

of stillborn children or of children who were known to have died in hospital, as in these cases the hospital records themselves provided all the necessary information.

The liveborn children whose sex was not recorded are known to have died in hospital in the neonatal period, so that further follow-up of these was not needed. The very few liveborn children for whom adequate records were not obtained may have been registered in districts other than those in which the hospital or the recorded address of the mother was situated, and their records could not be identified in the Central Register because, in many cases, there were too many entries that conceivably might have related to them. A few may have been missed because of a change of name at registration.

Information about the date and type of the mother's X-ray examination was obtained from the radiological records. All examinations directed at the mother's abdomen or pelvis were recorded if they had been made within nine calendar months of the date of delivery. On the basis of this information the women were classified into six categories according to the number and type of X-ray examinations to which they were exposed. The numbers of children born alive to women in each category, for whom full birth data were obtained, are shown in Table **24**, 3.

TABLE **24**, 3

Numbers of Liveborn Children Exposed to Various Types of Radiographic Examination in Utero

Exposure Category	No. of Liveborn Children		
	Male	Female	Total
A. Pelvimetry on one occasion only	7,864	6,900	14,768*
B. Pelvimetry on one occasion plus additional exposure	2,487	2,072	4,561*
C. Simple abdominal radiography on one occasion only	8,921	7,659	16,584*
D. Simple abdominal radiography on one occasion plus additional exposure other than from pelvimetry	1,149	1,017	2,166
E. Intravenous pyelography	291	262	553
F. Miscellaneous	270	264	534
Total	20,982	18,174	39,166*

* For 10 children the sex was not recorded—four each in categories A and C, and two in category B.

Identification of Leukaemia Deaths

The task of following up nearly 40,000 children until the age of 14 years to discover how many had died would have been extremely laborious. It was relatively simple, however, to discover how many had died of leukaemia, since we possessed copies of the death entries of all persons who had died of leukaemia in Great Britain from 1 January, 1945, to 31 December, 1958, which had been provided by the Registrars-General of England and Wales and of Scotland for the purpose of another inquiry. All that had to be done was to check the names of the children who had been irradiated against the names of the children who had died of leukaemia. If the child's first names and the first name of the father were alike on the two lists this was regarded as presumptive evidence that the irradiated child had died of leukaemia. The identity was, however, not considered to be established unless the occupation of the father was also alike and the addresses given at the time of birth and of death were the same. In all other circumstances—namely, of a lesser degree of similarity—inquiries were made from the hospital in which the child had died from leukaemia, or from the doctor who certified the death, about the date of birth of the child and the first names of the mother.

Calculation of the Expected Mortality

The mortality from leukaemia in childhood varies sharply with sex and age, and it also varied somewhat at each age during the period under investigation. We therefore had to estimate the number of children of each sex exposed to risk of death at each year of age during each of the years between 1945 and 1958. For this purpose children born in each calendar year were regarded as having been born at the mid-point of the year, and the numbers reaching each successive age were obtained by subtracting the numbers estimated to have been lost to the study during the course of the year. Since the identification of the children who died of leukaemia depended on the identification of the names of the child and of the parents given on the birth certificate, it is clear that adopted children would be liable to escape identification. All adopted children were therefore regarded as having been lost to the inquiry.

For children aged 1 year the loss rate was determined by adding the adoption rate to the infant mortality rate and the number of children of each sex lost to the study in the first year of life was then estimated by multiplying the number of entrants by this loss rate. For subsequent years the loss rate was obtained by adding the adoption rate to the corresponding age-specific death rate and the losses at each year of age were calculated by multiplying the loss rate by the average number of children estimated to have been alive throughout that year of life. For example, there were 916 living male children who were born in 1950 in the four London hospitals to mothers whose abdomen or pelvis was known to have been examined radiographically during the pregnancy. The male loss rate in the first year of life was 40.4 per 1,000 liveborn children (male infant mortality rate, 33.6, and male adoption rate at age 0–1 year, 6.8 per 1,000 liveborn children), so that the number of boys who reached the age of one year is calculated to be $916 - \dfrac{40.4}{1000} \times 916$—i.e. 879.0. The death rate and the adoption rate for boys aged 1–2 years in 1951 were 2.6 and 1.9 per 1,000 boys, so that the loss rate in the same group during this period was 4.5 per 1,000. Since the number of boys estimated at risk half-way through the year was 879.0 less half the number of losses, the total number of losses in the year (L) is $\left(\dfrac{4.5}{1000}\,879.0 - \dfrac{L}{2}\right)$, hence the number of losses was 3.9 and the number of boys who reached the age of two years is calculated to be 875.1.

Death rates from leukaemia for each sex and for each year of life were obtained for each calendar year between 1945 and 1958 by counting the number of the relevant death certificates in our possession and relating them to the published estimates of the corresponding populations. Finally, the numbers of deaths from leukaemia that could be expected to be found in our population of children irradiated *in utero* were calculated by multiplying the child-years at risk in each sex, age, and calendar year group by the corresponding leukaemia death rates. The total number of deaths from leukaemia was obtained by summing the results for all these sub-groups. Throughout the calculations the data for London and for Edinburgh were treated separately. The loss rates from death and adoption for England and Wales were, however, used for both sets of data, as sufficiently detailed data were not available for Scotland.

RESULTS

The number of children found to have died of leukaemia in the period 1945–58 was nine; the expected number was 10.5. Details of the nine cases are given in Table 24, 4. The numbers of deaths observed and expected among various groups of children are shown in Table 24, 5. In each group the observed and expected numbers are closely similar. It is perhaps particularly striking that there were four deaths from leukaemia among the 19,329 children exposed during pelvimetry, against 5.4 expected, and that there were five deaths among the 16,584 children exposed only in the course of one X-ray examination of the mother's abdomen, against 4.3 expected. All but one of the leukaemic children were exposed to radiation during the last four weeks of intra-uterine life; the exception was exposed in the last month but one. An exact calculation of the expected numbers of deaths among children exposed at various periods of intrauterine life has not been made; but data obtained for a 1 per cent sample show

TABLE **24,** 4

Details of Irradiation in utero *for Children Discovered to have Died of Leukaemia*

Date of Exposure	Cate-gory of Expos-ure*	Date of Birth	Interval between Exposure and Birth (Weeks)	Sex of Child	Age at Death (Years)	Type of Leukaemia
5/7/45	C	15/7/45	1	M	2	Acute lymphatic
11/7/45	C	27/7/45	2	F	9	Acute lymphatic
22/3/46	C	18/4/46	3	M	11	Unspecified
7/4/48	C	24/4/48	2	M	3	Aleukaemic
26/11/48	A	16/12/48	2	M	2	Acute lymphatic
18/8/49	C	10/10/49	7	F	1	Subacute
7/10/49	A	17/10/49	1	M	6	Acute lymphatic
22/8/52	A	31/8/52	1	M	4	Acute myeloid
10/11/52	A	27/11/52	2	M	3	Lymphatic

*A = Pelvimetry on one occasion only.
C = Simple abdominal radiography on one occasion only.

TABLE **24,** 5

Comparison Between Numbers of Deaths from Leukaemia Observed and Expected Divided by Age, Sex, Type of Irradiation, and Place of Residence

Category of Children	No. of Deaths from Leukaemia	
	Observed	Expected
Boys	7	6·2
Girls	2	4·4
Age less than 5 years	6	7·5
Age 5–13 years	3	3·0
Exposure to irradiation during pelvimetry (radiation groups A and B)	4	5·4
Exposure only to one simple X-ray examination (radiation group C)	5	4·3
Irradiation in Edinburgh	5	5·7
Irradiation in London	4	4·8
All children	9	10·5

that 50 per cent of the children were exposed only in the last four weeks, 38 per cent were first exposed in the preceding two months, 10 per cent were first exposed in the second trimester, and 2 per cent were first exposed in the first trimester.

It is clear from these data that the leukaemia mortality within the first 14 years of life was no greater among the group of children who were known to have been irradiated *in utero* than that for all children throughout the country who were born in the same years. Moreover, the leukaemia deaths were not disproportionately concentrated among those children who can be presumed to have received the heavier dose, nor among those children who were irradiated during the first part of intrauterine life. It should, however, be noted that few children were irradiated during the first three months, so that the inquiry provides little useful information about the extent of any possible risk in this period.

An incidental finding, which may be of some interest, is that the sex ratio among the irradiated children was substantially higher than normal. The sex ratio of liveborn children, shown in Table **24**,2 was 1.15 males to 1 female, whereas both for England and Wales and for Scotland the sex ratio for the years 1945 to 1956 was 1.06 to 1. An unusually high ratio was observed separately at each of the eight hospitals—the range being from 1.09 to 1 to 1.18 to 1—and in each of the years 1945 to 1956. The ratio was lower than average for the small number of children irradiated in 1956 who were born in 1957 (147 males to 144 females); but for the other 12 years the range was from 1.12 to 1 to 1.23 to 1. The most likely explanation of this high ratio would seem to be that the risk of a complicated delivery is higher for boys than for girls. Since the threat of a complicated delivery is one of the principal reasons for radiographic examination during pregnancy, this would result in a high male:female ratio among the children of irradiated mothers. There is no evident reason why the high proportion of boys in the series should have biased the results of the present inquiry.

DISCUSSION

Before discussing the results of this investigation we must consider whether they could have been influenced by any of several factors. First, was the technique employed adequate to identify all the cases of leukaemia that actually occurred in the population studied? This we have tested in two ways: (*a*) The records of a random sample of 50 of the children were re-examined to see if any errors had been made in recording the names of the children or of their parents; (*b*) A random sample of 50 deaths from leukaemia was selected (excluding those which referred to children born outside the period of the study) and the birth certificates of the children concerned were sought at the General Register Offices to see if the information recorded on these birth certificates would have enabled the child to be identified in the list of leukaemia deaths.

The first test revealed no inaccuracies in the data which had been extracted from the hospital records and the birth registers. The second test showed that in 46 instances the information given on the birth certificate was identical with that available to us in the copy of the death entry. In two instances there were minor differences in spelling which would not have resulted in any difficulty in identifying the child, had he been one of those who were studied. In one instance there was a serious difference in spelling, and in one the previous birth entry could not be traced because the child had been adopted. As already pointed out, it had been realized that cases might be missed because of adoption, and this was allowed for in calculating the number of expected deaths. The one example of a serious difference in spelling might have resulted in a failure to recognize that one of the children in our records had subsequently developed leukaemia. A small number of deaths may also have been missed because the children had emigrated, but this can hardly be more than a few per cent of the total for children under 15 years of age. It is possible, therefore, that the technique leads to an underestimate of the true incidence of leukaemia deaths by some 2 or 3 per cent. But even if the deficiency were as much as 10 per cent (which is very unlikely) the observed incidence of leukaemia among the irradiated children would still not exceed the national average.

Secondly, we may consider whether the results are distorted by the use of unsuitable data to calculate the expected mortality. Certainly it would have been preferable to compare the results with those obtained from a group of children born to unirradiated mothers from the same hospitals (although mothers who need to be X-rayed during pregnancy must differ from those who do not require such an examination and the comparison would not be ideal). Analysis of the leukaemia mortality for England and Wales and for Scotland has, however, shown that both the London and the Edinburgh leukaemia mortality rates are substantially above average for their respective countries (Hewitt, 1955; Court Brown, Doll, Spiers, Duffy, and McHugh, 1960); moreover, the Scottish mortality has been practically identical with that recorded in England and Wales. Unless, therefore, the children born at the hospitals included in this study were differentiated in some way which would have a major effect on their leukaemia mortality from all other children born in the same two cities, the method of comparison used in the study is more likely to have shown an excess among the irradiated children than the reverse.

Thirdly, it is possible that the dose of radiation received by the children in the present study may have been less than the average amount received from irradiation of the mother during pregnancy throughout the country. The eight hospitals which co-operated in the study were all metropolitan, and five of them were recognized for the teaching of obstetrics. The safety standards during radiological examination in these hospitals may therefore have been somewhat higher than average, and our results therefore not representative.

Fourthly, the number of cases of leukaemia that were observed is small and chance factors alone may have resulted in a fairly substantial risk being overlooked. If the effect of irradiation *in utero* were to raise the incidence of leukaemia by 50 per cent above the national average the expected number of cases in our inquiry would have been $\frac{150}{100} \times 10.5$, or 15.8. In these circumstances it would not be unreasonable to attribute to chance the fact that only nine cases were observed $(P = 0.04)$; but it is unlikely that the effect of irradiation could be much more. Had the effect been to double the risk, the probability of obtaining only nine observed cases (or less) would have been less than one in 300.

The results of this investigation may therefore be regarded as evidence that radiographic examination of the mother's abdomen during pregnancy does not induce leukaemia in the foetus, or that, if it does, the additional risk induced by the methods used in eight metropolitan hospitals is likely to be less than half the general risk to which children aged under 15 years are normally exposed throughout the country. On the other hand, we may note that there was no excess of observed deaths in those children who had been exposed to procedures likely to produce the largest irradiation dose and that no cases of leukaemia occurred among children who had been exposed in the first two trimesters of pregnancy. These results weigh against the belief that a substantial excess mortality was not observed among the irradiated children merely through the operations of chance.

The results obtained in other studies have generally been somewhat different. The first and most important of these, in regard to both size and scope, was that reported by Stewart, Webb, and Hewitt (1958). They traced and arranged an interview with the mothers of (1) 677 of the 792 children under 10 years of age who had been certified as having died of leukaemia in England and Wales during the period 1953–5, and (2) 739 of the 902 children under 10 years of age who had been certified as dying in the same period from other forms of cancer. They also arranged an interview with a control group of mothers whose children were still alive and who were matched with respect to sex and place and date of birth with the children who had died. A small part of the data was eliminated because the matched pair of mothers were interviewed by different investigators or one child was adopted, and the published results relate to a total of 1,299 pairs (in 619 of which one child had died of leukaemia). The principal results relate to the history of maternal irradiation, and are shown in Table 24, 6.

The most striking observation is that of a difference between the

TABLE **24,** 6

Frequency of Previous Radiographic Examination: Mothers of
1,299 Children who had Died of Cancer Compared with Mothers
of 1,299 Living Children (After Stewart, Webb, and Hewitt, 1958)

	X-ray Examination of					
	Abdomen			Other Part		
Period	No. of Mothers of Cancer Children	No. of Mothers of Control Children	Ratio	No. of Mothers of Cancer Children	No. of Mothers of Control Children	Ratio
Before marriage	44	26	1·69:1	335	275	1·22:1
Between marriage and relevant conception	109	121	0·90:1	213	184	1·16:1
During relevant pregnancy	178	93	1·91:1	117	100	1·17:1
Any period before birth of child	296	215	1·38:1	531	456	1·16:1

mothers of the children dying from cancer and the control mothers in respect of the frequency of abdominal X-ray examinations during the relevant pregnancy (178 to 93). The difference between the two proportions (13.7 per cent and 7.2 per cent) is statistically highly significant, and it was from this difference that Stewart and her colleagues concluded that children exposed *in utero* to X-rays were about twice as likely to die from cancer before the age of 10 years as other children.

The contrast depends, however, upon the controls being a representative sample of normal children, and it may be noted that about 40 per cent of the children who were first chosen for this purpose could not be used, principally because they had moved away from the area in which they were born. It may well be that this has not influenced the findings, but the possibility cannot be entirely excluded. Secondly, the result might be influenced by a difference between the responses of mothers whose children were dead and of mothers whose children were still alive. That there is such a difference is suggested by the data in Table **24, 6**. In all categories of exposure, with the exception of abdominal X-ray exposures between marriage and the relevant conception, the mothers of children with cancer indicated more frequent radiation exposure than the control mothers. It is reasonable to suppose that the mothers of dead children, and perhaps particularly of children dead from cancer, may recall the events of pregnancy more completely than the mothers of children who are alive and well, so that the results may, to some extent, be biased by a relative under-reporting of radiation exposures by the control mothers. We should note, however, that there was some correlation between (1) the magnitude of the ratio between the numbers exposed to abdominal irradiation and the number of X-ray films reported to have been taken, and (2) that the ratio was highest for mothers exposed during the first few months of pregnancy. This period includes that of major foetal organogenesis, when the susceptibility to induced malformations is high. Maybe the susceptibility to leukaemia induction will also be high during the same period, although, so far as we know, this is unsupported by experimental evidence.

The results of other studies are summarized in Table **24, 7**. A survey of the radiation exposure histories of children whose deaths had been ascribed to acute leukaemia in the State of California during 1955 and 1956 was reported by Kaplan (1958). He studied also the exposure histories of the closest sib and of the child's habitual playmate, and the histories of the parents. His results were equivocal. He found that the mothers of the leukaemic children gave a history of irradiation more often while they were carrying the leukaemic child than while they were carrying the child's sib; but there was less difference between the maternal radiation exposure when the leukaemic child was compared with his closest playmate.

TABLE **24,** 7

Frequency of Abdominal Irradiation During Pregnancy of Mothers of Cancer Children and Mothers of Control Children: Summary of Published Data*

Reference	Cancer Children		Control Children	
	Description of Group	Proportion of Mothers who Received Abdominal Irradiation During Pregnancy	Description of Group	Proportion of Mothers who Received Abdominal Irradiation During Pregnancy
Kjeldsberg (1957)	Children with leukaemia seen at Rikshospitalet, Oslo, 1946–56	5/55 (9·1%)	Healthy children	8/55 (14·5%)
Kaplan (1958)	Children dying of acute leukaemia in California, 1955–6	37/150 (24·7%) 34/125 (27·2%)	(a) Closest sib (b) Most habitual playmate	24/150 (16·0%) 27/125 (21·6%)
Polhemus and Koch (1959)	Children with leukaemia seen at the Children's Hospital, Los Angeles, 1950—7	72/251 (28·7%)	Children attending the Children's Hospital, Los Angeles, 1950–7 with other selected conditions	58/251 (23·1%)
Ford, Paterson and Trenting (1959)	Children dying of leukaemia under 10 years of age in Louisiana, 1951–5: (a) white (b) coloured	20/70 (28·6%) 1/8 —	Children dying of causes other than cancer under 10 years of age in Louisiana, 1951–5: (a) white (b) coloured	48/247 (19·4%) 8/59 —
MacMahon (1958)	Children dying of cancer under 10 years of age in New York City, and born in a specified maternity hospital, 1947–57	8/114 (7·3%)	1% sample of children born in one of 11 specified maternity hospitals, 1947–57, residents of New York City only	173/2,520 (7·3%)

* Excluding data of Stewart, Webb, and Hewitt (1958), shown in Table 24, 6, and the data of Murray, Heckel, and Hempelmann (1959), referred to in the text.

Polhemus and Koch (1959) obtained evidence of increased frequency of post-natal radiation exposure in children developing leukaemia, but found little indication of an excessive frequency of antenatal X-rays. They sent questionaries by post to the families of 317 children with leukaemia who had been seen at the Children's Hospital, Los Angeles, between January, 1950, and July, 1957, but obtained satisfactory data for only 251. For controls, the same number of children were chosen of a comparable social class, age, and birthplace who had attended the same hospital for other selected conditions. Of the leukaemic children 72 had been exposed *in utero* against 58 of the control children; for exposure to pelvimetry the relevant figures were 65 and 58. In contrast, there were substantial differences in the frequency of post-natal irradiation, particularly irradiation to the thymus in infancy (reported for 11 of the leukaemic and two of the control children).

Ford, Paterson, and Treuting (1959) reported the results of a survey of the radiation histories of all children under the age of 10 years certified to have died from leukaemia or some other form of cancer in Louisiana between 1951 and 1955. In this study the information was obtained from the practitioners who attended the births of the children. Data were obtained for 78 children who had died from leukaemia (including eight negro children), 74 children dying from other forms of cancer (including 13 negro children) and 306 control children who had died from other causes. The authors found that 21/78 leukaemic children (26.9 per cent) and 21/74 children dying from some other form of cancer (28.4 per cent) had been exposed *in utero* to X-rays, whereas 56/306 control children (18.3 per cent) had been so exposed. The data for white children, which are more suitable for comparison with British data, show that exposure to radiation *in utero* was reported by 20/70 children with leukaemia (28.6 per cent), 20/61 children with other forms of cancer (32.8 per cent), and 48/247 control children (19.4 per cent). The relative risk of developing cancer after exposure compared with the risk in the absence of exposure is 1.82 to 1 (that is, 40/91 : 48/199), which is close to the ratio of 2.06 to 1 obtained by Stewart and her colleagues. It should be noted that the American investigators also found that the ratio between the cancer and control children was highest for those who were exposed during procedures involving four or more X-ray films (8/152 against 5/306 or 3.2 : 1). The similarity of these findings to those obtained by Stewart, Webb, and Hewitt (1958) is striking.

The techniques used were, moreover, different in some important respects though they shared the characteristic that the data were obtained from persons who could have been influenced by knowledge of the subsequent fate of the child.

Kjeldsberg (1957) investigated the 68 children with leukaemia who had attended the children's clinic of Rikshospitalet in Oslo between 1946 and 1956. Data were obtained for 55 of them, and these were compared with the data for 55 living children of the same ages. The results showed a lower incidence of exposure *in utero* for the leukaemic children (9.1 per cent) than for the control children (14.5 per cent). The children in the control series were, however, born at a date later than the children with leukaemia, and radiographic examinations during pregnancy are likely to have changed in frequency with the passage of time.

Murray, Heckel, and Hempelmann (1959) interviewed the mothers of 65 out of the 75 residents of one county in New York State who died of leukaemia under the age of 20 years between 1940 and 1957. Three of the mothers (4.6 per cent) said that they had received pelvic or abdominal irradiation during the relevant pregnancy which was identical with the corresponding figure for 65 residents, matched for race, sex, age, and time of death, who had died from other causes. The relevant figures for sibs of leukaemic and control children were respectively 7/93 (7.5 per cent) and 2/82 (2.4 per cent).

A different type of study has been reported by MacMahon (1958). He examined a 1 per cent sample of the records of all children born alive in 11 selected maternity hospitals in New York City between 1947 and 1954. Of the 2,520 selected children 160 were excluded as the parents were not permanently resident in New York City. The hospital records of the remaining children were searched for evidence of X-ray examination of the mother during her pregnancy, and it was found that 173 of the children (7.3 per cent) had been exposed *in utero*. The death certificates were then reviewed of all the children who died under the age of 10 years in New York City during the period 1947–57 and whose deaths were attributed to leukaemia or some other form of cancer. These certificates include the date of birth, so that it was possible to trace the corresponding birth certificates. From these it was discovered that 114 of the children had been born in one or other of the 11 special maternity hospitals. Reference to the hospital records showed that eight of the children (7.3 per cent) had been exposed *in utero*. The data therefore provide no evidence for a special risk associated with diagnostic X-ray exposure during prenatal life. The number of cancer cases, however, is small, and a slight risk might well not have been demonstrated.* It is possible that the results might have been influenced by a differential migration out of New York City between children who had been exposed and children who had not. MacMahon tested this by sending a questionary to a number of mothers whose radiation history was known. Replies were received equally, irrespective of whether the women had been irradiated, but it is notable that 10 out of 37 mothers who were known to have had an abdominal X-ray examination during a particular pregnancy stated that they had not been examined in this way. This may perhaps be regarded as confirming the suggestion that information sought direct from mothers is likely to be of variable accuracy and that it could be influenced by knowledge of the fate of the child.

It is clear, therefore, that the existing evidence of the effect of irradiation *in utero* is conflicting. This is not surprising, since the carcinogenic effect of the doses used in diagnostic radiography is certainly not great and, with the small numbers of cases recorded in some of the studies, chance factors alone could have been sufficient to prevent its recognition. During the early part of intrauterine life the risk may be relatively high, but there is little evidence relating to this period. In the present study some 750 women were irradiated in the first three months of their pregnancy and none of the children developed leukaemia during an average follow-up of over six years, which clearly suggests no major risk even at this stage of pregnancy. For the full duration of pregnancy the magnitude of any risk from irradiation in metropolitan hospitals is unlikely to be more than 50 per cent of that normally incurred irrespective of radiographic examination. Even a small risk of this size would imply that the foetus was a great deal more susceptible to the induction of leukaemia than the adult. Estimates of the effect of radiation in the adult have suggested that a dose of 1 rad to the whole red marrow might produce about one case of leukaemia per million persons per annum for perhaps 10 years after the exposure. Since the amount of radiation received by the foetus from irradiation of the mother's abdomen is estimated to be of the order of 1 rad and the normal annual incidence of leukaemia in England and Wales under the age of 10 years is approximately 37 per million, it would follow, with a 50 per cent

* In 1961, MacMahon, with more data, has demonstrated some such risk.

increase, that the leukaemogenic effect of irradiation on the foetus would be about 20 times as great as on the adult irrespective of the relative sizes of the target tissue. If the difference in susceptibility was much less, the effect would in all probability escape recognition. In the light, however, of all the data it would seem that an increase of leukaemia among children due to radiographic examination of their mother's abdomen during the relevant pregnancy has not been established.

SUMMARY

Evidence of the leukaemogenic effect on the foetus of exposure to ionizing radiations *in utero* has been sought by comparing the leukaemia mortality in a group of children whose mothers were known to have been irradiated during the relevant pregnancy with that expected from the corresponding sex-and-age specific national mortality rates. Pregnant women who received diagnostic irradiation directed towards their abdomen or pelvis between 1945 and 1956 were identified in the records of the radiological departments of eight hospitals in London and Edinburgh. Information about the date of birth and sex of the child was obtained from the corresponding maternity records. If the child left hospital alive, his full name and the first names of his father were obtained from the local register or, in a few instances, from the Central Register of Births. The children who had died of leukaemia were discovered by comparing the children's names with the list of names of all the children who had died of leukaemia in Britain between 1945 and 1958.

Altogether information was obtained about 39,166 liveborn children whose mothers were known to have been subjected to abdominal or pelvic irradiation during their pregnancy. Among their children, nine were discovered to have died of leukaemia before the end of 1958. The expected number was estimated to be 10.5. There was no evidence of any disproportionate occurrence of leukaemia among the children who had been most heavily irradiated nor among the children who had been irradiated early in intrauterine life.

Published data on the leukaemogenic effect of irradiation *in utero* are conflicting. It is concluded that an increase of leukaemia among children due to radiographic examination of their mother's abdomen during the relevant pregnancy is not established.

REFERENCES

Court Brown, W. M., Doll, R., Spiers, F. W., Duffy, B. J., and McHugh, M. J. (1960). *Brit. med. J.* **i,** 1753.

Ford, D. D., Paterson, J. C. S., and Treuting, W. L. (1959). *J. nat. Cancer Inst.* **22,** 1093.

Hewitt, D. (1955). *Brit. J. prev. soc. Med.* **9,** 81.

Kaplan, H. S. (1958). *Amer. J. Roentgenol.* **80,** 696.

Kjeldsberg, H. (1957). *T. norske Laegeforen.* **77,** 1052.

MacMahon, B. (1958). Paper read to the American Pubic Health Association, December 1958.

Murray, R., Heckel, P., and Hempelmann, L. H. (1959). *New Engl. J. Med.* **261** 585.

Polhemus, D. W., and Koch, R. (1959). *Pediatrics,* **23,** 453.

Stewart, A., Webb, J., Giles, D., and Hewitt, D. (1956). *Lancet,* **ii,** 447.

Stewart, A., Webb, J., and Hewitt, D. (1958). *Brit. med. J.* **i,** 1495.

CHAPTER 25

STUDIES IN THE INCIDENCE OF CANCER IN A FACTORY HANDLING INORGANIC COMPOUNDS OF ARSENIC

IN investigating statistically the mortality experience of the factory under inquiry certain serious difficulties had to be faced. Excluding clerical workers the factory was relatively small, employing in all not very many more than 100 operatives; further, only a proportion of these would have been in contact with the chemical process and exposed to the specific risk. A long period of years was therefore essential to produce sufficient data to give reliable results. Data for any such period were, however, entirely lacking in the factory records. The information required was as follows: (*a*) a list of the male employees, divided according to their occupations, for each year from 1943 (the time of inquiry) back to 1900 or thereabouts; (*b*) the approximate dates of birth of these men so that the age constitution of the population at risk could be computed at different points of time between 1900 and 1943; (*c*) information regarding all deaths occurring in that period of time. Given these data the recorded numbers of deaths from different causes could then have been compared with the deaths which would have been expected to occur in a population of the stated size and age constitution if it had been experiencing during the passage of years the national, or local, rates of mortality. Comparison of observation with expectation would have revealed whether or not this group of workers, or some section of it, had experienced any abnormal rates of mortality.

This procedure could, however, not be followed since no details of the employees on the books over so long a period of time were available. A list of the deaths of employees was available and was believed to be comprehensive though lacking the cause of death in some cases. The necessary population figures, to relate to these deaths, were absent.

A different method of approach had, therefore, to be devised, and the only possible one was by means of proportional mortality rates,

(With E. Lewis Faning.) Reprinted from the *British Journal of Industrial Medicine*, 1948, **5**, 1.

that is, to see whether the proportion of deaths in these factory workers which was debited to cancer differed materially from the proportion found in other groups of workers in the same area. To acquire this material the following procedure was adopted. The factory was situated, and most of its employees lived, in a small country town within a specific births and deaths registration sub-district which contained no other factory of the same kind. By consulting the death registers of the area and studying the recorded occupations of the deceased it was, therefore, possible to identify with a high degree of accuracy the deaths of its employees which took place within that specified area. At the same time the deaths of males not so employed could be extracted from the same registers for comparison.

Residents of the town, whether employed in the factory or not, who died away from home would not, of course, appear in this sample. The difficulty here lay mainly in the removal to a hospital in another area, an adjacent town, of patients with certain illnesses. In the event of their death in hospital, registration would be effected in this town. These registers had, therefore, also to be consulted since the causes of death of patients removed to hospital might well be of considerable importance.

Basic Data from the Death Registers

In the registration sub-district of the town in which the factory was situated a complete study was made of the death registers over the years 1900 to 1943 inclusive, particulars being extracted for each recorded death of a male of age 20 and over. These particulars included the date of death, age at death, certified causes of death, and the occupation followed. The total number of such deaths was 2,063 but 367 of these, it was found, related to men who had died within the area but were not residents of it (in a Poor Law Union and a hospital). Such non-residents were not relevant to the inquiry, and excluding them left 1,696 deaths for further analysis. Of these 1,696 deaths, 64 had been workers in the specific factory and 1,632 employed in other pursuits. Tabulation of these deaths by year of occurrence showed that only three of the factory workers' deaths took place in the first decade of the period, 1900–1909.* In view of

---

* One died of phthisis, aged 28, in 1903; one died of sarcoma of the arm and recurrent sarcoma of the thorax, aged 56, in 1908; one died of epithelioma of the tongue, aged 42, in 1909.

the very small amount of data at this end of the time-scale it was decided to limit the collection of further data, and the analysis, to the subsequent years, 1910 to 1943.

The collection of further data took place in the adjacent town, mentioned above, the death registers of which revealed 14 cases of factory workers dying in the hospital there who were residents of the town containing the factory. Other occupations produced 153 such cases. In total, therefore, these searches gave rise to 75 deaths of factory workers between 1910 and 1943 and 1,412 deaths of other workers.

The list of deaths provided by the factory, and referred to above, gave a total of 88, so that there was a discrepancy of 13 between this figure and the 75 deaths identified in the registers. Two of those missing were known to be residents of the adjacent town, and to have died there, and one had died on active service in the war of 1914–18. The remaining 10 could not be traced. They may have lived and died in some other adjacent area; they may have been moved in their fatal illness to some more distant hospital. The three who were traced (living in the adjacent town and dying on active service) have not been included with the 75 known factory workers' deaths since the data for the other occupations used for comparison could include no such cases. The inclusion of such cases on one side and not on the other would not be just.

These other occupations were sub-divided into four broad groups, namely 319 agricultural workers, 701 skilled artisans or shop workers, 196 general labourers, and 196 other workers, mainly in professional, managerial, and clerical occupations. This last mixed group has been omitted, since on a social and industrial basis it is not comparable with the factory workers. The final data for comparison relate, therefore, to the 75 deaths of the factory workers and 1,216 deaths of other workers, sub-divided as described.

Comparison of Factory and Other Workers

In the absence of the actual numbers of men of different ages at risk of dying in these occupations, and in these years, no death *rates* can, as previously pointed out, be calculated. The comparisons are, therefore, limited to proportional mortality figures, that is, the proportion of the total recorded deaths which were certified as being due to specified causes.

The resulting figures are set out in this form in Table 25, 1 which

TABLE 25, 1

Number of Deaths in the Occupational Groups and their Proportional Distribution by Cause of Death

Cause of death	Absolute numbers of deaths				Percentage distribution			
	The specific factory workers	Agri-cultural workers	General labourers	Artisans and shop-workers	The specific factory workers	Agri-cultural workers	General labourers	Artisans and shop-workers
Diseases of heart and circulatory system	17	105	50	221	22·7	32·9	25·5	31·5
Diseases of the respiratory system	19	70	45	151	25·3	21·9	23·0	21·5
Diseases of nervous system	6	18	18	78	8·0	5·6	9·2	11·1
Disease of digestive and genito-urinary system	3	14	11	47	4·0	4·4	5·6	6·7
Infectious and general diseases	3	30	21	64	4·0	9·4	10·7	9·1
Violence, ill-defined and other causes	5	36	24	56	6·7	11·3	12·2	8·0
Cancer: all forms	22	46	27	84	29·3	14·4	13·8	12·0
Total	75	319	196	701	100·0	100·0	100·0	100·0

disregards the age at death and the period of time at which it took place. In this somewhat crude form the figures show that a considerably larger proportion of the deaths of the factory workers had been attributed to all forms of cancer than was the case with the other occupational groups, which, in this respect, closely resemble one another. Thus, approximately 29 per cent of the factory workers' deaths were from cancer, compared with 14, 14, and 12 per cent of the deaths of the agricultural labourers, general labourers, and artisans and shopworkers respectively. These differences are quite unlikely to have been due to chance, being with their standard errors as follows:

Factory workers excess over agricultural labourers .. .. 14.9 ± 4.8

Factory workers excess over general labourers .. .. 15.6 ± 5.2

Factory workers excess over artisans and shopworkers .. .. .. 17.4 ± 4.2

Taking the other three occupations as one group gives 157 of their 1,216 deaths, or 12.9 per cent, as due to cancer compared with the 22 in 75, or 29.3 per cent in the factory workers, a significant difference of 16.4 ± 4.1.

Analysis of Deaths by Period of Time and Age

This comparison, as pointed out, is somewhat crude in that it takes no account of the ages at which deaths took place in the comparative groups or of the secular period of time at thich they were certified. A finer comparison, taking each of these factors into account, is given in Tables **25**,2 and **25**,3. When so divided, the numbers necessarily become small, but they confirm the conclusions reached from the cruder comparison. Table **25**,2 shows that the proportional excess of cancer deaths in the factory workers is a consistent feature of each of the three periods of years 1910–19, 1920–9, and 1930–43. Tests of significance give: 1910–19, χ^2 2.43, $P = 0.12$; 1920–9, χ^2 2.61, $P = 0.11$; 1930–43, χ^2 6.84, P = 0.0009. Sum of $\chi^2 = 11.88$, P less than 0.01.

Table **25**,3 shows that it is apparent at ages under 55 (mainly ages 40 to 54) and at ages 55 to 69, but at ages 70 and over the two groups do not differ very much (the experience of the factory workers is here

TABLE **25**, 2

Number of Deaths Due to All Causes and the Number Registered as Cancer in Different Periods of Time

Period of time	Factory workers			Other 3 occupational groups		
	All causes	Cancer	% due to cancer	All causes	Cancer	% due to cancer
1910–19	14	4	28·6	350	39	11·1
1920–29	29	8	27·6	373	54	14·5
1930–43	32	10	31·3	493	64	13·0
Total	75	22	29·3	1,216	157	12·9

TABLE **25**, 3

Number of Deaths Due to All Causes and the Number Registered as Cancer at Different Ages

Age group	Factory workers			Other 3 occupational groups		
	All causes	Cancer	% due to cancer	All causes	Cancer	% due to cancer
Under 55*	29	8	27·6	268	30	11·2
55–69	33	12	36·4	386	64	16·6
70 and over	13	2	15·4	562	63	11·2
Total	75	22	29·3	1,216	157	12·9

* Majority at ages 40–54.

based upon 13 deaths only). Tests of significance give: Under 55, χ^2 4.92, P = 0.027; 55 to 69, χ^2 6.74, P = 0.0009; 70+, χ^2 0.0007, P = 0.99. Sum of χ^2 = 11.66, P less than 0.01.

A more detailed analysis was made taking both age and period of death into account as follows. The deaths from all causes of the factory workers were listed by period and age using the three periods given in Table **25**, 2 and the four age groups under 40, 40–54, 55–69, and 70+. Each group of these factory workers' deaths for a given period and given age were then divided into the numbers that would be 'expected' to be due to (*a*) cancer and (*b*) other causes, on the basis of the proportions shown by the other three occupational groups (combined) in that same period and same age group.* These 'expected' numbers were then summed for all periods and all ages. This form of standardization leads to the result that of the 75 factory workers' deaths 11 or 14.7 per cent would have been expected to be due to cancer, whereas there were in fact registered 22, or 29.3 per cent. The difference is slightly less than that shown by the preliminary crude comparison, namely 29.3 per cent to 12.9 per cent, but shows that that comparison is not seriously in error.

In spite of the rather small numbers involved it is clear that the factory workers as a whole have had between 1910 and 1943 a significantly greater proportion of their deaths attributed to cancer of all forms than is to be observed in other occupational groups in the same area.

Comparison of Workers within the Factory

A further and illuminating analysis could, however, be made by means of a broad sub-division of the deaths according to the actual occupations followed by the men *within* the factory. This division was based not upon the occupation given on the death certificate but upon the advice of the factory itself from available records and memory. The results show (Table **25**, 4) that there is no proportional excess at

TABLE **25**, 4

Proportion of Cancer Deaths in the Factory Population Distinguishing Type of Work

Description of work (by factory definition)	Cancer	All other causes of death	Total	% due to cancer
Chemical workers	16	25	41	39·0
Engineers and packers	3	7	10	30·0
Others (builders, printers, watchmen, carters, boxmakers, sundries)	3	21	24	12·5
Total	22	53	75	29·3

* For example, in 1920–29 there were 10 factory workers' deaths at ages 55–69. At these ages in 1920–29 there were 112 deaths in the other occupational groups, of which 24, or 21·4 per cent, were due to cancer. We should, therefore, 'expect' 2·14 of these 10 factory workers' deaths to be due to cancer, whereas 4 of them were so certified.

all of deaths attributed to cancer in those workers who would not be exposed to any specific hazards—builders, printers, box-makers, etc. Of the 24 deaths in this group three, or 12.5 per cent, were due to cancer, a figure very similar to those found in the other occupational groups of Table 25, 1. The excess proportion found for the factory as a whole is therefore derived, as Table 25, 4 shows, from the workers denoted as chemical workers (*i.e.* workers in the process), 39 per cent of whose deaths were certified as due to cancer, and from the small group of engineers and packers, of whose 10 deaths three were attributed to cancer. This differential incidence within the factory obviously adds considerably to the evidence for a real hazard. Statistical tests indicate a significant difference between the chemical workers and the general group of other occupations ($\chi^2 = 3.95$; P = .047), but not between the small group of engineers and packers and the latter ($\chi^2 = .53$; P = 0.47).

Analysis of Cancer Deaths by Site

In dealing with the bodily distribution of the observed cancer deaths, there is clearly too little material to allow a firm conclusion. In Table 25, 5 the deaths of the factory workers and the other three

TABLE 25, 5

Number of Deaths Due to Cancer According to Site

Site*	Absolute numbers		Percentages	
	Factory workers	Other 3 occupa-tional groups	Factory workers	Other 3 occupa-tional groups
Buccal cavity and pharynx	2	10	9·1	6·4
Digestive organs and peritoneum	5	91	22·7	58·0
Respiratory organs	7	25	31·8	15·9
Genito-urinary organs	2	13	9·1	8·3
Skin	3	2	13·6	1·3
Other sites or unspecified	3	16	13·6	10·2
Total	22	157	99·9	100·1

* In detail the sites involved under each heading were as follows. *Buccal cavity:* lip, tongue, mouth, jaw, pharynx. *Digestive:* oesophagus, stomach, splenic flexure, sigmoid flexure, large intestine, rectum, liver, gall bladder, pancreas, intestine undefined. *Respiratory:* larynx, lung, mediastinum, bronchus. *Genito-urinary:* kidney, suprarenal bladder, testis, penis, scrotum.

occupational groups have been put into broad site groups on the basis of the Registrar-General's tabulations. The result suggests a relative excess in the factory workers of cancers of the respiratory system and skin and a corresponding deficit in the digestive organs and peritoneum. An alternative approach gave as follows. It will be remembered that 22 cancer deaths were observed in the factory workers, whereas 11 were expected on the basis of the deaths recorded in the other three occupational groups. These 22 deaths were composed of five from cancer of the lung (including one of the bronchus), two from other respiratory sites (larynx and mediastinum), three from cancer of the skin, and 12 from cancer at other sites. The corresponding expected numbers, comprising the total 11, were 1.01 lung and bronchus, 1.43 other respiratory, 0.12 skin and 8.42 other sites. Some excess is apparent under each heading, but particularly, the small figures suggest, for the lung and skin. These eight deaths (lung and skin) all occurred in the 41 total deaths of the chemical workers.

In view of these results an attempt was made to extend the investigation to other factories similarly engaged. It proved, unfortunately, impossible to do so. The numbers employed were either so small as to be of no value whatever, or the factories were situated in large towns in which there could have been no means of identifying the deceased employees in the local death registers. This form of inquiry, the only possible approach to the problem, was dependent upon the unique situation of the factory in question.

CONCLUSIONS

1. The factory workers whose mortality experience has been analysed show in their deaths recorded in 1910–43 a proportional and significant excess of deaths attributed to cancer when compared with three other occupational groups living in the same area. The deaths of the former include 29 per cent attributed to cancer, and the latter 13 per cent. Standardization for age and period of time does not materially affect this comparison.

2. A proportional excess of cancer in the factory workers, and of much the same order, is consistently apparent in each of the three periods 1910–19, 1920–9, and 1930–43. It is present at ages under 55 and 55–69 but is small and insignificant at ages 70 and above.

3. The proportional excess is confined to workers in the chemical processes, including engineers and packers, and is entirely absent

from a general group of operatives in the same factory, such as
printers, box-makers, etc., who would be unlikely to be exposed to
any specific hazard.

4. The numbers are small when sub-divided by the site of growth,
but there is a suggestion in the figures that the factory workers have
been especially affected in the lung and skin.

CHAPTER 26

SNOW—AN APPRECIATION

IT has been said that 'The progress of Science renders useless the very books which have been the greatest aids to that progress. As those works are no longer useful, modern Youth is naturally inclined to believe they never had any value; it despises them and ridicules them if they happen to contain any superannuated material whatever'. That will surely never be the fate of a classic that must always fascinate and inspire the student of epidemiology and preventive medicine—John Snow's short treatise *On the Mode of Communication of Cholera*. It should be read once, wrote Wade Hampton Frost, 'as a story of exploration'—in that sense, I would add, it should be read quickly, for its fascination—'many times as a lesson in epidemiology'. In that sense, like all closely reasoned statistical studies, it must be taken slowly, carefully and critically with every piece of evidence weighed by the reader and its relevance studied.

What we now celebrate is the centenary of publication of the *second* edition of Snow's masterpiece. The first edition was published in 1849 and it may seem odd that we have, for this celebration, awaited the second. The answer is not so much that the first issue was slender both in size and content, to be swallowed up later in the much enlarged work of 1855, but that this early work could not, in fact, contain the main, and most convincing, part of the observations bearing on Snow's belief that cholera was water-borne. It could not contain that evidence for the very good reason that that evidence did not exist. Snow could not put his views, well developed as they were in 1849, to the critical test until the epidemic of 1854–55. His views were formed in the earlier year and were, as events proved, sound. But they lacked proof. It was the events in London in 1854 and 1855 that could provide the proof and to which Snow unsparingly devoted himself—letting, as Richardson says, nothing personal stand in the way of his scientific pursuits. The results were incorporated in the book of less than 150 pages and published in 1855, a work in the

Reprinted from the *Proceedings of the Royal Society of Medicine*, 1955, **48**, 1008.

preparation and publication of which, it was said, Snow 'spent more than £200 in hard cash, and realized in return scarcely so many shillings'.

THE THEORY

Omitting the illustrative cases, which were many, and the discussion which was full and lucid, the logical development of Snow's theory can be set out in half a dozen sentences taken (or adapted) from his early pages. Thus:

Innumerable examples show that cholera can be communicated from the sick to the healthy.

Diseases which are communicated from person to person are caused by some material which has the property of increasing and multiplying in the systems of the persons it attacks.

This material, or morbid matter, may be transmitted to a distance, e.g. on soiled linen; in other words proximity to the patient and to his 'emanations' is not essential.

Cholera invariably commences with an affection of the alimentary canal.

It follows that the morbid material producing cholera must be introduced into the alimentary canal and not through some other system, e.g. the lungs.

Thus runs the basic theory. And thus, from a consideration of the *pathology* of the disease, Snow first approaches its mode of communication.

THE FACTS

In support of this theory Snow believes that the instances in which minute quantities of the ejections and dejections of cholera patients must be swallowed are sufficiently numerous to account for the spread of the disease. He seeks to see whether the known facts of cholera fit in with the theory:

The disease is found to spread most where the facilities for this mode of communication are greatest—amongst the poor, eating, living and sleeping in cramped and crowded quarters. In the better kind of houses it hardly ever spreads from one member of the family to another.

Want of light in some of the dwellings of the poor has often been commented on as increasing the prevalence of cholera. Deficiency of light is a great obstacle to cleanliness; it prevents dirt from being seen and it must aid very much the contamination of the food with cholera evacuations.

On the other hand the *post-mortem* inspection of the bodies of cholera patients has hardly ever been followed by the disease, this being a duty that is necessarily followed by careful washing of the hands; and it is not the habit of medical men to be taking food on such an occasion.

These, and other facts that he advances are not incompatible with the theory but they are clearly insufficient to explain the characteristics of widespread epidemic cholera. And so Snow moves on.

If the cholera had no other means of communication . . . it would be constrained to confine itself chiefly to the crowded dwellings of the poor, and would be continually liable to die out accidentally in a place, for want of the opportunity to reach fresh victims; but there is often a way open for it to extend itself more widely, and to reach the well-to-do classes of the community; I allude to the mixture of the cholera evacuations with the water used for drinking.

The Water Supply

He illustrates his case against water by accounts of epidemics in London and the provinces, in the army in India and in the Black Sea fleet. I shall pass this evidence by, extremely convincing as some of it is, with but one (unconvincing) quotation. The drainage from cesspools had found its way into the well attached to some houses in a village near Bath and the cholera

became very fatal. The people complained of the water to the gentleman belonging to the property, who lived at Weston, in Bath, and he sent a surveyor, who reported that nothing was the matter. The tenants still complaining, the owner went himself, and on looking at the water and smelling it, he said that he could perceive nothing the matter with it. He was asked if he would taste it, and he drank a glass of it.

That, I regret to say, was the end of the poor owner; he was dead of cholera three days later. While, of course, that may be an admirable cautionary tale for 'gentlemen belonging to properties' it clearly adds no real evidence to Snow's thesis. The same sequence of events *could* have occurred if the epidemic had been one of plague with its very different mode of spread.

The Broad Street Pump

It is clearly impossible to celebrate the publication of Snow on Cholera without some reference to his most famous field study— that of the Broad Street Pump. Indeed I think it is necessary in this centenary year once more to point out that Snow's claim to fame does *not* rest upon the removal of a pump handle and a *post hoc propter hoc* argument which he would, I believe, have despised. Yet that belief is still widespread. It may well have its origin in Sir Benjamin Ward Richardson's fine memoir of Snow for this is what Richardson wrote:

On the evening of Thursday, September 7th, the vestrymen of St. James's were sitting in solemn consultation on the causes of the visitation. They might well be solemn, for such a panic possibly never existed in London since the days of the great plague. People fled from their homes as from instant death, leaving behind them, in their haste, all which before they valued most. While, then, the vestrymen were in solemn deliberation, they were called to consider a new suggestion. A stranger had asked, in modest speech, for a brief hearing. Dr. Snow, the stranger in question, was admitted and in few words explained his view of the 'head and front of the offending'. He had fixed his attention on the Broad Street pump as the source and centre of the calamity. He advised the removal of the pump-handle as the grand prescription. The vestry was incredulous, but had the good sense to carry out the advice. The pump-handle was removed, and the plague was stayed.

It is difficult to resist the final dramatic touch; it is almost sacrilege to attempt to debunk it. Yet perhaps it is fair in a centenary year to see what Snow himself wrote. He shows the sequence of events as determined by his inquiry into the 616 fatal attacks which I give below in slightly shortened form.

Date					No. of fatal attacks commencing on each day
August 26	..	..	..	..	1
27	..	..	..	..	1
28	..	..	..	..	1
29	..	..	..	..	1
30	..	..	..	..	8
31	..	..	..	..	56
September 1	..	..	..	..	143
2	..	..	..	..	116
3	..	..	..	..	54
4	..	..	..	..	46
5	..	..	..	..	36
6	..	..	..	..	20
7	..	..	..	..	28
8*	..	..	..	..	12
9	..	..	..	..	11
10	..	..	..	..	5
11	..	..	..	..	5
12	..	..	..	..	1
13	..	..	..	..	3
14–30	..	..	..	..	18
Date unknown	..	..	..	..	45

*Pump handle removed

Though conceivably there might have been a second peak in the curve, and though almost certainly some more deaths would have occurred if the pump handle had remained *in situ*, it is clear that the end of the epidemic was not dramatically determined by its removal. The deaths had already been declining from a very marked peak for at least five days.

Wholly recognizing these facts Snow himself wrote: 'There is no doubt that the mortality was much diminished . . . by the flight of the population, which commenced soon after the outbreak; but the attacks had so far diminished before the use of the water was stopped, that it is impossible to decide whether the well still contained the cholera poison in an active state, or whether, from some cause, the water had become free from it.' He never occupied the flimsy pedestal upon which some would place him.

His evidence lay principally in the geographical distribution of the deaths around the pump and in the fact, from his personal inquiries, that almost all the dead had used the pump water.* Taken alone, obviously more than one explanation could fit these facts but there were other, and very odd, observations which had to be fitted in at the same time. How was it that the inmates of the workhouse went almost unscathed though surrounded by houses in which deaths from cholera took place? The workhouse had its own water supply. That no cholera affected the 70 men employed in the local brewery hardly calls for even a rhetorical question and answer. On the other hand at the percussion cap factory where the only vintage supplied was two tubs of Broad Street pump water, 18 of 200 workpeople died. And then there was the astonishing case of the unfortunate widow at Hampstead whose custom it was to have a large bottle of the water brought to her daily and who, with her niece, perished of cholera in a cholera-free area. Snow was right, in my opinion, in regarding that event as 'perhaps the most conclusive of all in proving the connexion between the Broad Street pump and the outbreak'. But his whole 'build-up' of evidence is impressive and should be read in full.

While the scale of the Broad Street disaster and Snow's detailed analysis of it naturally command the limelight, he sets out less well-known but, in my opinion, equally convincing stories. Let, for

---

* In setting out this information Snow acknowledges the kindness of and the help given him by the Registrar-General of 1855. References in epidemiological papers of 1955 would suggest an inheritance of acquired characteristics.

instance, the reader study the events of 28 July to 13 August, 1849, in the 'genteel suburban dwellings' of Albion Terrace, Wandsworth Road, where 20 persons died in 10 houses and in one house six out of the seven inmates perished. What conceivably could be so local in its effects, leaving untouched 'the houses opposite to, behind, and in the same line, at each end of those in which the disease prevailed'? The answer was that they were supplied with water on the same plan, and after the storms of 26 July and 2 August it seems to have been a case almost of 'water, water everywhere, nor any drop to drink'.

VITAL STATISTICS

Another, and, indeed, perhaps the most important, link in the chain of argument lay in Snow's adept handling of the vital statistics of London in relation to its various water supplies. Very briefly, in 1832 the chief villain was the Southwark Water Company with its unfiltered supply from the Thames at London Bridge. In 1849 there is little to choose between the Southwark (now combined with the Vauxhall) and the Lambeth Companies in their capacity, in friendly rivalry, to kill their customers—at a rate of about 1 in 60. And, then, in 1852 the Lambeth Company removed their water-works to Thames Ditton, 'thus obtaining a supply of water quite free from the sewage of London'. The result is immediately reflected in the contrasting mortality rates of 1853. The rates are relatively high in districts served wholly by the Southwark and Vauxhall Company (114 deaths per 100,000), only half that level in districts served by both companies (60 deaths per 100,000) and nil in the three districts served wholly by the Lambeth Company. There follows in the epidemic of 1854, Snow's fantastic personal inquiry into every death taking place in the districts served by both companies—'where circumstances were so happily adapted for the inquiry' for 'the pipes of each Company go down all the streets, and into nearly all the courts and alleys', 'each Company supplies both rich and poor, both large house and small'. It is the almost perfect experiment.

Snow was not, however, able to take entire advantage of it. He could compare the absolute numbers of deaths but he did not know the number of houses served by the two water companies in the districts served by both and so could calculate no rates. There was a return of the total houses served by each Company but in using these he must bring into his comparison districts served by one *or* other Company only, thus somewhat vitiating the natural experiment. In a later publication (1856) he has acquired detailed population statistics and is able to reveal that *in every single sub-district* served by both Companies the cholera death-rate of the customers of the Southwark and Vauxhall Company was grossly higher than the rate of the customers of the Lambeth Company; in total the ratio was about 6 to 1. Frost considered that this later paper was 'not altogether essential to Snow's argument, which was already well established, but confirms it in detail and shows his keenness in statistical analysis'. Personally I think that is an underestimate of its importance. The sub-districts had, in fact, quite widely varying rates; the provision of an exposed-to-risk that allows the contrast of the water supplies *within* the sub-districts is almost fundamental. Snow must have bitterly regretted that he could not do it in his major work. However that may be, the contrast, whether in absolute numbers of deaths or in total districts, was so great as not to be mistaken.

None but the most stubborn, says Frost, could now deny the influence of contaminated water though the way in which it operated was still questioned. As Professor Mackintosh has observed, the stubborn were still quite thick on the ground. It is well to note, too, that the whole of Snow's case rested upon circumstantial evidence, almost entirely upon statistical observations and relationships. Even the not so stubborn were allergic to that kind of evidence—and are still allergic to it.

CONCLUSION

In conclusion let us, through the eyes of his friend Richardson, look at Snow one hundred years ago, in the epidemic of 1854.

'He laboured personally with untiring zeal. No one but those who knew him intimately can conceive how he laboured, at what cost, and at what risk. Wherever cholera was visitant, there he was in the midst. For the time he laid aside as much as possible the emoluments of practice; and when, even by early rising and late taking rest, he found that all that might be learned was not, from the physical labour implied, within the grasp of one man, he paid for qualified labour. The result of his endeavours, in so far as scientific satisfaction is a realization, was truly realized, in the discovery of the statistical fact, that of 286 fatal attacks of cholera, in 1854, occurring in the South districts of the metropolis, where one water company, the Southwark and Vauxhall, supplied water charged with the London faecal impurities, and another company, the Lambeth, supplied pure water, the proportion of fatal cases to each 10,000 houses was to the Southwark and Vauxhall Company's water 71, to the Lambeth 5.

To those who hold that statistics are dull I commend that simple comparison; to those who hold that the statistical approach is barren and unprofitable I commend Snow on Cholera. 'This disease', he concluded, 'may be rendered extremely rare, if indeed it may not be altogether banished from civilized countries.' How right he was. For close upon 100 years we have been free in this country from epidemic cholera, and it is a freedom which, basically, we owe to the logical thinking, acute observations and simple sums of Dr. John Snow.

BIBLIOGRAPHY

PUBLISHED WORKS OF SIR AUSTIN BRADFORD HILL

1925   Internal Migration and its effects upon the death rates: with special reference to the County of Essex. *Spec. Rep. Ser. med. Res. Coun. Lond.* No. **95**.

A physiological and economic study of the diets of workers in rural areas as compared with those of workers resident in urban districts. *J. Hyg.* **24**, 189.

A note on the correlation between birth and death rates with reference to Malthus's interpretation of their movements. *Ann. Eugen. Lond.* **1**, 244.

On the average longevity of physicians. *Brit. med. J.* **i**, 754.

1927   Artificial humidification in the cotton weaving industry. Its effect upon the sickness rates of weaving operatives. *Rep. industr. Hlth. Res. B.* Lond. No. **48**.

Cricket and its relation to the duration of life. *Lancet*, **ii**, 949.

1929   An investigation into the sickness experience of printers (with special reference to the incidence of tuberculosis). *Rep. industr. Hlth. Res. Bd.*, Lond. No. **54**.

An investigation of sickness in various industrial occupations. *J. R. statist. Soc.* **92**, 183.

1930   Sickness amongst operatives in Lancashire cotton spinning mills. *Rep. industr. Hlth. Res. Bd.*, Lond. No. **59**.

1931   Statistical appendix to report by H. M. M. Mackay and L. Goodfellow on Nutritional Anaemia in Infancy: with special reference to iron deficiency. *Spec. Rep. Ser. med. Res. Coun. Lond.* No. **157**.

1932   *The Lancet Commission on Nursing. Statistical Analysis of the Questionnaire issued to hospitals.* Final Report of the Commission. London: *Lancet.*

1933   Contributions to the experimental study of epidemiology. A study of cage age and resistance to environment. *J. Hyg.* **33**, 359.

Some aspects of the mortality from whooping-cough. *J. R. statist. Soc.* **96**, 240.

The inheritance of resistance to bacterial infection in animal species. *Spec. Rep. Ser. med. Res. Coun. Lond.* No. **196**.

1934   The trend of mortality in early childhood and in adolescence. *Annual Report, Chief Medical Officer, Ministry of Health, for the year* 1933, p. 17. London: H.M.S.O.

1935   Mortality from pernicious anaemia in England and Wales. *Lancet*, **i**, 43.

The present-day openings of medical practice. *Lancet*, **ii**, 512.

1936   Sickness amongst workers in alumina. *Lancet,* **ii,** 1478.

The recent trend in England and Wales of mortality from phthisis at young adult ages. *J. R. statist. Soc.* **99,** 247.

The enumeration of population at the meetings of the Society. *J. R. statist. Soc.* **99,** 162.

Experimental epidemiology. (With Greenwood, M., Topley, W. W. C., and Wilson, J.). *Spec. Rep. Ser. med. Res. Coun. Lond.* No. **209.**

Enteric fever in milk-borne and water-borne epidemics: a comparison of age and sex incidence. (With Mitra, K.). *Lancet,* **ii,** 589.

1937   *Principles of Medical Statistics.* London: Lancet.

An investigation into the sickness experience of London transport workers, with special reference to digestive disturbances. *Rep. Industr. Hlth. Res. Bd. Lond.* No. **79.**

Observations on the response of the pulse rate to exercise in healthy men. (With Magee, H. E., and Major, E.). *Lancet,* **ii,** 441.

1938   National nutrition and health. *Mother and Child, Lond.* **8,** 455.

Some observations on the weight and length of infants in the first year of life. (With Magee, H. E.). *Med. Offr.* **60,** 157, 167.

Mortality in childhood. (With Rao, B. M.). *Annual Report, Chief Medical Officer, Ministry of Health, for the year* 1937, p. 23. London: H.M.S.O.

1939   *Principles of Medical Statistics,* 2nd ed. London: Lancet.

Mortality from cancer of the skin in relation to mortality from cancer of other sites. An analysis of occupational mortality statistics of England and Wales. (With Conrad, K. K.). *Amer. J. Cancer,* **36,** 83.

The effect of withdrawing mice from an infected herd at varying intervals. (With Greenwood, M., Topley, W. W. C., and Wilson, J.). *J. Hyg.* **39,** 109.

Construction of an abridged life table. (With Hyder, M. G.). *Lancet,* **i,** 225.

A study of the nasopharyngeal bacterial flora of different groups of persons observed in London and S.E. England during the years 1930–37. (With Straker, E., and Lovell, R.). *Rep. publ. Hlth. med. Subj. Lond.* No. **90.**

Antistreptolysin S. titres in rheumatic fever. (With Todd, E. W. and Coburn, Alvin F.). *Lancet,* **ii,** 1213.

1940   The inheritance of resistance, demonstrated by the development of a strain of mice resistant to experimental inoculation with a bacterial endotoxin. (With Hatswell, J. M. and Topley, W. W. C.). *J. Hyg.* **40,** 538.

A study of the mortality rates of calves in 335 herds in England and Wales (together with some limited observations for Scotland). (With Lovell, R.). *J. Dairy Res.* **11,** 225.

1942   *Principles of Medical Statistics,* 3rd ed. London: Lancet.

1946   Statistics in Medicine. *Trans. Manchr. Statist. Soc.,* 1946–47.

1947 Statistics in the Medical Curriculum. *Brit. med. J.* **ii**, 366.

Reliability of psychiatric opinion in the Royal Air Force. Psychological disorders in flying personnel of the Royal Air Force investigated during the war, 1939–1945. (With Williams, D. J.). Air Ministry. Air Publication 3139, p. 308.

1948 Studies in the incidence of cancer in a factory handling inorganic compounds of arsenic. Mortality experience in the factory. (With Faning, E. Lewis). *Brit. J. industr. Med.* **5**, 2.

Principles of Medical Statistics, 4th ed. London: Lancet.

1949 Maternal rubella and congenital defects. (With Galloway, T. M.). *Lancet*, **i**, 299.

Poliomyelitis and the social environment. (With Martin, W. J.). *Brit. med. J.* **ii**, 357.

1950 Inoculation and Poliomyelitis. (With Knowelden, J.). *Brit. med. J.* **ii**, 1.

Smoking and carcinoma of the lung. (With Doll, R.). *Brit. med. J.* **ii**, 739.

Principles of Medical Statistics, 5th ed. London: Lancet.

Medical Statistics. In *Chambers Encyclopaedia*, vol. IX, pp. 209b–211b.

1951 The doctor's day and pay. The inaugural address of the President. *J. R. Statist. Soc.* ser. A. CXIV, Pt. I, 1–37.

The clinical trial. *Brit. med. Bull.* **7**, 278.

General principles of field surveys. The application of scientific methods to industrial and service medicine. *Medical Research Council Conference*, p. 7. London: H.M.S.O.

1952 Chemotherapy of pulmonary tuberculosis in young adults. An analysis of the combined results of three Medical Research Council trials. (With Daniels, Marc). *Brit. med. J.* **i**, 1162.

The clinical trial. *New Engl. J. Med.* **247**, 113.

A study of the aetiology of carcinoma of the lung. (With Doll, R.). *Brit. med. J.* **ii**, 1271.

Inoculation procedures as a provoking factor in poliomyelitis. *Papers and discussions presented at the Second International Poliomyelitis Conference*, p. 330. Philadelphia; Lippincott.

1953 Observation and experiment. The Cutter lecture in Preventive Medicine, Harvard University. *New Engl. J. Med.* **248**, 995.

The Philosophy of the Clinical Trial. The National Institutes of Health Annual Lectures 1953. Public Health Service Publications, No. **388.** Washington: U.S. Government Printing Office.

1954 Medical statistics and the design of experiment. *Proceedings, First World Conference on Medical Education*, London: Oxford University Press.

The mortality of doctors in relation to their smoking habits. A preliminary report. (With Doll, R.) *Brit. med. J.* **i**, 1451.

Poliomyelitis in England and Wales between the Wars. *Proc. R. Soc. Med.* **47**, 795.

1955   *Principles of Medical Statistics*, 6th ed. London: Lancet.

Snow—an appreciation. *Proc. R. Soc. Med.* **48**, 1004.

1956   Lung cancer and tobacco. (With Doll, R.). *Brit. med. J.* **ii**, 208.

Statistics in medical research. *Triangle*, **2**, 208.

Lung cancer and other causes of death in relation to smoking. A second report on the mortality of British doctors. (With Doll, R.). *Brit. med. J.* **ii**, 1071.

Recent statistics of carbon monoxide poisoning. Report to the Medical Research Council. *Brit. med. J.* **ii**, 1220.

1957   Deaths from poliomyelitis among British doctors. (With Doll, R.). *Brit. med. J.* **i**, 372.

The significance of cell-type in relation to the aetiology of lung cancer. (With Doll, R., and Kreyberg, L.). *Brit. J. Cancer*, **11**, 43.

1958   Virus diseases in pregnancy and congenital defects. (With Doll, R., Galloway, T. M., and Hughes, J. P. W.). *Brit. J. prev. soc. Med.* **12**, 1.

The Harben Lectures, 1957. The Experimental approach in preventive medicine. *J. R. Inst. publ. Hlth.* **21**, 177, 185 and 209.

1959   Lung Cancer mortality and the length of cigarette ends. An international comparison. (With Doll, R., Gray, P. G., and Parr, E. A.). *Brit. med. J.* **i**, 322.

Aims and ethics. In *Controlled Clinical Trials*. Oxford: Blackwell.

Conclusion—the statistician. In *Controlled Clinical Trials*. Oxford: Blackwell.

1960   Asian influenza in pregnancy and congenital defects. (With Doll, R., and Sakula, J.). *Brit. J. prev. soc. Med.* **14**, 167.

Incidence of leukaemia after exposure to diagnostic radiation *in utero*. (With Court Brown, W. M. and Doll, R.). *Brit. med. J.* **ii**, 1539.

A controlled clinical trial of long-term anticoagulant therapy in cerebro-vascular disease. (With Marshall, J., and Shaw, D. A.). *Quart. J. Med.* **29**, 597.

1961   *Principles of Medical Statistics*, 7th ed. London: Lancet.

SOME MEDICAL RESEARCH COUNCIL TRIALS OF TREATMENT AND VACCINES IN THE YEARS 1948 TO 1960

1948   Streptomycin treatment of pulmonary tuberculosis. *Brit. med. J.* **ii**, 769.

1950   Treatment of pulmonary tuberculosis with streptomycin and para-amino-salicylic acid. *Brit. med. J.* **ii**, 1073.

1952   The prevention of streptomycin resistance by combined chemotherapy. *Brit. med. J.* **i**, 1157.

The treatment of pulmonary tuberculosis with isoniazid. *Brit. med. J.* **ii**, 735.

1953 Isoniazid in the treatment of pulmonary tuberculosis. Second Report. *Brit. med. J.* **i,** 521.

Isoniazid in combination with streptomycin or with P.A.S. in the treatment of pulmonary tuberculosis. *Brit. med. J.* **ii,** 1005.

1954 A five-year assessment of patients in a controlled trial of streptomycin in pulmonary tuberculosis. *Quart. J. Med.* **23,** 347.

1955 Various combinations of isoniazid with streptomycin or with P.A.S. in the treatment of pulmonary tuberculosis. *Brit. med. J.* **i,** 435.

1954 A comparison of cortisone and codeine medication as an adjuvant to manipulation in rheumatoid arthritis. A report to the Joint Committee on Cortisone and ACTH in chronic rheumatic diseases of the M.R.C. and the Nuffield Foundation. *Brit. med. J.* **i,** 233.

A comparison of cortisone and aspirin in the treatment of early cases of rheumatoid arthritis. A report by the Joint Committee of the M.R.C. and the Nuffield Foundation on clinical trials of cortisone, ACTH and other therapeutic measures in chronic rheumatic diseases. *Brit. med. J.* **i,** 1223.

1955 A comparison of cortisone and aspirin in the treatment of early cases of rheumatoid arthritis. A second report by the Joint Committee of the M.R.C. and Nuffield Foundation on clinical trials of cortisone, ACTH and other therapeutic measures in chronic rheumatic diseases. *Brit. med. J.* **ii,** 695.

1957 A comparison of cortisone and prednisone in the treatment of rheumatoid arthritis. *Brit. med. J.* **ii,** 199.

1955 The treatment of acute rheumatic fever in children. A co-operative clinical trial of ACTH, cortisone and aspirin. A joint report by the Rheumatic Fever Working Party of the Medical Research Council of Great Britain and the Sub-committee of Principal Investigators of the American Council on Rheumatic Fever and Congenital Heart Disease, American Heart Association. *Brit. med. J.* **i,** 555.

1960 Evolution of rheumatic heart disease in children. Five-year report of a co-operative clinical trial of ACTH, cortisone and aspirin. A joint report by the Rheumatic Fever Working Party of the Medical Research Council of Great Britain and the Sub-committee of Principal Investigators of the American Council on Rheumatic Fever and Congenital Heart Disease, American Heart Association. *Brit. med. J.* **ii,** 1033.

1950 Clinical trials of antihistaminic drugs in the prevention and treatment of the common cold. *Brit. med. J.* **ii,** 425.

Gamma globulin in the prevention and attenuation of measles. Controlled trials in day and residential nurseries. *Lancet,* **ii,** 732.

1951   The prevention of whooping-cough by vaccination. *Brit. med. J.* **i,** 1464.

1956   Vaccination against whooping-cough. Relation between protection in children and results of laboratory tests. *Brit. med. J.* **ii,** 454.

1959   Vaccination against whooping-cough. *Brit. med. J.* **i,** 994.

1956   B.C.G. and vole bacillus vaccines in the prevention of tuberculosis in adolescents. *Brit. med. J.* **i,** 413.

1959   B.C.G. and vole bacillus vaccines in the prevention of tuberculosis in adolescents. Second report. *Brit. med. J.* **ii,** 379.

1953   Clinical trials of influenza vaccine. A progress report. *Brit. med. J.* **ii,** 1173.

1955   Antibody responses and clinical reactions with saline and oil adjuvant influenza virus vaccines. Second progress report. *Brit. med. J.* **ii,** 1229.

1957   Clinical trials of influenza vaccine. Third progress report. *Brit. med. J.* **ii,** 1.

1958   Trials of an Asian influenza vaccine. Fourth progress report. *Brit. med. J.* **i,** 415.

1957   The assessment of the British vaccine against poliomyelitis. *Brit. med. J.* **i,** 1271.

1956   Poliomyelitis and prophylactic inoculation against diphtheria, whooping-cough and smallpox. *Lancet,* **ii,** 1223.

Printed in Great Britain by Pickering & Inglis, Glasgow